Collector's
Encyclopedia of
Stangl
ARTWARE, LAMPS, and BIRDS
IDENTIFICATION
&
VALUES
Robert C. Runge, Jr.
cb
COLLECTOR BOOKS
A Division of Schroeder Publishing Co., Inc.

Front cover:
Silver Green #1037 Oval Lovebird lamp, $200.00 – 250.00; Terra Rose Green #3569 Dolphin Bowl, $275.00 – 300.00; Sunburst glaze #1389 candleholders, $225.00 – 275.00 per pair; #3625 Bird of Paradise, $2,200.00 – 2,800.00; Variegated Rust #3104 vase, $95.00 – 110.00.

Cover design by Beth Summers
Book design by Terri Hunter

COLLECTOR BOOKS
P.O. Box 3009
Paducah, Kentucky 42002-3009
www.collectorbooks.com

Searching For A Publisher?

Contents

Dedication

This book is dedicated to the memory of Martin Stangl, the man whose drive, vision and aptitude kept Stangl Pottery Company on a forward course for over 50 years. Also to Martin Stangl's daughters Martha, Christl, and Betty, who each in her own way has added greatly to the Stangl Pottery legend; and to Martin Stangl's sons-in-law, Merrill Bacheler and David Thomas, for their many marketing and engineering contributions to the company.

Johann Martin Stangl, 1881 – 1972

Marcena North (left) with Stangl designer Kay Hackett (right) during one of the Stangl weekends in Flemington, New Jersey.

In Memoriam

Marcena North, Fort Myers, Florida

Fondly Remembered

Marcena was one of those people who makes an instant impression and stays vividly in one's mind. She was one of the most energetic, enthusiastic, and dedicated Stangl collectors I have ever known. She was a delight to know!

She had a thirst for knowledge and wanted to know every detail about the pottery she collected. She seemed to be on a quest to have an example of every item made. Always seen with her Stangl reference books under her arm, friends often quipped that Marcena "bought by the page." She would point out her needs in each group of dinnerware or artware indicating what she did not yet have… but intended to!

Marcena made a pilgrimage twice a year from her Ft. Myers, Florida, home to attend nearly every Stangl weekend in Flemington. She was an aggressive bidder at the auctions and was always seen happily laden with bags and packages from her purchases at the shows and shops in Flemington. She was usually accompanied by her daughters on these trips, and we looked forward to sharing a meal and great conversation with these ladies. We miss those days, and the Stangl-world is definitely not the same without Marcena.

Rob was warmly welcomed into the North home and spent two days photographing her collection. This book could never have been as complete without Marcena's generous hospitality. We heartily thank her for her support of this effort and wish in some way that she could see the finished product.

We do know that she took one of her favorite Stangl birds with her.

Farewell, Marcena,
You are missed by all your friends.

Diana E. Bullock-Runge

Acknowledgments

This book would have been impossible without the assistance and unselfish sharing of many, many fantastic people.

First, I thank Diana, my colleague in research, best friend, partner, and wife, for the multitude of tireless hours she has devoted to research. Nearly all the many details of Fulper and Stangl history published here were uncovered by her. Diana has been steadfast and unfailing in her support of this work from beginning to end and has been with me every step of the way. She has made personal sacrifices to provide the encouragement, time, peanut butter sandwiches, and support necessary to complete this work.

I am indebted to my parents, Linda and Robert Runge, and brother and sister-in-law, Ralph and Colleen Runge, for assisting us by diving headlong into all our projects, no questions asked, and to my grandmother and lifelong friend, Loretta Javes, for being with me along the way.

I am very grateful to my dearest friend Kay Hackett for sharing her memories of Stangl and inspiring me to write this book. I wish to thank several other terrific friends whose help was invaluable: Charles and Patricia Walther for pointing me in the right direction, and Frank and Liz Kramar for their unending support and cherished friendship.

Without the generous assistance of a number of extraordinary individuals, this book would certainly never have been possible. I am genuinely grateful to Martin Stangl's daughters and sons-in-law for their tremendous assistance. I thank Merrill and Christl Stangl Bacheler and Dave and Betty Stangl Thomas for sharing with me their belongings to photograph, for extending hospitality, and for offering an abundance of detailed Stangl production knowledge.

I would like to express heartfelt thanks to the following Stangl employees. The vast amount of information and personal insight each graciously shared has added great depth and detail to this book.

Edward Alvater, Flemington Outlet manager, 1972 – 1978
Christl Stangl Bacheler, demonstrator, cataloging, decorator, 1935 – 1964
Martha Stangl Bacheler, Flemington Outlet manager, 1935 – 1943
Merrill Bacheler, demonstrator, Flemington Outlet manager, 1938 – 1964
Gloria Cardone, decorator, assistant to Irene Sarnecki, 1956 – 1978
Helen Orashan Cervenka, Flemington Outlet secretary, museum curator, 1965 – 1968
Evelyn Pyatt Crone, decorator, 1941 – 1948
Dorothy Denyse, decorator, 1948 – 1968
Agnes Douglass, Flemington Outlet sales clerk, 1948 – 1953
Norma (Nonny) Stockwell English, designer, 1944 – 1945
Edith Gambi, personnel, switchboard, 1950 – 1972
Florence Gardner, decorator, 1949 – 1978
Florence Dunn Glenn, decorator, 1948 – 1970
Kathleen (Kay) Kastner Hackett, designer, 1941 – 1965
Teresa Hawryluk, decorator, 1945 – 1978
Rose Herbeck, designer, 1967 – 1972
Rose Jacobs, decorator, 1946 – 1976
Charles Jankowski, ceramic engineer, 1964 – 1968
Mary Meyers Jones, secretary to Martin Stangl, 1929 – 1944
Paul Kavulic, kiln operator, 1969 – 1978
Rudolf Kleinebeckel, designer, sculptor, 1968 – 1978
Ruth Klenk, decorator, 1952 – 1956
David Koch, production control, shipping manager, 1873 – 1976
Gerrie Majeski, decorator, 1954 – 1968
Alice Maple, Flemington Outlet sales clerk, 1968 – 1978
Anné Fritsche Martin, Flemington Outlet potter, decorator, 1965
Walter McBride, jiggerman, supervisor, 1949 – 1978
Enez Mitzkewich, Flemington Outlet assistant manager, 1969 – 1978
Richard Nerges, jiggerman, 1963 – 1967
James Paul, general manager, 1964 – 1971
Clinton Peterman, accountant, 1942 – 1973
Irene Podayko, Flemington Outlet assistant manager, 1949 – 1964
Anne Pogranicy, office manager, 1946 – 1978
Jean Taylor Polasek, Flemington decorator, 1946 – 1948
Cleo Crawford Salerno, designer, 1942 – 1947
Alice Samsel, decorator, 1951 – 1978
Irene M. Sarnecki, designer, forelady of decorating, 1948 – 1978
William Smith, engineer's assistant, 1949 – 1956
Shirley Thatcher Spaciano, Flemington Outlet sales clerk, decorator, demonstrator, 1942 – 1962
David Thomas, general manager, engineer, 1945 – 1956
Betty Stangl Thomas, sculptor, decorator, 1939 – 1941
Josephine Tiffenbach, decorator, 1939 – 1941
Rosa Veglianetti, decorator, 1938 – 1976
Fred Walker, jiggerman, board carrier, 1948 – 1971
Geraldine West, engobe sprayer, 1951 – 1967
Ethel Weyman, decorator, 1947 – 1954
Lucia Zanetti Ziemba, Flemington Outlet, 1939 – 1944

I also wish to thank these family and descendants of Fulper and Stangl pottery employees for the information they have eagerly shared.

Eleanor Skelton, granddaughter of John Kunsman

Craig Ewing and Alaine Ewing, grandson and granddaughter of Gerald Ewing

Laura Teague Moore and Archie Teague, daughter and son of James Teague

I am especially indebted to the many fine Stangl collectors and dealers who enthusiastically shared information or loaned items for photography. Through the combined efforts of all, this project has been possible. Thanks to Bennett and Flossie Avila; Patricia Bacon; Dennis Barone; Jim Blanchard; Muriel Brannon; Bob and Shirley Bond; Dennis Boyd; Trish Claar; Scott Creighton; Bob and Tammie Cruser; Lynn Davis; Lynn Dezmain; Louis and Sally DiPlacido; Manning and Agnes Douglass; Barry Everett; Marion Farrell; Lulu Fuller; David and Deb Gainer; Steve Goodman; Skip and Dolores Hager; Brian and Christi Hahn; Gary Hanson; Patrick Harmon; Jim Horner; Ed and Shari Heinz; Loretta Javes; Ben and Pauline Jenson; Vera Kaufman; Janie King; Kevin and Nancy Klein; Frank and Liz Kramar; Peggy Kramar; Ed and Donna Ledoux; Gloria Logan; Bill Martin; Chris McGeehan; Johann and Chris McKee; Joe Miklos; Barbara Miller; Bob and Donna Miller; Connie Moore; David Negley; Jim and Barbara Nelson; Marcena North; Martin Parker; Todd Petersen; Wayne Pratt; Jason and Christina Price; Mark and Charity Rinker; Lee Rosbach; Luke and Nancy Ruepp; Bill Serviss and Susan Lewis; Bob Sherman; Ed Simpson; Lowell Snare; Ellsworth Snyder; David and Laura Solomon; John Arthur Timmons; Marge Voorhees; Wayne Weigand.

Special thanks to Ulysses Dietz of the Newark Museum; Roxanne Carkhuff of the Hunterdon County Historical Society; Terry Kinsey of McCoy Pottery Online; the staff of the Trentoniana Collection at the Trenton Public Library; Gay Taylor, Susan Gogan, Diane Wood, and Elizabeth Wilk of Wheaton Village Museum of American Glass; John Kane of Sperry, Zoda & Kane, patent attorneys for Stangl Pottery; the staff at the Newark Library; the staff at Zimmerli Art Museum; and the staff of the archival collection at the *Hunterdon County Democrat.*

Additional Information and Stangl Sources

Be sure to visit the Hill-Fulper-Stangl Potteries Museum in the old Stangl Pottery Outlet building, now Pfaltzgraff, Mine St., Flemington, New Jersey. The web address for the Hill-Fulper-Stangl Potteries Museum is www.stanglpottery.org.

Stangl Sources and Dinnerware Matching Services

Main Street Antique Center
156 Main St.
Flemington, NJ 08822

Grandpa's Trading Company
5403 15th Street East
Bradenton, FL 34203
941-756-7337

Ben & Floss Avila
157 Kingwood-Locktown Road
Stockton, NJ 08559-1221

Judy and Dan Meck
229 Hogestown Road
Mechanicsburg, PA 17055

Lynn Dezmain
Ephrata, PA
717-738-0896

For more information or specific questions regarding Stangl Pottery Artware or Dinnerware, please feel free to contact me at:

robrunge@stanglpottery.org
or
Robert C. Runge Jr.
PO Box 5427
Somerset, NJ 08875

For information concerning Stangl's Cigarette Boxes or Country Life or Kiddieware patterns, please contact:

Luke and Nancy Ruepp
PO Box 349
Lake Hiawatha, NJ 07034

Pertinent Web Addresses

Stangl Pottery
www.stanglpottery.org
Contains a great amount of current and historic information on Stangl Pottery, including Hill-Fulper- Stangl Museum doings and updates on recent Stangl and Fulper fakes.

The Stangl Bird Collectors Club
www.stanglbird.com
Features a website and free e-mail newsletter dedicated to the dissemination of knowledge concerning Stangl Bird collecting and late-breaking news concerning all aspects of Stangl.

Fulper Pottery
www.fulperpottery.org
The only web address wholly devoted to Fulper Pottery and the company's history.

From 1924 to 1978, Martin Stangl developed and produced, under several brand names, a great assortment of earthenware lamps, artware, figurines, dinnerware, and special-order products. It was Stangl's dinnerware that was manufactured in the greatest quantities with the hand-carved, hand-painted fruit and floral patterns most remembered and most widely collected today. Martin Stangl was innovative and instrumental in directing the course of the American ceramics industry. He introduced America's first full line of nationally distributed, open stock solid-color dinnerware under the Fulper Fayence brand in 1924. Stangl was also a major lamp manufacturer during the 1920s and 1930s and a prominent American ceramics supplier during World War II when imported ceramics were unavailable. Stangl Pottery was the leading American manufacturer of hand-decorated pottery bird figurines during the 1940s, smoking accessories during the 1950s, and brushed gold artware during the 1960s and 1970s.

This book lists nearly all of Stangl's art lines, figurines, lamps, and special-order products in all known glazes and finishes. However, because the length and breadth of Stangl production was so widespread and Martin Stangl was always developing new and different finishes for old tried and true shapes, nearly anything is possible! Should a Stangl topic (other than Stangl dinnerware) not be covered here, please feel free to contact me at robrunge@stanglpottery.org or Robert Runge, PO Box 5427, Somerset, NJ 08875. I will be happy to answer any questions or discuss new finds.

The values listed are average compilations gleaned from many nationwide sources. Even today, in this age of worldwide connection, the saleability of many Stangl lines can be very regional. An item that may sell repeatedly for $50.00 in Florida can be undesirable at half that price in New York. Also, the extreme high and low prices sometimes realized on Internet auctions such as eBay do not represent the retail values of Stangl items offered for sale at antiques shops and shows. Please bear in mind that the values published here are examples only and are not the standard for Stangl pottery pricing.

Each type of Stangl artware is divided into individual chapters and sections. Within each chapter and section, items are listed in numerical order, according to the shape numbers assigned them in original company records.

Hill Pottery

Flemington, New Jersey, was already a growing center of commerce when twenty-year-old Samuel Hill arrived with the purpose of setting up an earthenware manufactory in 1814. Samuel Hill had just completed his potter's apprenticeship with the Ephraim Mackay Pottery of New Brunswick, New Jersey, a producer of earthenware household and utility items. Hill was drawn to Flemington by his uncle Thomas Capnerhurst (the family name Capnerhurst was ultimately shortened to Capner) and by the prospect of useable deposits of red shale residual clay in and near Flemington. Several area brick manufacturers were already using this Flemington clay; one Flemington brickyard was operating as early as 1790.

Samuel Hill borrowed $800 from his uncle Thomas Capner and Thomas's son Joseph Capner to "add to capital already in possession of S. Hill for the singular purpose to construct and begin operation of an earthen ware manufactory." This was stated on a loan agreement between both Thomas and Joseph Capner and Samuel Hill dated June 16, 1814. By July 1814, Hill had purchased two and one-quarter acres of land at the corner of Mine Street and Main Street in Flemington and commenced building his pottery.

Portion of a Flemington borough pictorial map dated 1889 showing building #16, the location of Hill's original pottery. The building was known as Fulper Bros. Pottery in 1889. The large updraft kiln used for earthenware firing can be seen protruding through the roof line. The two Fulper family homes are the large and small houses in the upper left corner.

Although most collectors are familiar with Fulper and Stangl pottery products bearing the inscription, "Since 1805," historians believe that date was purely a bit of inventive advertising created by Wilson F. Fulper, Fulper Brothers Company sales manager, during the 1880s and 1890s. According to Snell's *History of Hunterdon and Somerset Counties, New Jersey*, published in 1881, "Samuel Hill built the pottery-works about 1815, operating them until his death, in 1858. He was born Aug. 13, 1793. His son William, the present postmaster, was born Feb. 13, 1822." What's more, there is absolutely no evidence of any pottery manufacturing at Mine and Main Streets in Flemington prior to Hill's arriving in 1814. It is also even more unlikely that Samuel Hill could have established anything in Flemington in 1805 because at that time he was still in New Brunswick and only twelve years old! The "1805" date first appears on an 1891 Fulper Bros & Co. sales list. At that time, Pfaltzgraff Pottery Company, Fulper's biggest competitor in stoneware, was declaring 1811 as their "founding date." Consequently, in order to claim the distinction of being America's oldest operating pottery, Fulper needed to predate Pfaltzgraff. The "1805" date seemed a good choice and looked good in ad copy. Wilson Fulper, with a liberal dose of creative license, demonstrates how it is possible to perpetuate a mythical founding date for nearly a century. Additional evidence of Fulper Pottery's advertising "embellishments" are documented farther along in this chapter.

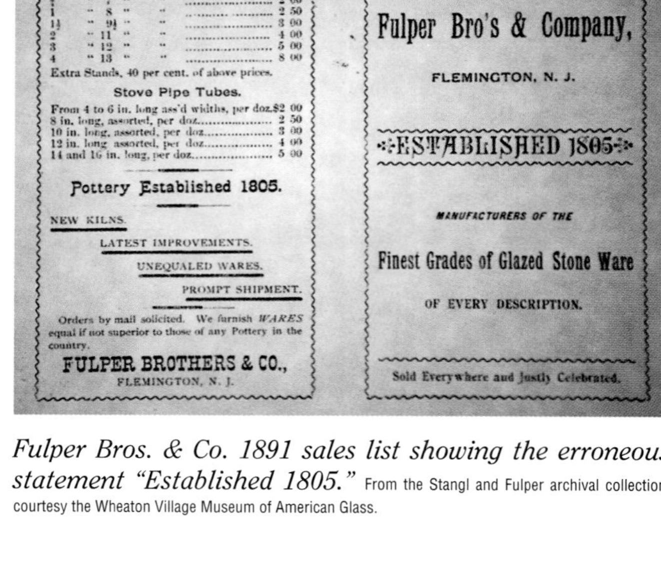

EARTHENWARE.

Earthen Flower Pots--with Stands.

Gal.	Inch		Price
1-16 Gal.,	3 inch,	per doz.	$ [illegible]
[illegible]	4		75
[illegible]	5		1 00
[illegible]	6		1 50
[illegible]	7		2 00
1	8		2 50
1½	9½		3 00
2	11		4 00
3	12		5 00
4	13		8 00

Extra Stands, 40 per cent. of above prices.

Stove Pipe Tubes.

From 4 to 6 in. long ass'd widths, per doz.	$2 00
8 in. long, assorted, per doz.	2 50
10 in. long, assorted, per doz.	3 00
12 in. long assorted, per doz.	4 00
14 and 16 in. long, per doz.	5 00

Pottery Established 1805.

NEW KILNS.

LATEST IMPROVEMENTS.

UNEQUALED WARES.

PROMPT SHIPMENT.

Orders by mail solicited. We furnish *WARES* equal if not superior to those of any Pottery in the country.

FULPER BROTHERS & CO.,
FLEMINGTON, N. J.

PRICE LIST.

Fulper Bro's & Company,

FLEMINGTON, N. J.

ESTABLISHED 1805

MANUFACTURERS OF THE

Finest Grades of Glazed Stone Ware

OF EVERY DESCRIPTION.

Sold Everywhere and Justly Celebrated.

Fulper Bros. & Co. 1891 sales list showing the erroneous statement "Established 1805." From the Stangl and Fulper archival collection, courtesy the Wheaton Village Museum of American Glass.

The products of Hill's pottery were lead-glazed redware utilitarian household and storage items as well as glazed and unglazed drain pipe. According to advertisements placed by Hill in the *Hunterdon Gazette* and *Farmer's Advertiser* during the 1820s and 1830s, Hill was shipping substantial quantities of earthenware pots and jars to the Trenton, New Brunswick, and Newark areas on a regular basis. This was in addition to the products being bought and used in Hunterdon County.

Drain pipe and drain tile produced by Hill Pottery of Flemington clay. These pipes were excavated from under the streets of Flemington, where many such examples continue to serve their original purpose draining the basements of some of Flemington's older homes. Courtesy of the Hill-Fulper-Stangl Museum.

Redware pot attributed to Samuel Hill. Courtesy of the Hill-Fulper-Stangl Museum.

Samuel Hill married Letitia Van Nest, also of Hunterdon County, on June 18, 1817. The 1850 Census of Manufacturers lists Samuel Hill & Son Pottery, as it was then called, with six employees. Among those were Samuel's son William Hill and Abraham Fulper, listed as a potter, age 35. Abraham, also called Abram, was born in Hunterdon County on April 7, 1815 to Jacob and Hanna Ruple Fulper. Very little documentation on Abraham Fulper's early life exits, but he married Jane Forker on December 26, 1839, and they had five sons, William H., George W., Wilson F., Edward B., and Charles D. Each one ultimately participated in the Flemington pottery business.

Cream pot made of earthenware clay with Albany Slip glazing, typical of wares produced by the pottery during the 1850s and 1860s. Courtesy of the Hill-Fulper-Stangl Museum.

Earthenware milk jug with Albany Slip glazing, also typical of wares produced during the 1850s and 1860s. From the Stangl and Fulper archival collection, courtesy of the Wheaton Village Museum of American Glass.

Stoneware Clay Comes to Flemington

Although Flemington's red shale clay was an original factor in drawing Samuel Hill to the area, it was not the best quality for manufacturing better-grade articles. In 1904, ninety years after Hill began potting in Flemington, state geologist Henry B. Krummel compiled his report "The Clays and Clay Industry of New Jersey," and stated of the Flemington clays, "A bed of loamy clay ranging from 3 to 7 feet in thickness is worked at Flemington, for the manufacture of common brick. The lower portion of the clay was derived directly from the Triassic red shale, while the upper few feet, which contain occasional pebbles of trap rock, were derived by wash from the steep slopes of a hill of trap rock a few rods west of the clay pits. Both clays are used and burn to a product of good red color and hard body, but they are too gritty for use in draintile." Because of the low quality of the Flemington clay, better clays such as stoneware were sought. None were available at a reasonable cost until the mid 1850s, after the Belvidere & Delaware Railroad completed its branch line to Flemington in 1854. This new rail line greatly reduced shipping costs of bulk materials, such as fuel and clay, allowing the pottery to expand its product line to include stoneware vessels. The rail connection also allowed inexpensive transportation to Trenton, then on to farther destinations such as Philadelphia and New York.

The stoneware clay used at the pottery was Amboy stoneware clay and was mined at the Raritan Formation along the Raritan River near Perth Amboy, Middlesex County, New Jersey. According to Dr. M. W. Twitchell, assistant state geologist in 1925, this was New Jersey's most important clay district producing a variety of high-quality clay types. The Amboy stoneware clay used by Fulper would be loaded on barges at Perth Amboy and then shipped up the Raritan River to New Brunswick. The barges were then hauled along the Delaware & Raritan Canal to Trenton where the clay was then shipped by rail on the Belvidere & Delaware Railroad to Flemington. Once the stoneware clays were affordably available, Fulper then installed a round downdraft kiln for firing the salt glazed stoneware products. The large updraft kiln continued in use for firing the earthenware products. Earthenware products were still made of the locally mined Flemington red shale earthenware clay, but on a much smaller scale than previously.

Depot of the Belvidere & Delaware Railroad in the early 1950s prior to the building's restoration. This line ultimately became a division of the Pennsylvania Railroad. A portion of the Fulper home on Mine Street can be seen at the extreme right of the photo.

Clay pit and clay mining operation at Mauer, Middlesex County, New Jersey. This clay pit was typical of the type that produced New Jersey's best quality stoneware clays. Note the pottery kilns in background to the right. Many New Jersey potters established themselves near their source of raw materials. Courtesy of the New Jersey State Chamber of Commerce.

Fulper & Son stoneware crock with cobalt decoration, exemplary of the wares made of Amboy stoneware clay after 1854. From the Stangl and Fulper archival collection, courtesy of the Wheaton Village Museum of American Glass.

Fulper Pottery

By 1860, Hill Pottery still employed six workers and was under the direction of Abraham Fulper and his son William H. Fulper. The primary output of the pottery was tile, industrial lead pots, and cream pots, as well as various other stoneware and earthenware products. William Hill was apparently not interested in the pottery business at all. Shortly after his father Samuel's death on April 7, 1858, William began selling the business and property to potter Abraham Fulper. Abraham Fulper acquired full possession of the pottery by 1864 and then called the company Fulper Pottery and then Fulper & Son. They continued manufacturing stoneware and earthenware crockery, earthenware drainpipe, tile, and lead pots throughout the 1860s. William Hill went on to become postmaster of Flemington.

Fulper stoneware molasses jug. From the Stangl and Fulper archival collection, courtesy of the Wheaton Village Museum of American Glass.

In 1863 the Central Railroad of New Jersey completed its branch line into Flemington, greatly opening up the metropolitan New York market to Fulper's products.

During the 1870s, Fulper's tile and lead pot business expanded so much that by 1880 Fulper & Son employed twelve, which included eight potters, two potter's apprentices and a bookkeeper. In 1880 the New Jersey State Agricultural Society awarded Fulper & Son Pottery a bronze medal for the consistent high quality of the pots they produced for the dairy industry. This was the first of eight medals and various prizes ultimately awarded to the Fulper Company for their quality of products during the decades to come.

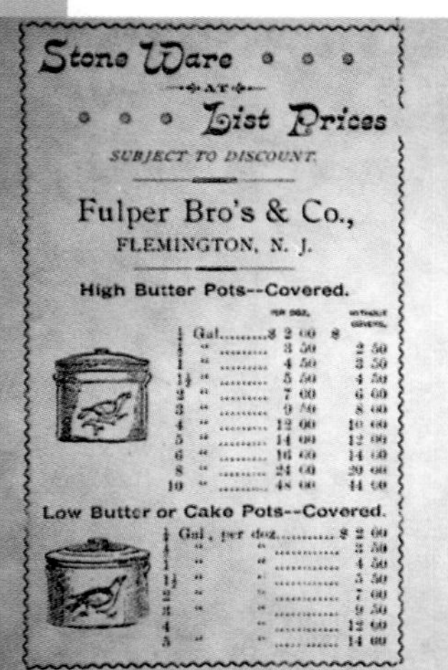

Stone Ware
AT
List Prices
SUBJECT TO DISCOUNT.

Fulper Bro's & Co.,
FLEMINGTON, N. J.

High Butter Pots--Covered.

Size	Per doz.	Without covers.
[illegible] Gal.	$2 00	$
[illegible] "	3 50	2 50
1 "	4 50	3 50
1½ "	5 50	4 50
2 "	7 00	6 00
3 "	9 50	8 00
4 "	12 00	10 00
5 "	14 00	12 00
6 "	16 00	14 00
8 "	24 00	20 00
10 "	48 00	44 00

Low Butter or Cake Pots--Covered.

[illegible] Gal., per doz.	$2 00
[illegible] " "	3 50
1 " "	4 50
1½ " "	5 50
2 " "	7 00
3 " "	9 50
4 " "	12 00
5 " "	14 00

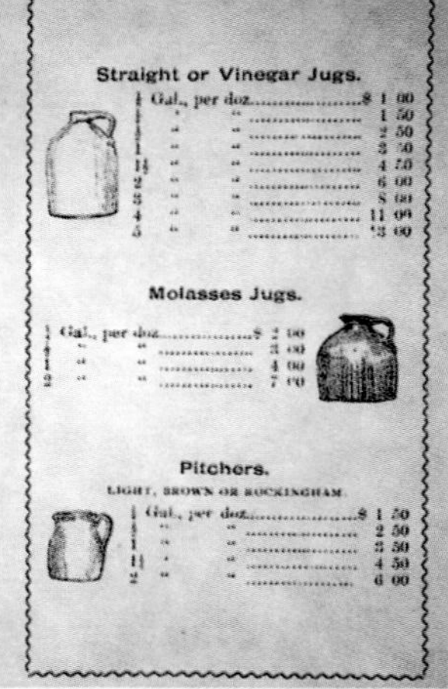

Straight or Vinegar Jugs.

[illegible] Gal., per doz.	$1 00
[illegible] " "	1 50
[illegible] " "	2 50
1 " "	3 50
1½ " "	4 50
2 " "	6 00
3 " "	8 00
4 " "	11 00
5 " "	13 00

Molasses Jugs.

[illegible] Gal., per doz.	$2 00
[illegible] " "	3 00
1 " "	4 00
2 " "	7 00

Pitchers.
LIGHT, BROWN OR ROCKINGHAM.

[illegible] Gal., per doz.	$1 50
[illegible] " "	2 50
1 " "	3 50
1½ " "	4 50
2 " "	6 00

Fulper Bros. Stone Ware price list, 1880s, showing some of their classic stoneware jugs and covered pots. From the Stangl and Fulper archival collection, courtesy the Wheaton Village Museum of American Glass.

Fulper Brothers

After Abraham Fulper's death in 1881, those of his five sons remaining in the pottery business changed the name to Fulper Bros. The output of the company continued to be tile and lead pots, with the addition of greater amounts of stoneware crockery and drainpipe as well as Albany slip glazed flowerpots for the florist industry and kitchen crockery of Rockingham and Yellow ware. The lead pots and stoneware crockery all continued to be hand-thrown on steam-powered, belt-driven potters' wheels, while most of the Rockingham and yellow ware articles were mold-formed. The Rockingham and Yellow ware lines included such items as spittoons, pitchers, mugs, chamber pots, mixing bowls, pie plates, and teapots in "Pineapple" and "Rebecca" shapes. Also advertised at that time were ornamental jardinieres in Majolica glazes Fulper called "Variegated Queensware." This would be Fulper's first foray into the artware field.

Fulper Bros. salt-glazed stoneware vinegar jug with a decorative cobalt motif. Courtesy of the Hunterdon County Historical Society.

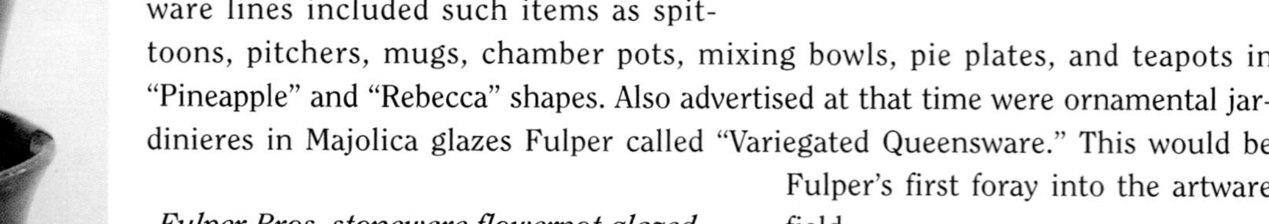

Fulper Bros. stoneware flowerpot glazed with Albany slip. Courtesy of the Hill-Fulper-Stangl Museum.

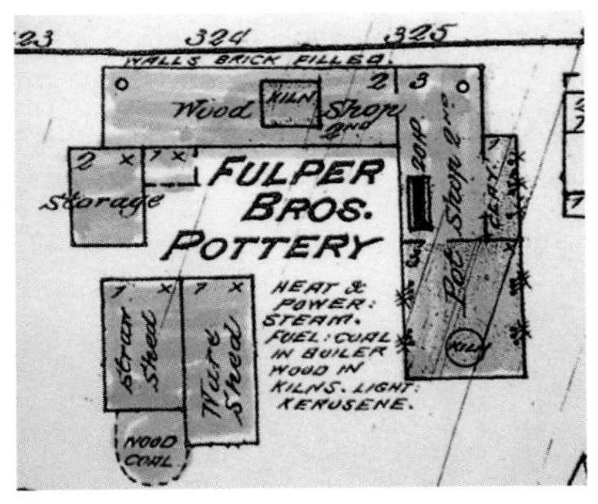

Sanborn Insurance map of 1885 showing the location and building configuration of Fulper Bros. Pottery.

According to the 1885 Sanborn Fire Insurance maps of Flemington Borough, Fulper Bros. used coal to fuel the steam boiler that powered the clay mixers and presses and potter's wheels, and wood was used exclusively to fire the kilns. Even though coal was less costly than wood at that time, wood-firing produced a bright, clear salt glaze that was more saleable than coal-fired salt glaze ware. Salt glaze, when fired with coal, always turned a murky dark gray-brown. Lighting in the factory at that time was provided by kerosene lamps.

By 1890, the building was expanded to nearly double its previous size. Another improvement was the fire-fighting apparatus, which was expanded to include 36 pails and one 150 foot hose. Also by 1890, earthenware production had ceased, and salt glazing was replaced with Bristol and Albany slip glazed products. Consequently, the large updraft kiln for earthenware firing was removed and replaced with two square wood-fired downdraft kilns, and the original round downdraft kiln used for salt glazing was replaced, thus bringing the total number of kilns to three.

Sanborn Insurance map of 1890, showing the building improvements done to the Fulper Bros. pottery.

Fulper's head potter, John Kunsman, initiated this kiln improvement. This would be the first of many advancements Kunsman would bring about at Fulper Pottery. He was well versed in stoneware production, as he had spent his early years working at his father's pottery in Johnsonville, Pennsylvania. The 1892 New Jersey Directory of Industry and Manufacture listed Fulper Pottery as having 19 employees, and by 1897, the pottery was producing 1,500 stoneware articles per day. While numerous articles continued to be hand-thrown, by this time production was switching more and more to jiggered and cast items. In addition, salt glazing was being replaced by Bristol glaze, which provided a brighter finish when fired with less costly fuels.

Lehigh Valley/Smith Pottery

Fulper was not the only stoneware manufacturer to operate in Flemington during the late nineteenth century. The Lehigh Valley Railroad completed its branch line from Flemington Junction to Main Street Flemington on August 4, 1884, and constructed an engine house. Then, according to the report of the Lehigh Valley Railroad Co. of November 30, 1886, "the Flemington Branch of the New Jersey Division has been extended a short distance and a passenger station and freight station built." In 1888, a 40 foot by 70 foot pottery with one kiln was constructed on railroad property east of the engine house, near the corner of Main Street and Park Avenue. It was typical of railroads during the nineteenth century to promote, and even sponsor, industry along their rights of way, thus ensuring a steady transportation business for themselves.

Known as the Lehigh Valley Pottery, this enterprise was leased and operated by two brothers, Oliver H. and Lincoln G. Smith. The Smiths were originally from Canada and served their apprenticeships at Fulper Pottery during the early 1880s. They established the Lehigh Valley Pottery at the completion of their apprenticeships. In 1890, to gain capital for expansion, the Smiths took on an investment partner, Hunterdon County merchant, farmer, and county surrogate, Charles Alpaugh. At that time the pottery building was expanded, more production equipment added and a second kiln constructed. The enterprise then became O. H. Smith and Bro. or Smith Bros. & Co. Both names seemed to be in use at the same time.

Lehigh Valley/Smith Pottery, 1890. Courtesy of the *Hunterdon County Democrat.*

Like Fulper, the Lehigh Valley Pottery also utilized Amboy stoneware clay. The New Jersey Division of the Lehigh Valley Railroad terminated at Perth Amboy, thus providing a direct line from the clay mines of the Raritan Formation to Flemington. By the 1890s, Fulper's Amboy stoneware clay was also shipped via the Lehigh Valley Railroad. The long route of bringing in clay via the Delaware & Raritan Canal and Belvidere & Delaware Railroad could no longer compete with the direct route of the Lehigh Valley. During a personal interview conducted by Todd Volpe in 1978 of William Hill Fulper III (great-grandson of Abraham Fulper), Mr. Fulper is quoted as saying: "I vividly remember watching two large dappled gray horses hauling a cart loaded with both imported and domestic clay from the Lehigh Valley train station, to the pottery, fondly known in Flemington as 'The Pot Shop'."

Patent drawing for Oliver Smith's improved water filter, dated 1893.

In 1891, Oliver Smith and his wife Matilda purchased the pottery property from the Lehigh Valley Railroad. Products at that time included typical stoneware crocks, jugs, pails, and pots. The *New Jersey Business Review* of 1891 stated that the Smiths "make a prominent specialty of fancy vases for decorating purposes which are admirable specimens of art pottery. Another specialty of this house is the 'Gate City Stone Water Filter,' which they manufacture in large quantities exclusively for the patent holder." The review also stated, "The capacity of the works is one kiln per week and an average force of 15 workmen is employed. Their products are shipped to wholesale dealers in New York, Baltimore, Philadelphia, Boston, Pittsburgh, and other large cities."

Oliver Smith attempted to improve on the Gate City Stone Water Filter. He was interested in accelerating the filtering cycle by pressurizing the water passing through the filter. He also redesigned the ice chamber, hoping to increase its efficiency. Oliver Smith's design was patented on April 4, 1893, but there is no evidence that this filter was ever put into production.

By 1894 the Lehigh Valley/Smith Pottery was suffering from the economic depression of 1893, and competition in the stoneware industry at that time was fierce. Oliver Smith was borrowing operating capital from another brother, Charles Smith, and John Creveling, a local businessman and trustee of the Bloomsbury National Bank. Finally, in 1895, the Fulpers purchased the Lehigh Valley/Smith pottery from the Smiths' creditors. With the purchase of this enterprise, Fulper acquired the patents and standing orders for the "Gate City Stone Water Filter" as well as an established artware line. According to local Flemington gossip, the Smiths continued working for the Fulpers for a short time, then returned to Canada to establish a pottery there. Fulper Pottery continued to operate the former Lehigh Valley/Smith Pottery on Main Street as a division of Fulper for a very short time, but then sold that property and concentrated all manufacturing at the original Mine Street location. For a very brief period after that, a private firm known as the Flemington Stoneware Company operated the old Lehigh/Smith pottery until the buildings burned in 1900.

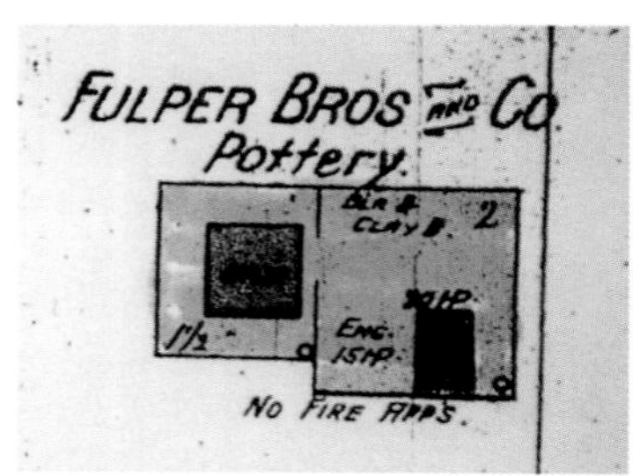

1896 Sanborn Insurance map showing the former Lehigh Valley/Smith Pottery buildings now operating as Fulper. Observe the notation beneath the building, "No Fire Apparatus;" would on-site fire-fighting equipment have perhaps saved the building in 1900? We shall never know.

The Famous Fulper Filter

Fulper Pottery continued production of the old Lehigh Valley/Smith Pottery's highly popular water filter, and ultimately re-developed it as the "Fulper Germ-Proof Water Filter." Fulper's Germ Proof filter was available in six sizes, ranging from three gallons up to eighteen gallons. The filters consisted of two Bristol glazed stoneware jars and a cover. The top jar held non-filtered water, which dripped through the patented porous "filter-stone" into the holding jar below. A removable ice chamber could also be purchased to keep the filtered water cool. Fulper's advertising stated "The 'Fulper' is the only germ-proof filter on the market — and the only filter that is advertised. It is at once the BEST and the BEST-KNOWN."

Fulper Germ Proof Filter, size No. 8, which had a 15-quart capacity and could filter 6 gallons of water per day. It retailed for $6.05 in 1905. Courtesy of the Hill-Fulper-Stangl Museum.

Fulper had contracted with Dr. J. Robert Moechel, Ph.D., Ph.M., analytical chemist and bacteriologist of Kansas City, Missouri, to test the Fulper Germ Proof Filter for effectiveness. The tests concluded that the filter was between 98.27% and 100% effective in filtering out various bacteria such as Typhoid bacilli, Bacillus coli commune, Bacillus violaceus, and Bacillus prodigiosus. Fulper then utilized these test results and a certification signed by Dr. Moechel in printed advertising, as well as in a trademark sometimes printed on the filters themselves.

Fulper's Germ Proof Filters were innovative and novel at that time due to their effectiveness in filtering and simplicity of use. All competitive filters relied on filtering devices that required maintenance or replacement on a regular basis. Some of the competing filters used rock, gravel, charcoal, cloth, or even sponges as filtering devices. These materials, when they did work, necessitated continual upkeep to remain functional. Fulper's "filter stone" was a ceramic product that only needed an occasional brushing and rinsing. This was the simplest and most economical filter on the market. For this reason Fulper's Germ Proof Filter won a bronze medal in 1902 at the South Carolina Interstate and West Indiana Exposition at Charleston, South Carolina, and another bronze medal in 1904 at the Louisiana Purchase Exposition at St. Louis, Missouri.

Fulper Germ Proof Filter trade booklet which included a complete report of Dr. Moechel's filter tests. Courtesy of the Hunterdon County Historical Society.

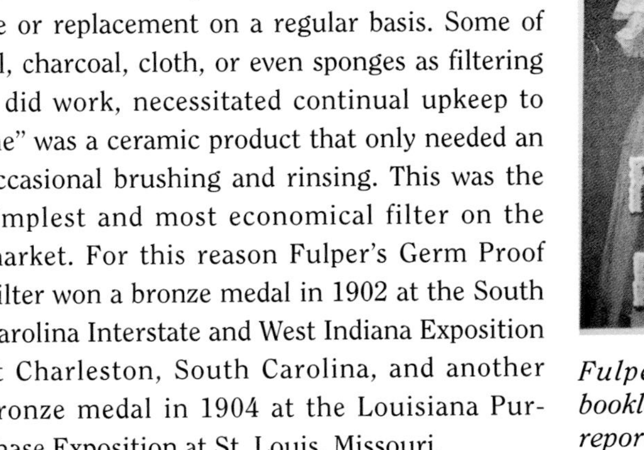

Mechanical trade card that demonstrates the effectiveness of Fulper's Germ Proof Filter, souvenir of the Louisiana Purchase Exposition, 1904.

Fulper's filters were exceedingly popular and provided clean, safe drinking water in both private homes and public places such as offices, schools, and railroad stations throughout the United States and South America through World War I.

In addition to the Germ Proof filters, Fulper was also producing an assortment of water coolers and Fulper Fire-Proof cooking ware from the 1890s until World War I. The water coolers ranged in size from two gallons to twelve gallons, featured nickel-plated bronze faucets and were decorated with cobalt bands and Bristol glaze. These were very popular items and were shipped to accounts throughout the United States.

Fulper water cooler. Courtesy of the Hill-Fulper-Stangl Museum.

A No. 5 Fulper water cooler (extreme right) in use at the Pleasant Plains School, Franklin Township (Somerset County), New Jersey, about 1905. Courtesy of the Franklin Township Historical Society.

Fulper's Fire-Proof cooking ware was made of stoneware glazed with dark brown Albany slip with contrasting bands of Bristol glaze. The assortment consisted of such items as casseroles, Dutch ovens, covered soups, bean pots, pie plates, game pans, and marmites. The Fulper Fire-Proof cookers were exceedingly popular, as the Albany slip glaze was resistant to crazing, and the heavy stoneware body easily withstood the rigors of coal- and gas-fired cooking ranges.

Fulper Fire-Proof cooking ware, marmite, and Dutch oven.
Courtesy of the Hill-Fulper-Stangl Museum.

Sanborn Fire Insurance map showing location and kilns of the Fulper Pottery Company, 1896.

Fulper Pottery Company and William H. Fulper II

From 1890 until 1899, the pottery was known as Fulper Bros. & Co. In 1899, it was incorporated as the Fulper Pottery Company. President of the company was George W. Fulper; vice president and plant manager was Edward B. Fulper with their nephew William H. Fulper II serving as secretary and treasurer. William Hill Fulper II was a graduate of the class of 1895 at Princeton University, where he had been a halfback on the football team. From April through October 1898 he had served as paymaster on the U.S.S. Resolute during the Spanish-American War. In this capacity, 26-year-old Fulper was the youngest naval officer to serve under Commodore Dewey during the war. His adventures as paymaster were chronicled in his letters home to family, which were then compiled and published as *The Diary of William H. Fulper, on Cruise of the U.S.S. "Resolute," With Forty Tons of Dynamite, During the War With Spain.*

DIARY

OF

WILLIAM H. FULPER,

ON

CRUISE OF THE U. S. S.

"RESOLUTE,"

WITH FORTY TONS OF DYNAMITE, DURING THE WAR WITH SPAIN.

PUBLISHED AS A CHRISTMAS SOUVENIR, DECEMBER 25TH, 1898.

TRENTON, N. J.:
PRESS OF THE J. L. MURPHY PUB. CO.
1899.

Title page of The Diary of William H. Fulper, on Cruise of the U.S.S. "Resolute."
Courtesy of the Hill-Fulper-Stangl Museum.

The U.S.S. Resolute off Portsmouth, New Hampshire, transporting Spanish prisoners of war in July 1898.
Courtesy of the United States Naval Historical Center Archives.

This volume was published by the J. L. Murphy Co. of New York, and was a popular war souvenir, widely given as gifts during the Christmas season of 1898. The creative genius and adventurous spirit of William Fulper would now be applied to guiding the destiny of the family's stoneware business.

By 1902, William H. Fulper II had taken the place of his uncle Edward B. Fulper as plant manager, thus allowing him additional authority over the Fulper product lines. Products at that time consisted primarily of the Germ Proof filters, water coolers, and cookware, with a small percentage of production devoted to artware, florist vases, jardinieres, and novelty souvenir items. Twenty-five workers were employed at that time.

Newspaper portrait of William H. Fulper II.

Fulper Pottery souvenir bank showing an ink print of Main Street, made for the 1909 Flemington Carnival.

Fulper Pottery souvenir miniature whiskey jug, hand-thrown by John Kunsman. Courtesy of the Avila Collection.

To accommodate the increased demand for the filters, coolers, and cookware, by 1902 two of the square downdraft kilns were replaced with improved round downdraft kilns, and a fourth improved downdraft kiln was also added. The warerooms were also expanded at that time, and the lighting was converted to electricity.

The years between 1902 and 1910 were witness to monumental changes at Fulper Pottery Company. It was during this time that production of Fulper Germ Proof water filters and Fire-Proof cooking vessels reached its zenith. To keep pace with demand, a fifth downdraft kiln was added, and all kilns were converted to burn coal, as the Bristol and Albany slip glazes were not adversely affected by coal firing as the salt glaze had been. In addition, a sixth kiln, used for decorating, was constructed at the rear of the building. The building itself was expanded at this time as well. The warerooms were doubled in size, a new packing wing was added, and an elevated tunnel was constructed to connect the new packing wing with an existing barn used as a warehouse for finished products and for straw and excelsior storage. Also, the Industrial Directory of New Jersey in 1906 listed Fulper Pottery Company as manufacturers of stoneware with a total of 55 employees.

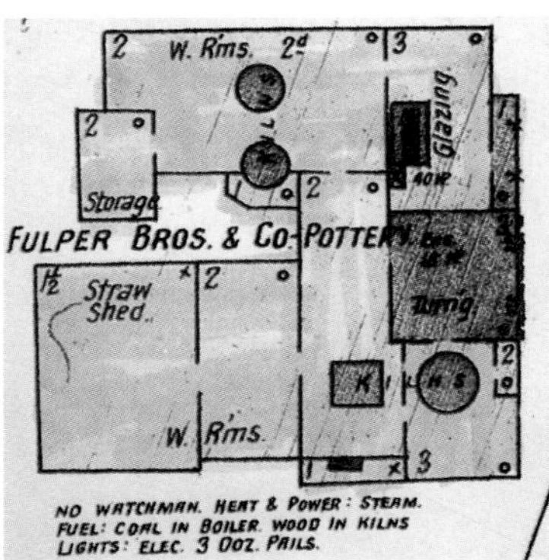

Sanborn Fire Insurance map showing location of the Fulper Pottery Company, 1902. The Sanborn Co. had updated the map to reflect the building configuration but had not yet updated the name to Fulper Pottery Company.

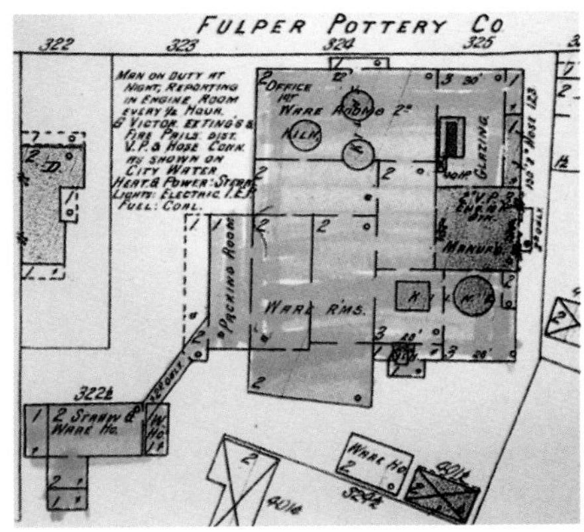

Sanborn Fire Insurance map showing location of the Fulper Pottery Company, 1910. The Fulper residences are to the left of the pottery buildings.

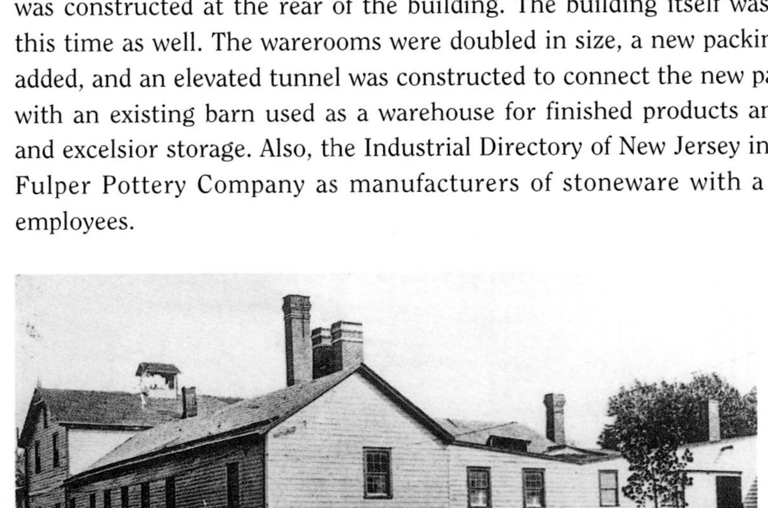

Fulper Pottery Company on Mine St., Flemington, 1909, photographed by noted local photographer Mary Sunderland. Notice that the chimneys of the efficient downdraft kilns are small and square, unlike the huge monolithic domes of updraft kilns. Courtesy of Merrill and Christl Stangl Bacheler.

Postcard view of the two Fulper family residences on Mine Street, Flemington, about 1910. These homes were later moved back from the street and remodeled. The Fulper Pottery factory building would be to the left of the small white house. Courtesy of the Hill-Fulper-Stangl Museum.

William Fulper's Artware

Always looking to future trends and projects and not relying solely on current successes, William Fulper was quite aware of the advances in household technology that would soon adversely impact his own industry. Even though Fulper Pottery was shipping thousands of Germ Proof filters worldwide, he knew that the very rapid advancements of indoor plumbing and affordable electric refrigeration would soon make his filters and water coolers obsolete. In addition to being a responsible business manager, William Fulper was a daring visionary with a practical imagination that he put to use developing new inventions or improving old ideas. Several of his inventions were granted patents, such as a water cooler for dispensing bottled water, which he developed with his uncle, George Fulper, in 1906, and a child's rocking amusement ride patented in 1914. During World War I, William Fulper was an assignor on patents filed by William Case, one being a self-righting warfare rocket, the other a centrifugal gun, patented in 1920 and 1921 respectively.

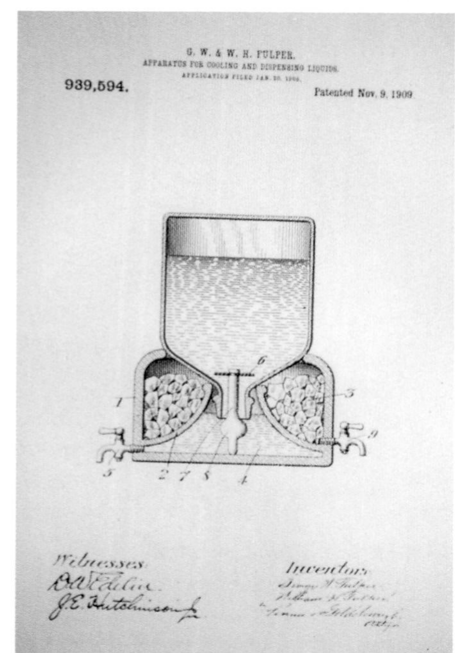

Patent drawing for George W. and William H. Fulper's water cooler.

As art pottery and the Arts and Crafts and Bungalow styles became increasingly popular, William Fulper desired to develop a distinctive and readily affordable line of art pottery that would complement America's burgeoning love for artistic pottery in both historic and modern styles, yet sustain the company once the Germ Proof filter sales began to lag. He also was drawn to the Arts and Crafts ideology of honesty in workmanship and that form should follow function, so he strove to develop a line of simple art shapes with glazes of strong character that would champion hand-craftsmanship.

A homey Arts and Crafts style bungalow, very popular during the first 20 years of the twentieth century, from House and Garden *magazine, 1911.*

As early as 1899, William Fulper was experimenting with artware shapes and glazes to improve upon the old Lehigh Valley/Smith Pottery art line. John Kunsman threw the shapes that were then glazed with Fulper's experimental glazes. These early art pieces were then displayed in one of the pottery's front windows and sold to passersby. Fulper's development of the art pottery was inspired by the growing popularity of using single-color flambé, mat or crystalline glazes as the vase decoration, as opposed to the late Victorian style of hand-painted floral and portraiture vase decorations. This "new" style of art pottery decoration was highly promoted by Charles Fergus Binns, director of the Trenton Technical School of Science and Art from 1898 to 1900, and then head of New York State School of Clay Working and Ceramics at Alfred University from 1900 to 1931. In addition to being an eminent instructor and widely published author on ceramics, Binns was also a celebrated potter well known for his organic, naturalistic glazes on stoneware. The single-color style of glazing was also popularized at the turn of the century by an increased appreciation for the ancient ceramics produced in China, Greece, and Persia. Wealthy collectors as well as public and private museums were amassing and displaying large collections of antique Oriental ceramics at that time.

An example of an Arts and Crafts dining room, from House and Garden *in 1911.*

A very early example of William Fulper's art pottery and glaze. This Oriental-style bottle vase was hand-turned by John Kunsman and glazed in an early form of William Fulper's Old Rose Matte. From the Stangl and Fulper archival collection, courtesy the Wheaton Village Museum of American Glass.

By 1904, William Fulper had developed an assortment of soft matte glazes, which were applied to John Kunsman's hand-thrown artware shapes. At the Louisiana Purchase Exposition at St. Louis that year, Fulper exhibited a large display of Germ Proof Filters, water coolers, and cooking ware, plus a minor showing of the new Fulper Art Pottery. It was there that Fulper's artware was awarded an Honorable Mention for "novelty in ceramic style."

Fulper then sought to improve the existing glazes and develop new ones by enlisting the aid of Dr. Cullen Parmelee, director of the Department of Clay Working and Ceramics at Rutgers University, New Brunswick, New Jersey. William Fulper and Dr. Parmelee strove to recreate several of the ancient Chinese flambé and crystalline glazes.

Vase-Kraft Artware

By 1909, Dr. Parmelee had developed enough glazes to allow William Fulper to confidently introduce the Vase-Kraft line of art pottery. The first Vase-Kraft glazes introduced included Famille Rose, Chinese Blue, Mirrored Black, Clair de Lune, Seladon, and Rouge Flambé. These were true re-creations of the ancient Chinese glazes and were applied to Classical Chinese and Greek styled shapes. John Tierney, head of the plaster shop, sculpted the models to create the molds for this artware. A study of the centuries-old ceramics at the Metropolitan Museum of Art was all the inspiration Tierney needed to create Fulper's new shapes.

One of the first Fulper Pottery Vase-Kraft ads, appeared in Women's Home Companion, *November 1909.* Courtesy of the Hill-Fulper-Stangl Museum.

The Vase-Kraft Clair de Lune glaze was a pale, soft moon-yellow, Seladon was a soft gray-green, and both glazes used ferric oxide as their primary colorant. Rouge Flambé was a re-creation of ancient China's most sought-after copper red. Fulper's Rouge Flambé usually featured splashes of brilliant ruby red throughout a crystalline background of green or bluish green.

Fulper Vase-Kraft #25 Lily Vase in Dr. Cullen Parmelee's extremely rare Rouge Flambé glaze. Courtesy of the Hill-Fulper-Stangl Museum.

The Clair de Lune, Seladon, and Rouge Flambé glazes required a reducing atmosphere in the kiln to create their unusual coloring. These glazes were extremely difficult to fire successfully, so were discontinued by 1910.

During autumn 1909, several ads touting the new Fulper Vase-Kraft pottery were run in various household magazines such as *Good Housekeeping* and *House and Garden.*

The ads featured a small assortment of inexpensive hand-thrown and slip-cast shapes glazed in "Old Rose Matte," one of the Famille Rose glazes. The Vase-Kraft Christmas assortment promotion of 1909 was quite successful, and as a result, the Vase-Kraft art line quickly grew in popularity.

During this time, Fulper often ran two concurrent ads in most magazines. In addition to the Vase-Kraft ad, a separate ad was also run featuring Fulper's Fire-Proof cookware, lest anyone forget what Fulper Pottery was truly known for at that time.

It was during this period that William Fulper began to fully utilize the great number of home-decorating magazines to promote his products and establish name recognition. Even though Fulper products were in fact stoneware, ad copy always described them as being "earthenware." Fulper believed that the earthenware name presented a much more urbane and sophisticated image. He wanted to thoroughly eliminate the popular notion that Fulper Pottery was known only for the salt glazed crockery of America's pioneer days. Fulper placed ads in *House and Garden, The International Studio, Arts and Decoration, Good Housekeeping, The Craftsman, Vogue, The Fra, Automobile Blue Book, Vanity Fair,* and several other decorating publications and trade journals. Fulper continued to advertise heavily throughout the 1910s and 1920s, often utilizing extreme imagination and creative license in those ads.

Economize CASSEROLE
on your
meat bills
by cooking
your foods in
"Fulper"
Earthenware Utensils
and follow the recipes as printed in the Free Book of Recipes which we send with every order for the
Home Assortment of Cookers
1 large Casserole and Cover
2 small Casseroles and Covers
1 large Chicken or Game Pan and Cover
1 Marmite (for Soups) and Cover
These 5 pieces for only $2, delivered Free. Make an Ideal Xmas Gift
Your guests will envy you the hot, tasty, savory viands, cooked and served in these five quaint snub-nosed dishes. They'll all want to learn how to cook and serve "En Casserole" and "En Marmite."
MARMITE
Send Us $2.00 Right Now, together with your Dealer's name; we will see that you get the Home Assortment at once. Be the first to serve a luncheon in this new style.
FULPER POTTERY CO.
Founded 1805
9 Main St., Flemington, N. J.
Reference: Dun's or Bradstreet's.

Fire-Proof cookware ad appearing in the December 1909 Good Housekeeping *magazine.*

No. 58 Ovoid Bowl
Mustard Matte with Brown & Black Flambe
92-194-223 $4.50
FULPER VASE-KRAFT
Shows many odd forms of Pottery in Exquisite Shades and Tones of Color, and makes a most beautiful and
APPRECIATED GIFT
Write for portfolio of Lamps, Bowls, Vases, Tea Sets, Stein Sets, Cider Sets and Tobacco Jars with description and prices shown
CHRISTMAS ORDERS
by mail promptly filled
Fulper Pottery Co. Founded 1805
27 Fulper Place, FLEMINGTON, N. J.

Fulper Vase-Kraft ad appearing in The Fine Arts Journal, *December, 1910.*

Vase-Kraft's First Gold Medal

As a new potter in the field of art pottery, Fulper Pottery Company was invited to display ware at the Exhibition of Industrial Arts held at the Chicago Art Institute in Chicago, Illinois, in 1910. Fulper's Vase-Kraft exhibit was awarded the Mrs. J. Ogden Armour sponsored gold medal prize. Some of the exhibitors competing with Fulper for this prize included such established and known potters as Frederick Walrath, Rookwood Pottery, Adelaide Alsop Robineau, and Durant Kilns. The Vase-Kraft pottery was appreciated as an innovative recreation of very popular ancient ceramic forms and stylish glazes. It was also noted that most of the Vase-Kraft articles were popularly priced. "Fulper's wares are affordable even to those of modest income," stated a brief write-up on the exhibition. This gold medal, the first awarded to Fulper's art pottery, impelled William Fulper to further develop the Vase-Kraft art line. William Fulper consequently decided that the pottery needed its own on-site technician to facilitate the development of new shapes and glazes. This would be much less difficult than trying to work with distant university professors, especially considering the problems encountered in trying to mass-produce several of Dr. Parmelee's glazes.

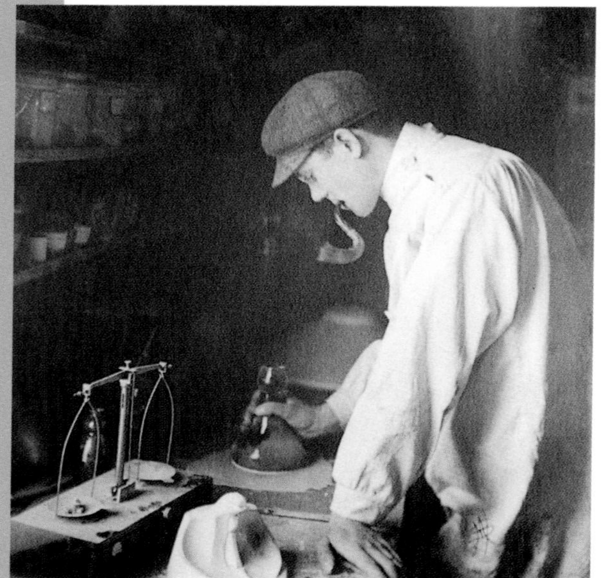

Technical superintendent Johann Martin Stangl in the laboratory at Fulper Pottery in 1910. In the foreground is the plaster model for one of Martin Stangl's first designs, the #54 fish match holder and ashtray.

Johann Martin Stangl

William Fulper would ultimately find his technician in Johann Martin Stangl. Born in Hof, Germany, Stangl studied ceramic engineering and design at the Bunzlau School of Industry and Applied Arts in Bunzlau, Germany, and graduated in 1908 with a master's degree in ceramic engineering. Martin Stangl was visiting a German friend in New Jersey during 1910 when he heard that a pottery in Flemington was searching for a ceramic technician. Thinking that he would work for a while in America, then return to Germany and start his own pottery, Stangl approached Fulper about the position. William Fulper was apparently impressed with Martin Stangl's resume because he immediately hired him as "Superintendent of Technical Department." A portion of the contract between Fulper and Stangl dated September 22, 1910 states: "In consideration of this contract between you and ourselves for three years of your service from this date as Superintendent of Technical Department of our Pottery you are to work up glazes and bodies for the best results to the company, use your best endeavors in all departments of ceramics for the good of the company. In consideration of your accepting this three-year contract, we agree to pay you a yearly salary of seven hundred eighty dollars ($780) per year, payable weekly fifteen dollars ($15) per week and a commission on art ware equal to 5% on actual sales and a commission of 2% on actual sales of Guaranteed Fire-Proof Cooking Ware. Commissions on glazed art ware and cooking ware payable monthly." Martin Stangl ultimately pursued his ceramic career in the United States and never did return to Germany except to visit family.

Fulper Vase-Kraft #67 four-handled ashtray in Mission Matte glaze, one of many Arts and Crafts shapes designed by Martin Stangl.

Martin Stangl immediately began developing new shapes, which were primarily a series of electric lamps, lighting fixtures, and vases greatly influenced by Arts and Crafts styles. Many of the shapes designed by Stangl were very bold and heavy, exemplifying earthiness and hand-craftsmanship and coordinating perfectly with the very popular Arts and Crafts and Bungalow styles of home decorating. Most of the Vase-Kraft items were mold cast, but several continued to be hand thrown, particularly the extra large "monumental" vases made specifically for exhibitions and museum displays.

New glazes were also introduced, many featuring mirrored colors, deep flambés, and highly figured crystalline surfaces. During a 1966 interview with author Robert Blasberg, Martin Stangl stated: "Fulper wanted me to create a line of artware for the factory. He was convinced there was money in it, in spite of the fiasco made by his first venture in the field. This ware had a red glaze of oriental character supplied by Professor Parmelee of Rutgers, and it required a reducing atmosphere to change the green to red. Nobody ever bought any of it, but the jobbers collected from the freight carriers when shipments arrived broken. So I did the designing for Fulper and he supplied the ideas in many cases." Martin Stangl also stated in the same interview: "At the time I began making artware for the factory in 1910, it was well known for specialties like battery supports and water coolers with a filter they got a professor out West to swear was germproof. Fulper's biggest line was heavy ware like the batter jugs Woolworth bought for 9 cents and sold for 10 cents. Each month everybody took two days off to prepare the Woolworth order, which was packed into vans drawn by big white horses."

Fulper's Vase-Kraft line of table lamps was in full production by late fall 1910 and was introduced that December. So novel was the concept of pottery lamps with pottery shades, William Fulper applied for a lamp patent on April 8, 1911. The patent was granted December 3, 1912. The Vase-Kraft table lamps and lighting fixtures were quite popular and continued to sell for nearly ten years.

William Fulper's patent for a pottery lamp and shade assembly, developed by himself and Martin Stangl.

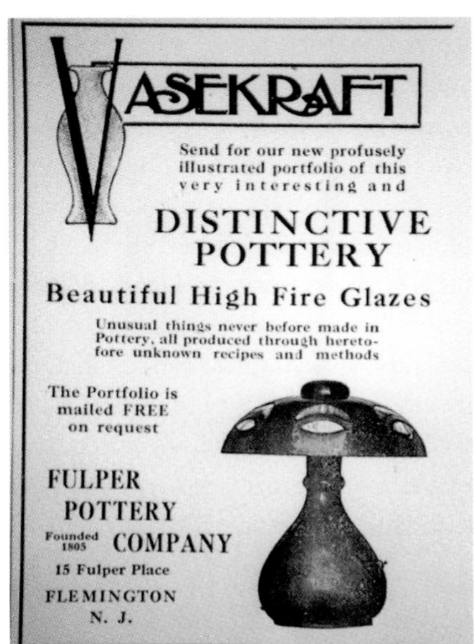

Fulper Vasekraft lamp ad, House and Garden, *December 1911. By 1911, the hyphen was removed from the name "Vase-Kraft," and it became simply "Vasekraft."* Courtesy of the Hill-Fulper-Stangl Museum.

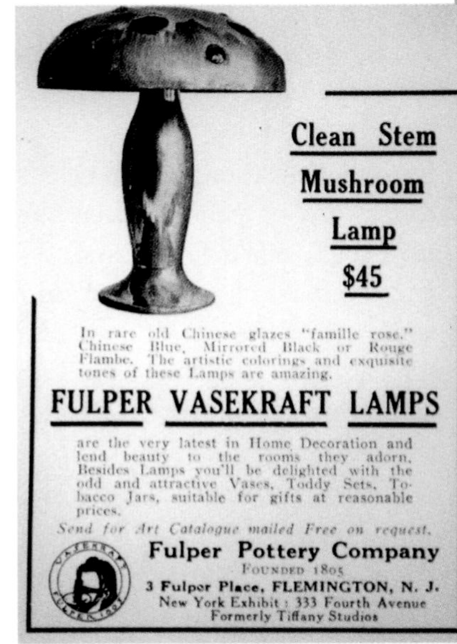

Fulper Vasekraft lamp ad, The International Studio, *December 1912.* Courtesy of the Hill-Fulper-Stangl Museum.

In 1911, Fulper Pottery leased a suite and set up a sales office and showroom at 333 Fourth Avenue, Manhattan, New York. This address had been the home of Tiffany Studios and Tiffany Glass Company since the 1880s. William Fulper maximized that fact to his best advantage on letterheads and ad copy, "New York Exhibit, formerly Tiffany Studios, 333 Fourth Ave.," even though Tiffany had vacated the building in 1904 — a full seven years prior to Fulper's lease.

The growing popularity of Fulper's Vasekraft lamps and artware prompted William Fulper to expand the artware department and promote Martin Stangl from technical superintendent to superintendent of pottery on October 19, 1911. William Fulper's memo of that date states: "M. Stangl, is Supt. of Pottery from this date, with control over all men including foremen."

The Prang Contract

Beginning in 1913, Fulper Pottery Company began producing art pottery shapes for the Prang Company of New York. Louis Prang was originally known for the color litho prints he produced during the nineteenth century. Louis Prang was a tireless leader in the advancement of art education. The standards for art education tools he set during his lifetime were continued by the Prang Company after his death. Prang's specialty was providing all materials and supplies necessary for art education and instruction for all school levels. From 1913 through 1929, the Prang Company sold Fulper artware shapes for use as still-life models for students to sketch or draw. Prang's 1924 catalog blurb stated this of Fulper's artware: "Most teachers have difficulty in securing drawing models that are inexpensive, yet beautiful in shape and attractive in color. These Prang Pottery Models were especially designed to meet this need. They offer variety and beauty in both shape and color and at the same time are inexpensive. They have been widely used for many years and give universal satisfaction. They are made expressly for us by one of the oldest and most famous Potteries in the United States. In addition to being used as drawing models, their shape and color as well as their perfect glazing enables them to be used as flower vases or for school room decoration. We offer five sets of these Pottery Models... The shape and general character of each of the pieces in each of the sets is shown in the accompanying illustrations. Each set is packed at the factory in a strong carton ready for shipment. We do not break sets."

Prang Pottery Models. Set I.

Prang Pottery Models. Set II.

Prang Pottery Models

MOST teachers have difficulty in securing drawing models that are inexpensive, yet beautiful in shape and attractive in color.

These Prang Pottery Models were especially designed to meet this need. They offer variety and beauty in both shape and color and at the same time are inexpensive. They have been widely used for many years and give universal satisfaction.

They are made expressly for us by one of the oldest and most famous Potteries in the United States. In addition to being used as drawing models, their shape and color as well as their perfect glazing enables them to be used as flower vases or for school room decoration.

Prang 1924 catalog illustration showing Fulper Pottery artware.

The Fulper shapes produced for Prang were all clearly marked "PRANG" on the bottom. Even though Prang's catalogs showed the original shapes first offered in 1913, the Prang assortments changed as older shapes were discontinued. The actual pieces provided in each Prang assortment were determined by Fulper, so not all pieces shown in Prang's catalogs were available. Because of this, the Prang Company added the following statement to the Fulper listing of the 1927 Prang catalog: "Assortments may vary — a uniform number of pieces — but different shapes in each set."

At the close of Martin Stangl's initial three-year contract with Fulper Pottery Company, he renewed his contract on September 26, 1913. This next contract was nearly identical to the original contract dated September 22, 1910. "In consideration of your services as Superintendent of factory and of technical department of our pottery, we agree to pay you yearly the salary of seven hundred eighty dollars ($780.00)... and a commission of four per cent (4%) on actual sales on all Vase Kraft pottery. In consideration of this salary and commission, you are to work up new glazes and bodies as needed; assist in designing and overseeing the general factory work, all for the benefit and advancement of the company. ...This contract can be cancelled by either party on ninety days notice." Even though Martin Stangl had been promoted to Superintendent of Pottery in 1911, his salary did not reflect the added responsibility of the position. The only compensatory increase he received in 1913 was a two percent raise in commission. Apparently, neither Martin Stangl nor William Fulper were completely satisfied with this contract as it contained the ninety-day notice cancellation clause. No such clause was in the original contract.

Stangl Departs Fulper

By 1914, Martin Stangl felt there would be no further advancement for him at Fulper Pottery Company, so he began pursuing positions elsewhere. A glowing letter of recommendation signed by William Fulper and dated April 27, 1914, states: "TO WHOM IT MAY CONCERN, This is to advise that Mr. Martin Stangl is resigning his position with us as Chemist and superintendent of plant, which position he has held with us for the last four years. We recommend him as a very competent man in handling all details of producing pottery; a splendid designer and modeler and an efficient Superintendent of the men and work. We believe he has no superior as Ceramic Chemist and will be glad to answer any inquiries concerning him. We are, very respectfully, FULPER POTTERY COMPANY."

During the first week of July 1914, Martin Stangl left Flemington for a position at Haeger Brick & Tile Co. in Dundee, Illinois. The July 1, 1914 issue of the *Hunterdon County Democrat* announced his exodus with the following "Mr. Martin Stangl, who for four years and a half has been superintendent of the Fulper Pottery here, will leave this week for Elgin, Ill., where he will be connected with the Haeger Brick & Tile Co., and produce a new line of pottery similar to the ware started here. Many of our people are familiar with the ware he introduced here. He has made many friends here who will regret that it is necessary for him to leave, but who will send with him many hopes for his success in his new field."

While at Haeger, Martin Stangl developed a line of earthen artware and glazes. In 1966 Martin Stangl had this to say about his move to Haeger: "I stayed longer (at Fulper) than either of us expected, but by 1914, I wasn't getting anywhere so I went to Haeger at Dundee, Ill. Their brickworks were no longer profitable and they wanted me to help them enter the ovenware field. I persuaded them to make artware instead. Artware! Today Haeger is our biggest competitor, and to think that they are still using the body I worked out for them during the war!" Martin Stangl came back to Flemington in December 1914 to marry his fiancee Elizabeth Case. Their honeymoon was the train trip returning to Dundee, where they then set up housekeeping.

Through the years, historians have tried to connect Stangl's Fulper and Haeger designs. Although a few of Martin Stangl's Vasekraft designs are similar to several he also developed at Haeger, they were not carried over from his Fulper days. In most cases, the designs bearing a resemblance were generic, popular stock shapes produced by many American and European pottery companies at that time. Some of the Fulper and Haeger shapes that have been compared were actually designed contemporaneously; Stangl was designing at Haeger in Dundee while Fulper's new designer John Kugler was creating independently of Stangl's influence in Flemington. Martin Stangl had this to say on the topic: "People are so funny. When I was at Haeger, buyers would bring me things I had done for Fulper and say 'Here, make us something like this.' Then when I returned to Fulper they would bring me Haeger items and ask for copies. I would never do it for them. What I do belongs to its time and place, in all cases."

A group of Haeger Art Pottery from the late 1910s through the 1920s. Not all of these shapes were designed by Martin Stangl, but he did develop all the glazes shown.

Meanwhile, Fulper's Vasekraft line was given an added boost by the publication of a glowing article titled "Vasekraft — An American Art Pottery" in *The Fine Arts Journal* in 1914. The article was authored by Evelyn Marie Stuart, editor of the Artistic Home Decoration department of *The Fine Arts Journal.* Miss Stuart was well respected for her detailed and informative articles on "home art." Miss Stuart's enthusiastic Fulper narrative praised the artistic and useful nature of Vasekraft glazes and shapes "One of the most distinguishing features of Vasekraft is the excellent taste displayed in its substantiality, which at once proclaims it as pottery making no pretense to a semblance of more delicate wares. Another distinctive feature is the individuality of each piece, no two being colored, spotted or streaked exactly alike, and yet another potent and enduring charm is the beauty, depth and richness of its many colored glazes." Miss Stuart also praised Fulper's array of functional items, "Not only in variety of beauty, however, but in variety of purpose as well, has Vasekraft taken a step in advance of most other forms of pottery, for it has been used effectively not only in vases,

Rare example of Fulper Vasekraft automobile horn in Butterscotch Flambé glaze, as mentioned by Evelyn Marie Stuart.
Courtesy of the Hill-Fulper-Stangl Museum.

steins, mugs, flagons and tea sets, but in lamps, lighting fixtures, automobile lights and horns. Its use in lamps is perhaps its strongest individual characteristic in the eyes of the general public." This article added greatly to the national popularity of Fulper's Vasekraft, which by then was being carried by major department and jewelry stores across the country.

Also during 1914, William Fulper hired designer John O.W. Kugler to add new shapes to the artware line. Many new forms were designed and produced, adding even more variety to the original assortment. Several of the new Kugler shapes featured naturalistic and Oriental motifs and designs molded in relief. The Vasekraft Mushroom and Cattail vases and Effigy fruit bowl are some of John Kugler's best-known designs.

John Tierney, foreman of the mold department, sculpted all of the models used to produce the molds for Fulper's shapes. John Kugler also designed at that time a great number of shallow bowls and figural flower frogs to satiate America's demand for vessels suitable for ikebana, Japanese-style flower arranging, which was enjoying a vogue at that time.

Popular Arts and Crafts styled Fulper Vasekraft #443 Cattail vase designed by John Kugler. From the Stangl and Fulper archival collection, courtesy the Wheaton Village Museum of American Glass.

So popular was Japanese ikebana, Fulper published a booklet on "how to arrange in the Japanese style" that was given out at Fulper retailers and showrooms. Every promotional effort was designed to keep the Fulper name in the minds of American decorators and homemakers. Also in vogue at that time were decorative figural "Book Ends" or "Book Blocks," both terms used simultaneously in Fulper's catalogs.

Illustration of a typical Japanese ikebana flower arrangement, from the May 1912 House and Garden.

Fulper also produced sculptural adaptations of artists' work other than John Kugler, such as the Sleepy Reader and Polar Bear bookends designed by Frederick G.R. Roth. Roth was an extremely talented artist and sculptor, known for his ability to capture the animal's personality and psychology in his animal studies. Two of his best-known statuary sculptures are the Columbia Lion in Baker Field, New York, and his monument to Balto the sled dog in Central Park, New York.

Fulper Vasekraft #492 "Bum the Pup" door stop, modeled after William Fulper's own English Bulldog. Courtesy of the Wayne Weigand Collection.

Fulper Vasekraft #442 flower tray and #496 canoe girl flower insert, both designed by John Kugler. Courtesy of the Hill-Fulper-Stangl Museum.

Vasekraft Artware Wins More Medals

John Kugler's new Vasekraft designs were featured in Fulper's 1914 showing at the Exhibition of Arts and Crafts at the Chicago Art Institute, where Fulper again won one of the Mrs. J. Ogden Armour Awards, this time a bronze medal. Fulper's next exhibit was in 1915 at the Panama Pacific International Exposition at San Francisco, California. Fulper Vasekraft lamps and vases shared exhibit space with Gustav Stickley's Craftsman furniture, an ideal blending of Fulper's Arts and Crafts deco-

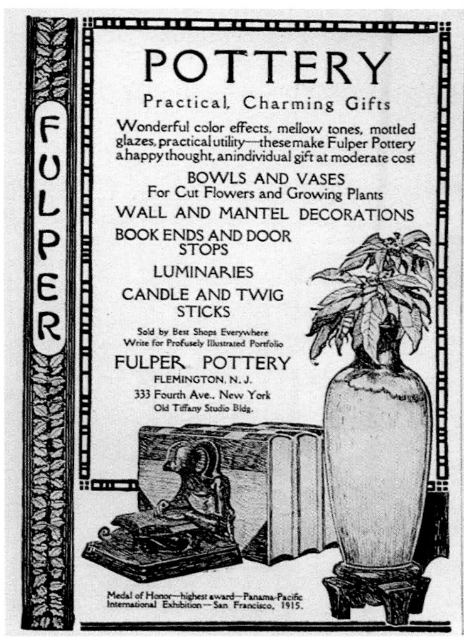

Fulper Pottery ad from the December 1915 The Decorator *magazine. Noted on the very bottom of the ad is the statement "Medal of Honor – highest award – Panama-Pacific – San Francisco, 1915."*

rative accessories with Stickley's Arts and Crafts furniture. It was this exhibit that won Fulper the gold Medal of Honor, "the highest possible award for ceramics." So proud was William Fulper of this achievement that he made sure the gold medal was mentioned in advertising, catalogs, and on paper labels affixed to Vasekraft pottery for the next several years.

Fulper Vasekraft catalog, 1916. Every page of this catalog makes mention of the winning of the Medal of Honor at the Panama Pacific International Exposition in 1915. Courtesy of the Donald Hall collection.

Fulper Brings Tourism to Flemington

By the mid 1910s, as automobiles were becoming a more and more commonplace mode of transport, Flemington often became the destination of auto outings. As the New Jersey State Highway Commission improved the state roads and trails, Flemington's accessibility from both New York and Philadelphia also improved. The Tuxedo Trail (now State Route 202) led motorists from Philadelphia through Flemington to northern New Jersey. Travelers from Manhattan, New York, could take the Lincoln Highway, also State Route 1 at the time, to New Brunswick, and from there the Amwell Road into Flemington.

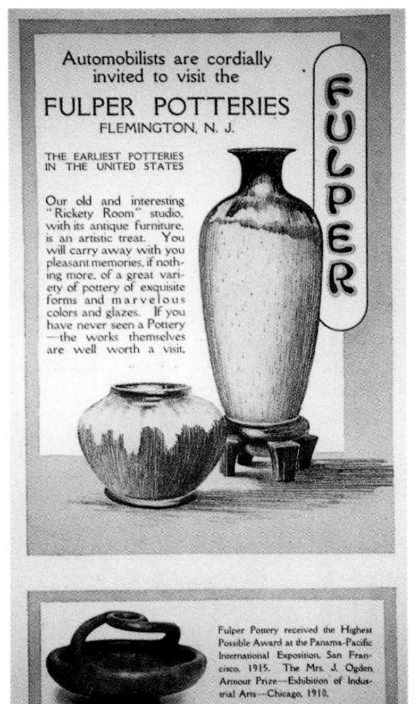

Fulper ad in Automobile Blue Book, 1917, promoting the Fulper factory and "Rickety Room" showroom as a travel destination. Courtesy of the Hill-Fulper-Stangl Museum.

Flemington's hotels were advertising Hunterdon County as "an idyllic motor destination for that long week-end" and "find that perfect rest from city noise and dirt." Fulper Pottery advertising also attempted to catch the motorist's eye. In the 1917 issue of Automobile Blue Book, an early travel guide, a full-page Fulper ad states: "Automobilists are cordially invited to visit the FULPER POTTERIES, Flemington, N.J." The ad goes on to describe Fulper's "Rickety Room" studio showroom, Flemington's very first "factory outlet." Flemington's next "factory outlet" came about in 1920 when the Flemington Cut Glass Company opened a retail showroom displaying first and second quality wares. By 1927, with the opening of the Flemington Fur Company, Flemington had become firmly established as a retail attraction and tourist destination. From these small beginnings, Flemington has become renowned for its name-brand factory outlets.

Martin Stangl and Fulper Porcelain Dolls

During World War I, the American doll industry was taking a major hit because Germany and France, practically the only producers of porcelain-bisque doll heads, were unable to supply American toy companies. One of the most prominent doll manufacturers, E.I. Horsman, contacted several potteries, including Haeger, hoping to convince them to initiate porcelain doll production. All refused, but Martin Stangl agreed to try to develop a porcelain body for doll heads. Martin Stangl stated in a 1966 interview with Robert Blasberg: "It was in 1918 that the largest doll manufacturer in America came to me at Dundee and asked me to go East and start a doll head factory." Several individuals and companies had already attempted to create a porcelain body comparable to German products, but were unsuccessful.

Martin Stangl successfully developed a porcelain formula equal to, and in some respects superior to, the porcelain from Europe. The secret to Martin Stangl's success where others had failed before him was in the grinding of the feldspar. For most ceramic applications, feldspar was ground for six to eight hours in a ball mill. The feldspar in Martin Stangl's porcelain formula was milled no less than 100 hours. Martin Stangl firmly believed that the finer the feldspar, the more translucent and vitreous the porcelain. After developing the porcelain body, Martin Stangl moved back to Flemington to seek financing for the porcelain venture and intended to set up shop on his own. Finding no ready backers, Stangl was invited by William Fulper to rejoin the company as factory manager and establish porcelain production with Fulper Pottery Company. Fulper was looking to branch into other ceramic lines at that time. American consumers had been in a general mood of nervousness since the beginning of the Great War in Europe. Consequently, Fulper's sales were down and production slowed. By 1918, Fulper's workforce had dropped to 39 from the high of 55 in 1906.

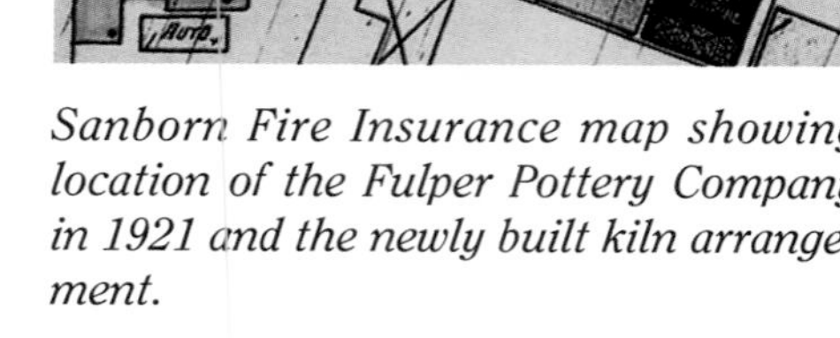

Sanborn Fire Insurance map showing location of the Fulper Pottery Company in 1921 and the newly built kiln arrangement.

With E.I. Horsman supplying start-up capital, Fulper revamped the factory for porcelain production in 1919. At that time all the kilns were replaced with three new large kilns for the cookware and artware firing and one large kiln, set off from the stoneware production, for the porcelain doll heads.

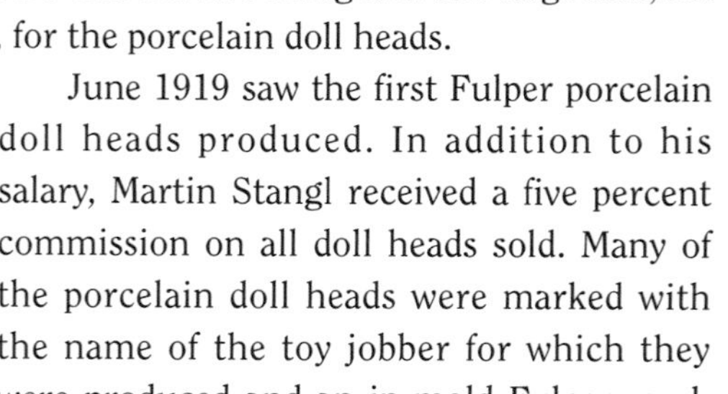

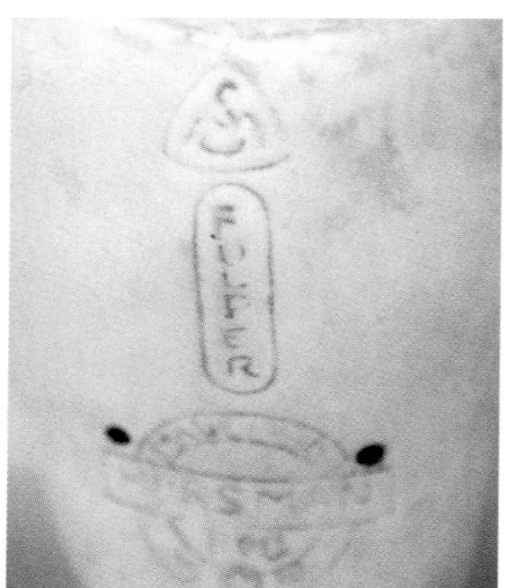

In-mold markings on a typical Fulper doll head made for the E.I. Horsman Doll Co. The Horsman trademark is on the bottom. Fulper in the center and Martin Stangl's monogram on the top. Courtesy of the Hill-Fulper-Stangl Museum.

June 1919 saw the first Fulper porcelain doll heads produced. In addition to his salary, Martin Stangl received a five percent commission on all doll heads sold. Many of the porcelain doll heads were marked with the name of the toy jobber for which they were produced and an in-mold Fulper mark and Martin Stangl's monogram. The monogram was there in deference to Martin Stangl's ownership of the porcelain body and guaranteed his five percent commission, as he had privately developed the porcelain prior to his return to Fulper and owned all rights to its use. Martin Stangl's monogram was incorporated in the markings of every piece of Fulper porcelain produced from 1919 through the early 1920s.

The doll heads were bisque porcelain and were decorated with fired-on china paints. Martin Stangl was responsible for the doll head production and decorating departments. Twenty women were initially hired and trained as decorators. Martin Stangl stated in his 1966 interview with Robert Blasberg: "Originally we made the shells of the heads only and decorated them. As it turned out, our best painter — she did eyelashes — was my wife's sister. We fitted them with eyes, teeth and tongues, and later we made a quantity of complete dolls." The doll heads were attached to cloth, kid leather or composition bodies by the toy companies who then distributed them to the retailers.

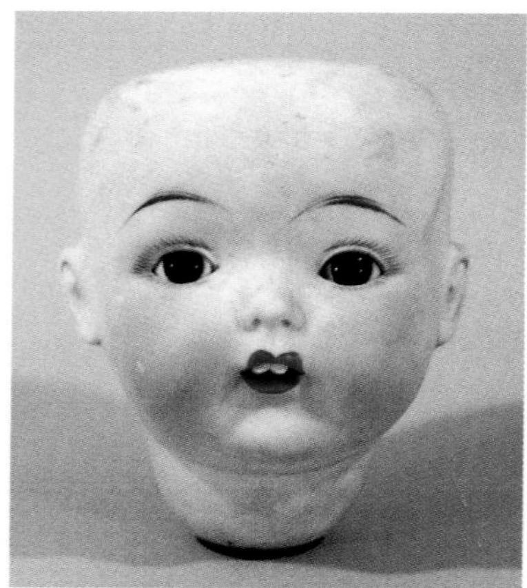

Fulper porcelain doll head. Courtesy of the Hill-Fulper-Stangl Museum.

By October 1919, increased competition caused Fulper and Horsman to part ways, and Fulper began selling to other doll companies, including Amberg Dolls, Colonial Doll Co., and American Bisque Doll Co. During peak demand, Fulper was producing 1,000 doll heads per day. Doll head production was a very lucrative product for the Fulper Pottery Company at that time. Also produced were life-sized children's heads for department store display mannequins.

Fulper Porcelain doll head on original jointed kid body with porcelain hands. Courtesy of the Hill-Fulper-Stangl Museum.

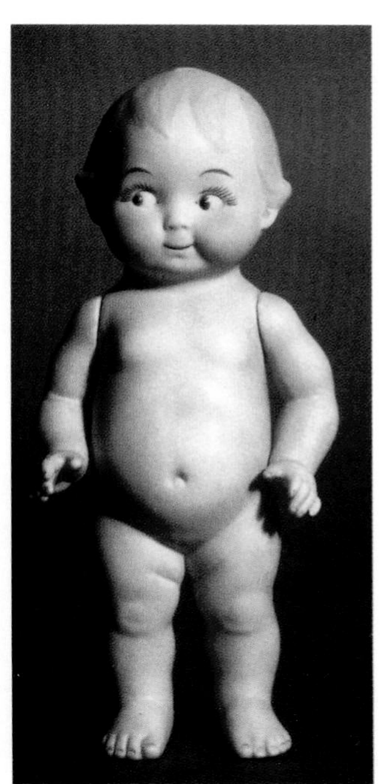

Peterkin 11" doll designed by Helen Trowbridge, produced by Fulper. This is one of the "complete" dolls referred to by Martin Stangl. Gifted to the Newark Museum, Newark, NJ, in 1920 by the Fulper Pottery Co., courtesy of the Newark Museum collection.

By late 1920, Germany was once again supplying American toy companies with inexpensive bisque doll heads, and the demand for American porcelain doll heads disappeared. Martin Stangl: "with the cheap labor of central Europe, it cost less to make an entire doll there than to fasten a pair of eyes inside an American Fulper head." By 1921, Fulper's porcelain doll production had ceased, and thousands of unsold Fulper doll heads remained in storage. By the late 1920s, space was at a premium at the Flemington plant, so the doll heads were moved to the Trenton factory where they were stored in the attic. Early in 1950, Martin Stangl claimed the mud and potholes in the driveway at the Trenton factory were ruining his new car, so he ordered the Fulper doll heads be used to fill the potholes. Once they were crushed and covered with asphalt, neither the doll heads nor the potholes bothered Martin Stangl again.

While the porcelain doll department was going strong and sales continued to climb during 1919 and early 1920, William Fulper moved the New York sales office and showroom from 333 Fourth Avenue to the new Ceramic and Glass building at 200 Fifth Avenue. Fulper also opened additional sales offices and showrooms at 40 Rue de Paradis, Paris, France; 46 Queen Victoria Street, London, England; Viale, 17 Magenta, Milan, Italy; and at 1364 Avenida De Mayo, Buenos Aires, Argentina, so as to promote Fulper Germ Proof filters and water coolers in less developed areas of the world. This was because just prior to World War I, the Fulper Germ Proof filters and water coolers were abruptly made obsolete in the United States by the rapid advancement of improved indoor plumbing and inexpensive electric refrigeration. Also, by 1920 demand for Fulper's Fire-Proof cookware ended with the development of heat-resistant glass cookware, and very cheap methods of aluminum cookware production.

The most popular decorating style of the late 1910s through the 1920s was Colonial Revival, which was executed in a wide variety of interpretations, as this 1919 photo attests.

During this same time, sales of the heavy Arts and Crafts Vasekraft products were declining as American decorative taste was changing. Coming into vogue just prior to World War I were styles based on English and Spanish motifs as well as historical revival styles such as Colonial, Empire, Beaux-Arts, and adaptations of Louis XVI styles. This was becoming the age of the revival of revivals!

The End of Vasekraft

The Arts and Crafts and Bungalow styles continued for a short time, but not in their original pure form. Interior decorators were now advocating lighter, brighter decorative themes, and furniture with ornamental turnings, carvings and applied decoration. By 1918, the Vasekraft name was discontinued, and the line simply became known as Fulper Pottery Artware. Although Fulper Pottery Artware was still a heavily glazed stoneware product, the ponderous Arts and Crafts shapes were discontinued as more graceful forms were developed and produced. The new designs introduced at that time were inspired by historical or English country styles.

New, lighter, brighter Fulper Pottery #541 Flower Flagon in Rainbow Flambé glaze; introduced in 1916 and produced through the early 1920s. Courtesy of the Hill-Fulper-Stangl Museum.

Even though Fulper is known today primarily for Vasekraft art pottery, Vasekraft was a relatively minor line in the history of Fulper Pottery Company. Fulper's prominence as an important American potter was a result of the success of the Germ Proof filters and porcelain doll heads. These were the moneymakers. The art pottery line was certainly popular but never could compete in sales or profitability with the water filters or doll heads.

Fulper could tolerate slower sales in the artware, cookware, and water filter departments as long as doll head production continued to take up the slack. However, with the drastic decline in doll head sales and the ending of the porcelain doll line in September 1921, the future appeared grim for the Fulper Pottery Company.

Fulper Porcelaines

It was the combined genius of William Fulper, Martin Stangl, John Kugler, and John Tierney that developed Fulper Pottery Company's next venture which gave the company the "shot in the arm" it needed. Capitalizing on America's growing desire for whimsical gift wares and utilizing Fulper's existing porcelain works and team of decorators, a line of quaint porcelain novelties was introduced in 1921. Simply called "Porcelains," the line featured figural perfume lamps and candy jars, decorative bells, atomizers, and powder jars. These were capricious, brightly colored, high quality items designed for sale in the better gift shops and department stores.

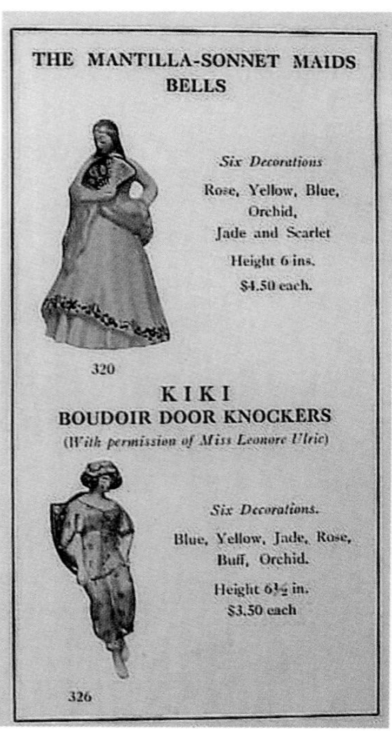

THE MANTILLA-SONNET MAIDS
BELLS

Six Decorations
Rose, Yellow, Blue, Orchid, Jade and Scarlet
Height 6 ins.
$4.50 each.

320

KIKI
BOUDOIR DOOR KNOCKERS
(*With permission of Miss Leonore Ulric*)

Six Decorations.
Blue, Yellow, Jade, Rose, Buff, Orchid.
Height 6½ in.
$3.50 each

326

A catalog page from Fulper's first "Porcelains" catalog, 1921. Featured are "The Mantilla" bell and "Kiki" door knocker. Courtesy of the Special Collections Library, Rutgers University.

Fulper Porcelain Ballet Girl perfume lamp. Courtesy of the Wayne Weigand collection.

John Tierney's sculpting of the original plaster model for the Ballet Girl perfume lamp. This model was used to cast the original mold for the Ballet Girl lamp shape.

John Kugler designed many of the figures, and John Tierney sculpted all the models. William Fulper's wife, Marietta Pierce Fulper, posed for many of the figurines. "Etta," as she was known, had been a professional dancer prior to her marriage to William Fulper in 1906. She belonged to the Gertrude Hoffman dance troupe and had been a member of the Florodora Sextette. She brought a certain coquettishness and expressive elegance to the figurine models for which she had posed. Anna Pavlova, the popular ballerina who was touring Europe and the United States during the 1920s, posed for the "Ballet Girl" perfume lamp.

Illustrator Tony Sarg also designed a series of figural candy and powder boxes featuring a cartoonish peasant woman. Tony Sarg was best known for his humorous and whimsical illustrations and marionettes, as well as for creating the giant balloons featured in many holiday parades, including Macy's Thanksgiving Day Parade, and much later in Stangl history, the Stoby mugs.

Broadway actress Lenore Ulric posed as her Kiki character from the 1921 Broadway production "Kiki" for John Tierney to model the "Kiki" boudoir door knocker.

Two of Tony Sarg's whimsical powder jars of the early 1920s. Courtesy of the Frank and Elizabeth Kramar collection.

During 1921, a major ad campaign was used to launch the Porcelains. The ad featured the Ballet Girl perfume lamp and the words "Direct From Paris! Lumier de Parfum" and again, "Direct From Paris!" in an attempt to capitalize on Americans' fascination with France, and especially with things Parisian. This was probably Fulper's most blatantly embellished ad copy, "direct from Paris," indeed! This was definitely only a hair's breadth away from serious false advertising. The Ballet Girl perfume lamp did become Fulper's best selling and most profitable porcelain. She was available in a great assortment of colors and color combinations and was continually produced from 1921 through 1929.

Fulper Porcelain Ballet Girl perfume lamp ad, "Direct From Paris!" as it appeared in December 1921. Courtesy of the Hill-Fulper-Stangl Museum.

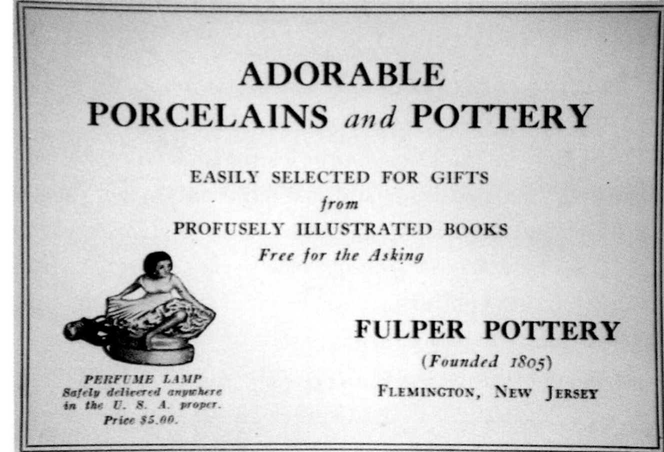

By 1924, Fulper's Porcelain advertising had been toned down considerably. Courtesy of the Hill-Fulper-Stangl Museum.

Imaginative advertising notwithstanding, the new porcelain giftware line was popular and successful but did not wholly replace doll head sales. To cut unnecessary costs, the Paris, London, Milan, and Buenos Aires offices were dropped by the end of 1922. In order to service the rapidly increasing West Coast markets, two new sales offices were opened in California. One office was at the San Fernando Building in Los Angeles and the other at the Furniture Exchange Building in San Francisco. Also at that time the New York office was moved from 200 Fifth Avenue (currently the International Toy Building) to 267-269 Fifth Avenue for a very brief time and then was moved to Room #726 at the new Ceramic, Glass and Giftware Building at 225 Fifth Avenue.

Partial view of the Fulper Pottery New York showroom display at #267 Fifth Avenue in late 1922. Courtesy of the Hill-Fulper-Stangl Museum.

Bullock's Department Store, Los Angeles, California, one of Fulper's West Coast retailers.

In 1923, the popular Porcelains line was expanded and renamed the more sophisticated "Fulper Porcelaines." The new shapes added at that time included elaborate figural and bird-inspired perfume and boudoir lamps.

In 1925, Fulper Pottery Company introduced the Fulper Decorated line of artware. Fulper Decorated items were usually whimsical or modern in style. They were made of Fulper's earthenware fayence body with solid-color glazes and decorated with the same fired-on china paints that decorated the Fulper Porcelaine products. Some of the Fulper Decorated items were painted with underglaze colors under the glaze.

The continued popularity of the Fulper Porcelaines and Fulper Decorated pottery products prompted several new introductions in 1925 and 1927. A number of these shapes featured the cartoon characters developed by Britain's cartoonist-illustrator "Fish," known for her popular cartoons in *Vanity Fair* and *Vogue*.

Fulper Decorated #901 coffee service, available during the 1920s.

Fulper Operates Briefly in Trenton

During the devastating potters' union strike of 1922 – 1923, many American potteries remained operational by hiring unskilled labor and installing automated machinery to replace the skilled union workers. This strike dealt a great blow to the Trenton, New Jersey, pottery industry as well as the potters' union. Skilled union workers found themselves permanently replaced by unskilled labor and mechanized processes or forced to work for reduced pay at non-union potteries. The strike and its aftermath also caused many of Trenton's pottery companies to close and never reopen, while others simply left New Jersey altogether and relocated in Ohio.

Fulper Pottery Company was non-union so continued to operate during the strike. William Fulper even closed the factory briefly in 1914 to prevent unionization at that time and was therefore able to continue operating during subsequent strikes. William Fulper and Martin Stangl both believed that if employees were treated fairly and paid adequate wages, their own contentment with the company would inhibit any desire to unionize. This policy of fairness on the part of Fulper and Stangl kept the company union-free until the late 1970s, long after the passing of both men.

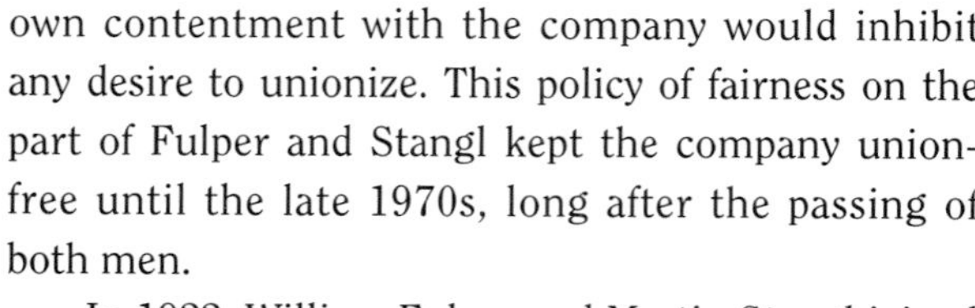

"Members of the New Jersey Clay Workers Association at the annual convention — in front of the new ceramics building, Rutgers College" as appeared in the 1922 Winter quarterly issue of The Ceramist. *Martin Stangl is in the second row, immediately behind the man with the white beard holding a hat.*

In 1922, William Fulper and Martin Stangl joined the newly formed New Jersey Clay Workers Association and attended nearly every one of the semi-annual conventions during the 1920s. It was at these conventions that Fulper and Stangl became acquainted with Enoch Mountford, general manager of Anchor Pottery in Trenton, New Jersey.

Early in 1923, Enoch Mountford approached Fulper with a proposal to utilize some of the production area at Anchor Pottery, then idle due to the potters' union strike. Fulper began leasing production space at Anchor to produce tobacco humidors. Thus, the Fulper Tobacco Jar Company division of Fulper Pottery Company was formed. Fulper employees were able to safely report to work at the Anchor factory because a court injunction prevented picketers from interfering with any pottery's operations.

Fulper Keramidor in Gunmetal Flambé glaze.
Courtesy of the Hill-Fulper-Stangl Museum.

The new tobacco jars, called "Fulper Keramidors," were novel in that they contained a built-in porous earthenware disk to maintain humidity. The porous disks employed the same patented technology that was used to produce Fulper's Germ Proof Filter 25 years earlier. The tobacco jars were launched with an ad campaign that lasted from April 1923 through July 1923. Typical ad copy read: "This most unique and beautiful piece of genuine Fulper Pottery is offered to the smoker. 6½" high and holds a pound of tobacco. Special Feature — the porous cylinder — fired into the top, which keeps contents at an even moisture, no sponge — no bother — Made in dull gun metal flambé — very decorative and useful for — the Den — Club or Home. Fulper Tobacco Jar Co. Trenton, New Jersey."

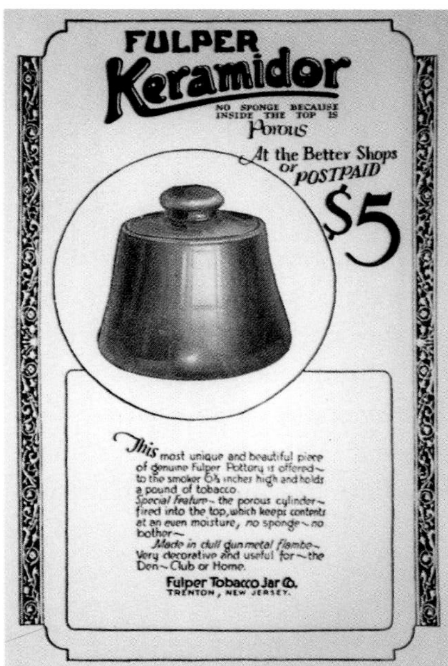

One of the several Fulper Keramidor ads published in various magazines during 1923. Courtesy of the Hill-Fulper-Stangl Museum.

Large paper label pasted to the bases of the Fulper Keramidor tobacco jars.

Earthenware "moisture cylinder" inside the lid of the Fulper Keramidor, molded with the Fulper trademark. Courtesy of the Hill-Fulper-Stangl Museum.

The tobacco jars were produced in one shape and one glaze only. They could be purchased for $5 in gift shops or department stores or ordered directly from Fulper at the Trenton address. For some of Fulper's larger accounts, a Grand Rapids furniture company was commissioned to produce oak smoking stands with a recess into which the tobacco jars fit. The complete set, a tobacco jar with an oak stand, retailed for $20.

By summer 1923, Fulper discontinued the Keramidor tobacco jar and again concentrated all production in Flemington. Although Fulper's 1923 association with Anchor Pottery was brief, it opened the door to a further, greater Trenton involvement in the future.

Fulper Pottery in Dire Circumstance — Martin Stangl Proposes Deliverance

Fulper's 1923 catalog of Fulper Pottery Artware featured over 200 different shapes in almost as many different glaze combinations. However, these were the same Arts and Crafts shapes and glazes that had always been in the line, with very few new introductions. By 1923, America's interest in the cumbersome artware shapes and earthy glazes had diminished to almost nil. Following America's economic panic of 1921, the only line receiving any interest and sales was Fulper's Porcelaines. Water filter and water cooler production had diminished drastically by World War I and Fire-Proof cookware production was reduced to a few pie plates and bean pots. William Fulper was desperately seeking a solution to save the ailing family business.

Old-timers of Flemington had long gossiped about the frequent and sometimes voluble personality clashes between William Fulper and Martin Stangl. In spite of their differences, both men had a deep and mutual respect for the other's creative and business genius. Martin Stangl, who always kept abreast of current popular trends, believed he had a solution for the ailing Fulper Pottery Company. He told William Fulper, "If you make me vice president, I will save the company." Martin Stangl was certain Fulper Pottery could profit from two major forces that had been influencing home decorating trends since just before World War I. These were the improved availability of inexpensive electrical power and the increased demand for color in household furnishings.

Martin Stangl's proposal to William Fulper included soliciting and developing more jobber accounts, introducing new lines of lighter-bodied, brightly colored decorative products, streamlining the Fulper Pottery Artware line, and discontinuing shapes that were no longer selling. Also planned was an ongoing promotional program directed toward retail consumers. William Fulper put aside any reservations he may have had about Martin Stangl's proposal "to save the company," for by 1924, changes at the pottery were well underway, and Martin Stangl was appointed vice president of Fulper Pottery Company. Consequently, 1924 marks the beginning of Stangl Pottery as its own entity, even though the Stangl Pottery brand name would not be implemented for several more years.

The first line of business for Martin Stangl was streamlining the Fulper Pottery Artware line by eliminating the shapes and glazes that were no longer selling and lowering prices in an attempt to initiate fresh sales. The new assortment for 1924 listed half the number of shapes offered in 1923 at an average price reduction of 20 percent. The new assortment in the 1924 catalog listed 110 of the most popular shapes available in only six standard glazes. Only the brightest, most vibrant glaze colors were retained. Fulper continued to offer 23 other glazes, but these were special-order and cost 50 percent more than the standard glazes.

Stangl Develops Fulper Fayence

Next on the list of Martin Stangl's objectives was the development of a brightly colored line of moderately priced pottery household accessories. The new line was made of a white earthenware body and glazed with bright, clear, solid-color glazes in Colonial Blue, Persian Yellow, Chinese Ivory, and Silver Green. This new line was formally introduced as "Fulper Fayence," and the shapes featured classically styled console sets, vases, and modern-styled dinnerware. This modern, solid-colored dinnerware in bright, vibrant hues quickly caught America's fancy and demand skyrocketed. Martin Stangl's Fulper Fayence dinnerware was considered "cutting-edge" not only because it was solid color but also because it was carried by department stores in complete sets and open stock. The shopper was able to purchase one or 100 pieces! Until that time, dinnerware was sold only in complete sets. If a homemaker broke any dinnerware, replacement pieces had to be ordered from the company that produced it, if indeed the pattern was still being produced. With department stores now selling sets as well as individual pieces of Fulper Fayence dinnerware, repeat sales and customer loyalty were promptly developed. Homemakers were now confident that replacement and additional pieces matching their dinnerware would be available, so they bought greedily this exciting, fresh dinnerware so vastly different from the fussy, blossom bedecked patterns of the past.

Fulper Fayence dinnerware pattern #901, America's first solid-colored, open stock dinnerware pattern.

Expansion in Flemington

Fulper Pottery had done special-order earthenware production in the past, so was certainly capable of manufacturing the new Fulper Fayence line with ease. Advance showings of the line during the fall of 1923 generated great interest and enough orders to warrant increased production. It soon became quite clear that more space was needed for its production. However, there was absolutely no room left for expansion at Fulper Pottery. All available buildings and land were utilized to their fullest.

Fulper Pottery Co. officer and stockholder, Judge George K. Large.

Enter William Fulper's longtime friend, Judge George K. Large, with a solution. What had begun as a neighboring business venture that failed ultimately became Fulper's immediate remedy. On June 14, 1916, Judge Large purchased nearly three acres of land from the Belvidere & Delaware division of the Pennsylvania Railroad adjacent to the freight depot at Mine Street, Flemington. In 1921 Judge Large sold a portion of the property at #48 Mine Street to Charles N. Darlington and T. Walter Hanum. Darlington and Hanum constructed a cement block building for manufacturing candy novelties and in May 1921 officially began operating the "D. & H. Confectionery Company."

By 1923, it was evident to Darlington and Hanum that no profit was to be realized from their venture, as they owed Judge Large nearly $10,000 for the property mortgage and construction costs. Therefore, Judge Large then offered his Mine Street property to Fulper for expansion. On February 21, 1924, William H. Fulper purchased the bankrupt D. & H. Confectionery Company and property. Also purchased by Fulper was the remainder of the original acreage purchased by Judge Large in 1916. In consideration for this deal, Judge Large became a stockholder in the Fulper Pottery Company at that time and ultimately served as vice president of the company from 1926 through the 1940s.

Plans for expansion were drawn up that included construction of four kilns and 11,000-square feet of additional production space. It was decided to expedite production by constructing only one kiln and one-third of the planned floor space during 1924, and the rest at a later date. Fulper immediately began construction at the former D. & H. Confectionery building. A blurb in the June

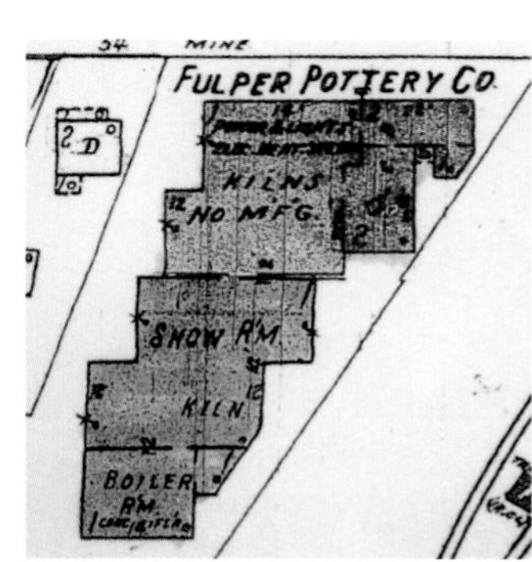

Sanborn Fire Insurance map showing location of Fulper Pottery's Plant #2. The pink shaded area indicates the D. & H. Confectionery and original 1924 addition. The blue shaded area represents the addition added in 1929 – 30.

1924 *The Ceramist* stated: "N.J., FLEMINGTON – The Fulper Pottery Co., manufacturer of art pottery, has acquired the property in the vicinity of its plant, previously used by the D. & H. Candy Co., to be remodeled and improved for an addition to its pottery. The extension, it is understood, will be equipped primarily for the production of a line of popular-priced art pottery. Work has been commenced on a one-story addition, 70x80 ft., to be used as a kiln shed; two new kilns will be constructed." Money for this expansion and development of the new line was procured by Martin and Elizabeth Stangl mortgaging their properties and William Fulper borrowing from the Flemington Building and Loan. All loans were repaid within a year.

By late summer 1924, the new facility was operational. It housed a bank of belt-driven potter's wheels, an expansive production area, and one kiln for firing the product. This building became known as Plant #2, while the original Fulper factory was called Plant #1. Plant #2 produced the brightly colored Fulper Fayence art and dinnerware, while the heavy Fulper Pottery Artware and whimsical Fulper Porcelaine and Fulper Decorated items continued to be produced at Plant #1.

Fulper Pottery Company's Plant #2 as seen from Mine Street, circa 1950.

John Kunsman Takes Fulper on the Road

Martin Stangl's next phase in attempting to save Fulper Pottery Company involved establishing consumer recognition with the Fulper Pottery name. To accomplish this, Martin Stangl enlisted the aid of Fulper's master potter John Kunsman. Kunsman had been with Fulper Pottery since 1888. He had begun as a potter, hand-throwing stoneware crocks and jugs, and was ultimately involved in factory improvements and developing several Fulper artware lines. Martin Stangl felt that John Kunsman's personable and easygoing personality made him an ideal candidate for publicly representing Fulper Pottery Company. In 1924 John Kunsman began demonstrating how pottery is made at prominent department stores and pottery exhibits across the country. The demonstrations were conducted as near to Flemington as New Brunswick, New Jersey, or as far away as Atlanta, Georgia or St. Louis, Missouri, but always at a retailer that carried Fulper Pottery Company products. Not only did this generate a consumer interest in pottery, but other retailers soon recognized John Kunsman's drawing power and, more importantly, the crowds he attracted to the well publicized demonstrations. These retailers also began to carry Fulper products, so that they too could host the popular John Kunsman demonstrations.

A 1920s view of the prominent Bamberger's Department Store, Newark, New Jersey.

John Kunsman demonstrating at a Fulper Pottery display at Bamberger's Department Store in 1925.
Courtesy of the Hill-Fulper-Stangl Museum.

Kunsman traveled with a potter's wheel, a small portable electric kiln, and enough clay and glazes needed to demonstrate the potter's art while promoting Fulper products. Demonstration items were produced in Fulper Pottery clay and glazes as well as Fulper Fayence clay and glazes. As he demonstrated, Kunsman explained to onlookers the ancient art of the potter, as well as modern ceramics production.

A pair of handmade double candlesticks produced by John Kunsman during pottery demonstrations. Courtesy of the Hill-Fulper-Stangl Museum.

Throughout the 1920s and 1930s, John Kunsman made many trips to distant department stores and exhibitions to promote Fulper products and demonstrate pot throwing. Some of the stores where he demonstrated were Bamberger's, S.S. Kresge, and Hahne's in Newark, and M.E. Blatt's in Atlantic City, New Jersey; Ovington's, R.H. Macy's, Nieman-Marcus, and Bloomingdale's in Manhattan, New York; John Wanamaker's and Strawbridge & Clothier's in Philadelphia and Hess's in Allentown, Pennsylvania; Hutzler Brother's in Baltimore, Maryland; Rich's in Atlanta, Georgia; Mendelssohn's in St. Louis, Missouri; L.B. Judson and Marshall Field in Chicago, Illinois; S.S. Kresge in Detroit, Michigan; Loveman's in Chattanooga, Tennessee; and Jordan Marsh in Boston, Massachusetts. Kunsman's demonstrations were very popular and always received great local press coverage, all of which was calculated to establish the Fulper Pottery name as a leader in American ceramics.

A group of miniature vase, jug, and flowerpot forms produced by John Kunsman at his pottery demonstrations. Courtesy of the Hill-Fulper-Stangl Museum.

Stangl Procures Jobber Accounts

Finally, we come to Martin Stangl's most important aspect of his deal with William Fulper to "save the company." During early 1924, while overseeing production of Fulper Fayence and the expansion at Plant #2, Martin Stangl also began developing a very large customer base of jobber accounts. Fulper Pottery had a few jobber accounts prior to 1923, such as the Prang Company beginning in 1913 and the toy and doll manufacturers during World War I. It was Martin Stangl's dynamic sales ability that expanded Fulper's commercial customer base during the 1920s. The jobber contracts negotiated by Stangl for ceramic products included importers, lamp companies, gift shops, department stores, food and spice packers, jewelers, metal wares producers, and cosmetics companies. For some companies, Fulper produced only one or two shapes, while for others hundreds of different shapes were produced. The jobber goods were made of all brands of Fulper's product lines, including Fulper Pottery Artware body and glazes, Fulper Porcelaine, and Fulper Fayence body and solid-color glazes.

Fulper Pottery Artware musical jug made for Ritz Manufacturing Enterprise.

Jars for cosmetics were produced for Kramer, Claudia, and R. Louis. Food and spice companies such as Patty's Studio, Mount Hope, E. C. Rich, Arden Farm, and Raffetto packed their products in Fulper containers. Ironically, Fulper produced more musical whiskey jugs and decanters for Sprague and Ritz Manufacturing Enterprise during Prohibition than at any other time in history.

Fulper also manufactured ceramic ashtray inserts for Ronson's Art Metal Works, Frankart, Inc., Nuart Metal Creations, Bronzart, and A.P.T. metal companies. For gift and department stores such as R.H. Macy, Bamberger's, S.S. Kresge, and Rena Rosenthal, anything from vases and lamps to cigarette boxes and novelty ashtrays were produced.

Candy dish insert produced by Fulper for Frankart, Inc., during the 1920s. Courtesy of the Negley collection.

Although Fulper Pottery Company was a rural Hunterdon County pottery, more of its products were shipped to distant cities than were sold in Flemington. During the 1920s, 90 percent of Fulper's output was sent to metropolitan jobbers and department stores, while only 10 percent was sold in Flemington.

Lamps

But it was lamps that Fulper produced in the greatest quantity. In the 10 years between 1924 and 1934, over 400 different lamp shapes were designed and produced for 20 different lamp, gift, and import companies. But why so many lamps?

America's table lamp craze had its beginnings shortly after the turn of the nineteenth century into the twentieth. From the 1880s until the early 1900s, many new and existing homes were being wired for electricity. However, only ceiling fixtures or wall brackets were used to provide light, as homes were not yet wired with electric outlets. Portable table lamps or electric appliances were powered by screwing the plug-end into the ceiling fixtures or wall brackets, so lamps and appliances could only be used directly under those fixtures. As a result, all manner of socket adapters and extension cords were developed as electric appliances became commonplace during the 1910s and homemakers sought to maximize the few outlets they had.

Two ads for the Benjamin "Two-Way Plug." Ads for such adapters were run in many magazines from 1910 to 1920.

As the Bungalow style of home construction spread across the nation, nearly all new homes were wired for electric lighting, and wall or floor outlets were becoming commonplace as homeowners demanded more convenient electric power. From 1911 to 1918 Fulper capitalized on this by producing Vasekraft table lamps and lighting fixtures.

By the mid 1910s as electric outlets now provided power to nearly every corner of a room, top decorators were advocating greater use of table lamps. The decorators' reasoning was that several properly shaded table lamps in a room imparted an even-shadowed and glare-free light that ceiling fixtures could not provide. At last, a world without eyestrain! Reading or needlework could now be done comfortably in the home any time of day or night. Glare-causing ceiling fixtures were becoming something to be shunned. This prompted a lamp craze that began just before World War I and lasted right through the 1930s.

Fulper Pottery Company 1916 catalog page showing a few of the Vasekraft lamps available.

At the beginning of the table lamp craze, the fashionable lamps to own were antique Chinese or Japanese vases drilled and fitted with silk shades. Carved Chinese jade or rose quartz statuary mounted on lamp bases were also popular. Many American import companies made their fortunes supplying America with Oriental antiques converted to lamps. As the true antiques became scarce, new Chinese reproductions were being imported as the craze for Chinese-styled lamps lasted well into the 1920s.

Demand for table lamps during the early 1920s was so great that nearly any vase became a candidate to be mounted as a lamp. Even Fulper Pottery was offering pre-drilled vases at that time. The 1925 catalog stated:

A 1930 ad for General Electric's Wiring System for home rewiring. Throughout the 1920s and early 1930s, General Electric advertised heavily in all home magazines advocating home rewiring "The General Electric Wiring System ... assures you plenty of outlets where you need them." Such ads propelled America's table lamp craze even further.

"Drilling is done before firing, requiring special factory handling for which there is a charge of 20%." Fulper also sold lamp adapters in three sizes for "Instantly converting Vases into Lamps without drilling."

By the mid 1920s, as suburban housing developments began springing up at the outskirts of nearly every American city, the lamp craze grew even more intense. All of the new homes were fully wired with electric wall outlets and very few ceiling fixtures. Many rooms now required a full complement of table lamps, which set off a demand that lamp companies could not satiate.

Import and gift companies were competing for the same lamp bases that traditional lighting companies were seeking. Metal, glass, and ceramics companies began producing articles made specifically to be lamp bases; and they could not keep up with the demand! By the late 1920s, Chinese lamp styles were still reigning, but Jazz Modern and Modernism (as Art Deco was called then) and handmade Italian styles were also in vogue. Fulper Pottery Company produced lamp bases in all these styles in their Fayence, Porcelaine, and Pottery body and glazes. Fulper could provide nearly any type, style, body, glaze or color needed by a jobber.

Fulper Pottery lamp adapter with brass stem and sockets with a Fulper Pottery vase that could become a lamp without being drilled. Courtesy of the Hill-Fulper-Stangl Museum.

A 1923 Colonial style living room with a Chinese table lamp on the davenport table, a smaller lamp on the writing desk, and a floor lamp seen reflected in the mirror on the right. There are no ceiling or wall fixtures, so table lamps are a necessity. Note also the Fulper Pottery Peacock bookends on the end table, the Fulper Pottery vase on the davenport table, and the Fulper Pottery candlesticks and bowl on the console table to the far right.

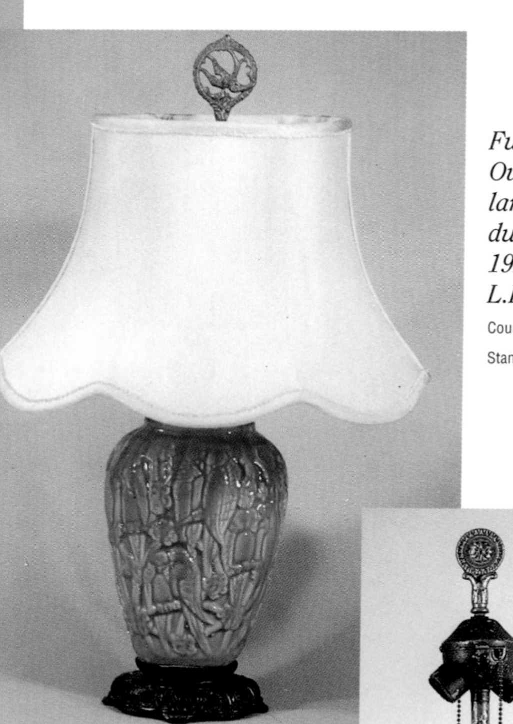

Fulper Fayence Oval Lovebirds lamp produced during the 1920s for the L.D. Bloch Co. Courtesy of the Hill-Fulper-Stangl Museum.

Fulper Pottery Egyptian lamp, late 1920s. Courtesy of the Bullock collection.

Martin Stangl Becomes President of Fulper Pottery Company

It was Martin Stangl's development of the extensive jobber accounts, and most particularly the lamp accounts, which did indeed "save" the Fulper Pottery Company during the 1920s. It was also the jobber accounts that enabled the company to remain solvent throughout the Great Depression of the 1930s.

In 1926 William Fulper appointed Martin Stangl president of the Fulper Pottery Company in consideration for Stangl's having saved the company from economic failure and re-establishing it as leader in American ceramics. At that time Judge George K. Large became vice president, and William Fulper assumed the positions of secretary and treasurer.

Fulper-Stangl Brand Introduced

Once Martin Stangl became president of Fulper Pottery in 1926, he and William Fulper instituted a new Fulper-Stangl trademark. This was an effective way to connect the Stangl name with the Fulper Pottery reputation for outstanding high quality. The Fulper-Stangl trademark was applied to new dinnerware shapes and artware lines. Even though the Fulper Fayence and Fulper-Stangl products were made of the same earthenware body and solid-color glazes, each line had its own style characteristics. The Fulper Fayence shapes were Classical and Oriental in style, while Fulper-Stangl shapes featured ultra modern and ultra primitive styles. The Fulper-Stangl trademark never replaced the Fulper Fayence brand name. Both logos were used simultaneously on solid-color glazed earthenware products from 1926 until 1929 when both logos were replaced with the Stangl trademark, which had been in use on several items since 1927.

Fulper Pottery Company Tries Trenton — Again

By 1926, demand for lamp bases and Fulper's new solid-color dinnerware had grown to such proportions that production space at Plants #1 and #2 suddenly became very limited. The insufficient and cramped manufacturing facilities threatened to seriously impact Fulper's meeting production deadlines. Additional manufacturing space was immediately sought and was found in the form of their old friend in Trenton, Anchor Pottery.

Anchor Pottery was located on Trenton's New York Avenue, 23 miles from the Flemington plants. The first pottery to occupy the Anchor site was the East Trenton Porcelain Company, begun by Imlah Moore in 1864. The company was purchased by Israel Lacey in 1884 and was renamed Anchor Pottery.

The 1906 Trenton City Directory listed Anchor Pottery as manufacturing dinnerware and toilet ware and employing 250 persons. Anchor produced white graniteware and semi-vitreous dinnerware with transfer decorations often trimmed with gold.

Trenton's famous slogan, "Trenton Makes — The World Takes," was erected in neon on the bridge spanning the Delaware River between Trenton, New Jersey, and Morrisville, Pennsylvania, in 1935. Even though Trenton is no longer the manufacturing center it once was, this legendary 330' x 9' sign continues to illuminate the Delaware River today.

Early 1900s "bird's eye view" of Trenton, showing the industrial district of East Trenton in the distance.

In 1907, Anchor began producing premiums for the Grand Union Tea Company and the Great Atlantic & Pacific Tea Company. This was a profitable business until lower tariffs on imported goods allowed greater competition from German and Japanese potteries. This foreign competition plus competition from Ohio potteries conspired with the potter's union strike of 1922 – 23 to deal a nasty blow from which Anchor Pottery never fully recovered. Depressed pottery sales were experienced nationally, as reported in the September 1925 *The Ceramist:* "...the general ware trade was experiencing 'rather poor' conditions and that potteries both at Trenton and the middle western states were operating at about 65 per cent capacity." In an effort to assuage this situation, the United States Potters Association was planning a "Buy American" campaign by targeting advertising to "...American housewives to interest them in American-made chinaware and semi-porcelain ware as a means of meeting foreign competition and bettering the slackening conditions in the pottery industry."

In 1926 Anchor Pottery secretly offered production space to Fulper Pottery, secretly, because it was feared that Anchor's contracts with the Grand Union and A&P Tea Companies would be jeopardized if it became known that Anchor's business was so poor that they had to sublet space just for additional operating income.

Secretly, Fulper Pottery moved a small contingent of potters to the Anchor Pottery buildings in Trenton and began producing the Fulper Fayence and Fulper-Stangl solid-color dinnerware in early 1926. Martin Stangl oversaw production at Trenton, while William Fulper managed the two plants in Flemington.

The Fulper Pottery Artware and Fulper Porcelaine lines continued to be produced at Plant #1, while Fulper Fayence and Fulper-Stangl solid-color earthenware artware was produced at Plant #2. Fulper's Plant #1 also continued to house the very popular tourist attraction, the "Rickety Room" showrooms. All brands of Fulper Pottery Company's various products were displayed and sold in the Rickety Room.

The popularly held explanation for moving dinnerware production to Trenton was William Fulper's alleged dislike for solid-color dinnerware. William Fulper's personal taste may have prevented him from using solid-colored dinnerware in his home, but he never would have entrusted Martin Stangl with the future of his family's business by promoting him to company president if he did not have full confidence in Stangl's dynamic business capabilities. In addition, William Fulper risked his home by mortgaging it to the Flemington Building and Loan to finance the move to Trenton and the development of the Fulper-Stangl product line (Martin Stangl also mortgaged his home for $2,500 for the same purpose). Are these the actions of a man with no faith in the products his company is producing?

Moreover, being a sound businessman himself, William Fulper recognized that there was much more profit to be had by moving dinnerware production to the Anchor facility than to expand at either of the properties in Flemington. The Anchor buildings were immediately available and already equipped with all the fixtures necessary for dinnerware production. With orders for the solid-color dinnerware backing up, there was simply no time to build additions in Flemington. The Anchor buildings also had three rail sidings and a canal slip, serviced by two separate railroad companies and an active canal. This greatly facilitated the receiving of raw material and coal and the shipping of finished products. Both Plant #1 and Plant #2 in Flemington required supplies to be trucked to and from rail platforms with greater handling expenses.

Anchor Pottery buildings as they appeared when Fulper Pottery Company began leasing space there in the 1920s. In the foreground is the Delaware and Raritan Canal.

As an incentive for employees living in the Flemington area to transfer to the Trenton plant, Martin Stangl supplied a jitney-bus to convey them from Flemington to Trenton and back. From the 1920s through the 1960s, this transportation service was provided by Stangl. After World War II Martin Stangl replaced the jitney-bus with station wagons. During the 1950s, as many as three station wagons were making the daily trips to and from Flemington. Some of Stangl's drivers over the years were Andy Koscis, Harry Slader, Clinton Peterman, and John Teyhen. During the times when there were only one or two employees commuting from Flemington to Trenton, Mr. Stangl simply carpooled with them in his own car.

Another Gold Medal for Fulper

In 1926, William Fulper and Martin Stangl began to re-establish Fulper Pottery Company as an exhibitor at prominent public expositions. Fulper Pottery participated in the Sesqui-Centennial International Exposition at Philadelphia, Pennsylvania that year, and won a gold medal for its art pottery display. An article in the November 1926 *The Ceramist* described the Fulper exhibit thus: "Another distinctive type of American art pottery exhibited was the product of works situated in Flemington, N.J. In innumerable appealing shapes, this ware distinguished for beauty and variety of glaze and delicate coloring did not depend upon applied design for charm or originality. In Chinese or Venetian blues, in violet or yellow flambé, in jade or cucumber green, in moss-rose, copperdust, café au lait, or black and buff, it all appealed by the soft blending of tints, individuality of finish, and exquisite form of vases, bowls, candlesticks, jugs, and the various objects to which the ceramic lends itself.

"With the main exhibit there was also a collection of interesting novelties in hand decorated porcelain, containing flower candlesticks, ash trays designed by a well-known cartoonist, perfume burners, lamps, and other articles that attracted by their originality." This was the eighth medal to be awarded to Fulper Pottery Company since the first was won in 1880. These are certainly proud achievements of which only a few American potteries can boast.

A brief overview of operations at Fulper was chronicled in a notice published in *The Ceramic Age* in May 1927. "Students in the sophomore and junior classes at Rutgers University, enrolled in the ceramics division, recently visited the Fulper Pottery at Flemington, N.J. The trip was made by automobile, under the direction of Messrs. Catlin and Henry, instructors in the department.

"The Fulper Pottery, occupying a two-story frame building near the center of the town, is devoted to three distinct lines of manufacture, china, stoneware, and a low-fired ware called 'Fayence.' The plant uses New Jersey clays for the production of the two last noted, while foreign clays are employed for the manufacture of china.

"The casting method is principally used at this plant, but some ware is jiggered. The stoneware and china are both biscuited before the glaze is applied and then are fired to a high temperature so the glaze and the ware mature at the same temperature. This is claimed to give a stronger product and lessen the chance of dunting. The kilns are sealed as soon as the firing has been completed and are allowed to cool very slowly.

"The 'Fayence' ware is a low-fired body with a very strong glaze, also low-fired. In this type of art pottery the colors are most perfectly developed because of the facility of control at the lower temperatures. Most of the novelty ware is made of this type."

The 1920s — Modernism and Primitive

During the late 1920s, two diametrically opposed styles of decoration were suddenly "up-to-the-minute" fashion. The style most remembered today is Art Deco, called "Modernism" and "Jazz Modern" at the time. The Modernism style was made popular by the Exposition Internationale des Arts Décoratifs et Industriels held in Paris in 1925 and embodied bold, colorful patterns, circles, rakish angles, and skyscraper motifs. In Europe, this style was adapted to all manner of objects, including furniture and home architecture. Buildings large and small and every piece of furniture and decorative accessory were fully enveloped in Modernism. The American version of the Modernism style was much less exaggerated and was primarily reserved for fabrics, decorative accessories, lamps, jewelry — and skyscrapers.

While the Modernism style was running full-tilt, the "Primitive" style began gaining in popularity. Just as the Arts & Crafts movement was a reaction to late Victorian overly-ornamented styles and the under-appreciation of handicrafts a generation earlier, America's fascination with handmade products during the late 1920s was a direct reaction against the widespread use of automated, mechanized factory production and the Jazz Modern "Machine Age." The penchant for Primitive styles was most evident in the textile, pottery, and glass industries. Hand-thrown pottery became all the rage. Old-time potters in the Seagrove, North Carolina area who had produced handmade wares for their own local use for generations, suddenly found New York jobbers and department store buyers clamoring for their products. Brightly decorated "Peasant Art" china was being shipped from England and Czechoslovakia in fantastic quantities. Colorful and unsophisticated pottery vases with sgraffito designs were brought from Spain, Portugal, and Italy. America could not seem to satisfy its desire for these homey, unsophisticated products.

An adaptation of American Modernism. Modernistic pieces, such as the low-slung club chairs and skyscraper bookcase, are mixed with American Colonial antiques. This is the type of Modernism interior many American designers advocated. Modernism fabrics, draperies, and accessories were often used to complete the modern theme.

Fulper Pottery produced wares in both Modernism and Primitive styles. Reuben Haley, of the Consolidated Glass Company in Coraopolis, Pennsylvania, designed a few of the Fulper-Stangl Modern-styled dinnerware and lamp shapes. Several years later, Haley also developed several Modernism designs for Muncie Pottery in Muncie, Indiana as well as the modern Ruba Rombic and primitive Catalonian glass designs produced at Consolidated Glass.

Fulper-Stangl Square Modern #1081 dinnerware designed by Reuben Haley in 1925.

The designer for Fulper's Fulper-Stangl brand of Primitive handmade artware was found right at home. After hand-turning Fulper's art and utility wares for nearly 40 years, no one could be more qualified to develop a handmade art line than John Kunsman. Simple, well-proportioned shapes showing clear evidence of being hand-wrought were developed and produced by Kunsman.

John Kunsman remained the primary potter of this line, but because of its astounding success, two additional potters were added in 1928 and two more in 1930. During the "Machine Age" of factory automation, it was still much more economical for potters to hand-throw these shapes than to have them mold-cast. John Kunsman liked to amaze onlookers by stating that he could throw as many as 300 flowerpots with attached saucers in eight hours, "...cheaper than they could be turned out by machinery." Margaret H. Fort, in an article written for *New Jersey Life* in 1931, had this to say about the Fulper-Stangl handmade artware: "Every one of these men is an artist, turning out I don't know how many different kinds of vases, lamps, figures and what-not in a day. Nowadays they have machines also that make these articles, but what surprised me was the fact that it is no cheaper or faster to use them. And hand-finished work is always so much more interesting."

An assortment of Fulper-Stangl handmade artware illustrating the variety of shapes developed by John Kunsman. Courtesy of the Hill-Fulper-Stangl Museum.

Fulper Pottery Company original promotional photo showing the newly designed #735 ten-piece table set in 1925.

Even with the addition of delicately styled forms and brighter glazes, Fulper Pottery Artware sales continued to weaken during the late 1920s. However, orders for brightly colored Fulper Fayence and Fulper-Stangl dinnerware and lamps persistently increased. Fulper's 1926 catalog showed a reduction of available shapes in both Fulper Pottery Artware and Fulper Porcelaines but listed additional new shapes in the Fulper Fayence line. To boost the lagging Fulper Pottery Artware, new shapes in both Primitive and Modern styles were introduced during 1927 and 1928.

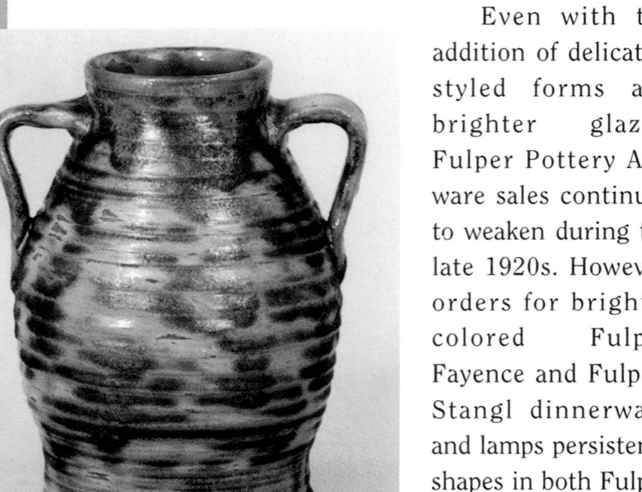

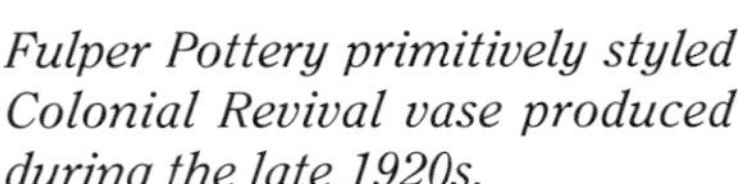

Fulper Pottery primitively styled Colonial Revival vase produced during the late 1920s.

Fulper Pottery #833 Modern Cat door stop introduced in 1928.

Fulper Pottery Modern vase, introduced in 1929.

Fulper Pottery Expands at Trenton

Near the end of 1927, Anchor Pottery Company closed forever, another victim of brutal competition from imported dinnerware and cheaper grades of dinnerware produced in Ohio. Since Anchor no longer had contracts to protect, it was now possible for Fulper Pottery to publicly proclaim its move to Trenton. An announcement in the June 1928 *The Ceramic Age* stated: "The Fulper Pottery Co., Flemington, N.J., manufacturer of art pottery, is now operating at the plant of the Anchor Pottery, Trenton, in which the company became interested a couple of months ago, as reported in these columns at that time. The Trenton plant is being run as a branch of the Flemington Works, and will develop large output of the well known Fulper art ware." Once Anchor had vacated the premises, Martin Stangl was then able to expand his operations and lease a bit more of the factory. Martin Stangl again mortgaged his home and property in Flemington to gain the additional $6,000 necessary for the expansion at Trenton and development of new Fulper Pottery Artware and Fulper Fayence shapes. By the end of 1927, a total of 81 people were employed between the Flemington and Trenton plants. The name of Fulper Pottery's Trenton facility soon became known as the "Fulper-Stangl Pottery," a name it continued to carry well into the 1950s. The Fulper Pottery Company was reorganized in 1955 and officially became the Stangl Pottery Company on December 28, 1955.

Fulper Pottery Company buildings, Trenton, NJ, front view, 1930. The packing house is on the left, the offices were in the small building to the right of the car. During the 1940s, Martin Stangl moved the offices to a second story addition that replaced the large kiln in the center of the photo. From the Stangl and Fulper archival collection, courtesy the Wheaton Village Museum of American Glass.

Fulper Pottery Company buildings, Trenton, NJ, 1930. The two gable-end buildings on the left housed the plaster shop, mold storage, casting, and jiggering operations. The low building to the right was the slip house that contained all the clay processing equipment. From the Stangl and Fulper archival collection, courtesy the Wheaton Village Museum of American Glass.

One of the Trenton pottery periodic kilns (above) being loaded with saggers containing glazed ware for firing. These kilns were fired with Pennsylvania soft coal, and it took approximately 48 hours from the sealing of the kiln for the fire to reach the desired temperature (most of Stangl's products matured between 1800° and 2200° F) and then cool enough to open the kiln again. Another periodic kiln (left) being loaded with dinnerware saggers; the kilnmen always carried full saggers on their heads and rarely dropped or jostled any! Note the stacks of saggers in the foreground and the ladder used inside the kiln to stack the saggers to the ceiling.

Fulper Pottery Company formally introduced the "Stangl Ware" brand of ceramic products in late 1927. Stangl Ware, which was marked with a Stangl Pottery gold-foil paper label, featured newly styled artware shapes. The Fulper Fayence and Fulper-Stangl brands continued as separate lines until 1929, when all three lines were consolidated into one line called "Stangl Pottery, made by Fulper Pottery Company."

Fulper Pottery and the International Exhibition of Contemporary Ceramic Art

Late 1928 saw Fulper Pottery Company once again become acknowledged by the true art world, something that had not happened since Fulper's early showings at the Chicago Art Institute during the 1910s. The American Federation of Arts invited Martin Stangl to provide a representative collection of Fulper products to be displayed in the "International Exhibition of Contemporary Ceramic Art." This exhibition displayed 400 of the foremost examples of ceramic design from the United States, England, France, Germany, Austria, Holland, Sweden, Czechoslovakia, and Denmark. It was intended to "keep the designer, the manufacturer, and the public abreast with current productions in the entire field of the industrial arts." Martin Stangl's contribution of Fulper Pottery products included their latest Modernism designs. Other American exhibitors were Adelaide Alsop Robineau, Henry Varnum Poor, American Encaustic Tiling Co., Charles F. Binns, Lenox, Inc., Leon Volkmar, and Pewabic Pottery. The exhibition opened at the Metropolitan Museum of Art in New York on October 2, 1928. It then traveled to prominent art museums in Philadelphia, Minneapolis, Cleveland, Baltimore, Detroit, Newark, and Pittsburgh. Nearly one million people had viewed this exhibit by the time its run was finished at the end of 1929. This exhibit was successful in that it truly brought about an appreciation for quality design in modern American industrial art. Due in part to this exhibition, the late 1920s became the infancy of the "designer age" as leaders in American industry were trying to convince manufacturers that better design and artistry of household products would help American companies compete against foreign imports. Instead of relying on in-house design staff (usually poorly trained or lacking talent), as most companies were doing, several firms began buying designs directly from competent and known freelance designers. This trend did not fully catch on until the early 1930s when American companies finally realized that to compete with foreign imports and survive the depression, quality designs were needed, thus launching the careers of such noted industrial designers as Raymond Loewy, Walter Dorwin Teague, Henry Dreyfus, Helen Dryden, and Russel Wright.

Fulper Pottery Mourns Loss of William H. Fulper II

In October 1928, Flemington was stunned by the sudden death of William Fulper. The following obituary for this talented and far-seeing man was published in *The Ceramic Age* October 1928. "William H. Fulper, of the Fulper Pottery Co., Flemington, N.J., died suddenly from a heart attack at his home in that city on Oct. 15, and his untimely passing has been a severe shock to his many friends in the ceramic industries throughout New Jersey and other parts of the country. Mr. Fulper was prominent in the art branch of the industry. He was the third in his family to head the Fulper Pottery C., which was established about 125 years ago. The plant has been noted for its artistic and original conceptions, and Mr. Fulper was responsible for many of these. A branch pottery recently was opened at Trenton, N.J. Mr. Fulper was 56 years of age at the time of his death and is survived by his wife, one son and a daughter. He was a member of the Metropolitan Museum of Art, the Boston Society of Arts and Crafts, American Ceramic Society, New Jersey Clay Workers Association and a number of other prominent organizations." William Fulper's widow, Etta Fulper, continued to serve in her husband's place as secretary and treasurer of Fulper Pottery Company for nearly 10 years after her husband's passing. By the late 1930s, Etta Fulper had retired and sold her interests in the pottery company to both Martin Stangl and Judge George K. Large.

During 1929, while the International Exhibition of Contemporary Art was touring across America, Fulper Pottery Company also exhibited wares a bit closer to home. From March 8 to March 16, 1929, Rutgers University, New Brunswick, New Jersey, hosted their first Exposition of New Jersey Ceramic Industries.

John Kunsman demonstrating at the Exposition of New Jersey Ceramic Industries, Rutgers University, New Brunswick, New Jersey, March 1929.

Housed in Rutgers' new Ceramics Building, 75 different New Jersey companies exhibited wares relating to the ceramics industry. Fulper Pottery displayed an assortment of Fulper-Stangl and Fulper Pottery artware and tile. Fulper's most popular contribution to the weeklong exposition was John Kunsman demonstrating at the potter's wheel.

"The Fulper Pottery Co., has a booth containing a number of interesting pieces of decorative Stangl pottery, much of it modern in design and feeling" stated the caption for this photo in the August 1930 The Ceramic Age. *This display was one of several put together by Trenton ceramic companies at the American Fair held at Atlantic City during July and August 1930.*

Fulper Pottery Company's display of Stangl Ware at the March 1931 Second Ceramic Exposition at Rutgers University, New Brunswick, New Jersey.

Fulper Pottery also participated in subsequent expositions, such as the American Fair at Atlantic City, and a prominent display of American Ceramics at the New Jersey State Museum in Trenton during 1930. Fulper Pottery Company also participated at the second and third Ceramic Expositions at Rutgers University in 1931 and 1933.

As the 1920s were drawing to a close, Fulper Pottery Company continued to sell heavily to jobbers. Most of the jobbers were still lamp or gift companies, but new jobber contracts were added regularly, such as the Raffetto account for "Rafco" honey jars added in 1927.

Three Fulper Pottery "Rafco" #743 honey jars made for Raffetto in 1927.

During the late 1920s, lamps counted for nearly one-third of production, with another third devoted to dinnerware. The remainder was divided between containers, ashtrays, vases, and gift novelties.

In 1929, Martin Stangl hired Heinrich Below as plant manager. Like Stangl, Heinrich Below was educated in Bavaria as a ceramic engineer. One of the first things he accomplished was the development of Fulper Pottery's uranium oxide based Tangerine and Rust glazes. These were very popular glaze colors and were used extensively until 1943, when the United States government took control of all commercial grade uranium oxide.

1929 — Stangl Pottery

Martin Stangl consolidated the Fulper Fayence, Fulper-Stangl, and Stangl Ware brands into a single line called Stangl Pottery in 1929. The Stangl Pottery line retained many of the Fulper Fayence and Fulper-Stangl items but primarily featured newly designed shapes. The revamped line was launched with an ad campaign featuring full-page advertising designed by Willie Preston. These ads were featured in ceramics and gift trade publications as well as the primary decorating magazines. A 1929 ad copy states: "Because of the increasing demand for brightly colored table ware and for low priced art pottery, the Fulper Pottery Company has perfected and offered to the public the now popular Stangl Ware which successfully meets both demands. The large variety of Stangl pottery consisting of useful articles of practical design offers an unusual selection of ware successfully combining art, utility and moderate price." This same blurb was also published in trade catalogs during the 1930s. Knowing the value of name recognition, all ads for the new Stangl Pottery line included the words "Made by Fulper Pottery" in oversize lettering. A similar ad campaign promoting Fulper Pottery Artware was run simultaneously in many of the same magazines.

During late summer 1929, a series of radio ads touting Fulper's Rickety Room as a destination for bargain hunters was broadcast over metropolitan New Jersey and New York from Newark's radio station WOR. This was a short-lived promotion, as the Rickety Room would soon cease to be.

Full-page ad featuring "Stangl Pottery, made by Fulper Pottery," from Art-In-Trade, *September 1929.* Courtesy of the Hill-Fulper-Stangl Museum.

1929 — Fulper's Great Fire

During the early morning of September 19, 1929, a fire broke out at the Fulper Pottery Company Plant #1. An employee, John Antes, discovered the fire at 5:30 am as he approached the building. He hurriedly told the night watchman, who himself had just discovered the blaze, then raced to pull the alarm box a half block away. The Flemington fire company was at the blaze within seven minutes of the call box alarm. Fire companies from neighboring Lambertville, Three Bridges, and Ringoes also responded. The four companies battled the blaze for three hours, using over three hundred thousand gallons of water. The fire was prevented from spreading to adjacent homes and businesses, but the factory could not be saved. Fulper's veteran potter Ed Wyckoff's home was only 20 feet from the burning factory. The firefighters valiantly saved his home, the only damage being blistered paint! Nearly the whole population of Flemington turned out to watch or assist. Etta Fulper was staying in Trenton during the disaster so was spared the tragedy of witnessing her late husband's life's work go up in smoke.

On a lighter note, Christl Stangl Bacheler, age ten at the time, remembers the blaze: "We helped get some of the furniture from Mrs. Fulper's home outside. She lived right next door to the factory, so everyone feared her house would burn also. The first thing I thought of when I heard the pottery was on fire was my bicycle. It was in one of the store rooms, and all I could think of was 'there goes my bike!'"

Martin Stangl was en route to a meeting in Boston during the disaster. Upon arriving, he was greeted with condolences upon the loss of the factory. He assumed his associates were "pulling his leg," as this was the first news of the disaster to reach him. He soon realized that it was no joke, the meeting was cut short, and Stangl returned to Flemington on the next train.

The entire Plant #1, portions of which dated back to 1814, was destroyed. All workspace and kilns that had been used for production of the Fulper Porcelaines and Fulper Pottery Artware were gone, as were the Rickety Room showrooms and much of the finished pottery that had been packed and waiting to be shipped. Sixty-five workers were left unemployed by the fire. Several workers had recently been hired to assist with the increased pre-holiday production. Positions were almost immediately provided for all employees at Plant #2 in Flemington as well as Fulper's Trenton factory. The company provided all transportation to and from Trenton.

It was ultimately concluded that the fire was electrical in origin. It was not related to the high temperatures of the kilns as had originally been supposed. Tragically, the building was insured for only about half its replacement value, so a greater loss was incurred than was at first estimated. But, the fireproof safe and file cabinets were undamaged, so all glaze formulas, business records, and product orders were saved. Some of the finished ware was salvaged as well. Also saved were nearly all the Fulper Pottery Artware molds and models, as they had been stored at Plant #2 when space became limited at Plant #1.

Martin Stangl and Judge George K. Large (who was acting treasurer in Etta Fulper's absence) seriously considered moving all operations to Trenton, closing even the small, one kiln Plant #2 in Flemington. The Trenton factory still had plenty of room for expansion, the only obstacle being the revamping of kilns for firing the Fulper Pottery Artware. Also, all production consolidated at one location would certainly add to the company's efficiency. Due to the limited acreage and downtown location of the original Plant #1, that site was never considered for rebuilding.

The Flemington Chamber of Commerce immediately endeavored to convince Martin Stangl and Judge Large to keep the Fulper Pottery Company in Flemington. The Chamber pleaded that Fulper Pottery should stay out of respect for "sentimentality and the pottery's 125-year relationship with Flemington." The Chamber of Commerce claimed primarily to be interested in preserving the jobs of the 65 employees. But as the employees were provided for and placed elsewhere within the Fulper Pottery Company, the Chamber's true reason for Fulper remaining in Flemington became apparent. The Chamber of Commerce was concerned that the loss of the Fulper Rickety Room showrooms as a tourist attraction would seriously impact the economy of Flemington, as Flemington had already begun to rely heavily on tourist trade. The concerns of the

Chamber of Commerce were stated in the *Hunterdon County Democrat* in 1929: "One of the greatest assets of the company is that it is widely advertised. The late William H. Fulper in his lifetime spent a large sum of money in advertising Fulper Pottery and the line is well known in every town over 5,000 in America" and "The community can ill afford to lose the Fulper plant. It has given Flemington renown among thousands who otherwise might not have heard of it" and "The loss to the community is very great. It has become a Mecca for tourists." The Chamber of Commerce even approached the owners of the vacant Empire Cut Glass building as a possible home for Fulper Pottery. Martin Stangl stated that he "would not consider its use, because in the first place kilns are required, and again, the factory is not designed for the most efficient operation as a pottery."

Martin Stangl and Judge Large finally agreed to remain in Flemington by adding the three kilns and greater production area to Plant #2 as planned in 1924. This was contingent upon the Flemington Chamber of Commerce endorsing the sale of $50,000 of seven percent Fulper Pottery Company preferred stock. However, construction would not begin until at least half the stock was sold. This announcement was made on October 10, 1929, nearly four weeks after the fire. Sale of the stock was begun immediately, but by November 7, 1929, nearly eight weeks after the fire, only $16,000 worth of stock had been sold. The *Hunterdon County Democrat* stated: "So far, the response from business men and employees of the company, two classes which are most affected, has not been gratifying." Martin Stangl was under extreme pressure by one of Fulper Pottery's largest accounts, threatening to cancel $20,000 worth of orders if delivery of Fulper Pottery Artware could not be done by early 1930. Fulper Pottery Company could ill afford to lose such an important account. If this order were cancelled, the Fulper Pottery Artware line would have simply been discontinued and the company moved to Trenton without further ado.

At last, enough stock was sold by the end of November to commence construction at Plant #2. The original kiln was adapted for higher temperature firing and was fired during the first week of December, 1929. Limited production was carried out during construction, and by February 1930 delivery of the first shipments of Fulper Pottery Artware was made. By the middle of 1930, the additions to Plant #2 were complete. However, only two additional kilns were constructed, bringing the total number of kilns to three. The total cost for the expansion, including building and equipment, was nearly $60,000. A small retail showroom to replace the old Rickety Room was also installed at the Flemington Plant #2.

Fulper Pottery Company Plant #2 in 1930, shortly after the 1929 – 30 expansion.

Fulper Pottery vase #4008, a post-fire design made at Flemington's Plant #2.

Advertising Crusade Conquers Loss of Factory

Martin Stangl feared that the rumors alleging Fulper Pottery Company not surviving the disastrous fire would do more to destroy his business than the actual fire itself. To dispel any lingering doubts about Fulper Pottery enduring beyond the 1929 fire, Martin Stangl blitzed the pottery and gift trade journals with Fulper Pottery ads from late 1929 through 1931. Much of the ad copy touted Fulper's new designs and long history.

While Willie Preston ads were still running, Martin Stangl hired Hungarian graphic artist Antony Lonkay to develop a series of ads, posters, and catalog covers for the company. Lonkay's designs were starkly progressive, utilizing the interplay of exaggerated shadow and light to illustrate the pottery shapes. The Lonkay ads began running in early 1930, and featured Fulper Pottery and Stangl Pottery products. Antony Lonkay ads were often run in the same journals with

Another post-fire design, Fulper Pottery #4058 Scrolled horn in Oxblood glaze, also made at Plant #2 in Flemington.

Willie Preston ads. Lonkay's Fulper Pottery posters were displayed at department stores and every trade show and exhibit Fulper Pottery participated in throughout the early 1930s. Antony Lonkay only had a six-month visa, so returned to Hungary before the end of 1930.

Another well-known artist involved with Stangl's advertising was noted photographer Margaret Bourke-White. During the early 1930s, she photographed several magazine cover layouts featuring Stangl Pottery. Miss Bourke-White is most remembered for creating daring photo-essays of skyscraper construction during the 1920s by dangling with her camera from steel girders hundreds of feet above New York streets.

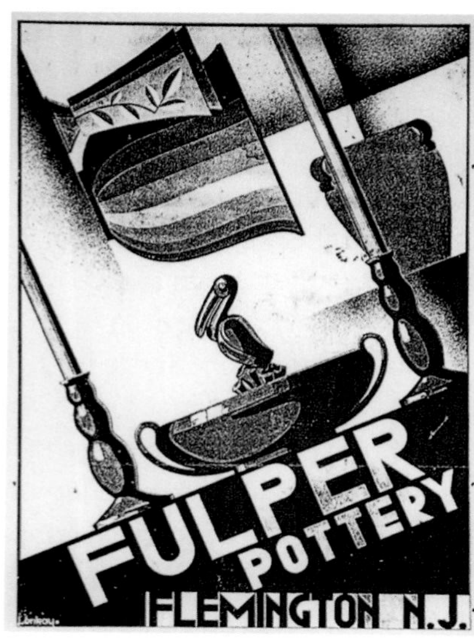

Antony Lonkay Fulper Pottery artware poster, 1930. Courtesy of the Wheaton Village Museum of American Glass.

Martin Stangl continued using the Antony Lonkay artwork style in subsequent poster and advertising designs, as this 1931 Stangl Pottery dinnerware poster attests.

Promotional poster based on a Delineator *magazine cover layout photographed by Margaret Bourke-White in 1934. The title reads "Stangl Dinnerware, as shown in Delineator, made by Fulper Pottery Company."* Courtesy of the Solomon collection.

The 1930s — Prospering During the Great Depression

At the dawn of the 1930s, America was just beginning to feel the calamity of the Great Depression. But as demand was increasing for solid-color kitchen and dinnerware, Fulper Pottery was not yet experiencing those woes. Martin Stangl stated in the *Ceramic Age* in January 1930, "We believe 1930 will be a very busy year for us. Orders received so far for 1930 delivery are considerably larger than they have been any previous year." In 1931, Martin Stangl insured the company's solvency by introducing what would become Fulper Pottery's most popular solid-color dinnerware pattern of the 1930s. The Colonial #1388 pattern was instantly successful and experienced increased sales throughout the 1930s and into the 1940s.

As dinnerware and lamp orders multiplied, Fulper Pottery Company continued to hire. In November 1931, the company reported increased holiday orders and 50 more employees had been added since 1930, bringing the total employees to 118. Fulper Pottery Company reported improved business for 1932 as well.

A minor setback occurred in December 1932, when fire once again plagued Fulper Pottery. *The Ceramic Age* in December 1932 reported the following: "Fire Damages Fulper Pottery. Early in December, fire occurred in a kiln shed and office building at the plant of the Fulper Pottery, New York Avenue, Trenton, N.J. The damage was slight and did not interfere with operations. Loss is reported at approximately $2,500. The plant is one of the oldest in the city, and was formerly known as the Anchor Pottery." The company quickly recovered structurally from what could have been as disastrous as the fire of 1929.

A few pieces of Stangl's most popular solid-color dinnerware pattern, #1388 Colonial.

Fulper's only production slump of the Depression occurred in early 1933; nearly 20 workers were laid off at that time. The event that turned the fortunes of Fulper Pottery Company, and the whole American ceramic and glassware industry was the passing of the Cullen bill legalizing beer on April 7, 1933. The ensuing demand for beer steins, pitchers, and bar ware was phenomenal, saving several companies that had been on the brink of financial failure. Fulper Pottery reported in the July 1933 *Ceramic Age* that they were experiencing "improved demand for mugs, steins and kindred wares, and a number of former employees at the local pottery have been reinstated." By 1934, Fulper's payroll was back up to 110 persons.

Fulper Pottery #4004 beer mug; sudden demand for these, and a variety of other styles of beer ware and accessories, certainly changed the destiny of many ceramic and glass companies during the depths of the Great Depression in 1933.

Style Trends Change During the 1930s

As the 1930s progressed, architectural and home decorating styles became simple and homey. Colonial continued to reign but with more formality and romanticism than was evident during the 1920s. The use of jarring, vibrant color was supplanted with pastel color schemes. Bright chintzes and fluffy chiffons became the fabrics of choice during the 1930s.

The two reasons for Fulper Pottery Company's overall prosperity during the depression years were that their product line was unique and well liked. Notably, Martin Stangl had great foresight in staying abreast of popular trends and adapting the product styles as tastes changed. While much of America's ceramics industry was suffering due to both foreign and domestic competition, Fulper Pottery Company was prospering as the only nationally distributed producer of solid-color dinnerware and kitchenware. Fulper Pottery experienced no real competition in this area until the mid 1930s when other American potters, such as Homer Laughlin, Metlox, and Bauer began to nationally market solid-color dinnerware. When the bold, angular, and "grotesque" Modernism forms of the 1920s fell from favor, Fulper Pottery was quick to produce articles of romantically styled classical and colonial design. Also, as America became enchanted with pottery garden animals, Martin Stangl immediately introduced a series of Fulper Pottery outdoor animals in 1930.

Modest but formal 1930s bedroom, with pastel walls, muted glazed chintz fabrics, and colonial furniture.

Fulper Pottery Garden Animal, the #874 Fox Terrier. Courtesy of the Wayne Weigand Collection.

In addition, as an increasing number of American companies were turning to automation and machine manufacturing, Martin Stangl began to emphasize the handmade qualities of Fulper and Stangl Pottery. "Handmade" and "hand-craftsmanship" were qualities that Martin Stangl promoted for nearly all his life.

Another Fulper Pottery Garden Animal #875 Small Duck, from 1930.

An example from Fulper Pottery's line of handmade artware, #1892 vase with applied rose, produced at Plant #2 in Flemington during 1934 only.

This colonial styled vase #1881 was also from the Fulper Pottery handmade artware line, produced at Plant #2 in Flemington during 1934 only.

Flemington, The Outlet and Lindbergh

Martin Stangl's business philosophy was "To be successful, you have to make something which no one else can, will, or wants to make, but that is attractive and saleable!" And succeed he did. But the final element in Fulper Pottery's equation to success during the Great Depression was the Flemington Outlet. Originally a small showroom in the Plant #2 building, the showroom was gradually expanded as sales of slightly imperfect Stangl brand dinnerware skyrocketed.

1950s photo of the front doors of Stangl's Flemington Outlet. Courtesy of the Hill-Fulper-Stangl Museum.

By 1934, sales of the heavy Fulper Pottery Artware had decreased to the point where the line was no longer showing a profit, even after the introduction of many new shapes that should have been marketable. Only 12 employees were producing the Fulper Pottery Artware at Flemington's Plant #2, while 94 persons were employed in the manufacture of Stangl Pottery at Trenton. At the end of 1934, the Fulper Pottery Artware was discontinued, and any Stangl Ware production remaining at Plant #2 was absorbed at the Trenton factory. Even though the Fulper Pottery Artware line was no longer produced, the company continued to be "Fulper Pottery, makers of Stangl Pottery" throughout the 1930s, '40s and '50s. By early 1935, the entire Plant #2 facility at Flemington was converted to retail showroom floor space and was managed by Martin Stangl's eldest daughter Martha. The building was thereafter known as the "Flemington Outlet." Weekend traffic at the Flemington Outlet during good weather, even throughout the economically bleak 1930s, often exceeded one thousand people!

As popular as Stangl's Flemington Outlet was, it could not compete with another Flemington attraction during the mid 1930s. For a few weeks in early 1935, Flemington suddenly became the center of the universe as the location of "The Trial of the Century." During January and February 1935, the Flemington courthouse was the scene of Bruno Richard Hauptman's trial for the kidnapping and murder of Charles and Anne Lindbergh's son. Crowds of reporters, celebrities, sightseers, souvenir hawkers, and just plain busybodies suddenly descended upon Flemington. Newspaper, radio, and newsreel reports made Flemington familiar to households across the nation. The hotels were beyond overflowing; desperate lodgers were paying up to $20 a night to camp on sofas or cots in crowded rooms. Many private citizens opened their homes to boarders. John Kunsman, whose home was across the street from the site of Fulper's Plant #1, rented rooms to radio reporter Walter Winchell and author Dorothy Kilgallen. Will Rogers, Martin Stangl's favorite actor, stayed at the Stangl home during the trial. Other celebrities in town at that time were Jack Benny, Robert L. Ripley, Damon Runyon, Adela Rogers St. John, and announcers Lowell Thomas and Gabriel Heatter. Many of these celebrities were already familiar with Hunterdon County, as they were frequent visitors to Colligan's Stockton Inn in Stockton, N.J., several miles southwest of Flemington on the banks of the Delaware River. This sudden influx of population certainly boosted Flemington's depression-era economy. Naturally, Martin Stangl's Flemington Outlet also benefited from the crowds. Many shoppers, discovering the Flemington Outlet for the first time during that 1935 trial, became loyal, repeat Stangl customers for years to come.

Late 1930s Trends — Early American and Moderne

During the mid 1930s, lamp production for the jobber market continued to be a staple for the company, but dinnerware sales far outdistanced all other lines. However in the artware line, Stangl's miniature vases gained great popularity during the 1930s. Prompted by the interest in John Kunsman's tiny pots thrown at demonstrations, Martin Stangl developed a complete line of miniature vases in a rainbow of colors. These items were wholesaled to carnivals and fairs, where they were used as prizes. Tourist attractions also purchased great quantities of the miniature vases and after applying decals with the name of the attraction, sold them as souvenirs. Cute, quaint, and fun, the miniature line has been a staple Stangl collectible for decades.

During the latter 1930s, styles in home decorating trends were again becoming divergent. One popular style, known as "Moderne," advocated sleek elegance, sophistication, and modern classicism. Soft, pastel colors and silvery tones were the accompaniment to the sleek shapes. The Moderne name and style both appeared in decorating magazines during the early 1930s and continued to grow in popularity, peaking just before World War II. Stangl developed several vase and lamp shapes with elegant lines and handles and soft, satin pastel glazes in keeping with the sophisticated Moderne trend. Many of Stangl's modern-styled vases and lamp shapes of the 1930s were designed by John Tierney.

The other major popular style of the late 1930s was a re-awakening of admiration for Early American and European peasant fashions. Bold, bright colors followed the peasant trend. Colorful accessories and maple furniture with braided rugs epitomized the late 1930s Early American styled home. Hand-painted Italian-styled pottery and dinnerware was becoming the ceramic of choice. Capo di Monte and Della Robbia type bric-a-brac was being imported from Europe by the ton to American decorators, gift shops, and furniture showrooms. Czechoslovakia, France, Italy, Spain, and Portugal were the largest producers of these ornamental items, with Japan supplying a portion of these ceramics as well.

Europe's Instability Affects American Markets

By the late 1930s, the "Buy American" campaign of several years before was finally getting some notice. Also, American designers were seeking to develop styles that were purely American or represented American historical motifs. But the popular ceramics continued to be brightly decorated peasant imports. Unfortunately for the importers, conditions were becoming unstable in European countries that normally imported to the United States. In 1936, Mussolini started marching troops around North Africa, and Spain embroiled itself in a civil war, causing American importers to reconsider trading with either Spain or Italy. By the end of 1938, Germany was beginning to occupy Czechoslovakia, greatly diminishing imports from that country to the United States. Importers, fearing the safety of their merchandise shipments, were reluctantly beginning to seek American manufacturers to supply the much loved peasant-type ceramics. The importers were accustomed to Americans' general disdain for American decorative accessories so were hesitant to attempt marketing American-made ceramics.

Stangl's Hand-Painted Dinnerware

Fulper Pottery had been producing hand-painted and underglaze-decorated products in very limited quantities, usually as special orders, since the 1920s. But in 1937, large-scale production of hand-decorated dinnerware was begun, prompted by the national demand for peasant ceramics. The motifs were originally silkscreened, then later stenciled onto each piece with powdered charcoal, and decorators applied the underglaze colors by following the charcoal outlines. Not one of Stangl's dinnerware patterns was ever decorated "freehand;" a predetermined stencil for each pattern was always followed. During the late 1930s, the hand-decorated dinnerware was but a small portion of Stangl's vast assortment of solid-color dinnerware and artware lines.

By 1938, the total number of employees producing Stangl's various products at the Trenton factory was 107, with seven sales clerks employed at the Flemington Outlet. Martha Stangl continued to

Two of Stangl's hand-painted dinnerware patterns of 1938, both designed by Gerald Ewing.

manage the outlet; assistant manager was her sister Christl Stangl. During the 1940s, the two Stangl sisters each married a brother from the Bacheler family. Martha married John Bacheler, a talented commercial artist, and Christl married Merrill Bacheler, who later became manager of the Flemington Outlet.

Stangl Responds to War in Europe with Dinnerware and Birds

By September 1939, Britain, France, and Canada had declared war on Germany, thereby beginning the Battle of the North Atlantic. Although the United States had announced a position of neutrality, during 1940 German U-boats began attacking merchant ships, severely hampering trans-Atlantic trade. In December 1941, Japan attacked the United States, causing the United States and Britain to declare war on Japan. So as not to feel left out, Germany then declared war on the United States. Germany immediately launched a U-boat offensive just off the eastern shore of the United States and by 1943 had sunk 27 merchant ships in the Atlantic.

Since it was no longer safe for trans-Atlantic shipping, American distributors and department stores were now forced to purchase the hand-painted peasant pottery from American potters. Martin Stangl then greatly expanded the hand-painted dinnerware lines. A few of the newly added dinnerware patterns were similar to those that had been available overseas, but most were freshly designed creations. Trade show advertising for Stangl's new dinnerware referred to the product as "Americana Hand Decorated Dinnerware." Americanism and patriotic pride were finally taking hold with America's retail consumers.

Stangl Develops Birds and Terra Rose

Always on top of popular trends, Martin Stangl developed a line of realistically sculpted and decorated animal and bird figurines in 1939. Many of the figurines were based on the American bird paintings of John James Audubon. Three sculptors had their turn at designing Stangl's bird figurines. The first of the series were designed and sculpted by John Tierney. August Jacob sculpted a number of birds during the early 1940s. August Jacob also sculpted bird figurines for Pennsbury Pottery of Morrisville, Pennsylvania, and Gort China of Metuchen, New Jersey, during the 1950s. Stangl's bird figurines of the late 1940s and early 1950s were designed and sculpted by both John Tierney and Herman Eichorn. By 1940, Stangl's pottery birds became immediately popular and demand for them soared! During World War II, the decorating staff was continually increased to keep up with orders for the figurines. A team of over 40 decorators was also set up at the Flemington Outlet just for pottery bird decorating.

In 1940 Fulper Pottery Company began producing the Terra Rose glaze finish. Developed by Martin Stangl, this finish combined boldly brushed metallic oxides with a semi-opaque glaze and imparted a look of antiquity to the shapes on which it was applied. Martin Stangl patented both the Terra Rose glazing process and the Terra Rose name. The name for Stangl's Terra Rose finish was an Americanized version of an ancient name for the color Venetian Red, Terra Rosa. Both the artist's color Venetian Red and Stangl's Terra Rose glaze relied on red iron oxide for their unique coloring. Terra Rose became a very popular finish and was utilized on several artware and dinnerware lines throughout the 1940s and 1950s.

While many of Fulper Pottery's jobber accounts had dwindled during the Depression, the onset of World War II created new accounts with new jobbers seeking to handle Stangl's hand-painted dinnerware lines. Stangl described exclusive jobber patterns with the term "private label." During and immediately after World War II, Stangl produced more private label dinnerware patterns than at any other time. Some of the more important jobbers handling Stangl's dinnerware during the 1940s were Carole Stupell, Frederik Lunning, Sak's Fifth Avenue, Fisher, Bruce & Co., and Russel Wright's American Way handicraft program.

Martin Stangl escorting Carole Stupell of Carole Stupell, Ltd., through the Trenton factory in August 1940. The potter is creating casseroles for the handmade Terra Rose finished #3506 Pie Crust dinnerware line. From the Stangl and Fulper archival collection, courtesy the Wheaton Village Museum of American Glass.

The greatest expense in developing any new ceramic line is the cost of the sculptor to create the models and the plaster shop to generate production molds. In order to finance the development of the new Terra Rose artware and pottery bird lines, Martin Stangl and Judge George K. Large once again borrowed on the Fulper Pottery Company during 1939 and 1942. The sale in 1940 of the vacant property where Plant #1 once stood to the New Jersey Telephone Company also added capital to develop the new lines.

Kay Hackett Arrives at Stangl Pottery

By the early 1940s, as hand-painted American dinnerware was becoming more popular, several other American potteries had also begun to manufacture hand-painted, white-bodied dinnerware. Martin Stangl knew that to keep ahead of the competition, he needed to develop something unique in the dinnerware lines. Taking a cue from the popularity of Italian ceramics and Early American styles, Stangl began experimenting with sgraffito-decorated dinnerware patterns. He believed designs similar to antique Pennsylvania Dutch red-ware pottery would be welcomed by American consumers.

In October 1941, Martin Stangl hired Kay Hackett as designer. Her experience with engobes, underglaze and sgraffito decoration was a factor in her obtaining this position. After several weeks of learning the operating procedures of Stangl Pottery and researching authentic Pennsylvania Dutch decoration, Kay Hackett began designing what would become Stangl's extremely popular "hand-carved, hand-painted" dinnerware and artware lines.

The first of the sgraffito-decorated patterns were introduced in January 1942. These patterns utilized a red-colored clay body with a thin coating of white clay, called "engobe," brushed over the surface of each piece. The motifs were carved into the engobe, and then hand-painted with bright underglaze colors. Stangl's hand-carved, hand-painted dinnerware and artware required much labor and handling of each piece so was more costly than the solid-color dinner and artware lines. These patterns were an instant success, the added cost was not a deterrent to sales. Stangl's hand-carved dinnerware patterns became increasingly popular from the 1940s right through the 1960s. Of all the lines produced by the company, the hand-carved, hand-painted dinnerware is most closely identified with the Stangl name even today.

Double Bird, one of Kay Hackett's earliest hand-carved, hand-painted dinnerware designs, introduced in 1942.

Stangl During War Time

Demand for Fulper Pottery Company's pottery bird figurines and hand-carved, hand-painted dinnerware was tremendous during World War II. Even with many pottery employees going into the services or defense work during the war (designer and decorating supervisor Gerald Ewing enlisted, Kay Hackett went to General Motors, and Merrill Bacheler to Eastern Aircraft), Fulper Pottery still retained 137 on the payroll. By 1943, Fulper Pottery received a United States government contract to produce high-grade porcelain bushings and insulators for the war effort. As a sideline to the insulator production, Martin Stangl introduced a line of realistically sculpted porcelain bird figurines. Accurately styled after Audubon's *Birds of America* watercolors, the porcelain figures were much more highly detailed and realistically colored than Stangl's pottery bird figurines. The porcelain birds were also much more costly than the pottery birds, so when the government defense contract ended, so went Stangl's porcelain birds.

However, there was a lasting benefit to the government porcelain bushing contract. In order to upgrade the production facility to standards set by the War Department, Fulper Pottery Company was provided with funds to replace the 14 old coal-fired, periodic kilns at the Trenton factory with two gas burning, continuous-fire tunnel kilns. The first tunnel kiln was completed in 1943 and replaced six of the periodic kilns. By 1945, the second tunnel kiln was operating, and the remaining eight periodic kilns were removed. Each kiln was 110 feet long and greatly increased Stangl's firing capability. The removal of the monolithic brick kilns also greatly opened up the floor plan, providing much needed work space. While the giant holes in the roofs left by the kilns were

A corner of the new conference room in 1949. Shown are designer Kay Hackett (on right) and her assistant testing the newly constructed "demonstration table." This table was used at department stores and trade shows to illustrate how each piece of Stangl's dinnerware was hand painted. Courtesy of Kay Hackett.

being repaired, Martin Stangl used that opportunity to add two floors and a gable near the main entrance to the building. Into this added space he put his own office, a large conference room, a design studio, kitchen, and dining room.

Wartime also spelled the end for the Stangl Pottery solid-color dinnerware and artware. When the United States government began restricting use of uranium oxide in 1943, Fulper Pottery could no longer produce the uranium-based Tangerine and Rust glazes. Martin Stangl felt that these two colors were integral to the whole solid-color line and were necessary to the color pallet. Articles glazed with the remaining colors were produced on a limited basis through 1943, but the original solid-color glazes were discontinued during 1944. Fortunately, demand for the hand-painted dinnerware and Terra Rose artware was increasing at a fantastic rate, so the company could survive without producing the solid-color lines.

A partial view of the design studio in 1957, Kay Hackett's office during her employ at Stangl Pottery. On the shelves are Antique Gold lamp and plate samples. Behind them, through the glass, is the conference room. Kay Hackett often met there with Mr. Stangl to discuss her latest design project. Courtesy of Kay Hackett.

Aerial view of Fulper Pottery's Trenton factory in the late 1940s after removal of the distinctive brick periodic kilns that formerly dominated the roof line. In addition to the kiln upgrade, Fulper Company's wartime prosperity also enabled the replacement of the ancient clay storage shed. The new shed is the flat-roofed building at the right end of the complex. New York Avenue is the street at the top of the photo; the Delaware and Raritan canal borders the factory at the bottom of the photo. Courtesy of the Wheaton Village Museum of American Glass.

During the post-war years, sales of the pottery bird figurines were abruptly diminished from their extreme demand during the war. Fulper Pottery no longer sold the quantity of birds it had during the war, but interest in the line remained strong enough to warrant adding shapes to the bird assortment. There was a boost in orders for Terra Rose artware at the time, as well as a steady increase in demand for the hand-carved, hand-painted dinnerware patterns. During the late 1940s, pottery lamps once again became popular, but never again did lamp production come near that of the 1920s and 1930s.

Traveling Demonstrations Continue

Throughout the 1930s, Martin Stangl continued the hands-on department store demonstrations first initiated in 1924. John Kunsman continued as the traveling potter until his retirement in 1938, after 50 years with the company. Martin Stangl's son-in-law, Merrill Bacheler continued the traveling department store demonstrations from 1938 until 1942, when wartime gas rationing temporarily discontinued the traveling demonstrations.

In 1949, Martin Stangl reinstated the traveling pottery demonstrations but with a difference. While men turning vases and pots conducted the old traveling demonstrations, with the new demonstrations an attractive woman explained the techniques of dinnerware production and demonstrated hand-painting. A large portable demonstration table was designed that displayed Stangl dinnerware in consecutive stages of production. Small leaflets explaining the display were distributed to patrons.

A rare example of Merrill Bacheler's skill with a potter's wheel, produced in 1942 at a department store demonstration. Courtesy of Merrill and Christl Stangl Bacheler.

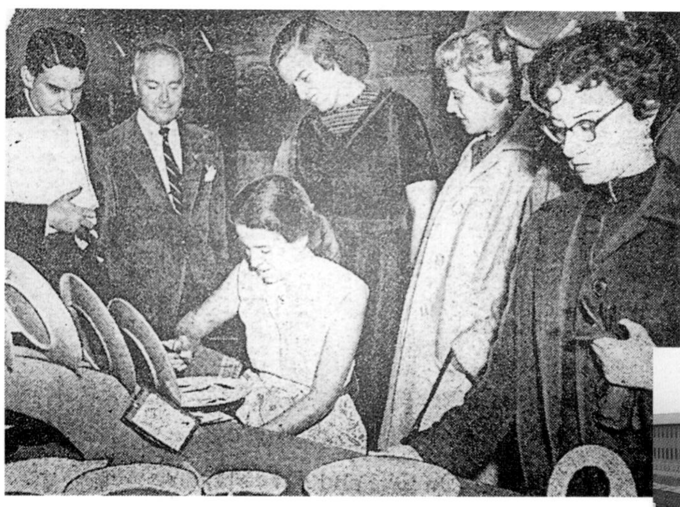

This news clipping from the October 19, 1953 Retailing Daily shows Kay Hackett demonstrating Stangl decorating at B. Altman's. Courtesy of Kay Hackett.

Stangl's designer, Kay Hackett, was the first hand-painting demonstrator. Several times per year during the early 1950s, she would demonstrate at department stores in New York and Philadelphia. B. Altman's on Fifth Avenue, New York, was a regular host to Stangl's hand-painting demonstrations. Throughout the 1950s and 1960s, other qualified employees, including Martin Stangl's own daughter Christl Stangl Bacheler, conducted the traveling demonstrations.

A view of the Trenton factory from the nearly completed Trenton Freeway (now U.S. Route #1), in 1954. Courtesy of the Trentoniana Collection of the Trenton Public Library, Trenton, New Jersey.

1950s — Modernization Brings New Lines to Stangl

The 1950s were among the most productive and innovative years for Stangl Pottery. During that decade the total number of employees reached an all-time high of 175! Also, production was streamlined, and several manual operations in the factory were eliminated by the addition of conveyors and other modern equipment.

Stangl's slip house in 1973. The filter press, which removes excess water from the clay, is on the left. On the right is the pug mill, which extrudes workable clay ready for manufacturing. From the Stangl and Fulper archival collection, courtesy the Wheaton Village Museum of American Glass.

Stangl's plates and cups were formed by jiggering. The "batter-out man," Leonard Bollman (left), presses the clay onto the plate molds for "jigger man" Walt McBride (right) in 1950. Courtesy of Dave Thomas.

Jiggering cups in 1955. Pugs of clay are on the left; plaster cup molds are on the rack behind the jigger man. Finished greenware cups are stacked on the conveyor to the right. This was one of the conveyors installed by Dave Thomas in the 1950s. Courtesy of Dave Thomas.

Hollow pieces, such as vases or teapots, were slip cast by pouring liquid clay into plaster molds. From Stangl's *A Portrait of Progress in Pottery*, copyright 1965.

Capillary action caused a wall of solid clay to form on the surface of the plaster mold. When the solid clay wall was the desired thickness, the excess liquid clay was poured from the mold, which was then inverted and left to dry, as demonstrated in this 1965 photo. From Stangl's *A Portrait of Progress in Pottery*, copyright 1965.

Worker draining and inverting molds in Stangl's casting room in 1973, virtually unchanged since the 1880s. From the Stangl and Fulper archival collection, courtesy the Wheaton Village Museum of American Glass.

A ware board of freshly unmolded vases on their way to the finishing department in 1973. From the Stangl and Fulper archival collection, courtesy the Wheaton Village Museum of American Glass.

Stangl's finishing department staff in 1950. Miss Inman (first woman on the left) was finishing department supervisor during the 1940s and 1950s. Fred Walker (young man on far right) carried ware boards full of pottery between the various departments until the mid 1950s when Dave Thomas's conveyors eliminated many board carriers. Walker was then promoted to jigger man. Courtesy of Dave Thomas.

Jenny finishing plates in 1950. Courtesy of Dave Thomas.

Some of the most notable changes made in the production of Stangl's dinnerware and artware during the 1950s were the conversion from hand-brushing engobe to spraying; and the introduction of colored engobes in 1952, and gold-decorated lines in 1955. Also during 1955, the name of the company was legally changed from Fulper Pottery Company to Stangl Pottery Company. While many other American potteries were foundering at this time, due to foreign imports and the increasing popularity of plastic dinnerware, Stangl was not only weathering the storm, but was prospering as well. Proving once again Martin Stangl's business philosophy, "To be successful, you have to make something which no one else can, will, or wants to make, but that is attractive and saleable!"

A close-up of Gerry West demonstrating engobe spraying in 1965. From Stangl's *A Portrait of Progress in Pottery*, copyright 1965.

Gerry West spraying engobe in 1950 on Dave Thomas and William Smith's new engobe wheel. Courtesy of Dave Thomas.

Martin Stangl's son-in-law and plant manager, Dave Thomas, with the assistance of William Smith, developed a process that enabled engobe to be sprayed on instead of hand-brushed. The spraying technique was perfected and put into use as early as 1950. This immediately lessened the amount of hand labor required for each piece. Hand-brushing of engobe was diminished but was not completely discontinued on regular production ware until mid 1952. Lamps produced for Mutual Sunset and several dinnerware patterns continued to have hand-brushed engobe through 1953, so can be found with either brushed or sprayed engobe.

Although Martin Stangl realized spraying engobe was a cost-saving improvement, he felt that the swirl of hand-brushed engobe on each piece represented hand-craftsmanship. He feared consumers would no longer be interested in buying Stangl dinnerware if it did not appear completely handmade. This turned out not to be true, for Stangl dinnerware patterns and art products became even more popular throughout the 1950s, in part due to the smooth white background created by sprayed engobe.

The engobe spraying process also made it possible to use colored engobes. A green engobe was introduced in 1952, and gray engobe was introduced in 1953. The colored engobes were very novel at that time, so Stangl was able to initially charge more for patterns with colored engobes, even though they cost no more to produce than similar patterns with white engobe. The gray engobe became background for Stangl's very popular line of Sportsmen's ashtrays and giftware. Other colored engobes that were used in later years at various times were coral, light gray, and dark yellow.

Greenware was placed on this two-story-high mangle to dry. After one revolution, the ware was dry enough to be handled and carved. Dave Thomas installed the mangle in the early 1950s. Courtesy of Dave Thomas.

Stangl's carving department in 1950. Dave Thomas's conveyor can be seen running straight between the carvers' stations. Courtesy of Dave Thomas.

Carving plates, 1950. Courtesy of Dave Thomas.

Kiln car loaded with bisque ware after emerging from the bisque tunnel kiln in 1952. Large fans were used to help quickly cool the ware for decorating. Courtesy of Dave Thomas.

Stangl's kilnmen, 1940, technically called "kiln draw-ers," stacked the old-style periodic kilns with saggers of ware. When firing was complete, they would "draw" (unload) the kiln, hence the name. Head draw-er, Wojeiech (George) Bac, second from right, holds the special reinforced cap which aided them in carrying fully loaded saggers on their heads so that their hands were free. Courtesy of Josephine Tiffenbach.

Rubber-stamping the Stangl trademark on creamers prior to being decorated in 1965. From Stangl's *A Portrait of Progress in Pottery,* copyright 1965.

Some of Stangl's carvers and decorators in 1950. Bill Warr (in front row) was designer and foreman of both departments during the late 1940s and early 1950s. Many old-time decorators can recall when it was so hot at the pottery during summer they had to soak their feet in tubs of ice-water just to keep cool. Courtesy of Dave Thomas.

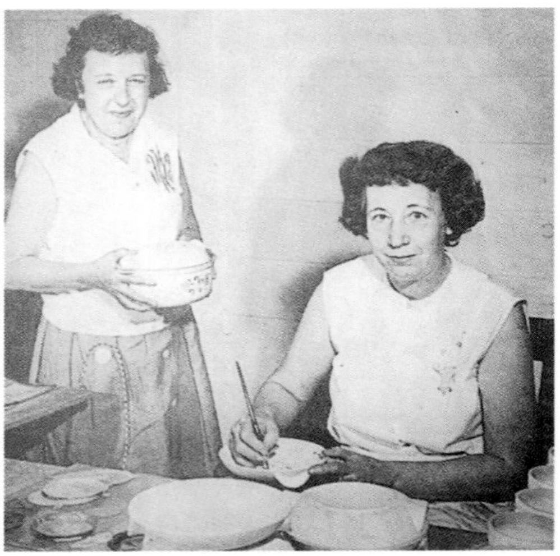

Two of Stangl's top decorators, Edna Swaine (left) and Maisie Swaine Boan (right), both began hand-painting Stangl's dinnerware in 1940 and continued through the 1960s. Courtesy of the Trentoniana Collection of the Trenton Public Library, Trenton, New Jersey.

The large "wheel" in the decorating department in 1950. Each decorator applied a single color to the piece and put it on the "wheel" where it traveled to the next decorator who added the next color, and so on. Very few Stangl patterns were decorated with this "assembly line" technique, as Martin Stangl liked to advertise the fact that Stangl dinnerware was hand-crafted by individual artists. Only inexpensive patterns needed in a hurry, such as Crocus and Golden Harvest, were decorated on the "wheel." Courtesy of Dave Thomas.

The Stangl decorating department in 1964. Another of Stangl's best decorators, Rosa Veglianetti, is in the foreground center. Rosa began decorating Stangl dinnerware and artware in 1938 and continued until Stangl Pottery closed in 1978. Her initials "R.V." or "R." can be found on many bird figurines and salad set patterns. Behind Rosa sit Edna Swaine and Maisie Boan. The glass-front cabinets in the back house all of the decorator samples used for referencing each pattern. This room and its contents were destroyed in the 1965 fire.

Stangl's entire decorating staff in 1952. Note the fellow on the left with the ware board on his head. His job was to keep the decorators supplied with bisque ware for them to decorate and carry away the decorated items to the glazing department. He could carry three full ware boards at one time, one in each hand and one on his head. Dave Thomas's conveyors eliminated some, but not all, hand-carrying of ware boards. Courtesy of Theresa Hawryluk.

In 1953, Stangl installed an electric rolling kiln for the low-temperature firing of red overglaze color on bird figurines such as cardinals and tanagers. In 1955, a second electric rolling kiln was added, and Stangl began using both kilns for firing metallic lusters. These rolling kilns were not stationary as were the large tunnel kilns. With the rolling kilns, ware was stacked on stationary firebrick tables, and the whole kiln was then rolled over the table and sealed for firing.

The first newly installed electric rolling kiln loaded for its initial test firing in July 1953. By the late 1950s there were three of these "gold kilns" installed at Stangl Pottery's Trenton factory. A fourth electric rolling kiln was also installed in the garage at the Flemington Outlet. Courtesy of Dave Thomas.

A decorator applying gold luster to a vase in 1965. From Stangl's *A Portrait of Progress in Pottery*, copyright 1965.

The first gold-decorated artware was Stangl's American Bone China developed in 1954. In 1956, several dinnerware patterns were introduced with platinum and 22-karat gold luster decorations, and in 1957 Stangl's dry-brushed Antique Gold finish was perfected. Ultimately, the brushed gold finishes became extraordinarily popular and were Stangl's most widely distributed artware decoration during the 1960s and 1970s. During the late 1970s, the electric kilns were also used for the firing of decals on the decal-decorated Christmas and Sportsmen's patterns produced at that time.

The sorting and shipping department in 1952. Mamie Wood (first woman on the left) was sorting and shipping supervisor during the 1950s. Courtesy of Dave Thomas.

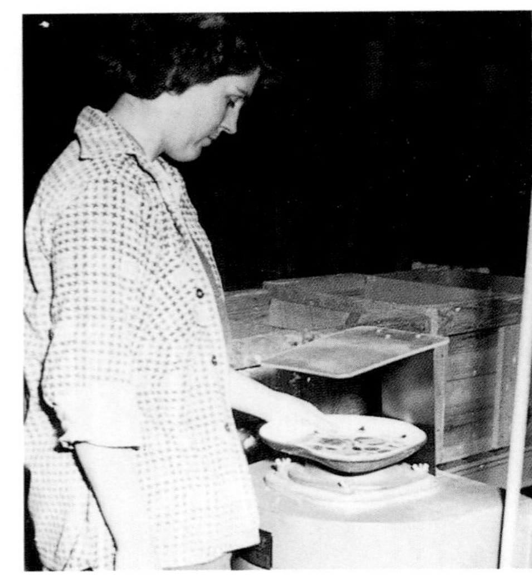

The sand-blast machine that etched Stangl's "second" mark on the backs of glazed dinnerware and artware. Courtesy of Dave Thomas.

If the 1950s were the most productive years for Stangl Pottery, the 1960s were certainly the most resourceful. New shapes, styles, and new methods of decoration were continually introduced. During the 1960s, patterns with molded decorations were developed, as were patterns with sponged motifs. New styles and shapes were developed in an ongoing effort to compete with the imported dinnerware products that continued to flood the American marketplace during that time. But in spite of the difficulties posed by foreign competition, Stangl continued to produce a unique product line that was always in demand. Even the Japanese attempted to copy Stangl's ware but fell miserably short with cheap-quality imitations.

Aerial view of Stangl's Flemington Outlet in 1942, showing James Teague's log cabin workshop on the left. Even during the gas rationing of World War II, Stangl's Flemington Outlet was a popular tourist spot, as evidenced by the number of autos in the parking lot. From the Stangl and Fulper archival collection, courtesy the Wheaton Village Museum of American Glass.

Stangl's Flemington Outlet Showrooms — Always Something Going On!

Beginning with the Flemington Outlet's opening in 1935, table display and decoration were always of primary importance. During the 1930s and 1940s, both Martha and Christl Stangl Bacheler arranged all the displays and table settings. Each table featured flatware and linens appropriate for the dinnerware patterns used. The setting was never complete until it was graced by a Stangl Pottery vase with an arrangement of fresh flowers grown by Martin Stangl himself.

Always an avid gardener, Martin Stangl cultivated several large plots of flowers and

Table settings at the Flemington Outlet in 1976. Town & Country is the featured dinnerware pattern. Courtesy of the Hill-Fulper-Stangl Museum.

Martin Stangl tending one of his garden plots and using a Stangl Pottery #2000 shape pitcher, of course! Courtesy of Dave and Betty Stangl Thomas.

even had a greenhouse constructed at the Flemington Outlet property so the showroom would have a continual supply of fresh blooms. During the Christmas season, Martin Stangl would have boughs of long-leaf pine and southern holly brought up from North Carolina to decorate the showroom.

The Flemington Outlet played a major role in maintaining cash flow for the pottery company. Martin Stangl threw nothing away; firsts, seconds, flawed pieces, tests, samples, and experiments were all sold through the outlet. By selling all of the various items that most potteries destroyed, Stangl was able to survive difficult times, such as the Great Depression during the 1930s, the recession following World War II, and the tremendous influx of imported dinnerware during the 1950s and 1960s. The only items *not* sold at the Flemington Outlet were damaged pieces. Anything suffering chips or cracks during manufacturing that could not be properly glazed over were sent to be destroyed. But sometimes even those pieces escaped destruction. Craig Ewing, whose grandfather Judiah Ewing worked at the Flemington Outlet during the 1930s, tells of his grandfather being "...ordered to destroy Stangl Pottery pieces with slight damage as they didn't want them sold. He was supposed to take them outside and smash them against a wall. This was during the Depression in the 1930s, and he thought that was terribly wasteful, so he sometimes gathered up some of the pieces and gave them away to several needy families in Flemington that otherwise didn't have any decent dinnerware to use in their homes. Could be that some rare pieces with slight damage exist today that otherwise would have been destroyed." Christl Stangl Bacheler also remembers the damaged pieces that were thrown away: "I guess I was nine or ten, and we walked past the pottery to and from school, and it used to be a kind of game for the kids in town to go out behind the pottery and see what was thrown in the pile where they dumped the unusable pieces. I remember digging through that pile and finding this or that and bringing home things, like a cup with a handle off. Daddy would say, 'What do you want with that? I'll give you a good one, that's no good with a handle off'. I think it was the challenge of finding a treasure in that pile that we kids really liked."

Stangl's Flemington Outlet sold a healthy amount of first-quality merchandise, but the Outlet was best known for its second-quality bargains. Because of Stangl Pottery's hand-crafted qualities, many of the minor flaws of the second-quality merchandise are nearly undetectable. Here is a little secret... promise not to tell... most of the merchandise sold at the Flemington Outlet as second-quality was actually first-quality. There was more profit and faster cash turnover in selling first-quality products as "seconds" at the Outlet than in selling them as first-quality to department stores. Martin Stangl would often remove first-quality products from department store orders and send them to Flemington just to keep the Outlet well stocked at all times. This practice caused great consternation with Stangl's shipping department. Mamie Wood, Stangl's shipping supervisor, was continually complaining that as soon as orders were picked, sorted, and ready to ship, Martin Stangl would come through and grab half of it for Flemington, subsequently delaying the shipment. Often, whenever a piece of Stangl Pottery is marked with a "second" backstamp, unless the piece is obviously flawed, chances are it was actually first-quality merchandise simply marked as a second so Martin Stangl could sell it at the Flemington Outlet.

From the very beginning, Martin Stangl had always sold specialty items at the Flemington Outlet that were not available to Stangl Pottery retailers. Some of these items were simply inexpensive pieces designed to generate cash flow, others were market tests, but most were merely second-quality merchandise. During the 1940s and early 1950s, badly flawed seconds were often decorated with French green, Blue #95, Orange, or no color at all. Artware green was used as a seconds treatment throughout the 1950s and early 1960s. These single color and brushed color seconds treatments were quickly and inexpensively produced, but not wildly popular. Stangl's bestselling seconds, naturally, were decorated with their most popular dinnerware motifs.

During the late 1940s and early 1950s, Martin Stangl began a campaign to redecorate the Flemington Outlet, to spruce up its quasi-industrial appearance, and make it more appealing to the hordes of visiting shoppers. In 1949 he installed the celebrated giant stoneware jar with gold leaf "Stangl Pottery." The jar was made by General Ceramics in New York and was originally designed for industrial acid storage.

Martin Stangl also began an extensive landscaping program at the Flemington Outlet. Because of his great appreciation for flora and greenery, he planted a variety of flowering trees and shrubs, accented with roses, evergreens, and flowering

The famous "Stangl Pottery" jar continues to guard the Flemington Outlet entrance today.

bulbs. Many of Martin Stangl's plantings are preserved and still bloom faithfully.

Indoors, Martin Stangl also did some sprucing up. In 1955, he replaced the old enormous boiler that used to heat and power the factory with a small, modern heating boiler in its own room addition. The old boiler room, which was quite large, then became the new "Seconds" room. After the room was painted, he had Kay Hackett spend several days in Flemington hand-painting popular dinnerware motifs on an oversize soffit along the top of the wall. Kay was able to keep proper proportion of the motifs by enlarging the bread tray stencil for each pattern to fit the space of the soffit.

Kay Hackett painting popular motifs on the soffit in the Flemington Outlet's former boiler room turned "Seconds" room in 1955. Courtesy of Kay Hackett.

Managers of the Flemington Outlet over the years were Martha Stangl Bacheler from 1935 until 1945, Martha's brother-in-law Merrill Bacheler from 1945 through 1964, Rae Killinger from 1964 until 1970, Doris Paetzel from 1970 through 1973, and Ed Alvater from 1973 until the company's closing in 1978. Some of the Outlet's assistant managers were Christl Stangl Bacheler (Martha's sister and Merrill's wife) during the late 1930s, Irene Podayko from 1949 to 1964, and Enez Mitzkewich from 1969 until 1978. At any given time during the 1950s and 1960s, the Flemington Outlet employed from 30 to 36 people.

The "Lights of Broadway" Come to the Flemington Outlet

Because Flemington was on the direct route from Manhattan, New York, to the celebrity weekend spot of Bucks County, Pennsylvania, Stangl's Flemington Outlet was often visited by many notable personalities. Frequent visitors included actress Ann Sothern, actor Ralph Bellamy, and comedienne Zasu Pitts. Playwrights George Kaufman and Moss Hart were known to have stopped at the Flemington showroom at least once, as were Clark Gable, Kitty Carlisle, Helen Hayes, and Damon Runyon.

There were also a few noted "celebs" with permanent or vacation homes in the Flemington area. One of the Outlet's frequent local luminaries during the 1940s and 1950s was popular Swing bandleader and host of his own television show, Paul Whiteman. He and his wife often purchased Stangl pottery at the outlet for their large farm overlooking the Delaware River near Stockton, New Jersey. Outlet manager Merrill Bacheler remembers: "Mrs. Whiteman would come in and buy what she needed. She always paid by check that he (Paul Whiteman) had signed. The signature was a drawing of Paul Whiteman's face, you know, that moon-face caricature he always used on his bandstand. But that was his legal signature, and the bank always cashed it!"

Anne Elstner Mathews, "Stella Dallas" on radio during the 1940s and 1950s, decorated her River's Edge restaurant in Lambertville, New Jersey, with Stangl dinnerware purchased at the Flemington Outlet.

Many of these "show biz" folks also frequented Colligan's Stockton Inn at Stockton, New Jersey. Colligan's was Martin Stangl's favorite dining spot as well; he conducted many business dinners in the Stockton Inn's dining rooms. Colligan's was a preferred weekend hangout for writers F. Scott Fitzgerald, Damon Runyon, Robert Benchley, and Dorothy Parker. It was also where Lorenz Hart and Richard Rodgers wrote the song "There's a Small Hotel" in 1933. Not only was the song written there, it was actually about Colligan's!

During the early 1930s, three young itinerant artists painted extensive murals depicting early Hunterdon County life on the walls of the dining rooms. One of these young artists was Kurt Weise, who ultimately became one of Martin Stangl's closest friends and designed a few Stangl dinnerware patterns, including Martin Stangl's own Farm Life.

When not immersed in pottery production, Martin Stangl enjoyed spending time with his family, particularly his grandchildren. In addition to his home in Flemington, Martin Stangl spent time at his farm in Hunterdon County and weekends at his house at Beach Haven, New Jersey.

A few pieces of Martin Stangl's personal dinnerware from his farm near Sergeantsville, New Jersey, designed by friend and artist, Kurt Weise.

Postcard view of Stangl's Flemington Outlet, taken during the early 1960s.

Stangl Pottery — Flemington's Factory Outlet Pioneer

Bargain conscious shoppers had been aware of Flemington's Flemington Fur, Flemington Cut Glass, and Stangl Outlet for many years. During the 1950s and 1960s, however, more and more weekend shoppers were visiting the Flemington area to take advantage of an increasing number of shops, outlets, and local attractions, such as the Black River & Western Railroad. Up to 3,000 customers per day had been known to shop at the Stangl Outlet during busy weekends and holidays. Local officials were concerned that chronic weekend traffic jams were becoming commonplace in and around Flemington.

During the early 1960s, interest in Stangl's Flemington Outlet was further stimulated by a full-page blurb in the local area guidebook *Follow Me!* The guidebook featured photos of each attraction with attractive model Martha Fischer. On the Stangl Pottery page, Miss Fischer poses with a Stangl flowerpot and basket of dinnerware. The caption reads: "Who hasn't heard of this famous name? Built around the original old kilns in Flemington are Stangl's own factory showrooms where all their lovely American designs are on display in endless variety."

Reproduction of the Stangl Pottery photo in the 1964 area guidebook, Follow Me! *showing Martha Fischer holding one of Stangl's celebrated egg basket shopping baskets.*

In order to capitalize on the increasing number of tourists visiting the outlet, numerous "Flemington Exclusives" were produced. Many of these "Exclusive" items were designed to coordinate with Stangl's bestselling dinnerware patterns. Others were simply novelty items or short-run dinnerware patterns. Often the "Flemington Exclusives" were inexpensively decorated, with little or no carving, and marked with the simple "second" mark and no pattern name.

A favorite Flemington item was the handled tidbit tray. These were produced at the Flemington Outlet by drilling holes in plates to accommodate standard inexpensive handles. In 1958, Merrill Bacheler instituted the practice of producing handled tidbits as a means to unload stacks of plates that were otherwise not selling. Any items that sat too long at the outlet were candidates for a handle, but 10" plates were most often used. Usually the tidbits were advertised at very low prices in order to draw additional customers to the Flemington Outlet. Sometimes tidbits were simply given to outlet customers during special promotions. Because of the vast quantities of tidbits produced at the Flemington Outlet, they are very common items at this time.

In addition to the handled tidbits, many 10" plates were also converted into clocks during the 1960s and 1970s. Clinton Peterman, Stangl Pottery accountant, would drill the appropriate size hole and affix the clock movements and numerals — this in addition to his duties as accountant!

A model poses in 1967 with Stangl's newest introductions, Sculptured Fruit dinnerware and Black Gold artware.

Courtesy of the Hill-Fulper-Stangl Museum.

Throughout its history, linens, glassware, and ceramics not produced by Stangl had always been sold at the Flemington Outlet. By the mid 1960s, Stangl began advertising that the Outlet stocked more than just Stangl Pottery, as this 1970 photo attests. Courtesy of the Hill-Fulper-Stangl Museum.

From the 1940s onward, prices for second-quality items were hand written on the back of each piece with green china markers. Flemington Outlet merchandise can sometimes still be found with the original price scrawled across the back in green wax! First-quality pieces were always priced using paper price tags and Stangl paper labels; the paper labels were applied only to firsts and Flemington exclusives.

Ceramics Awareness Promoted at the Flemington Outlet — James Teague, the Log Cabin, the Walk-In Kiln, and the Stangl Museum

James Teague's log cabin workshop and groundhog kiln at Flemington. Courtesy of the Hill-Fulper-Stangl Museum.

Martin Stangl was firm in his conviction that the Flemington Outlet should be more than just a retail store. His vision was that the Flemington Outlet be as recognized for its educational and enlightening qualities as it was for bargain pottery. Martin Stangl was continually initiating pottery demonstrations and educational displays at the Flemington Outlet. So firmly did Martin Stangl believe in the importance of public pottery demonstration, he installed a pot thrower to demonstrate daily at the Flemington Outlet. In 1939, Martin Stangl hired North Carolina potter James Goodwin Teague to demonstrate salt glaze stoneware production in Flemington. James Teague moved his family from Seagrove, North Carolina, where his forebears had been potters for generations, to Flemington. So that Teague could authentically demonstrate his craft, Martin Stangl also paid him to move his log cabin workshop and kiln to Flemington. Rather than disturb his existing workshop, Martin Stangl provided Teague with the materials to build a new cabin and groundhog kiln on his North Carolina farm, which was then disassembled and loaded on a railcar for shipment to Flemington. The log cabin was actually constructed of used electric line poles that Martin Stangl had purchased for pennies from the power and light company. Since the poles were of uniform size and weatherproofed with creosote, it was a simple matter for Teague to cut them to size and build the cabin.

By January 1940, James Teague had moved his family from North Carolina to Flemington. During the early part of 1940, Teague and a workforce provided by Martin Stangl reconstructed the log cabin and groundhog kiln on Stangl's Flemington Outlet property. Construction was finished by early spring 1940, and Teague immediately began hand-turning stoneware crocks, jugs, and vases in the North Carolina style.

Teague's stoneware pieces were marked with an impressed "Stangl Stoneware" mark, then fired and salt glazed in the stone groundhog kiln next to the cabin. Teague's demonstrations attracted crowds of Flemington Outlet visitors, especially during weekends. For nearly two years, James Teague produced Stangl Stoneware salt glazed pottery, before moving back to North Carolina shortly after the start of World War II. Martin Stangl closed the log cabin in early 1942; it was not reopened for pottery production again until the 1960s.

In 1950, one of Stangl's most memorable displays was installed at the Flemington Outlet. Outlet manager Merrill Bacheler designed a display explaining the various procedures and manufacturing processes of Stangl Ware and utilizing space that was otherwise wasted in the largest of the Outlet's kilns. The display was shown in a waist-high semi-circular glass showcase. The glass case housed a step-by-step illustration of every stage of Stangl's dinnerware and artware production. Printed commentary and photos showing actual factory processes lined the wall of the kiln.

Postcard view of the walk-in kiln display as it appeared in the early 1960s. Tables in the foreground display the most popular dinnerware patterns and a multitude of hand-painted pansy and flower ashtrays.

Some of the items from the original kiln display showing each step in the process of creating a Fruit and Flowers creamer, form casting the shape in the mold through engobing, carving, painting, and glazing. From the Stangl and Fulper archival collection, courtesy the Wheaton Village Museum of American Glass.

The walk-in Kiln Display was enjoyed by thousands of visitors to Stangl's Flemington Outlet showrooms from the time it opened in 1950 until Stangl's close in 1978. Even today, to nearly all Stangl patrons, the Kiln Display was always the most memorable part of their visit. The original Kiln Display was dismantled in 1978 when the Stangl Outlet property was sold to Pfaltzgraff. The walk-in kiln remained empty until early 2000 when the kiln was reopened and now houses the Hill-Fulper-Stangl Museum. For more on this museum, please see the Hill-Fulper-Stangl Museum section farther along in this chapter.

Fulper Pottery Company had always encouraged visitors to watch the manufacturing processes at the original Flemington Plant #1 and then at Plant #2 after 1929. Martin Stangl continued to promote the viewing of pottery making by shoppers when he installed James Teague's log cabin at the Flemington Outlet and at department store pottery demonstrations. During World War II, visitors were persuaded to view the Flemington Outlet decorating rooms and see how the pottery bird figurines were painted. During the 1950s and 1960s, a small team of decorators was set up at the Outlet to demonstrate hand-painting by decorating small pansy and leaf ashtrays in vibrant colors. The ashtrays were glazed and fired in an electric rolling kiln installed in the large garage on the Flemington Outlet property.

In 1961, Martin Stangl had a new building constructed at the south end of the Flemington Outlet property. The new building, called the Ceramic Workshop, housed potters conducting daily demonstrations. The items produced at the workshop were brightly colored flower and leaf ashtrays, card suit ashtrays, and diminutive flower-shaped buttons and jewelry. The workshop was open weekdays from 9 a.m. to 4 p.m., and was advertised on mimeographed bulletins sent to folks on Stangl's mailing list.

Stangl's new Ceramic Workshop as advertised on a mimeographed bulletin. Christl Stangl Bacheler drew the artwork on this bulletin. Courtesy of the Hill-Fulper-Stangl Museum.

In 1965 there occurred two momentous events in Stangl's history. The first was the 50th anniversary celebration of Fulper Pottery's winning the Award of Merit gold medal at the 1915 Panama Pacific Exposition. For the occasion, additional pottery demonstrations were planned, and a museum displaying the archival products of the Fulper and Stangl potteries was opened to the public. The new Stangl Museum, entitled "50 Years of Pottery," was installed in the former Ceramic Workshop building. The pottery demonstrations were moved to the garage and James Teague's log cabin, and the workshop was remodeled as a museum building. Many of the cabinets housing the museum's displays were Early American antiques collected by Martin Stangl. The museum's curator, Helen Cervenka, was on hand to answer any questions concerning the pottery on display.

Stangl Museum curator Helen Cervenka in front of a cabinet of Stangl Pottery birds in 1965. Courtesy of the Hill-Fulper-Stangl Museum, gift of Helen Cervenka.

Cover of the 1965 booklet Stangl, A Portrait of Progress in Pottery.

In 1965, the booklet *Stangl, A Portrait of Progress in Pottery* was published. This booklet, written by Stangl's general manager James Paul, outlined the history of the company and included a detailed account of Stangl's manufacturing procedures. This booklet was given to each Stangl Museum visitor during 1965.

Unfortunately, Stangl's museum lost its home as retail space became increasingly valuable. In 1968 the museum collection was inventoried and insured prior to its move from the Stangl Museum building. Homes were found for the displays in the Flemington Outlet main showroom building. By early 1968, the former Stangl Museum building became a lamp showroom.

Appraisal drawing of the Stangl Pottery Flemington Outlet Mine Street property in 1966. The main showrooms are shaded in pink, the log cabin is the small purple building. The next building, in blue, was the garage and carpenter shop. This building also housed the rolling kiln where the pansy ashtrays were fired. The small green building attached to the garage is Martin Stangl's greenhouse. The last building, shaded orange, was originally the Ceramic Workshop, then became the original 1965 Stangl Museum.

Aerial view of Stangl's Trenton factory immediately following the fire on August 25, 1965. Courtesy of James Paul.

1965 — Stangl's Great Fire

Stangl's second major event of 1965 was a calamity. On August 25, a fire destroyed nearly half of the Trenton facility. Wiped out were the warehouses jam-packed with inventory awaiting holiday shipment. Also destroyed was one of the two tunnel kilns, the design and decorating departments, the conference room, and offices. Because the fire started on the second floor near the office and safe, it was first surmised that a burglar had set the blaze in trying to open the safe. As it turned out, the safe had not been tampered with. The fire, like the 1929 fire in Flemington, was electrical in origin. It was later determined that

Interior view of the Trenton factory showing extensive fire damage, including warped steel floor supports and girders. These girders were installed during the 1940s when the periodic kilns were removed and Martin Stangl added a second floor to this section to house the new offices, conference room, and kitchen. Courtesy of Clinton Peterman.

an electric freezer in the factory kitchen caused a short circuit that started the blaze.

The surviving kiln was only partially damaged and was quickly repaired and put back in service. Also, the buildings housing the clay processing equipment were unaffected. Firefighters at the time stated that had the wind been from another direction, the whole complex would have been destroyed.

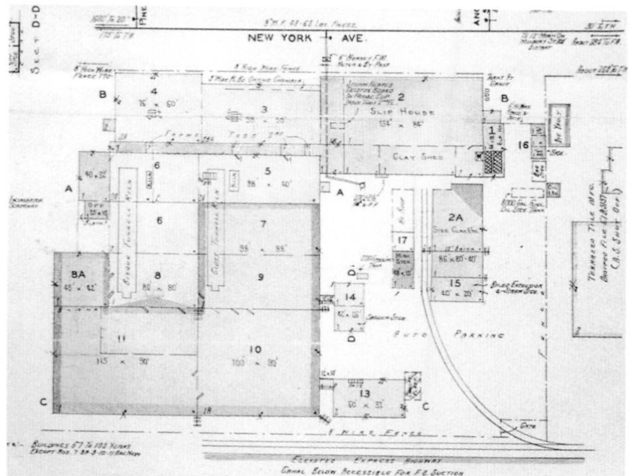

Fire insurance plan for Stangl's Trenton factory in 1966. Gray areas are the new construction after the fire; pink areas are the sections that survived the blaze.

Unlike the 1929 fire in Flemington, the building and equipment this time were insured for full value. Stangl Pottery accountant Clinton Peterman worked with the insurance company to speedily procure the funds necessary for rebuilding. Initially, 150 employees were put out of work. By October 1965, only six weeks after the fire, the plant was running limited production in the remaining buildings with 75 employees. Responsibility for rebuilding after the fire went to Stangl's general manager James Paul. By proper planning, James Paul was able to redesign the workspaces for more efficient operation and better utilization of space. By August 1966, nearly one year later, all employees had been called back to work, and Stangl Pottery was again fully operational.

1970s — An Era of Loss and Change

The decade of the 1970s saw significant changes in Stangl Pottery, both in operations at the Trenton plant and in the dinnerware itself. During the early 1970s, there was an ongoing endeavor to improve upon the Stangl lines and lower production costs as well.

The most tragic event concerning Stangl Pottery was the loss of Martin Stangl. Until the end of his life, Martin Stangl continued to personally direct Stangl operations in spite of failing eyesight and the general infirmities of an octogenarian. Martin Stangl was hospitalized with a heart attack in October 1971. Too spunky to allow himself complete incapacitation, Martin Stangl insisted on directing the company from his hospital bed. Nearly every day he required his chauffeur, John Teyhen, to bring key employees to the hospital to update him on operations. Designer Rose Herbeck was brought in on a regular basis to present him with her latest dinnerware designs. As it happened, Rose Herbeck was the last person to see Martin Stangl alive before he breathed his last breath on February 13, 1972.

Martin Stangl, 1888 – 1972

Frank Wheaton Takes Command

Because none of Martin Stangl's children were involved with the pottery at the time of his death, his will directed that the entire Stangl Pottery operation be sold. In June 1972, Frank Wheaton, owner of Wheaton Glass Company and Dorchester Industries in Millville, New Jersey, bought Stangl Pottery. Frank Wheaton had originally planned to use Stangl's Trenton plant for the production of pottery bottles for Avon, but later found he could have them produced more cheaply in Mexico.

Frank Wheaton fully intended to continue manufacturing a first-rate product line in keeping with the Stangl Pottery reputation. In July 1972, Michael P. Davis, new vice president of Stangl Pottery, sent the following letter to all retailers that carried Stangl products. It began: "Dear Stangl Dealer: We are pleased to announce that new ownership has undertaken the management of the Stangl Pottery Co. Mr. Frank Wheaton, Jr., President, Wheaton Industries, assumed ownership effective June 27, 1972. Both Mr. Wheaton and I are aware of the many uncertainties that have been associated with Stangl during the past few years. These uncertainties now belong to the past, and we at Stangl are enthusiastically looking to the future. You, our valued dealers, can now be assured of continuous management and policies designed to help you toward maximum profit growth with Stangl products. Our plans include programs in the area of national advertising and sales promotion, product and design development, and major improvements in sales representation and service. Any suggestions you may have in any of the above areas would be most welcome..." The letter was signed Michael P. Davis, Vice-President. Unbeknownst to Mr. Davis, very new to the company at that time, that under Martin Stangl's guidance the company faced no "uncertainties," had an established national advertising program and sales staff as well as a talented and innovative design team. Apparently, the "uncertainties" to which he was referring in his letter existed only during the four months between Martin Stangl's death and Frank Wheaton's purchasing the company. Because Martin Stangl had prepared no one to eventually succeed him, there was no one to assist the "Wheaton team" in understanding how Stangl Pottery had successfully operated for the past 50 years. Many of Frank Wheaton's managers assigned to Stangl Pottery were proficient in other aspects of the ceramics industry but were ill-equipped to maintain a profit with Stangl Pottery's labor-intensive hand-carved, hand-painted dinnerware lines.

A valiant effort was made to continue the Stangl tradition. Designers Rudy Kleinebeckel and Sandra Ward developed many new art and dinnerware lines during 1973 and 1974. Many of Stangl's older dinnerware patterns and Antique Gold artware continued to sell well, and sales of the new patterns began to increase. However, by the mid 1970s, rising production and labor costs and very cheap imported dinnerware were putting a terrific strain on the company. In efforts to reduce labor, Stangl Pottery management was exploring such economical production methods as white-bodied ware, transfer print motifs, silk-screen designs, and overglaze decals.

As sales started to spiral downward, Stangl Pottery began a yo-yo like practice of employee layoffs and rehiring. To lessen production labor, by 1975 all of Stangl's products were converted to a high-quality, white-colored body; Stangl's traditional red clay was no longer utilized. The use of a white body eliminated the need to apply engobe and speeded the greenware finishing process. For a short time after the body color transition, many white-bodied dinnerware patterns continued to be hand-carved. This added depth to the designs, but was soon stopped in order to eliminate even more labor-generated costs. With the change to white-bodied dinnerware production, Stangl Pottery instantly lost its unique identity. While this move may have seemed cost effective, Stangl customers who had been loyal to Stangl's red-bodied "hand-carved, hand-painted" dinnerware immediately stopped buying Stangl products. This extremely shortsighted move cost the company more in sales than it saved in labor! So the layoff and rehire yo-yo continued, resulting in an employee strike in 1976. Local 391 of the International Brotherhood of Pottery and Allied Workers called the strike in protest of the layoffs and "management deficiencies."

By the late 1970s, Frank Wheaton was having a very tough time keeping a handle on Stangl Pottery. Because he needed to spend nearly all of his time managing his vast holdings and glass factories employing 5,000 in Millville, 75 miles from Trenton, it was impossible for him to personally manage Stangl Pottery as Martin Stangl had done. Wheaton was required to trust managers to direct Stangl Pottery. Unfortunately, he could not find a single manager to competently run the company. During the six years Wheaton owned Stangl Pottery, he had a parade of management through Stangl's Trenton doors. If they weren't making shortsighted business decisions, they were alienating the employees or even "misdirecting" money and products. The only thing stable during Frank Wheaton's ownership of the company was the Flemington Outlet. One of his former managers was known to have said, "we could tell those Flemington tourists that 'dirt' was hand painted and they would buy it!"

By 1978, Stangl Pottery was one million dollars in debt. The workforce had diminished to 40, down from 150 in 1974. Japanese dinnerware was being sold more cheaply than it cost Stangl to produce dinnerware. The manufacturing equipment at the antiquated Trenton plant was in desperate need of replacement. The oldest part of the factory dated from the 1860s, and Anchor Pottery had installed all of the clay processing equipment during the early 1900s. So obsolete was the Stangl equipment that replacement would be an overwhelming expense.

Frank Wheaton was faced with a great dilemma. He certainly did not want to cut short the life of the venerable Stangl Pottery, America's second oldest continuously operating pottery. Yet he could not continue to throw good money after bad by trying to run Stangl Pottery through inexperienced or uncaring managers. Considering that he would have to invest an enormous amount of money to replace all the archaic production equipment at a time when the market for American ceramics was dismally bleak, the decision was made to close Stangl.

America's Oldest Pottery Purchases Stangl

In July of 1978, the Pfaltzgraff Company, operating in York, Pennsylvania since 1811, purchased the Flemington and Trenton properties, all inventory, and legal rights to the Stangl trademark. In October 1978 after the last of the outstanding orders had been filled, the Stangl Trenton factory was closed. By November 1978, all remaining Stangl wares had been liquidated from the Flemington Outlet, and Stangl Pottery was officially terminated. The closing of Stangl Pottery concluded a 164-year history of New Jersey ceramics and the ending of a truly unique American product. Nevertheless, it did not conquer the "essence" of Stangl.

Frank Wheaton Preserves Stangl Heritage

Frank Wheaton never abandoned his "hope" for Stangl Pottery. He planned to one day begin production of Stangl products again but in a manner that would allow him to control manufacturing. Because Frank Wheaton's true passion was American history, particularly New Jersey's early industrial heritage, he spent countless amounts of money and energy recreating an authentic early New Jersey industrial community. The Museum of American Glass and Wheaton Village in Millville, New Jersey, are enduring testimony to Wheaton's devotion to historic preservation.

During the waning months of 1978, Frank Wheaton had a team of movers carefully pack Stangl molds, models, records, stencils, ware boards, and even the electric rolling kilns for the 75-mile trek to Millville, requiring nearly 60 full-size tractor-trailer truckloads. It was the molds, representing over 60 years of Fulper and Stangl product lines that comprised the bulk of the move. Frank Wheaton was primarily interested in saving the block molds and case molds, the "master molds," from which production molds were made. The only production molds brought to Millville were for a few of the bird figurines and some of the dinnerware shapes. Upon arrival in Millville, two of the kilns and most of the Town & Country and Kiddieware production molds were set up for immediate use, but everything else was stored in Wheaton Glass Company warehouses.

Frank Wheaton's Royal Cumberland

During 1979 and 1980, Frank Wheaton contracted with the American division of Royal Copenhagen to produce dinnerware and vases inspired by Stangl motifs. Frank Wheaton set up a ceramics operation at one of his Dorchester Industries plants in Millville and brought in Stangl designer Irene Sarnecki to create several new motifs and instruct the new decorating staff. Frank Wheaton's new ceramics were trademarked "Royal Cumberland," named for the New Jersey county in which they were produced. The line featured adaptations of Stangl's Town & Country, Fruit, Grape, Holly, and Kiddieware dinnerware designs, and several bird and animal shapes. The Royal Cumberland pieces were made from Stangl molds, and the quality of the product was comparable to Stangl. However, by 1981, this incarnation of Stangl Pottery was also ended. The Stangl Pottery molds and equipment stored in the warehouses were left to languish into oblivion.

A few of Frank Wheaton's Royal Cumberland dinnerware patterns. The banding was hand-painted under the glaze, and the motifs were fired-on overglaze decals.

Frank Wheaton's Royal Cumberland 4" Tulip vase in cobalt glaze.

1990s and New Stangl

During 1991 and 1992, Frank Wheaton's grandson, Bob Shaw, attempted to re-establish the manufacturing of true Stangl products at the Royal Cumberland plant in Millville. With Frank Wheaton backing the project, Bob Shaw began producing items inspired by Stangl's wig stands, Kiddieware, Town & Country dinnerware, and hand-painted flowerpot lines. The articles were all cast using original Stangl molds retrieved from the warehouses. A few of the Kiddieware motifs were older Stangl designs, but most were newly created for this venture. The new Stangl product line was marked with a new variation of an old Stangl trademark. The "new Stangl" was marketed through several florist and gift shops.

Bob Shaw intended to ultimately produce a complete line of quality Stangl gift and dinnerware items, including Stangl lamps and pottery bird figurines. While the shapes and patterns resembled original Stangl products, the ceramic

A few examples of Bob Shaw's hand-painted "New Stangl" in a Town & Country finish.

materials available during the early 1990s precluded that the body, colors, and glazes did not approximate original Stangl quality. The colors lacked brilliance and usually did not match Stangl's original colors. Unfortunately, the Stangl collecting community was adverse to renewed production of Stangl-like ceramics. Even the New Stangl mark, a variation of the script Stangl trademark, was a cause for confusion. Only occasionally were pieces stamped "Millville," so antiques dealers of somewhat shady repute were selling "New Stangl" as original Stangl. The only merit collectors gave to Bob Shaw's New Stangl product line was to a series of wig stands artfully decorated as Betty Boop, Charlie Chaplin, pirates, and baseball players. By 1993, the high cost of skilled labor and difficulties encountered in producing a quality, hand-crafted product precipitated the end of Bob Shaw's New Stangl.

Millville warehouse, October 1997, thousands of Stangl molds stored on the second floor.

Stangl Pottery Mold Rescue 1997 – 1999

By Diana Bullock-Runge

In the fall of 1997, Rob Runge was offered the amazing opportunity as a Stangl Pottery historian and preservationist to relocate the original Stangl pottery molds. The molds had been warehoused in a turn-of-the-century brick factory building in Millville since the cessation of Stangl production in 1978.

The building was slated for demolition, time was running out, and Rob swiftly embarked on an aggressive Stangl mold rescue. Working exclusively for Frank Wheaton and the Wheaton Village Museum of American Glass, Rob and I purchased the entire contents of the warehouse so that preservation and distribution of the molds would be at our sole discretion. In addition, we were at the early planning stages of our Hill-Fulper-Stangl Museum and knew that the molds would play an important role in our future displays. Ultimately, many of the molds were distributed to the Trenton City Museum, the State Museum of New Jersey, and the Stangl Fulper Collectors Club. Most of the bird molds were donated to the Stangl Bird Collectors Club for preservation and historic displays. All molds were treated with silicone to render them unusable.

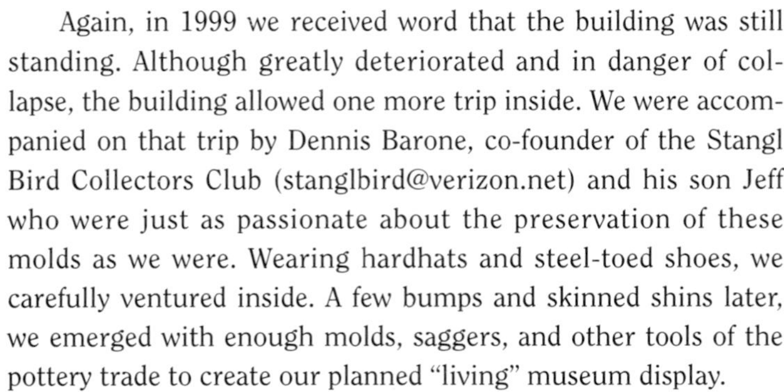

The utter expanse of the warehouse with stacks of Stangl molds.

We made several trips during that first year to rescue as many historically important molds as possible. The effects of 20 years of neglect, a leaking roof, and the improper packing in 1978 left many of the molds in slimy, wet condition, but there were still thousands that were spared from ruin. Considering the sheer tonnage of the plaster molds, the decision-making was difficult as to which molds to rescue for their historical significance.

Again, in 1999 we received word that the building was still standing. Although greatly deteriorated and in danger of collapse, the building allowed one more trip inside. We were accompanied on that trip by Dennis Barone, co-founder of the Stangl Bird Collectors Club (stanglbird@verizon.net) and his son Jeff who were just as passionate about the preservation of these molds as we were. Wearing hardhats and steel-toed shoes, we carefully ventured inside. A few bumps and skinned shins later, we emerged with enough molds, saggers, and other tools of the pottery trade to create our planned "living" museum display.

Mold rescuers Dennis Barone (left) and Diana Bullock (right) at work.

Stangl's original Flemington factory building and outlet store, now a Pfaltzgraff showroom. Two of the three original kilns are visible, with one of these now housing the Hill-Fulper-Stangl Potteries Museum.

The Establishment of the Hill-Fulper-Stangl Potteries Museum

By Diana Bullock-Runge

In the summer of 1999, following negotiations lasting nearly a year, Rob and I signed a contract with Pfaltzgraff Pottery Co., current owners of the original Stangl factory building in Flemington. This location is now a retail outlet store, but the original kilns are still in existence and situated within the selling area. The agreement we entered into with Pfaltzgraff was to create a museum inside the largest kiln and a "living demonstration" display in one of the smaller kilns. The largest kiln had housed the display of Stangl dinnerware and birds showing the many steps involved in the manufacturing process, set up by outlet manager Merrill Bacheler in 1950. These kilns are the only ones of this type still in existence in New Jersey, a surprising fact considering that New Jersey was the pottery capital in this country in the late nineteenth and early twentieth centuries. Stangl's is also considered the largest existing kiln left in the country.

In an effort to finance the design and construction of a museum display of Hill, Fulper, and Stangl pottery, Rob and I launched our first fundraising effort in May of 1999 by offering some of our personal pottery collection for sale on eBay. In June of 1999, we offered a Fulper and Stangl Museum lot, consisting of a signed and inscribed copy of Rob's first book, *Collector's Encyclopedia of Stangl Dinnerware;* an autographed photo of Stangl's top three designers, Kay Hackett, Irene Sarnecki, and Rose Herbeck; and a framed certificate stating that there would be a permanent plaque at the museum declaring that the winning bidder provided the "cornerstone" for this project. The lot was won by Frank and Liz Kramar of Elkton, Maryland. Our next fundraiser was in the form of Year 2000 Stangl Photo Calendars. There were four styles, Stangl Dinnerware, Stangl Kiddieware, Stangl Birds, and a biographical photo collage of Rose Herbeck's Life and Designs. These calendars sold for $20 and were successful in generating money for the museum fund.

Museum "cornerstone" benefactors Liz & Frank Kramar, holding Rob's first book.

Fundraising Year 2000 Stangl Photo Calendars.

By February 13, 2000, we had accumulated nearly $20,000 through our private fundraising efforts, enough to begin construction of the kiln display. We began by removing what remained of the rotted display platform installed in 1950 to leave the original brick walls ready for the work crew. Glass showcases were installed, generously provided by Paul Cona of Cona Antiques, Lafayette, New Jersey. Stangl designer Kay Hackett created an original floor medallion design for the display.

Diana and Rob with the original Flemington Outlet site plans, just prior to construction.

The Hill-Fulper-Stangl Museum Kiln Display grand opening celebration was held April 15, 2000. The dedication ceremony and ribbon cutting were officiated by Flemington Mayor Ken Kutscher and Hunterdon County Freeholder George Muller. The museum is now permanently open to the public six days a week, 9:30 to 5:30, and Saturdays 9:30 to 7:00. The Museum is located in the old Stangl Pottery Factory Showrooms, now Pfaltzgraff, at Mine St., Flemington, New Jersey.

Original floor medallion created by Stangl designer Kay Hackett for the Hill-Fulper-Stangl Museum.

A small portion of the gathering assembled at the base of the kiln as they await the grand opening festivities. Pictured from left to right are George Ringer, Nancy Ringer, Anita Stiles, Vladimir Herbeck, Rose Herbeck, and Nancy Geddes.

After the official opening of the museum display, nearly 200 visitors filed through the kiln. Pfaltzgraff reported record crowds visiting during the following week as well. Several former Stangl employees traveled to join the celebration, including Irene Podayko, Outlet asst. manager; Evelyn Crone, bird decorator; Dorothy Denyse, dinnerware decorator; Josephine Tiffenbach; and Charles Jankowski, Stangl's ceramic engineer.

Merrill and Christl Stangl Bacheler on the steps of the Walk-in Kiln Display conceived by Merrill 50 years before.

During the Grand Opening celebration, Kay Hackett gave a folio of her original Stangl Pottery sketches and renderings to the Museum. Daughter-in-law Mary McLaughlin looks on.

A view of some of the newly-filled cabinets of the Hill-Fulper-Stangl Potteries Museum during the grand opening.

The Ever-Popular Meet Me at the Kiln Educational Programs

January 2001 began the second year for Rob Runge's popular "Meet Me at the Kiln" program. Since the grand opening of the Hill-Fulper-Stangl Museum last year, Rob has presented his program to several local-interest groups. The program includes a slide show with images from the earliest days of the pottery and a personalized tour of the museum, which is housed inside the original Fulper/Stangl kiln. Rob then takes the group on a tour of the buildings and grounds to explain the manufacturing process.

Rob explaining the history of the log cabin and groundhog kiln constructed and used by North Carolina potter James Teague from 1940 to 1941.

One of the recently featured museum displays was called "A Bird's Eye View of Stangland." A large collection of Stangl birds was on loan to the museum from Frank and Liz Kramar. It included birds from the common to examples seldom seen. This bird display was followed by a special exhibit of Kay Hackett designs. It included examples of known production patterns as well as some of Kay's gorgeous sample pieces.

Recent acquisitions on display at the museum are shown throughout this book.

Martin Stangl relaxing at home during a rare break in his demanding schedule.

Key Personalities that Made Stangl Pottery Successful

Martin Stangl *was* Stangl Pottery. The innovations and direction he provided the company are chronicled throughout this history chapter. This section is concerned with the folks Martin Stangl relied on for their contributions and carrying out his directives.

Merrill and Christl at their home in 2001.

Merrill and Christl Stangl Bacheler

Christl Stangl, Martin Stangl's middle daughter, began working at Stangl's Trenton factory following graduation from high school in 1935. One of her first jobs in Trenton was to paint the "Stangl Pottery" logo on one of the buildings there. Christl reminisces, "Daddy must have thought I was the boy of the family because he put me way up there on a scaffold to paint this little sticker on the side of the building. But I did it! When it was done, it must have been about 15 feet square."

Christl was then required to create line drawings for each of Stangl's artware and dinnerware shapes to be used in company catalogs and mimeographed flyers and mailers. After attending college for interior design, Christl tried finding employment in the interior decorating field. Unable to obtain a job with a decorating firm, Christl accepted her father's offer of employment in 1938 as assistant manager of the Flemington Outlet. Her older sister Martha was the Flemington Outlet manager at that time. Christl put her decorating talents to use

A group of Flemington Outlet mimeographed flyers and ads, all drawn by Martha and Christl Stangl.

at the outlet by creating outstanding table settings and artware displays. Both Christl and Martha hand-drew all of the mimeograph advertising used at the Flemington Outlet.

In 1938, Merrill Bacheler began working at Stangl's Trenton factory. He soon became an important part of Stangl's sales team and did extensive traveling as a sales representative. Merrill also continued to supervise John Kunsman's traveling department store demonstrations.

Christl and Merrill were married in 1940. While raising their small children during the 1940s, Christl decorated birds at home in the evenings while the children slept. She also was in charge of the demonstrations and teas put on for group tours to the Flemington Outlet. Merrill worked at Eastern Aircraft in Trenton from 1942 through 1945 for the war effort. In the meantime, Martha Stangl married Merrill's brother, Jack Bacheler, a commercial artist. Martin Stangl wanted Jack to work at the pottery as a designer, but Jack chose not to abandon his established, successful art career.

Following World War II, Martha resigned at the Flemington Outlet, and Merrill Bacheler was offered the position of Outlet manager. Merrill possessed a degree in business management and with his sales experience was able to quickly take charge of the outlet. During this time, Christl helped occasionally at the outlet by conducting demonstrations and organizing group tours. She also conducted several decorating demonstrations at local New York and New Jersey department stores.

Decorating demonstration plate in Blueberry pattern created by Christl Stangl Bacheler at a B. Altman's demonstration in September 1960. Courtesy of the Robert Sherman collection.

Merrill Bacheler initiated many concepts during his time as Flemington Outlet manager, but his most remembered accomplishment was the popular walk-in kiln display. This display was built in response to the many Stangl Pottery shoppers asking, "How is it made?" Merrill utilized one of the most prominent features of the salesroom, the largest of the old brick periodic kilns no longer used. As Flemington's popularity as a tourist destination increased following World War II, Stangl's kilns became legendary novelties as fewer and fewer "old-timers" were left to recall New Jersey's "hey-day of clay" when such kilns were commonplace features of the clay districts.

Merrill Bacheler capitalized on the notoriety of the kilns by opening the largest as his "Walk-in Kiln Display." Within the kiln was installed a waist high, semi-circular display cabinet showing the various manufacturing steps required to produce Stangl's dinnerware and artware. On the wall were large photographs of actual Trenton factory production processes and signs explaining the procedures.

Christl and Merrill Bacheler retired from managing the Flemington Outlet in 1964.

Dave and Betty Stangl Thomas

Martin Stangl's youngest daughter Betty also worked at Stangl Pottery but at the Trenton factory rather than the Flemington Outlet. She spent time in each of the departments to learn the various processes. During the summer of 1939, Betty worked with John Tierney in the plaster shop where she designed and sculpted several artware shapes.

Candleholder designed by Betty Stangl Thomas in 1939. Courtesy of the Hill-Fulper-Stangl Museum.

Betty attended the New York State College of Ceramics at Alfred University where she earned degrees in ceramic arts and mechanical drawing. While at Alfred, Betty met Kay Kastner Hackett and was so impressed with Kay's talent, she insisted that her father hire Kay at Stangl Pottery, so Kay was hired as designer in 1941. Another of Betty's classmates, Cleo Crawford Salerno, was also hired by Stangl as a designer in 1942.

Betty Stangl Thomas in 1999.

David W. Thomas met and courted Betty Stangl while he too was an Alfred University student. After graduating in 1940 with a ceramic engineering degree, Dave worked in the refractory industry and then enlisted in the Flying Cadets during World War II. He and Betty were married in 1942 prior to his shipping out.

Martin Stangl hired Dave Thomas as ceramic engineer following World War II. Dave was engineer from 1945 until 1950 when Heinrich Below left Stangl Pottery to found Pennsbury Pottery.

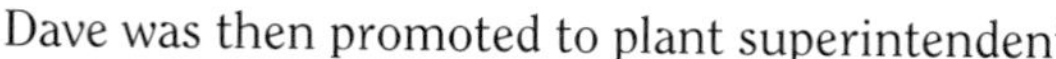

Dave was then promoted to plant superintendent.

Dave instituted many improvements at Stangl Pottery, such as using conveyors to expedite ware handling; the spraying of engobe to create a smooth, bright finish; improving durable clay bodies; and developing a number of glazes and artware lines.

Dave Thomas left Stangl Pottery in 1956 to purchase Ticer Pottery in Ohio and ultimately became a well-respected ceramics consultant to such firms as International Chemicals. The Thomases eventually retired to Florida where Dave launched Thomas Tiles, Inc., and Betty enjoys golf and raising prize-winning roses.

Dave Thomas poses in Stangl's clay storage bays during the early 1950s. Courtesy of Dave and Betty Stangl Thomas.

Aztec smoking set, one of the artware designs and glazes developed by Dave Thomas. Courtesy of Dave and Betty Stangl Thomas.

Gerald Ewing

Thanks to Alaine Ewing, Gerald Ewing's niece, we have the following information.

Gerald Ewing was born in Flemington, New Jersey, on December 29, 1915. He studied art in Trenton, attended the Guildhall School of Music and Drama in London, then Yale University. His early studies in painting and music led to an interest in lighting and the importance of lighting in the conception and development of architectural design.

Yearbook portrait photo of Gerald Ewing. Courtesy of Alaine Ewing.

Martin Stangl hired Gerald Ewing in 1937 as designer and as developer of a decorating department for Stangl's new hand-painted dinnerware line. Gerald Ewing created Stangl's silk-screened patterns, including Gazelle and May Feast. He also designed Stangl's wholly hand-painted dinnerware patterns during 1938. During the great demand for hand-painted dinnerware designs in 1939 and 1940, he and Ethel Kennedy developed several dinnerware patterns.

Gerald Ewing's Gazelle silk-screened dinnerware pattern of 1937.

At the outbreak of World War II, Gerald Ewing left Stangl Pottery to enlist and then served in the Army Engineer Intelligence. Following the war, he established himself as a lighting consultant and opened offices in both New York and Connecticut. Some of his work included the Department of Commerce Trade Affairs in Milan, Italy, and Paris, France. Gerald Ewing also developed much of the lighting at Colonial Williamsburg, Virginia. Gerald Ewing passed away in 1992 at the age of 77.

The #3200 Pear dinnerware pattern was a Gerald Ewing design and Stangl Pottery's first wholly hand-painted open stock dinnerware pattern.

Ranger, Gerald Ewing's best known Stangl dinnerware pattern, introduced in 1939.

Irene Sarnecki

Irene Sarnecki began her career with Stangl Pottery as a dinnerware decorator in 1948. She quickly showed her mettle by developing her own decorating techniques and within a few years was promoted to decorating supervisor. Irene relates: "I really worked hard for the decorators, 'The Girls' as we called them. If there was a pattern or something they wanted decorated at a certain amount per piece, I would tell Mr. Stangl that it was too difficult for the girls, he would have to raise the pay rate or scrap the design. And he would do it. There were a lot of designs that were scrapped because it wasn't worth the extra decorating cost… Sometimes in the summers when it was so hot, the decorating room was near one of the kilns, I would say to Mr. Stangl 'its too hot up there for the girls to work, they should have the afternoon off', and then about 35 of us would go up to Washington Crossing Park and play baseball. It was too hot to work, but not to play!"

Irene Sarnecki is still respected by her decorating staff, over 20 years since they last worked together. Here Irene (left) reminisces with two of her former decorators, Florence Dunn Glenn (center) and Florence Gardner (right) at a recent reunion.

During the times Stangl's design staff was overwhelmed with work, Martin Stangl called on Irene to develop motifs or patterns. She was instrumental in creating Stangl's wig stands, pitcher and bowl sets, and many short-run special-order items. Irene also designed several very popular dinnerware patterns, as well as nearly all of Martin Stangl's personal Christmas card coasters. "Mr. Stangl was always having me work on something. But sometimes we would argue about something, and he would tell me I was fired. So I would go out the front door of the pottery, walk around the other side of the building and come in the back door and go right back to work. I just kept busy with the decorating department and refused to do any of his special projects or design work. Then eventually we would speak again and I would do more designing."

Irene's primary accomplishment at Stangl Pottery was the relationship she developed with her decorating crew. She earned the respect and loyalty of the decorators with her fairness and her continuous protection of their interests. Irene is still in contact with many of Stangl's decorators today.

James Paul

In 1964, James Paul began as Stangl Pottery's sales manager. Eight salesmen were under his supervision, with 4,000 department, gift, and jewelry stores comprising the Stangl customer base. One of James Paul's first projects was to pen the tiny booklet *History of Stangl Pottery* in 1964. The booklet, which briefly outlined the history of the company, was distributed to Stangl Pottery retailers across the country. The following year, James Paul re-wrote his original *History of Stangl Pottery,* added photos, and re-titled the booklet *Stangl, A Portrait of Progress in Pottery* for Stangl's "50 Years of Pottery" celebration.

Because of James Paul's vast expertise and deft ability to research a problem and determine the best possible solution, he was quickly elevated to general manager. Several of his accomplishments as Stangl's general manager were the development and introduction of the Granada Gold and Black Gold finishes and the introduction of paper napkins printed with Stangl's popular dinnerware motifs by Fort Howard Paper Co. James Paul and Clinton Peterman together replaced the old "cash-box and sales slip" method of cashiering at the Flemington Outlet with a National Cash Register system of cash accounting, and profits at the outlet nearly doubled with the new system.

James Paul and Rose Herbeck during a recent get-together.

James Paul's greatest accomplishment for Stangl Pottery occurred in 1965. Following the disastrous Trenton factory fire in August that year, Martin Stangl entrusted the entire rebuilding process to James Paul. Martin Stangl was not disappointed. Through diligent research and planning, the rebuilt portions of the Trenton factory were greatly improved and much more efficient than the originals could ever have been. James Paul was also responsible for Stangl's hiring talented designer and sculptor Rudy Kleinebeckel and providing his transportation from Germany to Trenton in 1968. Even though it has been more than 30 years since his employ at Stangl Pottery, James Paul is still considered "Stangl Family" by those who worked beside him those many years ago.

Rose Herbeck

By Diana E. Bullock-Runge

Rose Herbeck was born November 25, 1921, in Germany, the daughter of a Danish piano teacher and a German educator and scientist. She graduated from the Bavarian State Ceramic College in Landshüt, Bavaria, with a Master of Arts degree in Ceramic Art and Science. She also took courses at the Munich Fine Arts Academy during 1941 and learned the art of mosaics.

During WWII, Rose endured the bombings in Munich and then met Vladimir Herbeck, an engineer from Moscow. They met by chance in the street, had a whirlwind romance, married, bought a kiln, and set up a pottery in an old horse stable. The Herbecks were in operation from 1945 – 1951. Vladimir handled the technical and electrical part while Rose handled the creative end. Her original and innovative designs were very popular and sold in the shops and department stores. Sometimes out of necessity, Rose bartered her pottery in exchange for milk, eggs, and other household items. Eventually things improved, and they had to hire some people to work the wheel and another to help with the painting. They worked day and night, with Rose painting for hours at a time.

A Herbeck-Keramik catalog sheet from 1948 showing some of Rose's original designs sold to German department stores. Courtesy of Rose and Vladimir Herbeck.

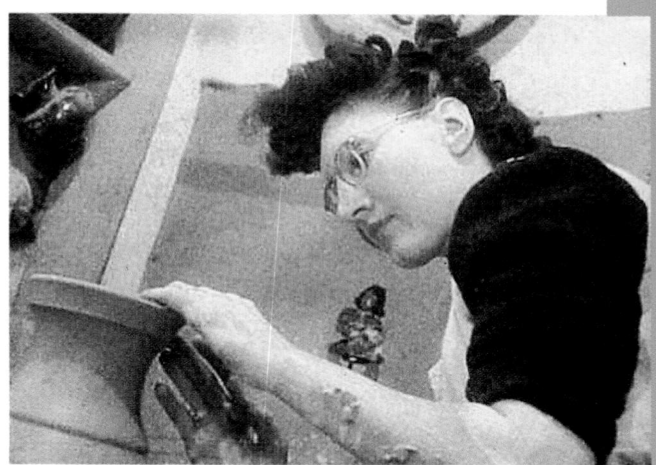

Rose working at the wheel in her studio in Germany, 1947. Courtesy of Rose and Vladimir Herbeck.

Because Germany had lost the war and the devaluation of the German mark (four to one) was devastating for the young couple, they immigrated to Toronto, Canada, with daughter Eva, age seven. Four years later, in 1957, they relocated to Trenton, New Jersey, and became United States citizens in 1962. Vladimir was plant engineer for Robertson Art Tile in Morrisville, Pennsylvania, and Rose was hired by an old family friend, Heinrich Below, at Pennsbury Pottery. She left there and worked for Edward Boehm at Boehm Porcelain for a time before going to Stangl in 1967 as a designer. Under Martin Stangl's watchful eye, Rose was expected to create a new design sample nearly every day. She was there for six years, so that adds up to a lot of original designs. Rose's sample designs are very sought after by collectors and depending on design, can easily sell as high as $200 – $300 each.

Rose has been a popular public speaker for many years and during one of her recent programs related the following: "When I was hired by Mr. Stangl during the 1960s, his company was at the height of success. He sold his ware — beautifully hand painted — to 4,000 stores in the USA. One hundred fifty people including 50 decorators worked in Trenton and Flemington. The Stangl outlet in Flemington, where 'seconds' and also my samples were sold cheap was a real success. People came from New York, Philadelphia, Trenton, and all around.

"When I came into the company, Mr. Stangl had just survived a devastating fire in 1965. Six factory buildings and offices in ashes! When I started there, he had just finished rebuilding. At that time, he had a lady fashion designer who had no idea of pottery techniques. She lasted only a few weeks. He wanted a ceramist. I was the answer! Mr. Stangl was delighted, especially since I was familiar with his trademark sgraffito technique, that I knew how to make glazes and that I knew the entire pottery business.

"At the start, Mr. Stangl told me to just put flowers on his dinner plates. Any flowers! Increasingly, he came up with specific ideas, certain flowers. More and more, he trusted my

One of Rose's popular design samples with a floral motif. Courtesy of Rose and Vladimir Herbeck.

taste. He also let me do more. I helped the sales manager to set up the very important annual International Ceramic Show in Atlantic City. I made, by hand, color-coordinated place mats for these shows all over the USA.

"I designed mugs, then just becoming very popular. I did tiles with various glazes and decors, both underglaze and glaze painted. I started the line of clay painting called Gingerbread. These pieces were only sold in Flemington and they sold fast.

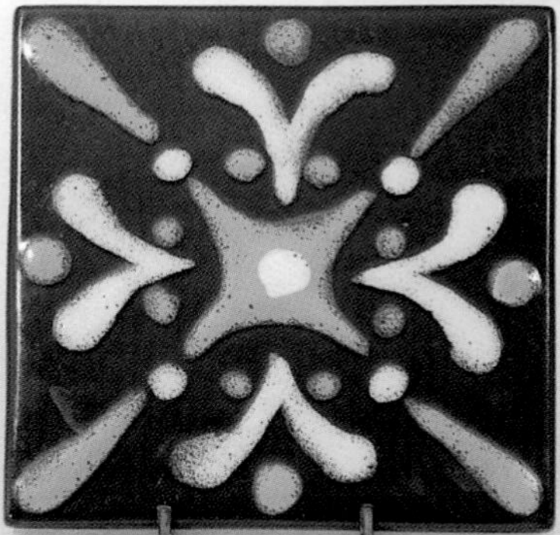

One of Rose Herbeck's Stangl Pottery ceramic tile designs. Courtesy of the Hill-Fulper-Stangl Museum.

"When I came into the company, Mr. Stangl was already rather old but was still fully involved. His whole life was his pottery until the end. Even in the hospital, he wanted to see new designs every day. Two days before he died in 1972, Mr. Stangl sent his chauffeur John to bring me to the hospital so he could look at my pottery. I was the last to see him. I was fired the next day by Mrs. Stangl, Vera, as she had no interest in the pottery and planned to sell it immediately."

A sampling of Rose's Gingerbread line.

Rose Herbeck's famous Colonial Rose pattern.

Following her career at Stangl, Rose was employed at the Engineering Department of Dow Jones Co., publisher of the *Wall Street Journal* newspaper. She was instrumental in establishing an art show there for over 800 employees. During that time she also produced a series of decorative tiles in polychrome glazes. Following her retirement from Dow Jones in 1988, Rose has spent several years as an educational speaker and recently has been producing watercolors from her home in Trenton, New Jersey.

Close-up of framed Kingfisher ceramic tile by Rose Herbeck

Kay Hackett

By Diana E. Bullock-Runge

Kay Hackett was born Kathleen Kastner in Batavia, New York. She began drawing at age eight and was given her first watercolor set at age ten. Then, when she was a teen, two townswomen who were patrons of the arts took notice. Impressed with Kay's talent, they provided the funds for art lessons. Soon after, she enrolled at the New York State College of Ceramics at Alfred University.

Graduation photo at Alfred University 1941. Courtesy of Kay Hackett.

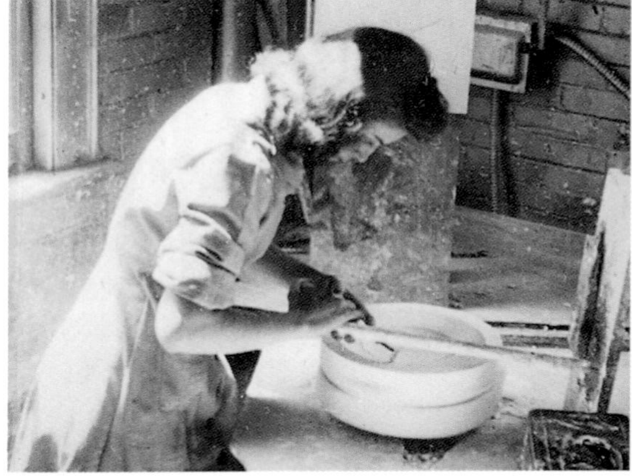

Kay working in her studio at Alfred University 1940. Courtesy of Kay Hackett.

Kay was a ceramic design major at Alfred. Her thesis was on various effects of glazes and firing using red body clays. A classmate of Kay's at the time, Betty Stangl, urged her father to hire Kay. The topic of her thesis drew interest from Martin Stangl as he was developing products using red clay and she already had experience in it. He originally offered her $20 a week but she held out for $25, taking a ten-week teaching position while she waited him out.

Kay arrived in Flemington in October 1941. She boarded with Christl and Merrill Bacheler, and the Stangl Pottery jitney bus provided Kay's daily transportation from Flemington to Trenton. For the first two weeks at Stangl, Kay worked in the decorating department in order to learn about the company. Following that brief stint, she went to the modeling shop to work with August Jacob. He was modeling Stangl artware at the time and had a studio of his own near the plaster shop.

Martin Stangl escorted Kay to the museum in Philadelphia to study early Pennsylvania Dutch style pottery, from which she patterned Tulips, Double Bird, and Single Bird from sketches she did right at the museum. This style of dinnerware was developed because Martin Stangl felt there was a market for an Early American style dinnerware to go with the style of decorating popular at the time (late '30s to early '40s). Within the same period, she designed Fruit and Garden Flower as well as some cigarette boxes.

Kay worked at Stangl for about two years. In 1943 with WWII at full tilt, Kay wanted to join the war effort but knew she would dislike the discipline of active service. Someone suggested that since she knew drafting, she might try working at General Motors in graphic engineering, a job that required her to illustrate the spare parts manual for the Grumman Avenger airplane. Kay married in 1944. Within a few years, two sons, Pat and Dave came along, and by 1947 she was working in advertising in Buffalo, New York, making $35 per week. At that time, she started doing free-lance work out of her attic and submitted designs to Stangl. Martin Stangl purchased six of her designs and paid $100 each.

Kay returned to work at Stangl in 1948 at triple her original pay. Her "attic" designs of Blueberry and the other small fruit patterns of Fig, Gooseberry, Cranberry, Kumquat, Lime, etc., were then being produced. Kay worked at Stangl Pottery continuously from 1948 until 1958 when her son, Marty Jr. was born. She did free-lance work for a while and some part-time work, but with three young children at home, it was difficult to work at the plant, so she submitted designs from home. In those years since 1941, she is credited with designing 40 dinnerware patterns that were put into production and over 100 miscellaneous novelty and artware items. Hundreds of her samples that were never put into actual production were sold at the Flemington Outlet. Many collectors today consider them the most prized of all Stangl products. Kay eventually left Stangl in 1965 to join her husband in their antique business.

Kay Hackett's original color rendering for her Pintail duck oval ashtray. Gift of Kay Hackett to the Hill-Fulper-Stangl Museum.

In year 2000, Kay briefly reopened her design studio and created a special-order item to be used as the floor medallion at the Hill-Fulper-Stangl Potteries Museum. Kay designed two motifs, different but uniquely "Kay Hackett." The motif chosen to grace the kiln floor is Pennsylvania Dutch inspired. The other, with two bluebirds, is very much like some of her early cigarette box designs.

This book follows the lives and deeds of the principals of Hill, Fulper, and Stangl potteries throughout 164 years of manufacturing. Our research brought us to their final resting place in Flemington.

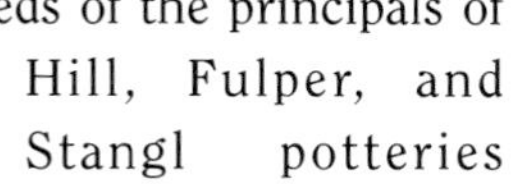

One of Kay's sample vase designs of the 1960s, this one with underglaze decoration on green body with Satin White glaze. Courtesy of Kay Hackett.

Kay's Egret vase, a sample she produced in the late 1940s.

Johann Martin Stangl, 1888 – 1972, still reigns over the hills and valleys of Hunterdon County from this spot at the Prospect Hill Cemetery in Flemington.

The original success of Stangl's hand-painted animals and birds resulted from several interconnected world events. During the 1930s, peasant-style ceramics were becoming increasingly popular as home decorating accessories. Capo di Monte and Della Robbia type bric-a-brac was being imported form Europe by the ton to American decorators, gift shops, and furniture showrooms. Czechoslovakia, France, Italy, Spain, and Portugal were the largest producers of these ornamental items. To a much lesser extent, Japan was supplying a portion of these ceramics as well. Included in the assortments of imported decorative objects were bird and animal figurines ranging from utterly whimsical to elegantly sublime. As the 1930s marched on, bird and animal figures became progressively more popular, but at the same time, Europe was becoming a less stable venue for international commerce. Importers, fearing the safety of their merchandise shipments, were then turning to American manufacturers to supply the much loved peasant-type ceramics.

As with all Stangl products, sizes of the animals can vary as much as ½" from one animal to the next.

Hand-Painted Animal Figurines, 1937 – 1978

Prototypes, 1937

In 1937, as a consequence to the growing market for American-produced figurines, Stangl Pottery began developing a line of small novelty animal figures. The first hand-painted animal figures believed to have been produced by Stangl were small characters full of whimsy. They were cast of white clay then lightly airbrushed with red iron oxide and hand-painted with black details. No records exist of these animals, but each one shown here was purchased at Martin Stangl's estate auction in 1973. According to the auctioneer, these animals had been in Martin Stangl's office since the 1940s. Also, during the Stangl Pottery mold rescue in 1998, a model for the Bear figurine mold was found among other 1930s era Stangl molds. However, these animals also resemble better-quality animals imported from Japan during the 1930s. At this time, only one each of the following animals is known to exist. Each measures about 2½" tall: Bear, Deer, Horse, Rabbit, Raccoon.

Bear from Martin Stangl's estate sale. Photo courtesy of the Bond collection.

Horse from Martin Stangl's estate sale. Photo courtesy of the Bond collection.

Rabbit from Martin Stangl's estate sale. Photo courtesy of the Bond collection.

Deer from Martin Stangl's estate sale. Photo courtesy of the Bond collection.

Raccoon from Martin Stangl's estate sale.

In December 1937, clearly documented prototype animals were produced. Several of the animal-shaped handles from the #3143 series of art vases were decorated with underglaze colors in order to test hand-painted animal figurine production. The animal handles decorated as figurines were the #3144 Pelican, #3146 Squirrel, #3148 Duck, #3158 Cat, and #3161 Dog. According to a memo from Martin Stangl to plant manager Heinrich Below dated December 18, 1937, twelve samples of each of the animal handle shapes were to be painted in various styles of underglaze decoration. After these prototype samples were evaluated, Martin Stangl decided that a newly designed line of simpler figurines would be produced and began the development of the #3178 Small Animals.

Prototype sample animals based on the #3146 3½" Squirrel vase handles.

Prototype sample animal based on the #3148 3¼" Duck vase handles.

Small Animals #3178 A-H

Sometimes, but incorrectly, called "prototype" animals, the #3178 Small Animals were a fully developed animal line that was produced for several years. Because Stangl's in-house sculptor John Tierney was busy sculpting other artware lines, Karl Hoffer sculpted the models for these figurines. The shapes were sculpted in whimsical, near caricature poses. The decorating was very minimal, usually just details in black underglaze color with clear glaze. Sometimes the #3178 animals were glazed with the tinted glazes used on Stangl's hand-painted dinnerware. Usually the animals produced with tinted glaze do not have the painted black details. Some of the animals were decorated with multicolor cold-paint polka dots for circus distribution. All of the #3178 animals were dotted, but the ones most often found are the Elephants and Percherons, giving them a festive, circus-like appearance. It is unusual to find the cold-paint polka dots still intact in good condition. The #3178 Small Animals were produced throughout the early 1940s. They were hastily decorated, with very little time and expense invested in their production. Martin Stangl considered them "low end" and sold them very inexpensively as carnival prizes and tourist trap souvenirs.

A white animal with black underglaze detail is the most common decoration. Tinted solid-color glazed animals and those with cold paint polka dots are harder to find, while animals with both tinted solid-color glaze and black underglaze detail are most elusive. These animals were not marked, but sometimes one can be found with a Stangl paper label still intact.

Several American and Japanese potteries produced knock-offs of these animals. The most common knock-offs were small animals attached to miniature planters and 4½" tall elephants of similar design. The styling and details of the Stangl animals is markedly different from that of the knock-offs.

Two #3178A Elkhounds, 3" black and white, showing the subtle variations in decorating. $200.00 – 250.00 each. Courtesy of the Robert and Tammie Cruser collection.

Two #3178A Elkhounds in tinted yellow and tinted pink glaze. $250.00 – 300.00 each. Courtesy of the Robert and Tammie Cruser collection.

Not Shown:

#3178A Elkhound, 3" polka dots. $350.00 – 400.00.

#3178B Pony, 3½" black and white. $250.00 – 300.00.

#3178B Pony, 3½" tinted glaze or polka dots. $350.00 – 400.00.

Four #3178B Ponies, hand-painted black and white, $250.00 – 300.00, and tinted yellow, pink, and blue glaze, $350.00 – 400.00 each. Courtesy of the Robert and Tammie Cruser collection.

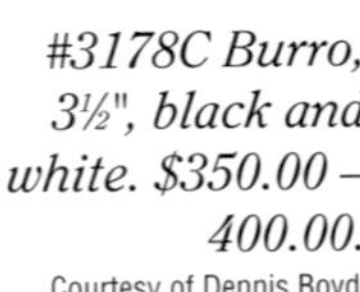

#3178C Burro, 3½", black and white. $350.00 – 400.00. Courtesy of Dennis Boyd.

#3178C Burro, 3½" tinted green glaze. $400.00 – 450.00. Courtesy of the Robert and Tammie Cruser collection.

#3178D Mule, 3½" tinted Parchment glaze with black underglaze decoration. $450.00 – 500.00. Courtesy of Dennis Boyd.

#3178E Giraffe, 3½" black and white. $350.00 – 400.00.

#3178F Percheron, 3" black and white. $150.00 – 200.00. Courtesy of the Robert and Tammie Cruser collection.

Three #3178F Percherons, 3" tinted yellow, pink, and green glazes. $275.00 – 325.00. Courtesy of the Robert and Tammie Cruser collection.

#3178F Percheron, 3" salt & pepper set. $300.00 – 350.00 per pair. Courtesy of the Robert and Tammie Cruser collection.

Not Shown:
#3178C Burro, 3½" polka dots. $400.00 – 450.00.
#3178D Mule, 3½" black and white. $300.00 – 350.00.
#3178D Mule, 3½" tinted glaze or polka dots. $400.00 – 450.00.
#3178E Giraffe, 3½" tinted glaze or polka dots. $400.00 – 450.00

#3178F Percheron, 3" polka dots. $275.00 – 325.00. Courtesy of the Robert and Shirley Bond collection.

#3178G Elephant, 2½" green tinted glaze, $300.00 – 350.00 each; black and white, $200.00 – 250.00 each. Courtesy of the Robert and Tammie Cruser collection.

#3178I Scotty, 3½" black and white. $350.00 – 400.00. Courtesy of the Robert and Tammie Cruser collection.

#3178H Squirrel, 3" tinted green and yellow glazes, $300.00 – 350.00 each; black and white, $250.00 – 300.00 each. Courtesy of the Robert and Tammie Cruser collection.

#3178J Gazelle, 3½" black and white. $250.00 – 300.00. Courtesy of the Wayne Weigand collection.

Not Shown:
#3178G Elephant, 2½" tinted glaze or polka dots. $300.00 – 350.00.
#3178H Squirrel, 3" tinted glaze or polka dots. $300.00 – 350.00.
#3178I Scotty, 3½" tinted glaze or polka dots. $425.00 – 475.00.
#3178J Gazelle, 3½" tinted glaze or polka dots. $300.00 – 350.00.

Hand-Decorated Animals

During the late 1930s, American decorators and gift-mongers continued to clamor for more sophisticated and colorful offerings as fewer shipments were coming from Europe and Japan. As a result, in 1939 Stangl Pottery developed a line of more realistically sculpted and decorated animal and bird figurines. This line included 11 animal figures and 11 bird figures (the bird figurines are listed in the Hand-Painted Bird section). The models for these figurines were sculpted by John Tierney. These animals were designed to be much more realistic than the #3178 Small Animal figures. The only animal to have been inspired by the #3178 Small Animal series was the #3244 Draft Horse. He is styled after, but not identical to, the #3178F Percheron.

In 1939 these new figurines were available hand-decorated in natural colors or in Turquoise Blue Crackled or Antique Ivory Crackled glazes. The Turquoise Blue Crackled and Antique Ivory Crackled glazes were discontinued before 1941, and are exceedingly rare. These animals continued to be produced in the hand-decorated natural colors throughout the 1940s. Some were also decorated with the Terra Rose colors of green, mauve or blue during 1941 only. Very rarely, some of these animals can be found decorated in yellow, pink, blue or green. Some of this series of miniature animal shapes were also produced briefly during 1973, and are nearly identical to the 1940s versions. The 1940s animals are much more common than the 1973 animals. Animals produced during the 1940s are rarely marked except for the occasional square gold-foil or silver and green foil paper label.

Paper label showing how many of these animals were marked.

Hand-Painted Animals, 1939 Introductions

In 1941, the manager of the Elmora Theater in Elizabeth, New Jersey special-ordered several hundred of the #3243 Wire Haired Dog decorated as "Asta," the dog belonging to Nick and Nora Charles in the "Thin Man" motion pictures. The "Asta" dog figurines were given away at Saturday matinee showings of the 1941 movie "Shadow of the Thin Man" starring William Powell, Myrna Loy, and of course, Asta!

#3243 Wire Haired Dog, 3¼" natural colors. $300.00 – 375.00.

Another #3243 Wire Haired Dog showing the variations of hand-decorating. Courtesy of the Frank and Elizabeth Kramar collection.

#3243 Wire Haired Dog, 3¼" decorated as "Asta." $700.00 – 800.00. Courtesy of the Dinmont collection.

#3244 Draft Horse, 3" dappled colors. $175.00 – 225.00. Courtesy of the Louis and Sarah DiPlacido collection.

#3244 Draft Horse, 3" marbled. $350.00 – 400.00. Courtesy of the Louis and Sarah DiPlacido collection.

In 1954, several of these animal shapes were reissued in pink or green marbled, but the marbled animals were simply Flemington Outlet novelties. Their production may not have encompassed all the animal shapes nor did it last for very long. The marbled products were developed by Dave Thomas in 1954 and were primarily a line of ashtrays. Marbled items were cast of colored slips swirled together in the molds. Two of the color combinations produced were light and dark green with cream, and pink and black with cream. In 1954, several of the Hand-Decorated Animal shapes were also cast of the marbled slips.

#3245 Rabbit, 2" natural colors. $300.00 – 375.00. Courtesy of the Robert and Tammie Cruser collection.

Not Shown:

#3243 Wire Haired Dog, 3¼" Crackled, Terra Rose, or Marbled. $450.00 – 500.00.

#3243 Wire Haired Dog, 3¼" yellow, pink, blue or green. $500.00 – 600.00.

#3244 Draft Horse, 3" Crackled or Terra Rose. $350.00 – 400.00.

#3244 Draft Horse, 3" yellow, pink, blue or green. $350.00 – 450.00.

#3245 Rabbit, 2" Crackled, Terra Rose, or Marbled. $450.00 – 500.00.

#3245 Rabbit, 2" yellow, pink, blue or green. $450.00 – 500.00.

#3246 Buffalo, 2½" Crackled, Terra Rose, or Marbled. $550.00 – 600.00.

#3246 Buffalo, 2½" yellow, pink, blue or green. $550.00 – 600.00.

#3246 Buffalo, 2½" natural colors. $450.00 – 500.00. Courtesy of the Frank and Elizabeth Kramar collection.

#3247 Gazelle, 3¾" natural colors. $300.00 – 350.00. Courtesy of the Frank and Elizabeth Kramar collection.

#3247 Giraffe, 3½" natural colors. $650.00 – 800.00. Courtesy of the Robert and Shirley Bond collection.

#3249 Elephant, 3" pink. $450.00 – 550.00. Courtesy of the Hill-Fulper-Stangl Museum.

The usual color of the #3249 Elephant can range from deep, glossy black with vibrant pink trim to a washed-out gray and muted pink. It is usually the wartime elephants that have pale coloring due to the molasses used in the underglaze colors at that time. Elephants with better color usually sell at the higher end of the scale.

#3249 Elephant, 3" natural colors, showing the variation of "black" color available. $225.00 – 300.00 each. Courtesy of the Jim Horner collection.

#3249 Elephant, 3" French Green. $450.00 – 550.00. Courtesy of the Frank and Elizabeth Kramar collection.

Not Shown:

#3247 Gazelle, 3¾" Crackled, Terra Rose, or Marbled. $450.00 – 500.00.
#3247 Gazelle, 3¾" yellow, pink, blue or green. $500.00 – 550.00.
#3247 Giraffe, 3½" Crackled, Terra Rose, or Marbled. $700.00 – 750.00.
#3247 Giraffe, 3½" yellow, pink, blue or green. $800.00 – 850.00.
#3249 Elephant, 3" yellow, pink, blue or green. $450.00 – 550.00.
#3249 Elephant, 3" Crackled, Terra Rose, or Marbled. $450.00 – 500.00.
#3272 Airedale Terrier, 2¼" Crackled, Terra Rose, or Marbled. $700.00 – 800.00.
#3272 Airedale Terrier, 2¼" yellow, pink, blue or green. $700.00 – 800.00.
#3277 Colt, 5" natural colors brown. $1,500.00 – 1,800.00.
#3277 Colt, 5" natural colors dappled white. $1,800.00 – 2,000.00.
#3277 Colt, 5" Crackled, Terra Rose, or Marbled. $1,800.00 – 2,000.00.
#3277 Colt, 5" yellow, pink, blue or green. $1,800.00 – 2,000.00.
#3278 Goat, 5" natural colors. $1,500.00 – 1,800.00.
#3278 Goat, 5" Crackled, Terra Rose, or Marbled. $1,800.00 – 2,000.00.
#3278 Goat, 5" yellow, pink, blue or green. $1,800.00 – 2,000.00.
#3279 Calf, 3½" natural colors. $800.00 – 1,000.00.
#3279 Calf, 3½" Crackled, Terra Rose, or Marbled. $1,000.00 – 1,200.00.
#3279 Calf, 3½" yellow, pink, blue or green. $1,000.00 – 1,200.00.

#3272 Airedale Terrier, 2¼" natural colors. $600.00 – 700.00. Courtesy of the Hill-Fulper-Stangl Museum.

#3280 Dog, 5¼" natural colors showing a typical variation of color. $400.00 – 450.00. Courtesy of the Wayne Weigand collection.

During the early 1940s, the sitting #3280 Dog, loosely resembling an English Setter, was usually decorated in tan sponged with black spots but was also infrequently produced in white with black sponging as well as Terra Rose green, blue or mauve.

#3280 Dog, 5¼" natural colors. $400.00 – 450.00. Courtesy of the Frank and Elizabeth Kramar collection.

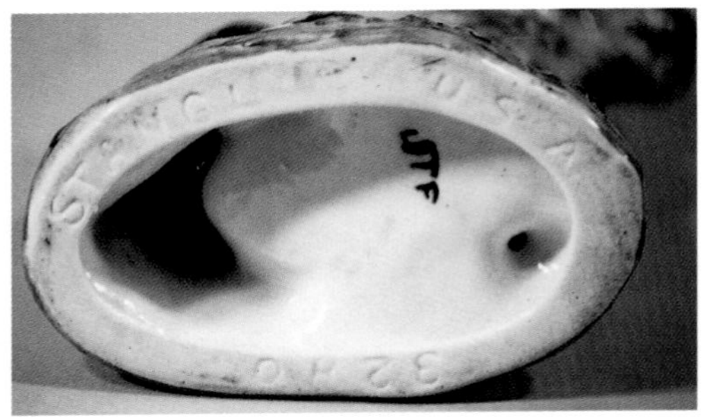

Characteristic base markings of the #3280 Dog figurine; this one was decorated by Jean Taylor Polasek at the Flemington Outlet during the mid 1940s.

Not Shown:
#3280 Dog, 5¼" white spotted, Crackled, Terra Rose, or Marbled. $550.00 – 600.00.
#3280 Dog, 5¼" yellow, pink, blue or green. $550.00 – 600.00.

Hand-Painted Animals, 1973 Introductions

In 1973 Stangl reintroduced several of the original 1940s Hand-Painted Animal shapes as part of their bird and animal assortment for that year. This group of animals included the #3244 Draft Horse (renamed "Horse"), #3245 Rabbit, #3246 Buffalo (renamed "Bison"), #3247 Gazelle, #3248 Giraffe, #3249 Elephant, and #3280 Dog. The 1973 animals were hand-painted in the same colors as the original 1940s animals. They were also decorated with Antique Gold, Granada Gold, and Black Gold and all-over solid gold luster, and like the 1940s animals, were also decorated in the more unusual underglaze colors yellow, pink, blue or green. Occasionally, the 1973 animals were marked with the name STANGL minutely hand-painted on the bottoms of the tiny feet of these figures and sometimes the date 1973 was also included. Usually these animals are unmarked or have only an oval gold-foil paper label.

Not Shown:
#3244 Draft Horse, 3", natural colors. $175.00 – 225.00.
#3244 Draft Horse, 3" yellow, pink, blue or green. $350.00 – 450.00.
#3244 Draft Horse, 3" Antique, Granada, Black Gold or all-over gold. $300.00 – 400.00.
#3245 Rabbit, 2", natural colors. $300.00 – 375.00.
#3245 Rabbit, 2" yellow, pink, blue or green. $450.00 – 500.00.
#3245 Rabbit, 2" Antique, Granada, Black Gold or all-over gold. $350.00 – 450.00.
#3246 Bison, 2½", natural colors. $450.00 – 500.00.
#3246 Bison, 2½" yellow, pink, blue or green. $550.00 – 600.00.
#3246 Bison, 2½" Antique, Granada, Black Gold or all-over gold. $350.00 – 450.00.
#3247 Giraffe, 3½", natural colors. $ 600.00 – 650.00.
#3247 Giraffe, 3½" yellow, pink, blue or green. $800.00 – 850.00.
#3247 Giraffe, 3½" Antique, Granada, Black Gold or all-over gold. $500.00 – 600.00.

#3249 Elephant, 3", natural colors. $300.00 – 350.00.
#3249 Elephant, 3" yellow, pink, blue or green. $450.00 – 550.00.
#3249 Elephant, 3" Antique, Granada, Black Gold or all-over gold. $350.00 – 450.00.
#3280 Dog, 5¼", natural colors. $450.00 – 500.00.
#3280 Dog, 5¼" yellow, pink, blue or green. $550.00 – 600.00.
#3280 Dog, 5¼" Antique, Granada, Black Gold or all-over gold. $450.00 – 550.00.

American Bison, 1940

In 1940, Martin Stangl had John Tierney create an American Bison figurine. This was a large figurine, 14" long and nearly 8" tall. Several examples of the American Bison were produced, one of which Martin Stangl displayed on his desk for many years. In 1965, Martin Stangl removed the figurine from his desk and placed it in his Stangl Museum in Flemington. By that stroke of fate, Martin Stangl's American Bison was spared destruction. When the Trenton factory burned in August 1965, Martin Stangl's office was completely destroyed in the conflagration, and the American bison would have gone as well. The American Bison remained with the museum archival collection of Hill, Fulper, and Stangl products and now resides at the Wheaton Village Museum of American Glass in Millville, New Jersey.

Not Shown:

American Bison figurine, 8"x14". $8,000.00 – 10,000.00.

Terra Rose Animal Match Holders, 1941

The #3243 Wire Haired Dog, #3244 Draft Horse, and #3245 Rabbit shapes were also used as the figures that decorated the #3533, #3534, and #3549 Rabbit, Dog, and Horse match holders. These three match holders were produced only during 1941, and were discontinued before the January 1942 price lists were printed. The Rabbit is much harder to find than either the Dog or the Horse match holders.

Above, base of the Terra Rose Animal match holder. Right, #3549 Horse match holder, 4¼" x 3½". $450.00 – 550.00.
Courtesy of the Robert and Shirley Bond collection.

Stangl's catalogs and price sheets stated that these match holders each had a "concealed receptacle in bottom for pack of paper matches." Much to the consternation of Stangl collectors, these match holders are too small to hold a pack of Stangl's own advertising matches! This is because the match holders were designed to hold 1½" wide standard paper book matches, the most widely used matchbook size. Stangl's Flemington Outlet was advertised with Lion Match Co.'s patented Feature Match Books, measuring a full 2" wide. The design of the Terra Rose match holders was based on the size of the most universal matchbooks available rather than the less obtainable 2" wide Feature matchbooks. Unfortunately, Martin Stangl gave no consideration to future pottery collectors who would like to display Flemington Outlet Feature matches in Terra Rose Match Holders!

Not Shown:

#3533 Rabbit match holder, 4¼" x 3". $550.00 – 600.00.
#3534 Dog match holder, 4¼" x 4". $450.00 – 550.00.

Hand-Painted Place Card Holders, 1941

During Kay Hackett's first few weeks of employment at Stangl Pottery during fall 1941, Martin Stangl required her to work in Stangl's plaster shop and learn the procedures there. It was during Kay's tenure in the plaster shop that August Jacob and Herman Eichorn sculpted Stangl's now legendary Horse head vase. One of Kay Hackett's projects in the plaster shop was to sculpt and create molds for a series of diminutive animal-shaped place card holders. Four figures were created: a horse, duck, squirrel, and an elephant. The squirrel and elephant are most lifelike, while the horse and duck are fancifully stylized. The elephant slightly resembles the #3249 Elephant figure but is much smaller.

The Place Card Animals were produced in both white and red clays. They were primarily decorated in simple floral or abstract motifs, but some of the solid-color glazes were tried on them as well. The Place Card Animal line was very short-

Two of Kay Hackett's Elephant place card holders, one red clay, the other white, with hand-painted flower motifs. $600.00 – 700.00 each. Courtesy of Kay Hackett.

Base of the Elephant place card holders.

lived, so these figures are extremely, extremely rare.

In 1954, casting employee Michael Palonski happened upon an old mold for the Duck place card holder and asked Harry Forker (Stangl's production foreman and Palonski's brother-in-law) if he could cast a few in the new marbled body. Harry Forker agreed and said he could keep them, so now several marbled place card Ducks exist.

Not Shown:

Duck Place Card Holder, 2". $600.00 – 700.00.

Elephant Place Card Holder, 2⅛". $600.00 – 700.00.

Horse Place Card Holder, 2½". $600.00 – 700.00.

Squirrel Place Card Holder, 2¼". $600.00 – 700.00.

Squirrel place card holder in unglazed bisque. $600.00 – 700.00. Courtesy of Kay Hackett.

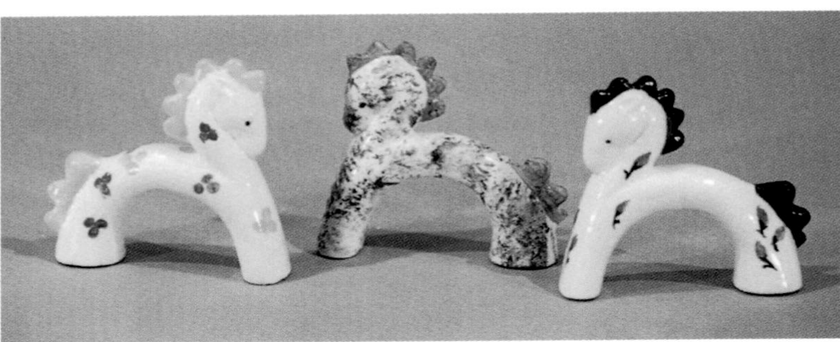

Three of Kay Hackett's Horse place card holders in a variety of motifs. $600.00 – 700.00 each. Courtesy of the Hill-Fulper-Stangl Museum.

Elephant #5281, 1973

In 1973, the #5281 5" Elephant was introduced. This Elephant was decorated with the brushed gold finishes and several single solid-colors such as Satin Tan, Satin Black, Gloss White, and all-over solid gold luster. Elephants with the Antique Gold finish are more popular than those with Granada or Black Gold. During the mid 1970s this little fellow was epoxied to matching brushed-gold ashtrays and advertised as "Dancing Elephant Ashtrays" at the Flemington Outlet.

#5281 Elephant, 5", Antique, Granada, Black Gold or all-over gold. $75.00 – 125.00. Courtesy of the Wayne Weigand collection.

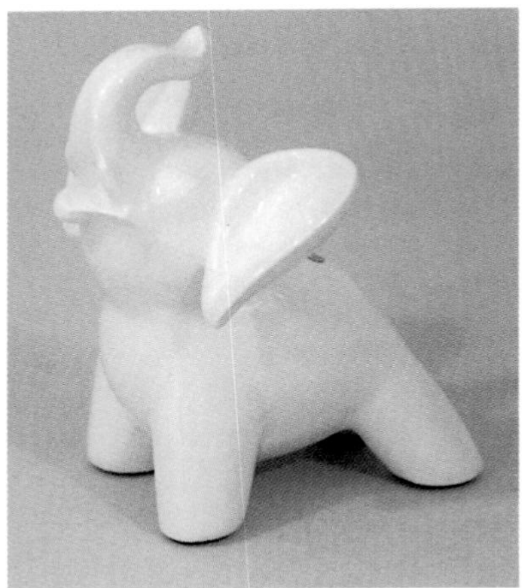

#5281 Elephant, 5", White, Black, Tan, Pink, Yellow, or Artware Green. $125.00 – 175.00. Courtesy of the Wayne Weigand collection.

#5281 Dancing Elephant Ashtray, Antique, Granada, Black Gold. $150.00 – 200.00.

Hand-Painted Novelty Animals, 1926 – 1978

These animal figures were primarily Flemington Outlet items and were not usually sold through Stangl's national catalogs.

Piggy Banks and Planters

The floral decorated #1076 Piggy Bank was originally made in solid-color glazes for Rena Rosenthal's New York gift shop in 1926. He became so popular during the 1920s that Stangl continued producing him throughout the 1930s in solid colors as a bank and planter. During the 1940s the #1076 Pig banks and planters were decorated with Stangl's Early Pennsylvania tulip motif and with that decoration became a solid seller at the Flemington Outlet until 1978. Throughout the 1940s and 1950s, the piggy banks were sold at the Flemington Outlet for only $1.00 each. Kay Hackett remembers tulip-decorated pig banks being shipped to the Flemington Outlet by the hundreds during the 1950s, selling out by the end of each weekend. Earlier pigs decorated with the Early Pennsylvania Tulip motif have hand-brushed engobe. These pigs usually are not marked "Stangl" but have the number 1076 carved on the bottom. By the late 1940s, the engobe was brushed heavier, giving a whiter appearance with fewer visible brush-marks. During the 1950s, the engobe was sprayed on, the tulips continued to be carved, and the Stangl backstamp was used to identify the pigs. For a very brief time during the early 1960s, a piggy bank was produced with a "Jeweled" decoration. In 1967 a red-clay bisque pig bank with carved embellishment was introduced and produced for two years. By 1966, some of the tulip decoration was no longer applied to portions of the pigs, such as the ears and forelegs. Also at that time, the tulips ceased to be carved, they were simply painted under the glaze with no carving. From 1970 until Stangl's closing in 1978, the pig banks were cast entirely of white clay. Stangl's advertising referred to the banks as both "Pig Banks" and "Piggy Banks" at various times throughout their years of production.

Early Pennsylvania Tulip #1076 B piggy bank showing the markings on the base.

During the 1930s and 1940s, the same #1076 Pig shape was produced as a planter and was called "cactus pot." These were decorated with solid-color glazes during the 1930s and early 1940s and were also decorated with the Early Pennsylvania Tulip motif throughout the 1940s. Numbers on the bottoms of the Pigs were #1076 "B" for "Bank" and #1076 "C" for "Cactus Pot."

The #1076 Pig shape was also adapted to a lamp shape with the number 1991 during the 1930s. The pig lamps were produced in solid colors during the 1930s and brushed Terra Rose colors during the 1940s and 1950s. In 1961, the #1991 pig lamp shape was adapted as a hand-painted children's lamp with the number 5086.

Other pig banks produced by Stangl were hand-thrown at pottery demonstrations at the Flemington Outlet during the 1960s and 1970s. These pigs were all handcrafted of red clay and decorated with bold abstract strokes of underglaze color. The poses and shapes of these pigs vary greatly as they were produced according to the whims of the college student potters employed to conduct the demonstrations. They are nearly always larger than the #1076 pig shape, measuring from six up to eight inches long and are usually were marked with the "STANGL" die-pressed mark. These handcrafted pigs are quite rare, as very few were produced during the Flemington Outlet demonstrations.

For more information also see the Lamp, Solid-Color, Sunburst, Stangl Stoneware, and Early Pennsylvania Artware sections.

#1076 Pig Bank, 4" Sunburst glaze, 1930 – 1934. $225.00 – 275.00. Courtesy of the Robert and Tammie Cruser collection.

#1076 Pig Bank and Cactus pots, 4" solid-color satin glazes, late 1930s. $120.00 – 150.00 each. Courtesy of the Robert and Tammie Cruser collection.

#1076 Pig Hors d'Oeuvre, 4", for Rena Rosenthal 1926 – 1929. $200.00 – 250.00. Courtesy of the Hill-Fulper-Stangl Museum.

#1076 Pig Bank and cactus Pot with brushed engobe and Early Pennsylvania Tulip decoration from the early 1940s. $125.00 – 150.00 each. Courtesy of the Robert and Tammie Cruser collection.

#1076 Pig Bank, 4" Terra Rose blue, green or mauve finishes, 1940 – 1961. $150.00 – 200.00. Courtesy of the Hill-Fulper-Stangl Museum.

#1076 Pig Bank, 4" brushed gold finishes, 1960 – 1978 (showing Antique Gold and Black Gold). $95.00 – 130.00 each.

#1076 Pig Bank, 4" Jeweled decoration, early 1960s only. $350.00 – 450.00. Courtesy of the Luke and Nancy Ruepp collection.

#1076 Pig Bank, 4", white body, floral decoration, not tulips, late 1970s only. $350.00 – 450.00. Courtesy of the Robert and Tammie Cruser collection.

Not Shown:

#1076 Pig Bank, 4" solid-color glazes, 1926 – 1945. $130.00 – 150.00.
#1076 Pig Cactus pot, 4" solid-color glazes, 1926 – 1945. $120.00 – 145.00.
#1076 Pig Bank, 4" gold luster over solid-color glazes, 1934 only. $275.00 – 300.00.
#1076 Pig Bank, 4" Tulip decoration, brushed engobe, carved decoration 1942 – 1952. $125.00 – 150.00.
#1076 Pig Bank, 4" Tulip decoration, carved decoration 1950 – 1966. $125.00 – 150.00.
#1076 Pig Bank, 4" Tulip decoration, fewer flowers, not carved 1966 – 1973. $100.00 – 125.00.
#1076 Pig Bank, 4" Tulip decoration, fewer flowers, white body 1970 – 1978. $100.00 – 125.00.
#1076-C Pig cactus pot, 4" Tulip decoration 1942 – 1945. $100.00 – 125.00.
#1076 Pig Cactus planter, 4" brushed gold finishes, 1960 – 1978. $95.00 – 130.00.

#5199 Pig Bank, 4" Red Bisque 1967 – 1969. $175.00 – 225.00. Courtesy of the Bullock collection.

Hand-thrown Pig Bank, die-pressed "STANGL," made at the Flemington Outlet log cabin, 1967 – 1971 only. $350.00 – 450.00.

#1991 Pig Lamp, 4" Terra Rose finishes, 1940 – 1961. $125.00 – 150.00. Courtesy of the Wayne Weigand collection.

Not Shown:

#1991 Pig Lamp, 4" Solid-Color glazes, 1935 – 1945. $125.00 – 160.00.

#1991 Pig Lamp, 4" Terra Rose finishes, 1940 – 1961. $100.00 – 125.00.

#1991 Pig Lamp, 4" brushed gold finishes, 1940 – 1961. $100.00 – 125.00.

#5086 Pig Children's Lamp, 5", pink or blue floral, 1961 only. $350.00 – 400.00.

Rear of 1930s hand-painted #2088 Baby Face Dog Bank.

Baby Face Dog

Stangl's #2088 Baby Face Dog was first produced in 1936 as a special-order item for the B&A gift company in 1936. The popular "Gyp" dog figurine inspired this figure. Gyp was a stylized puppy figurine that was manufactured by several companies in the form of cast iron paperweights or doorstops in several sizes during the 1920s and 1930s. Stangl produced the Baby Face Dog as both a bank and a figurine. It could be had in solid-color glazes or hand-painted. Stangl stopped producing the Baby Face Dog for B&A in 1937. The Baby Face Dog was reintroduced in 1965 for the Flemington Outlet. The 1965 versions are hand-painted and were produced as banks and figurines.

Front of 1930s hand-painted #2088 Baby Face Dog Bank, $300.00 – 400.00. Courtesy of the Frank and Elizabeth Kramar collection.

Not Shown:

#2088 Baby Face Dog bank, 4" solid-color 1930s. $300.00 – 400.00.

#2088 Baby Face Dog bank, 4" hand-painted 1930s. $300.00 – 400.00.

#2088 Baby Face Dog figurine, 4" hand-painted 1930s. $300.00 – 400.00.

#2088 Baby Face Dog bank, 4" hand-painted 1965. $200.00 – 300.00.

#2088 Baby Face Dog Bank, 4" hand-painted 1965. $200.00 – 300.00.

Nelson Lebo Dog

Throughout the 1960s and 1970s Stangl Pottery produced several ceramic lamp parts and ashtrays for the Nelson Lebo Company of Trenton, New Jersey. The "#1185 Water Dog," as Stangl called it, was first produced in 1966. These dogs were styled after English Staffordshire figurines resembling King Charles Spaniels. They stand 10¾" tall and were cast facing both right and left. The Nelson Lebo Company mounted them on wood platform lamp bases. The figures were cast of earthenware clay and decorated with underglaze colors and clear glaze. They were also made of vitreous china and glazed with opaque white glaze and left plain or decorated with overglaze colors.

#1185L Nelson Lebo Dog, left-facing (decorated), 10¾", 1966 – 1977. $450.00 – 550.00. Courtesy of the Frank and Elizabeth Kramar collection.

#1185R Nelson Lebo Dog, right-facing, 10¾", 1966 – 1977. $450.00 – 550.00. Courtesy of the Hill-Fulper-Stangl Museum.

#1185 Nelson Lebo Dog lamp, complete. $450.00 – 600.00. Courtesy of the Frank and Elizabeth Kramar collection.

Rabbit Cotton Holder

Another extremely popular Flemington Outlet animal novelty was the "Laughing Rabbit" cotton holder introduced in 1967. The Rabbit figure was a reintroduction of the #3109 Long-Eared Rabbit made as an air freshener dispenser for Airwick in 1937. The original 1930s #3109 Long-Eared Rabbit was glazed in solid-colors, while the 1967 version was gloss white with hand-painted pink #193 details. The Long-Eared Rabbit became very popular at the Flemington Outlet as a novelty cotton holder during the 1960s. He was also epoxied to 9" deviled egg dishes as well as 10" and 12" Pink Cosmos plates. He is most easily found as a cotton holder. Plates with the attached bunny are much harder to find. Other companies also produced similar rabbits. The competitors' rabbits are usually a bit shorter than Stangl's rabbit, and the body is heavier. The competitor's glaze is denser and off white while the Stangl rabbit is bright white with a clear gloss glaze. The competitors' rabbits also have an unglazed bottom that is flat with a prominent mold seam across it. The base of Stangl's rabbit has a raised "foot," and earlier rabbits have the number 3109 molded into the base. The competitors' rabbits have cold-painted pink details whereas Stangl's pink decoration is hand-painted under the glaze. Only a few of Stangl's #3109 Long-Eared Rabbits were decorated with cold-paint during the 1930s, but those are glazed in Stangl's solid colors, and the rabbits are clearly marked on the bases. In 1961 the #3109 Rabbit figure was adapted as a children's lamp and was decorated with pink or blue floral motifs. See also the Solid-Color Artware and Lamp sections for more information.

Typical base of Stangl's #3109 Long-Eared Rabbit showing the glazed concave base bearing number 3109.

Not Shown:

#3109 Long-Eared Rabbit Cotton Holder, 7½", white with pink underglaze ears and details, 1967 – 1970. $125.00 – 150.00.

#3109 Long-Eared Rabbit Deviled Egg Dish, 9"x7¾", 1967 – 1970. $150.00 – 175.00.

#3109 Long-Eared Rabbit Air Freshener, 7½", made for Airwick, solid-color glazes (this one Colonial Blue), 1937 – 1938. $175.00 – 200.00.

#3109 Long-Eared Rabbit Air Freshener, 7½", made for Airwick, solid-color glazes with intact original cold paint details (this one Ivory glaze), 1937 – 1938. $200.00 – 250.00. Courtesy of the Robert and Tammie Cruser collection.

#3109 Long-Eared Rabbit Server, 10" or 12"x7¾", 1967 – 1970. $150.00 – 175.00. Courtesy of the Jim and Barbara Nelson collection.

Lamp #5088 Rabbit (old #3109), 8", pink or blue floral decoration, 1961 – 1962. $500.00 – 550.00. Courtesy of Merrill and Christl Stangl Bacheler.

Owl, Pussycat and Pumpkin Candle Lamps

These novelty patio candle lamps were first introduced in 1965 and sold at the Flemington Outlet. They were produced in a variety of fashion glaze finishes such as Chartreuse Green, Dark Green, Canary Yellow, Pumpkin Orange, Peach, Cobalt Blue, Satin Tan, Black, and Gray. After the fire in August 1965, these novelty lamps were discontinued until 1973 when they were again produced, but in very limited quantities. At that time the Owls were decorated with Walnut Brown underglaze color swirled under the Brown Satin glaze, in addition to fashion solid-color glazes. The pumpkins were cast of white clay and glazed with Pumpkin Orange glaze. Pumpkins were produced both as candle lamps with the eyes and mouth cut out and as cookie jars, with the eyes and mouth left intact.

Owl candle lamp, yellow, 12". $150.00 – 200.00.

Group of Owl candle lamps in assorted fashion-color glazes. Courtesy of the Ed Simpson collection.

Pussycat candle lamp, Chartreuse Green, 13". $200.00 – 250.00. Courtesy of the Ed Simpson collection.

Pussycat candle lamps in assorted fashion-color glaze. Courtesy of the Ed Simpson collection.

Not Shown:

Pumpkin cookie jar, 9". $175.00 – 200.00.

Pumpkin candle lamp, 7". $150.00 – 200.00.

Pumpkin candle lamp, 9". $200.00 – 250.00. Courtesy of the Frank and Elizabeth Kramar collection.

Sitting Cat, Lying Cat, Deer

Stangl's 9" Sitting Cat figurine was introduced in 1973 with the brushed gold finishes and several single solid-colors such as Satin Tan, Satin Black, Gloss White, and all-over solid gold luster. The Sitting Cat was also produced in a pink-tinted slip with clear gloss glaze, sponged Blue Town & Country, and hand-painted as a Seal Point Siamese.

The smaller Lying Cat figurine was also produced during the 1970s in many of the same glazes and finishes as the 9" Sitting Cat. Stangl's Lying Cat was primarily used as a lamp figurine by Mutual Sunset but was also sold at the Flemington Outlet as a figurine.

The Deer figure was introduced in 1976, and was also a Mutual Sunset lamp figurine. The Deer was usually decorated with Pioneer Brown glaze but was hand-decorated in underglaze colors for the Flemington Outlet. Stangl's Sitting Cat, Lying Cat, and Deer figurines are rarely marked except with an occasional paper label or wax pencil price from the Flemington Outlet.

Lying Cat, 4"x6", any finish or glaze (this one is Pumpkin Orange). $375.00 – 450.00. Courtesy of the Frank and Elizabeth Kramar collection.

Group of Sitting Cats, 9", in Granada Gold, Antique Gold, and Black Gold. $250.00 – 350.00 each. Courtesy of the Wayne Weigand collection.

Sitting Cat, 9", Mandarin Red, $400.00 – 450.00. Courtesy of the Wayne Weigand collection.

Sitting Cat, 9", Town & Country Blue. $400.00 – 450.00.

Sitting Cat, 9", cast of pink clay. $275.00 – 300.00.

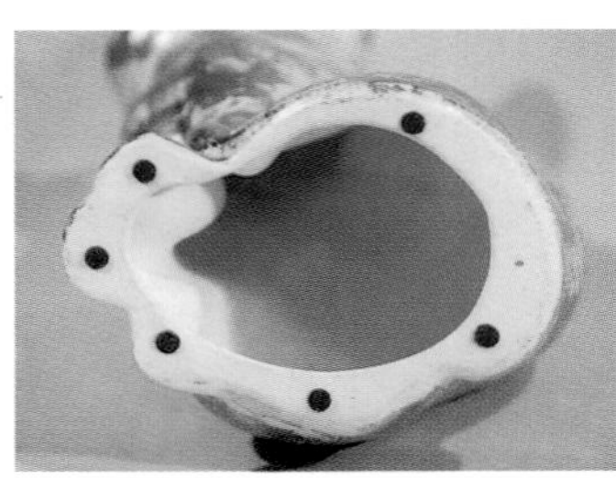

Base of the Sitting Cat, these are rarely marked.

Deer, 3½"x4¾", any finish or glaze. $275.00 – 300.00. Courtesy of the Frank and Elizabeth Kramar collection.

Not Shown:

Sitting Cat, 9", Antique, Granada, Black Gold or all-over gold. $250.00 – 350.00.

Sitting Cat, 9", white, black, tan or pink. $200.00 – 300.00.

Sitting Cat, 9", Seal Point Siamese. $600.00 – 700.00.

Sitting Cat, 9", Mandarin Red, Town & Country Blue. $400.00 – 450.00.

Hand-Painted Pottery Birds, 1939 – 1978 and beyond...

Stangl's hand-painted bird figurines are, and have been for generations, one of Stangl Pottery's most significant and widely recognized product lines. Second in popularity only to Stangl's hand-painted dinnerware lines, Stangl bird figurines continue to hold the interest of veteran pottery collectors as well as repeatedly attract new collectors to the field.

During 1939, Stangl's hand-painted pottery bird figurines were considered part of the hand-painted animal assortment. These early birds were primarily the shapes of domesticated fowl, chickens, ducks, and turkeys. Bluebirds and a penguin were the only non-domestic birds. At first, all figurines were available with the art glazes of Antique Ivory or Turquoise Crackled and Terra Rose, as well as hand-painted in "natural" colors.

Items glazed with the Turquoise and Antique Ivory Crackled glazes were dipped in a strong tea solution to further accentuate the crackling of the glaze. The crackling on these figurines can vary from all-over, even crazing to heavy crackling in one area, while another area exhibits very little crackling, all depending on how the item was glazed. Figurines that are turquoise or ivory colored but do not appear "crackled" are indeed Turquoise Crackled and Antique Ivory Crackled. These were simply sold at the Flemington Outlet without the tea treatment.

Popularity of the hand-painted naturally colored bird figurines quickly escalated, and the Turquoise, Ivory and Terra Rose "art glaze" finishes were dropped. Furthermore, it was soon apparent that brightly colored songbirds were much more popular than common old farm fowl. By 1940, so great was the demand for the hand-painted bird figurines that 29 additional bird shapes were introduced, including larger and more colorful birds. Because the demand for new shapes in all lines was so great, Martin Stangl hired another sculptor, August Jacob, to assist John Tierney in the design department. August Jacob had done freelance sculpting for Stangl in 1938 when he created the models for Stangl's Madonna vases. As with the Madonna vases, August Jacob's name appeared on each of the #3584 Large Cockatoo figurines produced, 1941 – 1948. His contract with Stangl paid a flat fee and percentage commission on each figurine sold. At the end of the contract, Jacob's name was removed from the molds.

A group of figurines in the Turquoise Crackled glaze. Courtesy of the Wayne Weigand collection.

Another group of birds in Antique Ivory Crackled glaze. Courtesy of the Wayne Weigand collection.

Martin Stangl instructed John Tierney and August Jacob to sculpt the new bird figurines after the Birds of America paintings by John James Audubon and drawings published by the National Audubon Society and Wilson's field guide. Ethel Kennedy, forelady of the dinnerware decorating department, "set" the colors of the bird figurines. By "setting" the colors, Ethel Kennedy determined which colors would be used and the exact brushstrokes needed to apply each color on each bird. All decorators were required to identically recreate Ethel Kennedy's coloring and brushstrokes so that all birds were consistently decorated. Subtle variations in color intensity were expected, but drastic color variations were not allowed. If a decorator strayed from the predetermined coloring, not only would she not be paid for that piece, but she would also be compelled to reimburse the company the cost of the item. For that reason, Stangl's decorators never took it upon themselves to use any creative license in their painting. All color changes were implemented by Martin Stangl either through his designers or heads of the decorating department. One of Stangl's bird decorators, Shirley Thatcher Spaciano, recalled the strict quality control this way: "I used to paint the pink cockatoos until I became cross-eyed! Then I would have trouble with the bird's eyes too. I don't know how many of those birds I had to wash off and start over because I would always paint the eyes square! Square eyes! Never would they have paid me for that!"

For a very brief time during 1940 and into 1941, Fulper Pottery produced a series of bird figurines for Russel Wright's American Way sales cooperative program. The American Way program was intended to promote American-made housewares and home furnishings. One of the primary selling points of this idealistic program was that all of the products were to be American inspired, American designed, and hand-crafted. The American Way products were sold exclusively at the most prominent department stores across the nation. The displays featured room settings of coordinated American Way furnishings and accessories. Eleanor Roosevelt hosted the formal opening of American Way at R.H. Macy's in New York on September 21, 1940.

Russel Wright felt that Stangl's hand-painted dinnerware and artware lines were well suited to this program, so in 1940, he contracted Fulper Pottery to produce three dinnerware patterns and a series of six bird figurines for the American Way program. The six birds were to be truly American, so were modeled closely following the poses in Audubon's Birds of America paintings. The six birds produced for American Way were the #3450 Passenger Pigeon, #3451 Willow Ptarmigan, #3452 Painted Bunting, #3453 Mountain Bluebird, #3454 Key West Quail Dove, and #3455 Shoveler Duck. All of the American Way bird shapes were sculpted by August Jacob. The American Way #3451 Willow Ptarmigan was decorated in light and dark color schemes representing the winter and summer plumage of the actual birds, as shown in Audubon's painting. These six birds were made exclusively for American Way during 1940 and 1941, and were marked with the American Way backstamp and the decorator's initials. Because of the large size and exacting detail of four of these birds, a quality control overseer would initial and code the figures before they were decorated. Sometimes the approval codes resemble limited edition numbers, but these were not "limited edition" figurines as both Martin Stangl and Russel Wright were interested in selling as many birds as possible. Besides, limiting production of decorative pottery was not a selling point during the 1940s. It would not be until the 1960s that importers would discover just how willing many people were to spend money on mass-produced "limited" editions.

Unfortunately, production of the American Way birds was unintentionally limited, as the American Way handicraft program failed and was ended during 1941. Martin Stangl continued to produce the American Way birds during the remainder of the 1940s, but as Stangl products bearing only the Stangl trademark. They no longer bore Russel Wright's American Way backstamp.

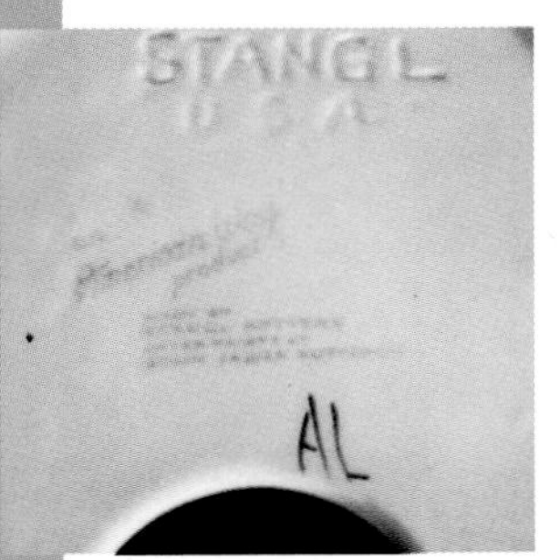

American Way backstamp, the decorator was Alberta Lee Burkhalter.

Twenty-three more bird figures were introduced in 1941, many of which were again modeled after Audubon paintings. In 1942, only seven new bird shapes were introduced, but during that year seven of the birds originally introduced in 1940 were re-styled. In 1942, Martin Stangl instructed John Tierney to re-sculpt the earlier designed Wrens, Orioles, and Cardinals to be more lifelike. The original bases of the Love Birds, Wrens, Orioles, and Double Cockatoos were very stylized waves or foliage and in some instances were too narrow and often toppled in the kiln. These bases were re-designed with more breadth and realistic perches of branches or leaves.

The unavailability of imported ceramics coupled with home decorating publications advocating the use of peasant-style pottery and figurines in home decor caused Stangl's hand-painted bird figurines to soar in popularity during World War II. The war that triggered demand for the birds also posed new obstacles for their production. Firstly, decorators in Trenton became scarce as women were needed to fill the positions of men serving in the armed forces or work in Trenton's defense plants. Secondly, materials necessary to bird production became scarce as they were commandeered for the war effort.

Stangl sidestepped Trenton's labor shortage by establishing a bird-decorating department at the Flemington Outlet since there were more women available for decorating in rural Hunterdon County than there were in Trenton at that time. Flemington's bird decorating department lasted from 1942 through 1946. Nearly 85 decorators had been employed at Flemington, but only about 30 decorated at the outlet at any given time. The foreladies of Flemington's decorating department were first Ruth Curtis and then Mary Lesson. The position was later taken over by Rae Killinger, who became manager of the entire Flemington Outlet during the 1960s. A portion of the Flemington decorating department was near the selling floor, and shoppers were encouraged to view the decorating process. Most of the decorating department, however, was on the second floor, away from the retail shopping area of the building. Many decorators still recall the pleasant working atmosphere in Flemington during that time. Shirley Thatcher Spaciano recalled: "There were about forty of us when I was there. We all chatted, and the radio was always on. Every morning, I still can hear it, 'Don McNeill's Breakfast Club!' Then later in the day, 'Broadcasting live from

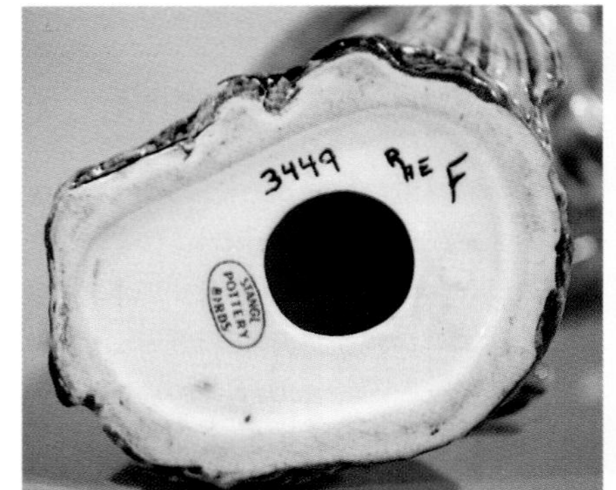

Base of bird decorated by Flemington supervisor Rae Killinger. Note the "F" indicating that this bird was decorated in Flemington. Courtesy of the Jim Horner collection.

beautiful Shawnee on the Delaware, it's Fred Waring and his Pennsylvanians!'"

Every bird decorated at Flemington was marked with each decorator's initials and an "F" to indicate Flemington. The birds were cast and fired to bisque at Trenton, then shipped to Flemington for painting. After decorating, the birds were then shipped back to Trenton for glazing and final firing. Only the smaller bird figurines were sent to the Flemington decorators. Stangl's larger, more complicated birds were produced in entirety at the Trenton factory.

Many Flemington decorators also worked from home, reporting to the Flemington Outlet to pick up birds and supplies and return completed birds. Even Martin Stangl's daughter, Christl Bacheler, decorated birds at home. She has recounted that she enjoyed the painting and could get quite a few finished at night while her young children were asleep. She remembers: "I painted so many yellow roosters that I never wanted to see a yellow rooster again!" Following are initials of many, but not all, of the Flemington decorators. There are duplicate initials belonging to different decorators as not all of the deco-

AA-F Ann Fitzpatrick Arnity
AS-F Ann Stone
BB-F Betty Butterfoss
BB-F Beth Boyd
BK-F Bertha Krause
BP-F Beth Painter
BP-F Betty Porter Connors
CB-F Christl Stangl Bacheler
CH-F Camilla Hunter
CS-F Cora Somers
CV-F Corinne Van Arsdale
DB-F Doris Boyd Case
DC-F Dot Cottrell
DD-F Dotty Denyse
DK-F Doris King Stout
DM-F Dale Morian
DS-F Dot Salter
DW-F Delores Wilson Greer
EB-F Eunice Boyd
EFB-F Elsa Barrick Miller
EG-F Edna Godfrey
EG-F Esther Gold Cohen
EK-F Elizabeth King Suydam
EM-F Edith Morgan Smith
EP-F Eleanor Pedrick Trout
EP-F Evelyn Pyatt Crone
EW-F Emma Waldron Santos
EW-F Edna Witlock
FH-F Faith Hommer Droppa
FM-F Florence Mazur
FS-F Florence Senderling Braugh
FS-F Florence Sutton Pegg
FM-F Frances Moore
GC-F Grace Cronce Hall
GH-F Grace Cronce Hall
GH-F Geraldine Hornbaker Toth
HC-F Henriette Cronce
HM-F Helene Morton
IF-F Ida French
IH-F Irma Hall
JA-F Jean Allegar
JAL-F Jean Leusenring Cole
JB-F Jean Briton
JG-F Jeanne Godley
JG-F Julia Galina Campbell
JH-F Jenny Pedrick Huffman
JJ-F Jeanette Jescwicz Norman
JL-F Jean Lechski LeBold
JL-F Jean Leusenring Cole
JT-F Jean Taylor Polasek
JV-F Josephine Van Roy
JW-F Jane Wurst
LM-F Lucy Mannon Sheetz
LS-F Laura Shaunsy Bailey
MB-F Mary Barrick
MB-F Marion Barry
MD-F Marion Dolter Stone
MDH-F Myrtle Hoffman
MG-F Meta Garrison
MH-F Margaret Higgins Hall
MH-F Mary Gulick Hawke
ML-F Maryanne Lawrence Humbert
ML-F Mary Lesson
ML-F Mary Longo
MM-F Margery Miles
MM-F Mildred Moody
MP-F Mary Pyatt Villani
MR-F Marion Riddle
MS-F Marion Stenabaugh
MT-F Marion Trimmer
MW-F Mary Walls
MW-F Mary Williamson
NR-F Nancy Reise Hooper
NT-F Norma Tarantola Rolla
OP-F Olga Polhemus
PH-F Peggy Hughes
RC-F Ruth Curtis
RAE-F Rae Killinger
RK-F Rae Killinger
RK-F Rose Kadezabek Schmid
RT-F Rose Tedeschi
ST-F Shirley Thatcher Spaciano
S-F Shirley Thatcher Spaciano
TV-F Trudy Van Eick
VG-F Vera Gordon Brainard
VL-F Virginia Lesson
VM-F Verna McPherson
VR-F Viola Reames
WB-F Wilhelmina Burkhardt

Following are initials belonging to a few of the Trenton bird decorators. This is certainly not a complete list but some of the more prolific decorators that have been identified. Some of the initials actually used on the birds are much more stylized than typesetting allows.

AES Annie Elizabeth Seabridge
AS Annie Elizabeth Seabridge
AL Albert Lee Burkhalter
AL Lillian Antonia Laird
AS Alice Samsel
BB Betty Bittner
D Doris Krisandra
D Dottie Denyse
D Florence Dunn Glenn
DD Dottie Denyse
DR Dora Ruggles
ED Ethel Denoravitch
EK Eleanor Kupiak
ES Edna Swaine
F Frances Hancock
FD Florence Dunn Glenn
FG Florence Gardener
G Josephine Grazikowski
H Helen Schill
JT Josephine Tiffenbach
MB Maisie Swaine Boan
MS Maisie Swaine Boan
MP Marion Plotz
MW Margaret Walsh

RC Ruth Clark
RK Ruth Klenk
R Rosa Veglianetti
RV Rosa Veglianetti
S Edna Swaine
S Shirley Thatcher Spaciano
SB Stella Bornyak
ST Shirley Thatcher Spaciano
T Theresa Hawryluk
V Veronica Malloy
µ Gloria Cardone

Hundreds of thousands of birds were decorated at the Flemington Outlet during World War II, so it is certainly understandable that some of those birds never made it "home" to Trenton for glazing and firing. Birds that became damaged at Flemington were disposed of in a dump behind the outlet building, but many of the errant birds simply remained with the home decorators and were never returned to the outlet. These unfinished birds often turn up as undecorated bisque (usually at New Jersey garage sales), but once in a while a decorated but unglazed bird figure is found. The unglazed color is very fragile so is usually partially rubbed off. Some unglazed birds have been found that were subsequently waxed, varnished or painted with oil colors, so the original underglaze color was protected. These are much more scarce than birds that are simply undecorated bisque.

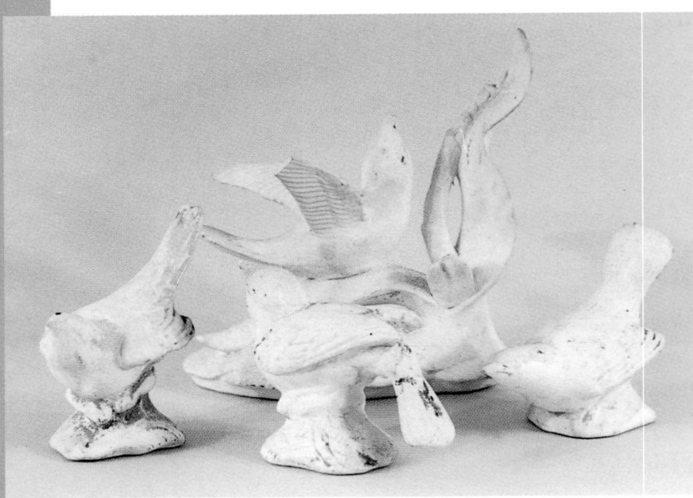

Group of undecorated bisque birds that had "flown" from the Flemington Outlet during World War II. The smaller birds are usually valued less than their fully decorated and glazed counterparts.

It is much more unusual to find large undecorated birds, such as the Chinese Pheasant, so they generally have a value equal to the fully decorated figures. The dealer sign was painted with underglaze color but was never glazed. It, too, is a rarity. Courtesy of the Weigand collection.

Decorated but unglazed birds from the Flemington Outlet. The underglaze color on these birds was protected with a coat of furniture wax, so they are in much better condition than the unglazed decorated birds not protected in some way. As with the undecorated bisque birds, small decorated but unglazed birds are less valuable than fully glazed versions, but larger, scarcer birds, such as the White Wing Crossbill, are valued equal to or more than their glazed counterparts. Courtesy of the Weigand collection.

Stangl's second impediment to wartime bird and animal production was the unavailability of glycerin, one of the primary components of ceramic underglaze color. During World War II glycerin was restricted for commercial use as it was also necessary for gunpowder and explosives production (such as nitro glycerin). Glycerin was used in underglaze color to provide a flowing brushable consistency for painting, and it did not affect the glaze or color during firing. Refined molasses was used as an acceptable glycerin substitute. However, molasses did adversely affect the colors by causing them to become pale in some instances and splotchy in others. Usually the blues and greens became splotchy while brown brushstrokes were indistinct. The colors most adversely affected were the pinks, reds, and sometimes black. These have always been unstable underglaze colors, but the molasses made them even more so. The slightest variation in kiln temperature or oxygen in the fire caused the color to almost disappear. This can be clearly seen on the #3405 Cockatoo figures. These birds were supposed to be a deep vibrant pink, but many of them decorated with molasses in the color came out of the kilns nearly white, with just a hint of pink remaining in the

Comparison of #3405D Cockatoo figurines decorated during World War II. The bird on left was decorated using color with molasses, causing the pink to fade out during firing. The bird on the right as the color was intended to look. Courtesy of the Wayne Weigand collection.

crevices of the feathers. Many of Stangl's birds produced during World War II are much paler and muted than birds produced afterward.

By 1943, August Jacob left Stangl Pottery. Jacob's assistant, Herman Eichorn, continued in Stangl's plaster shop sculpting on his own and assisting John Tierney. Herman Eichorn and John Tierney sculpted all of Stangl's bird figurines from 1943 onward. During 1943 and 1944 Stangl introduced 16 more bird figurines. As before, these figures were brightly colored and highly detailed. However, this would be the last large-scale bird introduction. After the end of World War II, the United Nations occupied Germany and Japan in order to restore industry and economy destroyed by the war. In both countries, ceramics industries were again established, and cheaper foreign ceramic products were once more available to the American market. The "bird madness" that kept Stangl's decorators busy during the war dwindled to nearly nothing by 1946. Fortunately for Stangl, the demand for birds was immediately replaced with a demand for hand-painted dinnerware. Returning servicemen eager to set up housekeeping with their war brides created a building boom and subsequent need for household furnishings. Without batting an eye, Martin Stangl simply minimized bird production as dinnerware production was increased. During 1946 the Flemington Outlet bird-decorating department was consolidated at the Trenton factory. By 1947, Martin Stangl discontinued many of the less popular birds, and 13 new birds were introduced during 1949, 1950 and 1952. The color patterns and brush-strokes used on these birds were "set" by Kay Hackett, as Ethel Kennedy had left the company by that time. In 1953, Kay Hackett reworked the colors on several of the red birds by replacing the Pink #160 underglaze color with scarlet overglaze color on such birds as the Woodpeckers, Crossbills, and Cardinals. Kay Hackett completely redesigned the colors of the Scarlet Tanagers by coloring them as Western Tanagers with yellow and black bodies with scarlet heads. Kay Hackett also used more vibrant colors on the bases and replaced the blue dogwood blossom set by Ethel Kennedy in 1944 with a more realistic ivory color. During the 1950s, Ethel Kennedy worked at Heinrich Below's Pennsbury Pottery and developed the colors for the bird figurines produced there.

The #3750D Western Tanager figurine without the scarlet overglaze color. Courtesy of the Weigand collection.

Occasionally, birds that should have been decorated with scarlet overglaze color were found to be defective and sold at the Flemington Outlet without the scarlet color. These birds will be gloss white where the scarlet color would have been. They are usually valued the same or a bit less than the same bird with its full complement of scarlet.

During 1955, Stangl introduced five new Herman Eichorn bird shapes to the figurine assortment. Eichorn was the lone sculptor on these figures as John Tierney had retired in 1954 after 50 years of service to the company. This group represents the final introductions of Stangl bird figurines. Although in "active" production for 10 years, only small quantities of these birds were produced during that 10-year span making these among the most highly valued of Stangl's birds.

By the late 1950s Stangl was actively producing 41 different bird shapes for department store sales. The number of available bird shapes had been reduced to 30 by 1963. Also at that time, Stangl began advertising the pottery bird figurines as "Stangl Birds of America." Even though only a limited number of bird shapes were available nationally, nearly all bird shapes were available at the Flemington Outlet. Throughout the 1950s and 1960s Stangl birds were on a semi-permanent half-price sale at the outlet. This sale was used as an advertising draw for many years.

Following the fire at the Trenton factory in 1965, only a limited number of the simpler bird shapes were produced. By the early 1970s, a few of the more complicated bird figures were again being produced, but in simplified forms. Details, such as flowers or leaves, which were cast separately and added on were no longer applied to the 1970s birds. Also, the decorating was simplified by using fewer, broader brush strokes. What the 1970s birds lacked in detail, they made up in color as the colors of the birds produced during the 1970s are always much more vivid and vibrant than any of the birds produced earlier. Also, birds produced during the 1970s were almost always marked with the year of production.

Martin Stangl was a firm believer in trademark name recognition, so nearly every Stangl bird figurine was clearly marked. During 1939, 1940, and 1941, most of the bird figures were marked only with a gold-foil paper label and an oval paper hang tag. Once the label and hang tag were removed, the bird was no longer marked, so Stangl began to use more permanent marks. Some birds, such as the #3405 Cockatoo and #3444 Cardinal, have STANGL, the number, and USA molded in the base of the figures, so these may not bear any other markings.

Early versions of birds that originally had "hollow bottoms," such as the #3273 Rooster, #3275 Turkey, and #3276 Bluebird, are now often found with no markings, or just the decorator's initials.

Hollow bottom of an early version of the #3276 Bluebird on the right, later version of the #3276 Bluebird with "flat bottom" on the left. Courtesy of the Kramar collection.

Stangl Pottery square hand-painted underglaze stamp, late 1930s – early 1940s.

Stangl Bird Marks

Many different back markings were used on the Stangl Pottery Birds. The first marks were Stangl's square underglaze rubberstamp mark. Underglaze decals were then introduced and used throughout the 1940s. The decals read "Stangl Pottery Birds" and were two sizes, 9/16" and 3/4". As production pace increased during the mid 1940s, Stangl began using rubberstamps to mark the birds. The first rubberstamp resembled the 9/16" underglaze decal. As bird production became more frenetic during the mid 1940s, more stamps were needed immediately, so the word Stangl in simple block letters 1/2" long was used. Birds decorated in Flemington were usually stamped in blue, while those decorated in Trenton were marked in brown. Following World War II, a 1/2" oval stamp with Stangl in all capital letters was introduced. Once foreign bird figurines were again available after the war, Stangl began stamping birds with a 3/8" long "Made in USA" stamp. Sporadically throughout production, the name Stangl was also hand-painted on the base of some birds. Birds produced during the 1970s can be found stamped with the Stangl name in script within an oval. Figurines produced specifically for the Mutual Sunset or Nelson Lebo lamp companies are rarely marked, except with an occasional gold-foil paper label.

Figurine identified with in-mold markings only, no underglaze stamps or decorators' initials, very common on birds produced during the very early 1940s.

Stangl Pottery Birds underglaze decal with shape number stamped in blue, used throughout the 1940s.

Partial sheet of Stangl's "Stangl Pottery Birds" underglaze decals.

Stangl's Terra Rose gold-foil paper label was used on birds sold at department stores during the early 1940s.

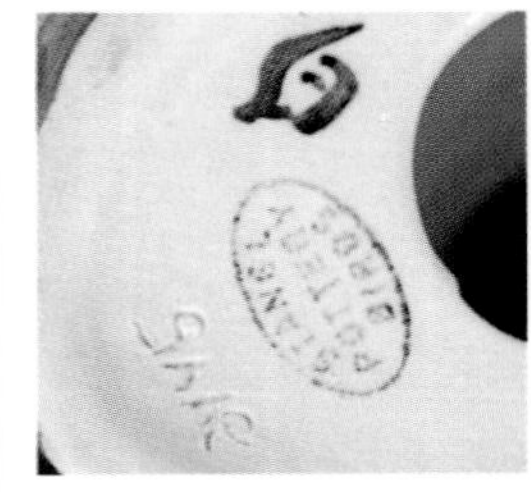

Stangl Pottery Birds underglaze stamp, sometimes with shape number inscribed in the wet clay, mid 1940s – 1960s.

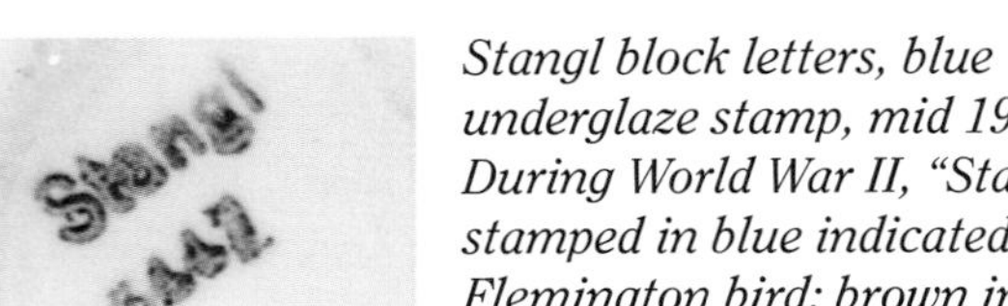

Stangl block letters, blue underglaze stamp, mid 1940s. During World War II, "Stangl" stamped in blue indicated a Flemington bird; brown indicated Trenton manufacture.

Stangl block letters, brown underglaze stamp, mid 1940s – 1970s.

Oval with Stangl in caps, late 1940s – 1970s, but used primarily during the 1960s. The broken oval "Made in USA" underglaze stamp was used primarily during the 1950s and 1960s.

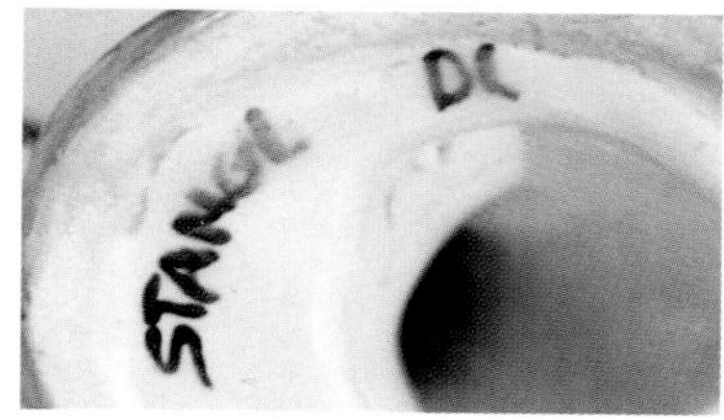

Hand-painted "Stangl," occasionally 1940s – 1970s.

Gold luster overglaze stamp, used on figurines with brushed gold finishes, 1950s – 1970s.

Oval underglaze stamp with Stangl in script, late 1960s – 1970s.

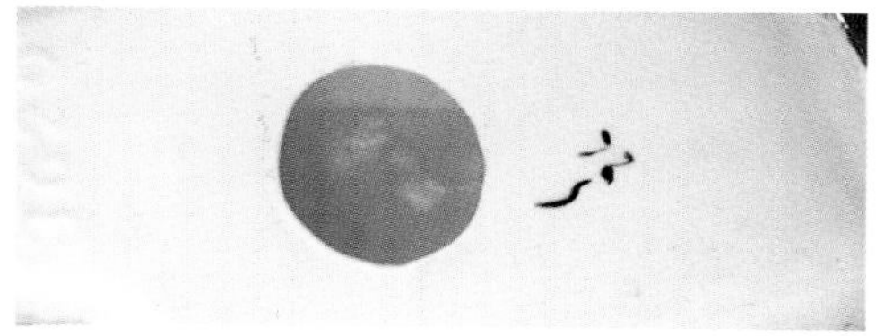

Dated bird, 1970s; this one is 1972.

Dated bird, 1970s; this one is 1976.

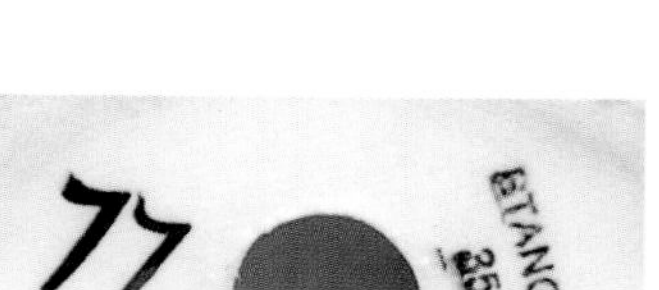

Stangl block letters in caps with registry mark, black underglaze stamp, mid 1975 – 1978, usually accompanied by year of manufacture date; this one is 1977.

In addition to the Stangl trademark, the figurines were marked with each decorator's initials. It was not artistic pride that prompted the decorators to initial each piece, but their desire to be paid! The initials were used for quality control and to determine payroll when decorators were being paid piecework. In 1952, decorators were paid 36¢ for each #3715 Blue Jay painted correctly. Other decorating prices at that time were 9¢ for each #3444 Cardinal, 13½¢ each #3490 Double Redstart, 18¢ each #3582 Double Parakeets, and 5½¢ each #3276 Bluebird. This was a very fair rate for the time. Any decorator of average ability painting at an average pace was able to produce enough pieces per day to earn the equivalent of the prevailing wage for that type of work. Birds with scarlet and black overglaze color were marked with two sets of initials, one set for the decorator that painted the underglaze colors and the other for the decorator that applied the scarlet overglaze color.

Also on the base of each bird will be the shape number. This number could be stamped under the glaze, carved into the clay while it was soft, hand-painted under the glaze, or cast into the piece as part of the mold as with #3444 Cardinals and #3635 Goldfinch groups. Each manner of applying the shape number was used throughout Stangl's bird production. Occasionally, an incorrect shape number was stamped or carved on a bird but generally does not affect the value. Once in a great while, a Stangl bird figurine was produced without a trademark, a shape number or a decorator's initials, but again this does not affect the value.

Original Stangl bird prices can sometimes still be found on the figurines. Most birds sold at the Flemington Outlet were sold as seconds (even if they were not flawed) so were priced with a green or black china marker on the unglazed foot of the base. First quality birds were usually marked with a paper price tag.

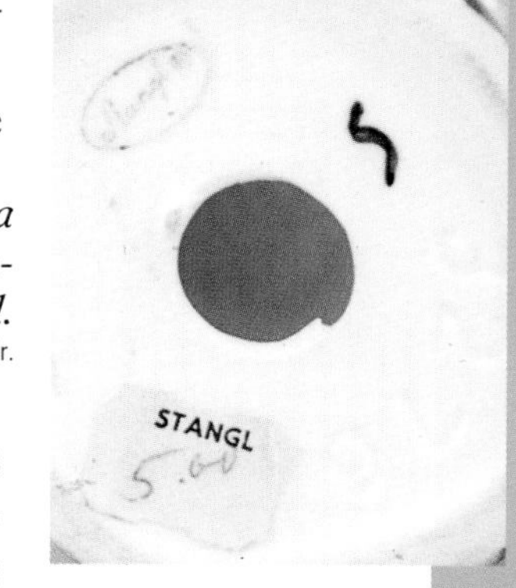

Paper price tag on a first-quality Flemington Outlet bird.
Courtesy of Robert C. Runge Sr.

Because many Stangl bird shapes were produced over a great period of time, many variations in weight and height can be found. Weight differences were caused by such variables as length of time the bird was in the mold and different components and formula of the clay slip itself. Variations in the types of clay used also caused variations in shrinkage, resulting in differences in height. The same bird shape can vary in height nearly ½". This size variation is typical of nearly all Stangl products and does not affect value.

The names of the birds listed here are the official names found in Stangl Pottery Company records or Martin Stangl's personal notes. The values stated are *only* for figurines in perfect condition with bright, well-painted colors. Birds with faded colors, glaze bubbles, factory flaws or repairs are valued considerably less.

1939 Introductions

In 1939, the shape #3250 represented only one duck figurine in the standing position, listed in Stangl sales sheets as "#3250 Wild Duck." During 1940, an additional five duck figures were designed and introduced as the #3250 A-F Decorative Duck series, and the #3250 Wild Duck became #3250A Standing Duck.

#3273 Rooster, 5½" 1939 – 1940. The earliest decoration on this rooster featured wings and tails predominately French Green and circular painted eyes. $550.00 – 650.00. Courtesy of the Wayne Weigand collection.

A slightly later version of the #3273 Rooster, 5½" with wings and tail more blue than green and a simple dot and brow eye, 1939 – 1942. $500.00 – 600.00.

#3274 Penguin, 5½" 1939 – 1942. $450.00 – 500.00. Courtesy of the Wayne Weigand collection.

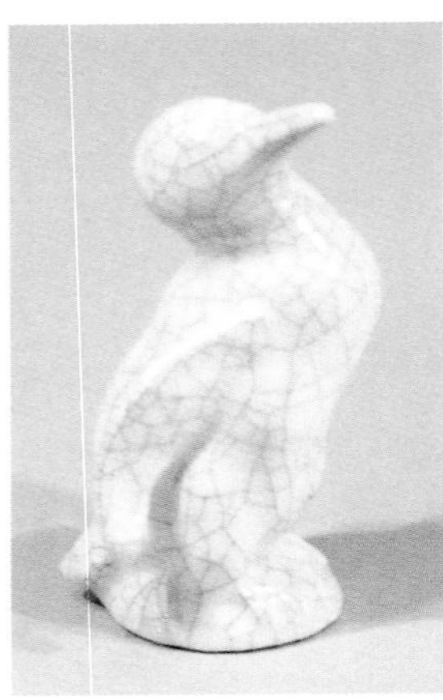

#3274 Penguin, 5½" Antique Ivory Crackled, 1940 only. $550.00 – 600.00. Courtesy of the Wayne Weigand collection.

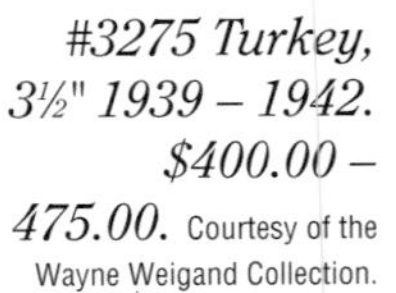

#3275 Turkey, 3½" 1939 – 1942. $400.00 – 475.00. Courtesy of the Wayne Weigand Collection.

The two styles of base on the #3275 Turkey figurine. The earlier open bottom (on right) was used during 1939; the style with a more closed bottom dates from 1940 – 1942.

Not Shown:

#3250 Wild Duck, 3½" renamed Standing Decorative Duck 1940, 1939 – 1944. $90.00 – 125.00.
#3250A Standing Decorative Duck, 3½" Antique Ivory or Turquoise Crackled 1940 only. $125.00 – 150.00.
#3250A Standing Decorative Duck, 3½" Terra Rose finish 1941 only. $60.00 – 90.00.
#3250A Standing Duck, 3½" brushed gold finishes 1965 – 1975. $45.00 – 60.00.
#3250A Standing Duck, 3½" salt or pepper shaker 1967 – 1970. $120.00 – 135.00.
#3273 Rooster, 5½" Antique Ivory or Turquoise Crackled 1940 only. $600.00 – 650.00.
#3273 Rooster, 5½" Terra Rose finish 1941 only. $600.00 – 650.00.
#3274 Penguin, 5½" Antique Ivory or Turquoise Crackled 1940 only. $550.00 – 600.00.
#3274 Penguin, 5½" Terra Rose finish 1941 only. $500.00 – 550.00.
#3275 Turkey, 3½" Antique Ivory or Turquoise Crackled 1940 only. $500.00 – 550.00.
#3275 Turkey, 3½" Terra Rose finish 1941 only. $450.00 – 500.00.

Detail of airbrushed color on a 1939 vintage #3276 Bluebird.

During 1939, the original modeling of the #3276 Bluebird figurines bore very minimal feather detail and were somewhat cartoonish in appearance. Also during that time, the #3276 Bluebirds were decorated by airbrushing blue underglaze color on the

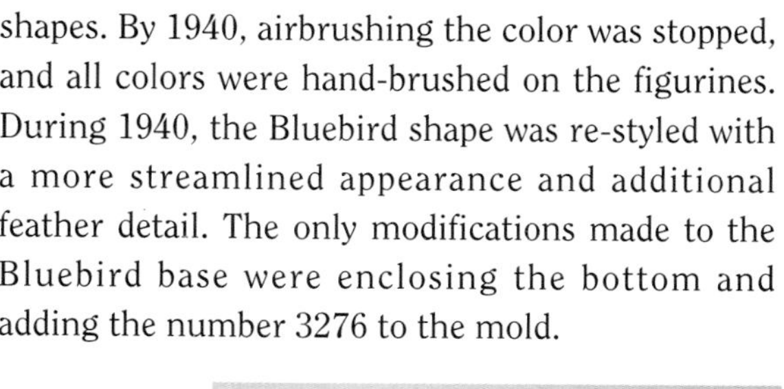

shapes. By 1940, airbrushing the color was stopped, and all colors were hand-brushed on the figurines. During 1940, the Bluebird shape was re-styled with a more streamlined appearance and additional feather detail. The only modifications made to the Bluebird base were enclosing the bottom and adding the number 3276 to the mold.

#3276 Bluebird, 5", original shape, airbrushed color, 1939 only. $180.00 – 200.00. Courtesy of the Frank and Elizabeth Kramar collection.

#3276 Bluebird, 5", re-styled shape, 1940 – 1978. $75.00 – 110.00. Courtesy of the Frank and Elizabeth Kramar collection.

#3276D Double Bluebird, 8½", original shape, airbrushed color, 1939 only. $250.00 – 275.00. Courtesy of the Frank and Elizabeth Kramar collection.

#3281 Duck, 4" originally named "Large Duck," mistakenly called "Momma Duck," 1939 – 1943. $600.00 – 700.00. Courtesy of the Wayne Weigand collection.

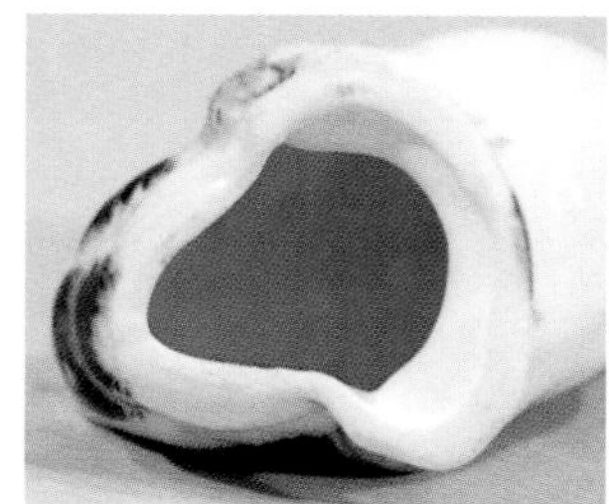

Open-style base of the #3281 4" Duck.

#3282 Bluebird salt and pepper shakers, 3", 1939 – 1943. $300.00 – 350.00 per set. Courtesy of the Wayne Weigand collection.

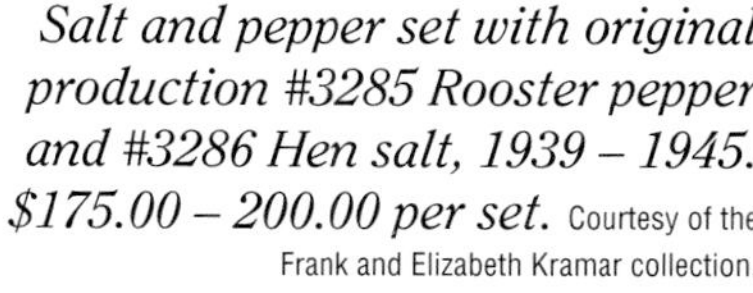

Salt and pepper set with original production #3285 Rooster pepper and #3286 Hen salt, 1939 – 1945. $175.00 – 200.00 per set. Courtesy of the Frank and Elizabeth Kramar collection.

Not Shown:

#3276 Bluebird, 5" Antique Ivory or Turquoise Crackled 1940 only. $200.00 – 250.00.

#3276D Double Bluebird, 8½" re-styled shape, 1940 – 1978. $150.00 – 200.00.

#3276D Double Bluebird, 8½" Antique Ivory or Turquoise Crackled 1940 only. $250.00 – 275.00.

#3281 Duck, 4" Antique Ivory or Turquoise Crackled 1940 only. $700.00 – 800.00.

#3285 Rooster pepper shaker, 4¼" white with black stippling, closed bottom, 1939 – 1945. $80.00 – 110.00.

Two #3285 Rooster pepper shakers, 4¼" solid-color glazes (Persian Yellow), 1939 – 1945. $80.00 – 100.00 each. Courtesy of the Wayne Weigand collection.

1960s era salt and pepper set, #3285 Rooster pepper and #3286 Hen salt. $150.00 – 200.00 per set. Courtesy of the Wayne Weigand collection.

Miniature Rooster #3287 and Miniature Hen #3288, 1939 – 1940. $100.00 – 125.00 each. Courtesy of the Wayne Weigand Collection.

Bases of the 1960s Rooster and Hen salt and pepper shakers.

The #3285 and #3286 Rooster and Hen Salt and Pepper shakers and the #3287 and #3286 Miniature Rooster and Hen shared the same basic shapes but featured different underglaze decorations. The colors of the #3287 and #3286 Miniature Rooster and Hen were decorated tan with black stippling while the #3285 and #3286 Rooster and Hen Salt and Pepper shakers were usually white with black stippling. Both the open-bottom figurines and closed-bottom shakers featured pink #160 combs, orange beaks and feet, with French Green bases. The #3287 and #3286 Miniature Rooster and Hen had open bases, while the bases of the salt and pepper shakers were each closed with a hole for a cork stopper. The tan decorated #3287 Miniature Rooster and #3286 Miniature Hen were discontinued during fall 1940, while the black and white stippled #3285 Rooster Pepper and #3286 Hen Salt shakers were produced through 1945. The #3285 and #3286 Rooster and Hen Salt and Pepper shakers were also produced with the single solid-color glazes of Colonial Blue, Persian Yellow, and Silver Green. Solid-color glazed Hen and Rooster shakers are somewhat harder to find than those decorated with the black and white stippling.

In 1967 Stangl reintroduced the #3285 and #3286 Rooster and Hen Salt and Pepper shaker shapes for the tourist trade at the Flemington Outlet. The 1967 Hen and Rooster shakers were bright white with pink #160 combs, orange beaks and feet, and Pomona Green bases. These shakers were identified with Stangl's rubber stoppers and sometimes paper labels. The bright white Hen and Rooster shakers were very popular at the Flemington Outlet and were produced throughout the late 1960s and early 1970s.

Not Shown:
#3285 Rooster pepper shaker, 4¼" white with green base, closed bottom, 1967 – 1970s. $75.00 – 90.00.
#3286 Hen salt shaker, 3" white with black stippling, closed bottom, 1939 – 1945. $80.00 – 110.00.
#3286 Hen salt shaker, 3" solid-color glazes, 1939 – 1945. $80.00 – 110.00.
#3286 Hen salt shaker, 3" white with green base, closed bottom, 1967 – 1970s. $75.00 – 90.00.
#3287 Miniature Rooster, 4¼" tan with black stippling, open bottom, 1939 – 1940. $100.00 – 125.00.
#3287 Miniature Rooster, 4¼" Antique Ivory or Turquoise Crackled, 1940 only. $130.00 – 150.00.
#3287 Miniature Rooster, 4¼" Terra Rose finish, 1941 only. $150.00 – 175.00.
#3288 Miniature Hen, 3" tan with black stippling, open bottom, 1939 – 1940. $100.00 – 125.00.
#3288 Miniature Hen, 3" Antique Ivory or Turquoise Crackled, 1940 only. $130.00 – 150.00.
#3288 Miniature Hen, 3" Terra Rose finish, 1941 only. $150.00 – 175.00.

Bases of the #3250 Duck salt and pepper.

#3250D Gazing Duck and #3250C Feeding Duck as 1960s era salt and pepper shakers. The colors are much more vibrant on the 1960s shakers than the colors on the 1940s figurines. $240.00 – 270.00 set. Courtesy of the Hill-Fulper-Stangl Museum.

Decorative Ducks #3250C and #3250D were also produced as salt and pepper shakers for the Flemington Outlet from 1967 through 1970. The #3250A Standing Duck was epoxied to egg plates during that time as well.

1940 Introductions

Stangl's six different #3250 Decorative Ducks in their various poses. Left to right: #3250E Drinking Duck, #3250A Standing Duck, #3250B Preening Duck, #3250D Gazing Duck, #3250F Quacking Duck, #3250C Feeding Duck. $90.00 – 125.00 each. Courtesy of the Wayne Weigand collection.

#3250A Standing Duck, 3½", black glaze (base for Black Gold finish, but no gold was applied), 1967 – 1975. $60.00 – 75.00. Courtesy of the Wayne Weigand collection.

#3250B Preening Duck, 2¾", brushed gold finishes, this one Green Lustre, 1965 – 1975. $45.00 – 60.00. Courtesy of the Luke and Nancy Ruepp collection.

A group of Decorative Ducks in an assortment of brushed gold finishes. $40.00 – 60.00 each. Courtesy of the Frank and Elizabeth Kramar collection.

Three Decorative Ducks in Terra Rose mauve and Terra Rose green. $60.00 – 90.00 each. Courtesy of the Frank and Elizabeth Kramar collection.

Not Shown:

#3250A Standing Decorative Duck, 3½" (originally Wild Duck in 1939), 1939 – 1944. $90.00 – 125.00.
#3250A Standing Decorative Duck, 3½" Antique Ivory or Turquoise Crackled, 1940 only. $125.00 – 150.00.
#3250A Standing Decorative Duck, 3½" Terra Rose finish, 1941 only. $60.00 – 90.00.
#3250A Standing Duck, 3½" brushed gold finishes, 1965 – 1975. $45.00 – 60.00.
#3250A Standing Duck, 3½" salt or pepper shaker, 1967 – 1970. $120.00 – 135.00.
#3250B Preening Decorative Duck, 2¾", 1940 – 1944. $75.00 – 100.00.
#3250B Preening Decorative Duck, 2¾" Terra Rose finish, 1941 only. $60.00 – 90.00.
#3250C Feeding Decorative Duck, 1¾", 1940 – 1944. $75.00 – 100.00.

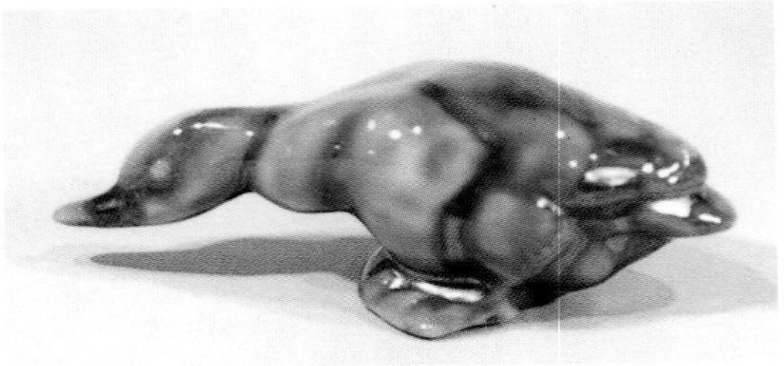

#3250C Feeding Decorative Duck, 1¾" Terra Rose finish 1941 only. $60.00 – 90.00. Courtesy of the Wayne Weigand collection.

#3399 Warbler, 5¼", 1940 only. $700.00 – 900.00. Courtesy of the Lynn Dezmain collection.

Two #3400 Love Birds, 4" original style, Terra Rose green and Terra Rose mauve finish, 1941 only. $150.00 – 200.00 each. Courtesy of the Wayne Weigand collection.

#3400 Love Bird, 4" original, 1940 – 1942. The base (above) was flat with no markings. $125.00 – 150.00. Courtesy of the Wayne Weigand collection.

#3400 Love Bird, 4" re-styled, 1942 – 1947 (base shown above). $95.00 – 110.00. Courtesy of the Wayne Weigand collection.

#3401 Wren, 3½" original, 1940 – 1942. $250.00 – 300.00. Courtesy of Dennis Barone.

Not Shown:

#3250C Feeding Duck, 1¾" brushed gold finishes, 1965 – 1975. $45.00 – 60.00.

#3250C Feeding Duck, 1¾" salt shaker, 1967 – 1970. $120.00 – 135.00.

#3250D Gazing Decorative Duck, 3¾", 1940 – 1944. $75.00 – 100.00.

#3250D Gazing Decorative Duck, 3¾" Terra Rose finish, 1941 only. $60.00 – 90.00.

#3250D Gazing Duck, 3¾" brushed gold finishes, 1965 – 1975. $45.00 – 60.00.

#3250D Gazing Duck, 3¾" pepper shaker, 1967 – 1970. $120.00 – 135.00.

#3250E Drinking Decorative Duck, 2¼", 1940 – 1944. $75.00 – 100.00.

#3250E Drinking Decorative Duck, 2¼", Terra Rose finish, 1941 only. $60.00 – 90.00.

#3250E Drinking Duck, 2¼ brushed gold finishes, 1965 – 1975. $45.00 – 60.00.

#3250F Quacking Decorative Duck, 3¾", 1940 – 1944. $75.00 – 100.00.

#3250F Quacking Decorative Duck, 3¾" Terra Rose finish, 1941 only. $60.00 – 90.00.

#3250F Quacking Duck, 3¾" brushed gold finishes, 1965 – 1975. $45.00 – 60.00.

#3399 Warbler, 5" Antique Ivory or Turquoise Crackled, 1940 only. $700.00 – 900.00.

#3400 Love Bird, 4" original, Antique Ivory or Turquoise Crackled, 1940 only. $150.00 – 200.00.

#3401 Wren, 3½" original, Antique Ivory or Turquoise Crackled, 1940 only. $300.00 – 350.00.

#3401 Wren, 3½" brushed gold finishes, 1968 – 1975. $50.00 – 75.00.

#3401 Wren, 3½" re-styled, 1942 – 1978. $60.00 – 75.00. Courtesy of the Wayne Weigand collection.

#3401D Double Wrens, 8" original, 1940 – 1942. $500.00 – 600.00. Courtesy of Dennis Barone.

#3401D Double Wrens, 8" re-styled, 1942 – 1978. $130.00 – 150.00. Courtesy of the Frank and Elizabeth Kramar collection.

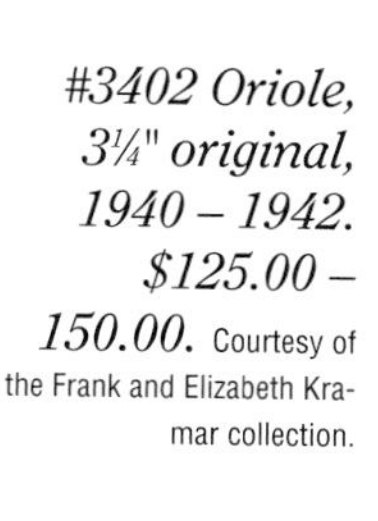

#3402 Oriole, 3¼" original, 1940 – 1942. $125.00 – 150.00. Courtesy of the Frank and Elizabeth Kramar collection.

#3402 Oriole, 3¼" re-styled, 1942 – 1978. $45.00 – 65.00. Courtesy of the Frank and Elizabeth Kramar collection.

#3402 Oriole, 3¼" Pompeii, 1971 only. $125.00 – 150.00. Courtesy of the Wayne Weigand Collection.

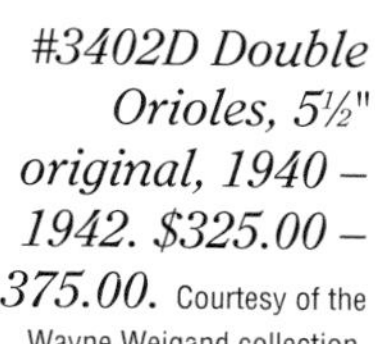

#3402D Double Orioles, 5½" original, 1940 – 1942. $325.00 – 375.00. Courtesy of the Wayne Weigand collection.

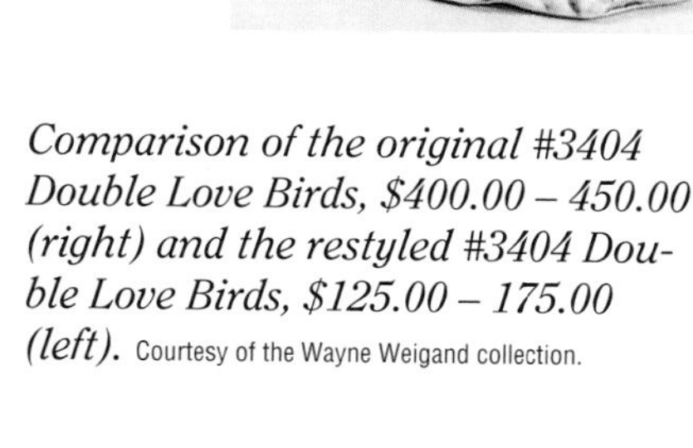

Comparison of the original #3404 Double Love Birds, $400.00 – 450.00 (right) and the restyled #3404 Double Love Birds, $125.00 – 175.00 (left). Courtesy of the Wayne Weigand collection.

#3402D Double Orioles, 5½" re-styled, 1942 – 1978. $100.00 – 125.00. Courtesy of the Frank and Elizabeth Kramar collection.

Not Shown:

#3401 Wren, 3½" Pompeii, 1971 only. $125.00 – 150.00.

#3401D Double Wrens, 8" Antique Ivory or Turquoise Crackled, 1940 only. $500.00 – 550.00.

#3402 Oriole, 3¼" Antique Ivory or Turquoise Crackled, 1940 only. $150.00 – 200.00.

#3402 Oriole, 3¼" brushed gold finishes, 1965 – 1975. $50.00 – 75.00.

#3402D Double Orioles, 5½" Antique Ivory or Turquoise Crackled, 1940 only. $400.00 – 450.00.

#3404 Double Love Birds, 5½" original, 1940 – 1942. $400.00 – 450.00.

#3404 Double Love Birds, 5½" Antique Ivory or Turquoise Crackled, 1940 only. $500.00 – 550.00.

#3404 Double Love Birds, 5½" re-styled, 1942 – 1947. $125.00 – 175.00.

The #3405 Cockatoo was originally called "Parrot" in 1940 and was tried with vibrant multicolor decoration. This multicolor scheme was dropped shortly in favor of the simpler pink decoration usually found on the #3405 birds.

Ethel Kennedy's original 1940 multicolor sample of the #3405 "Parrot." A variation of this decoration was used the following year on the #3580 Medium Cockatoo. Courtesy of the Louis and Sarah DiPlacido collection.

#3405 Cockatoo, 6" Antique Ivory or Turquoise Crackled, 1940 only. $165.00 – 185.00. Courtesy of the Bullock collection.

#3405 Cockatoo, 6" satin white, pastel colors, 1940 – 1943. $600.00 – 700.00. Courtesy of the Hill-Fulper-Stangl Museum.

Two #3405D Double Cockatoo figurines, 9½" original style, 1940 – 1942. $200.00 – 250.00 each. The one on the left is wartime era when molasses replaced glycerin in the underglaze colors which sometimes caused the pinks to "burn out" during firing. The one on the right is how the colors were intended to appear. Courtesy of the Wayne Weigand collection.

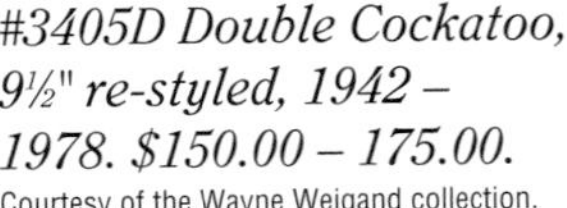

#3405D Double Cockatoo, 9½" re-styled, 1942 – 1978. $150.00 – 175.00. Courtesy of the Wayne Weigand collection.

#3406 Kingfisher, 3½" green, 1942 – 1965. $75.00 – 100.00. Courtesy of the Frank and Elizabeth Kramar collection.

#3406D Double Kingfisher, 5" blue, 1942 – 1944. $175.00 – 200.00. Courtesy of the Frank and Elizabeth Kramar collection.

Not Shown:

#3405 Cockatoo, 6" multicolored "Parrot" decoration, 1940 only. $700.00 – 800.00.

#3405 Cockatoo, 6" pink. $60.00 – 90.00.

#3405 Cockatoo, 6" Pompeii, 1971 only. $125.00 – 150.00.

#3405D Double Cockatoo, 9½" Antique Ivory or Turquoise Crackled, 1940 only. $250.00 – 300.00.

#3406 Kingfisher, 3½" blue, 1942 – 1944. $120.00 – 145.00.

#3406 Kingfisher, 3½" Antique Ivory or Turquoise Crackled, 1940 only. $125.00 – 150.00.

#3406D Double Kingfisher, 5" green, 1942 – 1965. $125.00 – 175.00.

#3406D Double Kingfisher, 5" Antique Ivory or Turquoise Crackled, 1940 only. $200.00 – 250.00.

Two #3407 Owls, 4¼" brown, 1940 – 1941, showing two variations of brown decoration. $450.00 – 500.00. Courtesy of the Wayne Weigand collection.

#3431 Standing Duck, 8", white with black stippling, $1,000.00 – 1,200.00; #3432 Running Duck, white with black stippling, $800.00 – 1,000.00.

#3408 Bird of Paradise, 5½", 1940 – 1978. $110.00 – 135.00. Courtesy of the Frank and Elizabeth Kramar collection.

The three duck shapes #3430, #3431, and #3432 were originally part of the Fulper Pottery Garden Animal line from early 1930s. New molds were made and the numbers updated for production of these three ducks as Stangl Pottery Birds in 1940. However, for a time, the figurines retained the old Fulper Garden Animal numbers, 871, 875, and 876, so can be found marked "Stangl" with old Fulper numbers. Even though length of production was the same for all three figures, the #3431 and #3432 Standing and Running Ducks are much more plentiful than the #3430 Large Duck.

#3432 Running Duck, 5", brown and green, $650.00 – 750.00; #3431 Standing Duck, 8", brown and green, $700.00 – 800.00.

Original Stangl Pottery catalog page dated July 1942, showing the #3430 22" Large Duck, $8,000.00 – 10,000.00; and #3433 16" Large Rooster, $4,000.00 – 5,000.00. From the Fulper and Stangl archival collection, courtesy the Wheaton Village Museum of American Glass.

Not Shown:

#3407 Owl, 4¼" white with black or gray speckling, 1940 – 1941. $550.00 – 600.00.

#3407 Owl, 4¼" Antique Ivory or Turquoise Crackled, 1940 only. $500.00 – 550.00.

#3407 Owl, 4¼" Terra Rose finish, 1941 only. $350.00 – 400.00.

#3408 Bird of Paradise, 5½" Antique Ivory or Turquoise Crackled, 1940 only. $300.00 – 350.00.

#3408 Bird of Paradise, 5½" Terra Rose finish, 1941 only. $300.00 – 350.00.

#3430 Large Duck, 22", 1940 – 1942. $8,000.00 – 10,000.00.

#3431 Standing Duck, 8", brown and green, 1940 – 1942. $700.00 – 800.00.

#3431 Standing Duck, 8", white with black stippling, 1940 – 1942. $1,000.00 – 1,200.00.

#3432 Running Duck, 5", brown and green, 1940 – 1942. $650.00 – 750.00.

#3432 Running Duck, 5", white with black stippling, 1940 – 1942. $800.00 – 1,000.00.

#3433 Large Rooster, 16", 1940 – 1942. $4,000.00 – 5,000.00.

#3433 Large Rooster, 16" Antique Ivory or Turquoise Crackled, 1940 only. $6,000.00 – 7,000.00.

The #3443 Flying Duck was originally decorated in vibrant airbrushed yellows, browns, and blues with hand-painted details. The airbrushed coloration was used only during 1940 and is exceptionally hard to find. This duck's colors were then changed to a choice of "green" or "gray" and were hand-painted, not airbrushed.

#3443 Flying Duck, 9", airbrushed colors, 1940 only. $700.00 – 800.00. Courtesy of the Wayne Weigand collection.

#3443 Flying Duck, 9" hand-painted gray, 1940 – 1958. $300.00 – 350.00. Courtesy of the Wayne Weigand collection.

The #3444 Cardinal probably experienced a more drastic evolution during its 38 years of production than any of Stangl's other bird figurines. The Cardinal's first incarnation featured a slim body on a plain stump with two acorns. These early Cardinals were originally airbrushed, not hand-painted, with crimson underglaze color. The original Cardinal figurine is often mistakenly referred to as a "female Cardinal." Stangl did not produce an actual female version of this bird.

#3443 Flying Duck, 9" hand-painted green, 1940 – 1958. $225.00 – 275.00. Courtesy of the Wayne Weigand collection.

#3443 Flying Duck, 9" Antique Gold, 1959 – 1962. $350.00 – 400.00. Courtesy of the Frank and Elizabeth Kramar collection.

The Cardinal was re-styled in 1941, his body was bulked up, his feathers were more defined, and his beak and crest were made more pronounced. A leaf was added to his base, and the acorns were now a separate casting. By this time the Cardinal was no longer airbrushed, but hand-painted with pink #160, a slightly darker red than the early crimson was. The Cardinal's next modification came in 1953 following Stangl's installation of an electric kiln for firing overglaze colors. The cardinal could now be decorated in a deep scarlet red overglaze color, a shade unattainable with underglaze colors. With hand-painted bright scarlet overglaze

#3544 Original Cardinals with airbrushed crimson underglaze color. Cardinal on the left was decorated with pre-World War II color suspended in glycerin while the bird on the right was decorated with wartime underglaze color with molasses. Birds with deeper, more intense colors are always more valuable than birds with the washed-out wartime colors. $150.00 – 225.00 each. Courtesy of the Frank and Elizabeth Kramar collection.

#3444 Cardinal on left is re-styled body with pink #160 hand-painted underglaze color, 1941 – 1953, $90.00 – 110.00; on right is #3444 Cardinal with re-styled body with scarlet and black overglaze decoration, 1953 – 1970, $95.00 – 130.00. Courtesy of the Wayne Weigand collection.

color and black detailing, this was the Cardinal's most realistic incarnation. By the 1970s, the Cardinal's brushstrokes were simplified, and much of his detail was eliminated. Also at that time the acorn casting was no longer applied to the base.

The final variation of the #3444 Cardinal (right). Details are eliminated such as the black mask around the eyes, feather definition, and applied acorns on the base. The colors were also simplified. $80.00 – 100.00. The bird on the left is the well-defined and detailed model produced from 1953 to 1970. Courtesy of the Kramar collection.

#3445 Medium Rooster, 9" gray, and #3456 Medium Hen, 7" gray, 1940 – 1947, $275.00 – 325.00 each. Courtesy of the Wayne Weigand collection.

#3445 Medium Rooster, 9" yellow, 1940 – 1958, $175.00 – 225.00 each, #3456 Medium Hen, 7" yellow, 1940 – 1958. $175.00 – 200.00 each. Courtesy of the Frank and Elizabeth Kramar collection.

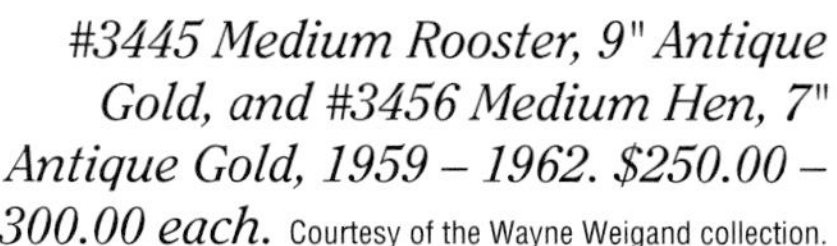

#3445 Medium Rooster, 9" Antique Gold, and #3456 Medium Hen, 7" Antique Gold, 1959 – 1962. $250.00 – 300.00 each. Courtesy of the Wayne Weigand collection.

Not Shown:

#3444 Cardinal, 6" original shape, airbrushed color, mistakenly called "female," 1940 – 1941. $150.00 – 225.00.
#3444 Cardinal, 6" original shape, Antique Ivory or Turquoise Crackled, 1940 only. $175.00 – 200.00.
#3444 Cardinal, 6½" re-styled shape, pink underglaze color, often called "glossy," 1941 – 1953. $90.00 – 110.00.
#3444 Cardinal, 6½" re-styled shape, red overglaze color, often called "matte," 1953 – 1970. $100.00 – 130.00.
#3444 Cardinal, 6½" final variation, no acorns and simplified decoration, red overglaze color, 1970 – 1978. $80.00 – 100.00.
#3445 Medium Rooster, 9" yellow, 1940 – 1958. $175.00 – 225.00.
#3445 Medium Rooster, 9" gray, 1940 – 1947. $275.00 – 325.00.
#3445 Medium Rooster, 9" Antique Gold, 1959 – 1962. $250.00 – 300.00.
#3456 Medium Hen, 7" yellow, 1940 – 1958. $175.00 – 200.00.
#3456 Medium Hen, 7" gray, 1940 – 1947. $275.00 – 325.00.
#3456 Medium Hen, 7" Antique Gold, 1959 – 1962. $250.00 – 300.00.

#3447 Yellow Warbler, 5", mistakenly called "Prothonotary Warbler," 1940 – 1965, early 1940s colors on the left, late 1940s – 1965 colors on the right. $60.00 – 90.00 each. Courtesy of the Frank and Elizabeth Kramar collection.

Two #3448 Blue headed Vireo showing the color variation available, 4½", 1940 – 1978. $60.00 – 90.00. Courtesy of the Frank and Elizabeth Kramar collection.

#3447 Yellow Warbler, 4½" American Bone China, 1954 only. $200.00 – 250.00. Courtesy of the Wayne Weigand collection.

Two #3449 Paroquet, 5½", early 1940s color on left, later 1940s color on right. This bird was based on Audubon's Carolina Parakeet eating a cocklebur seed, 1940 – 1947. $150.00 – 175.00. Courtesy of the Wayne Weigand collection.

Not Shown:

#3447 Yellow Warbler, 5", Antique Ivory or Turquoise Crackled 1940 only. $125.00 – 175.00.

#3448 Blue headed Vireo, 4½", Antique Ivory or Turquoise Crackled, 1940 only. $125.00 – 175.00.

#3449 Paroquet, 5½", Antique Ivory or Turquoise Crackled, 1940 only. $200.00 – 250.00.

Russel Wright's American Way Birds

Marked American Way during 1940 – 1941 only. Thereafter simply marked with a Stangl trademark.

#3450 Passenger Pigeon, 9"x18" marked American Way, 1940 – 1941. $2,000.00 – 2,250.00. Courtesy of the Frank and Elizabeth Kramar collection.

#3451 Willow Ptarmigan, 11"x11" marked American, Way 1940 – 1941. $3,500.00 – 4,000.00.

Not Shown:

#3450 Passenger Pigeon, 9"x18" marked Stangl, 1940 – 1947. $1,600.00 – 1,800.00.

#3451 Willow Ptarmigan, 11"x11", light or dark coloring, marked Stangl, 1940 – 1947. $2,800.00 – 3,200.00.

#3452 Painted Bunting, 5" marked American Way, 1940 – 1941. $200.00 – 250.00.

#3452 Painted Bunting, 5" marked Stangl, 1940 – 1965. $90.00 – 110.00. Courtesy of the Hill-Fulper-Stangl Museum.

#3453 Mountain Bluebird, 6¼" marked American Way, 1940 – 1941. $1,600.00 – 1,800.00.

#3454 Key West Quail Dove, 9" marked Stangl, 1940 – 1958. $225.00 – 275.00.

#3454 Key West Quail Dove, 9" two wings up, renumbered #5071, bright coloring, 1960 only. $1,500.00 – 1,800.00. Courtesy of the Wayne Weigand collection.

Not Shown:

#3453 Mountain Bluebird, 6¼" marked Stangl, 1940 – 1943. $1,000.00 – 1,300.00.

#3454 Key West Quail Dove, 9" marked American Way, 1940 – 1941. $600.00 – 800.00.

#3454 Key West Quail Dove, 9" two wings up, renumbered #5071, white, made for DeMoulen Bros. 1960 only. $800.00 – 1200.00.

#3455 Shoveler Duck, 12¼"x14" marked Stangl, 1940 – 1947. $2,000.00 – 2,500.00.

#3455 Shoveler Duck, 12¼"x14" marked American Way, 1940 – 1941. $3,000.00 – 3,500.00. Courtesy of the Frank and Elizabeth Kramar collection.

Stangl 1940 Introductions continued

#3456 Cerulean Warbler, 4¼", 1940 – 1960. $70.00 – 90.00.

#3457 Chinese Pheasant
7¼" X 15"
Price $15.00 Ea.

Original Stangl Pottery catalog page dated July 1942 showing the #3457 Chinese Pheasant. Note the original $15.00 retail price. Current value is $4,500.00 – 5,000.00. From the Stangl and Fulper archival collection, courtesy the Wheaton Village Museum of American Glass.

#3458 Mountain Quail, 7½", 1940 – 1943. $1,800.00 – 2,000.00. Courtesy of the Frank and Elizabeth Kramar collection.

Not Shown:

#3456 Cerulean Warbler, 4¼", Antique Ivory or Turquoise Crackled, 1940 only. $175.00 – 200.00.

#3456 Cerulean Warbler, 4", American Bone China, 1954 only. $200-250.00.

#3457 Chinese Pheasant, 7¼"x15", mistakenly called "Walking Pheasant," 1940 – 1943. $4,500.00 – 5,000.00.

#3459 Fish Hawk, 9½", renamed Tern 1941, mistakenly called "Falcon" or "Osprey," 1940 – 1943. $6,500.00 – 8,000.00. Courtesy of the Wayne Weigand collection.

1941 Introductions

Two #3490 American Redstarts, 9", pale wartime color on left, brighter postwar color on right, 1941 – 1965. This figurine was renamed Double Redstart by end of 1941, $175.00 – 225.00. Courtesy of the Frank and Elizabeth Kramar collection.

#3491 Hen Pheasant, 6¼"x11" wings up, 1941 – 1963. $150.00 – 175.00. Courtesy of the Wayne Weigand collection.

#3492 Cock Pheasant, 6¼"x11" wings down, 1941 – 1963. $175.00 – 225.00. Courtesy of the Wayne Weigand collection.

Antique Gold #3491 Hen Pheasant, 6¼"x11", $200.00 – 225.00 and #3492 Cock Pheasant, 6¼"x11", $225.00 – 250.00. Both produced 1959 – 1963. Courtesy of the Wayne Weigand collection.

#3518 Double White Headed Pigeons, 7½"x12½", 1941 – 1947. $850.00 – 1,200.00. Courtesy of the Jim Horner collection.

Not Shown:

#3519 Single White Headed Pigeon, 7½", 1941 only. $3,000.00 – 4,000.00.

The #3580 Cockatoo was originally produced during the 1940s in vibrant colors with variegated delicate shading. The head feathers of the Cockatoos were pierced to give each feather definition. During the 1950s and 1960s, the Cockatoo was decorated with the same colors but lacked the delicate shading. By the 1970s, the head feathers were no longer pierced, and the colors were heavy and almost opaque. The #3580 Cockatoo with pastel underglaze colors and Satin White glaze was produced only from 1941 to 1943.

#3580 Cockatoo (Medium), 8⅞" with delicate 1940s colors, 1941 – 1950. $175.00 – 200.00. Courtesy of the Wayne Weigand collection.

#3580 Cockatoo (Medium), 8⅞" with deep colors, 1970s. $150.00 – 175.00. Courtesy of the Wayne Weigand Collection.

#3580 Cockatoo (Medium), 8⅞" satin white, pastel colors, 1941 – 1943. $550.00 – 650.00. Courtesy of the Wayne Weigand collection.

#3581 Chickadee Group, 5½"x8½" brown and white, 1941 – 1965. $150.00 – 175.00. Courtesy of the Frank and Elizabeth Kramar collection.

#3581 Chickadee Group, 5½"x8½" black and white, 1970s only. $200.00 – 250.00. Courtesy of the Wayne Weigand collection.

#3582 Double Parakeets, 7" green, 1941 – 1978, $200.00 – 225.00, and #3582 Double Parakeets, 7" blue, 1941 – 1944, $275.00 – 300.00. Courtesy of the Frank and Elizabeth Kramar collection.

Not Shown:

#3580 Cockatoo (Medium), 8⅞" Terra Rose finish, 1941 only. $275.00 – 300.00.

#3582 Double Parakeets, 7" entirely bright green and Victoria Green, 1958 only. $375.00 – 400.00. Courtesy of the Frank and Elizabeth Kramar collection.

Two #3583 Parula Warblers showing early colors on left and 1970s colors on right, 4¼", 1941 – 1978. $60.00 – 80.00. Courtesy of the Frank and Elizabeth Kramar collection.

#3584 Large Cockatoo, 11⅜" bright colors, 1941 – 1963. $200.00 – 250.00. Courtesy of the Wayne Weigand collection.

#3584 Large Cockatoo, 11⅜" bright colors, in-molded with name "Jacob" (inset), 1941 – 1948. $275.00 – 300.00. Courtesy of the Frank and Elizabeth Kramar collection.

#3584 Large Cockatoo, 11⅜" satin white, pastel colors, 1941 – 1943. $800.00 – 1,000.00. Courtesy of the Wayne Weigand collection.

#3584 Large Cockatoo, 11⅜" Antique Gold, 1959 – 1962. $200.00 – 250.00. Courtesy of the Wayne Weigand collection.

#3585 Red Face Humming Bird, 3" renamed Rufous Humming Bird, bright colors, 1941 – 1965. $75.00 – 90.00. Courtesy of the Wayne Weigand collection.

#3585 Humming Bird, Black Gold, 3" brushed gold finishes, 1968 – 1975. $60.00 – 80.00. Courtesy of the Wayne Weigand collection.

Not Shown:
#3583 Parula Warbler 4¼" Pompeii, 1971 only. $125.00 – 150.00.
#3584 Large Cockatoo, 11⅜", all-over gold. $375.00 – 400.00.
#3585 Humming Bird, 3" Pompeii, 1971 only. $125.00 – 150.00.

#3586 Della Ware Pheasant (left), 9"x15½", bright colors, made for Fisher, Bruce & Co,. 1941 – 1947 (base shown in left inset). $1,200.00 – 1,400.00. Italian Majolica pheasant figurine (right) also made for Fisher, Bruce & Co. (base shown in right inset). The colors and pose are similar, but the Italian bird is chunkier and a bit smaller. This pheasant was an exclusive Fisher, Bruce & Co. shape, produced in Italy before and after World War II and produced by Stangl Pottery during the 1940s. Courtesy of the Wayne Weigand collection.

#3586 Della Ware Pheasant, 9"x16½", Terra Rose finish, Blue, 1941 – 1953. $700.00 – 900.00. Courtesy of the Jim Horner collection.

#3586 Della Ware Pheasant, 9"x16½", Terra Rose finish, Green, 1941 – 1953 (base shown in inset). $700.00 – 900.00. Courtesy of the Wayne Weigand collection.

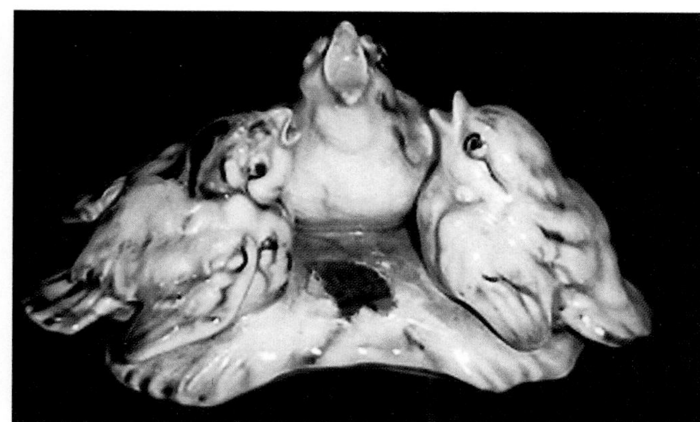

#3588 Birdling Group, 3"x5", 1941 only. $1,000.00 – 1,500.00. The number 3588 was also applied to a book block shape in late 1941. Courtesy of Lee Rosbach.

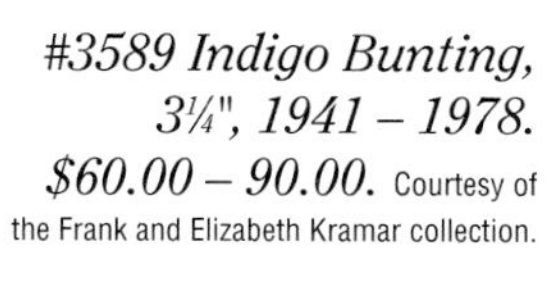

#3589 Indigo Bunting, 3¼", 1941 – 1978. $60.00 – 90.00. Courtesy of the Frank and Elizabeth Kramar collection.

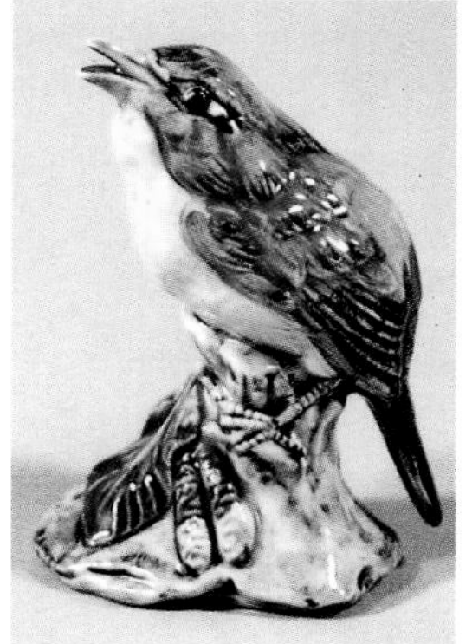

#3590 Chat, 4½", mistakenly called "Carolina Wren," 1941 – 1947. $150.00 – 175.00. Courtesy of the Frank and Elizabeth Kramar collection.

#3591 Brewer's Blackbird, 3½", 1941 – 1947. $175.00 – 200.00. Courtesy of the Wayne Weigand collection.

#3592 Titmouse, 2½", 1941 – 1978. $50.00 – 75.00. Courtesy of the Wayne Weigand collection.

#3593 Nuthatch, 2½", 1941 – 1978. $75.00 – 90.00. Courtesy of the Frank and Elizabeth Kramar collection.

Two #3594 Red Faced Warblers, showing the difference between wartime color with molasses (left) and pre- and post-war color with glycerin, 3", 1941 – 1947. $80.00 – 110.00 each. Courtesy of the Frank and Elizabeth Kramar collection.

#3595 Bobolink, 4¾", 1941 – 1947. $150.00 – 175.00. Courtesy of the Frank and Elizabeth Kramar collection.

#3596 Gray Cardinal, 4¾", 1941 – 1965. Pale wartime color with molasses on left, bright post-war color with glycerin on right. $80.00 – 110.00 each. Courtesy of the Wayne Weigand collection.

#3597 Wilson Warbler, 3½", 1941 – 1978. $50.00 – 65.00. Courtesy of the Wayne Weigand collection.

#3598 Kentucky Warbler, 3", original style on right, 1941 – 1848; re-styled on left, 1948 – 1978. $50.00 – 65.00 each. Courtesy of the Wayne Weigand collection.

#3598 Kentucky Warbler, 3" Antique Gold, $65.00 – 80.00. Courtesy of the Frank and Elizabeth Kramar collection.

Not Shown:

#3592 Titmouse, 2½", Pompeii, 1971 only. $125.00 – 150.00.

#3593 Nuthatch 2½", Pompeii, 1971 only. $125.00 – 150.00.

#3597 Wilson Warbler 3½" brushed gold finishes, 1968 – 1975. $65.00 – 80.00.

#3597 Wilson Warbler 3½" Pompeii, 1971 only. $125.00 – 150.00.

#3598 Kentucky Warbler, 3" brushed gold finishes, 1968 – 1975. $65.00 – 80.00.

#3599 Double Humming Bird, 8"x10½", 1941 – 1955. $300.00 – 375.00. Courtesy of the Wayne Weigand collection.

#3598 Kentucky Warbler, 3" Colonial Silver, $65.00 – 80.00. Courtesy of the Frank and Elizabeth Kramar collection.

Not Shown:

#3598 Kentucky Warbler, 3" Pompeii, 1971 only. $125.00 – 150.00.

1942 Introductions

#3625 Bird of Paradise, 13½", 1942 – 1947. $2,200.00 – 2,800.00.

#3626 Broadtail Humming Bird (blue flower), 6", 1942 – 1955. $150.00 – 175.00. Courtesy of the Wayne Weigand collection.

#3627 Rivoli Humming Bird, (pink flower), 6", 1942 – 1955. $150.00 – 175.00. Courtesy of the Frank and Elizabeth Kramar collection.

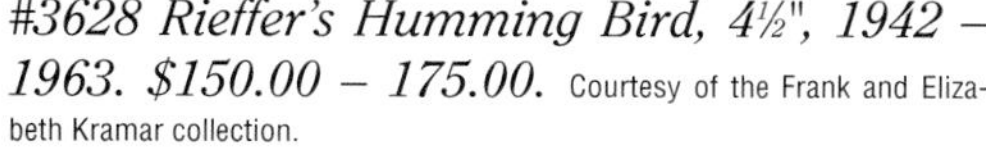

#3628 Rieffer's Humming Bird, 4½", 1942 – 1963. $150.00 – 175.00. Courtesy of the Frank and Elizabeth Kramar collection.

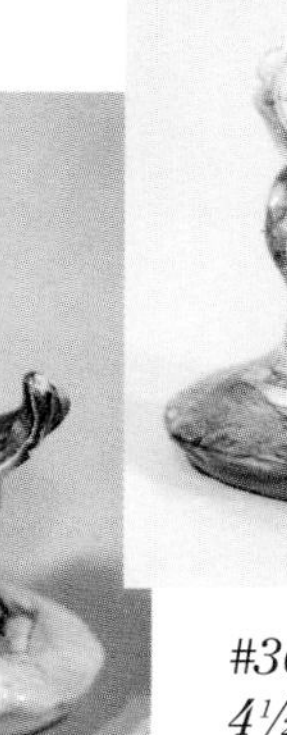

#3629 Broad Bill Humming Bird, 4½", 1942 – 1963. $150.00 – 175.00. Courtesy of the Wayne Weigand collection.

#3634 Allen's Humming Bird, 3½", 1942 – 1963. $85.00 – 120.00. Courtesy of the Wayne Weigand collection.

Not Shown:

#3635 Goldfinch Group, 4"x11½", three birds, tried during 1943 only. $700.00 – 800.00.

#3635 Goldfinch Group, 4"x11½", four birds, 1942 – 1978. $200.00 – 225.00. Courtesy of the Wayne Weigand collection.

1943 Introductions

#3715 Feeding Blue Jay, with peanut, 10¼", natural colors, 1943 – 1965. $700.00 – 800.00. Courtesy of the Wayne Weigand collection.

#3715 Feeding Blue Jay, with peanut, 10¼", Antique Gold, 1959 – 1963. $500.00 – 600.00. Courtesy of the Wayne Weigand collection.

#3716 Flying Blue Jay, with leaf, 10¼" natural colors, 1943 – 1965. $600.00 – 700.00. Courtesy of the Frank and Elizabeth Kramar collection.

Antique Gold #3716 Flying Blue Jay (foreground) and blue-brown Stoneware art glaze (mistakenly called "Fulper Glaze") #3716 Flying Blue Jay. Courtesy of the Louis and Sarah DiPlacido collection.

#3717 Double Blue Jay, 12½", 1943 – 1950. $3,500.00 – 4,000.00. Courtesy of the Wayne Weigand collection.

Briefly during 1965, the #3716, #3716, and #3717 Blue Jay shapes were produced of red clay and glazed with Stoneware art glazes Stangl was using on several lamps and the hand-thrown pots produced by Anné Fritsche in the log cabin. This glaze is often mistakenly called "Fulper Glaze," but was newly created in 1965 for the Log Cabin pottery items. The Stoneware art glazes were not produced after the fire at the Trenton factory in August 1965, so Blue Jays with these glazes are fairly scarce.

Not Shown:

#3715 Feeding Blue Jay, with peanut, 10¼" red clay body with blue-brown Stoneware art glaze (mistakenly called "Fulper Glaze"), 1965 only. $1,500.00 – 1,800.00.

#3715 Feeding Blue Jay, with peanut, 10¼" red clay body with yellow-brown Stoneware art glaze (mistakenly called "Yellow Fulper Glaze"), 1965 only. $1,800.00 – 2,000.00.

#3716 Flying Blue Jay, with leaf, 10¼", Antique Gold, 1959 – 1963. $500.00 – 600.00.

#3716 Flying Blue Jay, with leaf, 10¼" red clay body with blue-brown Stoneware art glaze (mistakenly called "Fulper Glaze"), 1965 only. $1,500.00 – 1,800.00.

#3716 Flying Blue Jay, with leaf, 10¼" red clay body with yellow-brown Stoneware art glaze (mistakenly called "Yellow Fulper Glaze"), 1965 only. $1,800.00 – 2,000.00.

#3717 Double Blue Jay, 12½" red clay body with blue-brown Stoneware art glaze (mistakenly called "Fulper Glaze"), 1965 only. $5,500.00 – 6000.00.

#3717 Double Blue Jay, 12½" red clay body with yellow-brown Stoneware art glaze (mistakenly called "Yellow Fulper Glaze"), 1965 only. $5,800.00 – 6,300.00.

#3746 Canary, right facing, rose flower, 6¼", 1944 – 1965. $200.00 – 250.00. Courtesy of the Frank and Elizabeth Kramar collection.

#3747 Canary, left facing, blue flower, 6¼", 1944 – 1965. $200.00 – 250.00. Courtesy of the Frank and Elizabeth Kramar collection.

#3749 Scarlet Tanager, 4¾", pink underglaze color, blue flower, 1944 – 1953. $375.00 – 400.00.

#3749 Western Tanager, 4¾", yellow and black with red overglaze color, tan flower, 1953 – 1978. $375.00 – 425.00.

#3750 Double Western Tanager, 8" yellow and black with red overglaze color, tan flower, 1953 – 1978. $550.00 – 625.00. Courtesy of the Frank and Elizabeth Kramar collection.

#3750 Double Scarlet Tanager, 8" pink underglaze color, blue or tan flower, 1944 – 1953. $475.00 – 550.00. Courtesy of the Wayne Weigand collection.

#3751 Red Headed Woodpecker, 6¼", red overglaze color, 1953 – 1978. $450.00 – 525.00. Courtesy of the Frank and Elizabeth Kramar collection.

#3752 Double Red Headed Woodpecker, 7¾", red overglaze color, introduced 1953. $550.00 – 625.00. Courtesy of the Frank and Elizabeth Kramar collection.

Not Shown:

#3748 White wing Crossbill group, 6", with 3 birds, 1944 only. $6,500.00 – 7,000.00.

#3751 Red Headed Woodpecker, 6¼", pink underglaze color, 1944 – 1953. $325.00 – 375.00.

#3752 Double Red Headed Woodpecker, 7¾", pink underglaze color, 1944 – 1953. $450.00 – 525.00.

#3753 White Wing Crossbill, 3½", 1944 – 1946. $2,500.00 – 3,000.00. Courtesy of the Wayne Weigand collection.

#3754 Double White wing Crossbill, 8¾", pink underglaze color, 1944 – 1953. $500.00 – 575.00. Courtesy of the Frank and Elizabeth Kramar collection.

#3755 Audubon Warbler, 4¼", black head and tail, pink flower, 1944 – 1965. $375.00 – 425.00. Courtesy of the Wayne Weigand collection.

#3755 Audubon Warbler, 4¼", blue head and tail, orange flower, 1954 – 1955. $425.00 – 525.00.

#3756 Double Audubon Warbler, 7¾", 1944 – 1965. $575.00 – 625.00. Courtesy of the Wayne Weigand collection.

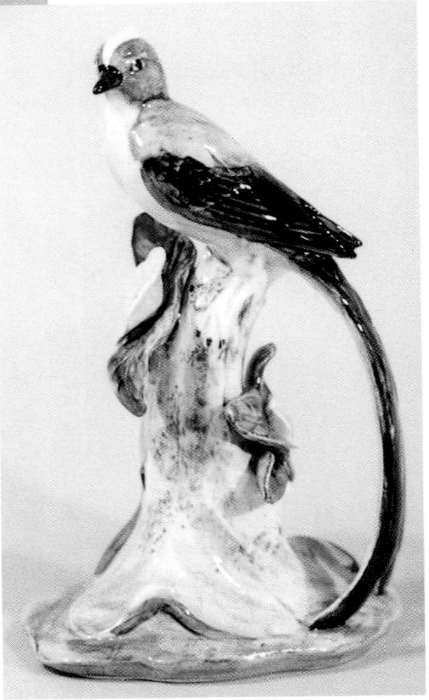

#3757 Scissor-Tailed Fly-catcher, 11", 1944 – 1955. $900.00 – 1,100.00. Courtesy of the Hill-Fulper-Stangl Museum.

#3757 Scissor-Tailed Flycatcher, 11", 1970 – 1978 (base, dated 1972, shown in inset). $900.00 – 1,100.00. Courtesy of the Wayne Weigand collection.

#3758 Magpie-Jay, 10¾", 1944 – 1955. $1,200.00 – 1,400.00.

Not Shown:

#3754 Double White wing Crossbill, 8¾", "Matte" red overglaze color, 1953 – 1978. $650.00 – 750.00.

1949 Introductions

While Audubon's bird prints were the inspiration for many of Stangl's bird figurines sculpted before and during World War II, Stangl's sculptors John Tierney and Herman Eichorn used standard modern bird guides and drawings published by the National Audubon Society for the bird poses produced after the war. Several of the Stangl bird species developed at that time were never even painted by John James Audubon. Some of these later bird introductions are among the most rare and valuable of Stangl's bird figurines.

#3810 Black Throated Warbler, 3½", mistakenly called "Blackpoll Warbler," 1949 – 1965. $150.00 – 200.00. Courtesy of the Frank and Elizabeth Kramar collection.

#3811 Chestnut Chickadee, 5", mistakenly called "Chestnut-Backed Chickadee," 1949 – 1965. $125.00 – 150.00. Courtesy of the Hill-Fulper-Stangl Museum.

#3812 Chestnut Warbler, 4", mistakenly called "Chestnut-Sided Warbler," 1949 – 1965. $125.00 – 150.00.

#3813 Crested Goldfinch, 5", mistakenly called "Evening Grosbeak," 1949 – 1965. $125.00 – 250.00. Courtesy of the Frank and Elizabeth Kramar collection.

#3814 Townsend Warbler, 3?", mistakenly called "Black-Throated Green Warbler," 1949 – 1965. $160.00 – 180.00. Courtesy of the Frank and Elizabeth Kramar collection.

#3815 Western Bluebird, 7", 1949 – 1965. $450.00 – 525.00. Courtesy of the Frank and Elizabeth Kramar collection.

1950 Introductions

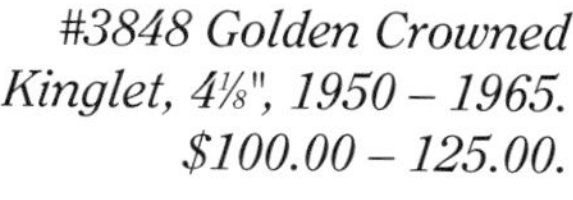

#3848 Golden Crowned Kinglet, 4⅛", 1950 – 1965. $100.00 – 125.00.

#3849 Prothonotary Warbler, 4", mistakenly called "Goldfinch," 1950 – 1965. $125.00 – 150.00. Courtesy of the Wayne Weigand collection.

#3850 Western Warbler, 4", mistakenly called "Yellow Warbler," 1950 – 1965. $150.00 – 175.00. Courtesy of the Frank and Elizabeth Kramar collection.

#3851 Red Breasted Nuthatch, 3¾", 1950 – 1965. $90.00 – 110.00. Courtesy of the Frank and Elizabeth Kramar collection.

#3852 Cliff Swallow, 3¾", 1950 – 1965. $125.00 – 165.00. Courtesy of the Wayne Weigand collection.

#3853 Kinglet Family 5½"x5", 1950 – 1955. $750.00 – 850.00. Courtesy of the Frank and Elizabeth Kramar collection.

1952 Introduction

#3868 Summer Tanager, 4", 1952 – 1965. $750.00 – 850.00.

1955 Introductions

#3921 Adult Verdin, 4½", 1955 – 1965. $1,200.00 – 1,500.00. Courtesy of the Frank and Elizabeth Kramar collection.

#3922 European Goldfinch, 4½", 1955 – 1965. $1,200.00 – 1,500.00. Courtesy of the Wayne Weigand collection.

#3923 Vermillion Flycatcher, 5¾", 1955 – 1965. $1,600.00 – 1,800.00. Courtesy of the Frank and Elizabeth Kramar collection.

#3925 Magnolia Warbler, 5¼", 1955 – 1965. $2,800.00 – 3,200.00. Courtesy of the Wayne Weigand collection.

#3924 Yellowthroat, 5½", mistakenly called "Yellow-Throated Warbler," 1955 – 1965. $700.00 – 800.00. Courtesy of the Frank and Elizabeth Kramar collection.

1961 Introduction

1960 Introductions

#5071 Key West Quail Dove, 9" two wings up, originally #3454, bright coloring, 1960 only. $1,500.00 – 1,800.00. Courtesy of the Wayne Weigand collection.

Not Shown:

#5071 Key West Quail Dove, 9" two wings up, originally #3454, gloss white, made for DeMoulen Bros., 1960 only. $800.00 – 1,200.00.

#5087 Duck, 3"x5" originally designed as a children's lamp, this duck was also produced as a figurine during the early 1960s. $450.00 – 500.00. Courtesy of the Hill-Fulper-Stangl Museum.

1967 Introductions, Made for the Flemington Outlet

#3250A Standing Duck Deviled Egg Dish, 1967 – 1970. $200.00 – 250.00. Courtesy of the Hill-Fulper-Stangl Museum.

Pair of #3250 Duck salt and pepper shakers, 1967 – 1970, $240.00 – 270.00 pair. Courtesy of the Hill-Fulper-Stangl Museum.

Not Shown:

#3250A Standing Duck, 3½" salt or pepper shaker, 1967 – 1970. $120.00 – 135.00.
#3250C Feeding Duck, 1¾" salt shaker, 1967 – 1970. $120.00 – 135.00.
#3250D Gazing Duck, 3¾" pepper shaker, 1967 – 1970. $120.00 – 135.00.
#3285 Rooster pepper shaker, 4¼" white with green base, closed bottom, 1967 – 1970s. $75.00 – 90.00.
#3286 Hen salt shaker, 3" white with green base, closed bottom, 1967 – 1970s. $75.00 – 90.00.
#3285 or 3286 Deviled Egg Dish, 9" with attached Rooster or Hen. $100.00 – 150.00.

#3286 Hen salt shaker and #3285 Rooster pepper shaker, $130.00 – 150.00 pair.

Hen Deviled Egg Dish, 9", $100.00 – 150.00.

Sometimes overstocked chicken or duck shakers were epoxied to the dishes, resulting in deviled egg dishes with shaker holes in the handles.

Not Shown:
#3285 or 3286 Server, Rooster or Hen attached to 10" or 12" Blue Dahlia or Pink Cosmos plates. $150.00 – 175.00.

Mutual Sunset Bird Figurines

Stangl produced the commanding #481 Mutual Sunset Rooster in various decorative treatments from 1967 through the 1970s. The Mutual Sunset Lamp Company, also of Trenton, mounted the rooster figurines on maple or walnut lamp bases for their wholesale trade. The rooster figures were made of red clay, white clay, and very heavy white vitreous china. Red clay roosters were decorated with silk glaze, black glaze or the brushed gold finishes. White clay roosters can be found in plain gloss white, brushed gold finishes or brightly painted with underglaze colors. The roosters made of the heavy vitreous china were either left bright white or hand-painted with fired-on overglaze colors.

The roosters were mounted on the bases facing both left and right. Left-facing roosters usually have a ½" notch ground at the base to accommodate the brass tube supporting the sockets. This notch was ground at Mutual Sunset and should be expected on left-mounted figures. Roosters mounted on their original Mutual Sunset lamp base usually sell for $100.00 – 150.00 more than unmounted figures.

#481 Mutual Sunset Rooster, 16", red clay with silk glaze. $1,000.00 – 1,200.00.
Courtesy of the Hill-Fulper-Stangl Museum.

#481 Mutual Sunset Rooster, 16", plain white or plain black. $1,000.00 – 1,200.00.
Courtesy of the Ed Simpson collection.

Not Shown:
#481 Mutual Sunset Rooster, 16", Antique, Granada or Black Gold. $1,000.00 – 1,200.00.

#481 Mutual Sunset Rooster, 16", white clay with bright underglaze colors. $2,000.00 – 2,200.00.

Lamp #481 Mutual Sunset Rooster, 16", with original mountings and shade, made for Mutual Sunset Lamp Co. 1960s – 1970s. $1,500.00 – 1,800.00.

#481 Mutual Sunset Rooster, 16", vitreous china with overglaze colors. $1,500.00 – 1,800.00.

Stangl also produced for Mutual Sunset a figure of two Red Tail Hawks on a tree stump. Like the #481 roosters, this figurine was made of antiqued red clay, red bisque, brushed gold finishes, and white clay with minimal decoration or white clay with fully detailed decoration. These figures were produced during the late 1960s and early 1970s.

Not Shown:

Mutual Sunset Red Tail Hawks, 9"x10", red clay Antiqued or bisque. $800.00 – 1,000.00.

Mutual Sunset Red Tail Hawks, 9"x10", brushed gold or minimal decoration. $800.00 – 1,000.00.

Mutual Sunset Red Tail Hawks, 9"x10", fully detailed decoration. $2,200.00 – 2,800.00. Courtesy of the Hill-Fulper-Stangl Museum.

#5253 Ashtray with Bird, 6", white with yellow and brown bird (above), $200.00 – 250.00. Green with blue and yellow bird (right), $250.00 – 300.00.

1971 Introduction

This little item was developed because Zephanelli Gift Importers, Inc. approached Stangl Pottery to produce a small "bird on a gourd" ashtray similar to Pennsbury's "Slick Chick" ashtray. No one was producing this item since Pennsbury had closed in 1970. The old #3896 Casual Ashtray shape was used as the "gourd," and the perching bird was taken from the #3635 Goldfinch group. The ashtrays were either plain white or hand-painted Pomona Green. The birds were usually decorated yellow and brown, but other colors were used, such as the blue and yellow shown. The #5253 Ashtray with Bird was produced during 1971 and 1972 only.

1972 Introductions: Terra Cotta Antiqued Birds

The Terra Cotta Antiqued bird figurines were produced only during 1972. These birds were cast of red clay and rather than glazed were brushed with an antiquing finish that accentuated the crisp detail of the figurines. To ensure good detail, the Terra Cotta Antiqued birds were only cast in new molds. As ceramic molds are used, they become worn and lose a great amount of detail. Most Stangl molds had a life span of about 100 castings before they were considered too worn to be used and were replaced. Stangl's plaster shop was kept busy continually creating new production molds. The Terra Cotta Antiqued birds were intended to complement the terra cotta hues of the patio ware popular at that time. However, by the end of 1972, the Terra Cotta Antiqued birds were discontinued.

Not Shown:
#3401 Single Wren. $250.00 – 300.00.
#3401D Double Wrens. $250.00 – 300.00.
#3402 Oriole. $250.00 – 300.00.
#3405 Cockatoo. $250.00 – 300.00.
#3447 Yellow Warbler. $250.00 – 300.00.
#3589 Indigo Bunting. $250.00 – 300.00.
#3592 Titmouse. $250.00 – 300.00.
#3593 Kentucky Warbler. $250.00 – 300.00.

Terra Cotta Antiqued #3583 Parula Warbler. $250.00 – 300.00. Courtesy of the Hill-Fulper-Stangl Museum.

1974 Introductions: Terra Cotta Decorator Birds

Stangl's Terra Cotta Decorator Birds were produced only during 1974. The figures were cast of red clay and epoxied on bases glazed with Onyx Black. The bird figures were unglazed bisque and did not have the antiqued finish of the Terra Cotta Antiqued birds. Nine Terra Cotta Decorator Birds were produced, and ranged in size from 5½" to 8½". The Terra Cotta Decorator Birds were discontinued by the end of 1974.

Not Shown:
B (#3401D) Double Wrens. $250.00 – 300.00.
C (#3447) Yellow Warbler. $250.00 – 300.00.
E (#3402) Oriole. $250.00 – 300.00.
G (#3593) Kentucky Warbler. $250.00 – 300.00.
I (#3592) Titmouse. $250.00 – 300.00.

Terra Cotta Decorator Bird figurines A (#3405) Cockatoo, $250.00 – 300.00; and D (#3401) Single Wren, $250.00 – 300.00. Courtesy of the Wayne Weigand collection.

Terra Cotta Decorator Bird figurine H (#3589) Indigo Bunting. $250.00 – 300.00. Courtesy of the Ed Simpson collection.

Terra Cotta Decorator Bird figurine F (#3583) Parula Warbler, $250.00 – 300.00. Courtesy of the Hill-Fulper-Stangl Museum.

1976 Re-Introductions

In 1976, Stangl "re-introduced" nine bird figurines for national distribution, even though bird figurines were never discontinued from the Flemington Outlet. The catalog numbering system was changed at that time. The catalog numbers ranged from 90 – 101 through 90 – 108. Stangl's ad copy stated, "Stangl reintroduces their famous BIRDS OF AMERICA. Many of these original pieces are now collectors items. Each piece dated with year of production. You will want to make these an important part of your gift selections." These nine are simply the birds offered nationally. Many other bird shapes were still being produced for the Flemington Outlet right up to Stangl's close in 1978. The year of production date was nothing new; Stangl had been dating bird figurines since 1970. The new numbers were used only for ordering and bookkeeping purposes. The figurines were not marked with the new catalog numbers, the shape numbers of these birds remained the same. The values for these later-production birds do not differ from the same birds of earlier vintage.

90-101 Cockatoo (#3405). $60.00 – 90.00.
90-102 Kentucky Warbler (#3598). $50.00 – 65.00.
90-103 Nuthatch (#3593). $75.00 – 90.00.
90-104 Oriole (#3402). $45.00 – 65.00.
90-105 Parula Warbler (#3583). $60.00 – 80.00.
90-106 Titmouse (#3592). $50.00 – 75.00.
90-107 Wilson Warbler (#3597). $50.00 – 65.00.
90-108 Wren (#3401). $50.00 – 65.00.

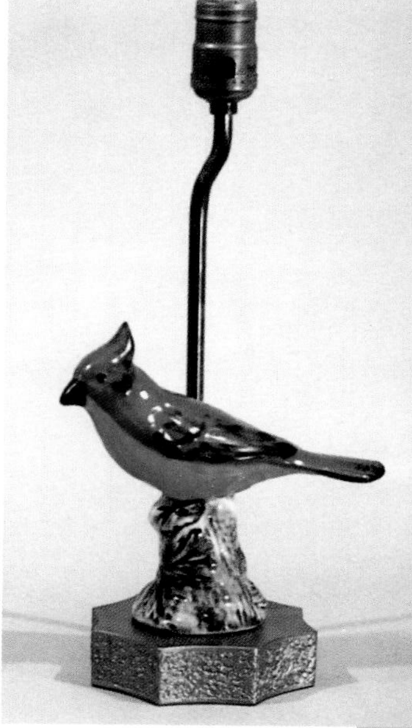

Cardinal lamp dating from the 1950s, $100.00 – 130.00. Courtesy of the Hill-Fulper-Stangl Museum.

Stangl Bird Lamps

Throughout the 1940s and 1950s, several lamp companies purchased Stangl bird figurines and mounted them on brass lamp bases. These were sold at better gift, department, and lamp stores. Nearly any Stangl bird can be found on a lamp base as the lamp companies used stock birds. These lamps are usually valued the same as the attached figurine.

The Mutual Sunset Rooster and Red Tail Hawks figurines were specifically produced for the Mutual Sunset Lamp Company. Mutual Sunset Rooster and Red Tail Hawks lamps are valued $100.00 – 150.00 more than the figures alone.

Stangl Bird Designer Samples, Test, and Seconds

Before going into production, the colors for each Stangl bird figurine were "set" (developed) by a Stangl designer and then approved by Martin Stangl. References such as drawings by Audubon, Wilson, and publications of the National Audubon Society were used to develop the colorings. Ethel Kennedy set the colors on all Stangl bird and animal figurines until 1948. Kay Hackett set the colors on the birds introduced from 1949 through the 1950s. The original bird figurine color samples were usually marked "SAMPLE" and sometimes were signed by the designer. These signed figurines are exceedingly rare, as only a handful of samples were ever produced for each bird shape. Values for designer sample birds can vary greatly and can range from double to nearly ten times the value of the same standard production bird figure.

Ethel Kennedy's sample for the #3405 "Parrot" (base, inset). Courtesy of the Hill-Fulper-Stangl Museum.

Kay Hackett's sample for #3848 Golden Crowned Kinglet (base, inset).

Kay Hackett's sample for the #3853 Kinglet Family (base, inset). Courtesy of the Jim Horner collection.

Occasionally, Stangl bird figures were used to test glazes or underglaze colors, such as the #3811 Chestnut Chickadee shown decorated only with Eye Black. Samples such as this usually sell for a little more than the bird would normally sell in usual colors.

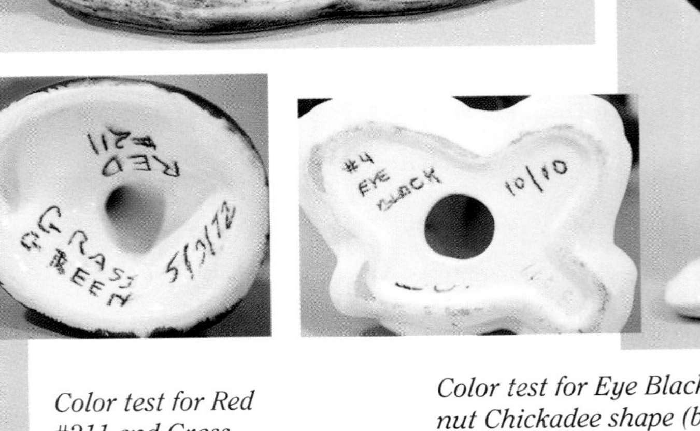

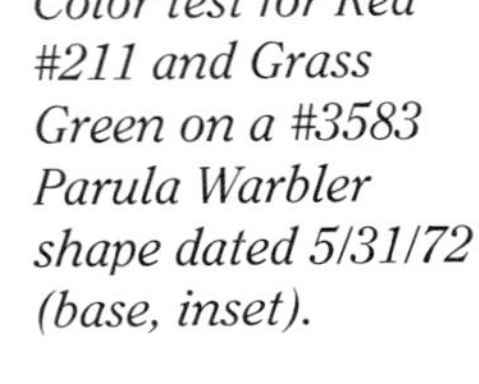

Color test for Red #211 and Grass Green on a #3583 Parula Warbler shape dated 5/31/72 (base, inset).

Color test for Eye Black from the 1950s on a #3811 Chestnut Chickadee shape (base, inset).

Vitreous china #3404 Double Love Birds (base, inset). Tests such as this usually sell for a bit more than the same bird would in typical earthenware body. Courtesy of the Wayne Weigand collection.

Other tests include the #3404 Double Love Birds cast of the same vitreous china clay usually used for the Mutual Sunset Roosters. This figurine was cast during the 1970s, and measures only 4½" tall, nearly ¾" shorter than the standard figure cast of earthenware clay. It too is worth a little more than a standard #3404 Double Love Birds figure.

Brushed blue seconds treatment on a #3590 Cockatoo. Courtesy of the Wayne Weigand collection.

Stangl did not usually apply seconds treatments to the bird figurines but simply painted seconds that were not too damaged in their usual colors and sold them at the Flemington Outlet. Occasionally, a simple color treatment would be applied to damaged pieces just to expedite the process, such as the blue hastily brushed on the #3590 Cockatoo.

Bird figures produced during the 1960s with the brushed gold finishes, and Terra Cotta Decorator Bird figurines were cast of red clay. Birds of poor quality that were not finished in brushed gold or epoxied to a Black Onyx base were sometimes sold as unglazed bisque seconds at the Flemington Outlet. These birds usually exhibit some sort of damage, most commonly a beak or tail nick. The red bisque birds should not be confused with the Terra Cotta Antiqued birds. The red bisque birds were usually cast from worn molds, so exhibit very little detail. The Terra Cotta Antiqued birds always

#3634 Allen's Humming Bird in red bisque. Courtesy of the Wayne Weigand collection.

show good detail, which is further enhanced by the burnished antiqued finish. Undamaged red bisque birds are valued about the same as those decorated with a brushed gold finish.

Stangl Bird Advertising

The Stangl Bird advertising item most coveted by collectors is the Stangl Birds dealer sign. With its sprightly pink Cockatoo, it is certainly a welcome addition to any bird collection. This sign was created in 1944 by Stangl's designer Cleo Salerno, and the original model was sculpted by Herman Eichorn. During the 1940s, the signs were provided free to any department or gift store ordering a bird assortment totaling $100 or more. The Stangl Bird signs were produced into the early 1950s but were no longer available after 1956. As with any retail selling aid, when the stores no longer carried Stangl birds, the leftover signs were simply thrown away.

Original Stangl Bird dealer sign, 1940s – 1950s. $3,000.00 – 3,500.00. Courtesy of the Weigand collection.

In 1993, the Stangl Bird Collectors Association commissioned 200 limited edition bird dealer signs to be produced by Bob Shaw of Wheaton Industries. The 1993 "Bird Plaques," as they were called, were cast from an original Stangl Bird sign mold. The Stangl Bird Collectors Association sold the signs for $50.00 each. They were all white with a gloss glaze and hand-painted on the back of each one were the words "Stangl Bird Collectors' Association, Limited Edition." Each "plaque" was numbered from "1" to "200." The backs of the limited edition signs had a "literature pocket," which Stangl's original Bird signs did not have. In 1999, the Stangl/Fulper Collectors Club had a number of the white limited edition signs decorated with overglaze colors to replicate the colors of the original Stangl Bird dealer signs.

Stangl Bird Collectors Association limited edition decorated "Bird Plaque" (back, inset). $100.00 – 125.00. Courtesy of the Jim Horner collection.

Not Shown:
"Bird Plaque," plain white. $50.00 – 75.00.

Paper Advertising

Throughout the 1940s and 1950s, Stangl advertised the pottery birds in many magazine ads that can still be found today. The average ad measures 2½" by 5" or 6" with a current value of $5.00 – 15.00.

Stangl Bird magazine ad, December 1941 Good Housekeeping. Courtesy of Gary Hanson.

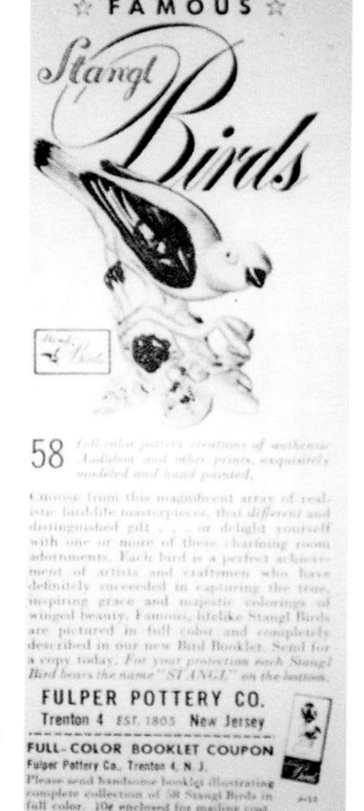

Stangl Bird magazine ad, December 1944. Courtesy of Gary Hanson.

Stangl Bird catalog, $150.00 – 200.00. Gift of Gary Hanson to the Hill-Fulper-Stangl Museum.

Stangl also offered catalogs, brochures, and flyers promoting the figurines. The catalogs were issued in 1944 and 1947. They feature 17 pages of the available figurines. The catalogs measure 3¾" x 9".

Several foldout brochures were also printed. The first brochure was entitled *Gay Birds* and was available during 1941 and 1942 and featured 27 birds. The next brochure advertised 55 birds in 1950 and measures 15½" x 16" unfolded. Both brochures were printed in color. Black and white folders were printed in the 1960s, and an 8½" x 11" glossy color sheet featuring Stangl's birds and Kiddieware was printed in 1976.

Not Shown:

Gay Birds brochure, 1941, color. $150.00 – 200.00.

Color fold-out brochure, 1950, color. $80.00 – 90.00.

Black and white price sheets, 1960s. $20.00 – 25.00.

Color sheet with Stangl Birds and Kiddieware, 1976. $35.00 – 45.00.

Stangl's 1940s booklet Attractive Settings for Your Table.

Stangl Pottery also advertised bird figurines in a full-color booklet called *Attractive Settings for your Table,* published by Stangl Pottery during the late 1940s. The featured table settings included Stangl bird figurines incorporated into the centerpieces.

Stangl's Yellow Tulip dinnerware pattern set with a centerpiece of Hen and Rooster figurines.

Royal Cumberland Birds and Animals

From 1979 through 1982, Frank Wheaton produced a series of bird and animal figurines for the American division of Royal Copenhagen. Wheaton's products were marketed under his Royal Cumberland trademark. The shapes were based on Stangl figurines but were produced without any of the applied leaf or flower details found on the Stangl originals. The Royal Cumberland birds were most commonly plain white or plain white with black eyes and sometimes with yellow beaks. Less often they can be found decorated in multicolors. Vibrant solid colors were also used, such as bright blue, cobalt blue, green, rose or yellow. Occasionally a Royal Cumberland bird will turn up decorated with all-over gold luster. The Royal Cumberland figurines are almost always clearly marked with a stamped "RC" or "Royal Cumberland." These figures are usually not collected on their own merit, but are merely casually collected because of their Stangl heritage.

Two groups of white Royal Cumberland birds with minimal decoration (two different marks in insets). Values shown on the following page. Courtesy of the Wayne Weigand collection.

#3250A Standing Duck, all white or minimal detail. $25.00 – 40.00. Courtesy of the Wayne Weigand collection.

#3401D Double Wrens, all white or minimal detail. $40.00 – 60.00. Courtesy of the Wayne Weigand collection.

Group of Royal Cumberland Cockatoos in vibrant glaze colors (base, inset). $400.00 – 450.00 each. Courtesy of the Wayne Weigand collection.

#3580 Cockatoo, all-over gold. $400.00 – 450.00. Courtesy of the Wayne Weigand collection.

Not Shown:

#3250A Standing Duck, bright color or gold. $65.00 – 80.00.
#3250B Preening Duck, all white or minimal detail. $25.00 – 40.00.
#3250B Preening Duck, bright color or gold. $65.00 – 80.00.
#3250C Feeding Duck, all white or minimal detail. $25.00 – 40.00.
#3250C Feeding Duck, bright color or gold. $65.00 – 80.00.
#3250D Gazing Duck, all white or minimal detail. $25.00 – 40.00.
#3250D Gazing Duck, bright color or gold. $65.00 – 80.00.
#3250E Quacking Duck, all white or minimal detail. $25.00 – 40.00.
#3250E Quacking Duck, bright color or gold. $65.00 – 80.00.
#3250F Drinking Duck, all white or minimal detail. $25.00 – 40.00.
#3250F Drinking Duck, bright color or gold. $65.00 – 80.00.
#3401S Single Wren, all white or minimal detail. $25.00 – 40.00.
#3401S Single Wren, bright color or gold. $65.00 – 80.00.
#3401D Double Wrens, bright color or gold. $100.00 – 125.00.
#3580 Cockatoo (medium), all white or minimal detail. $150.00 – 175.00.
#3580 Cockatoo (medium), bright color or gold. $400.00 – 450.00.
#3581 Chickadee group, all white or minimal detail. $100.00 – 125.00.
#3581 Chickadee group, bright color or gold. $125.00 – 150.00.
#3685 Goldfinch group, all white or minimal detail. $65.00 – 80.00.
#3685 Goldfinch group, bright color or gold. $125.00 – 150.00.
#3249 Elephant, 3", all white or minimal detail. $100.00 – 125.00.
#3249 Elephant, 3", bright color or gold. $130.00 – 165.00.
#5281 Elephant, 5", bright color or gold. $130.00 – 165.00.

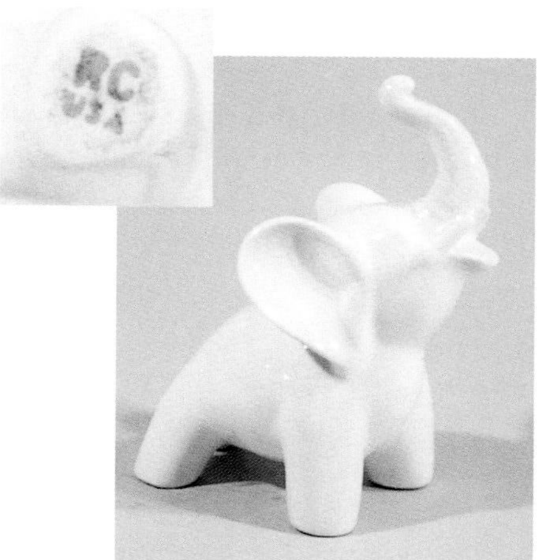

#5281 Elephant, 5", all white or minimal detail (mark, inset). $100.00 – 125.00. Courtesy of the Wayne Weigand collection.

Stangl Collector Series Bird Reproductions by Bill Estelle

Bill Estelle Stangl Collector Series #3590 Chat, 4½". Courtesy of the Wayne Weigand collection.

In 1985, Frank Wheaton offered the use of several Stangl bird molds to local ceramist Bill Estelle. Estelle produced ceramic greenware and bisque for the hobby ceramics industry. With Frank Wheaton's encouragement, Bill Estelle accumulated 100 bird molds from Wheaton's warehouses and began casting "Stangl" birds. These birds were sold undecorated as greenware or bisque to hobby ceramists. Bill Estelle and his wife Barbara decorated one each of 24 birds in underglaze colors to use as models when showing the undecorated birds. Each decorated bird was marked "Hand Painted by Bill Estelle, Stangl Collector Series." By 1988, demand for hobby ceramics bisque and greenware dwindled, and Bill Estelle pursued another career. He liquidated his molds and equipment and returned the Stangl bird molds to Frank Wheaton. The 24 birds decorated by Bill Estelle were also sold. They have since appeared at such South Jersey flea markets as Rancocas Woods, Cow Town, and Lambertville. An exact list of Bill Estelle decorated birds was not kept, but the following birds have been identified.

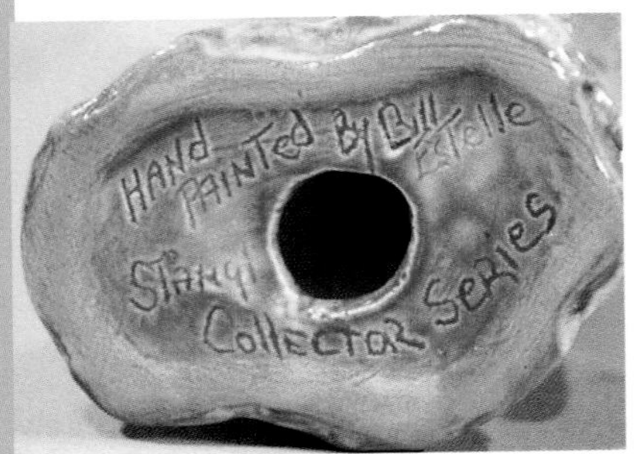

Mark used on the birds decorated by Bill Estelle.

- #3273 Rooster, 5½"
- #3276 Bluebird, 5"
- #3287 Rooster figurine, 4¼"
- #3288 Hen figurine, 3"
- #3400 Love Bird, 4" re-styled
- #3402 Oriole, 3¼" re-styled
- #3406 Kingfisher, 3½"
- #3431 Standing Duck, 8"
- #3432 Running Duck, 5"
- #3444 Cardinal, 6" re-styled
- #3492 Cock Pheasant, 6¼"x11"
- #3580 Cockatoo (Medium), 8⅞"
- #3590 Chat, 4½"
- #3596 Gray Cardinal, 4¾"
- #3598 Kentucky Warbler, 3"
- #3751 Red Headed Woodpecker, 6¼"
- #3848 Golden Crowned Kinglet, 4⅛"

Some of the undecorated birds produced by Bill Estelle were indeed purchased by hobby ceramists and decorated. These birds were not marked with the Stangl name nor stamped or carved with the Stangl shape number. They are usually decorated with glazes and colors so unlike anything Stangl used that there is very little danger of confusing them with authentic Stangl birds. Bill Estelle Stangl Collector Series birds have sold for about half that of original Stangl birds. Many collectors find them interesting but not valuable.

Wayne Weigand's Kramlik Porcelain Stangl Bird Reproductions

In 1994, Stangl Bird collector Wayne Weigand contracted Balint Kramlik to produce a limited edition series of Stangl bird shapes in porcelain. Kramlik, a recognized artist on two continents, was head of the decorating department at Herend, Hungary's most noted porcelain works, before immigrating to the United States in 1968. While still at Herend, Kramlik personally decorated a 48-piece coffee set for Pope John XXIII, for which he won several awards. Kramlik's work is also recognized and included in collections at the White House and the New Jersey State Museum.

Herend-inspired sample decoration on a #3273 Rooster. $700.00 – 900.00. Courtesy of the Wayne Weigand collection.

The porcelain birds produced by Balint Kramlik were limited to 30 of each shape. They were cast in Stangl molds and decorated in natural colors in great detail. The #3849 Prothonotary Warbler shape was decorated to represent the New Jersey state bird, the Goldfinch. The colors are vibrant, and nearly every feather appears to be painted on. Each Kramlik porcelain bird is marked "Made From a Stangl Mold" and signed "Balint Kramlik." Because they are porcelain, the birds are smaller than the Stangl earthenware originals. Kramlik also decorated a few samples of these birds in the traditional Hungarian style for which Herend is known. Samples decorated in the Herend style are valued several hundred dollars more than the naturally decorated production pieces.

Traditional Hungarian Herend sample decoration on two #3849 "Goldfinch" (Prothonotary Warbler) figurines. $600.00 – 800.00 each. Courtesy of the Wayne Weigand collection.

Since Balint Kramlik's retirement in 2001, collector interest in Kramlik porcelains has mushroomed and values for his sculptures, tiles, and Stangl-inspired figurines have increased accordingly. A complete set of Stangl Kramlik porcelain birds is on display at the Hill-Fulper-Stangl Museum in Flemington, New Jersey.

#3273 Rooster (base, inset). $475.00 – 525.00.

#3401 Wren. $375.00 – 425.00.

#3849 "Goldfinch" (Prothonotary Warbler). $275.00 – 325.00.

#3925 Magnolia Warbler (base, inset). $675.00 – 725.00.

Stangl Bird Dealer Sign (signature on back, inset). $725.00 – 800.00.

Stangl and Pennsbury Bird Fakes

During the 1990s, one or more talented hobby ceramists were producing ceramic bird figurines that intentionally replicated the Pennsbury and Stangl styles of decorating. These figurines were skillfully hand-painted with underglaze colors and bore "Pennsbury Pottery" or "Stangl" hand-painted on the bases. These items would easily be passed off as authentic Stangl or Pennsbury figurines if not for the fact that they are Holland Mold shapes, not Stangl or Pennsbury. Because of the excellent decorating of these figures and the deftly forged Stangl or Pennsbury trademarks, these counterfeits have been unwittingly purchased as genuine for sizeable amounts of money.

Holland Mold was begun by Frank Hollandonner in Trenton, New Jersey, in 1945 and produced molds for the hobby ceramics trade. Holland Mold also had a working relationship with both Stangl and Pennsbury potteries and occasionally did mold-work for them. However, neither Stangl nor Pennsbury would produce a Holland Mold shape as their own. During a conversation with Frank Hollandonner, he stated: "Yes, we did work for Pennsbury and Stangl, just casting or some sculpting when they needed help. We never used their designs and they didn't use ours. We hired our own designers and sculptors and all our designs were original and copyright protected. The Holland Mold name and copyright symbol are part of each mold; every one of our catalogs states that it was against the law to remove our name from the molds or cast pieces. We had a very good relationship with Stangl and Pennsbury and all of us being in the same community, so to speak, they wouldn't ruin our relationship by producing our designs with their names. It just wouldn't be done."

Hand-painted "Stangl" on the sham Turkey.

Holland Mold Turkey shaker counterfeiting a Stangl Turkey.

Every one of these Pennsbury and Stangl fakes found so far have had the Holland Mold name removed and bear a realistically forged Pennsbury or Stangl name. These items are truly fantasy pieces and were never produced by Pennsbury or Stangl. As a result of these forgeries listed below, several serious bird collectors have been accumulating Holland Mold catalogs to use as a reference in identifying fraudulently produced birds.

- Turkey, 3½"x3"
- Wood Duck Drake, 10¼"
- Wood Duck Hen, 8½"
- Golden Crowned Kinglet, 5"
- Bald Eagle, 14"x10¼"
- Quail Cock, 9"
- Quail Hen, 8¾"
- Pheasant Cock, 14"x10¾"
- Pheasant Hen, 12¼"x9½"
- Mallard Drake, 9"x12"
- Mallard Hen, 5½"x7½"
- Pheasant, 6¼"x4¾"

Holland Mold Pheasants decorated as Pennsbury and marked "Pennsbury Pottery." These items have no value other than as very well-executed home ceramics.

Holland Mold Quail decorated as Pennsbury and marked "Pennsbury Pottery." These items have no value other than as very well-executed home ceramics.

Stangl Porcelain Birds of America, 1944

"Stangl gives to Modern American Porcelain the Artistry of the Ages" so states Stangl's Porcelain Birds sales sheet. Stangl's Porcelain Birds of America figurines were truly an artistic achievement. Life-sized and lifelike, each figure was exquisitely detailed and decorated. "Stangl Porcelain Birds are true replicas. These twelve subjects, sculptured by Stangl in the likeness of seven outstanding birds of America, have been taken from natural life. Each bird reflects the careful research and study that Stangl craftsmen have given the authentic Audubon and other prints. The gay, hand-painted figures — lustrous and colorful — suggest the ultimate in distinctive home decoration for the table, mantel or shelf," says the sales sheet.

The Porcelain Birds of America were developed in response to the great popularity of Stangl's pottery bird figurines and Martin Stangl's belief that a figurine series of artistic superiority would be saleable. Martin Stangl was able to develop the porcelain birds as an accompaniment to the high-grade porcelain bushings and insulators the pottery was producing for the United States government. In 1943 Fulper Pottery received the contract to produce porcelain bushings and insulators for the war effort. Because of the defense work, Fulper Pottery was not directly affected by fuel and raw material rationing and was therefore able to continue producing dinnerware and artware products throughout the duration of World War II.

AUDUBON WARBLER

(Single and Double). Known from California and the Rio Grande, South. Has been seen in East. Habitat is primarily in evergreen forests and mountain villages. About five inches long. Five patches of yellow—crown, rump, flanks and throat.

FLYCATCHER

(Scissor-Tailed)

(Single): Breeds from Texas and Alaska and Louisiana. Habitat is open country where there are conspicuous perches. Length, about 14 inches. Has long forked tail, light head and red flanks. Tail spread suggests scissors.

SCARLET TANAGER

(Single and Double): Breeds from Saskatchewan and Nova Scotia to Alabama and Georgia. Habitat is woodlands, trees of village streets. Length about seven inches. Male is red and black. Greenish like female after breeding.

A portion of Stangl's original Porcelain Birds of America flyer showing four of the porcelain birds.

Introduced in 1944, the porcelain birds were the culmination of nearly one year of sculpting of plaster models by Stangl's sculptor John Tierney, assisted by Herman Eichorn. Because fine porcelain can be cast with great detail, Stangl's molds for these figures were created to impart as much detail as possible. Even more detail was added to each figurine by the individual hand-application of lifelike blossoms and leaves. Thirteen different figures were developed, but only 12 were offered to Stangl retailers. Stangl's 1944 Porcelain Birds of America flyer listed each bird with its accompanying flower and retail price. The thirteenth bird, which was not included on the flyer with the other porcelain birds, was the #3743 Parakeet. The Parakeet retailed for $125.00 in 1944. The Porcelain Birds of America were sold only at better department stores across the country. Relatively few were sold at Stangl's Flemington Outlet, but a permanent exhibit of the complete series of Porcelain Birds was on display at the Flemington showrooms from 1944 until the property was sold in 1978. This set of display birds was preserved by Frank Wheaton and has since passed to the Wheaton heirs.

1944 retail prices quoted from Stangl's Porcelain Birds of America flyer:

Audubon Warbler, Syringa, $35.00.

Audubon Warbler (double), Syringa, $75.00.

Crossbill, Yellow Rose, $50.00.

Crossbill (double), Yellow Rose, $125.00.

Robin, Orange Blossom, $150.00.

Robin (double), Orange Blossom, $250.00.

Scarlet Tanager, Pink Dogwood, $50.00.

Scarlet Tanager (double), Pink Dogwood, $100.00.

Red-Headed Woodpecker, Pink Wild Rose, $60.00.

Red-Headed Woodpecker (double), Pink Wild Rose, $125.00.

Magpie-Jay, Trumpet Vine, $175.00.

Scissor-Tailed flycatcher, Marsh Rose, $150.00.

Four more birds shown in Stangl's original Porcelain Birds of America flyer.

Norma Stockwell English, a graduate of Alfred University with a degree in ceramic design, was head of the porcelain bird decorating department. Norma English recalls the porcelain birds: "Our decorating room was upstairs. It used to be part of the regular decorating room, but Mr. Stangl moved the regular decorating room downstairs and expanded it when some of the old periodic kilns were removed. The old decorating room was divided up, we used part of it for the porcelain birds, the rest Mr. Stangl had made into a large showroom and dining room. Mr. Stangl had a cook that made lunch for the management and office staff, and lunch was served in that dining room.

"We had to be meticulous to decorate those porcelain birds, they required much more care than the pottery birds being decorated downstairs. But Mr. Stangl was selling them for much more than the pottery birds. We had to be careful not to contaminate the china paints with earthenware dust. Materials were so dear at that time; we couldn't afford to waste anything! I still don't understand why the Scarlet Tanager was painted with Western Tanager colors. Even the Audubon prints showed the colors we used on the Scarlet Tanager as belonging to the Western Tanager. The Western Tanager is undeniably a prettier bird, but why we didn't change the name from Scarlet Tanager I'll never know!

"For a time we couldn't keep up with the amount of birds we had to decorate. They kept making them because they were used to fill out the kilns when they were firing the government insulators. They were still firing the porcelain in one of the old periodic kilns at the time and had to have a full kiln to fire, so kept producing the porcelain birds. I know they were expensive, but we kept shipping them out. One day Mr. Stangl was so mad because one of the fellows in the packing barn sent out an order of porcelain birds that broke. After that Mr. Stangl personally instructed everyone how the birds were to be carefully wrapped in cotton batting before they were boxed. Every so often he would check up on how the birds were being packed and help pack them himself. He was always like that, not above anyone or above doing any job himself. I really enjoyed working there, partly because Mr. Stangl was someone you just automatically respected for who he was. He just had that type of charismatic personality.

"Mr. Stangl was very proud of the porcelain birds. He was also very proud to have the defense contract, but he certainly couldn't boast of that during the war! The porcelain birds pleased him because even at that time it was a great achievement for an American pottery to produce fine-quality porcelain and to have it recognized by the American public.

"I saw somewhere that someone guessed that we had produced less than 100 of the porcelain birds, or some such figure. I don't know where that came from, but I personally know from being there that that amount is utterly ridiculous! There were three or four of us decorating at any given time, and I remember averaging fifteen birds an hour, which was fewer than the other girls because I also had to keep them supplied with china paint and call the board carriers to come and take away what we finished and bring more when we needed. So that's about 300 to 400 birds per day that we decorated. And remember, we were producing these birds for over a year, so that adds up to thousands of the porcelain birds that were sold. I know that that is not nearly as many porcelain birds as the pottery birds they made. But, between the decorators in Trenton and the ones up there in Flemington, there were over 80 girls painting the pottery birds, and some of those girls could decorate nearly 100 of those birds an hour. That's a lot of pottery birds! That's why you can always find a pottery bird, there were just so many more of them made than porcelain birds. Besides, Mr. Stangl wouldn't have gone to all the expense of having the sculpting done and the molds made if he were only going to produce so few birds.

"Mr. Stangl did stop production of the porcelain birds when the government defense contract ended. They would have been too costly to produce without also producing the government insulators. I then became assistant designer to Cleo Salerno, her name was Crawford then, and I worked with her for almost a year, then I went to California to become a "real artist!" We just closed up that porcelain decorating room, and I was never in there again."

As years went on, display cabinets in the showroom hid the door to the porcelain bird decorating room. Nearly 20 years after porcelain bird production ended, Stangl designer Irene Sarnecki had opportunity to peek into the decorating room. She remembered the room being full of undecorated porcelain bird figures and paints and brushes left as though the decorators had left for just a moment but never returned. "It gave me an eerie feeling, seeing that room," she said. Sadly, that decorating room was completely destroyed by the fire in 1965. Being close to the storeroom where the fire started, it was one of the first areas in the factory to burn.

At this time, Scarlet Tanagers and Red-Headed Woodpeckers are the most plentiful. The Parakeet and the single and double Robin figures seem to be most elusive of Stangl's Porcelain Birds of America. Values are based on birds that are in absolutely pristine condition, with all beaks, wing tips, leaves, and blossoms intact.

#3724 Scarlet Tanager, double (mark, inset). $2,000.00 – 2,250.00.

#3725 Red-Headed Woodpecker, single. $3,000.00 – 3,500.00.

Not Shown:
#3723 Scarlet Tanager, single. $1,000.00 – 1,500.00.
#3726 White Winged Crossbill, single. $3,500.00 – 4,000.00.
#3727 White Winged Crossbill, double. $5,500.00 – 6,000.00.
#3728 Scissor-Tailed flycatcher. $8,500.00 – 9,000.00.
#3729 Red-Headed Woodpecker, double. $5,500.00 – 6,000.00.
#3739 Audubon Warbler, single. $5,500.00 – 6,500.00.
#3740 Audubon Warbler, double. $8,000.00 – 9,000.00.
#3741 Robin, single. $6,000.00 – 7,000.00.
#3742 Robin, double. $9,000.00 – 10,000.00.
#3743 Parakeet. $10,000.00 – 12,000.00.
Porcelain Birds of America flyer, 1944. $175.00 – 250.00.

#3738 Magpie-Jay. $7,500.00 – 8,000.00.

Fulper Pottery Company began producing Martin Stangl's recently developed solid-color glazed earthenware products at the newly opened Plant No. 2 in 1924. Bright, clear single-color glazes in popular shades propelled the line to renown. So successful was the solid-color glazed line, a third manufacturing facility was established in Trenton in 1926. During the 1920s, both locations were producing solid-color glazed dinnerware and artware. Sales and popularity of the solid-color glazed products ultimately surpassed the cumbersome Fulper Pottery brand of artware. During the 1920s, the solid-color products were sold as three distinct brand names. Fulper Fayence was the first name used in 1924, and was applied to classically styled artware and dinnerware. The Fulper-Stangl brand was introduced in 1926 and was ascribed to products of ultra-modern and primitive styles. As early as 1927, Martin Stangl was using the Stangl brand name on newly introduced solid-color glazed products. The Fulper Fayence and Fulper-Stangl brand names were in continual usage from their introductions until fire destroyed Fulper Plant No. 1 in September 1929. After the fire, many of the same solid-color glazed articles continued to be produced, but there was no longer a named style-differentiation. The Fulper Fayence and Fulper-Stangl brand names were dropped; all solid-color glazed products were now classified as "Stangl Pottery, made by Fulper Pottery Co."

The Stangl Pottery solid-color glazed artware increased in popularity throughout the 1930s. Toward the end of the 1930s, trends were changing and new pastel shades and satin finishes were introduced. The year 1943 was the end of Stangl's tangerine solid-color glaze. That year, the United States government restricted the use of commercial grade uranium and appropriated all uranium; this action immediately caused the discontinuance of Stangl's uranium-based tangerine glaze. Tangerine had been a staple of the solid-color glaze assortment since its introduction in 1929. By the mid 1940s, however, Stangl's solid-color glazed artware was being outdistanced in popularity by the relatively new hand-painted dinnerware and bird figurines and Terra Rose artware lines. In 1946, the last of the solid-color satin glazed artware shapes were fired. From time to time during the next three decades, a few lines of solid-color glazed articles were produced but never again in the great quantities that were manufactured from 1924 through 1945.

Colors and Value

A great quantity of different glazes were developed during the 1920s and 1930s. Some of the glazes became "standards" and were used extensively throughout the 1920s and 1930s. Other glazes were used less frequently, some to the point of rarity. Some of the glazes are rare because of greater cost so were ordered less frequently; some were special-order glazes exclusive to particular jobbers; and some were simply unpopular.

Theoretically, nearly every Stangl solid-color glaze could be available on nearly every Stangl shape. Rarely, however, were unusual glazes applied to artware. Most Stangl dealers simply ordered the standard artware colors offered at any given time, so rare glazes on Stangl artware are truly rare.

A crackle glaze finish could be had in any glaze color for an additional 10 percent of cost. Antiqued crackle glaze was available for an additional 20 percent. Rose Crackle was the most popular of the crackled glazes, Persian Yellow Crackle was second in popularity. Green and blue glazes were rarely crackled, but the finish was available. The crackling of a glaze was most often ordered on lamp bases and was rarely applied to vase shapes.

For glaze treatments such as Multi-Color, Sunburst, and Tropical Ware, please see those sections in the Hand-Decorated Artware, Giftware, and Novelties chapter.

Following are the standard and most common artware colors upon which current retail values are based. These are the colors most often found on Stangl's artware shapes.

Apple Green
Blue-of-the-Sky
Colonial Blue
Green Matte
Grey Matte
Ivory (gloss)
Persian Yellow
Rust
Satin Blue
Satin Brown
Satin Green
Satin White
Satin Yellow
Silver Green
Surf White
Tangerine
Turquoise

The following glazes were less used and are moderately difficult to find. Artware items glazed with these colors can sometimes, but not always, sell for a tiny bit more than the same items glazed with common "standard" glazes.

Aqua Blue
Black
Bronze Green
Champagne
Chinese Ivory
Dark Green
Dusty Pink
Eggplant
Glaze #85 (brown)
Leaf Green
Maize
Oyster White
Sand
Silk Blue

The following glazes are rare and have become very popular now. Value of items bearing such glazes can increase to nearly double that of items glazed in "standard" glazes. Most of these glazes were special-order and are normally found on lamp shapes rather than artware shapes.

Alice Blue	Lavender	Plum	Rose Crackle
Blue Matte	Ochre	Primitive Green	Turquoise Blue
Cobalt Blue	Orchid	Purple	Violet
Dove Gray	Oxblood	Rose Light	Yellow Orange
Ivory Antique	Pink Matte	Rose Dark	

Even though many shapes were discontinued or simply ceased production, that never stopped Martin Stangl from re-issuing long discontinued shapes in new glazes or finishes. The ending production dates are when the shapes were no longer listed in Fulper Pottery Company sales literature. It does not imply that those shapes were never produced again.

Fulper Fayence through Stangl, 1924 – 1978

1924 Introductions

Colonial Blue #904 Classic Candlestick, right, 7⅜", Fulper Fayence, 1924 – 1927. $70.00 – 95.00 each. From the Stangl and Fulper archival collection, courtesy the Wheaton Village Museum of American Glass.

Silver Green #906 Dolphin Candlesticks, 12" Fulper Fayence, 1924 – 1926 (base, inset). $400.00 – 500.00 pair. Courtesy of the Hill-Fulper-Stangl Museum.

Persian Yellow #907 Monk ashtray, 8" diameter, Fulper Fayence, 1924 – 1926. $350.00 – 375.00. Courtesy of the Hill-Fulper-Stangl Museum.

Not Shown:

#902L Tulip vase, 10", Fulper Fayence, 1924 – 1927. $65.00 – 80.00.
#902M Tulip vase, 8", Fulper Fayence, 1924 – 1927. $55.00 – 65.00.
#902S Tulip vase, 6", Fulper Fayence, 1924 – 1927. $40.00 – 50.00.
#903 Classic Candlestick, left, 7⅜", Fulper Fayence, 1924 – 1927. $70.00 – 95.00 each.
#905 Dolphin Console Bowl, 14" diameter, Fulper Fayence, 1924 – 1926. $200.00 – 250.00.
#908L Fruit Compote, 15¾" Fulper Fayence, 1924 – 1927. $150.00 – 200.00.
#908S Fruit Compote, 12" Fulper Fayence, 1924 – 1927. $125.00 – 175.00.
#909L Flower Bowl Insert, 5½" diameter, Fulper Fayence, 1924 – 1930. $25.00 – 35.00.
#909S Flower Bowl Insert, 3½" diameter, Fulper Fayence, 1924 – 1930. $20.00 – 25.00.
#910 Bouquet Console Bowl, 10" diameter, Fulper Fayence Decorated, 1924 – 1929. $175.00 – 200.00.
#910 Bouquet Candlesticks, 5½" diameter, handles Fulper Fayence Decorated, 1924 – 1929. $100.00 – 125.00 per pair.
#910 Bouquet Candlesticks, 5½" diameter, no handles Fulper Fayence Decorated, 1924 – 1929. $100.00 – 125.00 per pair.

Silver Green #910 Bouquet Console Set, Fulper Fayence Decorated 1924 – 1929. The bowls were available in Chinese Ivory, Colonial Blue, Persian Yellow or Silver Green, the base and candles were Chinese Ivory with hand-painted overglaze color china paint flowers. $275.00 – 325.00 per complete set. Courtesy of the Hill-Fulper-Stangl Museum.

Fulper Fayence #916 Wide Mouth vases. Left, Copper Green, 8", $50.00 – 60.00; right, Silver Green, 6", $35.00 – 45.00 (base, inset). Courtesy of the Hill-Fulper-Stangl Museum.

Stangl vase #2016 on left in Silver Green, $35.00 – 45.00; Fulper Fayence vase #934 on right in Rose, $70.00 – 80.00. Courtesy of the Hill-Fulper-Stangl Museum.

Bases of Stangl Vase #2016 on left and Fulper Fayence vase #934 on right.

Rose #919L Bud Vase, 8" with original Fulper Fayence gold-foil paper label. $100.00 – 125.00.

Not Shown:

#916EL Wide Mouth Vase, 12" Fulper Fayence, 1924 – 1930. $100.00 – 125.00.

#916L Wide Mouth Vase, 10" Fulper Fayence, 1924 – 1930. $60.00 – 75.00.

#916M Wide Mouth Vase, 8" Fulper Fayence, 1924 – 1930. $45.00 – 55.00.

#916S Wide Mouth Vase, 6" Fulper Fayence, 1924 – 1930. $35.00 – 45.00.

#919L Bud Vase, 8" Fulper Fayence, 1924 – 1930. $60.00 – 75.00.

#919S Bud Vase, 6" Fulper Fayence, 1924 – 1930. $45.00 – 55.00.

#920 Venetian Square Candlestick, square base , 10" Fulper Fayence, 1924 – 1925. $150.00 – 200.00 per pair.

#921 Roman Round Candlestick, round base, 9" Fulper Fayence, 1924 – 1925. $150.00 – 200.00 per pair.

#924 Venetian Square Console Bowl, square base, 12½" diameter Fulper Fayence, 1924 – 1925. $150.00 – 175.00.

#925 Roman Round Console Bowl, round base, 10½" diameter Fulper Fayence, 1924 – 1925. $150.00 – 175.00.

#927 Shouldered Vase, 8" Fulper Fayence, 1924 – 1925. $60.00 – 75.00.

#928L Console Bowl, 12" diameter, Fulper Fayence, 1924 – 1927. $150.00 – 175.00.

#928S Console Bowl, 9" diameter, Fulper Fayence, 1924 – 1927. $100.00 – 125.00.

#928L Candlesticks 13", Fulper Fayence, 1924 – 1927. $200.00 – 250.00 per pair.

#928S Candlesticks 10", Fulper Fayence, 1924 – 1927. $150.00 – 175.00 per pair.

#933 Vase, 3½" Fulper Fayence, 1924 – 1925 (same as Fulper Pottery #511). $85.00 – 95.00.

#934 Vase, 3¼" Fulper Fayence, 1924 – 1925 (later reintroduced as Fulper Pottery #825 in 1927 and Stangl #2016 in 1935). $70.00 – 85.00.

Fulper Fayence vase #935 on right, Colonial Blue, $70.00 – 85.00; Stangl vase #2020 on left in Silver Green, $35.00 – 45.00.

Difference in bases of the Fulper Fayence vase #935 on right, and Stangl vase #2020, left.

Colonial Blue #941 vase, 6", Fulper Fayence 1924 – 1927, also made as a lamp. $55.00 – 65.00.

Orchid #945S bowl, 6¾". $60.00 – 75.00.

Persian Yellow #944 vase, 12" Fulper Fayence, 1924 – 1925. $120.00 – 145.00. From the Stangl and Fulper archival collection, courtesy the Wheaton Village Museum of American Glass.

The Fulper Fayence #953 Card Suit ashtrays were originally produced only in Black and Rose glazes. Black and Rose glazes were no longer used on the Card Suit ashtrays by 1933. During the late 1930s, the #953 ashtrays were produced in transparent tinted glazes but were discontinued by World War II. The #953 Card Suit ashtrays were reintroduced again during the 1960s at the Flemington Outlet. At that time they were produced only at the Flemington Outlet Workshop and were glazed in a variety of tinted gloss colors or hand-painted decorations.

Black glaze #953 Club ashtray, 4¼", Black or Rose glaze only, Fulper Fayence, 1924 – 1933. $25.00 – 30.00.

Not Shown:

#935 Vase, 2¾" Fulper Fayence, 1924 – 1925 (later reintroduced as Stangl #2020). $70.00 – 85.00.

#936 vase, 10" Fulper Fayence, 1924 – 1925 (same as Fulper Pottery #585). $95.00 – 110.00.

#937 vase, 15" Fulper Fayence, 1924 – 1925 (same as Fulper Pottery #600). $175.00 – 200.00.

#938 vase, 14½" Fulper Fayence, 1924 – 1925 (same as Fulper Pottery #608). $190.00 – 225.00.

#939 vase, 11½" Fulper Fayence ,1924 – 1925 (same as Fulper Pottery #611). $120.00 – 145.00.

#945L bowl, 10½" Fulper Fayence, 1924 – 1927. $70.00 – 85.00.

#945M bowl, 8½" Fulper Fayence, 1924 – 1927. $60.00 – 75.00.

#945S bowl, 6¾" Fulper Fayence, 1924 – 1927. $45.00 – 55.00.

#952L powder jar, 6", Fulper Fayence, 1924 – 1927. $100.00 – 125.00.

#952M powder jar, 5", Fulper Fayence, 1924 – 1927. $95.00 – 110.00.

#952S powder jar, 4", Fulper Fayence, 1924 – 1927. $85.00 – 95.00.

#953 Diamond ashtray, 4¼", Black or Rose glaze only, Fulper Fayence, 1924 – 1933. $25.00 – 30.00.

#953 Heart ashtray, 4¼", Black or Rose glaze only, Fulper Fayence, 1924 – 1933. $25.00 – 30.00.

#953 Spade ashtray, 4¼", Black or Rose glaze only, Fulper Fayence, 1924 – 1933. $25.00 – 30.00.

Silver Green #956 oval jam jar, 6"x3½", for Rena Rosenthal, 1924 – 1928. $70.00 – 85.00.

Not Shown:

#956 underplate for oval jam jar for Rena Rosenthal, 1924 – 1928. $50.00 – 60.00.

1925 Introductions

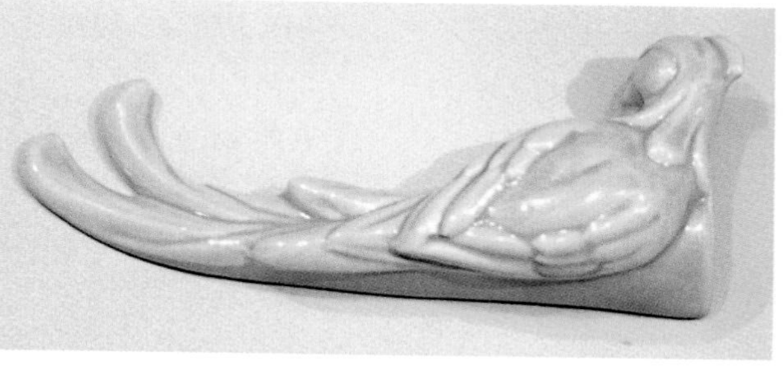

Silver Green #961 Bird wall pocket, left, 9", Fulper Fayence, 1925 – 1931. $275.00 – 300.00. Martin Stangl applied the number "961" to both the Fish ashtrays and this Bird wall pocket. Courtesy of the Hill-Fulper-Stangl Museum.

E.C. Rich #988-M Eight-Sided Jar in Silver Green with original cold-paint decoration. Originally packed with Rich's ginger preparations from 1925 – 1931. Because of the unusual ship motif, this jar is valued at $100.00 – 125.00. Undecorated Eight-Sided Jar, $55.00 – 65.00. Courtesy of the Hill-Fulper-Stangl Museum.

Group of Fulper Fayence #964 Fruit and 965 Butterfly candleholders. $40.00 – 50.00 per pair.

Not Shown:

#961A Dip novelty ashtray 4¾", Fish design, Fulper Fayence (same as Decorated #367A), 1925 only. $275.00 – 300.00.
#961B Sponge novelty ashtray 4¾", Fish design, Fulper Fayence (same as Decorated #367B), 1925 only. $275.00 – 300.00.
#961C Valentine novelty ashtray 4¾", Fish design, Fulper Fayence (same as Decorated #367C), 1925 only. $275.00 – 300.00.
#961D Pom novelty ashtray 4¾", Fish design, Fulper Fayence (same as Decorated #367D), 1925 only. $275.00 – 300.00.
#961E Messenger novelty ashtray 4¾", Fish design, Fulper Fayence (same as Decorated #367E), 1925 only. $275.00 – 300.00.
#961F Ring novelty ashtray 4¾", Fish design, Fulper Fayence (same as Decorated #367F), 1925 only. $275.00 – 300.00.
#962 Bird wall pocket, Right 9", Fulper Fayence 1925 – 1931. $250.00 – 300.00.
#963 Flower candleholders, 4"x2½", Fulper Fayence, 1925 – 1931. $40.00 – 50.00 per pair.
#964 Fruit candleholders, 4"x2½", Fulper Fayence, 1925 – 1931. $40.00 – 50.00 per pair.
#965 Butterfly candleholders, 4"x2½", Fulper Fayence, 1925 – 1931. $40.00 – 50.00 per pair.
#966A Dip novelty powder jar 5¼", Fish design, Fulper Fayence (same as Decorated #368A), 1925 only. $300.00 – 350.00.
#966B Sponge novelty powder jar 5¼", Fish design, Fulper Fayence (same as Decorated #368B), 1925 only. $300.00 – 350.00.
#966C Valentine novelty powder jar 5¼", Fish design, Fulper Fayence (same as Decorated #368C), 1925 only. $300.00 – 350.00.
#966D Pom novelty powder jar 5¼", Fish design, Fulper Fayence (same as Decorated #368D), 1925 only. $300.00 – 350.00.
#966E Messenger novelty powder jar 5¼", Fish design, Fulper Fayence (same as Decorated #368E), 1925 only. $300.00 – 350.00.
#966F Ring novelty powder jar 5¼", Fish design, Fulper Fayence (same as Decorated #368F), 1925 only. $300.00 – 350.00.
#986 vase, 10" made for L.D. Bloch, Fulper Fayence, 1925 – 1926. $85.00 – 95.00.
#988-L Eight-Sided Jar, 7½"x5" for E.C. Rich, Fulper Fayence, 1925 – 1931. $70.00 – 85.00.
#988-M Eight-Sided Jar, 5"x3½" for E.C. Rich, Fulper Fayence, 1925 – 1931. $55.00 – 65.00.
#988-S Six-Sided Jar, 4"x3¼" for E.C. Rich, Fulper Fayence, 1925 – 1931. $35.00 – 45.00.
#989 Grapes wall pocket, 8", Fulper Fayence, 1925 – 1928. $200.00 – 250.00.
#990 Spanish Figure flower holder, 8½" Fulper Fayence (same as Decorated #378), 1925 – 1927. $130.00 – 150.00.
#991 Turtle Girl flower holder, 5¾" Fulper Fayence (same as Decorated #379), 1925 – 1927. $95.00 – 130.00.
#994 upholstery ashtray 4¾", Fish design, Fulper Fayence (same as Decorated #380), 1925 only. $275.00 – 300.00.

Colonial Blue #997 Fruit wall pocket, 8" (left); Persian Yellow #998 Flowers wall pocket, 7½" (right). Both are Fulper Fayence, 1925 – 1931. $175.00 – 200.00 each. Courtesy of the Hill-Fulper-Stangl Museum.

Silver Green #1016 candy box 6"x4½", made for Bamberger's Dept. Store with original cold-paint decoration, Fulper Fayence, 1925 – 1929. $130.00 – 150.00.

Persian Yellow #1051 Donkey ashtray, Fulper Decorated, for Rena Rosenthal, 1925 – 1930. $225.00 – 275.00.

Silver Green #1050A Ribbed tobacco jar with walnut cover, 5½", part of smoking set for L.D. Bloch Co., 1925 – 1927. $130.00 – 150.00. Courtesy of the Hill-Fulper-Stangl Museum.

Three Raffetto #1005 Honey Jars glazed in Dark Rose, Silver Green, and Colonial Blue, showing some of the cold-paint decorations Fulper Pottery offered to jobber accounts. Fulper Fayence, 1925 – 1931. Intact cold-paint can add up to 50 percent to the value of a container. Large jar, $70.00 – 85.00; small jar, $40.00 – 50.00. Courtesy of the Bill Servis, Susan Lewis collection.

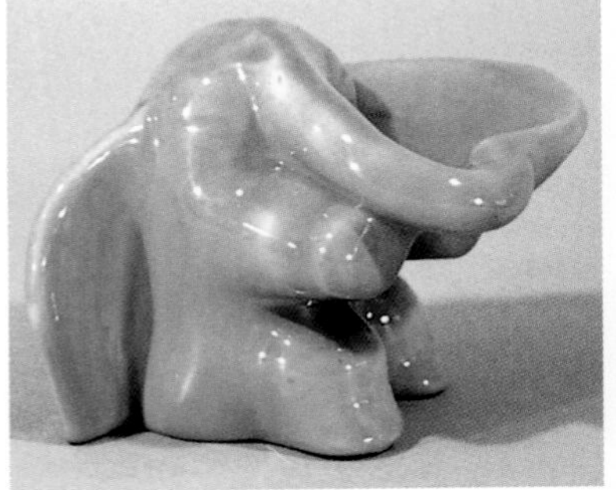

Silver Green #1052 Sitting Elephant ashtray, Fulper Fayence, for Rena Rosenthal, 1925 – 1932. $225.00 – 275.00. Courtesy of the Hill-Fulper-Stangl Museum.

Not Shown:

#999 Pipes of Pan flower holder, 5"x6" Fulper Fayence (same as Decorated #383), 1925 – 1927. $95.00 – 130.00.
#1005-L Honey Jar 5"x4½", made for Raffetto, Fulper Fayence, 1925 – 1931. $70.00 – 85.00.
#1005-S Honey Jar 3½"x3½", made for Raffetto, Fulper Fayence, 1925 – 1931. $40.00 – 50.00.
#1008 Musical Jug, with music box, made for Sprague, Sprague Brown glaze, 1925 – 1927. $95.00 – 130.00.
#1049 cosmetic cream jar, 16 oz., made for R. Louis, Fulper Fayence, 1925 – 1929. $100.00 – 125.00.
#1049 cosmetic cream jar, 8 oz., made for R. Louis, Fulper Fayence, 1925 – 1929. $60.00 – 75.00.
#1049 cosmetic cream jar, 4 oz., made for R. Louis, Fulper Fayence, 1925 – 1929. $35.00 – 45.00.
#1049 cosmetic cream jar, 2 oz., made for R. Louis, Fulper Fayence, 1925 – 1929. $30.00 – 35.00.
#1049 cosmetic cream jar, 1 oz., made for R. Louis, Fulper Fayence, 1925 – 1929. $25.00 – 30.00.
#1050B Ribbed cigarette jar, 3", part of smoking set for L.D. Bloch Co., 1925 – 1927. $65.00 – 80.00.
#1050C Ribbed cigarette box, part of smoking set for L.D. Bloch Co., 1925 – 1927. $130.00 – 150.00.
#1050D Ribbed pipe rest, part of smoking set for L.D. Bloch Co., 1925 – 1927. $65.00 – 80.00.
#1050E Ribbed ashtray, part of smoking set for L.D. Bloch Co., 1925 – 1927. $65.00 – 80.00.
#1053 Square cigarette box, for Rena Rosenthal, 1925 – 1926. $175.00 – 200.00.
#1057 Turtle ashtray, Fulper Fayence solid-color glazes, 1925 – 1930s. $175.00 – 200.00.

Orange overglaze color #1058 Lizard ashtray, Fulper Decorated, 1925 – 1927. $300.00 – 350.00. Courtesy of the Hill-Fulper-Stangl Museum.

1926 Introductions

Originally a special-order item for Rena Rosenthal during the 1920s, the #1076 Pig shape has been produced in a great variety of glazes and finishes from 1926 until the close of the company in 1978. For other finishes on the #1076 Pig, see also the sections on Brushed Gold, Sunburst, Early Pennsylvania Artware, and Hand-Painted Animal Figurines.

Silver Green #1049 R. Louis 1 oz. cosmetic jars with their original japanned tin box. Made for cosmetician R. Louis and marketed with his exclusive cosmetics at his Fifth Avenue Salon from 1925 – 1929. Jars, $25.00 – 30.00 each; tin box, $50.00 – 75.00.

Green Matte #1076 Pig Cactus pot and Tangerine #1076 Pig Bank. Courtesy of the Robert and Tammie Cruser collection.

Silver Green #1087 Nude Candlestick, 5", Fulper Fayence for Frankart, 1926 – 1927. $300.00 – 400.00 pair. Courtesy of the Hill-Fulper-Stangl Museum.

Not Shown:

#1076 Pig Bank, 4" solid-color glazes, 1926 – 1945. $130.00 – 150.00.
#1076 Pig Cactus pot, 4" solid-color glazes, 1929 – 1945. $120.00 – 145.00.
#1076 Pig Hors d'Oeuvre, 4", for Rena Rosenthal, 1926 – 1929. $190.00 – 225.00.
#1076 Pig Bank, 4" gold luster over solid-color glazes, 1934 only. $190.00 – 225.00.
#1077 Large Elephant figurine, 5½" x 6¼", for Rena Rosenthal (also made as a lamp), 1926 – 1928. $300.00 – 350.00.
#1078 Deer ashtray, 5" diameter, solid-color glazes, for Rena Rosenthal 1926 – 1935. $100.00 – 125.00.

1927 Introductions

Stangl first called the handmade items "Primitive." The items produced during 1927 were usually marked with a Fulper-Stangl gold-foil paper label. The presence of an undamaged complete Fulper-Stangl label can sometimes add $15.00 – $40.00 to the value. Please see the section on Fulper-Stangl Handmade Artware for photos of the handmade items.

Not Shown:

#1119L bowl, 8" Fulper-Stangl handmade, 1927 – 1930s. $80.00 – 90.00.
#1119S bowl, 7" Fulper-Stangl handmade, 1927 – 1930s. $65.00 – 80.00.
#1120L flower holder, 3½", 6 holes, Fulper-Stangl handmade, 1927 – 1930s. $20.00 – 25.00.
#1120S flower holder, 3", 5 holes, Fulper-Stangl handmade, 1927 – 1930s. $15.00 – 20.00.
#1121L Double Bulge vase, 12½" Fulper-Stangl handmade, 1927 – 1930s. $180.00 – 200.00.
#1121S Double Bulge vase, 10" Fulper-Stangl handmade, 1927 – 1930s. $150.00 – 175.00.
#1122 Band Rim vase, 8" Fulper-Stangl handmade, 1927 – 1930s. $100.00 – 125.00.
#1123 bottle, 9" Fulper-Stangl handmade, 1927 – 1930s. $130.00 – 150.00.
#1124 Slanting Handle vase, 7½" Fulper-Stangl handmade, 1927 – 1930s. $85.00 – 95.00.
#1125 rose bowl, 4"x6" Fulper-Stangl handmade, 1927 – 1930s. $65.00 – 80.00.

Rust #1124 Slanting Handle vase, 7½" Stangl mold-cast, 1932 – 1937. $65.00 – 80.00. Courtesy of the Chris McGeehan collection.

Apple Green #1126 Ball vase, 7½" Stangl mold-cast, 1932 – 1937. $65.00 – 80.00. Courtesy of the Brian and Cristi Hahn collection.

#1165 Round Ring Jar, Fulper Decorated, gold crackle luster, 1927 – 1929. $200.00 – 250.00. From the Stangl and Fulper archival collection, courtesy the Wheaton Village Museum of American Glass.

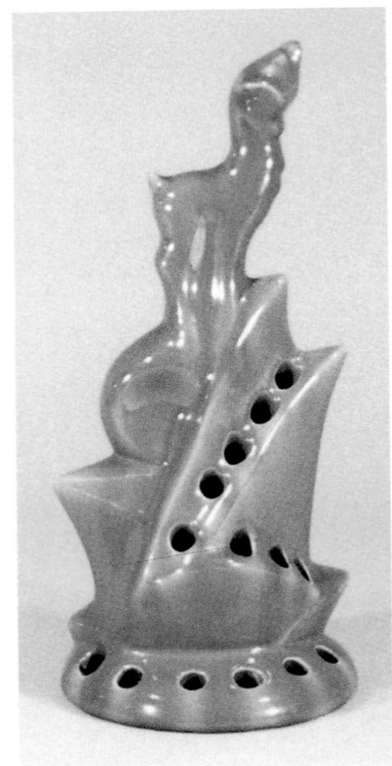

Colonial Blue #1169 Gazelle flower holder, 11½" (same as Fulper Pottery #820), 1927 – 1929. $200.00 – 250.00. Courtesy of the Hill-Fulper-Stangl Museum.

Silver Green #1168 Angular cigarette box, Fulper-Stangl solid-color glazes, (same as Fulper Decorated #392), 1927 – 1929. $290.00 – 325.00. From the Stangl and Fulper archival collection, courtesy the Wheaton Village Museum of American Glass.

Not Shown:

#1126 Ball vase, 7½" Fulper-Stangl handmade, (later reintroduced as Stangl #1907) 1927 – 1930s. $100.00 – 125.00.
#1127 Four-sided vase, 6½" Fulper-Stangl handmade, 1927 – 1930s. $120.00 – 145.00.
#1128L Double 4 handle vase, 8" Fulper-Stangl handmade, 1927 – 1930s. $150.00 – 175.00.
#1128S Double 4 handle vase, 4" Fulper-Stangl handmade, 1927 – 1930s. $95.00 – 110.00.
#1129L Double 3 handle vase, 8¾" Fulper-Stangl handmade, 1927 – 1930s. $110.00 – 135.00.
#1129S Double 3 handle vase, 5¾" Fulper-Stangl handmade, 1927 – 1930s. $85.00 – 95.00.
#1142 Angular ashtray, Fulper Fayence solid-color glazes, (same as Fulper Decorated #393) 1927 – 1929. $100.00 – 125.00.
#1143 Angular ashtray, Fulper Fayence solid-color glazes, (same as Fulper Decorated #395) 1927 – 1929. $100.00 – 125.00.
#1148L bowl, 8" Fulper-Stangl mold-cast, 1927 – 1929. $30.00 – 40.00.
#1148S bowl, 6" Fulper-Stangl mold-cast, 1927 – 1929. $25.00 – 35.00.
#1149L jar, 7½" Fulper-Stangl mold-cast, 1927 – 1929. $65.00 – 80.00.
#1149M jar, 5" Fulper-Stangl mold-cast, 1927 – 1929. $45.00 – 55.00.
#1149S jar, 4" Fulper-Stangl mold-cast, 1927 – 1929. $35.00 – 45.00.
#1150L flowerpot, 8" Fulper-Stangl handmade, 1927 – 1929. $95.00 – 110.00.
#1150M flowerpot, 6" Fulper-Stangl handmade, 1927 – 1929. $70.00 – 85.00.
#1150S flowerpot, 4" Fulper-Stangl handmade, 1927 – 1929s. $55.00 – 65.00.
#1153L vase, 9" Fulper-Stangl mold-cast, 1927 – 1929. $70.00 – 85.00.
#1153S vase, 6" Fulper-Stangl mold-cast, 1927 – 1929. $55.00 – 70.00.
#1154 bowl, plain, 10"x3" Fulper-Stangl mold-cast, 1927 – 1929. $55.00 – 70.00.
#1163 Square cigarette box, Fulper-Stangl solid-color glazes, (same as Fulper Decorated #394) 1927 – 1929. $290.00 – 325.00.
#1166 modern vase, 12"x10" Fulper-Stangl 1927 only. $130.00 – 150.00.
#1166 modern vase, 9"x7½" Fulper-Stangl 1927 only. $100.00 – 125.00.
#1166 modern vase, 6" Fulper-Stangl 1927 only. $85.00 – 95.00.

1928 Introductions

The brand name "Stangl Pottery" makes its debut during 1928. The Fulper Fayence and Fulper-Stangl brands were being phased out as Stangl Pottery gold-foil paper labels were applied to all new introductions. The Fulper Pottery and Fulper Porcelaines continued as strong sellers.

Blue Matte #1185L Square Modern vase, 9" Stangl Pottery, 1928 – 1930. $95.00 – 130.00. Courtesy of the Brian and Cristi Hahn collection.

Variegated Tangerine #1185S Square Modern vase, 6" Stangl Pottery, 1928 – 1930. This glaze available after 1929 only. $85.00 – 95.00.

Three #1187 Levin ½-pint pitchers in Tangerine, Silver Green and Colonial Blue. $30.00 – 40.00 each.

Tangerine with green lining #1188 Levin round bowls, 11", $175.00 – 200.00, and 6", $25.00 – 35.00. Courtesy of the Ben and Pauline Jensen collection.

Levin #1188 6" round Ringed bowl mounted on metal stand with nude figures. Bowl, $25.00 – 35.00. Courtesy of the Hill-Fulper-Stangl Museum.

Not Shown:

#1187EL pitcher, 2-quart, made for Levin, 1928 – 1930. $95.00 – 110.00.

#1187L pitcher, 1-quart, made for Levin, 1928 – 1930. $60.00 – 75.00.

#1187M pitcher, 1-pint, made for Levin, 1928 – 1930. $45.00 – 55.00.

#1187S pitcher, ½-pint, made for Levin, 1928 – 1930. $30.00 – 40.00.

#1188L round Ringed bowl, 11" made for Levin, 1928 – 1932. $175.00 – 200.00.

#1188M round bowl, 9" made for Levin, 1928 – 1932. $85.00 – 100.00.

#1188S round bowl, 6" made for Levin, 1928 – 1932. $25.00 – 35.00.

#1189 oval bowl, made for Levin, 1928 – 1930. $60.00 – 75.00.

#1190 6-sided bowl, footed 13½" made for Levin, 1928 – 1930. $175.00 – 200.00.

Blue Matte #1192 wall pocket, two birds, 5"x7" Stangl Pottery, 1928 – 1932. $275.00 – 300.00. Courtesy of the Hill-Fulper-Stangl Museum.

Silver Green #1191 twin candlestick, 6"x6" made for Levin, 1928 – 1930. $50.00 – 75.00 each.

Blue Matte #1200 square flowerpot, missing tray, 4" Stangl Pottery, 1928 – 1930. $35.00 – 45.00.

Silver Green #1201S oblong flowerpot & tray 6", Stangl Pottery, 1928 – 1930. $65.00 – 80.00. Courtesy of the Marcena North collection.

Not Shown:

#1193 bowl, 8-sided, flat, no foot, 12" Stangl Pottery, 1928 – 1930. $100.00 – 135.00.

#1200 square flowerpot & tray, 4" Stangl Pottery, 1928 – 1930. $60.00 – 75.00.

#1200C square candy jar & cover, 4" Stangl Pottery, 1928 – 1930. $130.00 – 160.00.

#1201L oblong flowerpot & tray 12", Stangl Pottery, 1928 – 1930. $100.00 – 125.00.

#1201M oblong flowerpot & tray 9", Stangl Pottery, 1928 – 1930. $80.00 – 90.00.

#1202 oblong bowl, 6-sided, footed, 12", Stangl Pottery, 1929 – 1934. $120.00 – 145.00.

Ivory Satin glazed Stangl Pottery "A.D. 1828" Flemington Courthouse book blocks, 5" tall, 1928 only. $600.00 – 700.00 pair. Courtesy of the Hunterdon County Historical Society.

Courthouse Book Blocks

In 1928, Flemington's neo-classical courthouse building celebrated its one hundredth anniversary. For the occasion, Fulper Pottery Company produced two styles of book blocks replicating the front portico of the courthouse. One was produced from Fulper Pottery clay and glazed with Fulper Ivory glaze. The other was a tad smaller and made of Stangl earthenware with Satin White glaze. The book blocks were named "A.D. 1828" in reference to the inscription on the marble date stone set into the front gable of the courthouse. The book blocks were produced for a short time during 1928 and sold locally in Flemington.

1929 Introductions

Sold under the Stangl trademark, usually marked only with a Stangl Pottery gold-foil paper label.

Not Shown:

#1213L Pleated flowerpot, 8" Stangl Pottery, 1929 – 1932. $60.00 – 75.00.

#1213M Pleated flowerpot, 6" Stangl Pottery, 1929 – 1932. $55.00 – 65.00.

#1233EL Crimp bowl, 10" Stangl handmade, 1929 – 1935. $120.00 – 145.00.

#1233L Crimp bowl, 8" Stangl handmade, 1929 – 1935. $80.00 – 100.00.

#1233M Crimp bowl, 6" Stangl handmade, 1929 – 1935. $70.00 – 85.00.

#1233S Crimp bowl, 5" Stangl handmade, 1929 – 1935. $60.00 – 75.00.

#1237 jar, 3 handles, 7½" ribbed, Stangl handmade, 1930 – 1935. $95.00 – 110.00.

#1237 jar, 3 handles, 7½" ribbed, Stangl handmade, 1930 – 1935. $95.00 – 110.00.

Silver Green #1213S Pleated flowerpot, 4" Stangl Pottery, 1929 – 1932. $35.00 – 45.00. Courtesy of the Hill-Fulper-Stangl Museum.

Apple Green #1211 Birds on rocks, flower holder, 10" Stangl Pottery, 1929 – 1932. $180.00 – 195.00.

Not Shown:

#1237 jar, 3 handles, 6" ribbed, Stangl handmade, 1929 – 1935. $85.00 – 95.00.

#1237 jar, 3 handles, 6" ribbed, mold-cast, 1933 – 1937. $65.00 – 80.00.

#1238L jar, 3 handles, 9" smooth, Stangl handmade, 1929 – 1935. $130.00 – 150.00.

#1238M jar, 3 handles, 6" smooth, Stangl handmade, 1929 – 1935. $65.00 – 80.00.

#1239 jar, 2 high-handles, 7" Stangl handmade, 1929 – 1935. $120.00 – 145.00.

Three #1237 3-handle jars, 6", handmade Apple Green (left), handmade Blue Matte, $80.00 – 90.00 each (center), and mold-cast Tangerine (right), ribbed, 1933 – 1937, $65.00 – 80.00.

1930 Introductions

Group of #1261 jardinieres, 5" dark Colonial Blue, 6" dark Persian Yellow, 4" Maize, and 3" Pink Matte. Courtesy of the Hill-Fulper-Stangl Museum.

Not Shown:

#1261 jardiniere, 8" Stangl mold-cast, 1930 – 1937. $35.00 – 45.00.
#1261 jardiniere, 6" Stangl mold-cast, 1930 – 1937. $25.00 – 35.00.
#1261 jardiniere, 5" Stangl mold-cast, 1930 – 1937. $25.00 – 30.00.
#1261 jardiniere, 4" Stangl mold-cast, 1930 – 1937. $20.00 – 25.00.
#1261 jardiniere, 3" Stangl mold-cast, 1930 – 1937. $20.00 – 25.00.
#1262 cigar cup/vase, 4"x3¾", for Art Metal Works, 1930. $55.00 – 65.00.
#1271L bowl, 2 handles, 9", 1930 only. $60.00 – 75.00.
#1271M bowl, 2 handles, 7", 1930 only. $40.00 – 50.00.
#1272 Zig-Zag bulb bowl, 5"x9", 1930 – 1935. $40.00 – 50.00.
#1273 6-sided bulb bowl, 7", 1930 – 1935. $45.00 – 55.00.
#1273 6-sided bulb bowl, 4", 1930 – 1935. $35.00 – 45.00.
#1274 hanging basket, 7"x3", Stangl handmade, 1930 – 1935. $75.00 – 95.00.
#1275 hanging basket, 3 handles 7"x4", 1930 – 1935. $75.00 – 95.00.
#1311 fruit bowl, supported by 3 female figures, 1930 only. $500.00 – 600.00.
#1315 Mandolin ashtray, 10" jazz musician, Stangl, 1930 – 1931. $350.00 – 400.00.
#1316 Saxophone ashtray, 10" jazz musician, Stangl, 1930 – 1931. $350.00 – 400.00.

Silver Green #1259 Bird ashtray & match holder 5¾"x 3¾", with ridged match striker along bird's head, 1929 – 1932. $200.00 – 250.00. Courtesy of the Hill-Fulper-Stangl Museum.

Silver Green #1253 Bee Hive honey jar, 4½"x4½", made for Mount Hope Farm, Williamstown, Mass. 1929 – 1930. $175.00 – 200.00.

Rust #1312 candleholder, male figures, 1930 only. $700.00 – 800.00 per pair. From the Stangl and Fulper archival collection, courtesy the Wheaton Village Museum of American Glass.

Oxblood #1317 Accordion ashtray, 10" jazz musician, Stangl, 1930 – 1931. $350.00 – 400.00. From the Stangl and Fulper archival collection, courtesy the Wheaton Village Museum of American Glass.

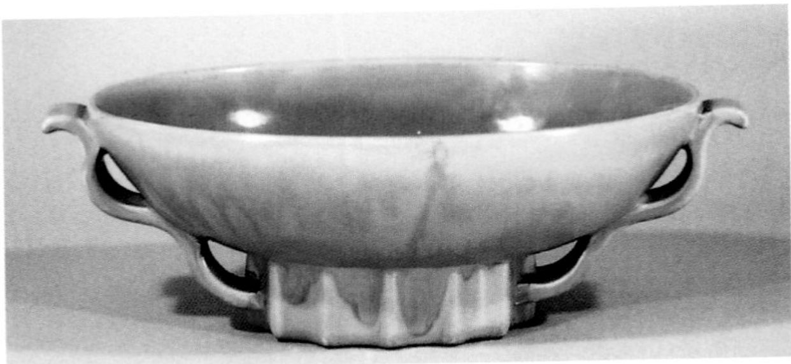

Blue-of-the-Sky #1319 oval bowl, 2 handles, 12", 1930 – 1935. $85.00 – 110.00.

Apple Green #1325 Crane flower holder, 9", 1930 – 1935. $200.00 – 225.00.

Oxblood #1323 Bird ashtray, 5½" diameter, 1930 – 1934. $130.00 – 150.00. Courtesy of the Hill-Fulper-Stangl Museum.

Apple Green #1328 vase, narrow, two handles at neck, 14" mold-cast, 1933 – 1938. $120.00 – 145.00.

Tangerine #1329 vase, wide 18" mold-cast, 1933 – 1938. $200.00 – 250.00. Courtesy of the Brian and Cristi Hahn collection.

Not Shown:

#1318 Horse ashtray and match holder, 5½" diameter, 1930 – 1931. $150.00 – 180.00.
#1319 oval bowl, 2 handles, 10", 1930 – 1935. $65.00 – 80.00.
#1320 Gazelle flower holder, 6", 1930 – 1935. $100.00 – 125.00.
#1320 Gazelle candleholder, 6", 1930 – 1935. $175.00 – 200.00 per pair
#1322 Elephant ashtray, 6" diameter, 1930 – 1934. $130.00 – 150.00.
#1324 Monkey ashtray, 5" diameter, 1930 – 1931. $190.00 – 225.00.
#1324 Monkey & Dog ashtray, 5" diameter, 1930 – 1931. $190.00 – 225.00.
#1327L vase, 11" Stangl handmade, 1930 – 1935. $120.00 – 145.00.
#1327M vase, 9" Stangl handmade, 1930 – 1935. $95.00 – 130.00.
#1328 vase, narrow 2 handles at neck 14" Stangl handmade, 1930 – 1933. $175.00 – 200.00.
#1329 vase, narrow 18" Stangl handmade, 1930 – 1933. $175.00 – 200.00.
#1329 vase, wide 18" Stangl handmade, 1930 – 1933. $350.00 – 375.00.
#1329-B vase 15" Stangl handmade, 1930 – 1933. $175.00 – 200.00.
#1329 vase, narrow 18" mold-cast, 1933 – 1938. $150.00 – 175.00.
#1329-B vase 15" mold-cast, 1933 – 1938. $130.00 – 150.00.

Black glaze #1360 scrolled candleholder, 10", 1930 – 1932. $175.00 – 190.00 pair.

Silver Green #1371 round candleholder, 3"x4", 1930 – 1934. $80.00 – 95.00 pair.

Anchor Pottery Shapes

During 1930, Stangl produced several old Anchor Pottery Victorian shapes in Stangl solid-color glazes and Sunburst glaze. These were produced simply as novelty pieces and sold at the Flemington Outlet. There was not a complete line of these shapes produced in these glazes.

Old Anchor Pottery shapes with Stangl glazes: Persian Yellow covered vegetable, $150.00 – 175.00 (left), and Colonial Blue large covered sugar, $80.00 – 90.00 (right).

Not Shown:

Anchor jug. $85.00 – 95.00.

Anchor small jardiniere. $70.00 – 85.00.

Anchor large jardiniere in Persian Yellow glaze, $100.00 – 125.00.

1931 Introductions

Not Shown:

#1380 ivy ball on chain, 4", 1931 only. $60.00 – 75.00.

#1381 ivy ball on stand, 6½", 1931 only. $100.00 – 125.00.

#1382 strawberry jar, 15" Stangl handmade, 1931 – 1935. $200.00 – 250.00.

#1382 strawberry jar, 12" Stangl handmade, 1931 – 1935. $130.00 – 150.00.

#1382 strawberry jar, 9" Stangl handmade, 1931 – 1935. $100.00 – 125.00.

#1382 strawberry jar, 8" Stangl handmade, 1931 – 1935. $95.00 – 110.00.

#1382 strawberry jar, 6" Stangl handmade, 1931 – 1935. $85.00 – 95.00.

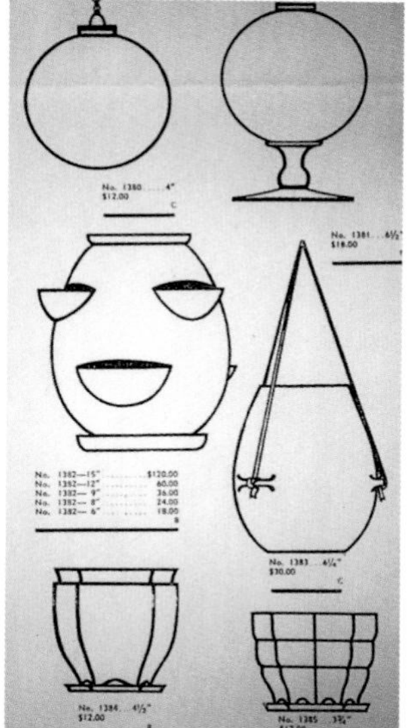

Page of 1931 Stangl Pottery catalog showing items #1380 through #1385. From the Stangl and Fulper archival collection, courtesy the Wheaton Village Museum of American Glass.

Silver Green #1382 strawberry jar, 6" mold-cast, 1933 – 1938. $60.00 – 75.00.

Apple Green #1384-C 6-sided candy jar with bird cover, 6", 1931 – 1932. $150.00 – 175.00.

Tangerine #1386 flower vase, 5¾", 1931 – 1935. $40.00 – 50.00. Courtesy of the Hill-Fulper-Stangl Museum.

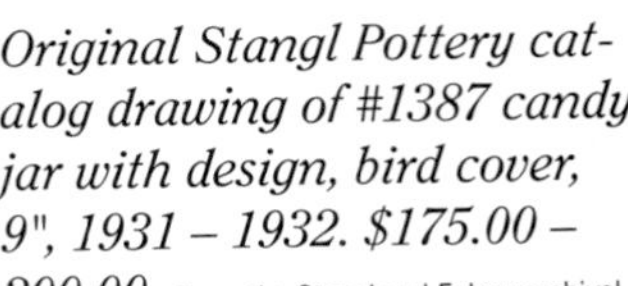
Original Stangl Pottery catalog drawing of #1387 candy jar with design, bird cover, 9", 1931 – 1932. $175.00 – 200.00. From the Stangl and Fulper archival collection, courtesy the Wheaton Village Museum of American Glass.

Silver Green #1388 candy jar, bird cover, 6"x5", part of Colonial dinnerware pattern, 1931 – 1932. $120.00 – 145.00.

Colonial Blue #1388 candy jar, 5"x5", part of Colonial dinnerware pattern, 1932 – 1938. $80.00 – 100.00.

Rust #1388 candleholder, 3½" part of Colonial dinnerware pattern, 1935 – 1944. $20.00 – 30.00 pair.

Satin Brown #1388 baking shell, also marketed as an ashtray, 1936 – 1942. $12.00 – 18.00.

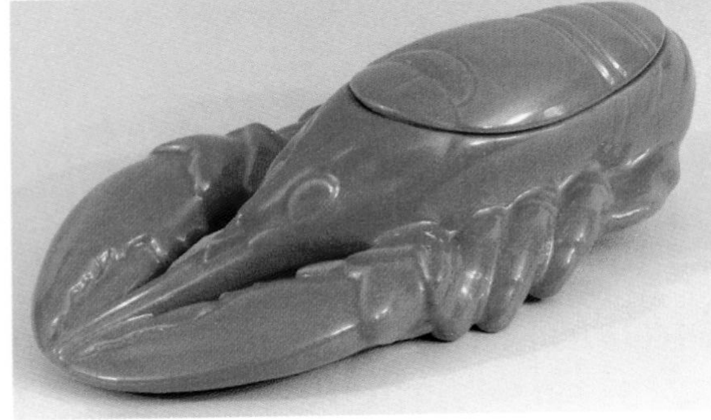
Tangerine Lobster covered dish, 12"x5½", 1931 only. $375.00 – 400.00. Courtesy of Merrill and Christl (Stangl) Bacheler.

Not Shown:

#1383 hanging bowl, 6¼", 1931 only. $85.00 – 95.00.
#1384 6-sided flowerpot, 4½", 1931 – 1932. $45.00 – 55.00.
#1384-A 6-sided ashtray with bird, 4", 1931 – 1932. $50.00 – 75.00.
#1385 8-sided flowerpot, 3¾", 1931 – 1932. $45.00 – 55.00.
#1388 cigarette box, 4½"x3½", part of Colonial dinnerware pattern, 1935 – 1943. $85.00 – 95.00.
#1388 ashtray 4", part of Colonial dinnerware pattern, 1935 – 1943. $20.00 – 25.00.
#1388 coaster ashtray 4", part of Colonial dinnerware pattern, 1933 – 1935. $25.00 – 30.00.
#1388 oval console bowl, 12"x8", part of Colonial dinnerware pattern, 1935 – 1943. $35.00 – 45.00.
#1388 triple candle, part of Colonial dinnerware pattern, 1936 – 1942. $75.00 – 85.00 each.
#1388 miniature jug, 2¼", 1938 – 1945. $20.00 – 25.00.

Original Stangl Pottery catalog drawing of #1390 compote, 3 handles, 7½" diameter, 1931 – 1932. $100.00 – 125.00. From the Stangl and Fulper archival collection, courtesy the Wheaton Village Museum of American Glass.

Apple Green #1391 twin candleholder, bird and flower, 6½", 1931 – 1933. $130.00 – 160.00.

Silver Green #1392-C candy jar with flower cover, 4½", 1931 – 1933. $110.00 – 135.00. Courtesy of the Hill-Fulper-Stangl Museum.

Silver Green #1392 low flowerpot, 3", 1931 – 1933. $35.00 – 45.00.

Persian Yellow #1393 compote, 3 birds, 7½", 1931 – 1933. $130.00 – 150.00.

Tangerine with Turquoise lining #1426L oval Japanese garden, 10½"x8½", 1931 – 1934. $60.00 – 75.00.

Persian Yellow #1394L Swan flowerpot, 9", $65.00 – 80.00, and Apple Green #1394M Swan flowerpot, 6", $45.00 – 55.00.

Not Shown:

#1389 candleholder, bird and flower, 7¾", 1931 – 1933. $130.00 – 160.00 pair.
#1394EL Swan flowerpot, 13", 1931 – 1940. $100.00 – 125.00.
#1394L Swan flowerpot, 9", 1931 – 1940. $65.00 – 80.00.
#1394M Swan flowerpot, 6", 1931 – 1940. $45.00 – 55.00.
#1394S Swan flowerpot, 4", 1931 – 1940. $30.00 – 40.00.
#1426S oval Japanese garden, 9"x6½", 1931 – 1934. $55.00 – 65.00.
#1427L oblong Japanese garden, 10½"x8½", 1931 – 1934. $60.00 – 75.00.
#1427S oblong Japanese garden, 8½"x6", 1931 – 1934. $55.00 – 65.00.

See also the section on Handmade Hand-Decorated Artware (page 242) for the following items.
#1453 rose bowl, 5½" Stangl handmade, 1931 – 1935. $55.00 – 65.00.
#1454 violet jar, 5¼" Stangl handmade, 1931 – 1935. $55.00 – 70.00.
#1455 ovoid vase, 5" Stangl handmade, 1931 – 1935. $60.00 – 75.00.
#1456 basket, 7" Stangl handmade, 1931 – 1935. $70.00 – 85.00.
#1457 low jar, 2 handles, 4¾" tall, Stangl handmade, 1931 – 1935. $80.00 – 100.00.
#1458 flower bowl, 7¼" diameter, Stangl handmade, 1931 – 1935. $70.00 – 85.00.
#1460 candleholder, 4 ½" Stangl handmade, 1931 – 1935. $65.00 – 80.00.
#1461 flower pot, attached saucer 4½" Stangl handmade, 1931 – 1935. $55.00 – 65.00.
#1462 flower vase, small neck, 6¾" Stangl handmade, 1931 – 1935. $60.00 – 75.00.
#1463 flower vase, tall neck, 8" Stangl handmade, 1931 – 1935. $80.00 – 90.00.
#1464 bowl, 6" diameter, Stangl handmade, 1931 – 1935. $60.00 – 75.00.
#1465 vase, straight top, 5½" Stangl handmade, 1931 – 1935. $60.00 – 75.00.
#1466 tall vase, 10¼" Stangl handmade, 1931 – 1935. $85.00 – 95.00.

The #1515 flowerpot/jardiniere shapes were developed as pot covers for the florist industry. They were designed to fit over standard clay flowerpot sizes commonly in use at the time. When first introduced in 1931, the pots were produced with a drainage hole and matching saucers. By 1934, the drainage holes and saucers were available only by special-order so there is now a shortage of saucers to pots.

#1515 jardiniere, 11", 1931 – 1938. $95.00 – 110.00.
#1515 jardiniere, 9", 1931 – 1938. $65.00 – 80.00.
#1515 jardiniere, 8", 1931 – 1938. $50.00 – 60.00.
#1515 jardiniere, 7", 1931 – 1938. $35.00 – 45.00.
#1515 jardiniere, 6½", 1931 – 1938. $35.00 – 45.00.
#1515 jardiniere, 5½", 1931 – 1938. $25.00 – 30.00.
#1515 jardiniere, 4½", 1931 – 1938. $15.00 – 20.00.
#1515 jardiniere, 3½", 1931 – 1938. $20.00 – 25.00.
#1515 jardiniere, low, 11", 1931 – 1938. $85.00 – 95.00.
#1515 jardiniere, low, 9", 1931 – 1938. $60.00 – 75.00.
#1515 jardiniere, 11", 1931 – 1938. $25.00 – 35.00.
#1515 saucer, 9", 1931 – 1938. $20.00 – 25.00.
#1515 saucer, 8", 1931 – 1938. $15.00 – 18.00.
#1515 saucer, 7", 1931 – 1938. $15.00 – 18.00.
#1515 saucer, 6½", 1931 – 1938. $15.00 – 20.00.
#1515 saucer, 5½", 1931 – 1938. $12.00 – 15.00.
#1515 saucer, 4½", 1931 – 1938. $10.00 – 12.00.
#1515 saucer, 3½", 1931 – 1938. $10.00 – 12.00.

Two #1515 jardinieres, Blue-of-the-Sky Matte, 6½", $35.00 – 45.00, and Apple Green, 8", $50.00 – 60.00.

Three #1452 Cereal Set 9" canisters with underglaze decorated floral motif and Parchment glaze, available 1933 – 1935. Martin Stangl designed this particular motif; he had done preliminary sketches of this floral device while still at Haeger Pottery during 1914 – 1918. Decorated, $85.00 – 95.00 each. Also produced in solid-color glazes, 1931 – 1935, $65.00 – 85.00 each.

Blue-of-the-Sky #1515 9" jardiniere with matching saucer. $85.00 – 100.00.

Acanthus Artware

See also the section on Decorated Acanthus Artware in the Hand-Decorated Artware chapter for more information on these shapes in combination glazes.

Group of Acanthus shapes: #1544 deep bowl, Turquoise, $40.00 – 50.00; #1540 oval vase, Yellow Orange, $60.00 – 75.00; #1549 candleholder, Ivory, $30.00 – 35.00; #1548 rose bowl, Satin White, $40.00 – 50.00.

Some shown on page 218:

#1537 Acanthus vase, 7", 1931 – 1935. $60.00 – 75.00.
#1540 Acanthus oval vase, 7"x7", 1931 – 1935. $60.00 – 75.00.
#1541 Acanthus oval vase, 9"x9", 1931 – 1935. $70.00 – 85.00.
#1542 Acanthus oval vase, 10"x7", 1931 – 1935. $80.00 – 90.00.
#1543 Acanthus deep bowl, 9"x4", 1931 – 1935. $60.00 – 75.00.
#1544 Acanthus deep bowl, 7½"x4", 1931 – 1935. $40.00 – 50.00.
#1545 Acanthus deep bowl, 14"x10", 1931 – 1935. $130.00 – 160.00.
#1546 Acanthus bud vase, 9½", 1931 – 1935. $60.00 – 75.00.
#1547 Acanthus bud vase, 7", 1931 – 1935. $55.00 – 70.00.
#1548 Acanthus rose bowl, 5½"x4½", 1931 – 1935. $40.00 – 50.00.
#1549 Acanthus candleholder, 4", 1931 – 1935. $70.00 – 85.00 pair.

1932 Introductions

The items #1570 – 1584 were special-order for Macy's Department Store in 1932. Some of the items, such as the #1574 swirl vase, #1575 and #1577 candleholders, and #1581 oval bowls, became part of Stangl's general product assortment during the latter 1930s. The #1570 flowerpots each have an internal "saucer" support ring that elevates the flowerpot and allows drainage.

Macy's #1570 6½" flowerpot in Apple Green glaze (interior support ring, inset). $40.00 – 50.00.

Not Shown:

Novelty Smoking Stands, #1567 Elephant table, 25"; #1568 Scotty table, 23"; #1569 Bear table, 26", 1932 only. $2,000.00 – $2,500.00 each.
#1570 flowerpot, 8¼" made for Macy's, 1932 only. $60.00 – 75.00.
#1570 flowerpot, 7½" made for Macy's, 1932 only. $55.00 – 65.00.
#1570 flowerpot, 6½" made for Macy's, 1932 only. $40.00 – 50.00.
#1571 round vase, 10" made for Macy's, 1932 only. $130.00 – 150.00.
#1572 oval bowl, 2 handles, 10" made for Macy's, 1932 only. $70.00 – 85.00.
#1572 oval bowl, 2 handles, 8" made for Macy's, 1932 only. $60.00 – 75.00.
#1573 candleholder, 2 handles, 5" made for Macy's, 1932 only. $80.00 – 100.00 pair.
#1573 candleholder, 2 handles, 4" made for Macy's, 1932 only. $85.00 – 95.00 pair.
#1574 Swirl vase, 12" made for Macy's, 1932 only. $130.00 – 150.00.
#1574 Swirl vase, 9" made for Macy's, 1932 – 1937. $65.00 – 80.00.
#1575 candleholder, 4" made for Macy's, 1932 – 1938. $85.00 – 95.00 pair.
#1576 bowl, 9" made for Macy's, 1932 only. $60.00 – 75.00.
#1577 candleholder, 7" made for Macy's, 1932 – 1938. $95.00 – 130.00 pair.
#1578 bud vase, 7" made for Macy's, 1932 only. $60.00 – 75.00.
#1579 flower vase, 9" made for Macy's, 1932 only. $70.00 – 85.00.
#1579 flower vase, 7" made for Macy's, 1932 only. $60.00 – 75.00.

Tangerine with Turquoise lining #1571 round vase, 8", made for Macy's 1932 only. $90.00 – 125.00.
Courtesy of the Brian and Cristi Hahn collection.

Maize with Ivory interior #1579 flower vase, 4½", made for Macy's, 1932 only. $55.00 – 65.00.

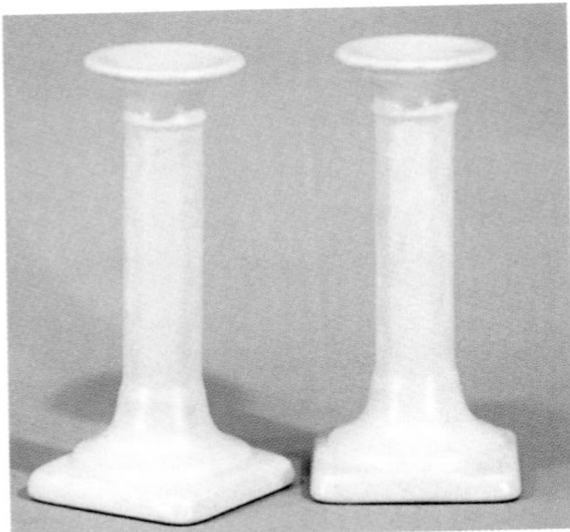

Satin White #1584 candleholders, square base, 7½", made for Macy's, 1932 only. $85.00 – 95.00 pair. Courtesy of the Hill-Fulper-Stangl Museum.

The handmade pieces nearly always have ridged "finger-marks" and applied handles and are sometimes marked with the hand-scrawled "Stangl." The mold-cast pieces are always smooth with cast handles and in-mold shape numbers.

In-mold mark on base of mold-cast #1588 tall jug.

Mold-cast #1588 tall jug on left in Apple Green glaze, $25.00 – 30.00, handmade #1588 tall jug on right in Tangerine, $40.00 – 50.00.

Hand-carved "Stangl Pottery" on the base of a handmade #1585 low jug.

Not Shown:
#1580 flower bowl on stand, 9", made for Macy's, 1932 only. $150.00 – 175.00.
#1581 oval bowl, 12", made for Macy's, 1932 – 1937. $60.00 – 75.00.
#1581 oval bowl, 8", made for Macy's, 1932 – 1937. $40.00 – 50.00.
#1582 round bowl, made for Macy's, 1932 only. $65.00 – 80.00.
#1583 bowl on square stand, 9", made for Macy's, 1932 only. $120.00 – 145.00.
#1585ES low jug, 3" Stangl handmade, 1932 – 1935. $25.00 – 35.00.
#1585S low jug, 3¾" Stangl handmade, 1932 – 1935. $30.00 – 40.00.
#1585 open sugar, 2½"x 3½" Stangl handmade, 1932 – 1935. $25.00 – 35.00.
#1586M low jug, 4" Stangl handmade, 1932 – 1935. $55.00 – 65.00.
#1587L low jug, 4¾" Stangl handmade, 1932 – 1935. $60.00 – 75.00.
#1588 tall jug, 4½" Stangl handmade, 1932 – 1935. $40.00 – 50.00.
#1585ES low jug, 3" mold-cast, 1933 – 1942. $20.00 – 25.00.
#1585S low jug, mold-cast, 3¾", 1933 – 1942. $20.00 – 25.00.
#1585 open sugar, mold-cast, 2½"x 3½", 1933 – 1942. $20.00 – 25.00.
#1588 tall jug, 4½" mold-cast, 1933 – 1942. $25.00 – 30.00.
#1590 Swirl sand jar, 15", 1932 – 1938. $200.00 – 275.00.
#1590 Swirl sand jar, 9", 1932 – 1938. $125.00 – 150.00.
#1592 Flared sand jar, 2 handles, 22", 1932 only. $500.00 – 600.00.
#1593 Rope handle sand jar, 16", 1932 – 1938. $375.00 – 400.00.

Turquoise glaze #1590 Swirl sand jar, 22", 1932 – 1938. $400.00 – 450.00. Courtesy of the Hill-Fulper-Stangl Museum.

Not Shown:

#1595 4-sided table, 24", 1932 only. $2,000.00 – 2,500.00.

#1596 round table, 24", 1932 only. $2,000.00 – 2,500.00.

#1634 bowl, 8¼" diameter, special-order for Bamberger's Department Store, Newark, New Jersey, 1932 – 1933. $85.00 – 95.00.

#1635 fluted vase large 6½", made for Bamberger's, 1932 – 1933. $130.00 – 160.00.

#1636 fluted vase small, 5", made for Bamberger's, 1932 – 1933. $110.00 – 135.00.

#1637 candleholder, 5", made for Bamberger's, 1932 – 1933. $70.00 – 85.00.

#1638 vase, 6", made for Bamberger's, 1932 – 1933. $85.00 – 95.00.

#1639 rose bowl, 5", made for Bamberger's, 1932 – 1933. $70.00 – 85.00.

Apple Green #1594 8-sided 24" table showing antlered deer. This particular table has been in the Stangl family for over 70 years. Christl Stangl Bacheler said, "That poor little table sat out on the patio for years! It's amazing how durable and weatherproof Stangl Ware really was!" $2,000.00 – 2,500.00. Courtesy of Merrill and Christl Stangl Bacheler.

1933 Introductions

The items #1640 to #1643 were special-order for Macy's Department Store. The #1640, #1642, and #1643 planters and flowerpots were also sold as Stangl Pottery catalog items throughout the 1930s. See the section on Macy's Hand-Painted Flowerpots and Vases (page 226), also produced during 1933.

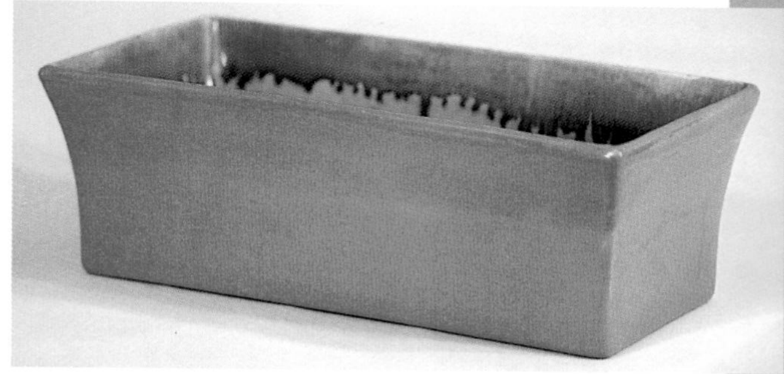

Tangerine with green lining #1640 flower box, 10"x4" made for Macy's 1933 – 1940. $60.00 – 75.00.

Not Shown:

#1641 vase, wide top, 9" made for Macy's, 1933 only. $85.00 – 95.00.

#1642 flowerpot, straight top, 8" made for Macy's, 1933 – 1940. $55.00 – 65.00.

#1642 flowerpot, straight top, 6" made for Macy's, 1933 – 1940. $45.00 – 55.00.

#1642 flowerpot, straight top, 5" made for Macy's, 1933 – 1940. $25.00 – 30.00.

#1642 flowerpot, straight top, 4" made for Macy's, 1933 – 1940. $20.00 – 25.00.

#1642 saucer, straight top, 8" made for Macy's, 1933 – 1940. $10.00 – 15.00.

#1642 saucer, straight top, 6" made for Macy's, 1933 – 1940. $8.00 – 12.00.

#1642 saucer, straight top, 5" made for Macy's, 1933 – 1940. $8.00 – 10.00.

#1642 saucer, straight top, 4" made for Macy's, 1933 – 1940. $6.00 – 8.00.

#1643 flowerpot, scroll top, 8" made for Macy's, 1933 – 1940. $55.00 – 65.00.

#1643 flowerpot, scroll top, 6" made for Macy's, 1933 – 1940. $45.00 – 55.00.

#1643 flowerpot, scroll top, 5" made for Macy's, 1933 – 1940. $25.00 – 30.00.

#1643 flowerpot, scroll top, 4" made for Macy's, 1933 – 1940. $20.00 – 25.00.

#1643 saucer, scroll top, 8" made for Macy's, 1933 – 1940. $10.00 – 15.00.

#1643 saucer, scroll top, 6" made for Macy's, 1933 – 1940. $8.00 – 12.00.

#1643 saucer, scroll top, 5" made for Macy's, 1933 – 1940. $8.00 – 10.00.

#1643 saucer, scroll top, 4" made for Macy's, 1933 – 1940. $6.00 – 8.00.

Macy's #1643 scroll top flowerpot and saucer in Tangerine. $30.00 – 40.00 per set.

#1644 Swirl sandwich tray, 12" with pottery handle, Stangl handmade, 1933 – 1935. $150.00 – 175.00.

#1645 Swirl sandwich plate, 8" Stangl handmade, 1933 – 1935. $30.00 – 40.00.

#1648 Step-back vase, 9" Stangl handmade, 1933 – 1935. $120.00 – 145.00.

#1649 Curvy vase, 9" Stangl handmade, 1933 – 1935. $110.00 – 135.00.

#1665 cylinder vase, 8" Stangl handmade, 1933 – 1935. $70.00 – 85.00.

#1666 Pitcher vase, 9½" Stangl handmade, 1933 – 1935. $95.00 – 115.00.

#1667 Cup vase, 7" Stangl handmade, 1933 – 1935. $85.00 – 95.00.

#1668 vase, handle, ring bottom, 9" Stangl handmade, 1933 – 1935. $120.00 – 145.00.

#1669 vase, handle, ring top, 7" Stangl handmade, 1933 – 1935. $110.00 – 135.00.

Not Shown:

#1683 vase, 8½", mold-cast, made for Macy's, 1933 only. $85.00 – 95.00.

#1670 vase, low handles, 7" Stangl handmade, 1933 – 1935. $95.00 – 110.00.

#1710 vase, 3 handles large, 9" Stangl handmade, 1933 – 1935. $125.00 – 145.00.

#1711 vase, 3 handles small, 6" Stangl handmade, 1933 – 1935. $75.00 – 85.00.

#1712 vase, 2 handles, 6" Stangl handmade, 1933 – 1935. $65.00 – 80.00.

Green Matte glaze #1712 vase, 2 handles, 6" mold-cast, 1935 – 1939. $55.00 – 65.00.

Modern Vases

See also the Hand-Decorated Artware, Giftware, and Novelties chapter for the following shapes decorated with the Sunburst glaze, or the Brushed Gold Decorated Artware chapter for these shapes finished with platinum or gold.

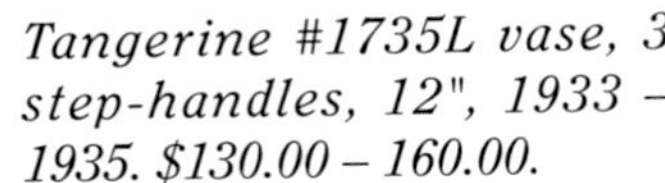

Tangerine #1735L vase, 3 step-handles, 12", 1933 – 1935. $130.00 – 160.00.

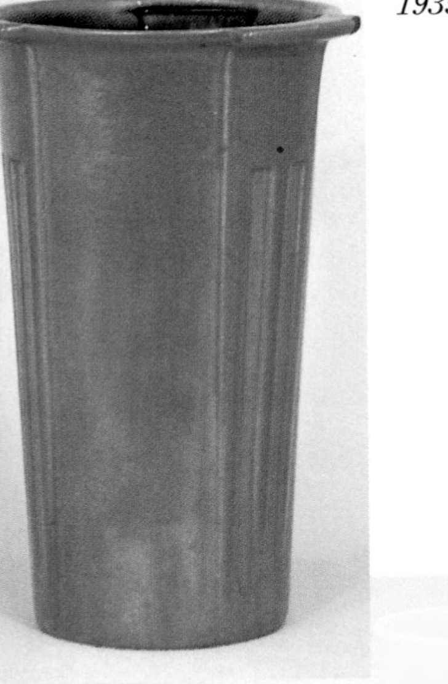

Rust #1735S vase, 3 step-handles, 9", 1933 – 1935. $85.00 – 95.00.
Courtesy of the Ben and Pauline Jensen collection.

Tangerine #1737 ball bowl, 3 handles, 6½", 1933 – 1935. $65.00 – 80.00.

Tangerine #1738 7½" bowl, and Maize #1739L 9½" vase, $100.00 – 125.00 each.
Courtesy of the Hill-Fulper-Stangl Museum.

Rust with Turquoise lining #1740 bowl, 3 step-feet, 9" diameter, 1933 – 1937. $85.00 – 95.00.

Not Shown:

#1733 cylinder vase, 2 flat handles, 12", 1933 only. $100.00 – 125.00.

#1733 cylinder vase, 2 flat handles, 10", 1933 only. $80.00 – 90.00.

#1733 cylinder vase, 2 flat handles, 6", 1933 only. $60.00 – 75.00.

#1734 cylinder vase, 2 flat handles, 8", 1933 only. $70.00 – 85.00.

#1736 vase, cone, 3 step-handles, 12", 1933 only. $130.00 – 160.00.

#1736 vase, cone, 3 step-handles, 10", 1933 only. $100.00 – 125.00.

#1736 vase, cone, 3 step-handles, 8", 1933 only. $80.00 – 90.00.

#1738 bowl, 3-groove foot, 7½" diameter, 1933 only. $100.00 – 125.00.

#1739L vase, 3-groove foot, 9¼" high, 1933 only. $100.00 – 125.00.

#1739S vase, 3-groove foot, 8" high, 1933 only. $80.00 – 100.00.

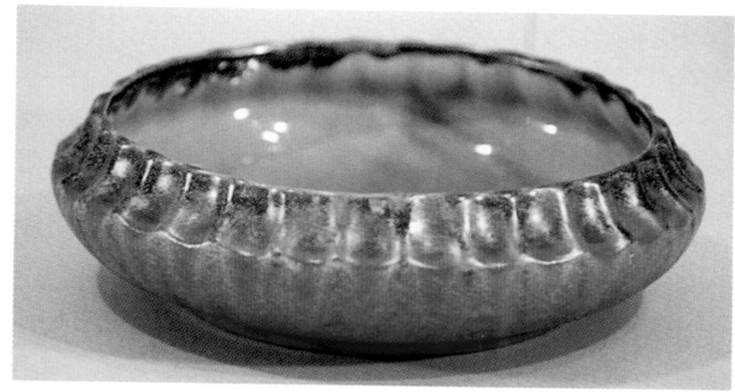

Variegated Rust with green lining #1741 bowl, pie crust rim, 8" diameter, 1933 – 1937. $55.00 – 65.00. Courtesy of the Marcena North collection.

The #1744 Wolf cigarette holder, #1745 Small Pig ashtrays, and #1746 Large Pig ashtrays were intended to be used together as smoking sets. The #1745 Small Pigs were ideal for bridge parties, while the #1746 Large Pig ashtrays were better suited to poker games where most participants smoked cigars.

The #1745 Small Pig ashtray shape was very popular during the late 1930s, and was consequently "mimicked" by other potteries. The most common #1745 Small Pig ashtray knock-offs were made of pink, blue or white clay with clear glaze or white clay with murky-colored glaze and are always marked with an in-mold "USA." Also, the face detail is less distinct on the knock-offs. Stangl's #1745 Small Pig ashtrays have well-defined eyes, nostrils, and mouths. Even if the glaze is thick, these features are usually evident. The knock-offs have only little indents for eyes, and the snout is much smaller than Stangl's. Overall, the glazing and workmanship of the knock-off pig ashtrays are greatly inferior to that of Stangl's #1745 Small Pig ashtrays.

#1744 Wolf cigarette holder, 9", Silver Green, made during 1933 only. $2,000.00 – 2,500.00. Courtesy of the Hill-Fulper-Stangl Museum.

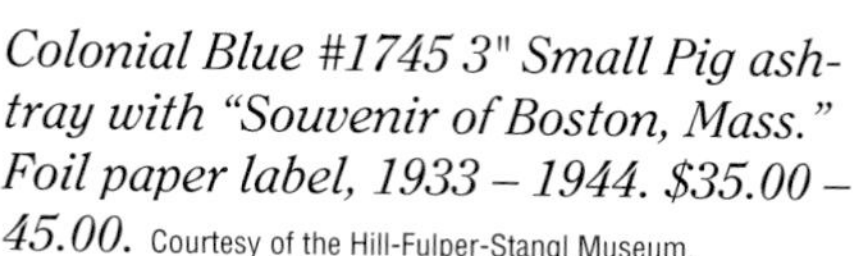

Colonial Blue #1745 3" Small Pig ashtray with "Souvenir of Boston, Mass." Foil paper label, 1933 – 1944. $35.00 – 45.00. Courtesy of the Hill-Fulper-Stangl Museum.

Two #1746 Large Pig ashtrays, Green Matte on left, Apple Green on right, 5½", 1933 – 1934. $150.00 – 175.00 each. Courtesy of the Robert and Tammie Cruser collection.

Comparison of Stangl's #1745 Small Pig ashtray face (left) and knock-off (right). Courtesy of the Cruser collection.

Silver Green #1749L Cabbage salad plate, 9", 1933 – 1934. $40.00 – 50.00 Courtesy of the Hill-Fulper-Stangl Museum.

Not Shown:

#1742 bowl, pie crust rim, 12" diameter, 1933 – 1937. $85.00 – 95.00.
#1743 bowl, oblong, 2 handles, 6¼"x4", 1933 only. $55.00 – 65.00.
#1747 Cabbage salad bowl, 1933 – 1934. $70.00 – 85.00.
#1748 Cabbage mayonnaise bowl, 1933 – 1934. $55.00 – 65.00.
#1749M Cabbage salad plate, 8", 1933 – 1934. $40.00 – 50.00.
#1751 bowl, oblong 8-sided, 16", 1933 – 1934. $100.00 – 125.00.
#1751 bowl, oblong 8-sided, 14", 1933 – 1934. $85.00 – 95.00.
#1757 bowl, 8"x3", 1933 – 1935. $65.00 – 80.00.

Satin White #1758 urn vase, 2 handles, 12", 1933 – 1939. $85.00 – 95.00. Courtesy of the Brian and Cristi Hahn collection.

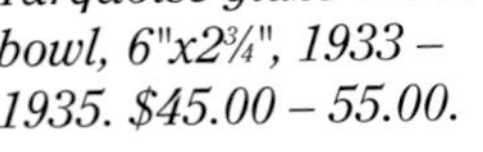

Turquoise glaze #1757 bowl, 6"x2¾", 1933 – 1935. $45.00 – 55.00.

Not Shown:

#1758 urn vase, 2 handles, 22", 1933 – 1937. $300.00 – 350.00.
#1758 urn vase, 2 handles, 16", 1933 – 1942. $175.00 – 200.00.
#1762 Tapering pitcher, 8" Stangl handmade, 1933 – 1935. $125.00 – 150.00.
#1763L vase, 5 indents, large, 8" Stangl handmade, 1933 – 1935. $150.00 – 175.00.
#1763S vase, 5 indents, small, 6" Stangl handmade, 1933 – 1935. $130.00 – 150.00.
#1764 vase, 5 indents, round 7" Stangl handmade, 1933 – 1935. $140.00 – 165.00.
#1765EL jardiniere, 9" Stangl handmade, 1933 – 1935. $120.00 – 145.00.
#1765L jardiniere, 7" Stangl handmade, 1933 – 1935. $70.00 – 85.00.
#1765M jardiniere, 5" Stangl handmade, 1933 – 1935. $55.00 – 65.00.
#1765S jardiniere, 4" Stangl handmade, 1933 – 1935. $40.00 – 50.00.

The #1765 jardinieres are similar to the #1238 three-handle jars, but the top rim is taller and the handles are thinner on the #1765 jardinieres.

Animal-shape Flowerpots

Made only during 1933 – 1935. See the section on Sunburst (pages 255 – 264) for these items with that glaze and more photos shown there.

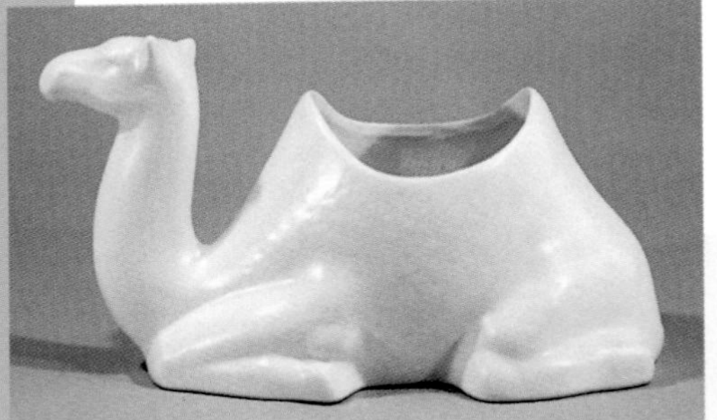

Satin White #1773 Camel flowerpot, 14", 1933 – 1935. $225.00 – 275.00.

Apple Green #1775 Scottie Dog flowerpot, 7½"x6", 1933 – 1935. $190.00 – 225.00. Courtesy of the Hill-Fulper-Stangl Museum.

Satin White #1777 Pig flowerpot, 5", 1933 – 1935. $200.00 – 225.00. Courtesy of the Bond collection.

Green Matte #1778 Sparrow flowerpot, 6½"x5", 1933 – 1935. $150.00 – 175.00.

Not Shown:

#1770 Fish flowerpot, 9", 1933 – 1935. $225.00 – 275.00.
#1771 Swan flowerpot, 10"x13", 1933 – 1936. $190.00 – 225.00.
#1772 Rabbit flowerpot, 1933 – 1935. $225.00 – 275.00.
#1776 Cow flowerpot, 5½"x6½", 1933 – 1935. $275.00 – 300.00.

Not Shown:

#1783 bud vase, 6" Stangl handmade, 1933 – 1935. $55.00 – 70.00.

#1784 candleholder, 6" Stangl handmade, 1933 – 1935. $100.00 – 125.00.

#1785 bowl, no handles, 3½" Stangl handmade, 1933 – 1935. $40.00 – 50.00.

#1791 vase, 2 handles, 4¼" Stangl handmade, 1933 – 1935. $50.00 – 60.00.

#1792EL flowerpot, 8" Stangl handmade, 1933 – 1934. $80.00 – 90.00.

#1792L flowerpot, 6" Stangl handmade, 1933 – 1934. $60.00 – 75.00.

#1792M flowerpot, 5" Stangl handmade, 1933 – 1934. $55.00 – 65.00.

#1792S flowerpot, 4" Stangl handmade, 1933 – 1934. $40.00 – 50.00.

#1792ES flowerpot, 3" Stangl handmade, 1933 – 1934. $35.00 – 45.00.

#1792 miniature flowerpot, 2½" Stangl handmade, 1925 – 1926. $60.00 – 75.00.

#1792 miniature flowerpot, 1¾" Stangl handmade, 1925 – 1926. $130.00 – 150.00.

#1792EL flowerpot, 8" mold-cast, 1934 – 1944. $45.00 – 55.00.

#1792L flowerpot, 6" mold-cast, 1934 – 1944. $35.00 – 45.00.

#1792M flowerpot, 5" mold-cast, 1934 – 1944. $25.00 – 35.00.

#1792S flowerpot, 4" mold-cast, 1934 – 1944. $20.00 – 25.00.

#1792ES flowerpot, 3" mold-cast, 1934 – 1944. $25.00 – 35.00.

#1792 miniature flowerpot, 2" mold-cast, 1934 – 1944. $25.00 – 35.00.

Group of mold-cast #1792 flowerpots.6", 4", and 2" miniature. Values listed on this page.

Tangerine #1783 bud vase, 6" mold-cast, 1935 – 1938. $45.00 – 55.00.

1934 Introductions

Solid-color glazed #1800 Cabbage Leaf servers produced during the 1930s have pottery twig-shape handles. Solid-color #1800 servers of the 1960s and 1970s were affixed with some type of metal tidbit handle. See also Cabbage #5197 on page 183.

Not Shown:

#1800 Cabbage Leaf round triple relish, 12½", 1934 – 1936. $35.00 – 45.00.

#1800 Cabbage Leaf double relish, 9½", 1934 – 1936. $20.00 – 25.00.

#1800 Cabbage Leaf single relish, 13", 1934 – 1936. $25.00 – 35.00.

#1800 Cabbage Leaf cake stand, 10", 1934 – 1936. $30.00 – 40.00.

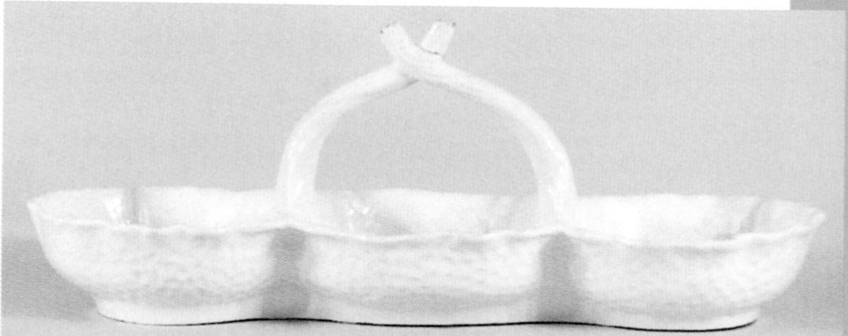

Ivory #1800 Cabbage Leaf oblong triple relish, 14", 1934 – 1936. $35.00 – 45.00.

The Selma Robb/Fisk Line

Early in 1934, the pottery and glassware sales brokerage firm Fisk, Marks & Rosenfeld, Inc., 98 Fifth Avenue, New York, contracted with Fulper Pottery Company to manufacture an exclusive art pottery line. The administrators of Fisk, Marks & Rosenfeld, Inc. were David Fisk, Harry Marks, and Allan Rosenfeld. They provided Fulper Pottery with the designs and glaze specifications for the artware and marketed it to gift and department stores under their exclusive Selma Robb brand name. Each piece was to be marked with the in-mold Selma Robb trade name and a gold-foil paper label.

Selma Robb in-mold trademark.

Original Selma Robb gold-foil paper label.

Early in 1935, Fisk, Marks & Rosenfeld, Inc. was reorganized. At that time, Harry Marks and Allan Rosenfeld left the company and Morton Fisk, David's brother, joined the firm which incorporated as Fisk & Fisk, Inc. By mid-1935, Morton and David Fisk (as Fisk & Fisk, Inc.) entered into a new contract with Fulper Pottery Company. At that time, the molds for the former Selma Robb shapes were re-tooled, and those shapes were then cast bearing the Fisk name. These shapes can therefore be found marked either "Selma Robb" or "Fisk."

The Selma Robb and Fisk artware products were never physically touched by either of those companies. Being strictly sales agents, Fisk, Marks & Rosenfeld, Inc., and later Fisk & Fisk, procured the orders from gift shop and department store retailers, Fulper produced the artware, shipped it to the gift shops and department stores, and invoiced the shops and stores directly. Fulper Pottery Company handled all the bookkeeping, received payment from the retailers, and then paid Fisk, Marks & Rosenfeld, Inc. or Fisk & Fisk 30% commission, earned for simply originating each sale. Fulper Pottery Company was prevented by contract to independently wholesale Fisk or Selma Robb items. Fulper Pottery was allowed, however, to retail Fisk and Selma Robb seconds at the Flemington Outlet.

In addition to the old Selma Robb shapes, Morton and David Fisk added seven more shapes to their Stangl Pottery "Fisk Line" in 1935 and six more shapes in 1936. Fulper Pottery Company ceased production of the "Fisk Line" during 1937.

These shapes can be found marked either "Selma Robb" or "Fisk." Value is the same for either. Presence of an original Selma Robb or Fisk paper label can add $20.00 – 30.00 to the value of a piece.

#1796S bowl, ball feet, 9", made for Fisk only, 1934 – 1937. $130.00 – 150.00. From the Stangl and Fulper archival collection, courtesy the Wheaton Village Museum of American Glass.

Surf White #1798 candleholders, 1¾"x4¼", made for Fisk only, 1934 – 1935. $130.00 – 150.00 pair. Courtesy of the Hill-Fulper-Stangl Museum.

Surf White #1806 tall candleholder, rope, 7½", for Selma Robb 1934 – 1935, for Fisk 1935 – 1937. $130.00 – 150.00 pair. Courtesy of the Hill-Fulper-Stangl Museum.

Apple Green #1810 vase, straight, leaves & berries, 8½", for Selma Robb 1934 – 1935, with original Selma Robb gold-foil paper label (ivory lining, inset). Also made for Fisk 1935 – 1937. $130.00 – 160.00. Courtesy of the Hill-Fulper-Stangl Museum.

Selma Robb and Fisk shapes introduced from 1934 through 1936 are listed in this section through shape #2081 on page 160.

Not Shown:

#1796L bowl, ball feet, 13", made for Fisk only, 1934 – 1937. $150.00 – 175.00.

#1801 vase, flare, rope, 7", for Selma Robb 1934 – 1935, for Fisk 1935 – 1937. $100.00 – 125.00.

#1802 oval bowl, flare, rope, 12"x7", for Selma Robb 1934 – 1935, for Fisk 1935 – 1937. $100.00 – 125.00.

#1803 footed vase, flare, rope, 15", for Selma Robb 1934 – 1935, for Fisk 1935 – 1937. $175.00 – 200.00.

#1804 ovoid vase, rope, 18", for Selma Robb 1934 – 1935, for Fisk 1935 – 1937. $175.00 – 200.00.

#1805 oval candleholder, 3½", for Selma Robb 1934 – 1935, for Fisk 1935 – 1937. $120.00 – 140.00 pair.

#1807 vase, flare, shell, 11", for Selma Robb 1934 – 1935, for Fisk 1935 – 1937. $130.00 – 150.00.

#1808 oval bowl, shell, 11"x7", for Selma Robb 1934 – 1935, for Fisk 1935 – 1937. $120.00 – 140.00.

#1809 round bowl, leaves & berries, 9", for Selma Robb 1934 – 1935, for Fisk 1935 – 1937. $95.00 – 130.00.

Rust glaze #1811 horn, 5½", for Selma Robb 1934 – 1935, for Fisk 1935 – 1937. $80.00 – 100.00.

Ivory #1818 vase, swirl ball, 5½", for Selma Robb 1934 – 1935, also for Fisk 1935 – 1937. $110.00 – 135.00. Courtesy of the Hill-Fulper-Stangl Museum.

Persian Yellow #1818 vase, swirl ball, 5½", for Selma Robb 1934 – 1935, also for Fisk 1935 – 1937. $110.00 – 135.00. Courtesy of the Hill-Fulper-Stangl Museum.

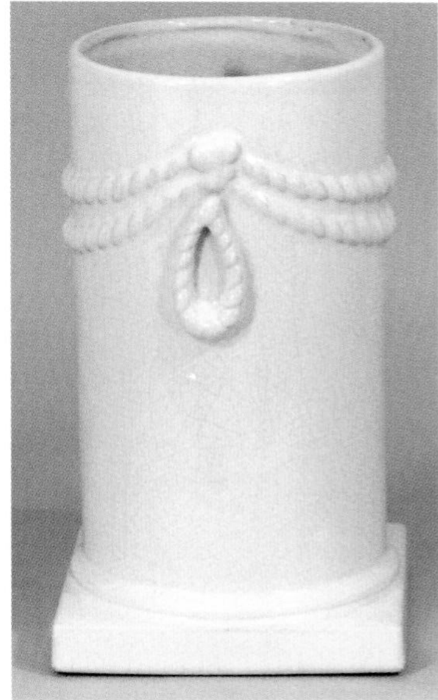

Ivory #2005 cylinder vase, rope, 9", made for Fisk only, 1935 – 1937. $130.00 – 160.00.

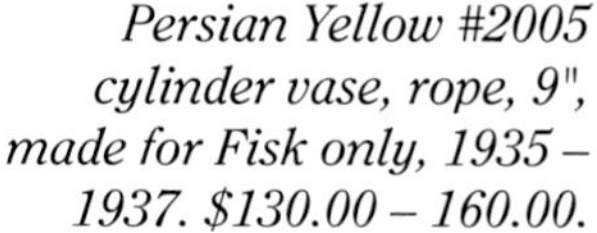

Persian Yellow #2005 cylinder vase, rope, 9", made for Fisk only, 1935 – 1937. $130.00 – 160.00.

Not Shown:

#1812 vase, urn, 2 handles, 13", for Selma Robb 1934 – 1935, for Fisk 1935 – 1937. $150.00 – 175.00.
#1813 oval bowl, 2 handles, 12"x8", for Selma Robb 1934 – 1935, for Fisk 1935 – 1937. $110.00 – 135.00.
#1814 urn, 2 handles, plain, 8", for Selma Robb 1934 – 1935, for Fisk 1935 – 1937. $120.00 – 145.00.
#1815 triple candleholder, 6½", for Selma Robb 1934 – 1935, for Fisk 1935 – 1937. $80.00 – 100.00 each.
#1816 urn, plain, ribbed, 9", for Selma Robb 1934 – 1935, for Fisk 1935 – 1937. $110.00 – 135.00.
#1817 vase, flare top, plain, 8", for Selma Robb 1934 – 1935, for Fisk 1935 – 1937. $110.00 – 135.00.
#1819 swirl, candleholder, 4", for Selma Robb 1934 – 1935, for Fisk 1935 – 1937. $100.00 – 125.00 pair.
#1820 bud vase, 7", for Selma Robb 1934 – 1935, for Fisk 1935 – 1937. $100.00 – 125.00.
#1821 candy jar with cover, 4¾", for Selma Robb 1934 – 1935, for Fisk 1935 – 1937. $150.00 – 175.00.
#2001 flowerpot, leaves, 5½", made for Fisk only, 1935 – 1937. $95.00 – 110.00.
#2002 ball vase, leaves, 10", made for Fisk only, 1935 – 1937. $120.00 – 145.00.
#2003 flare vase, leaves, 11", made for Fisk only, 1935 – 1937. $150.00 – 175.00.
#2004 oval vase, rope, 7", made for Fisk only, 1935 – 1937. $130.00 – 150.00.
#2006 urn vase, wave bands, 12", made for Fisk only, 1935 – 1937. $175.00 – 200.00.
#2007 bowl, wave bands, 12" diameter, made for Fisk only, 1935 – 1937. $120.00 – 145.00.
#2075 oblong vase, 8½", made for Fisk only, 1936 – 1937. $130.00 – 160.00.
#2076 oblong bowl, 8"x12", made for Fisk only, 1936 – 1937. $120.00 – 145.00.

Not Shown:

#2077 oblong candleholder, 3"x8", made for Fisk only, 1936 – 1937. $130.00 – 150.00 per pair.
#2078 round vase, 11", made for Fisk only, 1936 – 1937. $150.00 – 175.00.
#2079 round vase, draped, 8½", made for Fisk only, 1936 – 1937. $130.00 – 160.00.
#2081 square jar, 8", made for Fisk only, 1936 – 1937. $150.00 – 175.00.
#1852L basket, turned edge, 7½"x10½" Stangl handmade, 1934 – 1935. $160.00 – 185.00.
#1852M basket, turned edge, 6"x8" Stangl handmade, 1934 – 1935. $100.00 – 125.00.
#1852S basket, turned edge, 5½" Stangl handmade, 1934 – 1935. $95.00 – 110.00.
#1853 basket, sides in, 5" Stangl handmade, 1934 – 1935. $80.00 – 90.00.
#1853 basket, sides in, 5" mold-cast, 1935 – 1938. $50.00 – 60.00.
#1854 basket, scroll edge, 5" Stangl handmade, 1934 – 1935. $95.00 – 110.00.
#1855 vase, 2 handle, straight top, 10½" Stangl handmade, 1934 – 1935. $110.00 – 135.00.
#1856 vase, 2 handle, straight top, 7½" Stangl handmade, 1934 – 1935. $80.00 – 90.00.
#1857 vase, 2 handle, straight top, 5" Stangl handmade, 1934 – 1935. $85.00 – 100.00.
#1858 ball vase, neck ring, 2 handles, 6½" Stangl handmade, 1934 – 1935. $75.00 – 85.00.
#1859 vase, pinched top, 2 handles, 7½" Stangl handmade, 1934 – 1935. $100.00 – 135.00.
#1860 vase, pinched top, 2 handles, 3½" Stangl handmade, 1934 – 1935. $75.00 – 85.00.
#1861 pitcher vase, twisted handle, 9" Stangl handmade, 1934 – 1935. $135.00 – 165.00.
#1862 low vase, 3 handles, 4"x3½", Stangl handmade, 1934 – 1935. $35.00 – 45.00.
#1863 vase, flat ball, 3 feet, 3¾" Stangl handmade, 1934 – 1935. $80.00 – 90.00.
#1864 bowl, scroll turning in, 6½" Stangl handmade, 1934 – 1935. $65.00 – 80.00.
#1865 bowl, turned-over edge, 8½" Stangl handmade, 1934 – 1935. $70.00 – 85.00.
#1866 bowl, 3 double rope handles, 7½" Stangl handmade, 1934 – 1935. $125.00 – 150.00.
#1867 bowl, top turned in, 2 handles, 7½" Stangl handmade, 1934 – 1935. $85.00 – 95.00.
#1868 bowl, straight neck, Stangl handmade, 1934 – 1935. $65.00 – 80.00.

Uranium Matte #2080 urn, 2 handles, 10", made for Fisk only, 1936 – 1937. $150.00 – 175.00.

Flower Ware

Martin Stangl introduced the following line of flower blossom-shaped artware and dinnerware shapes in 1934 in combination glaze colors pink, blue, yellow, and purple. The combination glaze colors were very short lived, and these shapes were then produced only in single solid-color glazes. See also the section on Hand-Decorated Combination and Tropical Glazes (page 240). Although #1870 Daisy was a dinnerware pattern, some of the dinnerware accessories were classed as artware. Several of these shapes were also produced in the Terra Rose and brushed gold finishes (pages 349 – 366 and pages 328 – 348).

#1869 Cosmos bowl, 12", 1934 – 1940. $95.00 – 110.00.
#1870 Daisy candleholder, 4", 1934 – 1936. $85.00 – 95.00 pair.
#1870 Daisy oblong triple relish, 1934 – 1936. $35.00 – 45.00.
#1870 Daisy round triple relish, 1934 – 1936. $35.00 – 45.00.
#1870 Daisy double relish, 1934 – 1936. $20.00 – 25.00.
#1870 Daisy single relish, 13", 1934 – 1936. $25.00 – 35.00.
#1870 Daisy cake stand, 10", 1934 – 1936. $30.00 – 40.00.
#1871 Petunia bowl, 12", 1934 – 1936. $95.00 – 110.00.
#1872 Zinnia bowl, 10", 1934 – 1940. $70.00 – 85.00.

Tangerine #1875 Flower candleholders, $45.00 – 55.00 pair; Green Matte #1871 Petunia bowl, 12", $95.00 – 110.00; Variegated Rust #1873 Marsh Rose bowl, 14", $100.00 – 125.00; and Persian Yellow #1878S Tulip bowl, 4", $20.00 – 30.00.

#1873 Marsh Rose bowl, 14", 1934 – 1936. $100.00 – 125.00.
#1874 Wild Rose bowl, 8" (redesigned as #3410 in 1940). 1934 – 1940. $45.00 – 55.00.
#1875 Flower candleholder, 4" (redesigned as #3409 in 1940). 1934 – 1940. $45.00 – 55.00 pair.
#1876 Flower block insert, 4" 1934 – 1936. $55.00 – 65.00.
#1878EL Tulip bowl, 9", 1934 – 1935. $95.00 – 130.00.
#1878L Tulip bowl, 7", 1934 – 1945. $55.00 – 65.00.
#1878M Tulip bowl, 5½", 1934 – 1945. $35.00 – 45.00.
#1878S Tulip bowl, 4", 1934 – 1945. $20.00 – 45.00.
#1879 Phlox candleholder, 5½", 1934 – 1935. $120.00 – 145.00 pair.

1935 Introductions

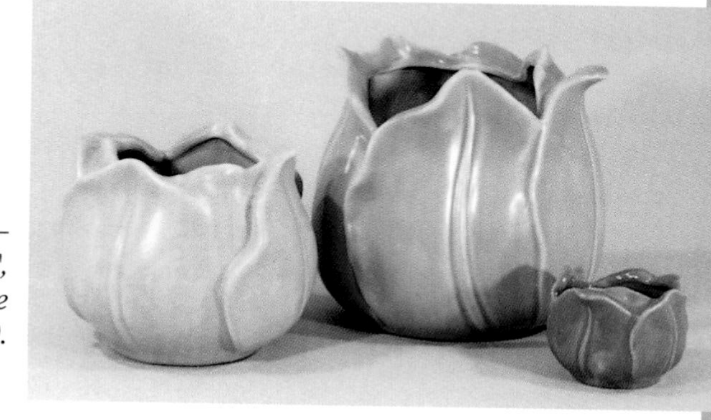

Satin Blue #1878S Tulip bowl, 4", $20.00 – 30.00; Satin Green #1878M Tulip bowl, 5½", $35.00 – 45.00; and Colonial Blue Miniature Tulip vase #3208, $40.00 – 50.00.

Tangerine #1903 vase, 3½", miniature, 1935 only. $190.00 – 225.00. Courtesy of the Hill-Fulper-Stangl Museum.

Blue-of-the-Sky #1905 Twist bud vase, 8", 1935 – 1940. $40.00 – 50.00.

Tangerine with green lining #1906 Scored Ribbed vase, 7½", 1935 – 1938. $65.00 – 80.00. Courtesy of the Ben and Pauline Jensen collection.

Blue-of-the-Sky #1912 vase, shell leaves, 7", 1935 – 1936. $80.00 – 90.00. Courtesy of the Marcena North collection.

Rust #1907S Ball vase, small, 5", and Silver Green #1908 Ball vase large, 9". Both vases based on the old shape #1126. Courtesy of the Marcena North collection.

Surf White #1917 Rabbit flowerpot, 9", 1935 only. $275.00 – 300.00. Courtesy of the Bill Servis, Susan Lewis collection.

Not Shown:
#1904 Twist vase, 9", 1935 – 1937. $70.00 – 85.00.
#1907M Ball vase, ridged, regular, 7" (based on shape #1126), 1935 – 1937. $65.00 – 80.00.
#1907S Ball vase, ridged, small, 5", 1935 – 1937. $65.00 – 80.00.
#1908 Ball vase, ridged, large, 9" (based on shape #1126), 1935 – 1937. $110.00 – 135.00.
#1909 Ball vase, diagonal cut, 8", 1935 only. $110.00 – 135.00.
#1910 bowl, ridged, 9" (based on shape #1126), 1935 only. $70.00 – 85.00.
#1911 ovoid vase, tall, ridged, 7¼" (based on shape #1126), 1935 – 1937. $70.00 – 85.00.
#1913 Twist Pitcher vase, 13½", 1935 – 1936. $200.00 – 250.00.
#1916 Triple Step vase, 12", 1935 only. $160.00 – 180.00.

Garden Center Vase and Bowl

Stangl's "Garden Center" vases and bowls were handmade during 1935 and 1936. The feature of these items is the built-in containers/inserts designed to "hold tall stems straight and make it easy to have artistic arrangements."

The Garden Center items became mold-cast production beginning in 1937. The handmade #1999 vases are smooth; the mold-cast items have molded artificial "finger marks" on the exteriors. The mold-cast #1919 bowls and #1999 vases were also available without the attached inserts. By 1940, the "Garden Center" items were discontinued, and these shapes were produced as "scrolled" vases and bowls, sans inserts.

Interior of #1999 Garden Center vase showing the internal container.

Alice Blue #1919 scrolled bowl, 7" mold-cast, 1937 – 1955. Alice Blue glaze available only during the 1930s. $25.00 – 30.00. Courtesy of the Hill-Fulper-Stangl Museum.

Not Shown:

#1919 Garden Center bowl, 10¼" Stangl handmade, 1935 – 1936. $85.00 – 95.00.
#1919 Garden Center bowl, 8½" Stangl handmade, 1935 – 1936. $70.00 – 85.00.
#1919 Garden Center bowl, 7" Stangl handmade, 1935 – 1936. $50.00 – 60.00.
#1919 Garden Center bowl, 10¼" mold-cast, 1937 – 1940. $35.00 – 45.00.
#1919 Garden Center bowl, 8½" mold-cast, 1937 – 1940. $25.00 – 30.00.
#1919 Garden Center bowl, 7" mold-cast, 1937 – 1940. $25.00 – 30.00.
#1919 scrolled bowl, 10" mold-cast, 1937 – 1955. $35.00 – 45.00.
#1919 scrolled bowl, 8½" mold-cast, 1937 – 1955. $25.00 – 30.00.
#1999 Garden Center vase, 11" Stangl handmade, 1935 – 1936. $110.00 – 135.00.
#1999 Garden Center vase, 9" Stangl handmade, 1935 – 1936. $95.00 – 110.00.
#1999 Garden Center vase, 7 Stangl handmade, 1935 – 1936. $80.00 – 90.00.
#1999 Garden Center vase, 11" mold-cast, 1937 – 1940. $45.00 – 55.00.
#1999 Garden Center vase, 9" mold-cast, 1937 – 1940. $35.00 – 45.00.
#1999 scroll top vase, 11" mold-cast, 1937 – 1945. $45.00 – 55.00.
#1999 scroll top vase, 9" mold-cast, 1937 – 1945. $35.00 – 45.00.
#1999 scroll top vase, 7" mold-cast, 1937 – 1945. $25.00 – 35.00.

Silver Green #1999 Garden Center vase, 7" mold-cast, 1937 – 1940. $25.00 – 35.00. Courtesy of the Brian and Cristi Hahn collection.

The following shapes were primarily decorated with Stangl's Tropical combination glazes. Please see the Hand-Decorated Combination and Tropical Glazes section (page 240) for these items with Tropical glazes. The following values are for items glazed in single solid-colors.

#1940 Raised Fruit salad bowl, 9", 1935 – 1940. $85.00 – 95.00.
#1940 Raised Fruit chop plate, 14", 1935 – 1940. $110.00 – 135.00.
#1940 Raised Fruit salad plate, 1935 – 1940. $35.00 – 45.00.
#1941 Striped footed bowl, 9", 1935 only. $70.00 – 85.00.
#1942 vase, 4 handles, 7", 1935 – 1936. $70.00 – 85.00.
#1943 Striped bowl with collar, 1935 only. $85.00 – 95.00.
#1944L Rope vase, 9", 1935 only. $100.00 – 125.00.
#1944S Rope vase, 7", 1935 – 1936. $85.00 – 95.00.
#1945 bowl, cut-out foot, 11", 1935 – 1936. $70.00 – 85.00.
#1945 candleholder, cut-out foot, 3½", 1935 – 1936. $70.00 – 85.00 pair.
#1946 Dotted compote, 7", 1935 only. $80.00 – 90.00.
#1947 Dotted bowl, 10", 1935 only. $85.00 – 95.00.
#1948 square jardiniere, 1935 only. $35.00 – 45.00.

Colonial Blue #1950 Birthday Cake ring with three candle cups, $75.00 – 90.00.

The Birthday rings were produced in five sizes and could be had with large or small cups. The candle cups were sold separately. They were produced in solid-color glazes from 1935 into the early 1940s. In 1965, the rings were reintroduced as "floral rings" in the Antique Gold finish.

#1950 Birthday Cake ring, 14", 1935 – 1942. $75.00 – 95.00.
#1950 Birthday Cake ring, 10", 1935 – 1942. $50.00 – 60.00.
#1950 Birthday Cake ring, 8", 1935 – 1942. $40.00 – 45.00.
#1950 Birthday Cake ring, 6", 1935 – 1942. $30.00 – 35.00.
#1950 Birthday Cake ring, 4", 1935 – 1942. $20.00 – 25.00.
#1950 candle cup, large, 1935 – 1942. $8.00 – 10.00 each.
#1950 candle cup, small, 1935 – 1942. $8.00 – 10.00 each.

Silver Green #1978 Manning Bowman hors d'oeuvre tray, 7" square, made for Manning Bowman appliances, 1935 – 1940. $15.00 – 20.00.

Gray #1997 Scallop water jug, 1935 – 1936. $175.00 – 200.00.

Colonial Blue #1998 Dog water jug, 1935 – 1936. $250.00 – 300.00.

Miniature Vases

Miniature and small vases suddenly became big business in 1935. Fulper Pottery Company had produced miniature and small vases as special-orders and for their own sales for many years, but the mid to late 1930s saw a great demand for the diminutive novelties. Many were wholesaled to tourist sites and roadside attractions to be sold as souvenirs to travelers. Occasionally these can still be found bearing decals stating the name of the attraction from which they were sold.

Many of the 1935 miniature vase introductions were diminutive versions of earlier Fulper and Stangl Pottery vase shapes. These shapes were chosen for their style compatibility, not their popularity, as some shapes were hardly produced in their original full-sized forms. Shapes #2016 and #2020 were actually larger than the 1920s era Fulper Fayence #934 and #935 vase shapes they were based on. The original 1935 miniature vase assortment included eight truly miniature vase shapes, five small vase shapes, and one miniature ashtray.

Values shown represent miniatures in "standard" solid-color glazes. Values can increase dramatically for miniature vases glazed in rare colors such as Purple, Blue-of-the-Sky, Oxblood, Rose, Orchid or Dusty Pink. The presence of an original Stangl Pottery gold-foil paper label can also sometimes, but not always, increase the value of a miniature by about $20.00 to $30.00.

See the section on Miniature Vases (pages 197 – 204) for photos and a complete list of miniatures, including information on miniature knock-offs made by other companies.

Not Shown:
#2009 miniature vase, 2 handles, 3½", based on Fulper #724, 1935 – 1936. $190.00 – 225.00.
#2010 miniature vase, 2", 1935 – 1938. $40.00 – 50.00.
#2011 miniature vase, 2", based on Fulper #643, 1935 – 1945. $25.00 – 35.00.
#2012 miniature vase, 2", based on vase #1817, 1935 – 1938. $35.00 – 45.00.
#2013 miniature vase, 2", based on vase #1916, 1935 only. $200.00 – 250.00.
#2014 miniature vase, 2", based on vase #1667, 1935 – 1938. $35.00 – 45.00.
#2015 miniature vase, 2", based on vase #1913, 1935 only. $200.00 – 250.00.
#2016 miniature vase, 3½", originally #934, 1935 – 1940. $35.00 – 45.00.
#2017 miniature vase, 3", based on Fulper #832, 1935 – 1940. $35.00 – 45.00.
#2018 miniature vase, 3½", based on Fulper #47, 1935 – 1940. $175.00 – 200.00.
#2019 miniature vase, 3", based on Fulper #452, 1935 – 1940. $40.00 – 50.00.

Not Shown:

#2020 miniature vase, 3", (originally #935), 1935 – 1940. $35.00 – 45.00.

#2021 miniature vase, 3", based on Fulper #701, 1935 – 1940. $35.00 – 45.00.

#2022 miniature shell ashtray, 3", 1935 – 1942. $20.00 – 25.00.

Variegated Rust #2025 vase, cylinder, rope decoration. 8", 1935 – 1936. $85.00 – 95.00. Courtesy of the Brian and Cristi Hahn collection.

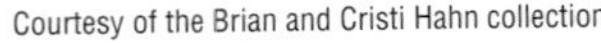

The following shapes were primarily decorated with Stangl's Tropical combination glazes. Please see the Hand-Decorated Combination and Tropical Glazes section (page 240) for these items with Tropical glazes. The following values are for items glazed in single solid-colors.

#2023 bowl, 3-footed, 7", 1935 – 1936. $85.00 – 95.00.

#2024 vase, scroll decoration, 7", 1935 – 1936. $85.00 – 95.00.

#2026 vase, scroll decoration, 8", 1935 – 1936. $85.00 – 95.00.

#2027 vase, 2 handles, 8", 1935 – 1936. $85.00 – 95.00.

#2028 pedestal bowl, wave decoration, 8", 1935 – 1936. $85.00 – 95.00.

1936 Introductions

Stangl's artware introductions for 1936 were distinguished by sweeping curves, decorative medallions, and elegant handles. The decorative medallions were not favored, but the elegant curves and handles continued to be characteristic of the artware shapes introduced throughout the late 1930s. Another late 1930s design element was the use of soft, pastel satin glazes. The satin glazes were the predominant finish on most of the artware shapes produced during the late 1930s and into the early 1940s. Consequently, items glazed with those colors are now quite common and usually sell at the low end of the price range. Certain satin colors, however, are harder to find and sometimes command better prices. Hard to find satin colors are Dusty Pink, Alice Blue, Silk Blue, and Champagne.

Persian Yellow #2039 vase, medallion insert, 8", 1936 – 1937. $110.00 – 135.00. Courtesy of the Bullock collection.

Colonial Blue #2040 vase, raised flowers, 9", 1936 only. $190.00 – 225.00. Courtesy of the Hill-Fulper-Stangl Museum.

Variegated Rust #2042 vase, wheat decoration, 8", 1936 only. $110.00 – 135.00. Courtesy of the Chris McGeehan collection.

Tangerine #2048 vase and Satin Yellow #2047 vase, 4½" tall. $35.00 – 50.00 each. Courtesy of the Ben and Pauline Jensen collection.

Not Shown:

#2041 vase, scroll handles, square base, 8", 1936 – 1937. $85.00 – 95.00.

#2043 vase, scroll handles, round vase, 9", 1936 only. $100.00 – 125.00.

#2047 Twist vase, 3 ball handles, 4½", 1936 – 1943. $40.00 – 50.00.

#2048 vase, 2 handles, square base, 4½", 1936 – 1943. $40.00 – 50.00.

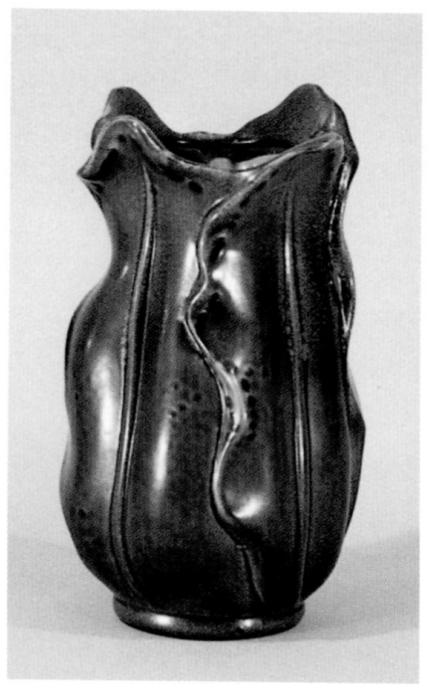

Rust glaze #2049 Tall Tulip vase, 12", 1936 – 1943. $85.00 – 95.00.

Satin White #2052 Round Scallop vase, 9½", 1936 – 1938. $60.00 – 75.00. Courtesy of the Marcena North collection.

Colonial Blue #2054 double candleholder, leaf center, 1936 – 1938. $110.00 – 135.00 each.

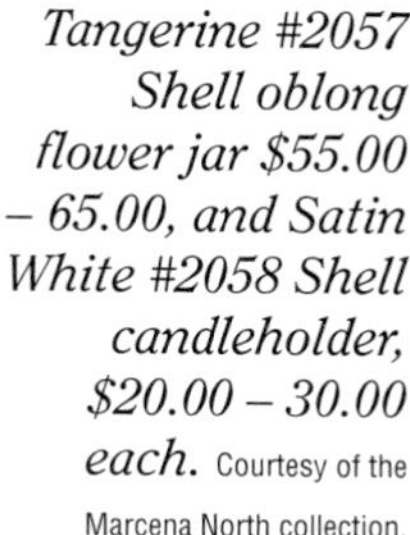

Tangerine #2057 Shell oblong flower jar $55.00 – 65.00, and Satin White #2058 Shell candleholder, $20.00 – 30.00 each. Courtesy of the Marcena North collection.

Satin White #2056 Scroll Horn vase, 6", 1936 – 1940. $18.00 – 22.00.

Colonial Blue #2062 Pointed bowl, 9", 1936 – 1937. $55.00 – 65.00.

Not Shown:

#2050 Round Scallop bowl, 8", 1936 – 1938. $30.00 – 40.00.
#2051 Round Scallop candleholder, 2½", 1936 – 1938. $35.00 – 45.00 pair.
#2053 Bowl, 3 footed, 12", 1936 – 1938. $70.00 – 85.00.
#2055 Horn double candleholder, 5½", 1936 only. $100.00 – 125.00 pair.
#2057 Shell oblong flower jar, 10"x4", 1936 – 1937. $55.00 – 65.00.
#2058 Shell candleholder, 4"x2", 1936 – 1937. $55.00 – 65.00 pair.
#2059 Scallop Oval candleholder, 4"x2", 1936 – 1938. $25.00 – 35.00 pair.
#2060 Cradle bowl, 7"x4", 1936 – 1938. $55.00 – 65.00.
#2061 Cradle candleholder, 3"x2", 1936 – 1938. $55.00 – 65.00 pair.
#2063 Pointed candleholder, 3½". $55.00 – 65.00 pair.

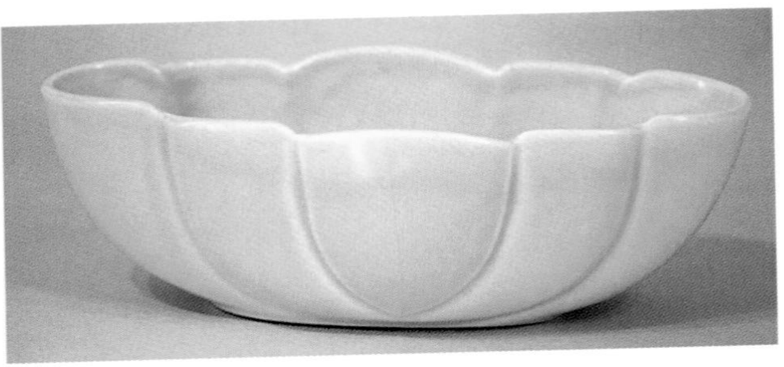

Satin Yellow #2064 Scallop Oval bowl, 9"x5", 1936 – 1938. $20.00 – 25.00. Courtesy of the Marcena North collection.

Silver Green #2068 Modern oblong vase, 8", 1936 only. $55.00 – 70.00. Courtesy of the Brian and Cristi Hahn collection.

Variegated Rust #2069 Leaf design bud vase, 6", 1936 only. $40.00 – 50.00. Courtesy of the Chris McGeehan collection.

Satin Green #2070 footed Ovoid vase, 15", 1936 – 1937. $275.00 – 300.00. Courtesy of the Robert and Tammie Cruser collection.

Not Shown:
#2065 Ornamental cylinder vase, 9", 1936 only. $175.00 – 200.00.
#2066 Capital vase, 8", 1936 only. $85.00 – 95.00.
#2067 Scallop vase, footed, 7", 1936 – 1937. $30.00 – 40.00.
#2071 Footed Modern vase, 10", 1936 only. $150.00 – 175.00.
#2072 High-footed Modern vase, 12", 1936 only. $175.00 – 200.00.
#2088 Baby Face Dog bank, 4", made for B&A Co., solid-color glazes 1937 only. $300.00 – 400.00.

Cosmos Line #2091

These pieces can occasionally be found in the solid gloss colors Colonial Blue, Persian Yellow, Silver Green, but were primarily produced in Satin Blue, Satin Green, Satin Yellow, Sand, Satin White, and Green Matte.

Cosmos #2091 Colonial Blue candleholder, $35.00 – 45.00 pair; Satin Yellow 12" flat bowl, $60.00 – 75.00; Satin Blue miniature bowl, $25.00 – 30.00; and Green 7" jardiniere, $35.00 – 45.00. Courtesy of the Marcena North collection.

Cosmos #2091 Sand 5" jardiniere, $25.00 – 35.00; Satin Blue 10" vase, $65.00 – 80.00; and Satin Yellow wall pocket, $100.00 – 125.00.

#2091 Cosmos low bowl, 14", 1936 – 1938. $70.00 – 85.00.
#2091 Cosmos low bowl, 7", 1936 – 1938. $35.00 – 45.00.
#2091 Cosmos low bowl, 6", 1937 – 1938. $25.00 – 35.00.
#2091 Cosmos jardiniere, large, 7", 1936 – 1937. $35.00 – 45.00.
#2091 Cosmos jardiniere, 5", 1936 – 1938. $25.00 – 35.00.
#2091 Cosmos vase, 10", 1936 – 1938. $65.00 – 80.00.
#2091 Cosmos bud vase, 7", 1936 – 1938. $55.00 – 65.00.
#2091 Cosmos candleholder, 4", 1936 – 1938. $35.00 – 45.00 pair.

#2091 Cosmos miniature bowl, 4", 1936 – 1938. $25.00 – 30.00.
#2091 Cosmos flat bowl, 12", 1936 – 1937. $60.00 – 75.00.
#2091 Cosmos wall pocket, 8", 1936 – 1943. $100.00 – 125.00.

Rhythmic Line #2092

Like the #2091 Cosmos Line, Rhythmic was infrequently glazed with Colonial Blue, Persian Yellow, and Silver Green, but was primarily produced in Satin Blue, Satin Green, Satin Brown, Satin White, and Green Matte. The low bowl and candleholder shapes produced through 1940 can also be found in Colonial Blue, Silver Green, and Satin Yellow. These items in the satin colors usually sell at the low end of or below the value.

Rhythmic #2092 Satin Blue 9" tall vase, $65.00 – 80.00; Satin Green 3¼" miniature vase, $25.00 – 30.00; and Green Matte basket, $60.00 – 75.00. Courtesy of the Marcena North collection.

Rhythmic #2092 Green Matte 6" small jar, $45.00 – 55.00; Satin Brown 11" tall vase, $65.00 – 80.00; and Satin White 3¼" candleholder, $35.00 – 45.00 pair. Courtesy of the Marcena North collection.

2092 Rhythmic low bowl, 7"x4½", 1936 – 1940. $25.00 – 35.00.
2092 Rhythmic candleholder, 3¼", 1936 – 1940. $35.00 – 45.00 pair.
2092 Rhythmic miniature vase, 3¼", 1936 – 1937. $25.00 – 30.00.
2092 Rhythmic tall vase, 11", 1936 – 1938. $65.00 – 80.00.
2092 Rhythmic tall vase, 9", 1937 only. $65.00 – 80.00.
2092 Rhythmic tall vase, 7", 1937 – 1938. $55.00 – 65.00.
2092 Rhythmic large jar, 9", 1936 – 1937. $65.00 – 80.00.
2092 Rhythmic small jar, 6", 1937 – 1938. $45.00 – 55.00.
2092 Rhythmic wall pocket, 6"x9", 1936 – 1937. $$120.00 – 145.00.
2092 Rhythmic basket, 6", 1936 only. $60.00 – 75.00.

Sasha cup in-mold marks.

Sasha Gourd Cups

During 1936, Fulper Pottery Company produced a line of special-order novelty cups for Sasha Katchamakoff, a Bulgarian citizen then residing in Los Angeles. The cups were gourd-shaped, their distinguishing feature being a peculiar animal head ornament on the end the handles. Mr. Katchamakoff was issued a patent for the cup shapes and handle ornament on May 19, 1936. Fulper Pottery Company produced the Katchamakoff handled gourd as simple cup, creamer, and sugar shapes. The name "SASHA" and "PAT. 99759" are molded into the base of each Katchamakoff item.

The cups were glazed with a series of special-ordered pastel satin glazes in mint green, canary yellow, light blue, and apricot. The green, apricot, and yellow satin glazes were only used on the "Sasha" cups and do not appear on other Stangl items.

Sasha cup in Satin Blue, $40.00 – 50.00; sugar in Persian Yellow, and creamer in Silver Green, $50.00 – 60.00 each.

However, the light satin blue is similar to Stangl's own Satin Blue glaze. These cups have also turned up in Satin White, Persian Yellow, and Silver Green. The Sasha cups were advertised and sold as sets of four with a wrought iron wall rack where they could be attractively displayed when not in use.

Sasha cup, 6½"x4", 1936 only. $40.00 – 50.00.
Sasha creamer, 6½"x4½", 1936 only. $50.00 – 60.00.
Sasha sugar, 7½"x4", 1936 only. $50.00 – 60.00.

1937 Introductions

Not Shown:
#3017 sand jar, grape medallion, 18", 1937 only. $375.00 – 450.00.
#3018 sand jar, modern handle, 18", 1937 – 1938. $350.00 – 400.00.
#3019 plant jar, modern handle, 9", 1937 – 1938. $65.00 – 80.00.

Pair of Scroll Leaf #3025 Tangerine tall candleholders, 5½", $130.00 – 150.00 pair. Courtesy of the Brian and Cristi Hahn collection.

Scroll Leaf Line #3020

Usually glazed in Satin White, Satin Blue, Satin Green, Tangerine, Rust, and Satin Brown. Items glazed in Rust or Tangerine are valued toward the high end of the price range.

Scroll Leaf #3020 7½" Rust large round bowl, $80.00 – 100.00; and #3024 Satin White bud vase, 5½", $45.00 – 55.00. Courtesy of the Ben and Pauline Jensen collection.

Satin Blue Scroll Leaf console set comprised of two #3027 2½" candleholders, $70.00 – 85.00 pair; and #3021 4" round bowl, $55.00 – 65.00. Courtesy of the Marcena North collection.

Not Shown:
#3020 Scroll Leaf round bowl, large, 7½", 1937 only. $80.00 – 100.00.
#3021 Scroll Leaf round bowl, medium, 4", 1937 only. $55.00 – 65.00.
#3022 Scroll Leaf medium vase, 9", 1937 only. $80.00 – 100.00.
#3023 Scroll Leaf small vase, 8", 1937 only. $80.00 – 90.00.
#3024 Scroll Leaf bud vase, 5½", 1937 only. $45.00 – 55.00.
#3025 Scroll Leaf tall candleholder, 5½", 1937 only. $130.00 – 150.00 pair.
#3026 Scroll Leaf round bowl, small, 2", 1937 only. $55.00 – 65.00.
#3027 Scroll Leaf candleholder, 2½", 1937 only. $70.00 – 85.00 pair.
#3028 Scroll Leaf low bowl, small, 6", 1937 only. $60.00 – 75.00.
#3029 Scroll Leaf low bowl, large, 9", 1937 only. $85.00 – 95.00.
#3030 Scroll Leaf floor jar, 17", 1937 only. $450.00 – 500.00.
#3031 Scroll Leaf flower holder insert, 4", 1937 only. $35.00 – 45.00.

Spiral Tangerine #3033 9½" tall vase, $70.00 – 85.00; Persian Yellow #3032 wall pocket, $100.00 – 125.00; and Satin Blue #3041 5" ashtray, $20.00 – 25.00. Courtesy of the Marcena North collection.

Spiral Line #3035

Originally called "Twist," this line was produced in Satin White, Satin Green, Persian Yellow, Tangerine, Dusty Pink, and Bronze Green. The Bronze Green and Tangerine glazes were used on these shapes during 1937. They were replaced with Satin Green and Dusty Pink for

1938. The items produced through 1940 can also be found in Colonial Blue, Silver Green, and Satin Yellow. Pieces glazed with Colonial Blue, Dusty Pink, and Tangerine usually sell at the higher end of the range. The other colors sell at the low end or lower.

#3032 Spiral wall pocket, 7", 1937 – 1938. $100.00 – 125.00.
#3033 Spiral tall vase, 9½", 1937 – 1938. $70.00 – 85.00.
#3034 Spiral medium vase, 7", 1937 – 1941. $55.00 – 65.00.
#3035 Spiral large bowl, 6½"x8", 1937 – 1938. $60.00 – 75.00.
#3036 Spiral low bowl, 4"x9", 1937 – 1940. $35.00 – 45.00.
#3037 Spiral low bowl, 3"x6" , 1937 – 1938. $25.00 – 35.00.
#3038 Spiral miniature bowl, 2½"x3", 1937 – 1938. $20.00 – 25.00.
#3039 Spiral candleholder, 2½"x3", 1937 – 1940. $35.00 – 45.00 pair.
#3040 Spiral flower block insert, 5", 1937 – 1938. $35.00 – 45.00.
#3041 Spiral ashtray, 5", 1937 – 1945. $20.00 – 25.00.
#3048 Spiral oval bowl, no handles, 6½"x4½", 1937 – 1938. $35.00 – 45.00.
#3056 Spiral oval bowl, with handles, 6½"x4½", 1937 – 1938. $45.00 – 55.00.

Three items in hard-to-find Bronze Green glaze: Spiral #3037 3"x6" low bowl, $25.00 – 35.00; Scroll #3043 candleholder bowl, $60.00 – 75.00; and Spiral #3038 miniature bowl, 2½"x3", $20.00 – 25.00. Courtesy of the Ben and Pauline Jensen collection.

Scroll Line #3042

This line was originally called "Curl." Its usual colors were Satin White, Satin Green, Persian Yellow, Dusty Pink, Bronze Green, and Tangerine. Bronze Green and Tangerine were used on these shapes during 1937. They were replaced with Satin Green and Dusty Pink for 1938. The items produced through 1940 can also be found in Colonial Blue, Silver Green, and Satin Yellow.

#3042 Scroll oval bowl, 10"x7", 1937 – 1940. $55.00 – 65.00.
#3043 Scroll oval candleholder bowl, 10", 1937 – 1940. $60.00 – 75.00.
#3044 Scroll miniature oval bowl, 5"x4", 1937 – 1938. $25.00 – 35.00.
#3045 Scroll round bowl, 7½", 1937 – 1938. $40.00 – 50.00.
#3046 Scroll candleholder, 3¾", 1937 – 1940. $40.00 – 50.00 pair.
#3047 Scroll 4-sided bowl, 10", 1937 – 1940. $60.00 – 75.00.

Pair of Scroll #3046 3¾" candleholders, Satin Green.

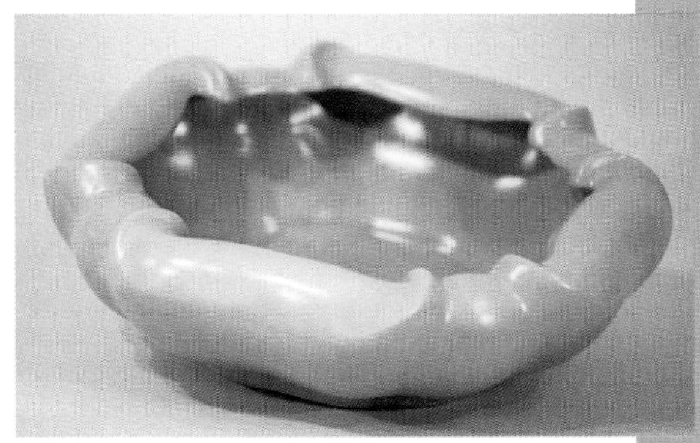

Scroll #3047 10" 4-sided bowl in Satin Blue, $60.00 – 75.00. Courtesy of the Marcena North collection.

Shade Pulls

Shade pulls were produced briefly during 1937 in a variety of satin and gloss glaze colors. They are usually not marked but sometimes have a gold-foil paper label.

Shade pulls #3077 Chinese in Persian Yellow , #3076 Queen in Silver Green, and #3075 King in Oxblood glaze, $100.00 – 125.00 each. Courtesy of the Dinmont collection.

Shade pull #3050 oval in Aqua Blue glaze, $45.00 – 55.00. Courtesy of the Frank and Elizabeth Kramar collection.

#3050 shade pull, oval, 2", 1937 only. $45.00 – 55.00.
#3051 shade pull, long, 2¾", 1937 only. $45.00 – 55.00.
#3052 shade pull, short, 2", 1937 only. $45.00 – 55.00.
#3075 shade pull, King, 3", 1937 only. $100.00 – 125.00.
#3076 shade pull, Queen, 2", 1937 only. $100.00 – 125.00.
#3077 shade pull, Chinese, 3½", 1937 only. $100.00 – 125.00.
#3078 shade pull, Evening Gown, 3½", 1937 only. $100.00 – 125.00.
#3079 shade pull, Maid, 3", 1937 only. $100.00 – 125.00.

Please see the section on Miniature Vases (page 197) for more information on these items.

#3053 miniature vase, long pitcher, 3", 1937 – 1943. $35.00 – 45.00.

#3054 miniature vase, ovoid, 3", 1937 – 1943. $35.00 – 45.00.

#3055 miniature vase, long neck, 3", 1937 – 1943. $35.00 – 45.00.

Colonial Blue #3084 Garden bowl, straight sides, 7"x5", 1937 – 1940. $35.00 – 45.00. Courtesy of the Marcena North collection.

Garden Bowls

The following Garden Bowls and matching candles were offered in Satin White, Silver Green, Satin Blue, Persian Yellow, and Colonial Blue. Other glaze colors were available as special-order at higher cost.

Satin Blue #3088 Garden bowl, oblong, six feet, 6"x4", 1937 only. $35.00 – 45.00. Courtesy of the Marcena North collection.

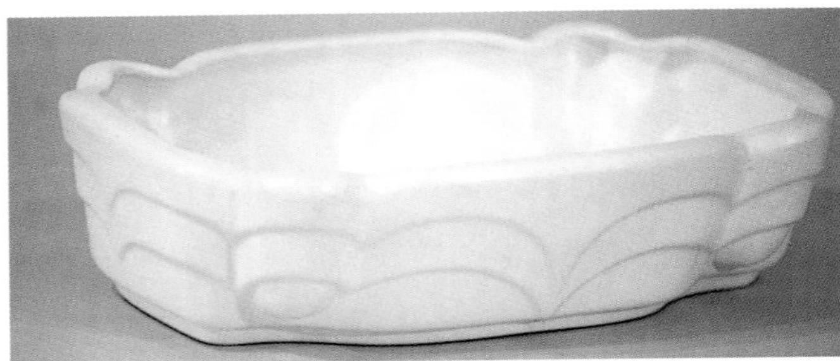

Satin White glaze #3092 Garden bowl, Garland, 12"x8", 1937 – 1940. $55.00 – 70.00. Courtesy of the Marcena North collection.

Persian Yellow #3096 Garden bowl, scroll sides, 1937 only. $40.00 – 50.00. Courtesy of the Marcena North collection.

Colonial Blue #3099 candleholder, French oval, 3"x2", 1937 – 1940. $35.00 – 45.00 pair.

Silver Green #3108 candleholder, scalloped, 3"x2", 1937 – 1940. $35.00 – 45.00 pair.

Not Shown:

#3082 Garden bowl, French oval, 7"x5", 1937 – 1940. $35.00 – 45.00.

#3083 Garden bowl, oblong, 6 feet, 7"x5", 1937 – 1940. $35.00 – 45.00.

#3085 Garden bowl, 3 wavy lines, 7"x5", 1937 only. $40.00 – 50.00.

#3086 Garden bowl, round, 3 feet, 6", 1937 only. $45.00 – 55.00.

#3087 candleholder, oblong, 6 feet, 3"x2", 1937 – 1940. $35.00 – 45.00 pair.

#3089 Garden bowl, French oval, 6"x4", 1937 only. $35.00 – 45.00.

#3090 Garden bowl, scalloped, 9"x5", 1937 only. $40.00 – 50.00.

#3091 Garden bowl, oblong, 9"x5", 1937 only. $40.00 – 50.00.

#3093 Garden bowl, double scalloped, 12"x8", 1937 – 1938. $55.00 – 70.00.

#3094 Garden bowl, Canoe oval, 6½"x 3¾", 1937 – 1938. $40.00 – 50.00.

#3095 Garden bowl, fluted, 6½", 1937 only. $40.00 – 50.00.

#3097 Garden bowl, oblong, 6½", 1937 only. $40.00 – 50.00.

The promotional colors for the following vases were Satin White, Satin Green, Satin Blue, Tangerine, Persian Yellow, Satin Yellow, Silk Blue, and Dusty Pink. Other colors, such as Silk Blue and Variegated Rust, could be special-ordered, but are extremely rare.

Tangerine with green lining #3101 lily vase, 6¾", 1937 only. $55.00 – 70.00. Courtesy of the Ben and Pauline Jensen collection.

Tangerine with green lining #3102 cylinder vase, 2 handles, 7", 1937 only. $70.00 – 85.00. Courtesy of the Ben and Pauline Jensen collection.

Satin Green #3103 vase, long neck and handles, 7¼", 1937 – 1941. $40.00 – 50.00. Courtesy of the Ben and Pauline Jensen collection.

Silk Blue #3104 vase, short neck and handles, 7", 1937 – 1939. $60.00 – 75.00. Courtesy of the Robert and Tammie Cruser collection.

Variegated Rust #3104 vase, short neck and handles, 7", 1937 – 1939. $95.00 – 110.00. Courtesy of Dave and Betty Stangl Thomas.

Satin Green #3104 vase, short neck and handles, 7", 1937 – 1939. $45.00 – 55.00.

Tangerine with green lining #3105 cylinder vase, fluted handles, 6½", 1937 only. $70.00 – 85.00. Courtesy of the Ben and Pauline Jensen collection.

Variegated Rust #3106 vase, cup shape, 2 handles, 6", 1937 only. $95.00 – 110.00. Courtesy of the Chris McGeehan collection.

Tangerine with green lining #3106 vase, cup shape, 2 handles, 6", 1937 only. $70.00 – 85.00. Courtesy of the Chris McGeehan collection.

New York Candleholder

Martin Stangl called the #3107 candlestick "New York candleholder," a special-order apparently for a New York retailer. Encircling the base of the candlestick is the Shakespearian quote, "How Far That Little Candle Throws His Beams!," excerpted from Act V of William Shakespeare's *Merchant of Venice*, as spoken by the character Portia, "See that lamp in my hall. How far that little candle throws his beams! So shines a good deed in a naughty world." Colonial Blue was the primary glaze used on this candlestick. Usually the only markings are the #3107 molded into the base, sometimes accompanied by a Stangl Pottery gold-foil paper label.

Colonial Blue #3107 New York candleholder, 3"x5½", 1937 – 1938. $55.00 – 65.00.

Airwick Long-Eared Rabbit

Stangl produced the #3109 Long-Eared Rabbit figure as an air freshener dispenser for Airwick in 1937. The Long-Eared Rabbit was glazed in solid-colors and sometimes was decorated with pink cold-paint ears and details.

Other companies also produced similar rabbits. The competitors' rabbits are usually a bit shorter than Stangl's rabbit, and the bodies are heavier. The competitor's glaze is denser and off-white while the Stangl rabbits were glazed with bright gloss solid-color glazes. The competitors' rabbits also have an unglazed bottom that is flat with a prominent mold seam across it. The base of Stangl's rabbit has a raised "foot" and earlier rabbits have the number 3109 molded into the base. A few of Stangl's #3109 Long-Eared Rabbits were decorated with cold-paint during the 1930s, but those are glazed in Stangl's solid-colors, and the rabbits are clearly marked with #3109 on the bases.

Silver Green #3109 Long-Eared Rabbit air freshener, 7½", made for Airwick, solid-color glazes, 1937 – 1938 (base, inset). $175.00 – 200.00.

In 1961, the #3109 Long-Eared Rabbit figure was adapted as a children's lamp and was decorated with pink or blue floral motifs. In 1967, the #3109 Long-Eared Rabbit shape was reintroduced for the Flemington Outlet in gloss white with hand-painted Pink #193 details. The Long-Eared Rabbit became very popular at the Flemington Outlet as a novelty cotton holder during the 1960s. He was also epoxied to 9" deviled egg dishes, as well as 10" and 12" Pink Cosmos plates. The 1960s decorated Long-Eared Rabbit is most easily found as a cotton holder, and plates with the attached bunny are much harder to find. See also the sections on Hand-Painted Animal Figurines and Lamps.

Ivory #3109 Long-Eared Rabbit air freshener with original pink cold-paint. $200.00 – 250.00. Courtesy of the Robert and Tammie Cruser collection.

Handled Flower Vases

The following vases were offered in the promotional colors Satin White, Satin Blue, Satin Green, Satin Yellow, Persian Yellow, Rust, Tangerine and Dusty Pink. Satin Blue, and Satin Green are most common. Rare colors, such as Variegated Rust or crystalline Zinc Green glaze, can nearly double the value of these vase shapes.

Three #3111 Handled flower vases, Satin White and Persian Yellow glazes, $60.00 – 75.00 each; very rare Zinc Green glaze, $145.00 – 175.00. Courtesy of the Chris McGeehan collection.

Satin Blue #3110 flower vase with handles, 6½", 1937 – 1938. $60.00 – 75.00. Courtesy of the Ben and Pauline Jensen collection.

Satin Blue #3111 flower vase with handles, 6½", 1937 – 1938. $60.00 – 75.00.

The following six 5½" tall vases were Satin White, Satin Blue, Satin Green, Satin Yellow, and Persian Yellow. They were also available in the colors Rust, Tangerine, and Dusty Pink for only six months during 1937, making those colors the most elusive and desirable on these shapes.

Satin Blue #3117 vase, footed, short neck, 5½", 1937 – 1938. $55.00 – 65.00.

Satin Blue vase #3112, Tangerine vase #3113, Satin Green vase #3114, Satin Blue vase #3115, and Tangerine vase #3116. Courtesy of the Ben and Pauline Jensen collection.

#3112 vase, footed, long neck, 5½", 1937 – 1942. $50.00 – 60.00.
#3113 vase, footed, scroll handles, 5½", 1937 – 1939. $60.00 – 75.00.
#3114 vase, squat, 5½", 1937 – 1942. $50.00 – 60.00.
#3115 vase, footed, wing handles, 5½", 1937 – 1939. $60.00 – 75.00.
#3116 vase, amphora, scroll handles, 5½", 1937 – 1938. $55.00 – 65.00.

Bulb Bowls

Not Shown:

#3133 irregular sides, 13"x3", 1937 – 1938. $85.00 – 95.00.
#3134 tree bark sides, 14"x3", 1937 – 1938. $100.00 – 125.00.

Tangerine #3132 round bulb bowl with tab handles, 14"x3", 1937 – 1938. $100.00 – 125.00.

Pen Trays

Four #3137 pen trays made for Toastmaster and glazed with Silver Green, Colonial Blue, Persian Yellow, and Tangerine. Two #3135 square bowls glazed in Satin White are in the right foreground. Courtesy of the Ben and Floss Avila collection.

#3135 square bowl, 1¼", 1937 only. $55.00 – 65.00.
#3136 round bowl, 1½", 1937 only. $55.00 – 65.00.
#3137 pen tray, 4½"x7½", made for Toastmaster, 1937 – 1945. $6.00 – 8.00.

Scalloped Vases

Martin Stangl called these "scalloped vases," produced in nearly all satin glazes.

1938 Introductions

Stangl's 1938 season was kicked off with a selection of 25 large vases, 11" to 18", with what Martin Stangl described as "fancy handles." Many were discontinued during 1938, but a few were produced through 1941. Most were glazed in Satin White, Silver Green, and Satin Blue, with an occasional Satin Yellow. The #3156 three-handle vase was also produced with Stangl's air-brush decorated treatment. See also the section on Hand-Decorated Artware (pages 237 – 239).

Dusty Pink #3139 scalloped vase with handles, 6½", 1937 – 1940. $50.00 – 60.00. Courtesy of the Brian and Cristi Hahn collection.

Satin White #3140 scalloped vase with handles, 7", 1937 – 1939. $50.00 – 60.00. Courtesy of the Brian and Cristi Hahn collection.

Satin Blue #3143 vase, ring handles, 12", 1938 only. $225.00 – 275.00. Courtesy of the Brian and Cristi Hahn collection.

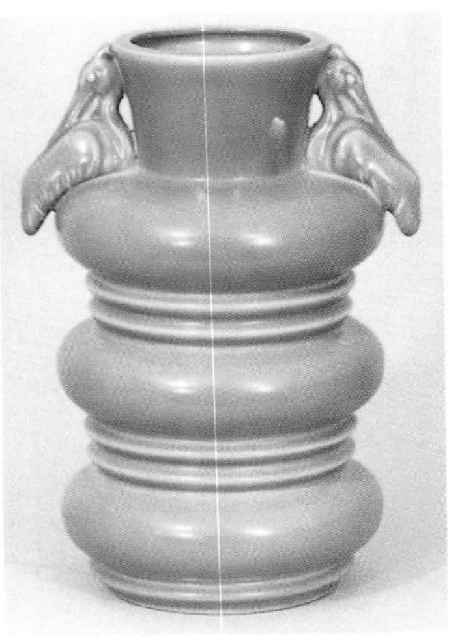

Satin Blue #3144 vase, Pelican handles, 12", 1938 only. $375.00 – 400.00.

Satin Blue #3145 vase, curly handles, 12", 1938 – 1940. $175.00 – 200.00. Courtesy of the Marcena North collection.

Satin Blue #3146 vase, Squirrel handles, 12", 1938 only. $375.00 – 400.00. Courtesy of the Bill Servis, Susan Lewis collection.

Satin Blue #3150 vase, short handles, 11", 1938 – 1941. $160.00 – 180.00.

Satin Green #3151 vase, point handles, 12", 1938 only. $175.00 – 200.00. Courtesy of the Bullock collection.

Not Shown:

#3147 vase, curly handles, 12", 1938 only. $200.00 – 250.00.

#3148 vase, Duck handles, 12". 1938 only. $300.00 – 350.00.

#3149 vase, long handles, 11", 1938 – 1941. $130.00 – 150.00.

Satin Blue #3152 vase, sweep handles, 11", 1938 – 1941. $160.00 – 180.00. Courtesy of the Marcena North collection.

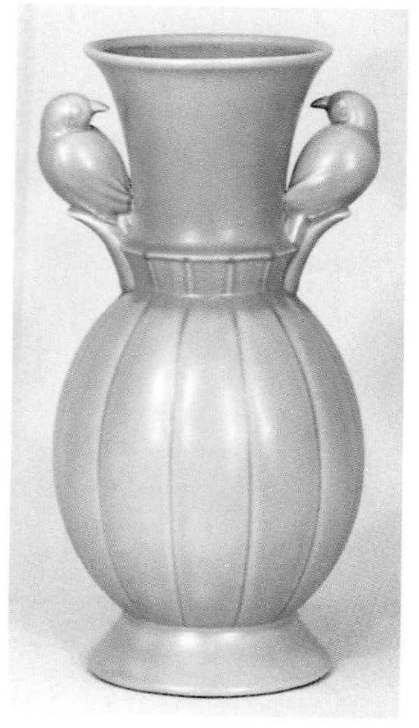

Silver Green #3154 vase, Bird handles, 13", 1938 only. $350.00 – 400.00. Courtesy of the Frank and Elizabeth Kramar collection.

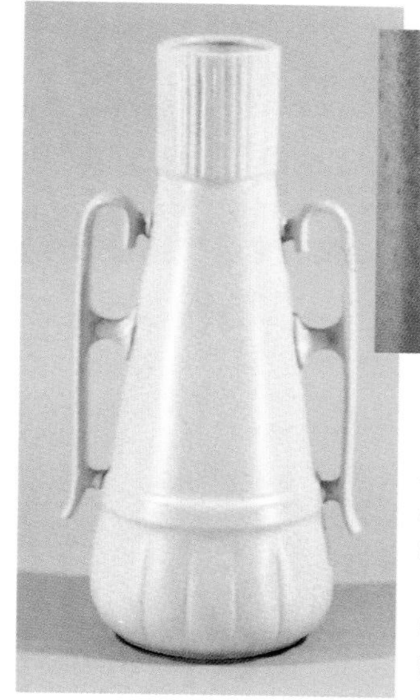

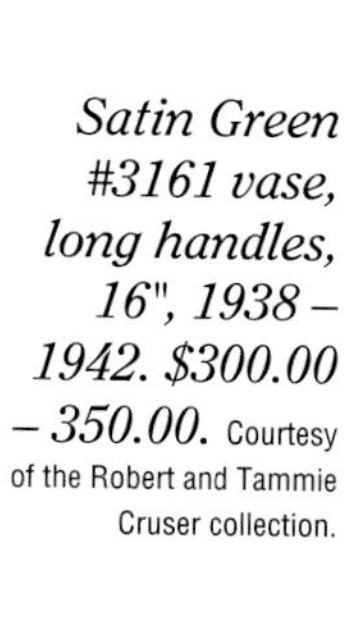

Champagne #3155 tapering vase, 15", 1938 – 1940 (close-up of the airbrushed red iron oxide "spritz" of the Champagne glaze, inset). $200.00 – 250.00. Courtesy of the Robert and Tammie Cruser collection.

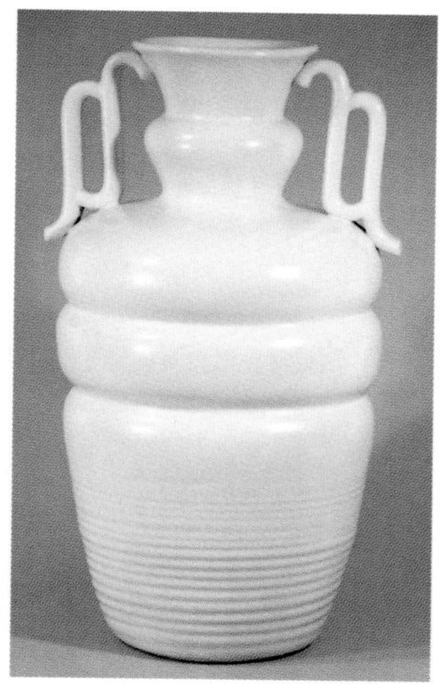

Satin White glaze #3159 vase, double sweep handles, 16", 1938 – 1940. $225.00 – 275.00. Courtesy of the Miklos collection.

Colonial Blue #3160 vase, Dog handles, 16", 1938 only. $430.00 – 475.00. Courtesy of the Bill Servis, Susan Lewis collection.

Satin Green #3161 vase, long handles, 16", 1938 – 1942. $300.00 – 350.00. Courtesy of the Robert and Tammie Cruser collection.

Satin Blue #3167 vase, small side handles, 18", 1938 – 1942. $275.00 – 300.00. Courtesy of the Robert and Tammie Cruser collection.

Not Shown:

#3153 vase, scallop, zigzag handles, 13", 1938 – 1941. $160.00 – 180.00.
#3156 vase, 3 handles, 15", 1938 only. $275.00 – 300.00.
#3157 vase, double long handles, 16", 1938 – 1942. $275.00 – 300.00.
#3158 vase, Cat handles, 16", 1938 only. $400.00 – 450.00.
#3162 vase, small double handles, 18", 1938 – 1940. $300.00 – 350.00.
#3163 vase, Peacock handles, 18", 1938 only. $400.00 – 450.00.
#3164 vase, small top handles, 16", 1938 – 1940. $275.00 – 300.00.
#3165 vase, leaf handles, 17", 1938 – 1942. $275.00 – 300.00.
#3166 vase, upsweep handles, 17", 1938 – 1942. $275.00 – 300.00.

The following shapes were briefly glazed in solid-color glazes, but are most often found in Stangl's Hand-Decorated finishes of Twilight Blue, Surf White, and Marigold Yellow. Please see the section on Hand-Decorated Artware (pages 237-239) for these items with the hand-decorated finishes. During 1939, the double handle shapes #3180 – #3185 were produced with Martin Stangl's "Rainbow" glaze finish. See page 253 for those items as well.

Group of vases, Colonial Blue #3188, 7½", with Silver Green vases #3187, 7½", and #3197, 4". Courtesy of the Marcena North collection.

Not Shown:

#3171 vase, scallop, zigzag handles, 7", 1938 – 1940. $35.00 – 45.00.

#3172 jug, scallop, zigzag handles, 7", 1938 – 1940. $35.00 – 45.00.

#3173 candleholder, scallop, zigzag handles, 4", 1938 – 1940. $55.00 – 65.00 per pair.

#3174 vase, scallop, zigzag handles, 4", 1938 – 1940. $35.00 – 45.00.

#3175 oval bowl, scallop, zigzag handles, 7½"x4", 1938 – 1940. $30.00 – 40.00.

#3181 vase, double handles, 7½"x2½", 1938 – 1939. $35.00 – 45.00.

#3182 vase, double handles, 7½"x3½", 1938 – 1939. $35.00 – 45.00.

#3183 vase, double handles, 4"x2½", 1938 – 1939. $30.00 – 40.00.

#3184 candleholder, double handles, 4"x2½", 1938 – 1939. $55.00 – 65.00 pair.

#3185 oval bowl, double handles, 8"x3½", 1938 – 1939. $35.00 – 45.00.

#3186 candleholder, 3 handles, 4", 1938 only. $95.00 – 110.00.

#3187 vase, 3 handles, 7¼", 1938 – 1940. $60.00 – 75.00.

#3188 vase with ribs, 7¼", 1938 – 1939. $60.00 – 75.00.

#3189 vase, ovoid with neck, 7¼", 1938 – 1940. $60.00 – 75.00.

#3190 vase, oval scalloped, 7½", 1938 – 1940. $45.00 – 55.00.

#3191 vase, oval scalloped, 9", 1938 – 1939. $70.00 – 85.00.

#3192 bowl, oval scalloped, 7½"x3", 1938 – 1939. $35.00 – 45.00.

#3193 bowl, oval scalloped, 6"x4", 1938 – 1939. $35.00 – 45.00.

#3194 bowl, oval scalloped, 9"x6", 1938 – 1939. $45.00 – 55.00.

#3195 bowl, oval scalloped, 12"x8", 1938 – 1939. $45.00 – 55.00.

#3196 candleholder, oval scalloped, 4", 1938 – 1939. $45.00 – 55.00 pair.

#3197 vase, oval scalloped, 4", 1938 – 1939. $35.00 – 45.00.

#3198 bowl, oval scalloped, 7½"x4½", 1938 – 1939. $35.00 – 45.00.

#3199 candleholder, with ribs, 4", 1938 only. $60.00 – 75.00 per pair.

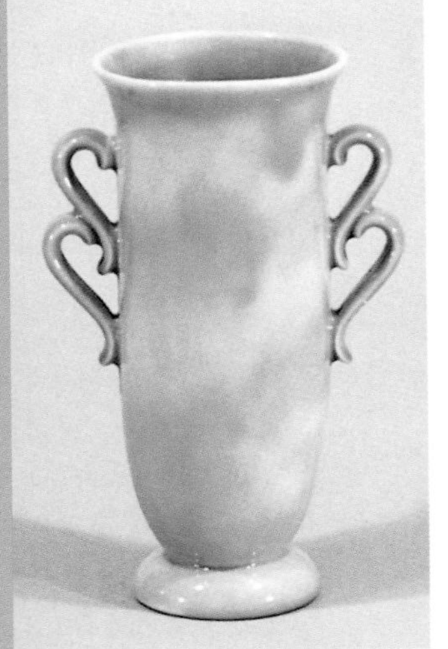

Silver Green #3180 vase, double handles, 9"x4½", 1938 – 1939. $40.00 – 50.00. Courtesy of the Brian and Cristi Hahn collection.

Silver Green #3176 jug, scallop, zigzag handles, 10", 1938 – 1940. $60.00 – 75.00.

Toastmaster Products

Stangl Pottery produced 8" square divided hors d'oeuvres trays with the Toastmaster logo for McGraw Electric Co. from 1938 to 1945. Also produced for McGraw Electric during that time were open and covered marmalade jars and #3137 pen trays, sold as relish dishes. McGraw Electric marketed these items with their Toastmaster toasters and appliances. The Toastmaster items were usually marked with in-mold "STANGL U.S.A."

Group of Toastmaster products produced by Stangl Pottery from 1938 to 1945.

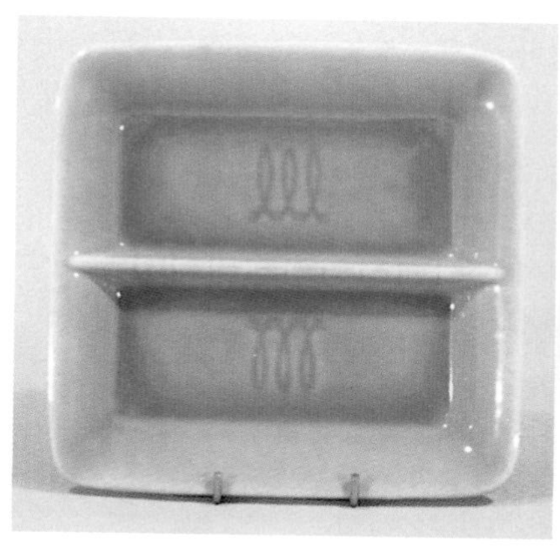

Silver Green Toastmaster divided hors d'oeuvres tray, 8" square, 1938 – 1945. $8.00 – 12.00. The square hors d'oeuvres trays were normally glazed Silver Green or Persian Yellow.

Persian Yellow and Tangerine Toastmaster open marmalades, 3¾"x2", 1938 – 1943. $10.00 – 15.00 each. Tangerine and Persian Yellow were the glaze colors specified by Toastmaster; other colors are scarce.

Toastmaster covered marmalade, 3½"x4", 1938 – 1945. $12.00 – 18.00. Toastmaster covered marmalade jars were normally glazed in Persian Yellow with Tangerine covers. Covered marmalades in other colors or color combinations are rare.

Rare Colonial Blue Toastmaster covered marmalade, 3½"x4". $25.00 – 35.00.

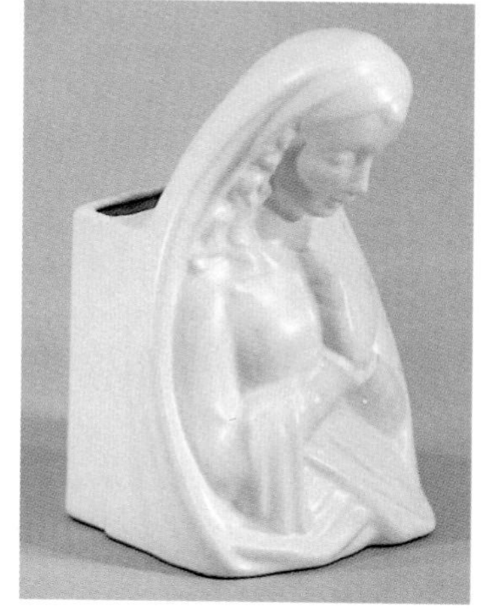

Satin White #3204 Madonna bust vase, 9", 1938 – 1941. $70.00 – 85.00.

Madonna Vases

Stangl advertised the Madonna vases as "Combination Madonnas and Vases." The Madonna vase shapes were sculpted by August Jacob, and Madonna vases cast from early molds bear his "AJ" cipher. During 1938, August Jacob was not employed by Fulper Pottery Company but worked as a freelance artist. He was paid a flat fee for each design produced and a percentage commission on every piece sold. Throughout the duration of Jacob's contract with Martin Stangl, items of his design were to be marked with his name or initials. At the end of each contract, Jacob's name or initials would be removed from the molds. The most recognized August Jacob commission piece is the #3584 Large Cockatoo bird figurine.

The Madonna vases were popular during the late 1930s and produced from 1938 through 1941. They were available primarily in plain Satin White but could also be special-ordered hand-painted with underglaze colors. See also the Hand-Decorated Madonna and Head Vases section (page 243).

Satin White Madonna vases, #3205 with hands clasped, 10", 1938 – 1941, $95.00 – 110.00, and #3206 with infant, 9½", 1938 – 1941, $95.00 – 110.00.
Courtesy of the Robert and Shirley Bond collection.

Miniatures

For complete information on miniature vases, see also that section (page 197).

Not Shown:

#3207 miniature tall tulip vase, 2¾", 1938 – 1945. $45.00 – 55.00.
#3208 miniature low tulip vase, 2¼", 1938 – 1945. $40.00 – 50.00.
#3209 miniature horn vase, 2¼", 1938 – 1945. $45.00 – 55.00.

Persian Yellow #3210 Bird ashtray, 4", 1938 – 1942. $50.00 – 60.00.

Satin Blue #3211 ball pitcher, 6" 1938 – 1945. $35.00 – 45.00.

Group of #3212 flat pitchers in Satin Blue, Satin Yellow, Satin White, and Satin Green, $22.00 – 28.00 each. Courtesy of the Marcena North collection.

Bright Satin Blue (almost a satin turquoise) #3214 streamlined pitcher, 8", 1938 – 1945. $45.00 – 55.00.

Satin Yellow #3214 streamlined pitcher, 8", 1938 – 1945. $45.00 – 55.00.

Satin Blue #3215 oval vase, 7", 1938 – 1940. $55.00 – 65.00. Courtesy of the Ben and Pauline Jensen collection.

Satin White #3216 horn vase, 8", 1938 – 1940. $55.00 – 65.00. Courtesy of the Ben and Pauline Jensen collection.

Satin White #3218 flare vase, 7", 1938 – 1941. $40.00 – 50.00. From the collection of Martha Runge.

Satin White #3219 oval vase, 7", 1938 – 1941. $35.00 – 45.00. Gifted to the Hill-Fulper-Stangl Museum by Charles and Patricia Walther.

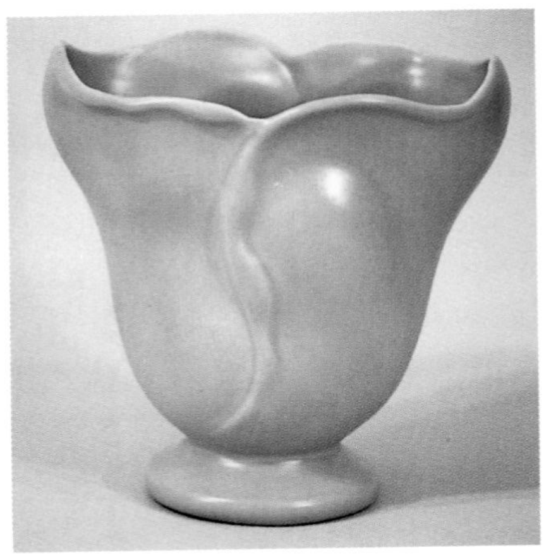

Satin Blue #3220 leaves vase, 7", 1938 – 1941, $50.00 – 60.00. Courtesy of the Ben and Pauline Jensen collection.

Not Shown:

#3211 miniature ball pitcher, 2¼", 1938 only. $100.00 – 125.00.
#3212 flat pitcher, 4"x7½", 1938 – 1944. $22.00 – 28.00.
#3213 short top pitcher, 7½", 1938 – 1940. $65.00 – 80.00.
#3217 scallop vase, 7", 1938 – 1943. $35.00 – 45.00.

Satin Yellow #3221 footed vase, 5½", 1938 – 1941. $55.00 – 65.00. Courtesy of the Marcena North collection.

Satin Blue #3222 points vase, 5½", 1938 – 1941. $55.00 – 65.00.

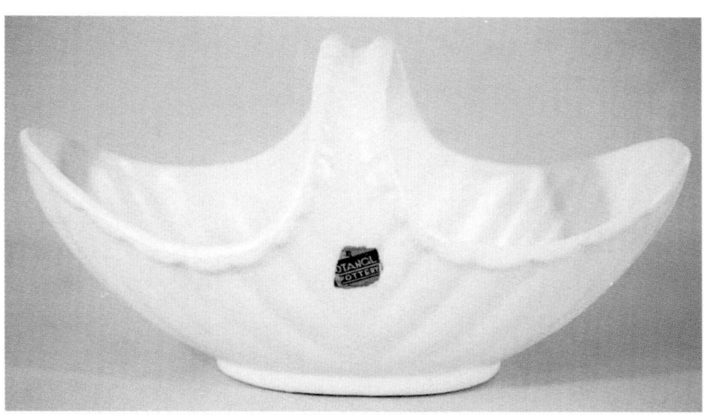

Satin White #3226 basket, 9"x4½", 1938 – 1943. $25.00 – 35.00.

Alice Blue #3226 basket, 9"x4½", 1938 – 1943. $60.00 – 75.00. Courtesy of the Frank and Elizabeth Kramar collection.

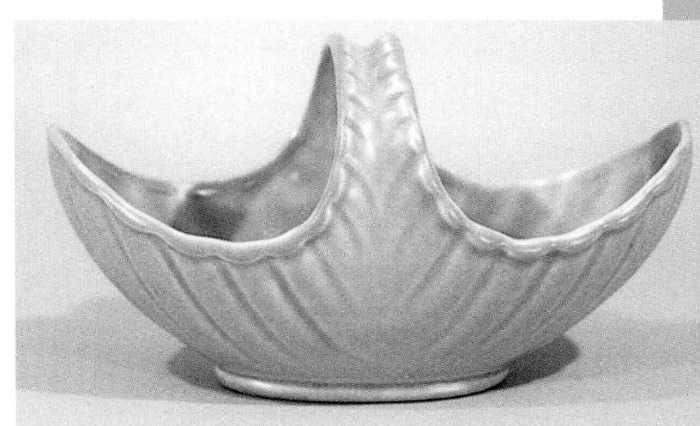

Satin Yellow #3228 leaf bowl, 7½"x4", 1938 – 1943. $45.00 – 55.00. Courtesy of the Ben and Pauline Jensen collection.

Satin Green #3229 bowl, 12", 1938 – 1942. $60.00 – 75.00.

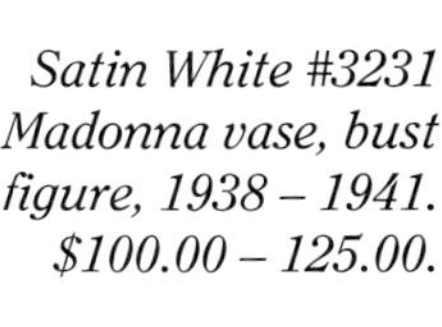

Satin White #3231 Madonna vase, bust figure, 1938 – 1941. $100.00 – 125.00.

Not Shown:

#3223 drape vase, 5½", 1938 – 1941. $60.00 – 75.00.
#3224 leaves vase, 5½", 1938 – 1941. $60.00 – 75.00.
#3225 basket, 7"x7", 1938 – 1943. $45.00 – 55.00.
#3227 bowl, 9"x4", 1938 – 1943. $30.00 – 40.00.
#3229 bowl, 9", 1938 – 1942. $40.00 – 50.00.
#3229 bowl, 6", 1938 – 1940. $40.00 – 50.00.
#3229 candleholder, 3¼", 1938 – 1940. $40.00 – 50.00 pair.

More Madonnas

Not Shown:

#3230 Madonna vase, full figure, 9¾", 1938 – 1941. $120.00 – 145.00.

Satin White #3232 Madonna vase, flat figure, 1938 – 1941. $95.00 – 110.00.

More Miniatures

Not Shown:

#3233 miniature ball jug, 2½" (#1388 shape), 1938 – 1945. $35.00 – 45.00.
#3234 miniature 2 handle vase, 3", 1938 – 1945. $35.00 – 45.00.
#3235 miniature swirl jug, 2½", 1938 – 1941. $45.00 – 55.00.

Wall Pockets

Satin Green #3236 wall pocket, leaves, 7", 1938 – 1941. $70.00 – 85.00. Courtesy of the Marcena North collection.

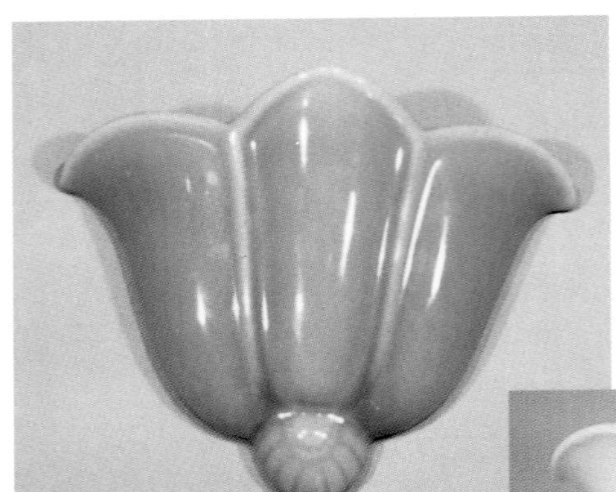

Silver Green #3237 wall pocket, scallop, 8"x5½", 1938 – 1940. $70.00 – 85.00. Courtesy of the Robert and Tammie Cruser collection.

Satin White #3238 wall pocket, snail, 9"x7", 1938 – 1940. $85.00 – 95.00. Courtesy of the Marcena North collection.

Not Shown:

#3239 Leaf candy dish/ashtray, 8"x7¾", 1938 – 1942. $25.00 – 35.00.

#3240 Shell candy dish/ashtray, 8"x7½", 1938 – 1942. $25.00 – 35.00.

#3241 Rectangle ashtray, 7"x6", 1938 – 1942. $25.00 – 30.00.

#3242 Three Arm candy dish/ashtray, 9" diameter, 1938 – 1942. $30.00 – 40.00.

1939 Introductions

Satin Blue #3251 basket, twist handle, 11"x6½", 1939 – 1943. $35.00 – 50.00. Courtesy of the Marcena North collection.

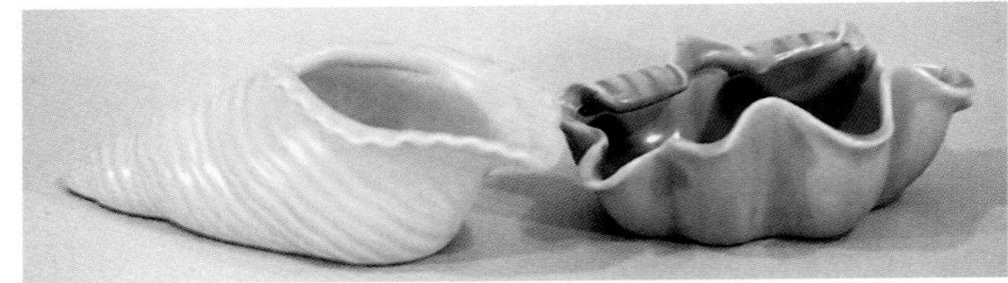

Satin Yellow #3255 horn shell bowl, $30.00 – 40.00; and Satin Green #3254 deep shell bowl, $25.00 – 30.00. Courtesy of the Marcena North collection.

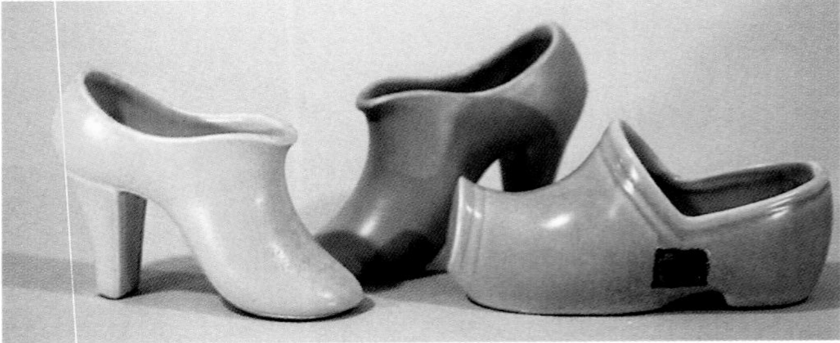

Two #3259 Lady slippers in Satin Yellow and Satin Blue, $55.00 – 65.00 each; with a Satin Green #3258 Dutch slipper with original paper label, $45.00 –55.00. Courtesy of the Ben and Floss Avila collection.

Not Shown:

#3252 basket, hat, 12"x6½", 1939 – 1942. $80.00 – 90.00.

#3253 basket, leaf and handle, 11"x6½", 1939 – 1942. $60.00 – 75.00.

#3254 bowl, deep shell, 2"x5", 1939 – 1942. $25.00 – 30.00.

#3255 bowl, horn shell, 2¼"x6½", 1939 – 1942. $30.00 – 40.00.

#3256 bowl, 3-sided scallop, 2¼"x5", 1939 – 1942. $20.00 – 25.00.

#3267 bowl, horn, 2¾"x5", 1939 – 1942. $20.00 – 25.00.

#3258 Dutch slipper, 2¼"x5", 1939 – 1942. $45.00 – 55.00.

#3259 Lady slipper, 3½"x5", 1939 – 1942. $55.00 – 65.00.

Satin Green #3260 vase, round, 2 curl handles, 7", 1939 – 1941. $85.00 – 95.00.

Satin Yellow #3261 vase, ovoid, 2 small handles, 1939 – 1941. $85.00 – 95.00. Courtesy of the Ben and Pauline Jensen collection.

Satin Blue #3263 vase, flared cup, 7", 1939 – 1942. $35.00 – 45.00.

Satin Blue #3266 vase, ovoid, small handles, 5½", 1939 – 1942. $40.00 – 50.00. Courtesy of the Brian and Cristi Hahn collection.

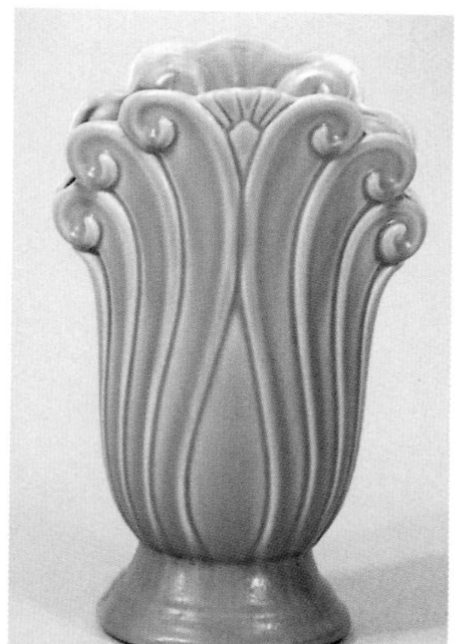

Satin Green #3268 vase, scroll top, 10", 1939 – 1941. $85.00 – 95.00. Courtesy of the Ben and Pauline Jensen collection.

Satin Green #3270 humidifier font, 1939 only. With original motor, $150.00 – 175.00. Courtesy of the Hunterdon County Historical Society.

Satin Blue #3283 scalloped bowl, 7", 1939 – 1944. $15.00 – 20.00. Courtesy of the Marcena North collection.

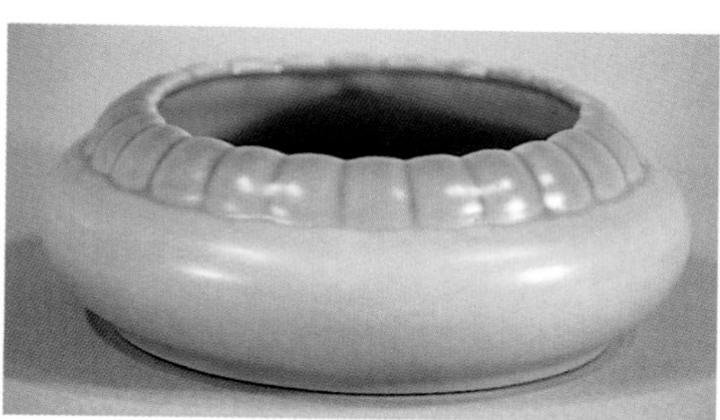

Satin Green #3284 pie crust bowl, 7", 1939 – 1940. $35.00 – 45.00. Courtesy of the Ben and Pauline Jensen collection.

Not Shown:

#3262 vase, petals and base, 7", 1939 – 1941. $45.00 – 55.00.

#3264 vase, modern, 9", 1939 – 1941. $85.00 – 95.00.

#3265 vase, round ribbed, rope base, 9", $70.00 – 85.00.

#3267 vase, cup, ovoid, 5½", 1939 – 1942. $35.00 – 45.00.

#3269 vase, petals, deep scallop top, 10", $60.00 – 75.00.

#3283 scalloped bowl, 11", 1939 – 1944. $35.00 – 45.00.

#3283 scalloped bowl, 9", 1939 – 1944. $20.00 – 25.00.

Silver Green #3412 stove candle warmer, solid-color glazes, 4½"x4½"x3¼", 1940 – 1941. See also page 354. $20.00 – 25.00.

1940 Introductions

Not Shown:

#3410 rose bowl, 10", 1940 – 1942. $30.00 – 40.00.

#3410 rose bowl, 9", 1940 – 1945. $25.00 – 30.00.

#3410 rose bowl, 7", 1940 – 1942. $25.00 – 30.00.

#3411 rose vase, 6½", 1940 – 1941. $65.00 – 80.00.

Tangerine #3410 rose candleholders, 3", 1940 – 1945 (Tangerine available only until 1943). $25.00 – 30.00 pair.

Head Vases

Stangl's head vases were normally glazed only in Satin White, but decorated head vases were produced. For decorated head vases, see also the Hand-Decorated Madonna and Head Vases section in the next chapter (page 243).

Not Shown:

#3418 Snood head vase, 6", 1940 – 1941. $95.00 – 120.00.

Satin White #3419 Curls head vase, 6", 1940 – 1941. $95.00 – 120.00.

Ribbed Scroll Bowls

Satin Green #3424 round ribbed scroll bowl, 7", 1940 – 1941. $25.00 – 35.00. Courtesy of the Marcena North collection.

Satin Green #3425 square ribbed scroll bowl, 7½"x7½", 1940 – 1941. $25.00 – 35.00. Courtesy of the Marcena North collection.

Not Shown:

#3423 Oblong ribbed scroll bowl, 11"x6", 1940 – 1941. $30.00 – 40.00.

1941 Introductions

Many of the shapes introduced in 1941 and 1942 are more commonly found in Stangl's Terra Rose finishes (see pages 349-366).

Satin Yellow #3511 tall watering pot, 10", 1941 – 1942. $190.00 – 225.00. Courtesy of the Marcena North collection.

Satin Blue #3517 Chinese shoe, 2"x5", 1941 – 1942. $45.00 – 55.00. Courtesy of the Ben and Floss Avila collection.

Satin Blue #3557 basket, 13½"x10", deep flutes, 1941 – 1943. $70.00 – 85.00. Courtesy of the Marcena North collection.

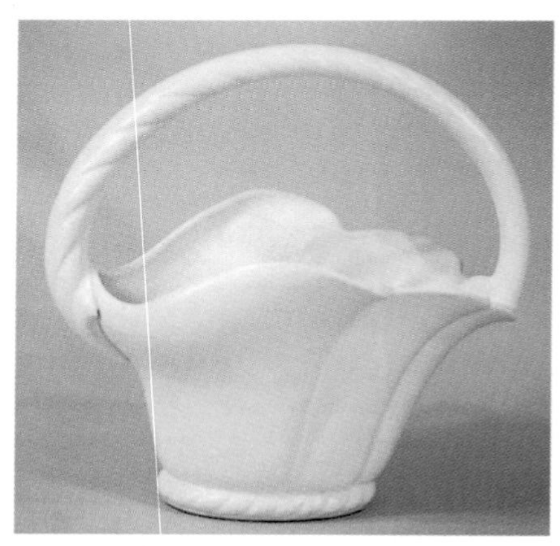

Satin White #3560 basket, round rope handle, 11", 1941 – 1943. $85.00 – 95.00. Courtesy of the Marcena North collection.

Not Shown:

#3510 round watering pot, 7¼", 1941 – 1942. $100.00 – 125.00.
#3555 basket, 13"x8½", 1941 only. $110.00 – 135.00.
#3558 bowl, rope handles, 11"x4½", 1941 – 1943. $50.00 – 60.00.
#3559 bowl, rope handles, 14"x5½", 1941 – 1943. $80.00 – 90.00.
#3561 basket, leaf handles, 11", 1941 – 1942. $85.00 – 95.00.
#3562 bowl, oblong leaf, 11½"x4½", 1941 – 1943. $35.00 – 45.00.

1942 Introductions

Not Shown:

#3612 vase, tall lily, 8", 1942 – 1943. $25.00 – 35.00.
#3614 vase, shell scroll base, 8½"x10½", 1942 – 1943. $100.00 – 125.00.
#3615 vase, scroll, 10½"x8¼", 1942 – 1943. $85.00 – 95.00.
#3616 basket, leaf, sweeping handle, 9½" high, 1942 – 1943. $70.00 – 85.00.
#3619 vase, leaf horn, 9¼", 1942 – 1943. $80.00 – 90.00.
#3620 bowl, lily of the valley, 5"x7", 1942 – 1943. $85.00 – 95.00.
#3621 small basket, 5½" high, 1942 – 1943. $35.00 – 45.00.
#3622 basket, flat handle, 7¾" high, 1942 – 1943. $85.00 – 95.00.
#3623 basket, scalloped, 9" high, 1942 – 1943. $55.00 – 65.00.
#3624 basket, twist handle, 9" high, 1942 – 1943. $80.00 – 90.00.
#3672 double Shell vase, 7½"x12", 1942 – 1943. $100.00 – 125.00.

Satin Blue #3675 vase, oval Morning Glory, 10", 1942 – 1943. $100.00 – 125.00.

1943 Introduction: Sailor Figurine

Colonial Blue Sailor figure, 9", 1943 only. $450.00 – 500.00.
From the Stangl and Fulper archival collection, courtesy the Wheaton Village Museum of American Glass.

1965 Introductions: Wall Console Sets

The #5169 boy & Fish and #5170 Ram's Head wall console sets were produced during 1965 in brushed gold finishes as well as in Satin White, Satin Black, and terra cotta bisque finishes.

#5169 Boy & Fish wall console set: boy 15"x6", bowl 8¼"x6½", 1965 only. $160.00 – 180.00.
#5169 boy only, 15"x6", $80.00 – 100.00.
#5169 bowl only, 8¼"x6½", $40.00 – 50.00.
#5170 Ram's Head wall console set: ram's head 12¾"x11½", bowl 7¼"x5½", 1965 only. $160.00 – 180.00.
#5170 ram's head only, 12¾"x11½". $80.00 – 100.00.
#5170 bowl only, 7¼"x5½". $40.00 – 50.00.

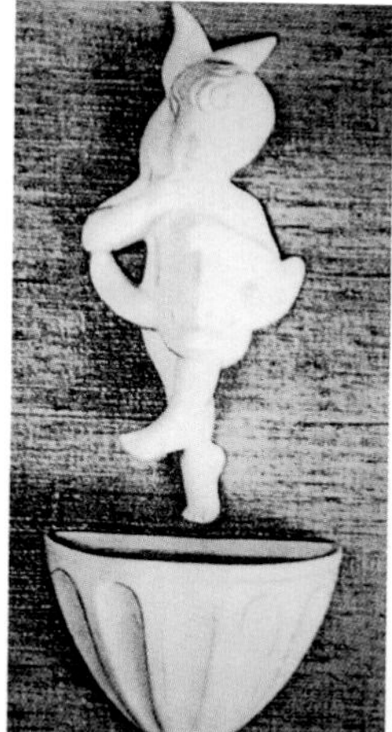

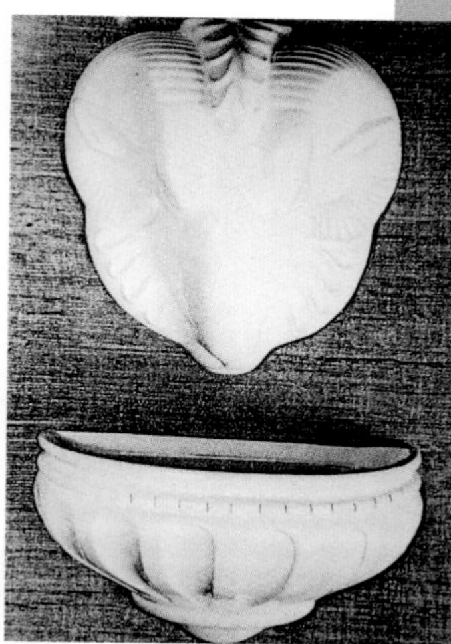

Original Stangl catalog pages showing #5169 Boy & Fish, and the #5170 Ram's Head wall console sets.

1967 Introductions: Cabbage #5197

In 1967 several old #1800 Cabbage Leaf shapes were brought back for gift shops and the Flemington Outlet. The 1967 reintroductions usually were marked with a #5197 underglaze stamp in addition to the old #1800 in-mold mark. The colors on the new issues were the fashion-color glazes Chartreuse Green, Canary Yellow, Art Ware Green, White, Dark Green, and Peach. Chartreuse Green and White are the colors most often found.

The #5197 Cabbage double relish servers were produced in great quantities from 1967 through the 1970s. The 1930s original #1800 Cabbage Leaf servers had pottery twig shape handles. The #5197 servers were affixed with a variety of inexpensive brass-tone metal handles.

#5197 Cabbage double relish, 9½", 1967 – 1970s. $6.00 – 10.00.
#5197 Cabbage round triple relish, 9½", 1967 – 1970s. $15.00 – 20.00.
#5197 Cabbage single relish, 13", 1967 – 1970s. $10.00 – 15.00.

Chartreuse Green #5197 Cabbage double relish, $6.00 – 10.00; and 10" plate, $12.00 – 18.00; with a gloss white #5197 Cabbage cup and saucer, $18.00 – 20.00.

1969 Introductions: New Serv-Ware

In 1969, Stangl introduced a line of serving items cast in red clay and in a durable, bright blue-white ovenproof glaze. Old tried-and-true server shapes were used for this new line. Sadly, Stangl's New Serv-Ware failed to capture the attention of the buyers at the January 1969 trade show, so the line was discontinued by February 1969.

Not Shown:
#1800-T triple leaf tray, 12" diameter, 1969 only. $20.00 – 25.00.
#1800-D double leaf tray, 8"x9½", 1969 only. $12.00 – 18.00.
#3410-9 flower bowl, 9", 1969 only. $25.00 – 30.00.
#3410-7 flower bowl, 7", 1969 only. $20.00 – 25.00.
#3546 apple tray, 13" diameter, 1969 only. $30.00 – 40.00.
#3779 leaf server, 7"x14½", 1969 only. $25.00 – 30.00.
#3781 triple shell tray, 12" diameter, 1969 only. $35.00 – 45.00.
#3782 double pear dish, 1969 only. $15.00 – 20.00.
#3783 single pear dish, 1969 only. $10.00 – 15.00.
#3784 double apple dish, 1969 only. $15.00 – 20.00.
#3785 single apple dish, 1969 only. $10.00 – 15.00.
#3788 heart dish, 8", 1969 only. $12.00 – 18.00.
#3857 clover server, 7", 1969 only. $25.00 – 30.00.
#3859 leaf server, 8", 1969 only. $12.00 – 18.00.
#4018 shell, 7½", 1969 only. $12.00 – 18.00.
#4019 shell, 9", 1969 only. $18.00 – 22.00.
#4020 shell, 10½", 1969 only. $22.00 – 28.00.
#4038 leaf server, 9"x13½", 1969 only. $25.00 – 30.00.

Stangl's New Serv-Ware #3784 Double Apple dish, $15.00 – 20.00.

#4039 leaf server, 8½"x12", 1969 only. $22.00 – 28.00.
#4041 leaf server, 13"x17", 1969 only. $40.00 – 50.00.
#4042 leaf server, 10"x16", 1969 only. $40.00 – 50.00.
#4065 bowl, 11" diameter, 1969 only. $25.00 – 30.00.
#5115-L oval bowl, 17½", 1969 only. $25.00 – 35.00.
#5115-M oval bowl, 14", 1969 only. $20.00 – 25.00.
#5115-S oval bowl, 11½", 1969 only. $12.00 – 18.00.
#5214 shell bowl, 7"x10", 1969 only. $25.00 – 30.00.

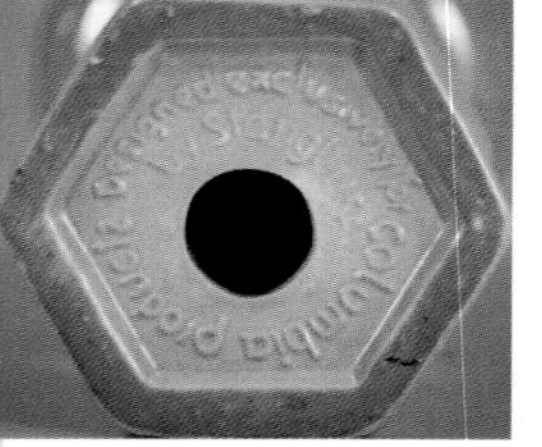

#5244 pillar candleholder, 5½", made for Columbia Products, 1971 – 1973 (base, inset). $25.00 – 30.00.

1971 Introductions: Columbia Products

The Columbia Products candleholders were made as special-order items for Columbia Products and were in-mold marked as such. They were produced with the brushed-gold finishes Antique Gold and Granada Gold and fashion-color glazes Dark Green, Chartreuse Green Canary Yellow, Tan, and Black.

1974 Introductions

Decorator Items

Stangl Pottery introduced these vases under the name "Decorator Items" in a variety of three solid-color glazes. Canary Yellow, Onyx Black, and Mandarin Red were the glazes available. Mandarin Red was actually a low temperature fired-on overglaze color, similar to the Tangerine overglaze color used on ashtray shapes during 1970. These vases were produced in these colors for less than a year and are now very rare. Items glazed in Mandarin Red usually sell for nearly double the value listed here.

#3979 vase, 9", 1974 only. $40.00 – 50.00.
#3981 vase, 6¾", 1974 only. $30.00 – 40.00.
#3993 vase, 13", 1974 only. $60.00 – 75.00.
#4007 vase, 7", 1974 only. $30.00 – 40.00.
Ginger Jar, 11¾", 1974 only. $85.00 – 95.00.

Original 1974 Stangl catalog page showing the "Decorator Items" assortment of vases.

Fashion-Color China Vases

Also introduced in 1974 was a series of popular vase shapes cast of heavy, vitreous "sanitary ware" china. These were glazed in the fashion colors Dark Green, Chartreuse Green, White, Peach, and Canary Yellow. These vases were primarily sold at the Flemington Outlet from 1974 through 1976. They can be identified by their extreme weight. Items cast of earthenware were also glazed with the fashion-color glazes and have the same values as the items made of vitreous china.

Three Fashion-Color #5133 spiral base china vases in Dark Green, Canary Yellow, and Chartreuse Green, $40.00 – 50.00 each. Courtesy of the Marcena North collection.

White #2032 handled bowl, 1974 – 1976. $35.00 – 45.00.

Not Shown:
#1906 urn vase, 7¾", 1974 – 1976. $45.00 – 55.00.
#3103 handled vase, 7½", 1974 – 1976. $35.00 – 45.00.
#3413 handled bowl, 10¼"x5½", 1974 – 1976. $25.00 – 35.00.
#3621 handled basket, 5½", 1974 – 1976. $25.00 – 35.00.
#3952 cylinder vase, 10". $25.00 – 35.00.
#3952 cylinder vase, 8". $25.00 – 30.00.
#3952 cylinder vase, 6". $25.00 – 30.00.
#3952 cylinder vase, 4". $20.00 – 25.00.
#5133 spiral base vase, 7¼", 1974 – 1976. $40.00 – 50.00.
#5134 cosmos vase, 7½", 1974 – 1976. $35.00 – 45.00.
#5144 tulip bowl, 4", 1974 – 1976. $25.00 – 30.00.
#5214 conch shell bowl, 7"x10", 1974 – 1976. $35.00 – 45.00.

White #4050 bud vase, 8", $25.00 – 35.00.

Chartreuse Green #5106 triple cylinder vase, 10"x5". $25.00 – 35.00.

Fulper-Stangl Handmade Artware, 1925 – 1935

The inspiration for Martin Stangl's line of Handmade artware is traced directly to the ancient pottery district of the Sandhills region surrounding Steeds, North Carolina (the name was changed to Seagrove in 1957). Pioneers originating from the Staffordshire pottery district in England settled this part of North Carolina in the 1740s and quickly took advantage of the abundant raw materials for pottery making. The initial products were soft earthenware with low-firing glazes. By the early 1800s, the Seagrove potters were producing high-quality salt glazed stoneware crocks, pots, and jugs. During the Civil War, potters of the area were under pressure by the Confederate Army to produce enough stoneware vessels for transporting food to the soldiers at the battlefields. Following the war, the Seagrove potters survived by farming and producing jugs for the whiskey distillers until the State of North Carolina implemented prohibition in 1908, thus ending the demand for whiskey jugs. A few of the potters augmented their farming efforts by producing pottery for the tourists at Pinehurst Resort, about 35 miles southeast of Seagrove. By the 1910s, Pinehurst Resort had played host to several noted golf championships and was frequented by such important personages as John D. Rockefeller, H.J. Heinz, and Annie Oakley. Also during the 1910s, Raleigh, North Carolina, artist/historian Jacques Busbee and his wife took an avid interest in the remaining potters of the Seagrove district and began documenting the products of both the existing as well as long-vanished potteries.

In order to help the Seagrove region financially and bring recognition to this fast-fading American folk-craft, the Busbees began purchasing local pottery and selling it in "The Village Store," a gift shop they established in Greenwich Village. By 1920, the remaining part-time Seagrove potters could not keep pace with the demand of the New York market, so in 192 Jacques Busbee opened his own pottery in Steeds (Seagrove). Called Jugtown Pottery, Busbee manned his works with descendants of the original Staffordshire settlers and produced re-creations of the wares produced during the Civil War era. From there he developed artistic pottery shapes and glazes based on the traditional craftsmanship, techniques, and materials of the area. Neighboring potteries soon began producing artistic pots and glazes as well. A singular achievement of some of the potters was the continued successful reduction firing of the difficult copper red and chrome red glazes. These glazes were so difficult to fire that few commercial potters outside of North Carolina attempted them at that time.

By 1922, the ardent passion for North Carolina pottery was fueled even more by the publication of a cover article in *House Beautiful.* By 1926, the North Carolina pottery craze had even caught the attention of the commercial ceramic industry. The January 1926 issue of *The Ceramist* stated: "Nothing has yet been said of the ornamental pottery industry of North Carolina. This industry was started in 1750, but has only within the past year commenced to become widely known outside of the state. The plants are small and their equipment crude but the demand for their products is so great in such art centers as New York and Chicago that it cannot be supplied. There are seven of these plants in the state. One of them, producing principally copper reds, is among the few potteries in the United States making this type of art ware. All the ware is turned on the wheel by native potters."

During the remainder of the 1920s, North Carolina pottery continued to be the focus of articles in several decorating, gift, and fashion publications. The pottery trade magazine *The Ceramic Age* requested Jacques Busbee himself to expound upon Jugtown pottery and the craze for North Carolina pottery. Busbee's article was published in the November 1929 issue and was prefaced with the following: "At the request of *The Ceramic Age,* Mr. Busbee, proprietor of the Jugtown Pottery at Steeds, N.C., has prepared this interesting sidelight of the famous district, from an historical standpoint, where Jugtown pottery is being manufactured. He paints a personal picture of charm of environment, showing how the revival of this pottery has brought prominence to the ceramic craft in the upper part of Moore County that had little short of expired a number of years ago. No traveler to these parts, and particularly those interested in ceramics, misses a call at the Jugtown Pottery, where is seen a replica of craftsmanship and tools as obtained in the early days of pottery in America." Thus, we come back to Fulper Pottery Company in 1926.

Always abreast of the latest ceramic trends, Martin Stangl was well aware of the increasing demand for North Carolina handmade pottery. In 1926, he began developing a line of folk-inspired, hand-turned pottery he called "Primitive." John Kunsman, who had been with Fulper Pottery since 1888 and had most recently been conducting traveling pottery demonstrations, became the principal potter and personally produced nearly all of the Handmade Artware during the 1920s. After hand-turning Fulper's art and utility wares for nearly 40 years, no one could be more qualified to develop a handmade art line than John Kunsman. Besides, he had been producing forerunners to the Handmade Artware line during his department store demonstrations. Nearly all of the shapes he turned at the demonstrations were diminutive forms that could be quickly worked up, yet have great effect. Some of the items were miniature versions of old Fulper shapes he had developed years before, while others were newly created and would become the models for the full-sized Handmade Artware line.

Fulper-Stangl gold-foil paper label on the bottom of a handmade vase, 1927 to 1929.

Stangl Pottery gold-foil paper label on the bottom of handmade pieces from 1929 to 1935.

Stangl's initial Handmade Artware assortment of full-size items was introduced in 1927. It was comprised of a variety of 16 vase and bowl shapes. Some were sleek, smooth, and modern with applied handles. Other shapes were simpler and textured with spiraling "finger marks" (actually produced with wooden tools) to indicate hand-crafting. These products were introduced as Fulper-Stangl brand and were marked only with Fulper-Stangl gold-foil paper labels, usually applied to the bottoms. Because these items were all turned on the potters' wheel, the bases are completely flat and bear no in-mold markings.

Martin Stangl's standard solid-color glazes were applied to the handmade shapes as well as newly developed glazes that replicated some of the earthy North Carolina finishes. Apple Green, Turquoise Blue, Primitive Green, Blue Matte, Blue Antique, Grey Matte, Violet, and Oxblood glazes were all developed during the late 1920s, primarily for the Handmade Artware products.

Martin Stangl truly sought to develop a vibrant red glaze akin to the North Carolina chrome and copper reds. However, chrome and copper could not be fired in the same oxidizing atmosphere as Stangl's other solid-color glazes, but glazes based on uranium oxide could. Uranium oxide had been a component of stable orange, red, and yellow colorants for the ceramic and glass industries since the 1830s. However, all formulae and processes were closely guarded secrets that never left the Bohemia region of Europe. Also, uranium oxide was too costly for typical ceramics production because the demand for radium for cancer treatments kept the cost of uranium at elevated levels. The discovery of high-quality radium-producing uranium by Belgium in 1921 caused a serious price reduction of American uranium in 1924, making commercial grade uranium oxide available at reasonable cost. Stangl began a search for someone well versed in uranium's use as a glaze colorant, and help in using the oxides arrived in the form of Heinrich Below. He had been educated in Bavaria as a ceramic engineer, like Stangl, and Below was knowledgeable of the closely guarded secrets of uranium glazing.

In 1929, Martin Stangl hired Heinrich Below as plant manager, a position he maintained until 1949. One of Below's first accomplishments was the development of Fulper Pottery's uranium oxide-based Tangerine and Rust glazes. These glazes very closely emulated the chrome and copper red glazes of North Carolina and were immediately popular. Soon after Stangl introduced the Tangerine glaze in 1929, other American potters (most notably Bauer of California and Homer Laughlin of West Virginia) followed suit with their own versions of "Uranium Red." The uranium red was an extremely popular glaze color and was used extensively until 1943 when the U. S. government took control of all commercial grade uranium oxide for development of nuclear weapons.

During the late 1920s, demand for the Handmade Artware snowballed to the point where John Kunsman was spending all his time mass-producing hand-turned artware, which left little time for the extremely popular traveling demonstrations. In 1928, two additional potters were hired for the Handmade Artware line and two more in 1930, allowing John Kunsman to divide his time between working on the handmade artware and doing traveling demonstrations.

By 1929, ten additional handmade artware shapes and a quantity of handmade lamp shapes were developed and introduced. From 1930 to 1935, over 95 simple, well-proportioned handmade shapes showing clear evidence of being handwrought were developed and produced. During the "Machine Age" of factory automation, it was still much more economical for potters to hand-throw these shapes than to have them mold-cast. John Kunsman liked to amaze onlookers by stating that he could throw as many as 300 flowerpots with attached saucers in eight hours, "cheaper than they could be turned out by machinery."

During the early 1930s, Martin Stangl eliminated some of the handmade shapes from the more "exclusive" Handmade Artware line and added them to slip-cast production. It was very costly to develop a new shape in slip-cast production due to the cost of producing plaster models, master molds, and production molds before the shape could even be market-tested. For this reason, Martin Stangl had molds made for only the most popular handmade shapes. Once they were slip-cast, he could no longer charge the same premium price he was getting for handmade shapes, but at the lower price-point could sell them in greater quantity. This also allowed the potters to produce more handmade shapes of a more profitable nature.

Following the destruction of Fulper Pottery Company Plant No. 1 by fire in 1929, all Fulper Fayence and Fulper-Stangl slip-cast production was moved to the Trenton factory. Production of Fulper Pottery Artware was hastily set up at the newly enlarged Plant No. 2 at Flemington, where the turning of Fulper-Stangl brand Handmade Artware continued. In spite of Martin Stangl's efforts to keep the line going, lackluster sales of Fulper Pottery Artware forced its termination in 1934. By 1935, all remaining production of handmade artware was moved from Flemington to Trenton. Even though the craze for North Carolina-styled handmade pottery was waning, having been replaced by a great demand for Italian peasant ceramics, Martin Stangl continued production of some of the handmade shapes well into the late 1930s rather than laying off his potters. By 1940, the potters were again kept busy creating hand-turned Italian-style Terra Rose dinnerware and serving pieces for Saks Fifth Avenue.

1930s era hand-scrawled "Stangl Pottery" on the base of a handmade jug,

During the 1920s and 1930s, many shapes were produced that appear handmade but were actually slip-cast. Those items are not listed here but can be found under the Solid-Color Artware section. Handmade Artware shapes that were later slip-cast are nearly always marked with an in-mold shape number and the name Stangl, and usually have detectable mold seams. The original handmade shapes have perfectly flat bottoms, no mold seams, and were almost never marked. Occasionally, handmade pieces were marked with the words "Stangl" or "Stangl Pottery" hand-scrawled into the base. The handmade shapes generally sell for a bit more than the same shapes that were slip-cast.

Please see also the sections on Multi-Color (pages 246 – 248), Sunburst (pages 255 – 265), and Tropical (pages 240 – 241) for additional finishes applied to the Handmade Artware items.

Pay careful attention to condition of this artware. Applied handles are prone to stress cracks, and the finger-formed ridges are particularly vulnerable to wear and chipping. It is easy to find pieces with slight damage but difficult to find pieces in mint condition. Values shown are for the easily-found colors of Colonial Blue, Persian Yellow, Silver Green, Apple Green, Green Matte, Satin White, Tangerine, and Rust. Pieces glazed with Blue Matte, Blue Antique, Grey Matte, and Yellow Orange sell for about 50% more than standard colors. Primitive Green, (a very rare spruce green) Purple, Rose, Turquoise Blue, Oxblood, Variegated Rust, Violet, or combination glazes can sell for up to double the value of standard colors.

1925 – 1926 Introductions

John Kunsman produced a large assortment of miniatures, handmade at traveling department store demonstrations. Because John Kunsman produced these items for over 10 years, a great variety of shapes can be found, and sizes can range from as small as 1½" inches to 4½". Some of the items, such as the flowerpot shape, were ultimately factory-produced in Flemington then later Trenton. The values shown here are only for the items handmade by John Kunsman.

Covered Jar, 4½" (demonstration shape). $165.00 – 200.00.
Flare vase, 3½" (original Fulper shape). $95.00 – 110.00.
Flare vase, 2¾" (original Fulper shape). $130.00 – 150.00.
Three-handle vase, 3½" (became #1124). $110.00 – 135.00.
Flowerpot, 1¾" (became #1792). $130.00 – 150.00.
Flowerpot, 2½" (became #1792). $60.00 – 75.00.
Basket, 4" (became Fulper #1888). $150.00 – 175.00.
Jug, 4" (original Fulper shape). $130.00 – 150.00.
Ruffled bowl, 3" (became #1919). $110.00 – 135.00.

An assortment of John Kunsman's handmade department store demonstration pieces, produced from 1925 through the mid 1930s. Courtesy of the Hill-Fulper-Stangl Museum.

1927 Introductions

The 1927 introductions were called "Primitive" and were usually marked with a Fulper-Stangl gold-foil paper label. The presence of an undamaged, complete Fulper-Stangl label can sometimes add from $15.00 to $40.00 to the value of the piece.

#1119L bowl, 8" Fulper-Stangl handmade, 1927 – 1930s. $80.00 – 90.00.
#1119S bowl, 7" Fulper-Stangl handmade, 1927 – 1930s. $65.00 – 80.00.
#1120L flower holder, 3½", 6 holes, Fulper-Stangl handmade, 1927 – 1930s. $20.00 – 25.00.
#1120S flower holder, 3", 5 holes, Fulper-Stangl handmade, 1927 – 1930s. $15.00 – 20.00.
#1121L Double Bulge vase, 12½" Fulper-Stangl handmade, 1927 – 1930s. $180.00 – 200.00.
#1123 bottle, 9" Fulper-Stangl handmade, 1927 – 1930s. $130.00 – 150.00.

John Kunsman handmade department store demonstration covered jar, 4½" to top of cover, Green Matte, 1925 – 1930s. $165.00 – 200.00.

Silver Green #1121S Double Bulge vase, 10" Fulper-Stangl handmade, 1927 – 1930s. $150.00 – 175.00.

Two #1122 Band Rim vases, 8", Colonial Blue and Silver Green, Fulper-Stangl handmade, 1927 – 1930s. $100.00 – 125.00 each.

Blue Matte #1119L 8" bowl with #1120L flower holder, $100.00 – 115.00 per set; and Persian Yellow #1119S bowl with #1120S flower holder, $80.00 – 100.00 per set.

The #1124 Slanting Handle vase was one of Stangl Pottery's most popular handmade shapes. This vase was in continual production from 1927 through the late 1930s, first as a handmade shape then as a mold-cast shape. The #1124 Slanting Handle vase can be found in more colors than almost any other handmade vase.

Silver Green #1124 Slanting Handle vase with original label, 7½" Fulper-Stangl handmade, 1927 – 1930s. $85.00 – 95.00. Courtesy of the Brian and Cristi Hahn collection.

Two #1124 Slanting Handle vases showing the difference between the hard-to-find Variegated Rust glaze (on left with white lining), $150.00 – 165.00; and the usual Rust glaze, on right, $85.00 – 95.00. Courtesy of the Chris McGeehan collection.

Group of #1124 Slanting Handle vases in Sunburst, Turquoise Blue, Persian Yellow, Rust, and Yellow Orange glazes.

Persian Yellow #1125 rose bowl, 4"x6" Fulper-Stangl handmade, 1927 – 1930s. $65.00 – 80.00. Courtesy of the Marcena North collection.

Grey Matte #1126 Ball vase, 7½" Fulper-Stangl handmade (later reintroduced as Stangl #1907), 1927 – 1930s. $100.00 – 125.00.

Apple Green #1126 Ball vase, 7½" Fulper-Stangl handmade (later reintroduced as Stangl #1907), 1927 – 1930s. $100.00 – 125.00. Courtesy of the Brian and Cristi Hahn collection.

Not Shown:

#1124 Slanting Handle vase, 7½" Stangl mold-cast, 1932 – 1937. $65.00 – 80.00.
#1128L Double 4-handle vase, 8" Fulper-Stangl handmade, 1927 – 1930s. $150.00 – 175.00.
#1128S Double 4-handle vase, 4" Fulper-Stangl handmade, 1927 – 1930s. $95.00 – 110.00.
#1129L Double 3-handle vase, 8¾" Fulper-Stangl handmade, 1927 – 1930s. $110.00 – 135.00.
#1129S Double 3-handle vase, 5¾" Fulper-Stangl handmade, 1927 – 1930s. $85.00 – 95.00.

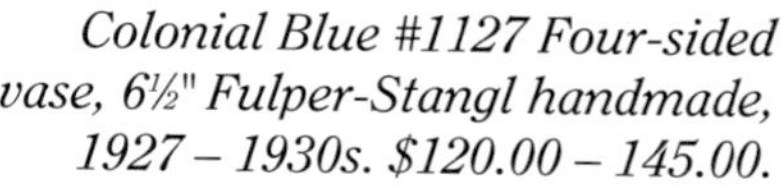

Colonial Blue #1127 Four-sided vase, 6½" Fulper-Stangl handmade, 1927 – 1930s. $120.00 – 145.00.

Not Shown:

#1150L flowerpot, 8" Fulper-Stangl handmade, 1927 – 1930s. $95.00 – 110.00.

#1150M flowerpot, 6" Fulper-Stangl handmade, 1927 – 1930s. $70.00 – 85.00.

#1150S flowerpot, 4" Fulper-Stangl handmade, 1927 – 1930s. $55.00 – 65.00.

1929 Introductions

Sold under the Stangl trademark, usually marked only with a Stangl Pottery gold-foil paper label.

Two #1129L 8¾" Double 3-handle vases, Silver Green and Grey Matte, $110.00 – 135.00 each; with a Persian Yellow #1129S 5¾" Double 3-handle vase, $85.00 – 95.00.

Silver Green #1233EL Crimp bowl, 10" Stangl handmade, 1929 – 1935. $120.00 – 145.00.

Three #1237 ribbed 3-handle jars, handmade Apple Green (left), handmade Blue Matte (center), $80.00 – 90.00 each; and mold-cast Tangerine (right), $65.00 – 80.00.

Group of handmade #1238 smooth 3-handle jars, Apple Green, Blue Matte, and Oxblood glazes on 6" jars, Violet glaze on 9" jar. Oxblood glaze and Violet glazes can increase the value of these jars up to 50%.

Tangerine with turquoise lining #1238L jar, 3-handles, 9" smooth, Stangl handmade, 1929 – 1935. $130.00 – 150.00.

Grey Matte #1238M jar, 3-handles, 6" smooth, Stangl handmade, 1929 – 1935. $80.00 – 90.00. Courtesy of the Brian and Cristi Hahn collection.

#1233L Crimp bowl, 8" Stangl handmade, 1929 – 1935. $80.00 – 100.00.

#1233M Crimp bowl, 6" Stangl handmade, 1929 – 1935. $70.00 – 85.00.

#1233S Crimp bowl, 5" Stangl handmade, 1929 – 1935. $60.00 – 75.00.

#1237 jar, 3-handles, 7½" ribbed, Stangl handmade, 1929 – 1935. $95.00 – 110.00.

#1237 jar, 3-handles, 7½" ribbed, mold-cast, 1933 – 1937. $65.00 – 80.00.

#1237 jar, 3-handles, 6" ribbed, Stangl handmade, 1929 – 1935. $80.00 – 90.00.

#1237 jar, 3-handles, 6" ribbed, mold-cast, 1933 – 1937. $65.00 – 80.00.

Two #1239 jar, 2 high-handles, 7" Stangl handmade, Apple Green and Silver Green, 1929 – 1935. $120.00 – 145.00 each. Courtesy of the Brian and Cristi Hahn collection.

1930 Introductions

Blue Matte #1274 hanging basket, 7"x3" Stangl handmade, 1930 – 1935. $100.00 – 125.00.

Tangerine #1327L vase, 11" Stangl handmade, 1930 – 1935. $120.00 – 145.00.

Tangerine #1328 vase, narrow 2 handles at neck 14" Stangl handmade, 1930 – 1933. $175.00 – 200.00. Courtesy of the Robert and Tammie Cruser collection.

Green Matte #1329 vase, wide 18" Stangl handmade, 1930 – 1933. $350.00 – 375.00. Courtesy of Merrill and Christl Stangl Bacheler.

Not Shown:

#1274 hanging basket, 3 handles 7"x4" Stangl handmade, 1930 – 1935. $120.00 – 145.00.
#1327M vase, 9" Stangl handmade, 1930 – 1935. $95.00 – 130.00.
#1328 vase, narrow 2 handles at neck 14" mold-cast, 1933 – 1938. $120.00 – 145.00.
#1329 vase, narrow 18" Stangl handmade, 1930 – 1933. $175.00 – 200.00.
#1329-B vase 15" Stangl handmade, 1930 – 1933. $175.00 – 200.00.
#1329 vase, narrow 18" mold-cast, 1933 – 1938. $150.00 – 175.00.
#1329 vase, wide 18" mold-cast, 1933 – 1938. $200.00 – 250.00.
#1329-B vase 15" mold-cast, 1933 – 1938. $130.00 – 150.00.

1931 Introductions

Not Shown:

#1382 strawberry jar, 15" Stangl handmade, 1931 – 1935. $200.00 – 250.00.
#1382 strawberry jar, 12" Stangl handmade, 1931 – 1935. $130.00 – 150.00.
#1382 strawberry jar, 9" Stangl handmade, 1931 – 1935. $100.00 – 125.00.
#1382 strawberry jar, 8" Stangl handmade, 1931 – 1935. $95.00 – 110.00.
#1382 strawberry jar, 6" mold-cast, 1933 – 1938. $60.00 – 75.00.

Silver Green #1382 strawberry jar, 6" Stangl handmade, 1931 – 1935. $85.00 – 95.00.

See also the sections on Decorated Handmade (pages 242 – 243) and Sunburst Artware (pages 255 – 264) for more photos of the following shapes.

#1453 rose bowl, 5½" Stangl handmade, 1931 – 1935. $55.00 – 65.00.
#1454 violet jar, 5¼" Stangl handmade, 1931 – 1935. $55.00 – 70.00.
#1456 basket, 7" Stangl handmade, 1931 – 1935. $70.00 – 85.00.
#1457 low jar, 2 handles, 4¾" tall, Stangl handmade, 1931 – 1935. $80.00 – 100.00.
#1458 flower bowl, 7¼" diameter, Stangl handmade, 1931 – 1935. $70.00 – 85.00.
#1460 candleholder, 4 ½" Stangl handmade, 1931 – 1935. $65.00 – 80.00.
#1461 flower pot, attached saucer 4½" Stangl handmade, 1931 – 1935. $55.00 – 65.00.
#1462 flower vase, small neck, 6¾" Stangl handmade, 1931 – 1935. $60.00 – 75.00.

Tangerine with green lining #1455 ovoid vase, 5" Stangl handmade, 1931 – 1935. $60.00 – 75.00.

#1464 bowl, 6" diameter, Stangl handmade, 1931 – 1935. $60.00 – 75.00.
#1465 vase, straight top, 5½" Stangl handmade, 1931 – 1935. $60.00 – 75.00.
#1466 tall vase, 10¼" Stangl handmade, 1931 – 1935. $85.00 – 95.00.

Green Matte #1463 flower vase, tall neck, 8" Stangl handmade, 1931 – 1935. $80.00 – 90.00.
Courtesy of the Brian and Cristi Hahn collection.

1932 Introductions

Group of Hand-Made Low Jugs, #1585S Silver Green, #1585ES Variegated Rust, #1587L Persian Yellow, and #1586M Tangerine with turquoise lining.

Not Shown:
#1585ES low jug, 3" Stangl handmade, 1932 – 1935. $25.00 – 35.00.
#1585S low jug, 3¾" Stangl handmade, 1932 – 1935. $30.00 – 40.00.

#1585 open sugar, 2½"x 3½" Stangl handmade, 1932 – 1935. $25.00 – 35.00.
#1586M low jug, 4" Stangl handmade, 1932 – 1935. $55.00 – 65.00.
#1587L low jug, 4¾" Stangl handmade, 1932 – 1935. $60.00 – 75.00.
#1588 tall jug, 4½" Stangl handmade, 1932 – 1935. $40.00 – 50.00.

Handmade pieces #1585 – #1588 nearly always have ridged "finger-marks" and applied handles and are sometimes marked with the hand-scrawled "Stangl." The mold-cast pieces are always smooth with cast handles and in-mold shape numbers.
#1585ES low jug, 3" mold-cast, 1933 – 1942. $20.00 – 25.00.
#1585S low jug, mold-cast, 3¾" 1933 – 1942. $20.00 – 25.00.
#1585 open sugar, mold-cast, 2½"x 3½" 1933 – 1942. $20.00 – 25.00.
#1588 tall jug, 4½" mold-cast, 1933 – 1942. $25.00 – 30.00.

These handmade items were for Bamberger's Department Store, Newark, New Jersey.

Not Shown:
#1636 fluted vase small, 5" made for Bamberger's, 1932 – 1933. $110.00 – 135.00.
#1637 candleholder, 5" made for Bamberger's, 1932 – 1933. $70.00 – 85.00.
#1639 rose bowl, 5" made for Bamberger's, 1932 – 1933. $70.00 – 85.00.

Rust with turquoise lining #1634 bowl, 8¼" diameter, made for Bamberger's, 1932 – 1933. $85.00 – 95.00.

Green Matte #1635 fluted vase large 6½", made for Bamberger's, 1932 – 1933. $130.00 – 160.00.

Variegated Tangerine #1638 vase, 6", made for Bamberger's, 1932 – 1933. $85.00 – 95.00.

Three #1645 Swirl sandwich plates in Tangerine, Rust, and Surf White, $30.00 – 40.00 each; with #1644 Swirl handled sandwich tray in Apple Green, $150.00 – 175.00.

Apple Green #1648 step-back vase, 9" Stangl handmade, 1933 – 1935. $120.00 – 145.00.

Silver Green #1649 Curvy vase, 9" Stangl handmade, 1933 – 1935. $110.00 – 135.00.

Apple Green #1665 cylinder vase, 8" Stangl handmade, 1933 – 1935. $70.00 – 85.00.

Green Matte #1666 Pitcher vase, 9½" Stangl handmade, 1933 – 1935. $95.00 – 115.00.

Green Matte #1667 cup vase, 7" Stangl handmade, 1933 – 1935. $85.00 – 95.00.

Apple Green #1668 vase, handle, ring bottom, 9" Stangl handmade, 1933 – 1935. $120.00 – 145.00.

Variegated Rust #1670 vase, low handles, 7" Stangl handmade, 1933 – 1935. $110.00 – 135.00. Courtesy of the Brian and Cristi Hahn collection.

Variegated Rust #1710 vase, 3 handles large, 9" Stangl handmade, 1933 – 1935. $125.00 – 145.00.

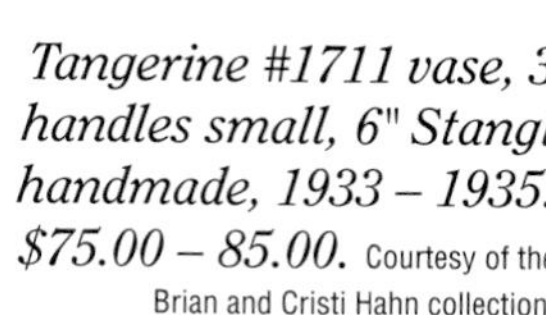

Tangerine #1711 vase, 3 handles small, 6" Stangl handmade, 1933 – 1935. $75.00 – 85.00. Courtesy of the Brian and Cristi Hahn collection.

Not Shown:

#1644 Swirl sandwich tray, 12" with pottery handle, 1933 – 1935. $150.00 – 175.00.
#1645 Swirl sandwich plate, 8" Stangl handmade, 1933 – 1935. $30.00 – 40.00.
#1669 vase, handle, ring top, 7" Stangl handmade, 1933 – 1935. $110.00 – 135.00.
#1712 vase, 2 handles, 6" Stangl handmade, 1933 – 1935. $65.00 – 80.00.
#1712 vase, 2 handles, 6" mold-cast, 1935 – 1939. $55.00 – 65.00.

Two #1712 vases, mold-cast in Green Matte glaze on left, $55.00 – 65.00; handmade in Rust glaze on right, $65.00 - 80.00.

Blue Matte #1763L vase, 5 indents, large, 8" Stangl handmade, 1933 – 1935. $150.00 – 175.00. Courtesy of the Jim and Barbara Nelson collection.

Silver Green #1763S vase, 5 indents, small, 6" Stangl handmade, 1933 – 1935. $130.00 – 150.00.

Tangerine #1764 vase, 5 indents, round 7" Stangl handmade, 1933 – 1935. $140.00 – 165.00.

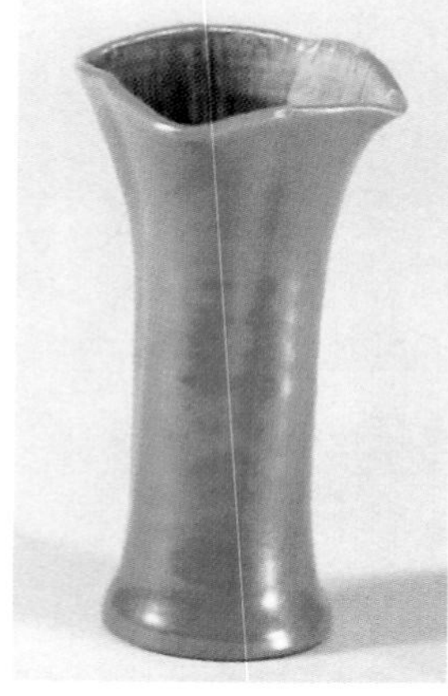

Tangerine with green lining #1783 bud vase, 6" Stangl handmade, 1933 – 1935. $55.00 – 70.00. Courtesy of the Brian and Cristi Hahn collection.

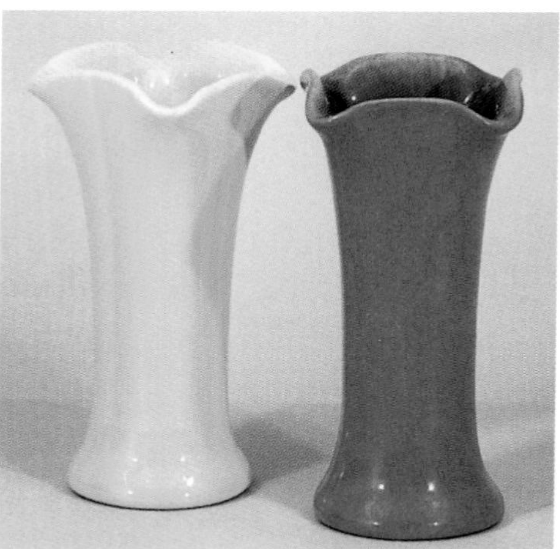

Two mold-cast #1783 bud vases, 6", Persian Yellow and Tangerine, 1935 – 1938. $40.00 – 50.00 each.

Black glaze #1784 candleholder, 6" Stangl handmade (also made as a lamp), 1933 – 1935. $100.00 – 125.00.

Rust glaze #1785 bowl, no handles, 3½" Stangl handmade, 1933 – 1935. $40.00 – 50.00.

Rust glaze #1791 vase, 2 handles, 4¼" Stangl handmade, 1933 – 1935. $50.00 – 60.00.

The #1765 jardinieres are similar to the #1238 three-handle jars, but the top rim is taller and the handles are thinner on the #1765 jardinieres.

Not Shown:

#1762 tapering pitcher, 8" Stangl handmade, 1933 – 1935. $125.00 – 150.00.
#1765EL jardiniere, 9" Stangl handmade, 1933 – 1935. $120.00 – 145.00.
#1765L jardiniere, 7" Stangl handmade, 1933 – 1935. $70.00 – 85.00.
#1765M jardiniere, 5" Stangl handmade, 1933 – 1935. $55.00 – 65.00.
#1765S jardiniere, 4" Stangl handmade, 1933 – 1935. $40.00 – 50.00.

Two #1792 5" flowerpots, mold-cast on left in Silver Green, $25.00 – 35.00; handmade on right in Colonial Blue, $55.00 – 65.00.

Bases of #1792 flowerpots, mold-cast on left and handmade on right.

Two #1792 flowerpots, Tangerine 6", on left, $60.00 – 75.00; Persian Yellow 3", on right, $35.00 – 45.00.

Not Shown:

#1792EL flowerpot, 8" Stangl handmade, 1933 – 1934. $80.00 – 90.00.
#1792L flowerpot, 6" Stangl handmade, 1933 – 1934. $60.00 – 75.00.
#1792M flowerpot, 5" Stangl handmade, 1933 – 1934. $55.00 – 65.00.
#1792S flowerpot, 4" Stangl handmade, 1933 – 1934. $40.00 – 50.00.
#1792ES flowerpot, 3" Stangl handmade, 1933 – 1934. $35.00 – 45.00.
#1792 miniature flowerpot, 2½" Stangl handmade, 1925 – 1926. $60.00 – 75.00.
#1792 miniature flowerpot, 1¾" Stangl handmade, 1925 – 1926. $130.00 – 150.00.
#1792EL flowerpot, 8" mold-cast, 1934 – 1944. $45.00 – 55.00.
#1792L flowerpot, 6" mold-cast, 1934 – 1944. $35.00 – 45.00.
#1792M flowerpot, 5" mold-cast, 1934 – 1944. $25.00 – 35.00.
#1792S flowerpot, 4" mold-cast, 1934 – 1944. $20.00 – 25.00.
#1792ES flowerpot, 3" mold-cast, 1934 – 1944. $25.00 – 35.00.
#1792 miniature flowerpot, 2" mold-cast, 1934 – 1944. $25.00 – 35.00.

1934 Introductions

Hand-made #1852 turned-edge baskets in Silver Green, 8" medium, on left, $100.00 – 125.00; 10" large, in center, $160.00 – 180.00; and 5½" small, on right, $95.00 – 110.00 .

Three handmade 5½" #1852 turned-edge baskets, Colonial Blue, Silver Green, and Persian Yellow, $95.00 – 110.00 each.

Not Shown:

#1852L basket, turned-edge, 7½"x10½" Stangl handmade, 1934 – 1935. $160.00 – 185.00.
#1852M basket, turned-edge, 6"x8" Stangl handmade, 1934 – 1935. $100.00 – 125.00.
#1852S basket, turned-edge, 5½" Stangl handmade, 1934 – 1935. $95.00 – 110.00.
#1853 basket, sides-in, 5" Stangl handmade, 1934 – 1935. $80.00 – 90.00.
#1853 basket, sides-in, 5" mold-cast, 1935 – 1938. $50.00 – 60.00.
#1854 basket, scroll-edge, 5" Stangl handmade, 1934 – 1935. $95.00 – 110.00.
#1855 vase, 2-handle, straight top, 10½" Stangl handmade, 1934 – 1935. $110.00 – 135.00.
#1856 vase, 2-handle, straight top, 7½" Stangl handmade, 1934 – 1935. $80.00 – 90.00.

Tangerine #1857 vase, 2-handle, straight top, 5" Stangl handmade, 1934 – 1935. $85.00 – 100.00. Courtesy of the Brian and Cristi Hahn collection.

Variegated Green Matte #1858 ball vase, neck ring, 2-handles, 6½" Stangl handmade, 1934 – 1935. $75.00 – 85.00.

Variegated Tangerine #1859 vase, pinched top, 2-handles, 7½" Stangl handmade, 1934 – 1935. $100.00 – 135.00.

Turquoise glaze #1860 vase, pinched top, 2-handles, 3½" Stangl handmade, 1934 – 1935. $60.00 – 75.00.

Two #1862 low vases, 3-handles, 4"x3½" in Variegated Rust and Variegated Green Matte glazes, Stangl handmade, 1934 – 1935. $35.00 – 45.00 each.

Rust glaze #1863 vase, flat ball, 3-feet, 3¾" Stangl handmade, 1934 – 1935. $80.00 – 90.00. Courtesy of the Chris McGeehan collection.

Tangerine #1864 bowl, scroll turning in, 6½" Stangl handmade, 1934 – 1935. $65.00 – 80.00.

Tangerine with turquoise lining #1865 bowl, turned-over edge, 8½" Stangl handmade, 1934 – 1935. $70.00 – 85.00.

Not Shown:

#1861 pitcher vase, twisted handle, 9" Stangl handmade, 1934 – 1935. $135.00 – 165.00.
#1866 bowl, 3 double rope handles, 7½" Stangl handmade, 1934 – 1935. $125.00 – 150.00.
#1867 bowl, top turned in, 2-handles, 7½" Stangl handmade, 1934 – 1935. $85.00 – 95.00.
#1868 bowl, straight neck, Stangl handmade, 1934 – 1935. $65.00 – 80.00.

1935 Introductions

Stangl's "Garden Center" vases and bowls were handmade during 1935 and 1936. The feature of these items is the built-in container/inserts designed to "hold tall stems straight and make it easy to have artistic arrangements." They became mold-cast production beginning in 1937. The handmade #1999 vases are smooth; the mold-cast items have molded "finger marks" on the exteriors. The mold-cast #1919 bowls and #1999 vases were also available without the attached inserts. By 1940, the "Garden Center" items were discontinued, and these shapes were produced sans inserts only.

Not Shown:

#1919 Garden Center bowl, 10¼" Stangl handmade, 1935 – 1936. $85.00 – 95.00.
#1919 Garden Center bowl, 8½" Stangl handmade, 1935 – 1936. $70.00 – 85.00.
#1919 Garden Center bowl, 7" Stangl handmade, 1935 – 1936. $50.00 – 60.00.
#1919 Garden Center bowl, 10¼" mold-cast, 1937 – 1940. $35.00 – 45.00.
#1919 Garden Center bowl, 8½" mold-cast, 1937 – 1940. $25.00 – 30.00.
#1919 Garden Center bowl, 7" mold-cast, 1937 – 1940. $25.00 – 30.00.
#1919 scrolled bowl, 10" mold-cast, 1937 – 1955. $35.00 – 45.00.
#1919 scrolled bowl, 8½" mold-cast, 1937 – 1955. $25.00 – 30.00.
#1919 scrolled bowl, 7" mold-cast, 1937 – 1955. $25.00 – 30.00.
#1999 Garden Center vase, 11" Stangl handmade, 1935 – 1936. $110.00 – 135.00.
#1999 Garden Center vase, 9" Stangl handmade, 1935 – 1936. $95.00 – 110.00.
#1999 Garden Center vase, 11" mold-cast, 1937 – 1940. $45.00 – 55.00.
#1999 Garden Center vase, 9" mold-cast, 1937 – 1940. $35.00 – 45.00.
#1999 Garden Center vase, 7" mold-cast, 1937 – 1940. $25.00 – 35.00.
#1999 scroll top vase, 11" mold-cast, 1937 – 1945. $45.00 – 55.00.
#1999 scroll top vase, 9" mold-cast, 1937 – 1945. $35.00 – 45.00.
#1999 scroll top vase, 7" mold-cast, 1937 – 1945. $25.00 – 35.00.

Colonial Blue #1999 Garden Center vase, 7" Stangl handmade, 1935 – 1936. $80.00 – 90.00.

Three handmade #1919 Garden Center bowls, 10¼" Variegated Rust $85.00 – 95.00; 7" Persian Yellow $50.00 – 60.00; 8½" Tangerine with green lining, showing the attached insert. $70.00 – 85.00.

Miniature Vases, 1924 – 1945

Stangl's first miniature vases were three small shapes introduced in 1924 as Fulper Fayence. These were smaller versions of Fulper Pottery brand shapes currently in production. The next miniatures were developed in 1925 as diminutive shapes produced by John Kunsman during his pottery demonstrations. For over 10 years, John Kunsman produced a large assortment of handmade miniatures at his traveling department store demonstrations. Consequently, a great variety of shapes can be found, and sizes can range from as small as 1½" inches to 4½". Some of the items, such as the flowerpot shape, were eventually factory produced in Flemington, then later in Trenton.

Throughout the 1920s and early 1930s, development of miniature vases was sporadic at best. However, miniature and small vases suddenly became big business in 1935. The mid to late 1930s saw a great demand for diminutive novelties. Many were wholesaled to carnivals, tourist sites, and roadside attractions to be sold as souvenirs to travelers. Occasionally these can still be found bearing decals stating the name of the attraction from which they were sold.

Original 1940s price tag on the bottom of a #1388 miniature jug. This jug sold for 25¢ at Chas. H. Bear & Co.

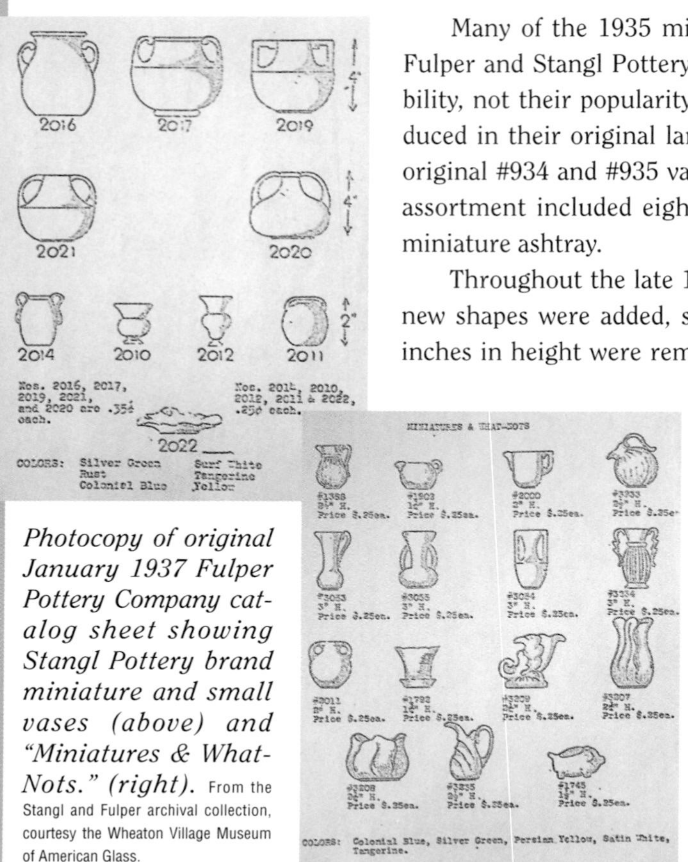

Photocopy of original January 1937 Fulper Pottery Company catalog sheet showing Stangl Pottery brand miniature and small vases (above) and "Miniatures & What-Nots." (right). From the Stangl and Fulper archival collection, courtesy the Wheaton Village Museum of American Glass.

Many of the 1935 miniature vase introductions were diminutive versions of earlier Fulper and Stangl Pottery vase shapes. These shapes were chosen for their style compatibility, not their popularity, as many of the shapes popular as miniatures were hardly produced in their original large size. Shapes #2016 and #2020 were actually larger than the original #934 and #935 vase shapes they were based on. The original 1935 miniature vase assortment included eight truly miniature vase shapes, five small vase shapes, and one miniature ashtray.

Throughout the late 1930s, the miniature vase assortment was finessed and modified, new shapes were added, slow sellers were removed. By 1939, all of the vases over three inches in height were removed from the line; the shapes that remained were truly miniatures. Stangl advertised this line as "Miniatures & What-Nots," the "what-nots" being non-vase items such as the #1745 pig ashtray, #1792 flowerpot, and the assortment of miniature pitchers and jugs.

With just a few exceptions, this assortment continued in production until 1943, then gradually declined until all miniatures were dropped in 1945.

Miniature Knock-Off Comparisons

Because of the extreme popularity of Stangl's miniature vases during the late 1930s and early 1940s, these shapes were constantly "mimicked" by other potteries. The miniature knock-offs usually exhibited inferior modeling and glazes. Some knock-offs were made of pink, blue, or white clay with clear glaze or white clay with murky-colored glaze and are marked with an in-mold "USA." The knock-off colors are generally murky and never match Stangl's known standard glaze colors. Workmanship and finish of the knock-offs are inferior to true Stangl miniatures. The most common #1745 Small Pig ashtray knock-offs are always marked with an in-mold "USA." Stangl's #1745 Small Pig ashtrays were never marked USA. In addition, the face detail is less distinct on the knock-offs. Stangl's #1745 Small Pig ashtrays have well-defined eyes, nostrils, and mouths. Even if the glaze is thick, these features are usually evident. The knock-offs have only little indents for eyes, and the snout is much smaller than Stangl's. Following are photo comparisons of Stangl miniatures and some of the more common knock-offs.

Values shown represent miniatures in "standard" solid-color glazes. Values can increase dramatically for miniature vases glazed in rare colors such as Purple, Blue-of-the-Sky, Oxblood, Rose, Orchid, or Dusty Pink. The presence of an original Stangl Pottery gold-foil paper label can also sometimes, but not always, increase the value of a miniature by about $10.00 to $30.00.

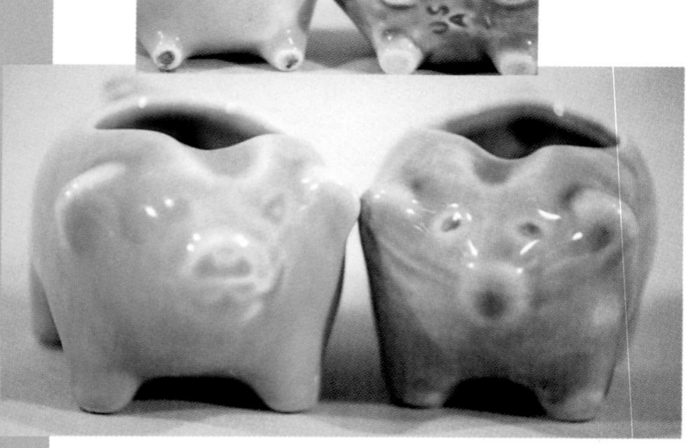

Comparison of Stangl's #1745 Small Pig ashtray face (left) and knock-off (right), with bases shown in inset. Courtesy of the Robert and Tammie Cruser collection.

Stangl miniature #2014 on left; knock-off on right. The base of the Stangl #2014 (inset) is always flat and unglazed. The knock-off is in-mold marked "USA."

Stangl miniature #1902 jug on left; knock-off on right. The Stangl #1902 miniature is always marked with in-mold "1902" (inset).

Stangl miniature #1388 jug on right; knock-off on left. The Stangl #1388 jug is marked with in-mold "1388 U.S.A." (inset).

Stangl miniature #2000 pitcher on right; knock-off on left. The knock-off is marked with in-mold "USA," Stangl #2000 pitcher is marked with in-mold "2000" (inset).

John Kunsman Handmade Miniatures, 1925 – 1930s

Not Shown:

The values shown here are only for the items handmade by John Kunsman.

Flare vase, 3½" (original Fulper shape). $95.00 – 110.00.

Flare vase, 2¾" (original Fulper shape). $130.00 – 150.00.

Flowerpot, 1¾" (became #1792). $130.00 – 150.00.

Flowerpot, 2½" (became #1792). $60.00 – 75.00.

Ruffled bowl, 3" (became #1919). $110.00 – 135.00.

John Kunsman handmade Colonial Blue Three-handle vase, 3½" (became #1124). $110.00 – 135.00.

Three John Kunsman handmade Flare vases, the 3½" ones glazed in Satin White and Turquoise glaze, $95.00 – 110.00 each, the shorter 2¾" vase glazed in Silver Green, $130.00 – 150.00.

John Kunsman handmade Flowerpots, 2½" in Silver Green, $60.00 – 75.00, 1¾" in Blue-of-the-Sky, $130.00 – 150.00.

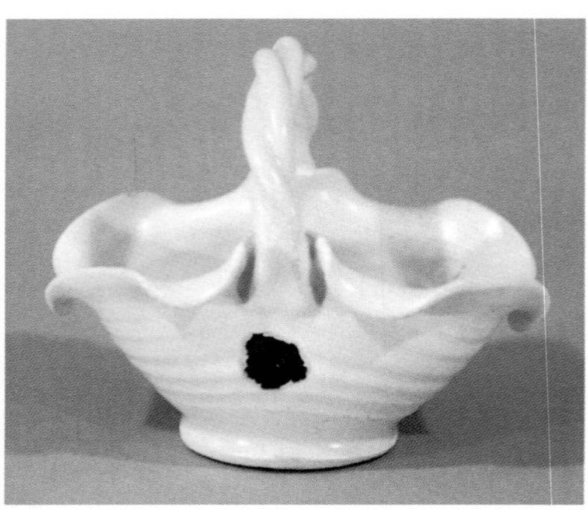

John Kunsman handmade Basket, 4", Satin White (became Fulper #1888). $150.00 – 175.00.

John Kunsman handmade Jug (base shown in inset), 4", Apple Green (original Fulper shape). $130.00 – 150.00.

Fulper Fayence Miniatures, 1924 – 1925

Not Shown:

#933 vase, 3½" Fulper Fayence (same as Fulper Pottery #511), 1924 – 1925. $55.00 – 65.00.

#934 vase, 3¼" Fulper Fayence (later reintroduced as Stangl#2016), 1924 – 1925. $55.00 – 65.00.

#935 vase, 2¾" Fulper Fayence (later reintroduced as Stangl#2020), 1924 – 1925. $55.00 – 65.00.

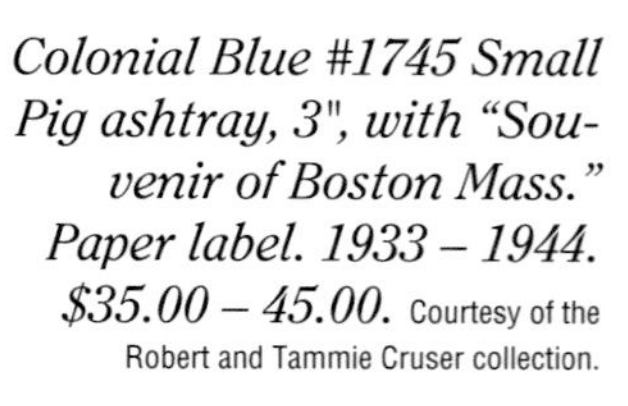

Comparison of Fulper Fayence #934 vase, 3¼" tall, Rose glaze on right, and the reintroduction of the same shape, Stangl Pottery #2016 vase, 3½" tall, Silver Green glaze on left. The #2016 vase had a glazed base (inset) and unglazed foot and bore the in-mold #2016. The #934 vase base was flat, unmarked, and unglazed.

Stangl Pottery Miniatures, 1930 – 1945

Not Shown:

#1792ES flowerpot, 3" mold-cast, 1934 – 1938. $25.00 – 35.00.

#1792 miniature flowerpot, 2" mold-cast, 1934 – 1938. $25.00 – 35.00.

#2014 vase, 2", (based on vase #1667), 1935 – 1938. $35.00 – 45.00.

Colonial Blue #1745 Small Pig ashtray, 3", with "Souvenir of Boston Mass." Paper label. 1933 – 1944. $35.00 – 45.00. Courtesy of the Robert and Tammie Cruser collection.

Persian Yellow #1271S bowl, 2 handles, miniature, 4½"x1¼", 1930 – 1933. $65.00 – 80.00. Courtesy of the Hill-Fulper-Stangl Museum.

Group of #1792 miniature flowerpots in Tangerine, Satin White, Colonial Blue, and Silver Green glazes, $25.00 – 35.00 each. Courtesy of the Robert and Tammie Cruser collection.

Tangerine #1903 vase, 3½", miniature, 1935 only. $190.00 – 225.00. Courtesy of the Hill-Fulper-Stangl Museum.

Persian Yellow #2009 vase, 2 handles, 3½" (based on Fulper #724), 1935 – 1936. $175.00 – 200.00. Courtesy of the Hill-Fulper-Stangl Museum.

Two #2009 3½" miniature vases, Tangerine on left, $175.00 – 200.00; Apple Green over Buff glaze on right, $350.00 – 400.00. Courtesy of the Robert and Tammie Cruser collection.

Group of miniature vases #2011 in Tangerine, Silver Green, Dusty Pink, Persian Yellow, and Colonial Blue, 2", 1935 – 1945. $35.00 – 45.00 each. Courtesy of the Robert and Tammie Cruser collection.

Group of miniature vases #2010 in Colonial Blue, Tangerine, and Tangerine with green lining glazes, 2", 1935 – 1938. $40.00 – 50.00 each. Courtesy of the Robert and Tammie Cruser collection.

Silver Green #2013 vase, 2", (based on vase #1916), 1935 only. $200.00 – 250.00. Courtesy of Blue Whale Antiques.

Group of miniature vases #2012 in Silver Green, Tangerine, and Satin White, 2", (based on vase #1817), 1935 – 1938. $35.00 – 45.00 each. Courtesy of the Robert and Tammie Cruser collection.

Persian Yellow Crackled #2014 vase, 2", (based on vase #1667), 1935 – 1938. $100.00 – 125.00. Courtesy of the Robert and Tammie Cruser collection.

Group of miniature vases #2014 in Colonial Blue, Satin White, Dusty Pink, and Silver Green, $35.00 – 45.00. Courtesy of the Robert and Tammie Cruser collection.

Three miniature vases #2018, based on the old Fulper shape #47 vase. These are in Variegated Tangerine, Persian Yellow, and Silver Green, $175.00 – 200.00 each. Courtesy of the Brian and Cristi Hahn collection.

Silver Green #2015 vase, 2", (based on vase #1913), 1935 only. $275.00 – 300.00. Courtesy of the Robert and Tammie Cruser collection.

Silver Green #2017 vase, 3", (based on Fulper #832), 1935 – 1940. $35.00 – 45.00.

Group of miniature long pitchers #3053 in Colonial Blue, Dusty Pink, Satin White, Persian Yellow, Silver Green, and Tangerine, $35.00 – 45.00 each. Courtesy of the Robert and Tammie Cruser collection.

Group of miniature ovoid vases #3054 in Tangerine, Colonial Blue, Silver Green, and Persian Yellow. $35.00 – 45.00 each. Courtesy of the Robert and Tammie Cruser collection.

Stangl small vases #2020 in Silver Green, #2016 in Satin White, #2021 in Rust, $35.00 – 45.00 each; and #2019 in Colonial Blue, $40.00 – 50.00. Courtesy of the Ben and Pauline Jensen collection.

Not Shown:
#2016 vase, 3½", (originally #934), 1935 – 1940. $35.00 – 45.00.
#2018 vase, 3½", (based on Fulper #47), 1935 – 1940. $175.00 – 200.00.
#2019 vase, 3", (based on Fulper #452), 1935 – 1940. $40.00 – 50.00.
#2020 vase, 3", (originally #935), 1935 – 1940. $35.00 – 45.00.
#2021 vase, 3", (based on Fulper #701), 1935 – 1940. $35.00 – 45.00.
#2022 shell ashtray, 3", 1935 – 1942. $20.00 – 25.00.
#2091 Cosmos miniature bowl, 4", 1936 – 1938. $25.00 – 30.00.
#2092 Rhythmic miniature vase, 3¼", 1936 – 1937. $25.00 – 30.00.
#3053 miniature long pitcher, 3", 1937 – 1943. $35.00 – 45.00.
#3054 miniature ovoid vase, 3",1937 – 1943. $35.00 – 45.00.

Colonial Blue #3055 miniature long neck vase, 3", 1937 – 1943. $35.00 – 45.00.

Group of miniature vases #3055 in Colonial Blue, Satin White, Tangerine, Persian Yellow, and Silver Green, $35.00 – 45.00 each. Courtesy of the Robert and Tammie Cruser collection.

Miniatures #2000 bowl, $25.00 – 35.00; jug, $20.00 – 25.00; and #2000 butter pat, $30.00 – 35.00. Courtesy of the Robert and Tammie Cruser collection.

Colonial Blue #1388 miniature bowl, 2½", 1938 – 1945. $25.00 – 35.00.

Silver Green #1902 miniature bowl and miniature jug, $25.00 – 35.00 each. Courtesy of the Robert and Tammie Cruser collection.

Colonial Blue #2000 miniature bowl, 2½", 1938 – 1945. $25.00 – 35.00.

Group of miniature jugs #1902, $25.00 – 35.00 each. Courtesy of the Robert and Tammie Cruser collection.

Group of miniature jugs #1388, 2¼", 1938 – 1945. $20.00 – 25.00 each. Courtesy of the Robert and Tammie Cruser collection.

Group of miniature jugs #2000 in Tangerine, Persian Yellow, Satin White, Aqua Blue, and Silver Green, $20.00 – 25.00 each. Courtesy of the Robert and Tammie Cruser collection.

Not Shown:

#1902 miniature jug, 1¼", 1938 – 1945. $25.00 – 35.00.

#1902 miniature bowl, 2½", 1938 – 1945. $25.00 – 35.00.

#2000 miniature jug, 2", 1938 – 1945. $20.00 – 25.00.

Group of miniature tall tulip vases #3207 in Tangerine, Silver Green, Colonial Blue, and Persian Yellow, 2¾", 1938 – 1945. $45.00 – 55.00 each. Courtesy of the Robert and Tammie Cruser collection.

Group of miniature low tulip vases #3208 in Persian Yellow, Colonial Blue, Aqua Blue, Silver Green, and Tangerine, $40.00 – 50.00 each. Courtesy of the Robert and Tammie Cruser collection.

Group of miniature horn vases #3209 in Tangerine, Silver Green, Satin White, Persian Yellow, and Colonial Blue, $45.00 – 55.00 each. Courtesy of the Robert and Tammie Cruser collection.

Satin White #3211 miniature ball pitcher, 2¼", 1938 only. $175.00 – 200.00. Courtesy of the Brian and Cristi Hahn collection.

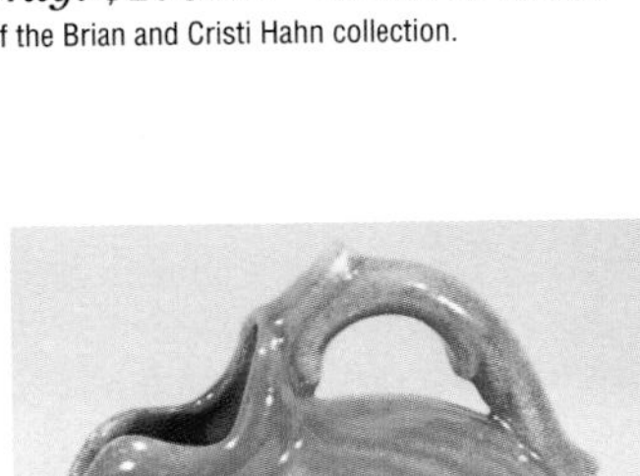

Tangerine #3233 miniature ball jug, 2½", (#1388 shape) 1938 – 1945. $35.00 – 45.00.

Group of miniature vases #3235 in Silver Green, Satin White, Tangerine, and Colonial Blue, 2½", 1938 – 1941. $45.00 – 55.00 each. Courtesy of the Robert and Tammie Cruser collection.

Group of miniature vases #3234 in Colonial Blue, Tangerine, Silver Green, and Persian Yellow, $35.00 – 45.00 each. Courtesy of the Robert and Tammie Cruser collection.

Not Shown:

#3208 miniature low tulip vase, 2¼", 1938 – 1945. $40.00 – 50.00.

#3209 miniature horn vase, 2¼", 1938 – 1945. $45.00 – 55.00.

#3234 miniature 2 handle vase, 3", 1938 – 1945. $35.00 – 45.00.

Dave Thomas's Marbled #3234 miniature 2 handle vase, 3", 1954 only. $275.00 – 300.00.

Antique French Crackle, 1970 – 1971

Antique French Crackle #3672 double shell vase, $100.00 – 125.00, and leaf server #3859, $15.00 – 20.00. Note detail of finish in inset of backstamp. Courtesy of the Hill-Fulper-Stangl Museum.

The Antique French Crackle finish was introduced in 1970 on Stangl's most popular artware shapes of the time. The finish was a satiny-white with an evenly patterned tracery of delicate crackling. The crackled glaze was further enhanced with a wash of dye. The Antique French Crackle glaze had actually been developed by Martin Stangl during the 1920s, when Fulper Pottery Company was noted for being the only American pottery able to produce quality crackle glazes. Stangl ads stated: "Stangl presents a dramatic patina with the authentic beauty of antique countryside charm. French Crackle, a complete collection in classic sculptured lines and contemporary stylings to compliment the latest trends in home decorating. These handcrafted giftables, glazed in a lacy network of fine lines, are true to the artistry of America's oldest pottery — a tradition since 1805." Regrettably, Antique French Crackle did not appeal to retail buyers, and was discontinued by 1971.

Not Shown:
dealer sign. $120.00 – 135.00.
#1906 urn vase 7¾". $40.00 – 50.00.
#2041 urn, footed Grecian 8". $40.00 – 50.00.
#3217 flared vase 7½". $35.00 – 45.00.
#3630 cigarette box 4½"x5½", flat top. $100.00 – 125.00.
#3630 coaster ashtray, 5". $20.00 – 25.00.
#3672 double shell vase, 7½"x11". $100.00 – 125.00.
#3688 vase, milk can, 7". $35.00 – 45.00.
#3782 double Pear dish, 7½"x7½". $15.00 – 20.00.
#3783 single Pear dish, 7½"x4". $15.00 – 20.00.
#3784 double Apple dish, 10"x5½". $15.00 – 20.00.
#3785 single Apple dish, 6". $15.00 – 20.00.
#3857 clover server, 7"x7½". $15.00 – 20.00.
#3859 leaf server, 8"x7". $15.00 – 20.00.
#4018 shell dish, small 7½". $20.00 – 25.00.
#4019 shell dish, medium 9?". $20.00 – 25.00.
#4020 shell dish, large 10½". $30.00 – 40.00.
#4037 ashtray, shell dish, 5"x5½". $15.00 – 20.00.
#4050 vase, bud 8" (Kay Hackett design). $30.00 – 40.00.
#4059 pitcher 6¼" (Kay Hackett design). $20.00 – 25.00.
#5023 vase, Phoenician 9¾" (Kay Hackett design). $45.00 – 55.00.
#5065 horn of plenty, small, 4½"x7¼" (orig. #3617). $25.00 – 35.00.
#5066 horn of plenty, large, 6½"x10" (orig. #3617). $40.00 – 50.00.
#5135 vase, flared 7½" (orig. # 2091). $35.00 – 45.00.
#5144 vase, Tulip, small 4" (orig. #1878S). $20.00 – 25.00.
#5146 leaf dish, ivy 8"x7¾"(orig. #3239). $15.00 – 20.00.
#5157-58 small pitcher & bowl set, 9"x12". $275.00 – 300.00.
#5190 vase, Chalice, 6¼". $20.00 – 25.00.

Antique Pitcher & Bowl Sets, 1965 – 1974

The #5157-58 Antique Pitcher & Bowl sets were introduced in 1965. Decorating supervisor Irene Sarnecki developed the Rose and Violet motifs that decorated the Pitcher & Bowl sets. The pitchers were #5157 and 9" tall; the bowls were #5158 and measured 15" in diameter. After dinner cup and saucer sets decorated with Rose or Violet motifs were produced during 1965 only. These were marketed as punch cups so the bowls could be used for serving punch.

After the 1965 fire, the Pitcher & Bowl sets were unavailable until 1967. From 1967 until 1972, the pitchers and bowls were produced with the Rose motif only. In 1972, the Violet motif was reintroduced, also the size of the bowl was reduced from 15" to 12" in diameter, and the pitcher was reduced from 11" to 9". The new, smaller Pitcher & Bowl sets were available with either roses or violets from 1972 until 1974 when Antique Pitcher & Bowl sets were discontinued altogether.

Not Shown:
Rose #5157-58 large pitcher & bowl set, 11"x15", 1965 – 1972. $290.00 – 325.00.
Rose #5157-58 small pitcher & bowl set, 9"x12", 1972 – 1974. $275.00 – 300.00.
Rose punch cup and saucer, 1965 only. $20.00 – 25.00.
Violet #5157-58 large pitcher & bowl set, 11"x15", 1965 only. $375.00 – 400.00.
Violet #5157-58 small pitcher & bowl set, 9"x12", 1972 – 1974. $300.00 – 350.00.
Violet punch cup and saucer, 1965 only. $60.00 – 75.00.

Rose large Pitcher & Bowl set. $290.00 – 325.00. Courtesy of the Jim and Barbara Nelson collection.

Violet large Pitcher & Bowl set. $375.00 – 400.00. Courtesy of the Jim and Barbara Nelson collection.

Rose punch cup and saucer. $20.00 – 25.00.

Violet small Pitcher & Bowl set. $300.00 – 350.00. Courtesy of the Bullock collection.

Appliqué, 1964 – 1965

The Appliqué line was advertised as "An exciting new range of giftware available in Blue or Jade green at fine stores everywhere." Appliqué featured a sprigged floral motif in white on a colored background. Jade green, dark green, and blue colored clays were used to cast the shapes of the Appliqué line. Dark green Appliqué was produced in the least amount, jade green and blue are much more plentiful. Appliqué was glazed with both clear gloss glaze and Satin White dinnerware glaze. Items with clear gloss glaze have bright, clear color and a highly reflective surface. The pieces glazed with Satin White dinnerware glaze have a subtle, muted color quality and a soft satiny texture. Appliqué was discontinued in 1965.

Appliqué dark green #4050 bud vase, light green #4060 pitcher, blue #5058 ashtray, and #4056 pitcher. Courtesy of the Marcena North collection.

Appliqué dark green #3666 ashtray, blue #4007 vase, and light green #4060 pitcher.

Not Shown:
#3666 ashtray, square 4½". $15.00 – 20.00.
#3898 cigarette box. $65.00 – 80.00.
#3996 cigarette holder, oval, 2½". $20.00 – 25.00.
#3997 ashtray, oval 3½". $15.00 – 20.00.
#4007 vase 6¾"x4¼". $20.00 – 25.00.
#4050 vase, bud 8". $25.00 – 30.00.
#4060 pitcher 5¼". $20.00 – 25.00.
#4056 pitcher 8¼". $25.00 – 30.00.
#5058 ashtray, round 7¼". $20.00 – 25.00.
#5152-7 vase, jug, small 7". $25.00 – 35.00.
#5152-9 vase, jug, medium 9". $30.00 – 40.00.
#5152-11 vase, jug, large 11". $45.00 – 55.00.
#5153 cigarette lighter, 4". $25.00 – 35.00.
#5154 ashtray, fluted, 7". $15.00 – 20.00.

Appliqué dealer sign. $150.00 – 175.00.

Aztec, 1963 – 1965

"A new group of gaily colored gift items, specially treated with a new satin glaze," stated Stangl's sales flyer for the new Aztec artware in 1963. The new glaze referred to was the Satin White dinnerware glaze, which debuted on Stangl's Blue Daisy dinnerware pattern also in 1963. The Aztec artware was decorated with wide bands of Walnut Brown and Dark Turquoise underglaze color and narrow stripes of Blue #95 underglaze color applied directly to the red body of the pieces. Narrow pinstripes of gold luster applied over the Satin White glaze completed the finish. Aztec artware was designed to complement the Blue Daisy dinnerware pattern, as the primary colors of both lines were Dark Turquoise, Walnut Brown, and Blue #95 under the Satin White glaze. Aztec was produced in limited quantities until the fire in August 1965 when it was discontinued.

Aztec A-4055 pitcher, A-5002 ashtray, and A-4059 pitcher. Courtesy of the Marcena North collection.

Not Shown:
#A-3630 coaster ashtray, 5". $20.00 – 25.00.
#A-3630 cigarette box 4½"x5½", flat top. $75.00 – 95.00.
#A-3898 cigarette box, fluted. $75.00 – 95.00.
#A-3898-5 ashtray, fluted 5". $15.00 – 20.00.
#A-3898-7 ashtray, fluted 7". $20.00 – 25.00.
#A-3972 ashtray, Flying Saucer 10", (Kay Hackett design). $35.00 – 45.00.
#A-3987 vase, urn 6". $$35.00 – 45.00.
#A-3989 vase 7¼". $35.00 – 45.00.
#A-3993 vase, urn 12". $80.00 – 100.00.
#A-4002 vase 6"x5". $30.00 – 40.00.
#A-4004 vase 5½"x4½". $30.00 – 40.00.
#A-4026 ashtray, conference table 11¼", (Kay Hackett design). $35.00 – 45.00.
#A-4028 bowl, 9" pedestal (orig. #3434 bowl) (Kay Hackett design). $35.00 – 45.00.
#A-4050 vase, bud 8" (Kay Hackett design). $35.00 – 45.00.
#A-4053 pitcher 12" (Kay Hackett design). $50.00 – 60.00.
#A-4055 pitcher 11¼" (Kay Hackett design). $35.00 – 45.00.
#A-4059 pitcher 6¼" (Kay Hackett design). $25.00 – 30.00.
#A-4060 pitcher 5¼" (Kay Hackett design). $20.00 – 25.00.
#A-4064 candleholders, pedestal 4" (Kay Hackett design). $25.00 – 30.00 pair.
#A-5002 ashtray, round 9¼" (Kay Hackett design). $25.00 – 35.00.
#A-5022 vase, 7¾" (Kay Hackett design). $35.00 – 45.00.
#A-5023 vase, Phoenician 9¾" (Kay Hackett design). $40.00 – 50.00.
#A-5093 vase, bud 5¾". $20.00 – 25.00.

Aztec #A-4007 vase 6¾"x4¼". $30.00 – 40.00.

Aztec #A-5063 bowl, footed (#5061), pierced 7". $25.00 – 35.00.

Bird-Shape Jug, 1953

Kay Hackett developed the Bird-Shape jug in 1953. The jug was originally designed with abstract motifs. However, the Bird-Shape jug was put in production in dark glazes with contrasting froth glaze. In 1954, the jug was also tried with Carnival, Lyric, and Amber-Glo dinnerware motifs. Kay Hackett's Bird-Shape jugs are now quite scarce.

Kay Hackett's Bird-Shape jug with black glaze with white frothing, one of the finishes in which this shape was produced (base, inset). Courtesy of Kay Hackett.

Kay Hackett's original photo of her Bird-Shape jug showing all phases of design, from original clay model sculpture through mold construction, greenware, bisque, and final finished product. Courtesy of Kay Hackett.

Not Shown:
Bird-Shape jug, 8", abstract motif, 1953 only. $175.00 – 200.00.
Bird-Shape jug, 8", froth glaze, 1953 only. $175.00 – 200.00.
Bird-Shape jug, 8", Lyric motif, 1954 only. $225.00 – 275.00.
Bird-Shape jug, 8", carnival or Amber-Glo, 1954 only. $175.00 – 200.00.

Bronze-Ware, 1978

Original Stangl Bronze-Ware catalog page, flyer, $8.00 – 12.00 each.

Bronze-Ware was the last product developed by Stangl Pottery. On January 1, 1978, this series of six decorative planters was introduced to commerce. "Dramatically different and truly new...a blend of metallic texture with majestic form creates striking beauty with maximum utility...six all-new quality containers that make plants and floral arrangements look expensive!" stated Stangl's Bronze-Ware flyer. The shapes were ultra-contemporary and textured with an orderly pattern of row upon row of gradating buttons. The Bronze-Ware glaze was a rich dark brown coppery color with a metallic luster. In addition to the Bronze-Ware glaze, the Bronze-Ware shapes were also glazed with Pioneer Brown, Winter Tan (peach), Harvest Yellow, and Summer Green. The Bronze-Ware line was discontinued several months before Stangl closed forever on November 1, 1978.

Bronze-Ware #5329-6002 long window planter, 16". $25.00 – 30.00.

Not Shown:
#5329-6001 flared planter, 11". $25.00 – 30.00.
#5329-6002 long window planter, 16". $25.00 – 30.00.
#5329-6003 console planter-bowl, 8". $25.00 – 30.00.
#5329-6004 window planter, 8". $25.00 – 30.00.
#5329-6005 round planter-bowl, 7½". $25.00 – 30.00.
#5329-6006 square planter-bowl, 6". $25.00 – 30.00.

Bronze-Ware #5329-6002 long window planter glazed in Harvest Yellow. $25.00 – 30.00.

Caribbean, 1968 – 1970

The Caribbean finish was a sponging together of transparent green and Caribbean Blue glazes. Stangl described it as "A stunning blend of blues and greens topped with a gloss glaze." Popular at first, the Caribbean fell from favor by 1969 and was discontinued in 1970. The Caribbean finish was also applied to lamp bases, so please see the Lamp chapter as well.

Not Shown:
#1953 ashtray, oblong 4¼". $15.00 – 20.00.
#1954 two compartment ashtray 4"x6". $15.00 – 20.00.
#2041 urn, footed Grecian 8". $35.00 – 45.00.
#2064 scalloped oval bowl 5"x9". $20.00 – 25.00.
#3410-9 bowl, Rose 9". $25.00 – 35.00.
#3410-7 bowl, Rose 7". $25.00 – 30.00.
#3630 cigarette box 4½"x5½", flat top. $75.00 – 95.00.
#3630 cigarette box 4½"x5½", quilt top. $75.00 – 95.00.
#3630 coaster ashtray, 5". $20.00 – 25.00.
#3676 covered candy dish, square, 4½"x5½". $30.00 – 40.00.
#3782 double Pear dish, 7½"x7½". $20.00 – 25.00.
#3783 single Pear dish, 7½"x4". $15.00 – 20.00.
#3784 double Apple dish, 10"x5½". $20.00 – 25.00.
#3785 single Apple dish, 6". $15.00 – 20.00.
#3857 clover server, 7"x7½". $20.00 – 25.00.
#3859 leaf server, 8"x7". $20.00 – 25.00.
#3898 cigarette box, fluted. $75.00 – 95.00.

Caribbean #2041 Grecian urn, $35.00 – 45.00; #1954 ashtray, $15.00 – 20.00; #5134 Cosmos vase, $30.00 – 40.00; and #5065 small horn of plenty, $25.00 – 35.00.
Courtesy of the Marcena North collection.

#3898-5 ashtray, fluted 5". $15.00 – 20.00.
#3898-7 ashtray, fluted 7". $20.00 – 25.00.
#3915 ashtray, square with round well 9", (Kay Hackett design). $30.00 – 40.00.
#4018 shell dish, small 7½". $20.00 – 25.00.
#4019 shell dish, medium 9⅝". $25.00 – 35.00.
#4020 shell dish, large 10½". $30.00 – 40.00.
#4021 compote 3½"x6½" (orig. #1388). $25.00 – 30.00.
#4025 vase, urn 7½". $25.00 – 35.00.
#4036 ashtray, leaf 6"x4½". $15.00 – 20.00.
#4037 ashtray, shell dish, 5"x5½". $15.00 – 20.00.
#4050 vase, bud 8" (Kay Hackett design). $25.00 – 35.00.
#4052 pitcher 14½" (Kay Hackett design). $40.00 – 50.00.
#4053 pitcher 12" (Kay Hackett design). $35.00 – 45.00.
#4054 pitcher 16" (Kay Hackett design). $45.00 – 55.00.
#4055 pitcher 11¼" (Kay Hackett design). $35.00 – 45.00.
#4056 pitcher 8¼" (Kay Hackett design). $25.00 – 35.00.
#4058 pitcher 7½" (Kay Hackett design). $25.00 – 30.00.
#4059 pitcher 6¼" (Kay Hackett design). $20.00 – 25.00.
#4060 pitcher 5¼" (Kay Hackett design). $20.00 – 25.00.
#4061 bowl, scalloped-ruffled 8" (Kay Hackett design). $25.00 – 30.00.
#4062 bowl, scalloped-ruffled 10¼" (Kay Hackett design). $25.00 – 35.00.
#5004 ashtray, rectangular, 12½"x6½" (Kay Hackett design). $25.00 – 35.00.
#5065 horn of plenty, small, 4½"x7¼" (orig. #3617). $25.00 – 35.00.
#5066 horn of plenty, large, 6½"x10" (orig. #3617). $35.00 – 45.00.
#5069 candleholders, ruffled, footed 3½"x 2". $20.00 – 25.00 pair.
#5093 vase, bud 5¾". $15.00 – 20.00.
#5097 ashtray, 6½"x4½". $15.00 – 20.00.
#5132 vase, flared 10½" (orig. #2091). $45.00 – 55.00.
#5134 vase, Cosmos 7½" (orig. #3413). $30.00 – 40.00.
#5135 vase, flared 7½" (orig. # 2091). $30.00 – 40.00.
#5138 candleholders, Rose 2½" (orig. #1875). $20.00 – 25.00 pair.
#5139 bowl, Cosmos 12" diameter (orig. #1869). $35.00 – 45.00.
#5144 vase, Tulip, small 4" (orig. #1878S). $20.00 – 25.00.
#5146 leaf dish, ivy 8"x7¾"(orig. #3239). $15.00 – 20.00.
#5151 Hearts & Flowers tidbit, 10". $8.00 – 12.00.
#5153 cigarette lighter, 4" (Kay Hackett design). $35.00 – 45.00.
#5156 Hearts & Flowers two-tier tidbit, 10"x6". $20.00 – 25.00.
#5173 ashtray, square, 4½". $15.00 – 20.00.
#5174 ashtray, square 7". $15.00 – 20.00.
#5174 ashtray, square, no rests, 7" made for Nelson Lebo Lamp Co. $15.00 – 20.00.
#5190 vase, Chalice, 6¼". $20.00 – 25.00.

Caribbean dealer sign. $160.00 – 180.00.

Caribbean bud vase #4050 and pitcher #4056. $25.00 – 35.00 each.

Caribbean #5023 vase, Phoenician 9¾" (Kay Hackett design). $45.00 – 55.00.

Caughley, 1964 – 1978

The Caughley dinnerware pattern was special-ordered by Tiffany & Company and was produced according to their specifications. The Caughley pattern was very popular and was continually produced from 1964 until the close of Stangl Pottery in 1978. Throughout that time, several artware items were produced with the Caughley finishes. Because

Blue Caughley dealer sign. $275.00 – 300.00.
Courtesy of Ed Alvater.

Tiffany distributed Caughley in several major cities and Stangl was allowed to sell Tiffany patterns in areas where there were no Tiffany stores, Caughley was well promoted across the nation. Some Caughley items were also backstamped with the name "Lord & Taylor" for that department store.

The front, back, and edge of red-bodied pieces were covered with white engobe; Tiffany wanted none of Stangl's distinctive red body to show. The decoration involved a two-step sponging process. The first color was sponged on lightly; a second, darker color was sponged over the first color. Both the front and back were entirely sponged with color. The finished piece of Caughley was to have as little white background showing as possible. The colors used for Blue Caughley were Blue #95 and Art Ware blue; Dark Green Caughley was Victoria green and Pomona green; Green Caughley was Victoria green and Green #1431; Yellow Caughley used Yellow and Orange. Pink Caughley and Brown Caughley each used a light, then heavy application of a single color. Pink Caughley was decorated with Pink #193, Brown Caughley with Walnut brown.

Green Caughley vanity tray, 7¼" square and 3" flowerpot. $20.00 – 25.00 each. Courtesy of the Ben and Floss Avila collection.

Blue Caughley 6" octagon tile. $30.00 – 40.00. Courtesy of the Luke and Nancy Ruepp collection.

When first introduced, Caughley was available only in Blue with a very limited number of shapes. By 1967, Pink Caughley and Dark Green Caughley were added, and the shape line was greatly expanded. During 1969, Pink Caughley was discontinued, and Dark Green Caughley was replaced with Green Caughley. Also during 1969, Yellow Caughley and Brown Caughley were introduced. Brown Caughley, however, was never in demand and lasted less than a year. Please see the Lamp chapter for lamps decorated with the Caughley motif.

	Blue	Pink, Green, Yellow
dealer sign.	$275.00 – 300.00	$200.00 – 250.00
ash tray, #3630 5" round	$20.00 – 25.00	$20.00 – 25.00
ash tray, #3898 5" fluted	$20.00 – 25.00	$20.00 – 25.00
ash tray, #3898 7" fluted	$25.00 – 35.00	$25.00 – 35.00
bean pot/cookie jar	$130.00 – 150.00	$65.00 – 80.00
bowl, #5300 Rose, 10½"	$60.00 – 75.00	$40.00 – 50.00
bowl, #5301 Rose, 8½"	$45.00 – 55.00	$30.00 – 40.00
bowl, #5302 Rose, 6"	$25.00 – 35.00	$20.00 – 25.00
cache pot, 7½" square	$100.00 – 125.00	$70.00 – 85.00
cache pot, 5½" square	$75.00 – 95.00	$60.00 – 75.00
candleholders #5138, 3" Rose, pair	$45.00 – 55.00	$25.00 – 35.00
candleholder, pillar #5244, 5½", Columbia shape	$45.00 – 55.00	$25.00 – 35.00
candleholder #5287, chamber-stick shape	$45.00 – 55.00	$30.00 – 40.00
candlestick #5299 7½" tall, pair	$120.00 – 135.00	$65.00 – 80.00
cigarette box #3630 flat top or quilt top	$100.00 – 125.00	$100.00 – 125.00
cigarette box #3898 fluted	$100.00 – 125.00	$100.00 – 125.00
cornucopia #5065 small, 4½"x7¼"	$40.00 – 50.00	$35.00 – 45.00
cornucopia #5066, large, 6½"x10"	$75.00 – 95.00	$55.00 – 65.00
dessert mold, fluted 6"	$45.00 – 55.00	$25.00 – 35.00
dessert mold, Turk's cap, 7½"	$50.00 – 60.00	$30.00 – 40.00
dog bowl, #5200	$100.00 – 125.00	$45.00 – 55.00
egg shape powder box, 5½"	$100.00 – 125.00	$65.00 – 80.00
flowerpot, 3"	$20.00 – 25.00	$20.00 – 25.00

flowerpot, 4"	$25.00 – 30.00	$25.00 – 30.00
flowerpot, 5"	$35.00 – 45.00	$30.00 – 40.00
flowerpot, 7"	$60.00 – 75.00	$40.00 – 50.00
ginger jar	$130.00 – 150.00	$100.00 – 125.00
planter, rolling pin, 13"	$150.00 – 165.00	$70.00 – 85.00
server, #3783 pear	$25.00 – 35.00	$20.00 – 25.00
server, #3785 apple	$25.00 – 35.00	$20.00 – 25.00
server, #3857 clover	$30.00 – 40.00	$25.00 – 30.00
server, dustpan shape	$75.00 – 95.00	$40.00 – 50.00
server, skillet shape	$65.00 – 80.00	$35.00 – 45.00
shaving mug	$60.00 – 75.00	$35.00 – 45.00
shell dish, 5"	$25.00 – 35.00	$25.00 – 30.00
shell dish, 7½"	$35.00 – 45.00	$30.00 – 40.00
soap dish, rectangular	$35.00 – 45.00	$30.00 – 40.00
spoon rest	$50.00 – 60.00	$25.00 – 35.00
tidbit, 10"	$20.00 – 25.00	$12.00 – 18.00
tile, 6" round, square or octagon	$30.00 – 40.00	$20.00 – 25.00
tissue box cover square, 6"	$65.00 – 80.00	$45.00 – 55.00
tissue box cover, rectangular	$65.00 – 80.00	$45.00 – 55.00
toothbrush holder, round	$65.00 – 80.00	$40.00 – 50.00
toothbrush holder, square, 4½" tall	$55.00 – 65.00	$25.00 – 30.00
tray, vanity 7¼" square	$35.00 – 45.00	$20.00 – 25.00
tray, 8¼" oval	$25.00 – 35.00	$20.00 – 25.00
vase, #3952 cylinder, 10"	$70.00 – 85.00	$55.00 – 65.00
vase, #3952 cylinder, 8"	$60.00 – 75.00	$45.00 – 55.00
vase, #3952 cylinder, 6"	$45.00 – 55.00	$40.00 – 50.00
vase, #3952 cylinder, 4"	$40.00 – 50.00	$35.00 – 45.00
vase, #4050, 8"	$60.00 – 75.00	$50.00 – 60.00
vase, #4055, 12"	$100.00 – 125.00	$55.00 – 65.00
vase #5106 triple cylinder, 10"x5"	$100.00 – 125.00	$55.00 – 65.00

Commemorative and Special-Order Plates

Stangl has produced various special-order or commemorative items since the 1920s. Ashtrays were usually the form these items took, but occasionally plate shapes were also used for commemorative items. See the *New Yorker Magazine* cartoon pieces, page 248.

Monogram Plates, 1939 – 1940

Monogram plates were made in several styles during 1939 and 1940. These plates would be decorated by Stangl's more talented decorators Gerald Ewing, John O'Brien, and Ethel Kennedy.

Not Shown:
Monogram plate, 14", 1939 – 1940. $300.00 – 350.00.
Monogram plate, 10", 1939 – 1940. $175.00 – 200.00.
Monogram plate, 9", 1939 – 1940. $150.00 – 175.00.
Monogram plate, 8", 1939 – 1940. $130.00 – 150.00.
Monogram plate, 6", 1939 – 1940. $100.00 – 125.00.

Monogram plates, 14" with "AGS" decorated by John O'Brien; 9" plate with "ESM" decorated by Gerald Ewing, both decorated in blue under Satin Blue glaze. Courtesy of the Hill-Fulper-Stangl Museum.

Jersey Shore Series, 1947 – 1948

Children's book illustrator and noted artist, Kurt Weise, was a close friend of the Stangl family. During the 1940s, he could often be found hanging about Stangl's Trenton factory chatting with Martin Stangl or kibitzing with designer Cleo Salerno.

Kurt Weise often created sketches, designs, and doodles while at the pottery. A few of the sketches piqued Martin Stangl's interest enough to have Cleo Salerno adapt them to dinnerware shapes. Martin Stangl's own Farm Life dinnerware pattern originated as a series of Kurt Weise sketches. The Jersey Shore 11" plates also began as Kurt Weise sketches. Kurt Weise created a series of sketches of New Jersey's Long Beach Island sights during a weekend visit to Martin Stangl's Beach Haven, New Jersey house. Martin Stangl so enjoyed Kurt Weise's beach vignettes, he had Cleo Salerno adapt eight of the sketches to 11" plate shapes, which he then called "Jersey Shore."

Each of Kurt Weise's sketch subjects can be found along the New Jersey coastline. Flounder are indigenous to the area, as are starfish, moon snails, channel whelks, and crown conch. Marlin and angelfish are native to tropical regions, but frequently will travel the Gulf Stream along the East Coast. Sailboats, fishing trawlers, and all manner of sea gulls can still be seen along New Jersey's shoreline.

The Jersey Shore plates were produced in limited quantities for the Flemington Outlet during 1947 and 1948. These plates were customarily stamped with the oval Terra Rose backstamp, but not all were marked. Although Cleo Salerno decorated the majority of these plates, other decorators were involved in their production as well. Cleo Salerno's original adaptation of the Jersey Shore series was decorated with a Dark Turquoise and Blue #95 wave device on the rims. Later versions were decorated with a simplified Blue #95 wave on the rims.

Stangl's Jersey Shore plates were produced in such small quantities, they are now extremely rare. The realistically rendered nautical subjects have generated considerable interest among collectors.

Not Shown:

Angelfish Jersey Shore 11" plate. $500.00 – 600.00.
Barnegat Lighthouse Jersey Shore 11" plate. $800.00 – 900.00.
Crown Conch Jersey Shore 11" plate. $400.00 – 450.00.
Flounder Jersey Shore 11" plate. $450.00 – 500.00.
Marlin & fishing boat Jersey Shore 11" plate. $500.00 – 600.00.
Sailboat Jersey Shore 11" plate. $500.00 – 600.00.
Sea Gull on piling Jersey Shore 11" plate. $450.00 – 500.00.
Shells & Starfish Jersey Shore 11" plate. $400.00 – 450.00.

The predicament of the little fisherman on this plate illustrates Kurt Weise's wry sense of humor. This was originally a sketch that Kurt had drawn for Cleo Salerno in 1944, which Cleo then immortalized by transferring to this plate. Although Cleo signed and dated the back of the plate, she reproduced Kurt Weise's signature on the front. Courtesy of Merrill and Christl Stangl Bacheler.

Jersey Shore Flounder and Sea Gull 11" plates. $450.00 – 500.00 each.

Jersey Shore Marlin and Sailboat 11" plates. $500.00 – 600.00 each.

Jersey Shore Shells & Starfish and Crown Conch 11" plates. $400.00 – 450.00 each.

Jersey Shore Barnegat lighthouse 11" plate with original rim treatment, Barnegat lighthouse 11" plate with simplified Blue #95 rim. $800.00 – 900.00 each

Authentic Pennsylvania Dutch Slip Ware, Early 1960s

During the early 1960s, Stangl's resident Flemington Outlet ceramic workshop potter created authentic reproductions of early Pennsylvania German redware. The redware shapes were coupe 9" and 10" deep plate shapes based on antique early Pennsylvania German originals. Edges of the plates were trimmed smooth or crimped with an antique coggle tool. The plates were primarily decorated with traditional slip trail abstract motifs on redware. A few rare plates were also decorated with horse, people or building subjects. All the Flemington Outlet Pennsylvania Dutch Slip Ware was marked with "Stangl Pottery, Flemington, N.J." hand-scrawled on the back of each piece. The Authentic Pennsylvania Dutch Slip Ware was discontinued during 1965 when the Ceramic Workshop building was converted to house the Stangl Pottery Museum.

Stangl's new Ceramic Workshop where the Pennsylvania Dutch Slip Ware was created as it was advertised on 1962 mimeographed bulletin. Christl Stangl Bacheler drew the artwork on this bulletin. Courtesy of the Hill-Fulper-Stangl Museum.

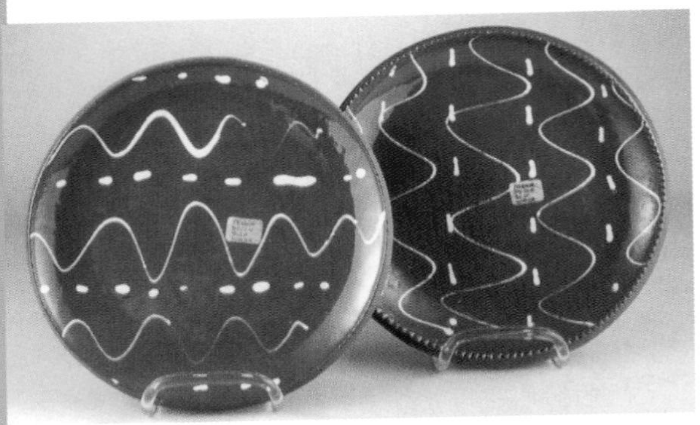

Two Pennsylvania Dutch Slip Ware plates with traditional decoration. The plate on the left has a smooth edge; the plate on the right has a coggled edge. These two plates were originally displayed in Martin Stangl's Stangl Pottery Museum in 1965, and still bear their hand-written museum tags "Penna. Dutch Slip Ware." $175.00 – 200.00 each. From the Stangl and Fulper archival collection, courtesy the Wheaton Village Museum of American Glass.

Hand-scrawled markings on the backs of Pennsylvania Dutch Slip Ware plates. From the Stangl and Fulper archival collection, courtesy the Wheaton Village Museum of American Glass.

Not Shown:

Pennsylvania Dutch Slip Ware plate, 10", abstract motif. $175.00 – 200.00.

Pennsylvania Dutch Slip Ware plate, 9", abstract motif. $160.00 – 180.00.

Pennsylvania Dutch Slip Ware plate, 10", horse or people motif. $375.00 – 400.00.

Pennsylvania Dutch Slip Ware plate, 9", horse or people motif. $375.00 – 400.00.

Victorian Lady or Gentleman, 1960s

The Victorian Lady and Gentleman 10" plates were decorative novelty pieces produced for the Flemington Outlet during the 1960s. Few of these were made and are now exceptionally difficult to find; both are valued about the same.

Victorian Gentleman 10" plate. $250.00 – 300.00 each.

Wedding and Anniversary Plates, 1967 – 1972

Rose Herbeck was the originator and decorator of Stangl's Wedding and Anniversary plates. Rose produced these plates from 1967 through 1972, and nearly all were marked with her "HR" cipher.

Patrons requesting personalized Wedding or Anniversary plates would order them at the Flemington Outlet. Generic Anniversary plates and non-specific plates with Colonial-style couples were simply produced for sale at the Flemington Outlet. Anniversary plates decorated with gold or silver luster are the least common and very desirable.

"Brian and Eve" 12" Wedding plate. $400.00 – 450.00. Courtesy of the Luke and Nancy Ruepp collection.

Rose Herbeck's signature on the back of plate shown above.

"Golden Anniversary," 10" plate. $200.00 – 300.00. Courtesy of the Luke and Nancy Ruepp collection.

Colonial Couple 10" coupe plate and "James R. Potter, Mary Jo Kellenbeck" 10" Wedding plate. $200.00 – 250.00 each. Courtesy of the Luke and Nancy Ruepp collection.

Colonial Couple 10" rim plate. $200.00 – 250.00.

Sgraffito decorated 25th Anniversary 10" plate. $200.00 – 250.00. Courtesy of the Luke and Nancy Ruepp collection.

Not Shown:
Wedding/Anniversary plate, 12". $400.00 – 450.00.
Wedding/Anniversary plate, 10". $200.00 – 250.00.
Wedding/Anniversary plate, 12" with gold trim. $400.00 – 500.00.
Wedding/Anniversary plate, 10" with gold trim. $200.00 – 300.00.
Colonial couple plate, 10", $200.00 – 250.00.

Solebury National Bank, 1971

After the 1970 close of Pennsbury Pottery in Morrisville, Pennsylvania, the Solebury National Bank of Lahaska, Pennsylvania asked Stangl Pottery to produce an item for them similar to one previously done by Pennsbury. During the 1960s, Pennsbury had produced a small promotional ashtray for the Solebury National Bank depicting a local canal scene with a bridge, canal boat, and mules. The Pennsbury ashtrays were molded with the decoration and hand-painted. Stangl began producing a version of that ashtray for the Solebury National Bank in 1971. Stangl's Solebury Bank ashtray was on a #5242 Croyden 6" plate that was spun with Tan underglaze color. The motifs on the Stangl pieces were hand-carved, not molded, as on the Pennsbury ashtrays. The hand-carved motifs add an unsophisticated quality that is absent from the Pennsbury Solebury National Bank ashtrays. Stangl Pottery discontinued these 6" plate/ashtrays by 1972.

Solebury National Bank 6" plate, 1971 only. $25.00 – 35.00. Courtesy of the Brian and Cristi Hahn collection.

Bahamas Independence Commemorative Plate, 1973

Stangl produced these plates to commemorate the Commonwealth of the Bahamas independence from British rule in 1973. The plates were decorated with well-known Bahamian symbols, pink Flamingos and blue water. These plates are very hard to find here since nearly all were shipped to The Bahamas in 1973.

Bahamas Independence commemorative plate, 10". $375.00 – 400.00. Courtesy of the Hill-Fulper-Stangl Museum.

Flemington Outlet Transfer Plates

The Flemington Outlet plates were produced very briefly in 1965, and then were mass-produced in large quantities from 1974 to 1978. The 1965 plates are red body; the 1970s plates were produced on white-bodied shapes. The plates were decorated using an underglaze transfer process with a popular view of the Flemington Outlet buildings. The underglaze transfer colors were black, yellow or blue. A variety of glazes were applied to these plates, including Satin Yellow, Satin Blue, Ivory Satin, and clear gloss. These plates were rarely marked. The name and image of the Outlet on the front was considered sufficient to identify these pieces as Stangl products.

Flemington Outlet Transfer plate from 1965 on a red-bodied Tiara shape plate, extremely rare. $275.00 – 300.00.

Flemington Outlet white-bodied 9" Transfer plate, blue design with clear glaze. $175.00 – 200.00. Courtesy of the Frank and Elizabeth Kramar collection.

Flemington Outlet white-bodied 8" Transfer plate, blue design with Satin Yellow glaze. $175.00 – 200.00. Courtesy of the Frank and Elizabeth Kramar collection.

Not Shown:

Flemington Outlet plate, 10", $200.00 – 250.00.

Flemington Outlet plate, 9". $175.00 – 200.00.

Flemington Outlet plate, 8" or 8¼" $175.00 – 200.00.

Groveville School Commemorative Plate

The Groveville School plate was made for the seventieth anniversary of the Groveville School in Groveville, New Jersey. The plates were the scalloped Queen Anne shape and were decorated with an underglaze transfer print of the Groveville school building.

Groveville School Commemorative Plate, underglaze transfer with platinum trim, 1972 only. $$95.00 – 110.00.

Brendan Byrne Violet Tray

Stangl Pottery produced 250 Violet decorated vanity trays for the New Jersey Statehouse in 1976. The 7¼" square vanity trays were hand-painted with the New Jersey state flower and stamped with a facsimile of Governor Brendan Byrne's signature. Several trays were also produced with the violet only and no signature.

Violet vanity tray, 7¼" square, with Governor Brendan Byrne's signature, 1976. $175.00 – 200.00.

Not Shown:

Violet tray, 7¼" square, violet only, 1976. $75.00 – 90.00.

Cylinder Vases, 1954 – 1978

Stangl first tried decorated cylinder vases during 1954. These vases were 5" tall, tumbler-shaped, and decorated to match popular dinnerware patterns Thistle, Magnolia, Golden Harvest, and Pink Lily. By the end of 1954, these vases were dropped.

Thistle tumbler-shape cylinder vase, 5", 1954 only. $150.00 – 175.00.

Golden Harvest tumbler-shape cylinder vase, 5", 1954 only. $80.00 – 100.00.

In 1956, a new series of decorated #3952 cylinder vases in four sizes was introduced. Kay Hackett developed several decorative motifs for these vases; two motifs were based on the Amber-Glo and Windfall dinnerware patterns. The #3952 cylinder vases were produced with these motifs through the late 1950s. The 4" size #3952 cylinder vase is the least common size.

During the mid 1960s, other popular finishes were applied to these shapes. In the late 1960s through the 1970s, the 10", 6", and 4" cylinder vases were attached together and decorated with popular finishes and the fashion-color glazes Dark Green, Chartreuse Green, Canary Yellow or White.

Photograph taken by Kay Hackett of her original samples of the #3952 Cascade vases. This photo was taken in her studio at Stangl's Trenton factory on April 27, 1956. Courtesy of Kay Hackett.

Not Shown:
#3952 cylinder vase, 10", Cascade, 1956 – 1959. $60.00 – 75.00.
#3952 cylinder vase, 8", Cascade, 1956 – 1959. $55.00 – 65.00.
#3952 cylinder vase, 6", Cascade, 1956 – 1959. $35.00 – 45.00.
#3952 cylinder vase, 4", Cascade, 1956 – 1959. $50.00 – 60.00.
#3952 cylinder vase, 10", Amber-Glo, 1956 – 1959. $55.00 – 65.00.
#3952 cylinder vase, 8", Amber-Glo, 1956 – 1959. $45.00 – 55.00.
#3952 cylinder vase, 6", Amber-Glo, 1956 – 1959. $35.00 – 45.00.
#3952 cylinder vase, 4", Amber-Glo, 1956 – 1959. $35.00 – 45.00.

Amber-Glo 10" cylinder vase on left with Cascade 8" cylinder vase on right. $55.00 – 65.00 each. Courtesy of the Hill-Fulper Stangl Museum.

Three Windfall cylinder vases, 4", 6", $35.00 – 45.00 each; and 10". $55.00 – 65.00. Courtesy of the Marcena North collection.

#3952 cylinder vase, 10", Windfall, 1956 – 1959. $55.00 – 65.00.
#3952 cylinder vase, 8", Windfall, 1956 – 1959. $45.00 – 55.00.
#3952 cylinder vase, 6", Windfall, 1956 – 1959. $35.00 – 45.00.
#3952 cylinder vase, 4", Windfall, 1956 – 1959. $35.00 – 45.00.
#3952 cylinder vase, 10", dry-brushed engobe, 1956 only. $70.00 – 85.00.
#3952 cylinder vase, 8", dry-brushed engobe, 1956 only. $60.00 – 75.00.
#3952 cylinder vase, 6", dry-brushed engobe, 1956 only. $55.00 – 65.00.
#3952 cylinder vase, 4", dry-brushed engobe, 1956 only. $50.00 – 60.00.
#3952 cylinder vase, 10", Blue Caughley, 1964 – 1968. $70.00 – 85.00.
#3952 cylinder vase, 8", Blue Caughley, 1964 – 1968. $60.00 – 75.00.
#3952 cylinder vase, 6", Blue Caughley, 1964 – 1968. $45.00 – 55.00.
#3952 cylinder vase, 4", Blue Caughley, 1964 – 1968. $40.00 – 50.00.
#5106 triple cylinder vase, 10"x5", Blue Caughley, 1964 – 1968. $100.00 – 125.00.
#3952 cylinder vase, 10", Caughley, 1964 – 1968. $55.00 – 65.00.
#3952 cylinder vase, 8", Caughley, 1964 – 1968. $45.00 – 55.00.
#3952 cylinder vase, 6", Caughley, 1964 – 1968. $40.00 – 50.00.
#3952 cylinder vase, 4", Caughley, 1964 – 1968. $35.00 – 45.00.
#5106 triple cylinder vase, 10"x5", Caughley, 1964 – 1968. $55.00 – 65.00.
#3952 cylinder vase, 10", Stangl Stoneware glaze, 1965 only. $70.00 – 85.00.
#3952 cylinder vase, 8", Stangl Stoneware glaze, 1965 only. $60.00 – 75.00.
#3952 cylinder vase, 6", Stangl Stoneware glaze, 1965 only. $55.00 – 65.00.
#3952 cylinder vase, 4", Stangl Stoneware glaze, 1965 only. $40.00 – 50.00.
#5106 triple cylinder vase, 10"x5", Stangl Stoneware glaze, 1965 only. $85.00 – 95.00.
#3952 cylinder vase, 10", Mediterranean, 1965 – 1967. $60.00 – 75.00.
#3952 cylinder vase, 8", Mediterranean, 1965 – 1967. $50.00 – 60.00.
#3952 cylinder vase, 6", Mediterranean, 1965 – 1967. $45.00 – 55.00.
#3952 cylinder vase, 4", Mediterranean, 1965 – 1967. $30.00 – 40.00.
#5106 triple cylinder vase, 10"x5", Mediterranean, 1965 – 1967. $55.00 – 65.00.

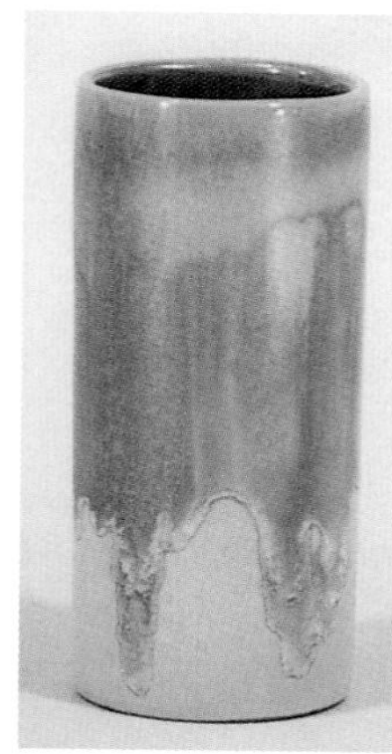

Cylinder vase, 6", glazed in green Stangl Stoneware glaze. $55.00 – 65.00. Courtesy of the Hill-Fulper-Stangl Museum.

Four dry-brushed engobe cylinder vases, 8", $60.00 – 75.00; 4", $50.00 – 60.00; 10", $70.00 – 85.00; and 6", $55.00 – 65.00; made only briefly during 1956. Courtesy of the Marcena North collection.

Mediterranean #5106 triple cylinder vase. $55.00 – 65.00. Courtesy of the Ben and Pauline Jensen collection.

#3952 cylinder vase, 10", Antique Gold, 1961 – 1962. $40.00 – 50.00.
#3952 cylinder vase, 8", Antique Gold, 1961 – 1962. $30.00 – 40.00.
#3952 cylinder vase, 6", Antique Gold, 1961 – 1962. $25.00 – 30.00.
#3952 cylinder vase, 4", Antique Gold, 1961 – 1962. $25.00 – 30.00.
#5106 triple cylinder vase, 10"x5", brushed gold finish, 1970 – 1977. $35.00 – 45.00.
#5106 vase, cylinder 10", Golden Glo, 1962 only. $35.00 – 45.00.
#5107 vase, cylinder 8", Golden Glo, 1962 only. $25.00 – 35.00.
#5108 vase, cylinder 6", Golden Glo, 1962 only. $20.00 – 25.00.
#5109 vase, cylinder 4", Golden Glo, 1962 only. $20.00 – 25.00.
#3952 cylinder vase, 10", Fashion-Colors, 1972 – 1977. $25.00 – 35.00.
#3952 cylinder vase, 8", Fashion-Colors, 1972 – 1977. $25.00 – 30.00.
#3952 cylinder vase, 6", Fashion-Colors, 1972 – 1977. $25.00 – 30.00.
#3952 cylinder vase, 4", Fashion-Colors, 1972 – 1977. $20.00 – 25.00.
#5106 triple cylinder vase, 10"x5", Fashion-Colors, 1972 – 1977. $30.00 – 40.00.

Fashion-color glazed Chartreuse #5106 triple cylinder vase. $30.00 – 40.00.

Decorated Acanthus Artware, 1934 – 1935

Stangl's popular acanthus Artware shapes were available decorated with two-color glaze combinations as special-order during 1934 and 1935. The bodies of the shapes were usually glazed in an opaque matte color with the ornamental leaves glazed in a transparent gloss color. The contrasting textures added dimension to the stylish Acanthus shapes. Some of the glaze combinations were Pink Matte with a gloss Dark Pink, Turquoise with Leaf Green, Rust with gloss Uranium Orange or Uranium Yellow glazes.

Acanthus #1540 7" vase decorated with Pink Matte and gloss Dark Pink. $125.00 – 150.00. Courtesy of the Marcena North collection.

The Decorated Acanthus finish required accurate hand application to produce the desired results and was therefore costly. Few accounts ordered the line because of the added cost, resulting in very a small number of the items being produced.

Acanthus #1543 9"x4" deep bowl glazed in Rust glaze with gloss Uranium Orange. $85.00 – 95.00. Courtesy of the Marcena North collection.

Not Shown:

#1537 Acanthus vase, 7", 1934 – 1935. $85.00 – 95.00.

#1540 Acanthus oval vase, 7"x7", 1934 – 1935. $80.00 – 100.00.

#1541 Acanthus oval vase, 9"x9", 1934 – 1935. $100.00 – 125.00.

#1542 Acanthus oval vase, 10"x7", 1934 – 1935. $110.00 – 135.00.

#1543 Acanthus deep bowl, 9"x4", 1934 – 1935. $85.00 – 95.00.

#1544 Acanthus deep bowl, 7½"x4", 1934 – 1935. $60.00 – 75.00.

#1545 Acanthus deep bowl, 14"x10", 1934 – 1935. $175.00 – 200.00.

#1546 Acanthus bud vase, 9½", 1934 – 1935. $80.00 – 100.00.

#1547 Acanthus bud vase, 7", 1934 – 1935. $70.00 – 85.00.

#1548 Acanthus rose bowl, 5½"x4½", 1934 – 1935. $55.00 – 70.00.

#1549 Acanthus candleholder, 4", 1934 – 1935. $110.00 – 135.00 pair.

Acanthus #1540 7" vase decorated with Rust on the body and Uranium Yellow leaves. $80.00 – 100.00. Courtesy of the Brian and Cristi Hahn collection.

This #1540 Acanthus vase is not decorated, but simply glazed in the highly variegated Yellow Orange glaze. $60.00 – 75.00.

Decorated Baskets, 1974

During 1974, the 5½" tall #3621 basket was decorated with a variety of floral motifs designed by Sandra Ward. The color of the flowers matched the color of the band on the handle.

Not Shown:

#3621 basket, 5½", Pink blossoms. $45.00 – 55.00.
#3621 basket, 5½", Pink tulips. $55.00 – 65.00.
#3621 basket, 5½", Purple violets. $60.00 – 75.00.
#3621 basket, 5½", Red blossoms. $50.00 – 60.00.
#3621 basket, 5½", Red tulips. $60.00 – 75.00.
#3621 basket, 5½", Turquoise blossoms. $40.00 – 50.00.
#3621 basket, 5½", Yellow blossoms. $45.00 – 55.00.
#3621 basket, 5½", Yellow tulips. $60.00 – 75.00.

Basket #3621, 5½", Orchid blossoms. $45.00 – 55.00.

Della-Ware & Lunning "Fancy Pieces," 1942

During 1942, Stangl produced several specialty items for Fisher, Bruce & Co. and Frederik Lunning. Stangl referred to these items, decorated to coordinate with the distributors' dinnerware patterns, as "Fancy Pieces." The Lunning shapes included the #3605 candy jar, #3607 vase, #3608 salad bowl, and #3609 hors d'oeuvres and were decorated with Lunning's Double Bird and Single Bird dinnerware patterns. Produced in very limited quantities, the pieces could be ordered by Frederik Lunning at any time during the 1940s. They were marked with the Lunning backstamp; seconds will have the backstamp obliterated, usually with black glaze. Single Bird is at the lower end of the range, Double Bird at the higher.

Della-Ware Festival #3576 14" fluted bowl. $160.00 – 180.00.

Lunning Shapes

#3605 candy jar, 4½" high. $200.00 – 250.00
#3608 large salad bowl, 12½" diameter. $150.00 –250.00
#3607 vase, 3 corner, 8¾" tall. $200.00 –250.00
#3609 tray, hors d'oeuvres, 13" diameter. $275.00 – 400.00

The Fisher, Bruce & Co. "fancy pieces" were handmade and decorated with their Della-Ware dinnerware patterns, Festival, Laurita, and El Rosa. Added to the line later in 1942, the #3714 candy dish was not handmade. It was also the only shape retained when the original Della-Ware "fancy pieces" were discontinued by the end of 1942. This dish was also produced with the Red Cherry motif in 1947. The Fisher, Bruce & Co. pieces are marked with the Della-Ware underglaze backstamp.

Della-Ware Festival #3714 candy dish. $35.00 – 45.00.

Della-Ware Festival #3576 12" round tray. $150.00 – 165.00.

Della-Ware Shapes

Not Shown:

#3575 round tray, 12", 1942 only. $150.00 – 165.00.
#3576 fluted bowl, 14", 1942 only. $160.00 – 180.00.
#3577 fluted bowl, 12", 1942 only. $110.00 – 135.00.
#3714 candy dish, 8", 1942 – 1948. $35.00 – 45.00.
#3714 candy dish, 8", Red Cherry, 1947 – 1948. $40.00 – 50.00.

The Garden Flower #3714 candy dish, 8", was not produced for Fisher, Bruce & Co., but distributed through Stangl's own retail accounts, 1942 only. $70.00 – 85.00.

Early Pennsylvania Artware, 1942 – 1948

The Early Pennsylvania Artware was developed to coordinate with Stangl's very popular Pennsylvania Dutch-inspired dinnerware patterns. Kay Hackett designed all the Pennsylvania Dutch patterns after her trip to the Philadelphia Museum where she studied authentic early American and Pennsylvania German decorative motifs.

Group of Stangl's Early Pennsylvania Artware including a #3689 6" covered jar, $65.00 – 80.00; #3696 ovoid 9" vase, $80.00 – 90.00; and #3682 5" ball vase, $40.00 – 50.00. Courtesy of the Marcena North collection.

As during the 1920s, Early American-styled home furnishings were extremely popular during the late 1930s and throughout the 1940s. Also popular at that time were European Peasant-style home accessories. Prior to Spain's civil war and Mussolini's actions in Italy, both those countries exported thousands of pieces of "Peasant-Ware" to the United States per year. By 1940, shipments of European Peasant ceramics were severely diminished. Additionally, American popular taste was swinging fully toward styles that were historically American, further strengthening the popularity of Colonial, Early American and Federal styles of home decoration.

By combining hand-decorated Early American Pennsylvania Dutch decorative motifs with modern, sophisticated artware forms, Martin Stangl and Kay Hackett were able to create a truly American "Peasant-Ware!" The hand-brushed engobe, hand-carved motifs, and bright, bold underglaze colors on well-designed shapes caused Stangl's Early Pennsylvania Artware to become tremendously popular.

Group of Stangl's Early Pennsylvania Artware including a #3691 5" ball vase with neck, $40.00 – 50.00; #3681 11" vase, $85.00 – 95.00; #3266 5½" ovoid vase, $30.00 – 40.00; and #3258 Dutch shoe, $30.00 – 40.00. Courtesy of the Marcena North collection.

The Early Pennsylvania Artware line consisted of vases, bowls, candleholders, flowerpots, candy boxes, lamps, and cigarette sets. The primary decoration was a conventionalized tulip motif. It was available in a choice of three colors, Blue #95, Pink #160 or Dark Yellow. Pennsylvania Dutch Green and Victoria Green completed the designs. The background was always an artistically rendered, hand-brushed swirl of engobe. Early Pennsylvania Artware was usually marked with Stangl's Terra Rose underglaze stamp, except for the few pieces made for Fisher, Bruce & Co., which were marked with the Della-Ware backstamp.

Stangl's original Early Pennsylvania Artware advertising sheets included cigarette sets, flowerpots, and piggy banks with other artware shapes. While technically Early Pennsylvania Artware, complete descriptions of these items are in the Cigarette Box chapter and Flowerpot and Novelty Animal sections.

Group of Stangl's Early Pennsylvania Artware including a #3510 7¼" round watering pot, $130.00 – 150.00; #3229 9" bowl, $40.00 – 50.00; and #3211 6" pitcher vase, $50.00 – 60.00. Courtesy of the Marcena North collection.

Two Early Pennsylvania Artware #1076 pig banks. $125.00 – 150.00 each. Courtesy of the Robert and Tammie Cruser collection.

Most of the Early Pennsylvania Artware line was discontinued by 1948. The #1076B Piggy Bank was the only Early Pennsylvania Artware item kept from oblivion. Throughout the 1940s, the 1076B Pig Bank was produced with hand-brushed engobe. The earlier hand-brushed pigs usually are not marked "Stangl" but have the number 1076 carved on the bottom. By the late 1940s, the engobe was brushed heavier, giving a whiter appearance with fewer visible brush-marks. Beginning in the

1950s, the banks were produced with sprayed engobe and retained the original Early Pennsylvania tulip hand-carved and hand-painted motif. Also beginning during the 1950s, the Stangl backstamp was used to identify the pigs. The piggy banks were produced throughout the 1950s, 1960s, and 1970s, bearing blue, pink or yellow tulips. For a very brief time during the early 1960s, a piggy bank was produced with a "Jeweled" decoration. In 1967, a red-clay bisque pig bank with carved embellishment was introduced and produced for two years. For many years, Tulip-decorated banks were a staple at the Flemington Outlet and were sold by the hundreds each weekend for $1.00 each. By 1966, the price began to increase, and the carving was dropped from the motif. By 1970, the pig banks were no longer cast of red clay with engobe but were cast entirely of white clay, and the two smaller tulip blossoms were eliminated. During 1972 and 1973, the piggy banks retailed nationally at $5.25 each. In 1974, the price increased to $6.00. After 1975, the piggies were no longer sold nationally but were sold only at the Flemington Outlet. Currently, Stangl's #1076B Piggy Bank shape is highly collectible in all finishes and decorations.

During the 1930s and 1940s, the same #1076 Pig shape was produced as planters and were called "cactus pots." These were decorated with solid-color glazes during the 1930s and early 1940s and were also decorated with the Early Pennsylvania Tulip motif throughout the 1940s. Numbers on the bottoms of the Pigs were #1076 B for "Bank" and #1076 C for "Cactus Pot." Please also see the sections on Solid-Color Artware, Hand-Painted Animal Figurines, and Flowerpots.

Not Shown:

#1643 flowerpot, 5" scallop-top. $30.00 – 40.00.

#1643 flowerpot, 6" scallop-top. $40.00 – 50.00.

#1643 flowerpot, 7" scallop-top. $60.00 – 75.00.

#1643 flowerpot, 8" scallop-top. $70.00 – 85.00.

#1076 Pig Bank, 4" Tulip decoration, carved decoration, 1950 – 1966. $125.00 – 150.00.

#1076 Pig Bank, 4" Tulip decoration, fewer flowers, not carved, 1966 – 1973. $100.00 – 125.00.

#1076 Pig Bank, 4" Tulip decoration, fewer flowers, white body, 1970 – 1978. $100.00 – 125.00.

#1076 Pig Bank, 4" Terra Rose finishes, 1940 – 1961. $150.00 – 200.00.

#1076 Pig Bank, 4" Jeweled decoration, early 1960s only. $350.00 – 450.00.

#5199 Pig Bank, 4" Red Bisque, 1967 – 1969. $1750.00 – 225.00.

#3211 pitcher vase, 6". $50.00 – 60.00.

#3229 bowl, 12½". $50.00 – 60.00.

Early Pennsylvania Artware #1643 flowerpot, 4" scallop-top. $30.00 – 40.00.

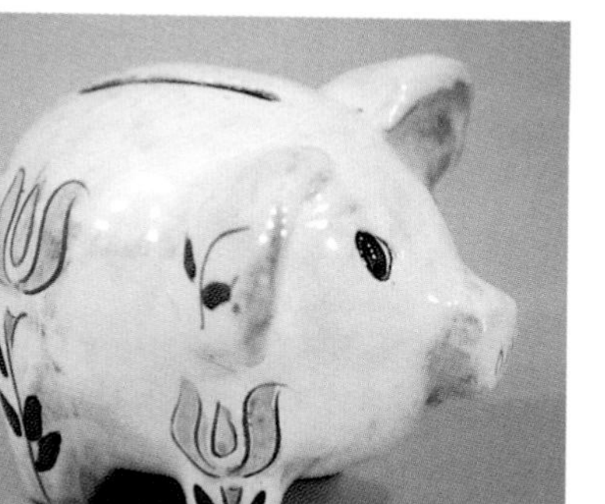

Early Pennsylvania Artware #1076-B Pig Bank, 4" Tulip decoration, brushed engobe, carved decoration 1942 – 1952. $125.00 – 150.00. Courtesy of the Robert and Tammie Cruser collection.

Early Pennsylvania Artware #1076-C Pig cactus pot, 4". $125.00 – 150.00. Courtesy of the Marcena North collection.

Early Pennsylvania Artware #3229 candleholders, 3½". $35.00 – 45.00 pair.

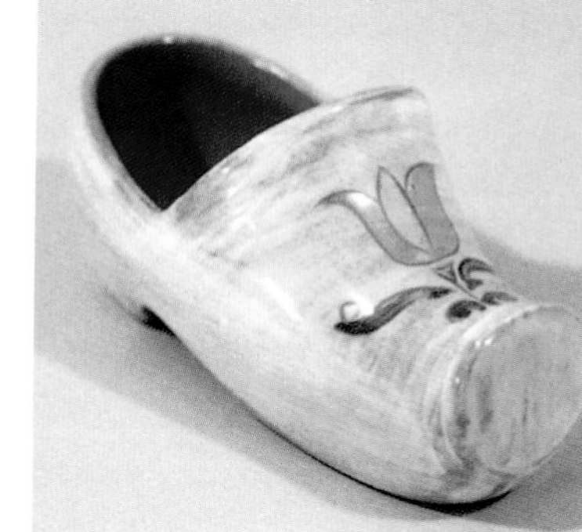

Early Pennsylvania Artware #3258 Dutch shoe, 2¾"x5". $30.00 – 40.00.

Early Pennsylvania Artware #3229 bowl, 9". $40.00 – 50.00.

Early Pennsylvania Artware #3266 vase, ovoid, handles, 5½". $30.00 – 40.00.

Early Pennsylvania Artware #3510 round watering pot, 7¼". $130.00 – 150.00.

Early Pennsylvania Artware #3676 candy jar, bird knob, 4½"x5½". Sometimes marked "Della-Ware." $60.00 – 75.00.

Early Pennsylvania Artware #3683 vase, flared, 7". $55.00 – 65.00.

Early Pennsylvania Artware yellow #3684 candy jar with cover, 4"x7". $70.00 – 85.00.

Early Pennsylvania Artware blue #3684 candy jar with cover, 4"x7". $85.00 – 95.00. Courtesy of the Luke and Nancy Ruepp collection.

Early Pennsylvania Artware #3685 vase, ovoid, 7". $55.00 – 65.00. Courtesy of the Luke and Nancy Ruepp collection.

Early Pennsylvania Artware #3688 vase, milk can, 7". $55.00 – 65.00. Courtesy of the Luke and Nancy Ruepp collection.

Not Shown:

#3511 tall watering pot, 10". $190.00 – 225.00.
#3681 vase, 11". $85.00 – 95.00.
#3682 vase, ball, 5". $40.00 – 50.00.
#3686 low bowl, round, 10". $55.00 – 65.00.
#3687 candleholders, 3½". $35.00 – 45.00 pair.
#3689 jar with cover, 6". $65.00 – 80.00.
#3690 vase, scalloped, 9". $55.00 – 65.00.

Early Pennsylvania Artware #3691 vase, ball with neck, 5". $40.00 – 50.00. Courtesy of the Luke and Nancy Ruepp collection.

Early Pennsylvania Artware oval bowls #3692, 7" and #3693, 9". $30.00 – 45.00 each. Courtesy of the Luke and Nancy Ruepp collection.

Early Pennsylvania Artware #3695 low bowl, oblong, 11"x7". $60.00 – 75.00.

#3692 oval bowl, 7" long. $30.00 – 40.00.
#3693 oval bowl, 9" long. $35.00 – 45.00.
#3694 vase, ovoid, 5". $40.00 – 50.00.

Early Pennsylvania Artware #3696 vase, ovoid, 9". $80.00 – 90.00.

Engobe Decorated Artware, "Gingerbread," 1967 – 1972

A 10" and two 8" Rose Herbeck Engobe Decorated "Gingerbread" plates decorated with popular building and bird motifs. 8" plates, $100.00 – 150.00 each; 10" plate, $150.00 – 200.00. Courtesy of Rose Herbeck.

Rose Herbeck developed the decorative Engobe Decorated plates and art pieces specifically for the Flemington Outlet. The motifs and style of decoration were based on antique, peasant-type pottery of Rose Herbeck's native Germany. The red clay shapes were decorated with colored engobes using a rubber syringe. These were usually glazed with clear glaze, but occasionally Cobalt Blue, Manganese Brown, Copper Green or Transparent Yellow glazes were used for variety. Because these pieces resemble icing-decorated cookies, collectors have come to call this line "Gingerbread."

The Engobe Decorated motifs were applied to a multitude of dinnerware and artware shapes. The most common shapes were plates in various sizes. Ashtrays and artware shapes were produced but in limited quantities. The old Pennsylvania Dutch Slip Ware deep plate shapes of the early 1960s were resurrected for Rose Herbeck's "Gingerbread" decoration and became known as "pie plates." The coggle tool was also dusted off and used to create a coggled edge on many of the Engobe Decorated "Gingerbread" pie plates.

Engobe Decorated 10" "pie plate" with coggled edge. $50.00 – 60.00.

Stangl's Engobe Decorated "Gingerbread" items were very popular at the Flemington Outlet and were produced steadily from 1967 until 1972. Rose Herbeck and her assistant were the only persons involved in the production of this ware. Values shown are for standard production "Gingerbread" items produced by Rose Herbeck or her

Pair of #5069 candleholders, $100.00 – 125.00 pair; with a #4061 8" flared bowl, $50.00 – 60.00, all decorated by Rose Herbeck.

Rose Herbeck's "HR" signature found on the items she herself decorated.

assistant. Because of her compelling personality, collectors have begun to covet Rose's Engobe Decorated articles signed with her "HR" cipher. Unusual "Gingerbread" pieces signed by Rose can sell for up to double the values shown here.

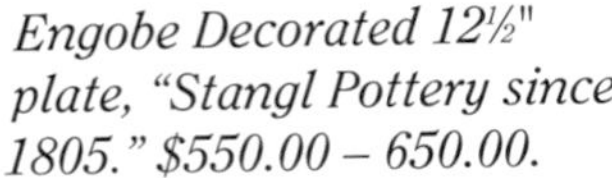

Engobe Decorated 12½" plate, "Stangl Pottery since 1805." $550.00 – 650.00.

Diminutive Engobe Decorated Cosmos ashtray decorated by Rose Herbeck, $60.00 – 75.00, with an unusual variation of her signature on back shown in inset. Courtesy of the Luke and Nancy Ruepp collection.

Group of Engobe Decorated pieces, 8" plate with buildings, $100.00 – 150.00; 12" plate with floral rim, $55.00 – 65.00; mug, $70.00 – 85.00; and 10" pie plate, $50.00 – 60.00. The 8" plate and mug were decorated by Rose Herbeck.

	Rim Motifs	All-Over Florals	Birds or Buildings
ashtray, large	$50.00 – 60.00	$50.00 – 60.00	$50.00 – 60.00
ashtray, small	$25.00 – 35.00	$25.00 – 35.00	$25.00 – 35.00
bowl, 10" #4062 flared	$20.00 – 25.00	$40.00 – 50.00	$60.00 – 75.00
bowl, 8" #4061 flared	$20.00 – 25.00	$30.00 – 40.00	$35.00 – 45.00
cake stand	$20.00 – 25.00	$30.00 – 40.00	$40.00 – 50.00
candleholder #5069, pair	$100.00 – 125.00	$100.00 – 125.00	$100.00 – 125.00
mug, 2-cup	$70.00 – 85.00	$70.00 – 85.00	$70.00 – 85.00
pie plate, 10"	$25.00 – 35.00	$50.00 – 60.00	$85.00 – 95.00
pie plate, 9"	$25.00 – 35.00	$45.00 – 55.00	$70.00 – 85.00
plate, 12½" chop	$55.00 – 65.00	$60.00 – 75.00	$110.00 – 135.00
plate, 10"	$25.00 – 30.00	$40.00 – 50.00	$70.00 – 85.00
plate, 8"	$15.00 – 20.00	$25.00 – 35.00	$55.00 – 65.00
plate, 6"	$15.00 – 20.00	$25.00 – 30.00	$45.00 – 55.00

Three "weeping gold" style experimental finishes in Black Gold, Antique Gold, and Granada Gold, early 1970s. $130.00 – 150.00 each. Courtesy of the Wayne Weigand Collection.

Experiments, Samples, and Tests

Because Martin Stangl used the Flemington Outlet to sell the sample, test, and experimental pieces that most companies would have destroyed, many of these items exist today. Values for experimental glaze tests and sample vases can range greatly. Attractive and interesting items always sell for much more than dull and unattractive samples and glaze tests.

Artware Samples

Stangl was continually developing new artware decorations and decorative processes. Examples of some sample artware finishes that were never produced follow.

Vase #5104 with sample banded decoration in Aztec style, 1960s. $80.00 – 135.00. Courtesy of the Frank and Elizabeth Kramar collection.

Irene Sarnecki experimental Town & Country finish, red and dark blue sponged under Silk White glaze on #5066 large cornucopia shape. Signed by Irene Sarnecki and dated 1976. $130.00 – 150.00.

Glaze Experiments

During the 1930s and 1970s, when solid-color glazes were most popular, Stangl experimented with a multitude of new glaze formulae. Experimental glazes were applied to artware shapes and marked with identifying numbers and application techniques. The #4050 bud vase shape was a favorite for glaze experiments during the 1970s because it was large enough to exhibit the glaze, and the various slopes and curves of the shape revealed inherent flaws the glaze might possess.

Cobalt blue with white froth glaze experiment on #4050 bud vase shape, 1970s. $60.00 – 85.00. Base, marked "290 G under 293/0" in inset. Courtesy of the Brian and Cristi Hahn collection.

Experimental sponged black and turquoise glaze finish on 9½" vase #3979, 1970s. Base marked "319B, 323D" in inset. $70.00 – 95.00. Courtesy of Beatrice Levine.

Vase #4049 with experimental curdled white and tan glaze, 1970s. Base, marked "309 Dipped, 309A Sponged over" in inset. $60.00 – 85.00. Courtesy of the Hill-Fulper-Stangl Museum.

Color and Glaze Tests

Stangl's lab was continually testing each new shipment or batch of glaze, color, and ceramic materials for quality control and compatibility. Color test plates or saucers are the most plentiful of the lab tests as these were sometimes produced daily, depending on the amount of color to be tested. Glaze tests were very similar to color tests but were generally marked with the glaze number rather than a color name.

Group of color tests: 8" 3-color test plate, $30.00 – 40.00; single-color test saucer with "s" on front, $6.00 – 8.00; 9" 2-color test plate, $40.00 – 50.00; 4-color test saucer, $15.00 – 20.00; and 8" 3-color test plate, $30.00 – 40.00.

Color test plates were usually done on saucers or 6" plates, although larger plates and hollow-ware pieces were also used. Color test pieces were decorated with swirls, bands or abstract brush strokes and always had information on the front or back pertaining to the glaze or color being tested. An "S" on the front of some pieces indicated a test "sample." Larger glaze and color test plates with interesting designs or plates with multiple colors are always valued higher than small, single-color pieces.

BLUE #95
YELLOW
FX. GREEN
1/11/51

Typical color test markings used during the late 1940s and into the 1950s.

Test rubber-stamp mark sometimes used on glaze test plates.

Plates with one to nine colors tested:
test plate, 10". $45.00 – 95.00
test plate, 9". $35.00 – 70.00
test plate, 8". $30.00 – 55.00
test plate, 6". $10.00 – 20.00
test saucer, $6.00 – 15.00

Plates with ten or more colors tested:
test plate, 12½". $200.00 – 250.00
test plate, 11". $200.00 – 250.00
test plate, 10". $100.00 – 200.00
test plate, 9". $80.00 – 125.00

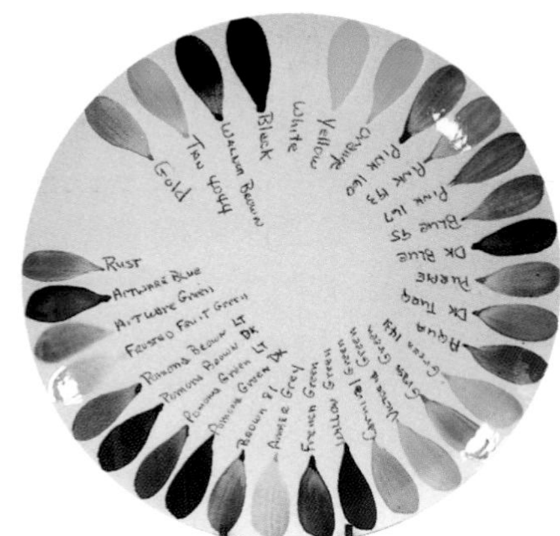

Color Test 10" plate with 31 colors. $175.00 – 200.00.

Flowerpots, Planters, and Patio Ware, 1933 – 1978

Macy's Hand-Painted Flowerpots and Vases, 1933

Fulper Pottery Company's first hand-painted underglaze color flowerpots were made for the R.H. Macy department store in New York during 1933. Macy's was an important account and had been purchasing both general line and special-order Fulper and Stangl products since the 1920s. In 1933, Macy's pottery buyer, William Bradley, special-ordered a series of exclusive artware in both hand-decorated underglaze colors and solid-color glazes. The hand-decorated items were for a special spring promotion and were not produced again afterward.

The shapes included the #1640 flower box, #1641 wide top vase, #1642 straight flowerpot, #1643 scallop flowerpot, and #1683 vase. The hand-painted shapes were decorated with plaid or floral patterns under Stangl's Parchment glaze. The #1643 scallop flowerpot was the only shape decorated with the floral motif. The other four shapes were all decorated with plaids, and the #1640 flower box was also decorated with stripes. The plaids were available in four color choices. They were blue horizontal bands with brown and red vertical stripes: yellow bands with black and red stripes; green bands with yellow and blue stripes; and red bands with green and brown stripes. The plaid pattern used on the vases was more intricate and used the colors red, blue, green, yellow, and brown. The floral motif was a spray of single roses and was available in blue, yellow or rose with green foliage and brown stems. The flowerpot saucers and rims were banded with the same color as the flowers.

The Macy's hand-painted artware was produced only during 1933 in limited quantities, so it is now quite rare. The same shapes continued to be produced in solid-color glazes for several years afterward and are comparatively common. See also the Solid-Color Artware chapter for those items. Values for the Macy's hand-painted flowerpots include the matching hand-painted saucer. Flowerpots missing the saucer usually sell at about half that of complete flowerpot and saucer sets.

Macy's #1640 flower box, 10"x4"x3½" high, plaid or striped. $120.00 – 135.00. Photo shows the red band and green and brown stripe plaid pattern. Courtesy of the Hill-Fulper-Stangl Museum.

Macy's #1683 vase, 8¼", plaid. $130.00 – 150.00. Courtesy of the Hill-Fulper-Stangl Museum.

Not Shown:
#1641 vase, wide-top, 9" plaid. $130.00 – 150.00.
#1642 flowerpot, & saucer 6" straight-top, plaid. $75.00 – 95.00.
#1642 flowerpot, & saucer 5" straight-top, plaid. $60.00 – 75.00.
#1642 flowerpot & saucer, 4" straight-top, plaid. $50.00 – 60.00.
#1643 flowerpot, & saucer 5" scallop-top, floral. $60.00 – 75.00.
#1643 flowerpot, & saucer 4" scallop-top, floral. $50.00 – 60.00.

Macy's #1643 flowerpot, & saucer 6" scallop-top, floral. $75.00 – 95.00. Courtesy of the Ruepp collection.

Early Pennsylvania Artware Flowerpots, 1942 – 1947

The rustic Early Pennsylvania Artware finish adorned several flowerpot and planter shapes. Each piece was cast of red clay and brushed with a thin wash of white engobe. The tulip motif was hand-carved then hand-painted in pink, yellow or blue with Pennsylvania Dutch Green underglaze colors. See also the complete section on Early Pennsylvania Artware (page 220).

Not Shown:

#1643 flowerpot, 8" scallop-top. $70.00 – 85.00.
#1643 flowerpot, 7" scallop-top. $60.00 – 75.00.
#1643 flowerpot, 6" scallop-top. $40.00 – 50.00.
#1643 flowerpot, 5" scallop-top. $30.00 – 40.00.
#1643 flowerpot, 4" scallop-top. $30.00 – 40.00.

#1076-C Pig cactus pot, 4". $100.00 – 150.00. Courtesy of the Robert and Tammie Cruser collection.

Two Early Pennsylvania Artware #1643 flowerpots, 4" and 5". $30.00 – 40.00 each. Courtesy of the Luke and Nancy Ruepp collection.

Della-Ware Flowerpots, 1942 – 1953

In 1942, Stangl began producing two styles of flowerpots with an assortment of hand-carved, hand-painted floral motifs for Fisher, Bruce & Co. The flowerpots were #3661 plain rim and #3662 fluted rim shapes and were stamped with the Fisher, Bruce & Co. Della-Ware backstamp. The floral motifs were all designed by Kay Hackett and included red or yellow Single Tulip, red Triple Tulip, red Cosmos, orange Calendula, and orange Nasturtium with Pennsylvania Dutch Green and Victoria Green leaves. There was also a Pennsylvania Dutch Green band on the top interior rim of each pot. The motifs were hand-carved and hand-painted on three sides of the Della-Ware flowerpots.

The Della-Ware flowerpots were produced in four sizes, 4½", 5½", 6½", and 8½" in diameter. The very large 8½" sized flowerpot shape was discontinued by 1943 and is now very hard to find. Engobe was hand-brushed on the exterior and inside the top edge of the pots. After Stangl began spraying engobe in 1950, the exteriors were sprayed with engobe while the inside top edges continued to be hand-brushed. In 1953, Stangl's contract with Fisher, Bruce & Co. ended, and the Della-Ware flowerpots were discontinued. Values for the different Della-Ware flowerpot motifs are all about the same. The red Triple Tulip seems the most difficult to find so often sells for more than the other motifs.

Three Della-Ware #3661 plain rim flowerpots, 8½" with Single Tulip, $75.00 – 85.00; 8½" with Triple Tulip, $85.00 – 95.00; and 5½" with Calendula, $35.00 – 45.00.

#3661 plain rim, 8½". $75.00 – 85.00.
#3661 plain rim, 6½". $50.00 – 60.00.
#3661 plain rim, 5½". $35.00 – 45.00.
#3661 plain rim, 4½". $25.00 – 35.00.
#3662 fluted rim, 8½". $75.00 – 85.00.
#3662 fluted rim, 6½". $50.00 – 60.00.
#3662 fluted rim, 5½". $35.00 – 45.00.
#3662 fluted rim, 4½". $25.00 – 35.00.

Three Della-Ware #3662 fluted rim flowerpots, 5½" with Single Tulip, $35.00 – 45.00; 8½" with Cosmos, $75.00 – 85.00; and 4½" with Nasturtium, $25.00 – 35.00.

Terra Rose Flowerpots, 1943 – 1955

Flowerpots decorated with bold swirls of Terra Rose Green, Blue or Mauve were made in relatively small quantities during the late 1940s and early 1950s.

Not Shown:

#3661 plain rim, 8½". $60.00 – 70.00.
#3661 plain rim, 6½". $40.00 – 50.00.
#3661 plain rim, 5½". $25.00 – 35.00.
#3661 plain rim, 4½". $20.00 – 30.00.
#3662 fluted rim, 8½". $60.00 – 70.00.

Terra Rose Mauve #2001 raised leaf design, 5½". $45.00 – 55.00.

#3662 fluted rim, 6½". $40.00 – 50.00.
#3662 fluted rim, 5½". $25.00 – 35.00.
#3662 fluted rim, 4½". $20.00 – 30.00.

Red Rose 4" hand-carved, $25.00 – 30.00, 3" not carved, $10.00 – 15.00; Red Tulip 7", $55.00 – 65.00; Yellow Tulip 3" not carved, $10.00 – 15.00; 5" not carved, $15.00 – 20.00; Yellow Tulip 3" votive candle (far right) 1973 only, $20.00 – 25.00.

Stangl Hand-Painted Flowerpots and Porch and Patio Ware, 1953 – 1977

Stangl continued to produce an assortment of decorated #3661 plain rim pots after the ending of the Fisher, Bruce & Co. contract in 1953 but with several changes. A small 3" diameter flowerpot size was added, and the interior engobe was eliminated from the pots. However, the interior band of green was retained. The motifs used on the flowerpots included the old Della-Ware single Yellow Tulip and newly developed (by Kay Hackett) Yellow Rose, Red Rose, and Red Daisy motifs. Each pot was decorated with only two motifs, not three as were on the Della-Ware pots, and the green was changed from Pennsylvania Dutch Green to Willow Green. The hand-carved Red Daisy and Yellow Rose motifs were produced only during 1953, but Yellow Rose was brought back again briefly in 1975.

Comparison of two Yellow Single Tulip flowerpots. A pre-1965 5" pot with carved motif and interior band is on right, $25.00 – 35.00; and a late-1960s 4" pot is on the left. $12.00 – 18.00.

The 3" flowerpot size was discontinued in 1956 and brought back again in 1960. From 1961 through 1965, #1792 ruffled shape flowerpot saucers were produced to coordinate with the Yellow Tulip and Red Rose flowerpots. The saucers were 4", 5", and 7" in diameter. After the fire in 1965, the flowerpot motifs were no longer carved. The pots were still red clay with white engobe, but the decoration was simply painted on. Also at that time, the #1792 saucers were discontinued. In 1966, the second motif and interior band was eliminated from each pot; the flowerpots were decorated on one side only from then on.

In 1972, several new decorations were added to the #3661 flowerpot line. Included in the new designs were sponged Caughley in blue, green or yellow; vertical stripes on the rims of the pots or horizontal stripes on the sides in Blue (Dark Turquoise), Red (Pink #160), Mustard (Old Gold), and Olive (Pomona Green). Occasionally, atypical colors were used during this time such as red on Tulip and yellow on Rose.

Original 1964 Stangl Flemington Outlet advertising mailer showing some of the birdhouse and patio lamp shapes available. Courtesy of the Hill-Fulper-Stangl Museum.

Also in 1972, the Porch and Patio series was introduced. This line consisted of unglazed terra cotta birdhouses and bird feeders. This was actually a reintroduction of the birdhouse and bird feeder shapes as they were originally introduced in 1964 and had been discontinued since 1965. The hanging patio lamps, bird houses, and bird feeders had "roofs" glazed in brown during 1964. The 1970s incarnations of these items had roofs glazed in gray.

Patio votive candles were also introduced during 1973. They came in three styles, which were the #3661 3" Yellow Tulip flowerpot with a green band instead of yellow, a flowerpot mug with the Chicory dinnerware motif, and a flowerpot mug with the Susan dinnerware motif. These mugs and flowerpots were sent to Wheaton's candle company in Tuckahoe, New Jersey, to be filled with wax then shipped back to the Stangl Trenton factory for distribution.

Group of Terra White flowerpots. 1975 only. 4", $20.00 – 25.00; 7", $30.00 – 40.00; 3", $15.00 – 20.00; 5", $25.00 – 30.00. Courtesy of the Luke and Nancy Ruepp collection.

During 1974, the 5" hanging flowerpot, birdhouses, bird feeders, and patio lamps were discontinued, and new flowerpot shapes and decorations were developed to meet the sudden demand for decorative planters during the 1970s. At this time, the Terra White treatment was introduced. Items in Terra White were cast or jiggered of a slightly swirled mixture of red and white colored clays, reminiscent of Dave Thomas' Marbled treatment of 1954. Terra White flowerpots were glazed, while Terra White hanging flowerpots were left in an unglazed bisque state.

In 1975, all decorated flowerpots were converted to white body so they could simply be cast of white clay without having to apply the sprayed engobe. Two new flowerpot shapes, called "cache pots," were introduced in 1975. Five hand-painted motifs designed by Sandra Ward were also introduced at that time. In addition, the hanging flowerpot shape was produced in white clay without a saucer, decorated in Art Ware Blue, Victoria Green or Yellow underglaze color and promoted as "hanging planters." During September 1974 only, the #3661 flowerpots were produced with plain white glaze.

During 1975, the flowerpot line was reworked, and new decorations were tried. Some of the trials were pots with textured surfaces, such as tree bark, fabric, and wicker. Also, dark brown manganese glaze, called Crock Pot Brown, was tried in various patterns. The Town & Country sponged finishes were added to the flowerpot assortment, and saucers for both the flowerpots and pail shaped cache pots were added at that time. The saucers were plain white with clear gloss glaze. By December 1975, all terra cotta hanging baskets, flowerpots, and planters were discontinued, as were the bowl-shaped cache pots.

Original catalog sheet showing Stangl's new flowerpot introductions for 1977. Courtesy of the Hill-Fulper-Stangl Museum.

At the end of 1976, just in time for introduction in January 1977, six new flowerpot motifs designed by Sandra Ward were introduced. These were applied only to the #3661 flowerpot shape; the pail shape cachepot was discontinued at that time. The assortment consisted of four sizes of the #3661 flowerpot shape available in seventeen different decorations. They comprised five colors of Town & Country, four different stripe colors, and eight different floral motifs. This was the final flowerpot assortment; it remained unchanged until Stangl ceased production in 1978.

Not Shown:

#3661 flowerpot Red Daisy, hand-carved, 3", 1953 – 1965. $40.00 – 50.00.
#3661 flowerpot Red Daisy, hand-carved, 4", 1953 – 1965. $50.00 – 60.00.
#3661 flowerpot Red Daisy, hand-carved, 5", 1953 – 1965. $55.00 – 70.00.
#3661 flowerpot Red Daisy, hand-carved, 7", 1953 – 1965. $65.00 – 80.00.
#3661 flowerpot Red Rose, hand-carved, 3", 1953 – 1965. $20.00 – 25.00.
#3661 flowerpot Red Rose, hand-carved, 4", 1953 – 1965. $25.00 – 30.00.
#3661 flowerpot Red Rose, hand-carved, 5", 1953 – 1965. $25.00 – 35.00.
#3661 flowerpot Red Rose, hand-carved, 7", 1953 – 1965. $30.00 – 40.00.
#3661 flowerpot Red Rose, 3", not carved, 1966 – 1978. $10.00 – 15.00.
#3661 flowerpot Red Rose, 4", not carved, 1966 – 1978. $12.00 – 18.00.
#3661 flowerpot Red Rose, 5", not carved, 1966 – 1978. $15.00 – 20.00.
#3661 flowerpot Red Rose, 7", not carved, 1966 – 1978. $20.00 – 25.00.
#3661 flowerpot Yellow Rose, hand-carved, 3", 1953 – 1965. $35.00 – 45.00.
#3661 flowerpot Yellow Rose, hand-carved, 4", 1953 – 1965. $45.00 – 55.00.
#3661 flowerpot Yellow Rose, hand-carved, 5", 1953 – 1965. $55.00 – 65.00.
#3661 flowerpot Yellow Rose, hand-carved, 7", 1953 – 1965. $60.00 – 75.00.
#3661 flowerpot Yellow Rose, 3", not carved, 1975 only. $20.00 – 25.00.
#3661 flowerpot Yellow Rose, 4", not carved, 1975 only. $25.00 – 30.00.
#3661 flowerpot Yellow Rose, 5", not carved, 1975 only. $35.00 – 45.00.
#3661 flowerpot Yellow Rose, 7", not carved, 1975 only. $45.00 – 55.00.
#3661 flowerpot Yellow Tulip, hand-carved, 3", 1953 – 1965. $20.00 – 25.00.

Stangl's rare Red Daisy 5" flowerpot. Red Daisy flowerpots sell for about double Red Rose flowerpots. $50.00 – 65.00. Courtesy of the Luke and Nancy Ruepp collection.

Two Red Rose flowerpots, pot on the left from the 1960s, 4" not carved, $12.00 – 18.00; pot on the right from the 1950s, 3" hand-carved, $20.00 – 25.00.

Yellow Rose 7" flowerpot from 1975. $45.00 – 55.00.

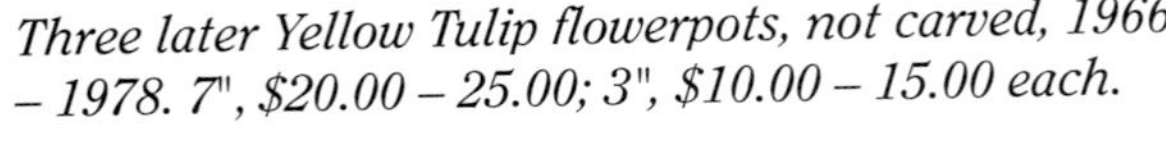

Three later Yellow Tulip flowerpots, not carved, 1966 – 1978. 7", $20.00 – 25.00; 3", $10.00 – 15.00 each.

#3661 flowerpot Yellow Tulip, hand-carved, 4", 1953 – 1965. $25.00 – 30.00.
#3661 flowerpot Yellow Tulip, hand-carved, 5", 1953 – 1965. $25.00 – 35.00.
#3661 flowerpot Yellow Tulip, hand-carved, 7", 1953 – 1965. $30.00 – 40.00.
#3661 flowerpot Yellow Tulip, 3", not carved, 1966 – 1978. $10.00 – 15.00.
#3661 flowerpot Yellow Tulip, 4", not carved, 1966 – 1978. $12.00 – 18.00.
#3661 flowerpot Yellow Tulip, 5", not carved, 1966 – 1978. $15.00 – 20.00.
#3661 flowerpot Yellow Tulip, 7", not carved, 1966 – 1978. $20.00 – 25.00.
#3661 flowerpot Yellow Tulip, 3", green band, votive candle 1973 only. $20.00 – 25.00.
#3661 flowerpot Red Tulip, 3", 1973 only. $25.00 – 30.00.
#3661 flowerpot Red Tulip, 4", 1973 only. $25.00 – 35.00.
#3661 flowerpot Red Tulip, 5", 1973 only. $45.00 – 55.00.
#3661 flowerpot Red Tulip, 7", 1973 only. $55.00 – 65.00.
#3661 flowerpot Blue Tulip, 3", 1975 – 1976. $25.00 – 30.00.
#3661 flowerpot Blue Tulip, 4", 1975 – 1976. $30.00 – 35.00.
#3661 flowerpot Blue Tulip, 5", 1975 – 1976. $45.00 – 55.00.
#3661 flowerpot Blue Tulip, 7", 1975 – 1976. $55.00 – 65.00.

Hard-to-find 7" Red Tulip flowerpot. $55.00 – 65.00.

#4071 Antique Gold fluted flowerpot, 4" (orig. #3662) 1959 – 1963. $20.00 – 25.00.
#4071 Antique Gold fluted flowerpot, 5" (orig. #3662) 1959 – 1963. $20.00 – 25.00.
#4071 Antique Gold fluted flowerpot, 7" (orig. #3662) 1959 – 1963. $25.00 – 35.00.
#3661 flowerpot Striped, 3", 1972 – 1978. $10.00 – 15.00.
#3661 flowerpot Striped, 4", 1972 – 1978. $12.00 – 18.00.
#3661 flowerpot Striped, 5", 1972 – 1978. $15.00 – 20.00.
#3661 flowerpot Striped, 7", 1972 – 1978. $20.00 – 25.00.
#3661 flowerpot Caughley, Blue, 3", 1972 – 1976. $20.00 – 25.00.
#3661 flowerpot Caughley, Blue, 4", 1972 – 1976. $25.00 – 30.00.
#3661 flowerpot Caughley, Blue, 5", 1972 – 1976. $35.00 – 45.00.
#3661 flowerpot Caughley, Blue, 7", 1972 – 1976. $60.00 – 75.00.
#3661 flowerpot Caughley, Green or Yellow, 3", 1972 – 1976. $20.00 – 25.00.
#3661 flowerpot Caughley, Green or Yellow, 4", 1972 – 1976. $25.00 – 30.00.
#3661 flowerpot Caughley, Green or Yellow, 5", 1972 – 1976. $30.00 – 40.00.
#3661 flowerpot Caughley, Green or Yellow, 7", 1972 – 1976. $40.00 – 50.00.
#3661 flowerpot plain white, 3", 1974 only. $10.00 – 15.00.
#3661 flowerpot plain white, 4", 1974 only. $12.00 – 18.00.
#3661 flowerpot plain white, 5", 1974 only. $15.00 – 20.00.

Three Blue Tulip flowerpots, even more desirable than Red Tulip. Blue Tulip flowerpots were decorated with Dark Turquoise, like the two on the left, or Blue #95 as on the right. 7", $55.00 – 65.00; 3" $25.00 – 30.00; 4", $30.00 – 35.00.

#3661 flowerpot plain white, 7", 1974 only. $20.00 – 25.00.
#3661 flowerpot Terra White, 3", 1975 only. $15.00 – 20.00.
#3661 flowerpot Terra White, 4", 1975 only. $20.00 – 25.00.
#3661 flowerpot Terra White, 5", 1975 only. $25.00 – 30.00.
#3661 flowerpot Terra White, 7", 1975 only. $30.00 – 40.00.

Antique Gold #4071 fluted flowerpot. $25.00 – 35.00.

Three Caughley flowerpots. 7" Green, $40.00 – 50.00; 3" Blue, $20.00 – 25.00; 4" Blue, $25.00 – 30.00.

Courtesy of the Ben and Floss Avila collection.

#3661 flowerpot Crock Pot Brown, 3", 1975 only. $20.00 – 25.00.
#3661 flowerpot Crock Pot Brown, 4", 1975 only. $25.00 – 30.00.
#3661 flowerpot Crock Pot Brown, 5", 1975 only. $25.00 – 35.00.
#3661 flowerpot Crock Pot Brown, 7", 1975 only. $35.00 – 45.00.
#3661 flowerpot Town & Country Blue, 3", 1976 – 1978. $20.00 – 25.00.
#3661 flowerpot Town & Country Blue, 4", 1976 – 1978. $25.00 – 30.00.
#3661 flowerpot Town & Country Blue, 5", 1976 – 1978. $35.00 – 45.00.
#3661 flowerpot Town & Country Blue, 7", 1976 – 1978. $55.00 – 65.00.
#3661 flowerpot Town & Country Green or Yellow, 3", 1976 – 1978. $20.00 – 25.00.
#3661 flowerpot Town & Country Green or Yellow, 4", 1976 – 1978. $20.00 – 25.00.
#3661 flowerpot Town & Country Green or Yellow, 5", 1976 – 1978. $25.00 – 30.00.
#3661 flowerpot Town & Country Green or Yellow, 7", 1976 – 1978. $25.00 – 35.00.
#3661 flowerpot Town & Country Brown or Honey, 3", 1976 – 1978. $10.00 – 15.00.
#3661 flowerpot Town & Country Brown or Honey, 4", 1976 – 1978. $15.00 – 20.00.
#3661 flowerpot Town & Country Brown or Honey, 5", 1976 – 1978. $20.00 – 25.00.
#3661 flowerpot Town & Country Brown or Honey, 7", 1976 – 1978. $25.00 – 30.00.
#3661 flowerpot Blue Flower, 3", 1977 – 1978. $25.00 – 35.00.
#3661 flowerpot Blue Flower, 4", 1977 – 1978. $30.00 – 40.00.
#3661 flowerpot Blue Flower, 5", 1977 – 1978. $40.00 – 50.00.
#3661 flowerpot Blue Flower, 7", 1977 – 1978. $55.00 – 70.00.
#3661 flowerpot Golden Iris, 3", 1977 – 1978. $20.00 – 25.00.
#3661 flowerpot Golden Iris, 4", 1977 – 1978. $25.00 – 30.00.
#3661 flowerpot Golden Iris, 5", 1977 – 1978. $30.00 – 40.00.
#3661 flowerpot Golden Iris, 7", 1977 – 1978. $45.00 – 55.00.
#3661 flowerpot Pine Cone, 3", 1977 – 1978. $20.00 – 25.00.
#3661 flowerpot Pine Cone, 4", 1977 – 1978. $25.00 – 30.00.
#3661 flowerpot Pine Cone, 5", 1977 – 1978. $30.00 – 40.00.
#3661 flowerpot Pine Cone, 7", 1977 – 1978. $45.00 – 55.00.
#3661 flowerpot Sun Flower, 3", 1977 – 1978. $20.00 – 25.00.
#3661 flowerpot Sun Flower, 4", 1977 – 1978. $25.00 – 35.00.
#3661 flowerpot Sun Flower, 5", 1977 – 1978. $35.00 – 45.00.
#3661 flowerpot Sun Flower, 7", 1977 – 1978. $45.00 – 55.00.
#3661 flowerpot Wild Golden Rose, 3", 1977 – 1978. $25.00 – 30.00.
#3661 flowerpot Wild Golden Rose, 4", 1977 – 1978. $25.00 – 35.00.
#3661 flowerpot Wild Golden Rose, 5", 1977 – 1978. $35.00 – 45.00.
#3661 flowerpot Wild Golden Rose, 7", 1977 – 1978. $55.00 – 65.00.
#3661 flowerpot Violet, 3", 1977 – 1978. $25.00 – 35.00.
#3661 flowerpot Violet, 4", 1977 – 1978. $30.00 – 40.00.
#3661 flowerpot Violet, 5", 1977 – 1978. $40.00 – 50.00.
#3661 flowerpot Violet, 7", 1977 – 1978. $55.00 – 70.00.

Two Terra White flowerpots, 1975 only. 7", $30.00 – 40.00; 4", $20.00 – 25.00. Courtesy of the Marcena North collection.

Flowerpot with Blue Flower motif. 4", 1977 – 1978, $30.00 – 40.00. Courtesy of the Marcena North collection.

Two Pine Cone flowerpots, 1977 – 1978. 4", $25.00 – 30.00; 7", $45.00 – 55.00. Courtesy of the Marcena North collection.

Two Sun Flower flowerpots, 1977 – 1978. 7", $45.00 – 55.00; 5", $35.00 – 45.00. Courtesy of the Marcena North collection.

Flowerpot with Violet motif, 5", 1977 – 1978. $40.00 – 50.00. Courtesy of the Marcena North collection.

Bowl cache pot in Rosebud pattern. 9", 1975 only. $50.00 – 60.00. Courtesy of the Marcena North collection.

cache pot, bowl shape, 6½" Rosebud, 1975 only. $25.00 – 35.00.
cache pot, bowl shape, 8" Rosebud, 1975 only. $35.00 – 45.00.
cache pot, bowl shape, 9" Rosebud, 1975 only. $50.00 – 60.00.
cache pot, bowl shape, 6½" Trees, 1975 only. $25.00 – 30.00.
cache pot, bowl shape, 8" Trees, 1975 only. $25.00 – 35.00.
cache pot, bowl shape, 9" Trees, 1975 only. $35.00 – 45.00.
cache pot, bowl shape, 6½" Violet, 1975 only. $35.00 – 45.00.
cache pot, bowl shape, 8" Violet, 1975 only. $45.00 – 55.00.
cache pot, bowl shape, 9" Violet, 1975 only. $65.00 – 80.00.
cache pot, pail shape, 6½" Posies, 1975 – 1976. $30.00 – 40.00.
cache pot, pail shape, 8" Posies, 1975 – 1976. $40.00 – 50.00.
cache pot, pail shape, 9" Posies, 1975 – 1976. $55.00 – 65.00.
cache pot, pail shape, 6½" Butterfly, 1975 – 1976. $25.00 – 35.00.
cache pot, pail shape, 8" Butterfly, 1975 – 1976. $35.00 – 45.00.
cache pot, pail shape, 9" Butterfly, 1975 – 1976. $55.00 – 65.00.
cache pot, pail shape, 6½" Bamboo, 1975 – 1976. $25.00 – 30.00.
cache pot, pail shape, 8" Bamboo, 1975 – 1976. $25.00 – 35.00.
cache pot, pail shape, 9" Bamboo, 1975 – 1976. $35.00 – 45.00.
cache pot, pail shape, 6½" Paisley, 1976 only. $35.00 – 45.00.
cache pot, pail shape, 8" Paisley, 1976 only. $45.00 – 55.00.
cache pot, pail shape, 9" Paisley, 1976 only. $65.00 – 80.00.
cache pot, square, 5½" Caughley, Blue, 1975 only. $75.00 – 95.00.
cache pot, square, 5½" Caughley, Green or Yellow, 1975 only. $60.00 – 75.00.
cache pot, square, 7½" Caughley, Blue, 1975 only. $100.00 – 125.00.
cache pot, square, 7½" Caughley, Green or Yellow, 1975 only. $70.00 – 85.00.
cache pot, square, 5½" Fruit , 1975 only. $70.00 – 85.00.
cache pot, square, 7½" Fruit , 1975 only. $120.00 – 145.00.
cache pot, square, 5½" Orchard Song , 1975 only. $35.00 – 45.00.
cache pot, square, 7½" Orchard Song , 1975 only. $60.00 – 75.00.
flowerpot mug 3", Chicory motif votive candle, 1973 only. $35.00 – 45.00.

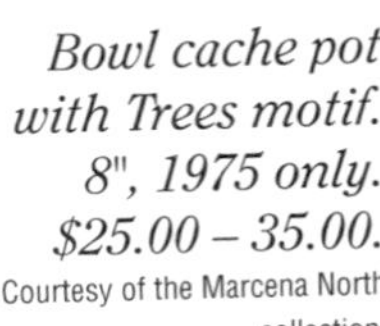

Bowl cache pot with Trees motif. 8", 1975 only. $25.00 – 35.00. Courtesy of the Marcena North collection.

Violet bowl cache pot, 9", 1975 only, $65.00 – 80.00; and flowerpot, 1977 – 1978, 4", $30.00 – 40.00.

Two pail cache pots in Butterflies, 1975 – 1976. 6½", $25.00 – 35.00; 8", $35.00 – 45.00. Courtesy of the Marcena North collection.

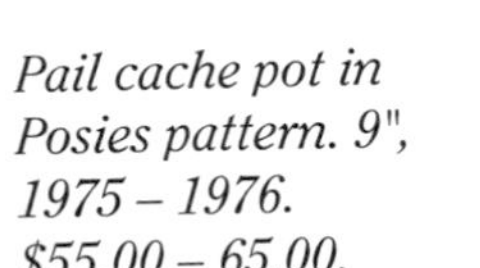

Pail cache pot in Posies pattern. 9", 1975 – 1976. $55.00 – 65.00. Courtesy of the Marcena North collection.

Fruit pattern square cache pot, 1975 only. $120.00 – 145.00. Courtesy of Scott Creighton.

Susan motif flowerpot mug votive candle, 3", 1973 only. $25.00 – 35.00. Courtesy of the Luke and Nancy Ruepp collection.

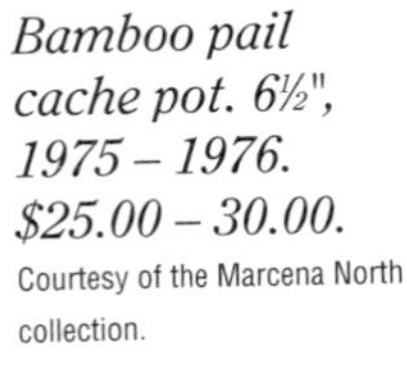

Bamboo pail cache pot. 6½", 1975 – 1976. $25.00 – 30.00. Courtesy of the Marcena North collection.

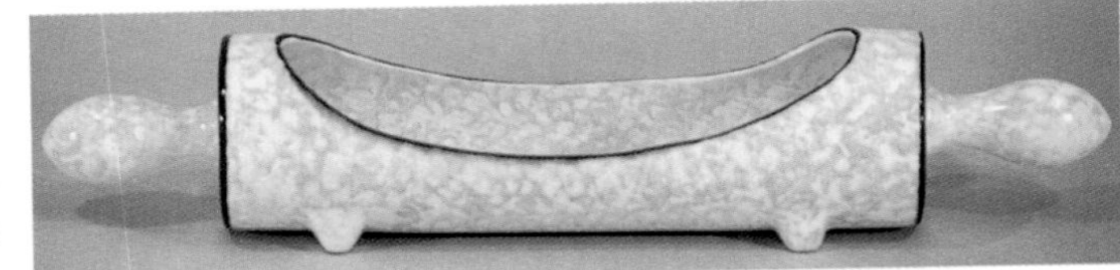

Yellow Town & Country rolling pin planter. 13", 1976 only. $70.00 – 85.00. Courtesy of the Ben and Floss Avila collection.

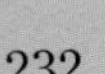

planter, rolling pin, 13", Caughley, Blue, 1976 only. $150.00 – 165.00.
planter, rolling pin, 13", Caughley, Green or Yellow, 1976 only. $70.00 – 85.00.
planter, rolling pin, 13", Town & Country, Blue, 1976 only. $150.00 – 165.00.
planter, rolling pin, 13", Town & Country, Green or Yellow, 1976 only. $70.00 – 85.00.
planter, rolling pin, 13", Town & Country, Brown or Honey, 1976 only. $60.00 – 75.00.
hanging planter, 9", Blue, 1975 only. $35.00 – 45.00.
hanging planter, 9", Yellow or Green, 1975 only. $25.00 – 35.00.
hanging planter, 7½", Blue, 1975 only. $30.00 – 40.00.
hanging planter, 7½", Yellow or Green, 1975 only. $25.00 – 30.00.
hanging ivy planter, 6½"x8", 1973 only. $30.00 – 40.00.
hanging ivy planter, 3½"x4½", 1973 only. $25.00 – 30.00.
hanging flowerpot, 12½"x8", 1973 – 1975. $50.00 – 60.00.
hanging flowerpot, 10½"x6½", 1973 – 1975. $45.00 – 55.00.
hanging flowerpot, 9"x5¾", 1973 – 1975. $35.00 – 45.00.
hanging flowerpot, 7½"x5", 1973 – 1975. $25.00 – 35.00.
hanging flowerpot, 5"x3", 1973 only. $25.00 – 30.00.
hanging flowerpot, Terra White, 9"x5¾", 1975 only. $45.00 – 55.00.
hanging flowerpot, Terra White, 7½"x5", 1975 only. $35.00 – 45.00.
hanging basket, 8"x4¾", 1975 only. $35.00 – 45.00.
hanging basket, 9"x5½", 1975 only. $45.00 – 55.00.
strawberry planter, 8½""x9½", 6 pockets, 1973 – 1975. $45.00 – 55.00.
strawberry planter, 10"x10½", 8 pockets, 1973 – 1975. $60.00 – 75.00.
cactus planter, 8"x 5½", 3 pockets, 1975 only. $30.00 – 40.00.
cactus planter, 10¾"x7½", 4 pockets, 1975 only. $40.00 – 50.00.
bird feeder, 5"x5½", brown roof, 1964 – 1965. $30.00 – 40.00.
bird feeder, 5"x5½", gray roof, 1972 – 1974. $25.00 – 30.00.
bird feeder, 7¼"x6", brown roof, 1964 – 1965. $40.00 – 50.00.
bird feeder, 7¼"x6", gray roof, 1972 – 1974. $25.00 – 35.00.
bird feeder, extra large, 11¾"x6", 1973 – 1974. $35.00 – 45.00.
bird house, 5"x6½", 3 holes, brown roof, 1964 – 1965. $35.00 – 45.00.
bird house, 5"x6½", 1 hole, gray roof, 1972 – 1974. $25.00 – 30.00.
bird house, 7½"x7", brown roof, 1964 – 1965. $45.00 – 55.00.
bird house, 7½"x7", gray roof, 1972 – 1974. $30.00 – 40.00.
patio lamp, 8", 1973 – 1974. $45.00 – 55.00.
patio lamp, 9¼", 1973 – 1974. $45.00 – 55.00.
patio lamp, 10¾", 1973 – 1974. $45.00 – 55.00.
hanging lamp, brown roof, 5½"x6½", 1964 – 1965. $30.00 – 40.00.
hanging lamp, gray roof, 5½"x6½", 1972 – 1974. $25.00 – 35.00.

Yellow 9" hanging planter with jute twine hanger, 1975 only. $25.00 – 35.00.

Porch and Patio items, bird feeder, 7¼"x6", $30.00 – 40.00, and hanging lamp, 5½"x 6½", $25.00 – 35.00, both with gray roof, 1972 – 1974. Birdhouse in center with three holes is 1964 – 1965 original, 5"x6½", $35.00 – 45.00.

Hanging ivy planter, bisque terra cotta. 3½"x4½", 1973 only. $25.00 – 30.00. From the Stangl and Fulper archival collection, courtesy the Wheaton Village Museum of American Glass.

Unusual Porch and Patio bird house glazed brown with white roof. 5" x 6½", 1964 sample. $45.00 – 55.00. Courtesy of the Ben and Floss Avila collection.

Unusual patio lamp in all-white glaze, 5½"x6½", 1964 sample. $45.00 – 55.00. From the Stangl and Fulper archival collection, courtesy the Wheaton Village Museum of American Glass.

Bisque terra cotta with gray glaze patio ashtray, 8" round, 1973 – 1974. $25.00 – 35.00.

Bob Shaw Reproduction Hand-Painted Flowerpots, 1991 – 1992

Bob Shaw Town & Country flowerpots produced during 1991 – 1992 (base, inset).

During 1991 and 1992, Frank Wheaton's grandson, Bob Shaw, produced a line of hand-painted flowerpots duplicating Stangl's Town & Country and Tulip flowerpot motifs. Original Stangl molds were used for this line. The decorating was well done and closely replicated the Stangl originals. The new Town & Country colors were not as vibrant as the originals. However, the Tulip motifs were attractively done in blue, pink, yellow, or lavender. The new items were produced in Millville, New Jersey, not Trenton or Flemington. They are usually marked with a trademark newly designed for this venture. At this time, many Stangl collectors continue to treat many of the items produced by Bob Shaw with disdain. They are looked upon as fakes designed to intentionally fool collectors, so at this time have very little value.

Fulper Decorated Pottery, 1924 – 1929

#346 Chin Toy perfume bottle, 5" Fulper Decorated Pottery (also produced in Porcelaine) 1924 – 1929. $400.00 – 450.00. Courtesy of the Hill-Fulper-Stangl Museum.

Fulper Fayence decorated #901 after-dinner coffee set, vibrant Modernism motif, late 1920s. Coffee pot, $500.00 – 600.00; creamer, $75.00 – 95.00; covered sugar, $100.00 – 125.00; after-dinner cup & saucer, $75.00 – 95.00. Courtesy of the Hill-Fulper-Stangl Museum.

During the 1920s, Fulper Pottery Company produced several "brands" of ceramic items. Best-known is the Fulper Pottery line of heavy glazed artware, descended from the Vasekraft line of the 1910s. Also produced at that time were Fulper Porcelaine decorated china novelties, Fulper Fayence classically styled solid-color glazed dinnerware and vases, Fulper-Stangl solid-color glazed primitive and modern designed artware and novelties, and Fulper Decorated Pottery. The Fulper Decorated Pottery items were just that, decorated. The items were produced of earthenware clay and were decorated with hand-painted underglaze colors or fired-on overglaze china paint colors. The Fulper Decorated items were sold under the Fulper brand name and were marked with the Fulper trademark. They were sometimes numbered within the Fulper Porcelaine series of numbers and sometimes within the Fulper Fayence series of numbers. The same china paint colors were concurrently being used on the Fulper Porcelaines. Fulper Decorated items, however, were not porcelain, but were made of the Fulper Fayence earthenware body and solid-color glazes. The decorative overglaze colors were applied over the Fulper Fayence base glaze, usually Silver Green or Chinese Ivory. The Fulper backstamp on these items was fired-on over the glaze, it is therefore possible to remove this mark with abrasive. Some shapes were produced both "decorated" and "undecorated." Undecorated pieces were given a different number and sold under the Fulper Fayence brand name, but occasionally Fulper Fayence items were decorated as well. The Fulper Decorated Pottery line was discontinued in 1929 when Fulper's Plant No.1 was destroyed by fire that September.

Not Shown:

#910 Bouquet Console Bowl, 10" diameter, Fulper Fayence Decorated 1924 – 1929. $175.00 – 200.00.

#910 Bouquet Candlesticks, 5½" diameter, handles, Fulper Fayence Decorated 1924 – 1929. $100.00 – 125.00 pair.

#910 Bouquet Candlesticks, 5½" diameter, no handles, Fulper Fayence Decorated 1924 – 1929. $100.00 – 125.00 pair.

#910 Bouquet Console Set, Fulper Fayence Decorated 1924 – 1929. $275.00 – 325.00 per set. Courtesy of the Hill-Fulper-Stangl Museum.

"FISH" Decorated Pottery Novelties

In 1925, Fulper Pottery Company introduced a series of Fulper Decorated pottery novelty items designed by English cartoonist Ann H. Fish. Ann Fish's cartoons had been featured in such magazines as *Vanity Fair* and *Vogue* from 1915 throughout the 1920s. She was popular for her ability to capture the innocence and ingenuous qualities of the flapper era. Fulper's Fish designs featured novelty boudoir lamps, powder boxes, inkwells and ashtrays. They were produced primarily in Fulper Decorated pottery, but some of the Fish shapes were also produced in Fulper Fayence solid-color glazes. The items designed by Ann Fish each bear a facsimile of her "Fish" signature. Unfortunately, she was not able to come from England to sign the novelty items herself, so the pieces were actually signed "Fish" by Martin Stangl's sister-in-law. Fulper's advertising stated: "Designed by 'FISH,' famed in *Vogue* and *Vanity Fair.* These items are copyrighted and are made exclusively in pottery by Fulper Pottery Company — hand-decorated ash trays by 'FISH' — at $2.00 each. Individually boxed. Label specially drawn by 'FISH.'" While none of the Fulper Pottery Fish items are easy to find, many of these pieces were produced through 1929 and are more plentiful than the same shapes in Fulper Fayence solid-color glazes.

Close-up of the "Fish" signature.

Please see the Solid-Color Artware chapter for solid-color Fulper Fayence and Fulper-Stangl items.

Not Shown:

#367A Dip novelty ashtray 4¾", Fish design, Fulper Decorated (same as solid-color #961A) 1925 – 1929. $500.00 – 600.00.

#367B Sponge novelty ashtray 4¾", Fish design, Fulper Decorated (same as solid-color #961B) 1925 – 1929. $500.00 – 600.00.

#367C Valentine novelty ashtray 4¾", Fish design, Fulper Decorated (same as solid-color #961C) 1925 – 1929. $500.00 – 600.00.

#367D Pom novelty ashtray 4¾", Fish design, Fulper Decorated (same as solid-color #961D) 1925 – 1929. $500.00 – 600.00.

#367E Messenger novelty ashtray 4¾", Fish design, Fulper Decorated (same as solid-color #961E) 1925 – 1929. $500.00 – 600.00.

#367F Ring novelty ashtray 4¾", Fish design, Fulper Decorated (same as solid-color #961F) 1925 – 1929. $500.00 – 600.00.

#368A Dip novelty powder jar 5¼", Fish design, Fulper Decorated (same as solid-color #966A) 1925 – 1929. $800.00 – 900.00.

#368B Sponge novelty powder jar 5¼", Fish design, Fulper Decorated (same as solid-color #966B) 1925 – 1929. $800.00 – 900.00.

#368C Valentine novelty powder jar 5¼", Fish design, Fulper Decorated (same as solid-color #966C) 1925 – 1929. $800.00 – 900.00.

1925 Fulper catalog page showing Fish #367 novelty ashtrays.

Original 1925 ad showing the Fulper Decorated "Fish" designed Ginnie and Lonesome lamps. Courtesy of the Hill-Fulper-Stangl Museum.

#368D Pom novelty powder jar 5¼", Fish design, Fulper Decorated (same as solid-color #966D) 1925 – 1929. $800.00 – 900.00.

#368E Messenger novelty powder jar 5¼", Fish design, Fulper Decorated (same as solid-color #966E) 1925 – 1929. $800.00 – 900.00.

#368F Ring novelty powder jar 5¼", Fish design, Fulper Decorated (same as solid-color #966F) 1925 – 1929. $800.00 – 900.00.

#370 Ginnie lamp, 7" Fish design, Fulper Decorated, 1925 – 1928. $1,200.00 – 1,500.00.

#371 Lonesome lamp, 7" Fish design, Fulper Decorated, 1925 – 1928. $1,200.00 – 1,500.00.

#380 upholstery ashtray 4¾", Fish design, Fulper Decorated (same as solid-color #994) 1925 – 1929. $600.00 – 700.00.

#381A Maid novelty ashtray 4¼"x6", Fish design, Fulper Decorated 1925 – 1929. $600.00 – 700.00.

#381B Pekinese novelty ashtray 4¼"x6", Fish design, Fulper Decorated 1925 – 1929. $600.00 – 700.00.

#381C Wading novelty ashtray 4¼"x6", Fish design, Fulper Decorated 1925 – 1929. $600.00 – 700.00.

Fulper Decorated #382A Hatbox novelty inkstand, 4½", Fish design, 1925 – 1929. $1,200.00 – 1,500.00. Courtesy of the Ben and Floss Avila collection.

Fulper Decorated #382C Reader novelty inkstand, 4½" Fish design, 1925 – 1929. $1,200.00 – 1,500.00. Courtesy of the Hill-Fulper-Stangl Museum.

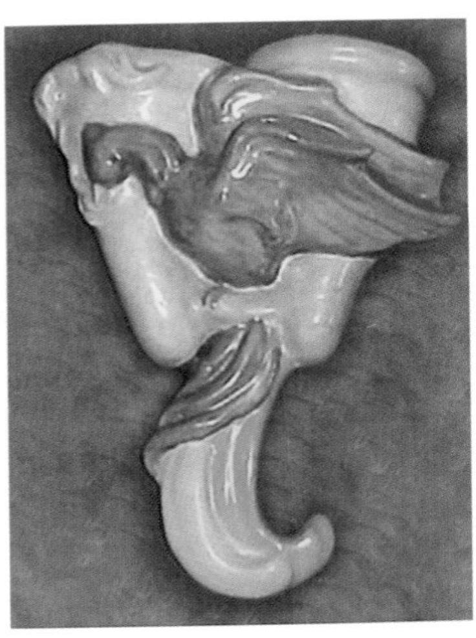

Fulper Decorated #374 Double Bird wall pocket, 9½", 1925 – 1929. $300.00 – 350.00. Courtesy of the Frank and Elizabeth Kramar collection.

Fulper Decorated #377 Corner wall pocket, 10", underglaze decorated 1925 – 1929. $200.00 – 250.00. Courtesy of the Hill-Fulper-Stangl Museum.

Fulper Decorated Pottery #383 Flower Holder, Pipes of Pan, 5"x6" 1925 – 1929. $300.00 – 350.00.

Fulper Decorated #1022 Oblong cigarette box in fired-on hand-painted black and orange color, for Rena Rosenthal, 1925 – 1926. $375.00 – 400.00.

Two Fulper Decorated #1085 cosmetic jars, 2½"x2¼", made for Kramer, 1926 – 1927, Silver Green with fired-on black overglaze color. $130.00 – 160.00 each.

Fulper Decorated #1058 Lizard ashtray in fired-on Mandarin Red color, 1925 – 1927 (base, inset). $300.00 – 350.00. Courtesy of the Hill-Fulper-Stangl Museum.

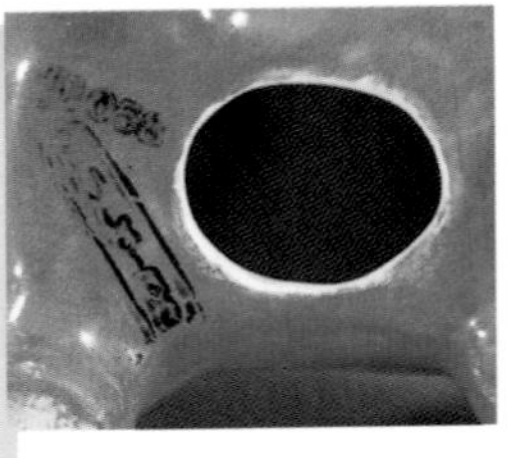

Not Shown:

#382B Winged Cupid novelty inkstand, 4½" Fish design, Fulper Decorated, 1925 – 1929. $1,200.00 – 1,500.00.

#386 Messenger novelty cigar box, Fish design, Fulper Decorated, 1926 – 1928. $1,200.00 – 1,500.00.

#387 Barmaid novelty cigar box, Fish design, Fulper Decorated, 1926 – 1928. $1,200.00 – 1,500.00.

#391 Butler novelty sander or potpourri, Fish design, Fulper Decorated, 1926 – 1928. $800.00 – 900.00.

#378 Flower holder, Spanish Figure, 8½" Fulper Decorated, 1925 – 1929. $350.00 – 400.00.

#379 Flower holder, Turtle Girl, 5¾" Fulper Decorated, 1925 – 1929. $300.00 – 350.00.

#1051 Donkey ashtray, Fulper Decorated, for Rena Rosenthal. $225.00 – 275.00.

#1059 Combination ashtray, Fulper Decorated, 1925 – 1926. $200.00 – 250.00.

#1085 Cosmetic jar 2½"x2¼" Fulper Decorated, made for Kramer 1926 – 1927. $130.00 – 160.00.

#393 Angular ashtray, Fulper Decorated (same as solid-color #1142), 1927 – 1929. $200.00 – 250.00.

Fulper Decorated #395 Angular ashtray (same as #1143), 1927 – 1929. $200.00 – 250.00. From the Stangl and Fulper archival collection, courtesy the Wheaton Village Museum of American Glass.

Fulper Decorated #394 Square cigarette box (same as #1163), 1927 – 1929. $450.00 – 500.00. From the Stangl and Fulper archival collection, courtesy the Wheaton Village Museum of American Glass.

Fulper Decorated #1165 Round Ring Jar, green crackle luster, 1927 – 1929. $200.00 – 250.00. Courtesy of the Hill-Fulper-Stangl Museum.

Fulper Decorated #392 Angular cigarette box, Silver Green with black (same as #1168), 1927 – 1929. $400.00 – 450.00. Courtesy of the Hill-Fulper-Stangl Museum.

Fulper Decorated #392 Angular cigarette box, Chinese Ivory with red & black (same as #1168), 1927 – 1929. $450.00 – 500.00. From the Stangl and Fulper archival collection, courtesy the Wheaton Village Museum of American Glass.

Hand-Decorated Artware, 1938 – 1940

Three items showing the Hand-Decorated finishes Surf White, Twilight Blue, and Marigold Yellow.

Floral Plaid dinnerware pattern with #3046 Scroll, and #3087 oblong candleholders decorated to match. $45.00 – 55.00 pair.

Martin Stangl developed the "Hand-Decorated Artware" line in response to the demand for multi-hued pastel giftware. The Hand-Decorated Artware was available in three varieties; Marigold Yellow, Surf White, and Twilight Blue. The finishes were airbrushed glaze colors over hand-painted details. Twilight Blue was Blue #95 hand-painted under Satin Blue glaze. Marigold Yellow was Dark Green and Satin Yellow airbrushed together. The Surf White finish was hand-painted with yellow under the airbrushed glazes Satin White and Satin Turquoise. During the early 1930s, Stangl used a glaze very similar to Satin White, which was also called "Surf White." Essentially, Satin White and the early Surf White are the same, but there is no relationship concerning the early Surf White solid-color glaze and the hand-decorated Surf White finish used between 1938 and 1940.

From 1939 through 1945, candleholders were decorated to match hand-painted dinnerware patterns with hand-painted colors under satin glazes. The #1388, #3087 oblong, and #3046 Scroll candleholder shapes were decorated with dinnerware patterns, and usually have the dinnerware pattern number hand-painted on the base. Depending on the pattern, values for the dinnerware-decorated candleholders can vary greatly, from about $50.00 per pair for Floral Plaid up to $200.00 per pair for Ranger.

A similar technique was also used to decorate some of the #5000 series lamp shapes during 1938. Please see the chapter on Lamps for hand-decorated lamps.

Hand-decorated #3087 oblong candleholders in the Valencia dinnerware pattern. $60.00 – 75.00 pair. Courtesy of the Ben and Floss Avila collection.

Hand-Decorated Surf White #3156 vase, three handles, 15", 1938 only. $350.00 – 375.00.

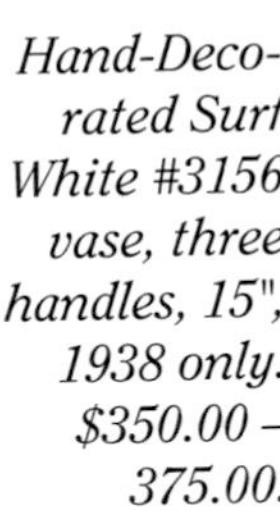

Hand-Decorated Surf White #3172 7" scallop jug, $50.00 – 60.00, with #3176 10" scallop jug in light Marigold Yellow, $100.00 – 125.00. Courtesy of the Brian and Cristi Hahn collection.

Hand-Decorated Twilight Blue #3172 scallop jug, $50.00 – 60.00; #3175 scallop oval bowl, $45.00 – 60.00; and #3171 scallop vase, $55.00 – 65.00. Courtesy of the Marcena North collection.

Hand-Decorated #3185 oval bowl in Surf White, $75.00 – 90.00; #3184 candleholder in Rainbow, $60.00 – 75.00; and #3182 7½" vase in Twilight Blue, $95.00 – 110.00. Courtesy of the Marcena North collection.

Hand-Decorated Marigold Yellow #3172 jug, scallop, zigzag handles, 7", 1938 – 1940. $50.00 – 60.00.

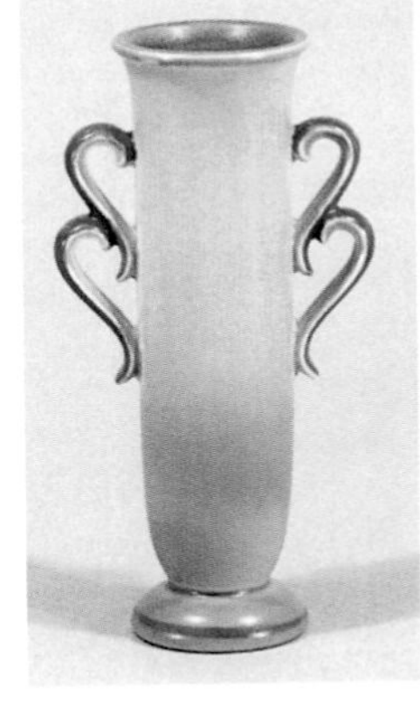

Hand-Decorated Twilight Blue #3182 vase, double handles, 7½"x2½", 1938 – 1939. $75.00 – 90.00. Courtesy of the Brian and Cristi Hahn collection.

Not Shown:

#3153 vase, scallop, zigzag handles, 13", 1938 – 1940. $200.00 – 250.00.
#3171 vase, scallop, zigzag handles, 7", 1938 – 1940. $55.00 – 65.00.
#3173 candleholder, scallop, zigzag handles, 4", 1938 – 1940. $60.00 – 80.00 pair.
#3174 bud vase, scallop, zigzag handles, 4", 1938 – 1940. $40.00 – 50.00.
#3175 oval bowl, scallop, zigzag handles, 7½"x4", 1938 – 1940. $45.00 – 60.00.
#3176 jug, scallop, zigzag handles, 10", 1938 – 1940. $100.00 – 125.00.
#3180 vase, double handles, 9"x4½", 1938 – 1939. $90.00 – 110.00.
#3181 vase, double handles, 7½"x3½", 1938 – 1939. $80.00 – 95.00.
#3183 vase, double handles, 4"x2½", 1938 – 1939. $40.00 – 50.00.
#3184 candleholder, double handles, 4"x2½", 1938 – 1939. $60.00 – 80.00 pair.
#3185 oval bowl, double handles, 8"x3½"x5", 1938 – 1939. $75.00 – 90.00.
#3186 candleholder, 3 handles, 4", 1938 only. $175.00 – 200.00 pair.

Hand-Decorated Surf White #3187 vase, 3 handles, 7¼", 1938 – 1940. $50.00 – 75.00.

Hand-Decorated Surf White #3188 vase with ribs, 7¼", 1938 – 1939. $70.00 – 80.00. Courtesy of the Brian and Cristi Hahn collection.

Hand-Decorated Twilight Blue #3189 vase, ovoid with neck, 7¼", 1938 – 1940. $50.00 – 75.00. Courtesy of the Brian and Cristi Hahn collection.

Hand-Decorated Surf White #3191 oval scalloped 9" vase, $95.00 – 110.00; #3196 oval scalloped 4" candleholders, $50.00 – 75.00 pair; and #3195 12" oval scalloped bowl, $70.00 – 85.00. Courtesy of the Marcena North collection.

Hand-Decorated Twilight Blue #3199 candleholder, with ribs, 4", 1938 only. $95.00 – 110.00 pair.

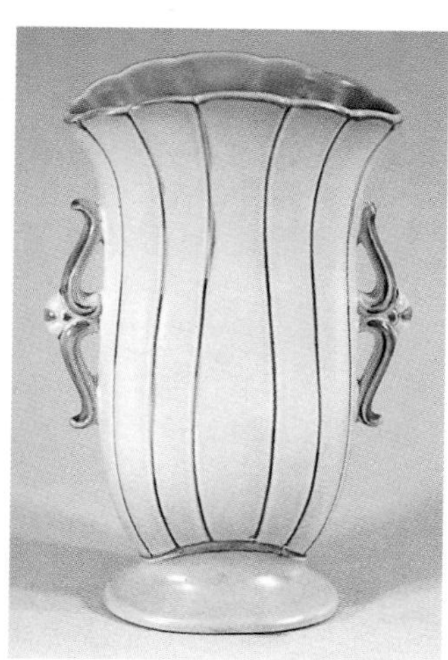

Hand-Decorated Twilight Blue #3191 vase, oval scalloped, 9", 1938 – 1939. $95.00 – 110.00. Courtesy of the Bullock collection.

Hand-Decorated Marigold Yellow #3197 oval scalloped 4" vase, $40.00 – 50.00, and #3190 oval scalloped 7½" vase, $55.00 – 65.00.

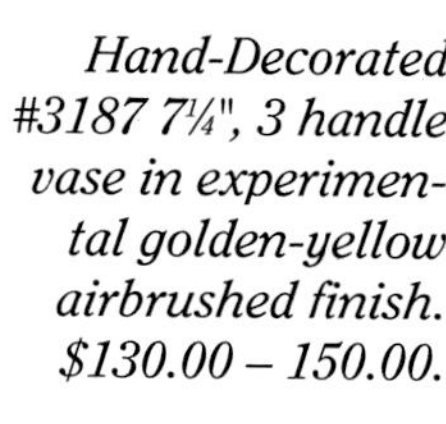

Hand-Decorated #3187 7¼", 3 handle vase in experimental golden-yellow airbrushed finish. $130.00 – 150.00.

Hand-Decorated #3172 scallop 7" jug in experimental plum and blue airbrushed finish. $130.00 – 150.00.

Not Shown:

#3190 vase, oval scalloped, 7½", 1938 – 1940. $55.00 – 65.00.
#3192 bowl, oval scalloped, 7½"x3"x2", 1938 – 1939. $45.00 – 55.00.
#3193 bowl, oval scalloped, 6"x4"x3", 1938 – 1939. $50.00 – 60.00.
#3194 bowl, oval scalloped, 9"x6"x4½", 1938 – 1939. $60.00 – 70.00.
#3195 bowl, oval scalloped, 12"x8", 1938 – 1939. $70.00 – 85.00.
#3196 candleholder, oval scalloped, 4", 1938 – 1939. $50.00 – 75.00 pair.
#3197 vase, oval scalloped, 4", 1938 – 1939. $40.00 – 50.00.
#3198 bowl, oval scalloped, 7½"x4½", 1938 – 1939. $60.00 – 75.00.

Hand-Decorated Combination and Tropical Glazes, 1934 – 1936

Flower Ware

Martin Stangl introduced the following line of flower blossom-shaped artware and dinnerware shapes in 1934 in combination glaze colors pink, blue, yellow, and purple. The combination glaze colors were hand-applied by spray, brush, and rubber syringe. The combination glaze treatment was very short-lived, but these shapes continued in production for several more years with single solid-color glazes. Although #1870 Daisy was a dinnerware pattern, some of the dinnerware accessories were classed as artware. Flower Ware items must have at least two different glaze colors on the exterior to be Combination Glazed. Vases with contrasting Silver Green interiors and Rust or Tangerine exteriors are not Combination Glaze.

Combination glazed #1875 Flower candleholder glazed in yellow and purple with Colonial Blue dribbling, $150.00 – 165.00 pair. Courtesy of the Hill-Fulper-Stangl Museum.

Also see several of these shapes produced in the Terra Rose and brushed gold finishes, as well as the Solid-Color chapter for these shapes in those finishes.

Not Shown:

#1869 Cosmos bowl, 12", 1934 only. $175.00 – 200.00.
#1870 Daisy candleholder, 4", 1934 only. $170.00 – 195.00 pair.
#1870 Daisy oblong triple relish, 1934 only. $130.00 – 150.00.
#1870 Daisy round triple relish, 1934 only. $130.00 – 150.00.
#1870 Daisy double relish, 1934 only. $110.00 – 135.00.
#1870 Daisy single relish, 13", 1934 only. $110.00 – 135.00.
#1870 Daisy cake stand, 10", 1934 only. $150.00 – 175.00.
#1871 Petunia bowl, 12", 1934 only. $190.00 – 225.00.
#1872 Zinnia bowl, 10", 1934 only. $175.00 – 200.00.
#1873 Marsh Rose bowl, 14", 1934 only. $200.00 – 250.00.
#1874 Wild Rose bowl, 8" 1934 only. $150.00 – 175.00.
#1875 Flower candleholder, 4" 1934 only. $150.00 – 165.00 pair.
#1876 Flower block insert, 4" 1934 only. $110.00 – 135.00.
#1878EL Tulip bowl, 9", 1934 only. $190.00 – 225.00.
#1878L Tulip bowl, 7", 1934 only. $165.00 – 185.00.
#1878M Tulip bowl, 5½", 1934 only. $130.00 – 150.00.
#1878S Tulip bowl, 4", 1934 only. $130.00 – 150.00.
#1879 Phlox candleholder, 5½", 1934 only. $200.00 – 250.00 pair.

1942 1944 2024
2023 1945 2025
2026 2027 2028

		Price each list
1942	Vase, 4 handles	$3.50
1944-7"	Vase, Criss Cross decor.	3.00
1944-9"	" " " "	5.00
2024-7"	Vase	2.50
2023-7"	Bowl, 3 feet	2.00
1945	Bowl, cut out foot	2.50
1945	Candleholder	.75
2025-5"	Vase, Cylinder	3.00
2026-8"	Vase	3.00
2027-8"	Vase	3.00
2028-8"	Bowl, footed	3.00

COLORS:
Blue & Yellow
Blue & Tangerine
Dark Green & Eggplant
Oyster White & Eggplant

JANUARY 1, 1936 PAGE 63

Stangl 1936 Tropical Ware catalog page showing several shapes.

Tropical Ware

Stangl's Tropical Ware was a line of vases and lamps featuring handles and interiors in glazes contrasting the main body glaze. Typical glaze combinations were Colonial Blue with Persian Yellow, Colonial Blue with Tangerine, Dark Green with Eggplant, and Oyster White with Eggplant. Other glaze combinations could also be had as special-orders for a premium price.

Tropical Ware shapes were all mold-cast in primitive and modern styles. Several of the shapes featured handles and adornments that appeared handmade but were in fact mold-cast.

The following shapes were primarily decorated with Stangl's Tropical combination glazes during 1935 and 1936 but were also glazed with single solid-color glazes as well. See the Solid-Color chapter for these items glazed in solid-color glazes. See also the Lamp chapter for lamp shapes decorated with Tropical combination glazes.

Not Shown:

#1940 Raised Fruit salad bowl, 9", 1935 – 1936. $110.00 – 135.00.
#1940 Raised Fruit chop plate, 14", 1935 – 1936. $150.00 – 175.00.
#1940 Raised Fruit salad plate, 1935 – 1936. $60.00 – 75.00.
#1941 Striped footed bowl, 9", 1935 only. $175.00 – 200.00.

Tropical Ware #1942 Tangerine & Blue vase, 4 handles, 7", 1935 – 1936. $175.00 – 200.00. Courtesy of the Chris McGeehan collection.

Tropical Ware #1942 Blue & Yellow vase, 4 handles, 7", 1935 – 1936. $175.00 – 200.00. Courtesy of the Chris McGeehan collection.

Tropical Ware #1944S Eggplant & Oyster White Rope vase, 7", 1935 – 1936. $170.00 – 195.00. Courtesy of the Marcena North collection.

Tropical Ware #1945 Eggplant & Oyster White bowl, cut-out foot, 11", 1935 – 1936. $170.00 – 195.00. Courtesy of the Brian and Cristi Hahn collection.

Tropical Ware #2023 Blue & Yellow bowl, 3-footed, 7", 1935 – 1936. $170.00 – 195.00. Courtesy of the Ben and Pauline Jensen collection.

Tropical Ware #2024 Tangerine & Blue vase, scroll decoration, 7", 1935 – 1936. $165.00 – 185.00.

Tropical Ware #2024 Eggplant & Oyster White vase, scroll decoration, 7", 1935 – 1936. $165.00 – 185.00.

Special-order Tropical Ware ashtray for the Restaurant Mayan, New York. Eggplant & Aqua glaze, 1935 only. $190.00 – 225.00 (base, inset). Courtesy of the Hill-Fulper-Stangl Museum.

Not Shown:

#1943 Striped bowl with collar, 1935 only. $175.00 – 200.00.
#1944L Rope vase, 9", 1935 only. $190.00 – 225.00.
#1945 candleholder, cut-out foot, 3½", 1935 – 1936. $80.00 – 125.00 pair.
#1946 Dotted compote, 7", 1935 only. $190.00 – 225.00.
#1947 Dotted bowl, 10", 1935 only. $190.00 – 225.00.
#1948 square jardiniere, 1935 only. $175.00 – 200.00.
#2025 vase, cylinder, rope decoration. 8", 1935 – 1936. $170.00 – 195.00.
#2026 vase, scroll decoration, 8", 1935 – 1936. $170.00 – 195.00.
#2027 vase, 2 handles, 8", 1935 – 1936. $170.00 – 195.00.
#2028 pedestal bowl, wave decoration, 8", 1935 – 1936. $165.00 – 185.00.

Handmade Hand-Decorated Artware, 1931 – 1932

Martin Stangl had been producing "glaze-decorated" finishes as special-order for lamps since the mid 1920s. In 1931, he combined the hand-decorated aspect of glaze-decorating with hand-thrown artware forms to create the Handmade Hand-Decorated Artware line.

For this line a new series of smooth-sided handmade shapes were designed. These shapes were then glaze-decorated with stylized floral motifs requiring a two-fire glazing process. The motif was first painted in wax resist on the unglazed bisque shapes. The interiors were then flushed with Silver Green or Turquoise glaze and the exteriors sprayed with Tangerine or Rust then fired. During the initial firing, the wax burned away, leaving an unglazed motif. The unglazed area was then decorated with colored glazes and fired a second time. Three glaze colors were used for the floral motifs, Uranium Yellow, Cobalt Blue, and Leaf Green. These colors were chosen for their tendency to stay put where they were applied and not run and blend into surrounding areas, particularly on vertical surfaces. Tangerine is the usual background glaze on these items. Rust was used very infrequently but is valued the same as items glazed with Tangerine.

Because the Handmade Hand-Decorated shapes were hand-thrown, they are rarely marked.

Not Shown:
#1453 rose bowl, 5½", handmade, 1931 only. $175.00 – 225.00.
#1454 violet jar, 5¼", handmade, 1931 only. $185.00 – 245.00.
#1455 ovoid vase, 5", handmade, 1931 only. $185.00 – 245.00.
#1457 low jar, 2 handles, 4¾" tall, 8" diameter, handmade, 1931 only. $200.00 – 250.00.
#1458 flower bowl, 7¼" diameter, handmade, 1931 only. $180.00 – 200.00.
#1459, cone vase, 9", handmade, 1931 – 1934. $325.00 – 375.00.
#1460 candleholder, 4½", handmade, 1931 only. $150.00 – 175.00 each.
#1464 bowl, 6" diameter, handmade, 1931 only. $180.00 – 225.00.

Handmade Hand-Decorated #1456 basket, 7", Tangerine glaze, 1931 only. $300.00 – 350.00. Courtesy of the Hill-Fulper-Stangl Museum.

Handmade Hand-Decorated #1456 basket, 7", with "Albany," Tangerine glaze. A special-order souvenir for Albany, NY, 1931 only. $275.00 – 300.00. Courtesy of the Brian and Cristi Hahn collection.

Handmade Hand-Decorated #1461 flower pot, attached saucer, 4½", Tangerine glaze, 1931 only. $175.00 – 225.00. Courtesy of the Hill-Fulper-Stangl Museum.

Handmade Hand-Decorated #1462 flower vase, small neck, 6¾", Rust glaze, 1931 only. $275.00 – 325.00.

Handmade Hand-Decorated #1465 vase, straight top, 5½", Tangerine glaze, 1931 only. $175.00 – 225.00. Courtesy of the Hill-Fulper-Stangl Museum.

Handmade Hand-Decorated #1463 tall-neck vase with handles, 8", Tangerine glaze, 1931 only. $300.00 – 350.00. Courtesy of the Brian and Cristi Hahn collection.

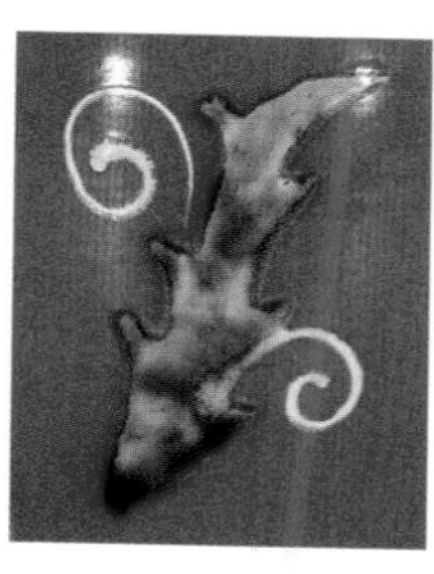

Handmade Hand-Decorated #1466 tall vase (left), 10¼", Tangerine glaze, 1931 only. Leaf motif on the back (above) is also on the backs of many of the Handmade Hand-Decorated artware shapes. $375.00 – 425.00. Courtesy of the Hill-Fulper-Stangl Museum.

Handmade Hand-Decorated #1585ES low jug, 3", made as a special-order souvenir for the Buck Hill Falls resort in Pennsylvania. Decorated with their "BHF" and pine tree motif. Rust glaze, 1932 only. $50.00 – 60.00.

Hand-scrawled "Stangl" usually found on the bases of the Buck Hill Falls Handmade Hand-Decorated jugs.

#1466 tall vase, 12½", handmade, 1931 only. $450.00 – 550.00.
#1588 tall jug, 4½", Stangl handmade, 1932 only. $100.00 – 125.00.

Hand-Decorated Madonna and Head Vases, 1938 – 1941

Decorated Madonna Vases

Madonna and Head vases were normally produced only in Satin White glaze. See also the Solid-Color chapter for plain Satin White Madonna and Head vases. Decorated Madonna vases are exceptionally rare as they were produced as special-orders only. The decorated Madonnas were usually hand-painted with traditional blue or purple underglaze colors under Satin White glaze.

Not Shown:

#3204 Madonna bust vase, 9", 1938 – 1941. $175.00 – 200.00.
#3205 Madonna vase with hands, 10", 1938 – 1941. $175.00 – 200.00.
#3206 Madonna vase with infant, 9½", 1938 – 1941. $175.00 – 200.00.
#3230 Madonna vase, full figure, 9¾", 1938 – 1941. $175.00 – 200.00.
#3231 Madonna vase, bust figure, 1938 – 1941. $175.00 – 200.00.
#3233 Madonna vase, flat figure, 1938 – 1941. $175.00 – 200.00.

Hand-Decorated #3205 Madonna vase with hands, 10", 1938 – 1941. $175.00 – 200.00.

Decorated Head Vases

The decorated #3419 Curls head vase was glazed with Satin White with underglaze color on the fabric of her dress. Likewise, the #3418 Snood head vase was glazed Satin White but with underglaze color on the dress and the snood. The usual colors used on the head vases are Blue #95 and Art Ware Green.

Decorated #3418 Snood head vase, 6", Satin White with Blue #95, 1941 only (back, inset). $195.00 – 235.00. Courtesy of the Hill-Fulper-Stangl Museum.

Two #3419 Curls head vases, 6", Satin White glaze decorated with Lavender underglaze color (left), and Art Ware Green (right), 1941 only. $195.00 – 235.00 each. From the Stangl and Fulper archival collection, courtesy the Wheaton Village Museum of American Glass.

Head vases decorated with Satin White and a single color are very hard to find, but not rare. Stangl's truly rare decorated Snood and Curls head vases were hand-painted with multiple realistic colors. Only a very few special-ordered fully decorated head vases were produced during 1941.

Fully decorated #3419 Curls head vase. The dress was hand-painted with Art Ware Green and the hair with manganese stain (the color used on the Terra Rose Mauve finish) under the Ivory Satin glaze. The lips and eyes are fired-on overglaze color (back, inset). $500.00 – 600.00 each.

Mediterranean, 1965 – 1972

Developed by Kay Hackett, Stangl's Mediterranean artware finish was introduced in 1965 and was instantly popular. Contemporary advertising stated: "A sublime blend of rich blues and greens truly reflecting the brilliant colors of the ageless Mediterranean." The transparent colors Art Ware Blue and Art Ware Green were sponged together on each piece, creating a blue-green blend that was given crystal clarity and depth with clear gloss glaze.

The combination of deep blue and green was a fashion color-blend that was very popular throughout the 1960s, ensuring the success of the Mediterranean artware finish. So popular did this finish become, it was applied to dinnerware shapes in 1966 and became the Mediterranean dinnerware pattern. However, by early 1968, the blue-green fad had faded; much of the Mediterranean artware was discontinued. Mediterranean dinnerware and an assortment of Mediterranean ashtrays remained in production. But even the ashtrays were discontinued in 1972. The Mediterranean finish was also applied to lamp bases, so please see the Lamp chapter as well.

Not Shown:
dealer sign. $130.00 – 150.00.
#3630 cigarette box, 4½"x5½", flat top. $75.00 – 95.00.
#3630 cigarette box, 4½"x5½", quilt top. $75.00 – 95.00.
#3630 coaster ashtray, 5". $20.00 – 25.00.
#3781 triple Shell tray, 12" diameter. $35.00 – 45.00.
#3782 double Pear dish, 7½"x7½". $20.00 – 25.00.
#3783 single Pear dish, 7½"x4". $15.00 – 20.00.
#3784 double Apple dish, 10"x5½". $20.00 – 25.00.
#3785 single Apple dish, 6". $15.00 – 20.00.
#3786 square snack dish, 4½". $15.00 – 20.00.
#3787 heart dish, 6". $15.00 – 20.00.
#3788 heart dish, 8". $20.00 – 25.00.
#3898 cigarette box, fluted. $85.00 – 95.00.
#3898-5 ashtray, fluted, 5". $15.00 – 20.00.
#3898-7 ashtray, fluted, 7". $20.00 – 25.00.
#3904L ashtray, Safety, 9¼"x5", (Ed Pettingil design). $25.00 – 30.00.
#3906 ashtray, notched, free form, 5½", (Ed Pettingil design). $12.00 – 18.00.
#3914 ashtray, square with square well, 9", (Kay Hackett design). $30.00 – 40.00.
#3915 ashtray, square with round well, 9", (Kay Hackett design). $30.00 – 40.00.
#3938M ashtray, Safety, free form, 7½", (Ed Pettingil design). $20.00 – 25.00.
#3926 ashtray, oval, plain, 10¾"x8", (Kay Hackett design). $25.00 – 35.00.
#3942 ashtray, Safety, oval, 8½"x7", (Ed Pettingil design). $20.00 – 25.00.
#3952 cylinder vase, 10". $60.00 – 75.00.
#3952 cylinder vase, 8". $50.00 – 60.00.
#3952 cylinder vase, 6". $45.00 – 55.00.

Mediterranean #5106 triple cylinder vase, 10"x5". $40.00 – 50.00. Courtesy of the North collection.

#3952 cylinder vase, 4". $30.00 – 40.00.
#3972 ashtray, Flying Saucer 10", (Kay Hackett design). $25.00 – 35.00.
#3973 ashtray, round 8½"x2⅛", (Kay Hackett design). $25.00 – 30.00.
#3977M ashtray, Safety, semi-oval 7½"x6¼", (Kay Hackett design). $25.00 – 30.00.
#3980 bowl, 8¼" diameter. $25.00 – 35.00.
#3987 vase, urn 6". $35.00 – 45.00.
#4018 shell dish, small 7½". $20.00 – 25.00.
#4019 shell dish, medium 9½". $25.00 – 35.00.
#4020 shell dish, large 10½". $30.00 – 40.00.
#4021 compote 3½"x6½" (orig. #1388). $25.00 – 30.00.
#4025 vase, urn 7½". $35.00 – 45.00.
#4026 ashtray, conference table 11¼", (Kay Hackett design). $45.00 – 55.00.
#4027 ashtray 12½" (Kay Hackett design). $55.00 – 65.00.
#4028 bowl, 9" pedestal (orig. #3434 bowl) (Kay Hackett design). $45.00 – 55.00.
#4029 bowl, 10" pedestal (orig. #3774 bowl) (Kay Hackett design). $45.00 – 55.00.
#4032 ashtray, leaf 5½"x4". $15.00 – 20.00.
#4033 ashtray, Cosmos 5½". $15.00 – 20.00.
#4034 ashtray, leaf 6½"x4". $15.00 – 20.00.
#4035 ashtray, leaf, Ivy 5¼"x4¼". $15.00 – 20.00.
#4036 ashtray, leaf 6"x4½". $20.00 – 25.00.
#4037 ashtray, shell dish, 5"x5½". $15.00 – 20.00.
#4050 vase, bud 8" (Kay Hackett design). $30.00 – 40.00.
#4052 pitcher 14½" (Kay Hackett design). $55.00 – 65.00.
#4053 pitcher 12" (Kay Hackett design). $50.00 – 60.00.
#4054 pitcher 16" (Kay Hackett design). $60.00 – 75.00.
#4055 pitcher 11¼" (Kay Hackett design). $55.00 – 65.00.
#4056 pitcher 8¼" (Kay Hackett design). $40.00 – 50.00.
#4058 pitcher 7½" (Kay Hackett design). $35.00 – 45.00.
#4059 pitcher 6¼" (Kay Hackett design). $30.00 – 40.00.
#4060 pitcher 5¼" (Kay Hackett design). $25.00 – 35.00.
#4061 bowl, scalloped-ruffled 8" (Kay Hackett design). $35.00 – 45.00.
#4062 bowl, scalloped-ruffled 10¼" (Kay Hackett design). $45.00 – 55.00.
#5002 ashtray, round 9¼" (Kay Hackett design). $25.00 – 35.00.
#5004 ashtray, rectangular, 12½"x6½" (Kay Hackett design). $30.00 – 40.00.
#5017 ashtray, triangular 7½"x6⅜"(orig. #3906). $12.00 – 18.00.
#5023 vase, Phoenician 9¾" (Kay Hackett design). $50.00 – 60.00.
#5033 swan planter L, 6¾"x8½"(orig. #1394). $55.00 – 65.00.
#5034 swan planter M, 5" high (orig. #1394). $40.00 – 50.00.
#5035 swan planter, SM, 3½" high (orig. #1394). $25.00 – 30.00.
#5056 ashtray, round 4⅝" (orig. #1955). $20.00 – 25.00.
#5057 ashtray, 5⅜" (orig. #1957). $20.00 – 25.00.
#5058 ashtray, round 7¼", plain. $25.00 – 35.00.
#5060 ashtray, round 8¼". $25.00 – 35.00.
#5065 horn of plenty, small, 4½"x7¼" (orig. #3617). $30.00 – 40.00.
#5066 horn of plenty, large, 6½"x10" (orig. #3617). $45.00 – 55.00.
#5069 candleholders, ruffled, footed 3½"x 2". $20.00 – 25.00 pair.
#5093 vase, bud 5¾". $20.00 – 25.00.
#5097 ashtray, 6½"x4½". $20.00 – 25.00.
#5106 triple cylinder vase, 10"x5". $40.00 – 50.00.
#5116S ashtray, Safety oval 6". $15.00 – 20.00.
#5116M ashtray, Safety oval 7". $15.00 – 20.00.

Mediterranean #3630 cigarette box 4½"x5½", flat top. $75.00 – 95.00.
Courtesy of the Luke and Nancy Ruepp collection.

#5132 vase, flared 10½" (orig. #2091). $60.00 – 75.00.
#5134 vase, Cosmos 7½" (orig. #3413). $45.00 – 55.00.
#5135 vase, flared 7½" (orig. # 2091). $45.00 – 55.00.
#5138 candleholders, Rose 2½" (orig. #1875). $20.00 – 25.00 pair.
#5139 bowl, Cosmos 12" diameter (orig. #1869). $60.00 – 75.00.
#5146 leaf dish, ivy 8"x7¾"(orig. #3239). $25.00 – 30.00.
#5151 Hearts & Flowers tidbit, 10". $10.00 – 15.00.
#5153 cigarette lighter, 4" (Kay Hackett design). $35.00 – 45.00.
#5156 Hearts & Flowers two-tier tidbit, 10"x6". $25.00 – 30.00.
#5174 ashtray, square 7". $25.00 – 30.00.
#5174 ashtray, square, no rests, 7" made for Nelson Lebo Lamp Co. $25.00 – 30.00.
tile, 6" round, square or hexagon. $20.00 – 25.00.

Multi-Color Decorated Artware, 1927 – 1931

In 1927 Martin Stangl introduced his Multi-Color glaze as a special-order lamp finish and limited line of artware. Glazes similar to Multi-Color were available as special-orders on Fulper Fayence items since 1924, but were not as dynamic or bold as Multi-Color in 1927. Multi-Color was available in Light, a Chinese Ivory base glaze, or Dark, a Silver Green base glaze. Over these base glazes, other glaze colors were dribbled using rubber syringes. Dribbled glazes were Persian Yellow, Colonial Blue, and Rose. Once fired, the glazes would blend and flow together, creating a dappled and drip effect with thick areas where the layers of glaze had mixed. On some lamps, Persian Yellow or Rose was used as a base glaze with other colors dribbled over. Sometimes Violet or Purple glazes can be found as a dribbled color on lamps.

Multi-Color Light #1153L vase with Chinese Ivory base glaze and Rose, Persian Yellow, and Silver Green dribbled glazes (base, inset). $225.00 – 275.00.

Glazing prices were calculated by the square inch of pottery during the 1920s and 1930s. In 1928, single solid-color glazes were 6¢ per square inch while Multi-Color gaze was 8¢ per square inch. The additional cost of 2¢ per square inch made enough difference in overall cost to prevent many retailers from ordering the Multi-Color finish. By 1929, the price for Multi-Color and Sunburst glazes dropped to 7½¢ per square inch, but Multi-Color remained a special-order glaze.

The shapes of the Multi-Color art line were mold-cast in a handmade primitive style of stacking rings. The #1150 flowerpot, however, was not mold-cast, but hand-thrown. As John Kunsman stated in a 1931 interview with Margaret H. Fort, he was able to hand-turn those flowerpots more cheaply than could be mold-cast. Consequently, the #1150 flowerpots were hand-thrown while the rest of the Multi-Color shapes were slip-cast.

Multi-Color Dark bowls #1148S 6", $60.00 – 75.00 (left); and #1148L 8", $100.00 – 125.00 (right), showing the variations of the Multi-Color finish. Base (inset) shows the heavy drips of the various glazes converging. Because of the accumulation of glaze, the foot was ground on many of the Multi-Color pieces.

Stangl's Multi-Color shapes were usually unmarked, but sometimes can be found with the Fulper-Stangl die-pressed oval mark, or a Fulper-Stangl or Stangl Pottery gold-foil paper label.

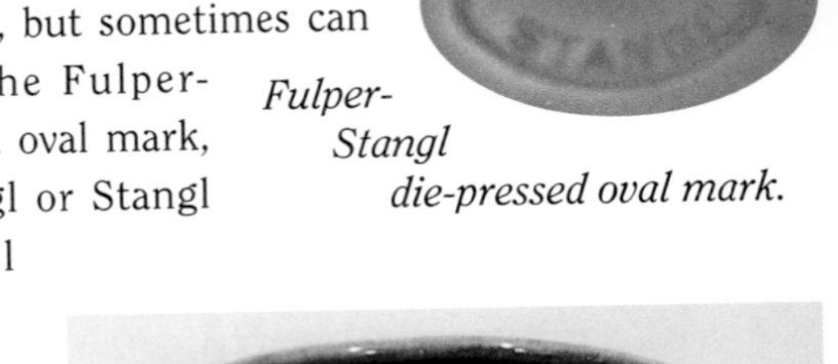

Fulper-Stangl die-pressed oval mark.

The Multi-Color art line consisting of shapes #1148 through #1157 was only produced from 1927 to 1929, but the Multi-Color glaze treatment was available as a special-order finish on lamps and artware shapes into the 1930s. See also the Lamp chapter for more details.

Multi-Color Dark #1148L bowl, 8" Fulper-Stangl mold-cast, 1927 – 1929. $100.00 – 125.00.

Multi-Color Dark #1148S bowl, 6" Fulper-Stangl mold-cast, 1927 – 1929. $60.00 – 75.00.

Multi-Color Light #1149L jar, 7½" Fulper-Stangl mold-cast, 1927 – 1929. $170.00 – 195.00.

Multi-Color Dark #1149M jar, 5½" Fulper-Stangl mold-cast, 1927 – 1929. $95.00 – 130.00.

Frankart Smoking Stand No. T330, 25½" tall, with Fulper-Stangl 6" Multi-Color #1148 ash bowl. Ash bowl only (inset), for Frankart, 1927 – 1934. $190.00 – 225.00. Courtesy of the Negley collection.

Multi-Color Dark #1150S flowerpot, 4" Fulper-Stangl handmade, 1927 – 1929s. $70.00 – 95.00.

Multi-Color Dark #1156 lamp, 7" (same as solid-color lamp #1083) $225.00 – 275.00.

Multi-Color Light and Dark #1153L vases, 9½" Fulper-Stangl mold-cast, 1927 – 1929. $225.00 – 275.00 each.

Multi-Color Yellow #1157 lamp, 5" (same as solid-color lamp #1084) $190.00 – 225.00.

Multi-Color Dark #1262 cigar cup/vase, 4"x3¾", for Art Metal Works, 1930 – 1931. $60.00 – 75.00.

Not Shown:

#1149S jar, 4" Fulper-Stangl mold-cast, 1927 – 1929. $95.00 – 110.00.
#1150L flowerpot, 8" Fulper-Stangl handmade, 1927 – 1929. $130.00 – 150.00.
#1150M flowerpot, 6" Fulper-Stangl handmade, 1927 – 1929. $90.00 – 110.00.
#1153S vase, 7½" Fulper-Stangl mold-cast, 1927 – 1929. $175.00 – 200.00.
#1153S vase, 5½" Fulper-Stangl mold-cast, 1927 – 1929. $150.00 – 175.00.
#1154 bowl, plain, 10"x3" Fulper-Stangl mold-cast, 1927 – 1929. $95.00 – 110.00.
#1177 lamp, 6" (same as vase #1153) $200.00 – 250.00.
#1178 lamp, 9" (same as vase #1153) $275.00 – 300.00.
#1222 lamp, Colonial, 6¼". $275.00 – 300.00.

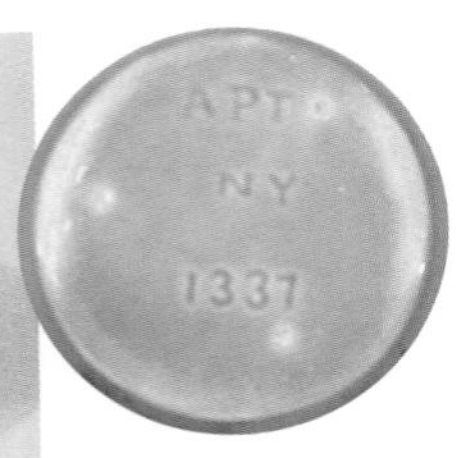

Multi-Color Dark #1337 round ashtray, 4", for APT, NY, 1930 – 1931 (base, inset). $80.00 – 95.00.

New Yorker Magazine Cartoon Pieces, 1950

New Yorker 12" chop plate, "Start the lesson, Teacher! I'm all ears!" $400.00 – 450.00. Courtesy of Dave and Betty Stangl Thomas.

During 1950, plant supervisor Dave Thomas developed a line of novelty items decorated with approximately 100 different motifs based on cartoons and drawings from *The New Yorker* magazine. Most of these items had brushed engobe and a wide band of color on the rims. Many of the cartoon motifs were somewhat risqué; cartoons depicting partial nudity and sexual innuendo were typical decorations.

Dave Thomas had hoped that *The New Yorker* would be intrigued by these items and market them in conjunction with the magazines. *The New Yorker,* however, was not interested, so the project was dropped and all the cartoon pieces were sold through the Flemington Outlet.

New Yorker 12" chop plate with Herbert Hoover caricature. $350.00 – 375.00. Courtesy of the Hill-Fulper-Stangl Museum.

New Yorker 12" chop plate, "Have you seen an occulist (sic)?" $400.00 – 500.00.

New Yorker 12" chop plate, "They're amazing!" $400.00 – 500.00. Courtesy of Dave and Betty Stangl Thomas.

New Yorker cartoon tile, "A simple 'yes' or 'no' will be sufficient, Madame." $200.00 – 250.00. Courtesy of Dave and Betty Stangl Thomas.

New Yorker cartoon tile, "Plumbing emergency." $200.00 – 250.00. Courtesy of Dave and Betty Stangl Thomas.

New Yorker cartoon tile, "Saaaaay… there's a fast one!" $200.00 – 250.00. Courtesy of Dave and Betty Stangl Thomas.

Not Shown:
beer mug, 1950 only. $190.00 – 225.00.
cigarette box, 1950 only. $900.00 – 1,000.00.
coaster ashtray, 1950 only. $200.00 – 250.00.
pitcher, 2 quart, 1950 only. $450.00 – 500.00.
plate, 12" chop, 1950 only. $350.00 – 500.00.
plate, 10", 1950 only. $200.00 – 275.00.
teapot bank, 1950 only. $450.00 – 500.00.
tile, 8"x8", 1950 only. $200.00 – 250.00.
tile, 6"x6", 1950 only. $200.00 – 250.00.

New Yorker cigarette box. $900.00 – $1,000.00. Courtesy of the Robert Sherman collection.

New Yorker cartoon beer mug, "Start the lesson, Teacher, I'm all ears." $200.00 – 225.00. Courtesy of the Marcena North collection.

Oyster Plates, 1973 – 1974

Stangl produced novelty oyster plates during 1973 and 1974. These plates were decorated with Dark Turquoise, Pink #193, Old Gold, Yellow, or Aqua Green underglaze colors. Plain white undecorated oyster plates were also produced.

Pink oyster plates were usually produced for the Port Norris Oyster House. Two Port Norris backstamps were used. The plates were stamped "Hand Painted for Port Norris Oyster House, Port Norris, N. J." or "Handcrafted, Port Norris Oyster Co., Port Norris, N.J." The blue, gold, and green plates were marked with a typical Stangl mark, sometimes accompanied by the Potters' Union mark. Although not scarce, Stangl's oyster plates are highly collectible.

Oyster plate with Aqua Green decoration. $275.00 – 300.00.

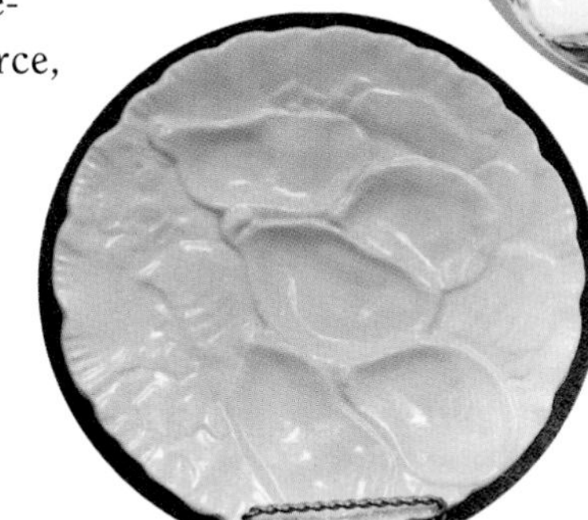

Undecorated oyster plate. $80.00 – 100.00. Courtesy of the Ed Simpson collection.

Not Shown:

oyster plate, 9" Dark Turquoise. $290.00 – 325.00.
oyster plate, 9" Aqua Green. $275.00 – 300.00.
oyster plate, 9" Pink #193. $290.00 – 325.00.
oyster plate, 9" Old Gold. $225.00 – 275.00.
oyster plate, 9" Yellow. $300.00 – 350.00.
oyster plate, 9" undecorated. $80.00 – 100.00.

Patrician, 1978

Stangl's Patrician Ceramic Bathware was introduced on January 1, 1978. This line of bath accessories came in four refreshing pastel colors with a textured white glaze. To produce the Patrician finish, each piece was sprayed with pastel blue, tan, yellow or green engobe, and then sprayed with an opaque pebbly white glaze. Interiors were sprayed with clear gloss glaze. The patrician shapes were a mix of old tried and true designs, such as the #4055 pitcher, and newer shapes developed for the Town & Country line in 1975. Stangl Pottery claimed that Patrician was: "Dramatically different and truly new... a blend of texture and form creating striking beauty with maximum utility... a complete line of quality ceramic bathware featuring white highlights over matte-colors of CAMEO-BLUE, SUN-TAN, MINT-GREEN, and LEMON-YELLOW." Patrician was a popular line and would have continued in production if Stangl Pottery had remained in business beyond November 1978.

Original 1978 Stangl Patrician catalog sheet showing a variety of Patrician shapes.

Not Shown:

#5328-626 vanity tray, 7½". $20.00 – 25.00.
#5328-650 pitcher & bowl set, pitcher, 12" (orig. #4055) bowl, 12" (orig. #5157). $70.00 – 85.00.
#5328-652 tumbler, 6 oz. $20.00 – 25.00.
#5328-653 bathtub ashtray. $35.00 – 45.00.
#5328-658 shaving mug. $20.00 – 25.00.
#5328-659 soap dish, rectangular. $20.00 – 25.00.
#5328- 660 tissue box cover, rectangular. $35.00 – 45.00.
#5328- 661 toothbrush holder, round. $30.00 – 40.00.
#5328-662 tumbler, 8 oz. $20.00 – 25.00.
#5328-663 toothbrush holder, square, 4½" tall. $20.00 – 25.00.
#5328-664 shell dish, 5". $20.00 – 25.00.
#5328-665 shell dish, 7½". $20.00 – 25.00.
#5328-666 bud vase, 11" . $25.00 – 30.00.
#5328-667 egg shape powder box, 5½". $50.00 – 60.00.
#5328-668 square tissue dispenser, 6" . $35.00 – 45.00.

Patrician dealer sign. $75.00 – 95.00. Courtesy of Ed Alvater.

Patrician #5328-652 6 oz. tumbler and #5328-626 7½" vanity tray. $20.00 – 25.00 each.

Patrician #5328-667 egg shape powder box, 5½". $50.00 – 60.00. Courtesy of the Luke and Nancy Ruepp collection.

Pebblestone, 1972 – 1973

Group of Amber Pebblestone artware. Courtesy of the Brian and Cristi Hahn collection.

"Pebblestone giftware created by Stangl designers is individually hand-crafted and hand-decorated by Stangl artists to bring nature's beauty into your home. Carefree natural pebble texture available in flowing earth tones of Amber, Jade or Blue. Each piece uniquely complements any décor, makes an ideal gift," stated Stangl's Pebblestone literature. The Pebblestone artware finish was introduced as a lamp finish in 1965, but was used infrequently. Pebblestone was brought back as an artware finish in 1972 in response to the "naturalistic" decorating trend of the early 1970s. Pebblestone had actually been developed by Kay Hackett 10 years earlier; it simply took that long for decorating fashion to catch up with her genius. The finish was created by sponging Silk glaze over the metallic oxide based colors Art Ware Green, Art Ware Blue, and Art Ware Mauve. The intermittent puddling and pooling of the sponged Silk glaze created the pebbly texture of Pebblestone. The interiors were glazed with Satin Back glaze. The Pebblestone finish was discontinued by January 1973.

Stangl's 1973 Pebblestone sales sheet. Courtesy of the Hill-Fulper-Stangl Museum.

Pebblestone Blue #3774 tray, 15". $25.00 – 30.00. Courtesy of the Bill Servis, Susan Lewis collection.

Pebblestone Blue #3981 vase, bud 6¾". $35.00 – 45.00. Courtesy of the Marcena North collection.

Not Shown:

dealer sign. $100.00 – 125.00.

#3926 ashtray, oval, plain, 10¾"x8", (Kay Hackett design). $20.00 – 25.00.

#3983 bowl, 9". $25.00 – 35.00.

#3979 vase, 9". $35.00 – 45.00.

#3993 vase, urn, 13". $70.00 – 85.00.

#3999 vase, bottle, large 15". $70.00 – 85.00.

#4007 vase, 6¾". $25.00 – 35.00.

#4049 vase, bud 9¼" (Kay Hackett design). $45.00 – 55.00.

#5115S bowl, oval footed 11¼". $20.00 – 25.00.

#5270 candy dish, round knob, 7" (orig. #3684). $25.00 – 35.00.

#5271 ashtray, 7¼". $25.00 – 30.00.

Pebblestone Amber #5157, #5158 small pitcher & bowl set, 9"x12", 1968 – 1974. $200.00 – 250.00. Courtesy of the Marcena North collection.

#5272 candleholder, multi-tapers, 7½". $25.00 – 35.00.
#5273 candleholder, pillar, 5". $20.00 – 25.00.
#5274 bottle vase, 8½", (Rose Herbeck design). $45.00 – 55.00.

Pompeii, 1971

Developed by John Ridgeway, Stangl's ceramic engineer at the time, the Pompeii finish decorated a great variety of giftware shapes such as serve-ware, candy dishes, and even birds. Although John Ridgeway created the glazing technique, Rose Herbeck worked out the color combinations for the Pompeii finishes that were put into production.

The Pompeii glaze treatment was created by dry-brushing streaks of underglaze color on the item to be decorated, then glazing with Silk glaze. The application of Silk glaze softened the colors and gave the red body a beige-pink hue. The Tan Pompeii finish was dry-brushed with Hardened Blue underglaze color directly over the bare red body of each piece. Pieces decorated with Blue Pompeii were swirled with Dark Turquoise underglaze color then dry-brushed with Hardened Blue. Yellow Pompeii featured Yellow underglaze color swirled under the dry-brushed Hardened Blue. Yellow Pompeii was tried for a very short time, but was not produced in quantity. Usually, the interiors of Pompeii vases were sprayed with white engobe for a clean, finished appearance.

Pompeii group with Tan Pompeii #5190 6¼" chalice vase, $20.00 – 25.00; Blue Pompeii #5139 12" Cosmos bowl $45.00 – 55.00; and Tan Pompeii #3217 7½" flared vase, $50.00 – 60.00. Courtesy of the Marcena North collection.

The #5231 and #5232 jiggered ashtray and #5233 pipe knockout ashtray shapes were developed in 1971 because of the increasing demand for smaller, heavier ashtrays. The era of the oversized conference table ashtrays was over; moderate size, substantial heft, and earthy finishes were essential for smart smoking accessories during the early 1970s. The heavy, jiggered ashtrays lent themselves well to the rustic Pompeii finishes. A limited assortment of Stangl's smaller bird figurines was briefly decorated with Blue Pompeii and Tan Pompeii during early 1971. This was very short-lived, making Pompeii birds exceedingly hard to find now. The Pompeii finishes were not quite as popular as had been anticipated. The entire Pompeii line was discontinued by November 1971, less than one year after introduction.

Not Shown:
dealer sign. $130.00 – 160.00.
#1905 vase, bud, 7½". $30.00 – 35.00.
#1906 vase, urn, 7¾". $35.00 – 45.00.
#2041 vase, Grecian urn, 8". $40.00 – 50.00.
#2064 bowl, scalloped, 5"x9". $20.00 – 25.00.
#3217 vase, flared, 7½". $50.00 – 60.00.
#3410-7 bowl, rose, 7". $20.00 – 25.00.
#3410-9 bowl, rose, 9". $25.00 – 35.00.
#3621 basket, 5½". $25.00 – 30.00.
#3630 cigarette box, flat top. $95.00 – 110.00.
#3630 coaster ashtray, 5". $20.00 – 25.00.
#3672 vase, double shell. $75.00 – 85.00.
#3676 covered candy, 5¾"x 4". $40.00 – 50.00.
#3688 vase, milk can, 7". $30.00 – 40.00.
#3782 dish, double pear. $20.00 – 25.00.
#3783 dish, single pear. $15.00 – 20.00.
#3784 dish, double apple. $20.00 – 25.00.
#3785 dish, single apple. $15.00 – 20.00.
#3857 dish, clover, 7". $15.00 – 20.00.
#3859 dish, leaf, 8". $15.00 – 20.00.

Blue Pompeii #5188 covered candy, 7"x 4½". $25.00 – 35.00. Courtesy of the Marcena North collection.

#3898 cigarette box, fluted. $95.00 – 110.00.
#3898 #3898-5 ashtray, fluted 5". $15.00 – 20.00.
#3915 ashtray, square, 9". $20.00 – 25.00.
#3942 ashtray, oval, 8½"x 7". $15.00 – 20.00.
#3972 ashtray, round, 10". $20.00 – 25.00.
#4018 dish, shell, 7½". $20.00 – 25.00.
#4026 ashtray, round, 11½". $20.00 – 25.00.
#4033 ashtray, flower, 5½". $15.00 – 20.00.
#4034 ashtray, leaf, 6½". $15.00 – 20.00.
#4036 ashtray, leaf, 6". $15.00 – 20.00.
#4037 ashtray, shell, 5"x 5½". $15.00 – 20.00.
#4038 dish, leaf, 9"x 13½". $20.00 – 25.00.
#4050 vase, bud, 8". $35.00 – 45.00.
#4055 pitcher, 11½". $45.00 – 55.00.
#4056 pitcher, 8¾". $30.00 – 40.00.
#4059 pitcher, 6¼". $20.00 – 25.00.
#4060 pitcher, 5¼". $20.00 – 25.00.
#5004 ashtray, 12½"x 6½". $20.00 – 25.00.
#5023 vase, 9¾". $25.00 – 30.00.
#5034 planter, swan, 5". $35.00 – 45.00.
#5060 ashtray, round, 8". $20.00 – 25.00.
#5065 horn of plenty, 4½"x 7¾". $30.00 – 35.00.
#5066 horn of plenty, 6½"x 10". $60.00 – 75.00.
#5069 candleholder, 2", pair. $20.00 – 25.00.
#5075 ashtray, prism, 6"x 4". $20.00 – 25.00.
#5093 vase, bud, 5¾". $15.00 – 20.00.
#5097 ashtray, apple, 6½"x 4½". $15.00 – 20.00.
#5115-S tray, footed, 11¼". $15.00 – 20.00.
#5115-M tray, footed, 14". $20.00 – 25.00.
#5115-L tray, footed. $35.00 – 40.00.
#5133 vase, spiral base, 7½". $35.00 – 45.00.
#5134 vase, cosmos, 7½". $30.00 – 40.00.
#5135 vase, cosmos flared, 7½". $25.00 – 35.00.
#5139 bowl, cosmos, 12". $45.00 – 55.00.
#5144 bowl, tulip, 4". $25.00 – 35.00.
#5145 bowl, tulip, 5½". $30.00 – 40.00.
#5146 dish, ivy leaf, 8". $20.00 – 25.00.
#5151 tidbit, 10" Hearts & Flowers. $10.00 – 15.00.
#5153 cigarette lighter, 4". $35.00 – 45.00.
#5156 tidbit, two-tier, 10"x 6" Hearts & Flowers. $20.00 – 25.00.
#5174 ashtray, square, 7". $15.00 – 20.00.
#5180 candy jar, fruit, 7"x 4". $45.00 – 55.00.
#5188 covered candy, 7"x 4½". $25.00 – 35.00.
#5190 vase, chalice, 6¼". $20.00 – 25.00.
#5194 candleholder, #1388, pair. $20.00 – 25.00.
#5213 dish, footed shell, 3". $15.00 – 20.00.
#5231 jiggered ashtray, 4". $20.00 – 25.00.
#5232 jiggered ashtray, 6". $20.00 – 25.00.
#5233 pipe knockout ashtray, 8". $25.00 – 35.00.

Tan Pompeii #5093 5¾" bud vase, $15.00 – 20.00; and Blue Pompeii #5232 6" jiggered ashtray, $20.00 – 25.00.

Pompeii Birds:

Not shown:

#3592 Titmouse. $125.00 – 150.00.
#3593 Nuthatch. $125.00 – 150.00.
#3597 Wilson Warbler. $125.00 – 150.00.
#3583 Parula Warbler. $125.00 – 150.00.
#3401 Wren. $125.00 – 150.00.
#3585 Hummingbird. $125.00 – 150.00.
#3402 Oriole. $125.00 – 150.00.
#3405 Cockatoo. $125.00 – 150.00.

Rainbow Artware, 1939

In 1939, Martin Stangl developed his "Rainbow" artware glaze finish. Rainbow was similar in appearance to Stangl's earlier Sunburst glaze, but the application of colors differed. Sunburst used the airbrushed opaque glazes Tangerine, Silver Green, Black, and sometimes Persian Yellow. The Rainbow finish was applications of Silver Green, Uranium Yellow, and Tangerine to create the "rainbow" effect. The placement of colors of Rainbow was opposite that of Sunburst. Sunburst colors always started with Tangerine on the top, then Silver Green or Persian Yellow in the center and Black on the bottom. The Rainbow finish began with Silver Green at the top, Uranium Yellow in the center and ending with Tangerine on the bottom. Uranium Yellow was more transparent and golden-hued than Persian Yellow. The Rainbow finish has been mistakenly called "Blended."

In production, the #3180-#3185 double handle shapes were the only ones sprayed with Rainbow, but several other shapes were also used to test the Rainbow process. Christl Stangl Bacheler remembers how proud her father was to show her his newly developed Rainbow Artware, "Daddy called me into his office where he had a couple of ware boards full of this yellow, green and orange pottery he was calling Rainbow. He asked me what I thought of it, I actually thought it was ugly, but I told him I hoped it would sell. He seemed to think it would, but I don't remember seeing it after that, so I guess it didn't go over too well." Stangl's Rainbow Artware was in active production for only several weeks during 1939.

Not Shown:
#3180 vase, double handles, 9"x4½", 1939. $190.00 – 225.00.
#3181 vase, double handles, 7½"x2½", 1939. $150.00 – 175.00.
#3182 vase, double handles, 7½"x3½", 1939. $150.00 – 175.00.
#3183 vase, double handles, 4"x2½", 1939. $60.00 – 75.00.
#3184 candleholder, double handles, 4"x2½", 1939. $130.00 – 150.00 pair.
#3185 oval bowl, double handles, 8"x3½"x5", 1939. $150.00 – 175.00.

Rainbow #3183 vase, double handles, 4"x2½", 1939. $60.00 – 75.00.
Courtesy of the Brian and Cristi Hahn collection.

Scandinavia, 1965

The Scandinavia finish relied on the simple contrasts of black underglaze color sponged over Stangl's red clay for its effectiveness. Developed during the era of sponged motifs, Scandinavia was never as popular as the sponged blue Mediterranean and Caribbean finishes. Scandinavia was discontinued during 1965. Because it was such a short-lived pattern, complete lists of the shapes decorated with this finish were not maintained; more items than what are listed here will probably turn up.

Not Shown:
dealer sign. $100.00 – 125.00.
#1953 ashtray, oblong 4¼". $15.00 – 20.00.
#1954 two compartment ashtray 4"x6". $15.00 – 20.00.
#1956 ashtray, round 4¼". $20.00 – 25.00.
#1999 vase 7". $40.00 – 50.00.
#2016 vase, 3¾". $25.00 – 30.00.
#2019 vase, 3". $25.00 – 30.00.
#2041 urn, footed Grecian 8". $35.00 – 45.00.
#2048 urn, 3". $25.00 – 30.00.
#2050 scalloped bowl 8" diameter. $25.00 – 35.00.
#2052 scalloped vase 9½". $30.00 – 40.00.
#2064 scalloped oval bowl 5"x9". $20.00 – 25.00.
#2067 scalloped vase 7". $35.00 – 45.00.
#2071 vase, tall footed 10½". $75.00 – 95.00.
#2074 ashtray, 6". $25.00 – 35.00.
#2089 ashtray, Scotty dog 4½"x5", 1965 – 1967. $60.00 – 80.00.
#3044 ashtray Scroll, 4"x5". $20.00 – 25.00.

Scandinavia #5156 Hearts & Flowers 10" tidbit, $10.00 – 15.00, and 11½" vase #4055, $35.00 – 45.00.

#3630 coaster ashtray, 5". $20.00 – 25.00.
#3630 cigarette box 4½"x5½", flat top. $95.00 – 110.00.
#3676 covered candy dish, square, 4½"x5½", $25.00 – 30.00.
#3898 cigarette box, fluted. $95.00 – 110.00.
#3898-5 ashtray, fluted 5". $15.00 – 20.00.
#3898-7 ashtray, fluted 7". $20.00 – 25.00.
#3972 ashtray, Flying Saucer 10" (Kay Hackett design). $35.00 – 45.00.
#3987 vase, urn 6". $25.00 – 35.00.
#3989 vase 7¼". $25.00 – 35.00.
#3993 vase, urn 12". $80.00 – 90.00.
#4002 vase 6"x5". $25.00 – 35.00.
#4004 vase 5½"x4½". $25.00 – 35.00.
#4007 vase 6¾"x4¼". $25.00 – 35.00.
#4026 ashtray, conference table 11¼", (Kay Hackett design). $35.00 – 45.00.
#4028 bowl, 9" pedestal (orig. #3434 bowl) (Kay Hackett design). $35.00 – 45.00.
#4050 vase, bud 8" (Kay Hackett design). $30.00 – 40.00.
#4053 pitcher 12" (Kay Hackett design). $35.00 – 45.00.
#4055 pitcher 11¼" (Kay Hackett design). $35.00 – 45.00.
#4059 pitcher 6¼" (Kay Hackett design). $25.00 – 30.00.
#4060 pitcher 5¼" (Kay Hackett design). $20.00 – 25.00.
#4064 candleholders, pedestal 4" (Kay Hackett design). $25.00 – 30.00 pair.
#5002 ashtray, round 9¼" (Kay Hackett design). $25.00 – 35.00.
#5022 vase, 7¾" (Kay Hackett design). $35.00 – 45.00.
#5023 vase, Phoenician 9¾" (Kay Hackett design). $35.00 – 45.00.
#5063 bowl, footed (#5061), pierced 7". $20.00 – 25.00.
#5093 vase, bud 5¾". $20.00 – 25.00.
#5156 Hearts & Flowers tidbit, 10". $10.00 – 15.00.
#5172 ashtray, pipe and cigar 7"x9". $25.00 – 30.00.
#5173 ashtray, square, 4½". $15.00 – 20.00.
#5174 ashtray, square 7". $20.00 – 25.00.

Stangl Stoneware Tiles, 1971

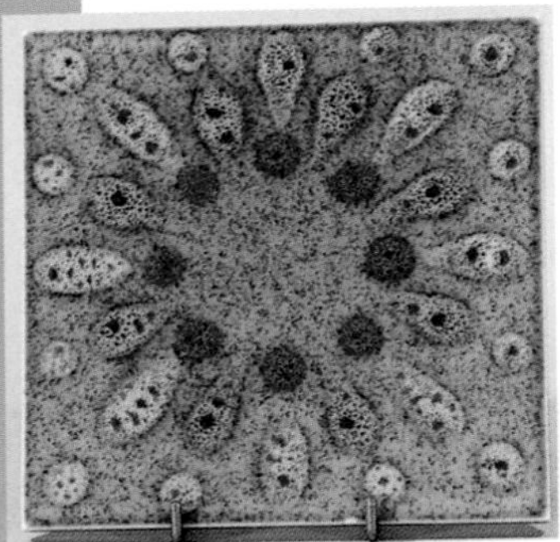

Unproduced Rose Herbeck glaze-on-glaze tile sample in green and blue.

Glaze-On-Glaze Stangl Stoneware Tiles

Rose Herbeck developed the glaze-on-glaze decorative treatment used on the square Stangl Stoneware tiles #5237 – #5240. Colored glazes were applied with a rubber syringe over the background glaze. Each glaze-on-glaze tile design was assigned its own number. Most of the tiles were red-bodied with an in-mold "Stangl Stoneware" mark. Additional tile blanks for the glaze-on-glaze tiles were bought from Wenczel Tile; these tiles bear the Wenczel name and were also backstamped with a Stangl logo. According to sources, the glaze-on-glaze tiles were discontinued after only a few weeks because the decorating supervisor refused to teach the technique to the decorators, stating it was "too complicated for them to learn."

Back of red-bodied Stangl Stoneware tile.

Not Shown:
#5238 - pink and white decoration. $50.00 – 60.00.
#5239 - brown and white heart decoration. $50.00 – 60.00.
#5240 - orange and yellow heart decoration. $50.00 – 60.00.

Back of a glaze-on-glaze tile blank purchased from Wenczel Tile Co.

Glaze-on-glaze tile #5237, brown glaze, yellow and orange decoration. $50.00 – 60.00.

Hand-Painted Stangl Stoneware Tiles

After the glaze-on-glaze tiles were discontinued, Rose Herbeck designed a series of hand-painted tile motifs intended to coordinate with "Stangl Stoneware" dinnerware patterns. The motifs were applied to both 6" octagonal and square tile blanks. The tiles were decorated with various underglaze colors and glazed with either Tan or Gray speckled "stoneware" dinnerware glazes. The octagonal tile motifs were simple geometrics or abstract florals. The octagonal tiles were sold primarily at the Flemington Outlet.

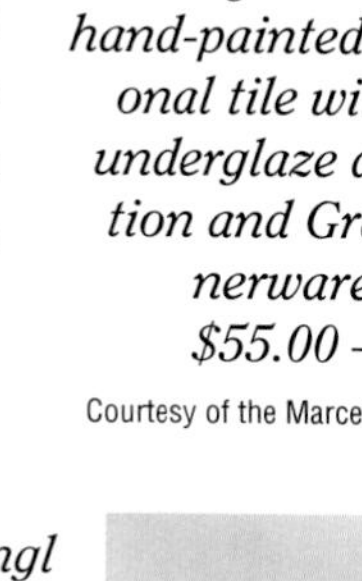

Stangl Stoneware hand-painted octagonal tile with blue underglaze decoration and Gray dinnerware glaze. $55.00 – 65.00. Courtesy of the Marcena North collection.

Two Stangl Stoneware hand-painted octagonal tiles with Tan dinnerware glaze. $40.00 – 50.00 each.

Two Stangl Stoneware hand-painted square tiles with Tan dinnerware glaze, $40.00 – 50.00 each. Courtesy of the Luke and Nancy Ruepp collection.

Not Shown:
octagonal tile, 6" gray glaze, blue decoration. $55.00 – 65.00.
octagonal tile, 6" tan glaze, brown decoration. $40.00 – 50.00.
square tile, 6" gray glaze, blue decoration. $55.00 – 65.00.
square tile, 6" tan glaze, brown decoration. $40.00 – 50.00.

Sunburst Decorated Artware, 1929 – 1934

Sunburst was a multicolored glaze treatment, not unlike Stangl's Multi-Color, but was a scintillating combination of vibrant color rather than the pastels of Multi-Color. The application of Sunburst differed from Multi-Color as well. Where Multi-Color glazes were hand-dripped over a base glaze, the Sunburst glazes were sprayed on each shape in slightly overlapping bands. First, the interior of each piece of Sunburst was flushed with Silver Green. A band of Tangerine was sprayed along the top third of the piece, followed by a band of Silver Green sprayed around the middle. The bottom and base were then sprayed with Black. Each color overlapped its neighboring glaze slightly, creating a blending effect from one color to the next. The overlapping Tangerine and Silver Green glazes bring about a rusty brown color, and the overlapping Silver Green and Black create variegated blue.

Two Sunburst mold-cast #1237 7½" jars, usual Sunburst on left, Sunburst with Persian Yellow on right. Courtesy of the Brian and Cristi Hahn collection.

Most Sunburst vase interiors were usually glazed in Turquoise or Silver Green. Interiors of Sunburst bowls can be found glazed in Black, Silver Green, or Turquoise, or in the Sunburst as well.

On some items, particularly the #1388 dinnerware shapes, drops of Persian Yellow were applied with a rubber syringe to certain areas. Drops of Persian Yellow can sometimes add a few dollars to the value, but only if the drops are vibrant and intact. Very faint drops of Persian Yellow that have dissipated into the neighboring glazes do not affect the value.

From 1932 to 1934, Sunburst shapes could also be ordered with the middle band sprayed with Persian Yellow instead of Silver Green. This created a vibrant, eye-catching, bright yellow effect that is now hard to find and coveted by many collectors. Sunburst items with the bright Persian Yellow midsections can sometimes sell for nearly double that of the same piece with the typical Tangerine/Silver Green/Black Sunburst glaze.

Occasionally, dark Sunburst was produced without the Silver Green middle band. The Tangerine and Black glazes blended together in the center of the piece with no bright color between them. Items with this finish are considered less attractive and usually sell for much less than typically glazed Sunburst with Silver Green or Persian Yellow.

By spraying the Sunburst glazes, Martin Stangl prevented the heavy, lumpy glaze drips that plagued the Multi-Color finish. The individual Sunburst glazes were sprayed on just heavily enough to create a slight flowing effect, but not so heavy as to cause excessive, bulging lumps of glaze. Sunburst was not dipped in successive vats of glaze as has been theorized.

Another Sunburst myth is that heavy glaze on the base obliterates identifying marks. In reality, most Sunburst items were simply not marked. Handmade Sunburst items are rarely marked Stangl or handmade. Many mold-cast items from the late 1920s and early 1930s were unmarked, including Sunburst. Any in-mold or die-pressed markings on Sunburst items can clearly be seen through the Black glaze.

Items glazed with Tangerine or Rust exteriors and Turquoise or Silver Green interiors are *not* Sunburst and are valued the same as single solid-color glazed items.

Black-glazed base of a #1388 candy dish, plainly showing the in-mold "1388."

Sunburst #1076-C Pig Cactus pot (left) and #1076-B Pig Bank (right), 4" each, 1929 – 1934. $190.00 – 250.00 each. Note the Persian Yellow near the nose of the #1076-C Pig Cactus pot. Courtesy of the Robert and Tammie Cruser collection.

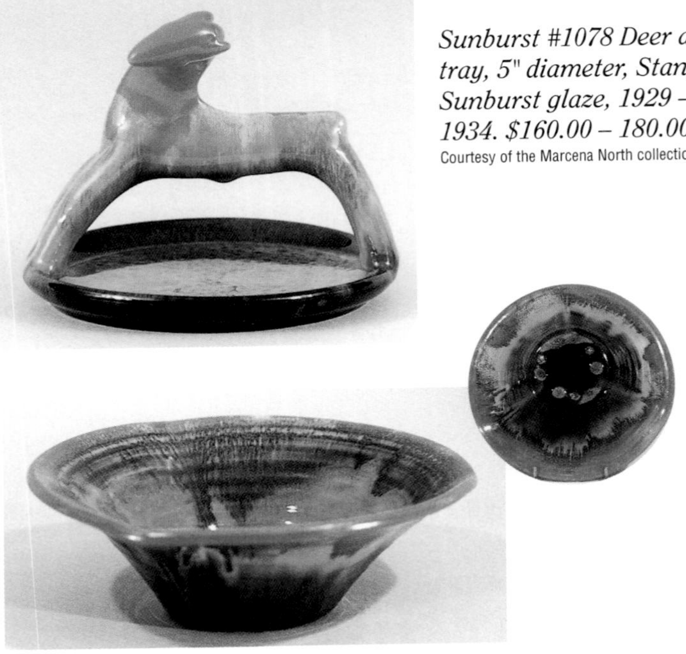

Sunburst #1078 Deer ashtray, 5" diameter, Stangl Sunburst glaze, 1929 – 1934. $160.00 – 180.00. Courtesy of the Marcena North collection.

Sunburst #1119L bowl, 8", handmade, 1929 – 1934. Note also the stilt and grinding marks left when excess glaze was ground from the base (inset). $110.00 – 135.00. Courtesy of the Hill-Fulper-Stangl Museum.

Sunburst #1124 Slanting Handle vase, 7½" handmade, 1929 – 1932. $110.00 – 135.00.

Not Shown:

#1076 Pig Hors d'Oeuvre, 4", for Rena Rosenthal, 1929 only. $275.00 – 300.00.
#1076 Pig Cactus pot, 4", 1929 – 1934. $190.00 – 250.00.
#1119S bowl, 7" handmade, 1929 – 1934. $110.00 – 135.00.
#1120L flower holder, 3½", 6 holes, handmade, 1929 – 1932. $50.00 – 60.00.
#1120S flower holder, 3", 5 holes, handmade, 1929 – 1932. $50.00 – 60.00.
#1121L Double Bulge vase, 12½" handmade, 1929 only. $275.00 – 300.00.
#1121S Double Bulge vase, 10" handmade, 1929 only. $200.00 – 250.00.
#1122 Band Rim vase, 8" handmade, 1929 only. $190.00 – 225.00.
#1123 bottle, 9" handmade, 1929 only. $190.00 – 225.00.
#1124 Slanting Handle vase, 7½" mold-cast, 1932 – 1934. $85.00 – 95.00.
#1125 rose bowl, 4"x6" handmade, 1929 – 1934. $65.00 – 80.00

Sunburst #1126 Ball vase, 7½" handmade, 1929 – 1934. $110.00 – 135.00.

Dark Sunburst #1126 Ball vase, 7½" handmade, 1929 – 1934. $110.00 – 135.00.

Sunburst #1129L Double three-handle vase, 8¾" handmade, 1929 only. $190.00 – 225.00.

Sunburst #1148L bowl, 8" mold-cast, 1929 – 1932. $70.00 – 85.00.

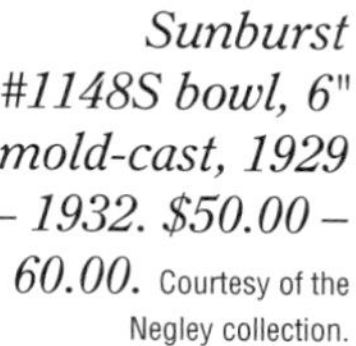

Sunburst #1148S bowl, 6" mold-cast, 1929 – 1932. $50.00 – 60.00. Courtesy of the Negley collection.

Sunburst #1150L flowerpot, 8" handmade, 1929 – 1934. $120.00 – 145.00.

Sunburst #1150S flowerpot, 4" handmade, 1929 – 1934. $60.00 – 70.00. Courtesy of the Hill-Fulper-Stangl Museum.

Sunburst #1185L Square Modern vase, 9" Stangl Pottery, 1929 – 1930. $175.00 – 200.00. Courtesy of the Brian and Cristi Hahn collection.

Sunburst #1188L round bowl, 11" made for Levin, 1929 – 1932. $160.00 – 180.00. Courtesy of the Hill-Fulper-Stangl Museum.

Sunburst #1185S Square Modern vase, 6" Stangl Pottery, 1929 – 1930. $150.00 – 175.00.

#1127 Four-sided vase, 6½" handmade, 1929 only. $175.00 – 200.00.
#1128L Double 4 handle vase, 8" handmade, 1929 only. $200.00 – 250.00.
#1128S Double 4 handle vase, 4" handmade, 1929 only. $190.00 – 225.00.
#1129S Double 3 handle vase, 5¾" handmade, 1929 only. $175.00 – 200.00.
#1150M flowerpot, 6" handmade, 1929 – 1934. $70.00 – 85.00.
#1169 Gazelle flower holder, 11½", 1929 only. $250.00 – 300.00.
#1188M round bowl, 9" made for Levin, 1928 – 1932. $120.00 – 145.00.
#1188S round bowl, 6" made for Levin, 1929 – 1932. $60.00 – 75.00.
#1189 oval bowl, made for Levin, 1929 – 1930. $130.00 – 150.00.
#1190 8-sided round bowl, footed 13½" made for Levin, 1929 – 1934. $275.00 – 300.00.
#1191 twin candlestick, 6"x6" made for Levin, 1929 – 1930. $100.00 – 125.00.
#1192 wall pocket, 2 birds, 5"x7" Stangl Pottery, 1929 – 1930. $290.00 – 325.00.
#1193 bowl, 8-sided, flat, no foot, 12" Stangl Pottery, 1929 only. $150.00 – 175.00.
#1200 square flowerpot & tray, 4" Stangl Pottery, 1929 – 1932. $100.00 – 125.00.

Sunburst with Persian Yellow #1202 oblong bowl, 6-sided, footed, 15"x10½"x4", Stangl Pottery, 1929 – 1934. $290.00 – 325.00. Courtesy of the Robert and Tammie Cruser collection.

Sunburst #1233EL Crimp bowl, 10" handmade, 1929 – 1934. $175.00 – 200.00.

Sunburst #1237 jar, 3 handles, 7½" ribbed, handmade, 1929 – 1934. $130.00 – 160.00.

Persian Yellow Sunburst #1237 jar, 3 handles, 7½" ribbed, with yellow, 1934 only. $200.00 – 250.00. Courtesy of the Brian and Cristi Hahn collection.

Sunburst #1238L jar, 3 handles, 9" smooth, handmade, 1929 – 1934. $200.00 – 250.00.

#1200C square candy jar & cover, 4" Stangl Pottery, 1929 – 1932. $170.00 – 195.00.
#1201L oblong flowerpot & tray 12", Stangl Pottery, 1929 – 1930. $130.00 – 160.00.
#1201M oblong flowerpot & tray 9", Stangl Pottery, 1929 – 1930. $100.00 – 125.00.
#1211 Birds on rocks, flower holder, 10" Stangl Pottery, 1929 – 1932. $190.00 – 225.00.
#1213L Pleated flowerpot, 8" Stangl Pottery, 1929 – 1932. $85.00 – 95.00.
#1213M Pleated flowerpot, 6" Stangl Pottery, 1929 – 1932. $70.00 – 85.00.
#1233L Crimp bowl, 8" handmade, 1929 – 1934. $150.00 – 175.00.
#1233M Crimp bowl, 6" handmade, 1929 – 1934. $80.00 – 100.00.
#1233S Crimp bowl, 5" handmade, 1929 – 1934. $85.00 – 95.00.
#1237 jar, 3 handles, 7½" ribbed, mold-cast, 1933 – 1934. $130.00 – 160.00.
#1237 jar, 3 handles, 6" ribbed, handmade, 1929 – 1934. $130.00 – 160.00.
#1238L jar, 3 handles, 9" smooth, with yellow, handmade, 1929 – 1934. $375.00 – 400.00.
#1238M jar, 3 handles, 6" smooth, handmade, 1929 – 1934. $130.00 – 160.00.
#1238M jar, 3 handles, 6" smooth, with yellow handmade, 1934 only. $200.00 – 250.00.
#1239 jar, 2 high-handles, 7" handmade, 1929 – 1934. $175.00 – 200.00.
#1259 Bird ashtray & match holder 5¾"x 3¾", with ridged match striker along bird's head, 1929 – 1932. $300.00 – 350.00.
#1261 jardiniere, 5" mold-cast, 1930 – 1934. $50.00 – 60.00.
#1261 jardiniere, 4" mold-cast, 1930 – 1934. $40.00 – 50.00.
#1261 jardiniere, 3" mold-cast, 1930 – 1934. $35.00 – 45.00.
#1273 6-sided bulb bowl, 7", 1930 – 1935. $85.00 – 95.00.

Sunburst #1261 jardiniere, 8" mold-cast, 1930 – 1934. $85.00 – 95.00. Courtesy of the Chris McGeehan collection.

Sunburst #1261 jardiniere, 6" mold-cast, 1930 – 1934. $65.00 – 80.00.

Sunburst #1273 6-sided bulb bowl, 4", 1930 – 1935. $60.00 – 75.00.

Sunburst #1274 hanging basket, 7"x3" handmade, 1930 – 1934. $175.00 – 200.00.

Sunburst #1320 Gazelle flower holder, 6", 1930 – 1934. $180.00 – 225.00.

Sunburst #1322 Elephant ashtray, 6" diameter, Sunburst glaze, 1930 – 1934. $400.00 – 450.00.

Sunburst #1323 Bird ashtray, 5½" diameter, 1930 – 1934. $200.00 – 250.00. Courtesy of the Chris McGeehan collection.

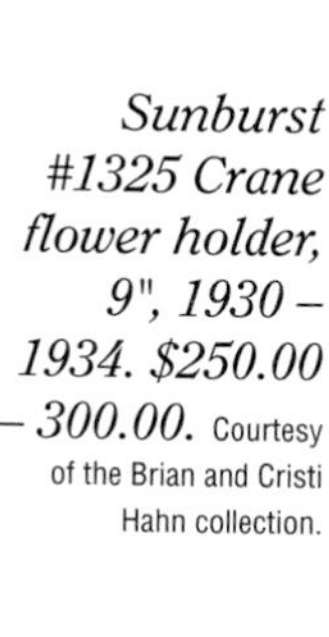

Sunburst #1325 Crane flower holder, 9", 1930 – 1934. $250.00 – 300.00. Courtesy of the Brian and Cristi Hahn collection.

Sunburst #1327 vase, 11" handmade, 1930 – 1934. $225.00 – 275.00. Courtesy of the Frank and Elizabeth Kramar collection.

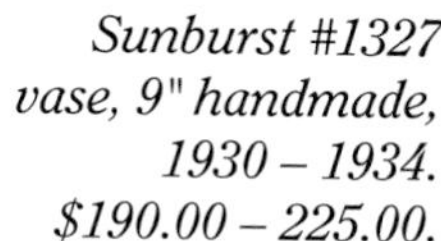

Sunburst #1327 vase, 9" handmade, 1930 – 1934. $190.00 – 225.00.

Sunburst #1328 vase, narrow 2 handles at neck, 14" mold-cast, 1933 – 1934. $275.00 – 325.00. Courtesy of the Chris McGeehan collection.

#1274 hanging basket, 3 handles 7"x4" handmade, 1930 – 1934. $175.00 – 200.00.
#1311 fruit bowl, supported by 3 female figures, 1930 only. $500.00 – 600.00.
#1312 candleholder, male figures, 1930 only. $500.00 – 600.00 pair.
#1318 Horse ashtray and match holder, 5½" diameter, 1930 – 1931. $375.00 – 400.00.
#1319 oval bowl, 2 handles, 12", 1930 – 1934. $190.00 – 225.00.
#1319 oval bowl, 2 handles, 10", 1930 – 1934. $150.00 – 175.00.
#1320 Gazelle candleholder, 6", 1930 – 1934. $250.00 – 300.00 pair.
#1324 Monkey ashtray, 5" diameter, 1930 – 1931. $400.00 – 500.00.
#1324 Monkey & Dog ashtray, 5" diameter, 1930 – 1931. $400.00 – 500.00.
#1328 vase, narrow 2 handles at neck 14" handmade, 1930 – 1933. $275.00 – 325.00.

#1329 vase, narrow 18" Stangl handmade, 1930 – 1933. $700.00 – 800.00.
#1329 vase, wide 18" Stangl handmade, 1930 – 1933. $850.00 – 950.00.
#1329-B vase 15" Stangl handmade, 1930 – 1933. $400.00 – 450.00.
#1329 vase, wide 18" mold-cast, 1933 – 1934. $850.00 – 950.00.
#1329-B vase 15" mold-cast, 1933 – 1934. $400.00 – 450.00.
#1360 scrolled candleholder, 10", 1930 – 1932. $190.00 – 225.00 pair.
#1371 round candleholder, 3"x4", 1930 – 1934. $120.00 – 145.00 pair.

Sunburst #1329 vase, narrow 18" mold-cast, 1933 – 1934. $700.00 – 800.00. Courtesy of the Robert and Tammie Cruser collection.

Anchor Pottery Shapes

During 1930, Stangl produced several old Anchor Pottery Victorian shapes in Stangl solid-color glazes and Sunburst glaze. These were produced as novelty pieces and sold at the Flemington Outlet. There was not a complete line of these shapes produced in these glazes.

Sunburst glaze Anchor Pottery covered vegetable shape, cover missing. $180.00 – 225.00.

Original Stangl Pottery catalog drawing of #1387 candy jar with design, bird cover, 9", 1931 – 1932. In Sunburst glaze, $375.00 – 400.00. From the Stangl and Fulper archival collection, courtesy the Wheaton Village Museum of American Glass.

Sunburst #1386 flower vase, 5¾", 1931 – 1934. $85.00 – 95.00.

Sunburst #1388 candy jar, 5"x5" part of Colonial dinnerware pattern, 1932 – 1934. $160.00 – 180.00.

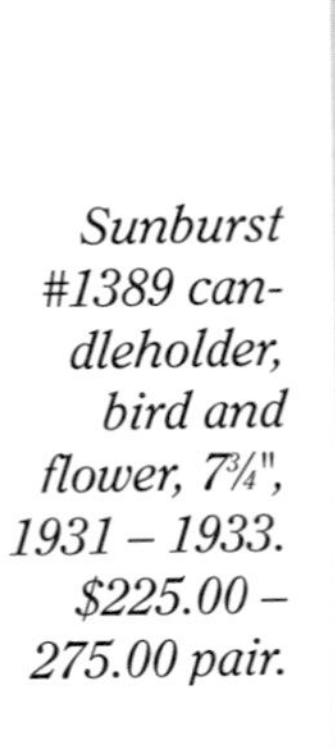

Sunburst #1391 twin candleholder, bird and flower, 6½", 1931 – 1933. $190.00 – 225.00.

Sunburst #1389 candleholder, bird and flower, 7¾", 1931 – 1933. $225.00 – 275.00 pair.

Not Shown:

Anchor large covered sugar, 1930 only. $190.00 – 225.00.
Anchor jug, 1930 only. $175.00 – 200.00.
Anchor covered vegetable, 1930 only. $225.00 – 275.00.
Anchor jardiniere, 1930 only. $275.00 – 300.00.
#1380 ivy ball on chain, 4", 1931 only. $190.00 – 225.00.
#1381 ivy ball on stand, 6½", 1931 only. $275.00 – 300.00.
#1382 strawberry jar, 15" handmade, 1931 – 1934. $275.00 – 300.00.
#1382 strawberry jar, 12" handmade, 1931 – 1934. $200.00 – 250.00.
#1382 strawberry jar, 9" handmade, 1931 – 1934. $175.00 – 200.00.
#1382 strawberry jar, 8" handmade, 1931 – 1934. $160.00 – 180.00.
#1382 strawberry jar, 6" handmade, 1931 – 1934. $130.00 – 150.00.
#1382 strawberry jar, 6" mold-cast, 1933 – 1934. $130.00 – 150.00.
#1383 hanging bowl, 6¼", 1931 only. $225.00 – 275.00.
#1384 6-sided flowerpot, 4½", 1931 – 1932. $130.00 – 150.00.
#1384-A 6-sided ashtray with bird, 4", for APT, NY, Sunburst glaze, 1931 – 1932. $85.00 – 95.00.
#1384-C 6-sided candy jar with bird cover, 6", 1931 – 1932. $290.00 – 325.00.
#1385 8-sided flowerpot, 3¾", 1931 – 1932. $130.00 – 150.00.
#1388 candy jar, bird cover, 6"x5", part of Colonial dinnerware pattern, 1931 – 1932. $200.00 – 250.00.

Sunburst #1392 low flowerpot with design, 3", 1931 – 1933. $100.00 – 125.00.

Sunburst #1393 compote, 3 birds, 7½", 1931 – 1933. $275.00 – 300.00.

Sunburst #1460 candleholder, 4½" handmade, 1931 – 1934. $100.00 – 125.00. Courtesy of the Marcena North collection.

Two Sunburst #1426L oval Japanese garden bowls, 10½"x8½", 1931 – 1934. $120.00 – 145.00 each. Courtesy of the McGeehan collection.

Sunburst #1456 basket, 7" handmade, 1931 – 1934. $190.00 – 225.00. Courtesy of the Brian and Cristi Hahn collection.

Sunburst #1466 tall vase, 10¼" handmade, 1931 – 1934. $200.00 – 250.00. Courtesy of the Hill-Fulper-Stangl Museum.

Sunburst #1457 low jar, 2 handles, 4¾" tall, handmade, 1931 – 1934. $190.00 – 225.00.

#1390 compote, 3 handles, 7½" diameter, 1931 – 1932. $225.00 – 275.00.
#1392-C candy jar with flower cover, 4½", 1931 – 1933. $200.00 – 250.00.
#1394EL Swan flowerpot, 13", 1931 – 1934. $275.00 – 300.00.
#1394L Swan flowerpot, 9", 1931 – 1934. $190.00 – 225.00.
#1394M Swan flowerpot, 6", 1931 – 1934. $150.00 – 175.00.
#1394S Swan flowerpot, 4", 1931 – 1934. $80.00 – 100.00.
#1426S oval Japanese garden, 9"x6½", 1931 – 1934. $110.00 – 135.00.
#1427L oblong Japanese garden, 10½"x8½", 1931 – 1934. $120.00 – 145.00.
#1427S oblong Japanese garden, 8½"x6", 1931 – 1934. $100.00 – 125.00.
#1453 rose bowl, 5½" handmade, 1931 – 1934. $120.00 – 145.00.
#1454 violet jar, 5¼" handmade, 1931 – 1934. $120.00 – 145.00.
#1455 ovoid vase, 5" handmade, 1931 – 1934. $120.00 – 145.00.
#1458 flower bowl, 7¼" diameter, handmade, 1931 – 1934. $130.00 – 150.00.
#1459, cone vase, 9", handmade, 1931 – 1934. $225.00 – 275.00.
#1461 flower pot, attached saucer 4½" handmade, 1931 – 1934. $100.00 – 125.00.
#1462 flower vase, small neck, 6¾" handmade, 1931 – 1934. $120.00 – 145.00.
#1463 flower vase, tall neck, 8" handmade, 1931 – 1934. $175.00 – 200.00.

Sunburst #1464 bowl, 6" diameter, handmade, 1931 – 1934. $100.00 – 125.00.

#1465 vase, straight top, 5½" handmade, 1931 – 1934. $120.00 – 145.00.
#1466 tall vase, 12½" handmade, 1931 – 1934. $300.00 – 350.00.
#1515 jardiniere, 11", 1931 – 1934. $190.00 – 225.00.
#1515 jardiniere, 9", 1931 – 1934. $150.00 – 175.00.
#1515 jardiniere, 8", 1931 – 1934. $100.00 – 125.00.
#1515 jardiniere, 7", 1931 – 1934. $80.00 – 100.00.
#1515 jardiniere, 6½", 1931 – 1934. $80.00 – 100.00.
#1515 jardiniere, 5½", 1931 – 1934. $60.00 – 75.00.
#1515 jardiniere, 4½", 1931 – 1934. $40.00 – 50.00.
#1515 jardiniere, 3½", 1931 – 1934. $40.00 – 50.00.
#1515 jardiniere, low, 11", 1931 – 1934. $170.00 – 190.00.
#1515 jardiniere, low, 9", 1931 – 1934. $150.00 – 175.00.
#1515 saucer, 11", 1931 – 1934. $35.00 – 45.00.
#1515 saucer, 9", 1931 – 1934. $30.00 – 40.00.
#1515 saucer, 8", 1931 – 1934. $25.00 – 35.00.
#1515 saucer, 7", 1931 – 1934. $20.00 – 25.00.
#1515 saucer, 6½", 1931 – 1934. $20.00 – 25.00.
#1515 saucer, 5½", 1931 – 1934. $20.00 – 25.00.
#1515 saucer, 4½", 1931 – 1934. $20.00 – 25.00.
#1515 saucer, 3½", 1931 – 1934. $20.00 – 25.00.
#1537 Acanthus vase, 7", 1931 – 1934. $100.00 – 125.00.
#1540 Acanthus oval vase, 7"x7", 1931 – 1934. $120.00 – 145.00.
#1542 Acanthus oval vase, 10"x7", 1931 – 1934. $150.00 – 165.00.
#1543 Acanthus deep bowl, 9x4", 1931 – 1934. $120.00 – 145.00.
#1544 Acanthus deep bowl, 7½"x4", 1931 – 1934. $110.00 – 135.00.
#1545 Acanthus deep bowl, 14"x10", 1931 – 1934. $190.00 – 225.00.
#1546 Acanthus bud vase, 9½", 1931 – 1934. $120.00 – 145.00.
#1549 Acanthus candleholder, 4", 1931 – 1934. $95.00 – 130.00 pair.
#1570 flowerpot, 8¼" made for Macy's, 1932 – 1934. $120.00 – 145.00.
#1570 flowerpot, 6½" made for Macy's, 1932 – 1934. $100.00 – 125.00.
#1571 round vase, 10" made for Macy's 1932 only. $175.00 – 200.00.
#1571 round vase, 8" made for Macy's 1932 only. $165.00 – 185.00.
#1572 oval bowl, 2 handles, 10" made for Macy's 1932 only. $165.00 – 185.00.
#1572 oval bowl, 2 handles, 8" made for Macy's 1932 only. $120.00 – 145.00.
#1573 candleholder, 2 handles, 5" made for Macy's 1932 only. $175.00 – 200.00 pair.
#1573 candleholder, 2 handles, 4" made for Macy's 1932 only. $150.00 – 175.00 pair.
#1574 Swirl vase, 12" made for Macy's 1932 only. $175.00 – 200.00.
#1574 Swirl vase, 9" made for Macy's 1932 – 1937. $165.00 – 185.00.
#1575 candleholder, 4" made for Macy's 1932 – 1934. $130.00 – 150.00 pair.
#1576 bowl, 9" made for Macy's 1932 only. $110.00 – 135.00.
#1577 candleholder 7" made for Macy's 1932 – 1934. $175.00 – 200.00 pair.
#1578 bud vase, 7" made for Macy's 1932 only. $110.00 – 135.00.
#1579 flower vase, 9" made for Macy's 1932 only. $130.00 – 160.00.
#1579 flower vase, 7" made for Macy's 1932 only. $120.00 – 145.00.
#1579 flower vase, 4½" made for Macy's 1932 only. $100.00 – 125.00.
#1580 flower bowl on stand, 9" made for Macy's 1932 only. $175.00 – 200.00.
#1581 oval bowl, 12" made for Macy's, 1932 – 1937. $170.00 – 190.00.
#1581 oval bowl, 8" made for Macy's, 1932 – 1937. $150.00 – 165.00.
#1582 round bowl, made for Macy's 1932 only. $110.00 – 135.00.
#1583 bowl on square stand, 9" made for Macy's 1932 only. $175.00 – 200.00.
#1584 candleholder, square base, 7½" made for Macy's 1932 only. $175.00 – 200.00 pair.
#1590 Swirl sand jar, 22", 1932 – 1934. $1000.00 – 1,200.00.

Base of a Sunburst glazed #1466 handmade tall vase marked "Wenczel Tile Co." Stangl Pottery and Wenczel Tile were close neighbors and often produced special-order items for one another. Value with Wenczel name, $350.00 – 375.00. Courtesy of the Hill-Fulper-Stangl Museum.

Sunburst with Persian Yellow #1515 jardiniere, 8", 1931 – 1934. $170.00 – 195.00. Courtesy of the Hill-Fulper-Stangl Museum.

Sunburst #1541 Acanthus oval vase, 9"x9", 1931 – 1934. $150.00 – 165.00.

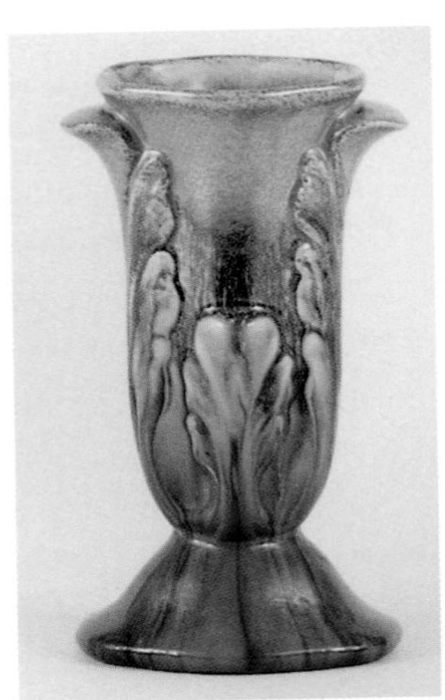

Sunburst #1547 Acanthus bud vase, 7", 1931 – 1934. $100.00 – 125.00.

#1590 Swirl sand jar, 15", 1932 – 1934. $900.00 – 1,000.00.
#1590 Swirl sand jar, 9", 1932 – 1934. $275.00 – 300.00.
#1592 Flared sand jar, 2 handles, 22" 1932 only. $1100.00 – 1,300.00.
#1593 Rope handle sand jar, 16", 1932 – 1934. $900.00 – 1,000.00.
#1634 bowl, 8¼" diameter, made for Bamberger's, 1932 – 1933. $110.00 – 135.00.
#1635 fluted vase large 6½" made for Bamberger's, 1932 – 1933. $175.00 – 200.00.
#1637 candleholder, 5" made for Bamberger's, 1932 – 1933. $110.00 – 135.00.
#1638 vase, 6" made for Bamberger's, 1932 – 1933. $120.00 – 145.00.
#1639 rose bowl, 5" made for Bamberger's, 1932 – 1933. $120.00 – 145.00.
#1648 Step-back vase, 9" handmade, 1933 – 1934. $165.00 – 185.00.
#1649 Curvy vase, 9" handmade, 1933 – 1934. $165.00 – 185.00.
#1665 cylinder vase, 8" handmade, 1933 – 1934. $130.00 – 160.00.
#1667 Cup vase, 7" Stangl handmade, 1933 – 1934. $160.00 – 180.00.
#1669 vase, handle, ring top, 7" handmade, 1933 – 1934. $175.00 – 200.00.
#1670 vase, low handles, 7" handmade, 1933 – 1934. $175.00 – 200.00.
#1712 vase, 2 handles, 6" handmade, 1933 – 1934. $130.00 – 150.00.
#1733 cylinder vase, 2 flat handles, 12" 1933 only. $200.00 – 250.00.
#1733 cylinder vase, 2 flat handles, 10" 1933 only. $175.00 – 200.00.
#1733 cylinder vase, 2 flat handles, 6" 1933 only. $165.00 – 185.00.
#1734 cylinder vase, 2 flat handles, 8" 1933 only. $170.00 – 195.00.
#1735 vase, 3 step-handles, 12", 1933 – 1934. $200.00 – 250.00.
#1735 vase, 3 step-handles, 9", 1933 – 1934. $175.00 – 200.00.
#1736 vase, cone, 3 step-handles, 12" 1933 only. $225.00 – 275.00.
#1736 vase, cone, 3 step-handles, 10". $200.00 – 250.00.
#1736 vase, cone, 3 step-handles, 8" 1933 only. $190.00 – 225.00.
#1737 ball bowl, 3 handles, 6½", 1933 – 1934. $170.00 – 195.00.
#1738 bowl, 3-groove foot, 7½" diameter, 1933 only. $170.00 – 195.00.
#1739 vase, 3-groove foot, 9" 1933 only. $190.00 – 225.00.
#1739 vase, 3-groove foot, 8" 1933 only. $175.00 – 200.00.
#1740 bowl, 3 step-feet, 9" diameter, 1933 only. $175.00 – 200.00.
#1741 bowl, pie crust rim, 8" diameter, 1933 – 1937. $130.00 – 150.00.
#1742 bowl, pie crust rim, 12" diameter, 1933 – 1937. $175.00 – 200.00.
#1743 bowl, oblong, 2 handles, 6¼"x4" 1933 only. $150.00 – 175.00.

Sunburst #1548 Acanthus rose bowl, 5½"x4½", 1931 – 1934. $110.00 – 130.00. Courtesy of the Brian and Cristi Hahn collection.

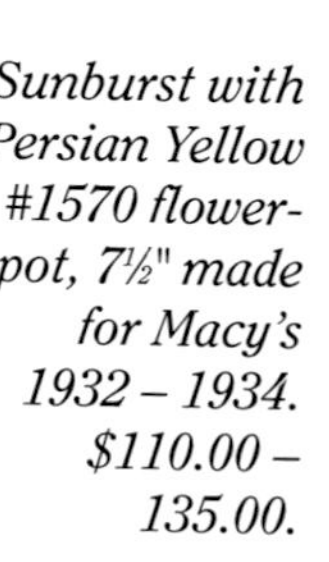

Sunburst with Persian Yellow #1570 flower-pot, 7½" made for Macy's 1932 – 1934. $110.00 – 135.00.

Sunburst #1636 fluted vase small, 5" made for Bamberger's 1932 – 1933. $170.00 – 190.00. Courtesy of the Chris McGeehan collection.

Sunburst #1666 Pitcher vase, 9½" Stangl handmade, 1933 – 1934. $175.00 – 200.00.

Sunburst #1668 vase, handle, ring bottom, 9" Stangl handmade, 1933 – 1934. $175.00 – 200.00.

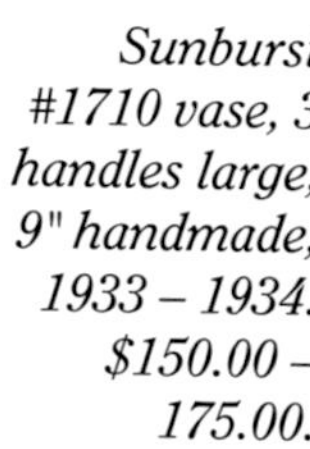

Sunburst #1710 vase, 3 handles large, 9" handmade, 1933 – 1934. $150.00 – 175.00.

Sunburst #1711 vase, three handles, small, 6", handmade, 1933 – 1934. $110.00 – 135.00.

Sunburst #1751 bowl, oblong, 8-sided, 16", 1933 – 1934. $200.00 – 250.00.

Sunburst with Persian Yellow #1758 urn vase, two handles, 12", 1933 – 1934. $225.00 – 275.00.

Sunburst #1765L jardiniere, 7", Stangl handmade, 1933 – 1934. $160.00 – 180.00.

Sunburst with Persian Yellow #1771 Swan flowerpot, 10"x13", 1933 – 1934. $400.00 – 450.00.

Sunburst with Persian Yellow #1770 Fish flowerpot, 9", 1933 – 1934. $500.00 – 600.00.

Sunburst #1773 Camel flowerpot, 14", 1933 – 1934. $225.00 – 275.00.

#1751 bowl, oblong 8-sided, 14", 1933 – 1934. $175.00 – 200.00.
#1757 bowl, 8"x3", 1933 – 1934. $150.00 – 165.00.
#1757 bowl, 6"x2¾", 1933 – 1934. $120.00 – 140.00.
#1758 urn vase, 2 handles, 22", 1933 – 1934. $600.00 – 700.00.
#1758 urn vase, 2 handles, 16", 1933 – 1934. $300.00 – 350.00.
#1758 urn vase, 2 handles, 12", 1933 – 1934. $175.00 – 200.00.
#1762 tapering pitcher, 8" handmade, 1933 – 1934. $175.00 – 200.00.
#1763L vase, 5 indents, large, 8" handmade, 1933 – 1934. $200.00 – 250.00.
#1763S vase, 5 indents, small, 6" handmade, 1933 – 1934. $195.00 – 210.00.
#1764 vase, 5 indents, round 7" handmade, 1933 – 1934. $200.00 – 250.00.

The #1765 jardinieres are similar to the #1238 three-handle jars, but the top rim is taller and the handles are thinner on the #1765 jardinieres.

#1765EL jardiniere, 9" Stangl handmade, 1933 – 1934. $200.00 – 250.00.
#1765M jardiniere, 5" Stangl handmade, 1933 – 1934. $100.00 – 125.00.
#1765S jardiniere, 4" Stangl handmade, 1933 – 1934. $80.00 – 100.00.
#1771 Swan flowerpot, 10"x13", 1933 – 1934. $400.00 – 450.00.
#1772 Rabbit flowerpot, 1933 – 1934. $400.00 – 450.00.

Sunburst with Persian Yellow #1773 Camel flowerpot, 14", 1933 – 1934. $400.00 – 500.00. Courtesy of the Jim Horner collection.

Sunburst with Persian Yellow #1776 Cow flowerpot, 5½"x6½", 1933 – 1934. $500.00 – 600.00.

#1775 Scottie Dog flowerpot, 7½"x6", 1933 – 1934. $400.00 – 500.00.
#1777 Pig flowerpot, 5", 1933 – 1934. $300.00 – 350.00.
#1778 Sparrow flowerpot, 6½"x5", 1933 – 1934. $225.00 – 275.00.
#1783 bud vase, 6" handmade or mold-cast, 1933 – 1934. $95.00 – 130.00.
#1784 candleholder, 6" Stangl handmade, 1933 – 1934. $95.00 – 130.00.
#1785 bowl, no handles, 3½" Stangl handmade, 1933 – 1934. $95.00 – 110.00.
#1852L basket, turned edge, 7½"x10½" handmade, 1934 only. $200.00 – 250.00.
#1852M basket, turned edge, 6"x8" handmade, 1934 only. $190.00 – 225.00.
#1852S basket, turned edge, 5½" handmade, 1934 only. $150.00 – 175.00.
#1853 basket, sides in, 5" handmade, 1934 only. $$110.00 – 135.00.
#1854 basket, scroll edge, 5" handmade, 1934 only. $165.00 – 185.00.
#1855 vase, 2 handle, straight top, 10½" handmade, 1934 only. $175.00 – 200.00.
#1856 vase, 2 handle, straight top, 7½" handmade, 1934 only. $160.00 – 180.00.
#1857 vase, 2 handle, straight top, 5" handmade, 1934 only. $130.00 – 150.00.
#1858 ball vase, neck ring, 2 handles, 6½" handmade, 1934 only. $150.00 – 175.00.
#1859 vase, pinched top, 2 handles, 7½" handmade, 1934 only. $175.00 – 200.00.
#1860 vase, pinched top, 2 handles, 3½" handmade, 1934 only. $130.00 – 150.00.
#1861 pitcher vase, twisted handle, 9" handmade, 1934 only. $175.00 – 200.00.
#1862 low vase, 3 handles, 4"x3½", handmade, 1934 only. $95.00 – 110.00.
#1863 vase, flat ball, 3 feet, 3¾" handmade, 1934 only. $130.00 – 150.00.
#1864 bowl, scroll turning in, 6½" handmade, 1934 only. $110.00 – 135.00.
#1865 bowl, turned-over edge, 8½" handmade, 1934 only. $120.00 – 145.00.
#1866 bowl, 3 double rope handles, 7½" handmade, 1934 only. $170.00 – 195.00.
#1867 bowl, top turned in, 2 handles, 7½" handmade, 1934 only. $170.00 – 195.00.
#1868 bowl, straight neck, handmade, 1934 only. $130.00 – 160.00.

Sunburst #1791 vase, two handles, 4¼", Stangl handmade, 1933 – 1934. $110.00 – 135.00.

Town & Country, 1974 – 1978

Stangl's Town & Country was developed and introduced in 1974 as a dinnerware pattern. It was the brainchild of Stangl's production manager at the time, Roberts Roemer; the Town & Country shapes were designed by Stangl's sculptor, Rudy Kleinebeckel, and the colors were developed by Irene Sarnecki, head of the decorating department. The pattern was inspired by nineteenth century enamel kitchenware. Underglaze color was sponged over the white body of the shapes to re-create the appearance of enameled ware. The original colors introduced in 1974 were Blue, Green, Crimson, Black, and Yellow. Crimson was discontinued during 1974, and Brown replaced Black in 1975. Honey-colored Town & Country was introduced in 1977.

The Town & Country dinnerware pattern was immediately popular, so additional items were developed in both dinnerware and artware shapes. New shapes decorated with the Town & Country finish were introduced throughout 1975 and 1976, culminating in the introduction of the Town & Country bath accessories introduced at the end of 1976.

Original 1977 Town & Country bath accessories sales sheet.

Blue continues to be the most popular Town & Country color. Green and Yellow are next in popularity and are valued at the high end of the range. Brown and Honey are least popular and are usually very slow sellers, even at the low end of the value range. Please see the Lamp chapter for Town & Country lamps.

	Blue	Brown, Green, Honey, Yellow
dealer sign	$160.00 – 180.00	$100.00 – 125.00
ashtray, #1953, 4¼"	$25.00 – 35.00	$15.00 – 20.00
ashtray, #3942, 8½"	$35.00 – 45.00	$20.00 – 25.00
ashtray, bathtub shape	$50.00 – 60.00	$40.00 – 50.00
basket, #3621, 5½"	$70.00 – 85.00	$50.00 – 60.00
bean pot/cookie jar	$130.00 – 150.00	$35.00 – 45.00
bowl, #5300 Rose, 9"	$60.00 – 75.00	$30.00 – 40.00
bowl, #5301 Rose, 7"	$45.00 – 55.00	$25.00 – 30.00
bowl, #5302 Rose, 5"	$25.00 – 35.00	$20.00 – 25.00
cake stand, 10⅝"	$35.00 – 45.00	$20.00 – 25.00
cake stand/chip & dip, 12½" round	$120.00 – 135.00	$55.00 – 65.00
candleholders, 3" Rose, #5138, pair	$35.00 – 45.00	$25.00 – 30.00
candleholder #5287, chamber-stick shape	$40.00 – 50.00	$25.00 – 35.00
candlestick #5299 7½" tall, pair	$100.00 – 125.00	$55.00 – 65.00
canister, #3688 milk can, cork cover	$55.00 – 65.00	$25.00 – 35.00
canister, #5262 milk can shape with ceramic lid	$130.00 – 150.00	$65.00 – 80.00
chamber pot, handled	$100.00 – 125.00	$50.00 – 60.00
citrus juicer with mug	$100.00 – 125.00	$55.00 – 65.00
clock, 10⅝" round	$35.00 – 45.00	$25.00 – 30.00
clock, skillet shape	$65.00 – 80.00	$35.00 – 45.00
cookie jar, 6¼" diameter, milk can shape	$150.00 – 175.00	$60.00 – 75.00
cornucopia #5065 small, 4½"x7¼"	$65.00 – 80.00	$30.00 – 40.00
cornucopia #5066, large, 6½"x10"	$100.00 – 125.00	$50.00 – 60.00
dessert mold, fluted 6"	$35.00 – 45.00	$25.00 – 30.00
dessert mold, Turk's cap, 7½"	$50.00 – 60.00	$25.00 – 35.00
egg shape powder box, 5½"	$100.00 – 125.00	$60.00 – 75.00
flowerpot, 3"	$20.00 – 25.00	$20.00 – 25.00
flowerpot, 4"	$25.00 – 30.00	$20.00 – 25.00
flowerpot, 5"	$35.00 – 45.00	$25.00 – 30.00
flowerpot, 7"	$55.00 – 65.00	$25.00 – 35.00
ginger jar	$120.00 – 135.00	$70.00 – 85.00
pitcher & bowl set, large, straight sides	$190.00 – 225.00	$150.00 – 175.00
pitcher & bowl set, small, ribbed sides	$175.00 – 200.00	$100.00 – 125.00
planter, French Phone #5303, 8½"x6½"	$175.00 – 200.00	$130.00 – 150.00
planter, rolling pin, 13"	$150.00 – 165.00	$70.00 – 85.00
salad fork	$100.00 – 125.00	$60.00 – 75.00
salad spoon	$100.00 – 125.00	$60.00 – 75.00
server, #3783 pear	$25.00 – 35.00	$20.00 – 25.00
server, #3785 apple	$25.00 – 35.00	$20.00 – 25.00
server, #3857 clover	$30.00 – 40.00	$25.00 – 30.00
server, dustpan shape	$75.00 – 95.00	$40.00 – 50.00
server, skillet shape	$60.00 – 75.00	$25.00 – 35.00
shaving mug	$50.00 – 60.00	$25.00 – 35.00
shell dish, 5"	$25.00 – 35.00	$20.00 – 25.00
shell dish, 7½"	$35.00 – 45.00	$25.00 – 30.00
soap dish, rectangular	$35.00 – 45.00	$25.00 – 35.00
spoon rest	$45.00 – 55.00	$25.00 – 35.00

tidbit, 10⅝"	$20.00 – 25.00	$15.00 – 20.00
tile, 6" round, square or hexagon	$30.00 – 40.00	$20.00 – 25.00
tissue box cover square, 6"	$65.00 – 80.00	$45.00 – 55.00
tissue box cover, rectangular	$65.00 – 80.00	$45.00 – 55.00
toothbrush holder, round	$55.00 – 65.00	$30.00 – 40.00
toothbrush holder, square, 4½" tall	$40.00 – 50.00	$20.00 – 25.00
tray, vanity 7¼" square	$35.00 – 45.00	$20.00 – 25.00
tray, 8¼" oval	$25.00 – 35.00	$15.00 – 20.00
tumbler, 8 oz.	$40.00 – 50.00	$20.00 – 25.00
tumbler, 9 oz.	$30.00 – 40.00	$15.00 – 20.00
vase, 6¾" #3981	$60.00 – 75.00	$35.00 – 45.00
vase, 8" #4050	$60.00 – 75.00	$35.00 – 45.00
vase, triple cylinder, 10"x5" #5106	$80.00 – 100.00	$40.00 – 50.00
vase, 12" #4055	$80.00 – 100.00	$40.00 – 50.00
wall pocket	$80.00 – 100.00	$40.00 – 50.00

Town & Country bath accessories in experimental pink sponging. Produced in limited quantity during 1976 only. Courtesy of the Simpson collection.

Town & Country Yellow #5299 candlesticks, $55.00 – 65.00; Blue flowerpot, 5", $25.00 – 30.00; and Brown tumbler, 9 oz., $15.00 – 18.00. Courtesy of the Ben and Floss Avila collection.

Town & Country Blue dealer sign. $160.00 – 180.00. Courtesy of Ed Alvater.

Town & Country Brown ginger jar. $70.00 – 80.00. Courtesy of the Jim Horner collection.

Town & Country Yellow 6" octagonal tile. $20.00 – 25.00. Courtesy of the Luke and Nancy Ruepp collection.

Town & Country Brown straight-sided large pitcher & bowl set. $150.00 – 165.00. Courtesy of the Jim Horner collection.

Wheatonware Exclusives, 1972 – 1974

During the early 1970s, Frank Wheaton produced a line of novelty items designated as "Wheatonware Exclusives." These items were produced at the Stangl plant in Trenton and distributed through Wheatonware, Inc. at Millville, New Jersey.

Aladdin's Lamp

The first Wheatonware item was the #5171 Aladdin's Lamp. The Aladdin's Lamp was originally produced only during 1965. Frank Wheaton brought it back in 1972 with the only difference being the 1972 lamps were marked "A Wheatonware Exclusive by Stangl Pottery." Frank Wheaton even resurrected the printed Aladdin's Lamp insert with the Arabian Nights fable and lamp instructions but changed the Stangl Pottery name and address to Wheatonware, Inc.

Wheatonware Exclusive Aladdin's Lamp. $25.00 – 35.00.

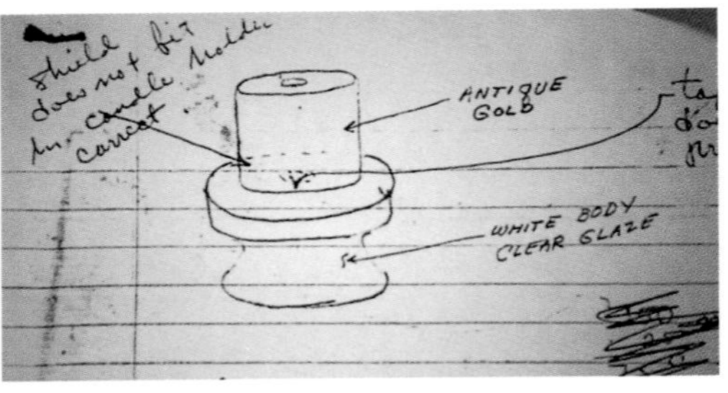

Rudy Kleinebeckel's original drawing for the Wheatonware Candleholder, produced in Antique Gold and White. $50.00 – 60.00.

Wheatonware Candleholder

The next group of Wheatonware Exclusives was produced during 1973. Rudy Kleinebeckel designed a candleholder that was Antique Gold on the top and plain gloss white on the base. Only one thousand of the Wheatonware Candleholders were produced.

Wheatonware Bath Sets

Also produced during 1973 were Wheatonware Exclusive Bath Sets. These were comprised of a 6½" Tulip soap dish, 3" Tulip votive candle, and a glass jar of "Air-Puff" bath salts with a ceramic Tulip stopper. The Tulip soap dish, votive, and stopper were designed by Rudy Kleinebeckel during June 1973. The soap dishes and votives were marked "A Wheatonware Exclusive" while the stoppers were unmarked.

The votive candleholders were filled with wax at the Wheaton Candle Co. in Tuckahoe, New Jersey, and the glass bath salt jars were produced by Wheaton Glass Co. in Millville. Only 2,000 bath sets complete with glass jar and wax votive were produced. One thousand were decorated in red (Pink #160), and the other thousand were decorated in yellow (Dark Yellow). The complete bath sets were not sold at the Stangl Flemington Outlet; they were distributed solely by Wheatonware, Inc. at Millville. However, a few odd Tulip soap dishes, votives without wax, and stoppers with no glass jars were sold at the Flemington Outlet. Some of the soap dishes and votive candleholders were marketed at the Flemington Outlet as cigarette cup and ashtray sets.

Complete Wheatonware Exclusive Bath Set with original velvet ribbon, unused wax votive and "Air-Puff" bath salts. Complete set, $190.00 – 225.00. Courtesy of the Hill-Fulper-Stangl Museum.

Not Shown:

Tulip soap dish, 6½". $25.00 – 35.00.
Tulip votive candleholder, 3". $25.00 – 35.00.
Tulip stopper, 2½". $20.00 – 25.00.

Wheatonware Exclusive backstamp.

White Grape, 1967 – 1968

The design of the White Grape dinnerware and artware pattern was a collaboration between Stangl designers Rose Herbeck and Rudy Kleinebeckel. It was loosely styled after Wedgwood's Queen's Ware style of decoration. White Grape used a pale blue clay body with grape embellishments cast in white clay. Mr. Stangl had high expectations for this pattern and initiated an extensive advertising campaign with full-color, full-page glossy ads placed in national bride and decorating magazines. Full-color price lists were also printed. Regrettably, White Grape was not adorned with 1967's "fashion colors" so did not attract the interest of dinnerware retailers at the fall 1966 trade shows. Consequently, White Grape was discontinued on January 1, 1968. Although classically and timelessly styled, very little White Grape was produced.

Not Shown:

ashtray, 7". $25.00 – 35.00.
coaster ashtray, 5". $25.00 – 35.00.
cake plate, 11" footed. $35.00 – 45.00.
candy dish, covered. $85.00 – 95.00.
cigarette box. $125.00 – 145.00.
compote, 6". $20.00 – 25.00.
jewel box, 5". $45.00 – 55.00.
jewel box, 2¾". $35.00 – 45.00.
vase, fan shape. $70.00 – 85.00.

White Grape 2¾" jewel box, $35.00 – 45.00; 12" chop plate, $65.00 – 80.00; and covered candy dish, $85.00 – 95.00.

Wig & Hat Stands, 1965 – 1974

Martin Stangl developed the #5168 wig stand shape in 1965 and always referred to the piece as a "hat and wig stand." The wig stands were decorated with a feminine face and originally sold only to several wig and millinery boutiques. A New York haberdasher ordered several masculine wig stands, so those were produced also. The wig stands became immediately popular, so Martin Stangl began selling them to regular Stangl accounts and at the Flemington Outlet. Irene Sarnecki was the primary wig stand decorator, but a few were painted by other decorators. Blonde and brunette were the principal hair colors. A few wig stands decorated with truly red hair, a deep auburn-pink, were produced and are quite rare. Also rare are masculine wig stands. These were available only as special-order or very infrequently at the Flemington Outlet.

The original wig stands produced for the boutiques were on round ceramic bases and are usually not marked. The wig stands made for national distribution and the Flemington Outlet were mounted on a dark-stained wood base. A screw and toggle keep the wood base affixed to the wig stand, and sometimes the bases have been removed. The name STANGL was branded into the rear of the wood base. Occasionally, the wig stands were also marked with a large 2" gold-foil paper label affixed at the back near the base. All wig stands were discontinued in 1974.

During 1967 and 1968, wig stands were drilled and sold to the Mutual Sunset Lamp Co. as lamp bases. Some wig stand lamps were also sold at the Flemington Outlet. Blonde and brunette were the usual wig stand lamp decorations, however, at least two male wig stand lamps are known.

Large gold-foil paper label on a wig stand. Courtesy of Ed and Donna Ledoux.

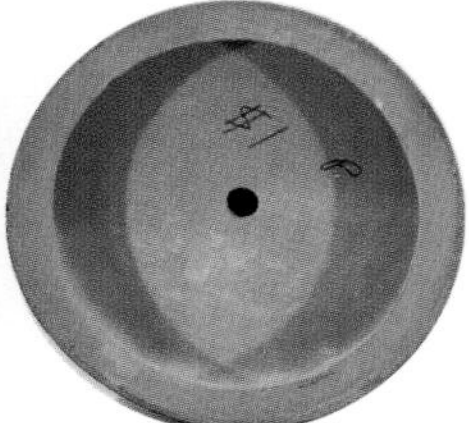

Bottom of a ceramic base with original Flemington Outlet $1.00 price in green marker.

Brunette Wig stand #5168, ceramic base. Blonde or brunette. $300.00 – 350.00. Courtesy of the Marcena North collection.

Lamp #5168, Wig Stand, made for Mutual Sunset Lamp Co. 1965 – 1970. $300.00 – 350.00. Courtesy of the Frank and Elizabeth Kramar collection.

Not Shown:

wig stand #5168, ceramic base, masculine. $2,000.00 – 2,500.00.
wig stand #5168, ceramic base, auburn-pink, $900.00 – 1,000.00.
wig stand #5168, wood base, auburn-pink. $800.00 – 900.00.
wig stand lamp #5168, female. $300.00 – 350.00.
wig stand lamp #5168, masculine. $2,000.00 – 2,500.00.
wig stand advertising postcard. $10.00 – 15.00.

Blonde wig stand #5168, wood base. Blonde or brunette. $250.00 – 300.00. Courtesy of Ed and Donna Ledoux.

Masculine wig stand #5168, wood base. $1,500.00 – 2,000.00. Courtesy of the Marcena North collection.

Advertising postcard showing blonde and brunette wig stands used during the late 1960s. Courtesy of the Hill-Fulper-Stangl Museum.

Bob Shaw Reproduction Wig Stands, 1991 – 1992

Bob Shaw wig stand, Gentleman decoration. Bob Shaw character wig stands. $500.00 – 650.00 each. Courtesy of the Luke and Nancy Ruepp collection.

During 1991 and 1992, Frank Wheaton's grandson, Bob Shaw, produced a line of hand-painted wig stands inspired by Stangl's original wig and hat stands. Actual Stangl molds were used to cast these wig stands, but the motifs were new and wholly original. The motifs were based on such personalities as Betty Boop, Charlie McCarthy, Charlie Chaplin, pirates, baseball players, gamblers, flappers, and purely whimsical characters. The decorating was expertly done and rivals even the originals decorated by Irene Sarnecki. These wig stands were not mounted on bases and very few of them were marked. The new items were produced in Millville, New Jersey, not Trenton or Flemington. Very few of the Bob Shaw wig stands were produced, and the clever characterizations and skilled decorating have caused these wig stands to become highly valued.

Wig Stand Knockoffs

During the 1980s, Hiatt House pottery of Cresco, PA produced male and female wig stands closely resembling those produced by Stangl. The Hiatt House wig stands were made of a vitreous china, not earthenware as were the Stangl and Shaw wig stands. The Hiatt House wig stands were slightly smaller than Stangl's and were not mounted on bases. They are usually clearly marked with the Hiatt House backstamp.

Mark used on Hiatt House wig stands. Courtesy of the Wayne Weigand collection.

Hiatt House male and female wig stands. Courtesy of the Wayne Weigand collection.

Flemington Outlet Workshop Flowers

Produced sporadically at Flemington Outlet workshop or Log Cabin demonstrations throughout the 1960s, these were realistically hand-formed ceramic blossoms hand-painted in vibrant colors. A variety of imaginative blossoms were created, but most common were tulips, roses, and bluebells. Many of the blossom colors mimic the colors of the flower ashtrays also produced at the Flemington Outlet at that time. Each blossom was epoxied to better-quality plastic stems with leaves. Because the blossoms were earthenware, the thin edges are very susceptible to chips and nicks. It is extremely rare to find these with no damage, so very minor nicks are acceptable to most collectors.

Group of Flemington Outlet workshop yellow tulips and roses, 1960s. $50.00 – 75.00 each. Courtesy of Beatrice Levine.

America's youth reacted to the tragedies of World War I by rebelling against established social conventions, not unlike the youth of the 1960s opposing the United States involvement in Vietnam. The most visible changes following World War I was seen in the behavior of young women. By 1920, young ladies were cutting their hair in short, boyish styles, wearing makeup, exposing their legs as hemlines became shorter, and adopting loose-fitting, masculine-styled fashions without corsets. During the 1920s, wild jazz dance parties, drinking, public smoking, and unchaperoned dating were indulged in by both American males and females. Frowned upon by the older generations earlier, by the late 1920s these activities had become tolerable, even acceptable.

The most pervasive social change of the 1920s was the approval of smoking. Before World War I, women were not allowed to smoke, and men smoked only away from women. By the early 1920s, smoking had become so widespread that smoking was now acceptable in public as well as at home. By this time, every proper living room was equipped with at least one cigarette box and a set of ashtrays. The modern hostess of the 1920s would be dreadfully remiss not offering her guests a Fatima or Chesterfield with their coffee. Smoking accessories became very chic as housewarming and hostess gifts. While the game of Mah Jong was the reigning fad, novelty smoking sets and ashtrays of Chinese style were the gift of choice. As bridge and pinochle replaced Mah Jong, smoking accessories decorated with card suits became popular gifts.

The popularity of smoking accessories for the home continued through the 1930s, though not as strongly as during the 1920s. During the 1940s, a renewed interest in cigarette sets continued to grow, leading to the development of large conference table styled ashtrays. By the 1950s, the popularity of smoking sets and ashtrays rivaled that of the 1920s. Cigarette boxes, individual ashtrays, and super-sized ashtrays lost their appeal during the 1960s, but medium-sized ashtrays in decorator colors were in great demand through the 1970s. The anti-smoking campaigns begun during the 1960s started to make smoking "politically incorrect" by the 1990s, which in turn prompted a passion for collecting obsolete smoking accessories. Cigarette boxes and decorative ashtrays continue to be one of the hottest categories of Stangl collecting, second only to bird figurines.

Cigarette Boxes and Smokers Giftware, 1920s – 1930s

From 1924 through the early 1930s, Fulper Pottery Company produced a very wide variety of cigarette boxes and smoking accessories. Many of the novelty items were special-order designs for a number of gift shops and import companies, such as Rena Rosenthal and L.D. Bloch. Several metal novelty manufacturers, including Frankart and Ronson's Art Metal Works, used Fulper Fayence ashtray inserts with their ash stands and sculptures.

During the 1920s, many of the cigarette box and ashtray shapes were decorated with fired-on overglaze china paint colors. These same colors were concurrently being used on the Fulper Porcelaines. The Fulper Decorated items were sold under the Fulper brand name and were marked with the Fulper trademark. They were sometimes numbered within the Fulper Porcelaine series of numbers and sometimes within the Fulper Fayence series of numbers. These items, however, were not porcelain but were made of the Fulper Fayence earthenware body and solid-color glazes. The decorative overglaze colors were applied over the Fulper Fayence base glaze, usually Silver Green or Chinese Ivory. The Fulper backstamp on these items was also fired-on over the glaze. It is therefore possible to remove this mark with abrasive. Undecorated pieces were sold under the Fulper Fayence brand name. The smoking items were usually glazed with Chinese Ivory, Persian Yellow or Silver Green, the most popular solid colors of the early 1920s. Other solid-color glazes such as Colonial Blue or Rose were also used but are found much less frequently. The solid-color glazed "undecorated" items were normally left unmarked or were occasionally affixed with a Fulper Pottery paper label or Fulper Fayence or Fulper-Stangl gold-foil paper label.

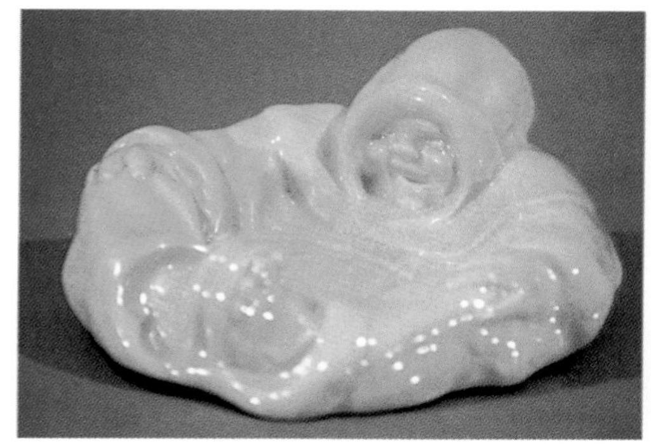

Persian Yellow #907 Monk ashtray, 8" diameter, Fulper Fayence 1924 – 1926. $350.00 – 375.00. Courtesy of the Hill-Fulper-Stangl Museum.

1924 Introductions

Not Shown:

#940 cigarette box, square, Fulper Fayence, 1924 – 1926. $70.00 – 85.00.

#943 Smocoaster (combination coaster and ashtray), Fulper Fayence, 1924 – 1926. $70.00 – 85.00.

#950 individual ashtray, oblong, Fulper Fayence, 1924 – 1926. $45.00 – 55.00.

The Fulper Fayence #953 Card Suit ashtrays were originally produced only in Black and Rose glazes. Black and Rose glazes were no longer used on the Card Suit ashtrays by 1933. During the late 1930s, the #953 ashtrays were produced in transparent tinted glazes but were discontinued by World War II. The #953 Card Suit ashtrays were reintroduced again during the 1960s at the Flemington Outlet. At that time, they were produced only at the Flemington Outlet Ceramic Workshop and were glazed in a variety of tinted gloss colors or hand-painted decorations.

Black Fulper Fayence #953 Card Suit Club ashtray, 4¼" Black or Rose glaze, 1924 – 1933. $25.00 – 30.00.

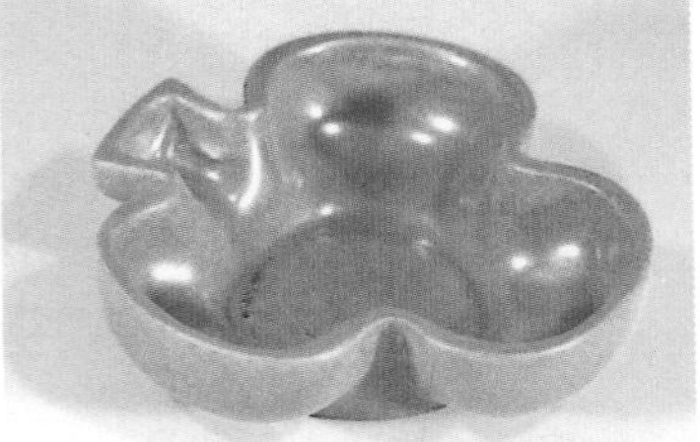

After 1929, other glaze colors were applied to the Card Suit ashtrays. Tangerine #953 Card Suit Club ashtray, 4¼", 1929 – 1933. $25.00 – 30.00.

Set of four #953 Card Suit ashtrays, tinted glazes, produced at the Flemington Outlet Workshop during the 1960s. $15.00 – 20.00 each.

Rena Rosenthal

Rena Rosenthal opened her exclusive gift and decorating shop at 520 Madison Avenue in New York in 1919. She provided the elite of Manhattan with the latest in decorative accoutrements throughout the 1920s and 1930s. Rena Rosenthal stocked her shelves with only the latest creations of the most noted designers and always stayed ahead of the current trends. She was very particular of the merchandise she carried; she would not tolerate anything that did not meet the "Rena Rosenthal Standard." Beginning in 1924, Rena Rosenthal began ordering exclusive designs from Fulper Pottery Company, thus beginning a relationship that lasted well into the 1930s. Throughout the 1920s, Fulper Pottery produced a multitude of decorator and gift items for Rena Rosenthal; particular favorites were jam jars and smoking accessories. Many of the designs were innovative or whimsical in style and usually featured hand-painted decoration.

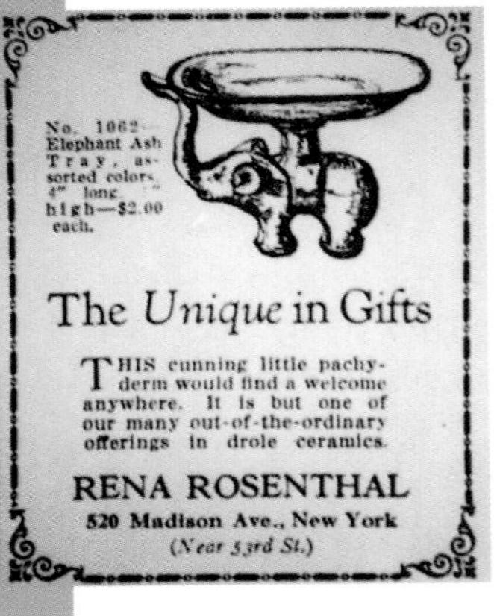

No. 1062 Elephant Ash Tray, assorted colors, 4" long high—$2.00 each.

The *Unique* in Gifts

THIS cunning little pachyderm would find a welcome anywhere. It is but one of our many out-of-the-ordinary offerings in drole ceramics.

RENA ROSENTHAL
520 Madison Ave., New York
(Near 53rd St.)

Original Rena Rosenthal ad showing the #992 Elephant Ashtray. Rena Rosenthal advertised this ashtray at various times from 1925 through 1928.

#992 elephant ashtray, 4"x3", for Rena Rosenthal, 1925 – 1927. $250.00 – 300.00.

1925 Introductions

"Fish" Novelty Ashtrays

In 1925, Fulper Pottery Company introduced a series of Fulper Decorated pottery novelty items designed by English cartoonist Ann H. Fish. Ann Fish's cartoons had been featured in such magazines as *Vanity Fair* and *Vogue* from 1915 through the 1920s. She was known for her ability to capture the innocence and ingenuous qualities of the flapper era. Fulper's Fish designs featured novelty boudoir lamps, powder boxes, inkwells, and ashtrays. They were produced primarily in Fulper Decorated pottery, but some of the Fish shapes were also produced in Fulper Fayence solid-color glazes. The items designed by Ann Fish each bear a facsimile of her "Fish" signature. Unfortunately, she was not able to come from England to sign the novelty items herself, so the pieces were actually signed "Fish" by Martin Stangl's sister-in-law. Fulper's advertising stated: "Designed by 'Fish,' famed in *Vogue* and *Vanity Fair.* These items are copyrighted and are made exclusively in pottery by Fulper Pottery Company — hand-decorated ashtrays by 'Fish' — at $2.00 each. Individually boxed. Label specially drawn by 'Fish.'" While none of the Fulper Pottery Fish items are easy to find, many of these pieces were produced through 1929 and are more plentiful than the same shapes in Fulper Fayence solid-color glazes.

Not Shown:

#367A Dip novelty ashtray 4¾", Fish design, Fulper Decorated (same as #961A), 1925 – 1929. $500.00 – 600.00.

#961A Dip novelty ashtray 4¾", Fish design, Fulper Fayence solid-color glazes (same as #367A), 1925. $275.00 – 300.00.

#367B Sponge novelty ashtray 4¾", Fish design, Fulper Decorated (same as #961B), 1925 – 1929. $500.00 – 600.00.

#961B Sponge novelty ashtray 4¾", Fish design, Fulper Fayence solid-color glazes (same as #367B), 1925. $275.00 – 300.00.

#367C Valentine novelty ashtray 4¾", Fish design, Fulper Decorated (same as #961C), 1925 – 1929. $500.00 – 600.00.

#961C Valentine novelty ashtray 4¾", Fish design, Fulper Fayence solid-color glazes (same as #367C), 1925. $275.00 – 300.00.

#367D Pom novelty ashtray 4¾", Fish design, Fulper Decorated (same as #961D), 1925 – 1929. $500.00 – 600.00.

#961D Pom novelty ashtray 4¾", Fish design, Fulper Fayence solid-color glazes (same as #367D), 1925. $275.00 – 300.00.

#367E Messenger novelty ashtray 4¾", Fish design, Fulper Decorated (same as #961E), 1925 – 1929. $500.00 – 600.00.

#961E Messenger novelty ashtray 4¾", Fish design, Fulper Fayence solid-color glazes (same as #367E), 1925. $275.00 – 300.00.

#367F Ring novelty ashtray 4¾", Fish design, Fulper Decorated (same as #961F), 1925 – 1929. $500.00 – 600.00.

#961F Ring novelty ashtray 4¾", Fish design, Fulper Fayence solid-color glazes (same as #367F), 1925. $275.00 – 300.00.

#380 upholstery ashtray 4¾", Fish design, Fulper Decorated (same as #994), 1925 – 1929. $600.00 – 700.00.

#994 upholstery ashtray 4¾", Fish design, Fulper Fayence solid-color glazes (same as #380), 1925. $275.00 – 300.00.

#381A Maid novelty ashtray 4¼"x6", Fish design, Fulper Decorated 1925 – 1929. $600.00 – 700.00.

#381B Pekinese novelty ashtray 4¼"x6", Fish design, Fulper Decorated 1925 – 1929. $600.00 – 700.00.

#381C Wading novelty ashtray 4¼"x6", Fish design, Fulper Decorated 1925 – 1929. $600.00 – 700.00.

#386 Messenger novelty cigar box, Fish design, Fulper Decorated, 1926 – 1928. $1,200.00 – 1,500.00.

#387 Barmaid novelty cigar box, Fish design, Fulper Decorated, 1926 – 1928. $1,200.00 – 1,500.00.

#1050B Ribbed cigarette jar, 3", part of smoking set for L.D. Bloch Co., 1925 – 1927. $65.00 – 80.00.

#1050C Ribbed cigarette box, part of smoking set for L.D. Bloch Co., 1925 – 1927. $130.00 – 150.00.

#1050D Ribbed pipe rest, part of smoking set for L.D. Bloch Co., 1925 – 1927. $65.00 – 80.00.

#1050E Ribbed ashtray, part of smoking set for L.D. Bloch Co., 1925 – 1927. $65.00 – 80.00.

#1053 Square cigarette box, for Rena Rosenthal, 1925 – 1926. $175.00 – 200.00.

Fulper Decorated #1022 Oblong cigarette box in orange and black fired-on color, lid doubles as ashtray, made for Rena Rosenthal, 1925 – 1926. $375.00 – 400.00.

Silver Green #1050A Ribbed tobacco jar, 5½" with walnut top, part of smoking set for L.D. Bloch Co. (matches lamp #979, also made for Bloch), 1925 – 1927. $130.00 – 150.00. Courtesy of the Hill-Fulper-Stangl Museum.

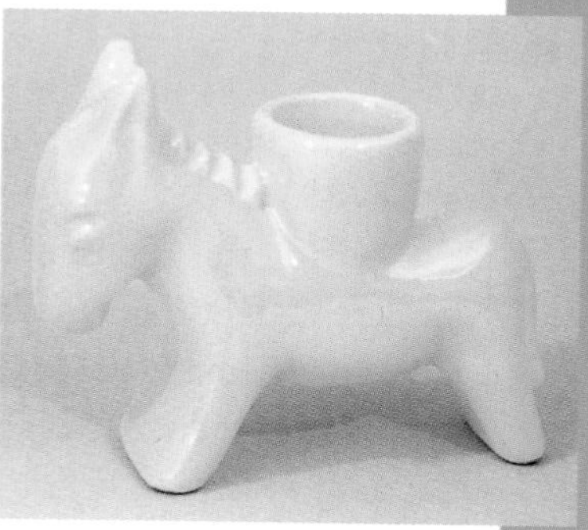

Persian Yellow #1051 Donkey ashtray, Fulper Decorated, for Rena Rosenthal, 1925 – 1930. $225.00 – 275.00.

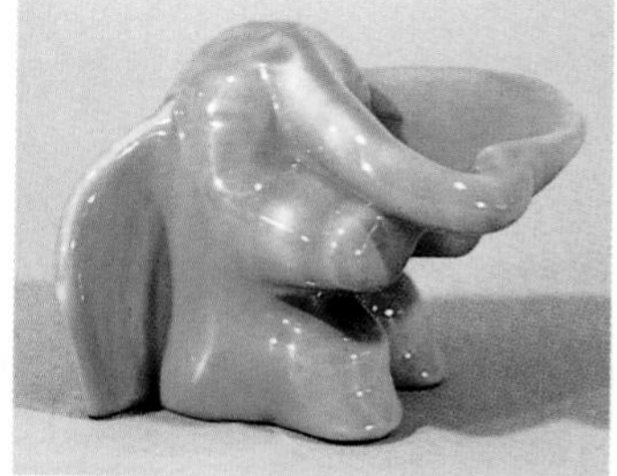

Silver Green #1052 Sitting Elephant ashtray, Fulper Fayence, for Rena Rosenthal, 1925 – 1932. $225.00 – 275.00. Courtesy of the Hill-Fulper-Stangl Museum.

Surf White #1057 Turtle ashtray, Fulper Fayence solid-color glazes, 1925 – 1930s. $175.00 – 200.00. Courtesy of the Bill Servis, Susan Lewis collection.

Fulper Decorated #1058 Lizard ashtray, in fired-on Mandarin Red color, 1925 – 1927. $300.00 – 350.00. Courtesy of the Hill-Fulper-Stangl Museum.

#1059 Combination ashtray, Fulper Decorated, 1925 – 1926. $200.00 – 250.00.

#1078 Deer ashtray, 5" diameter, Fulper Fayence solid-color glazes, for Rena Rosenthal 1926 – 1935. $100.00 – 125.00.

Sunburst glaze #1078 Deer ashtray, 5" diameter, 1929 – 1935. $160.00 – 180.00. Courtesy of the Marcena North collection.

Frankart, Inc.

Frankart, Inc. was organized as a corporation in 1922 for the manufacture and distribution of cast metal sculptures and accessories. The items were cast of white metal alloys and finished in a variety of patinated and polished finishes. All of Frankart's designs were originally developed and sculpted by Arthur von Frankenberg, who also held the copyright and patent rights. The style of the Frankart figures was typical 1920s modernism, with nearly every design featuring at least one nude female form. A few of the statuettes were more comical in nature and were styled after caricatures of golfers, cowboys, or animals. Many of the items produced by Frankart were smoking accessories with glass or ceramic ashtray inserts. All of Frankart's ceramic inserts were produced by Fulper Pottery Company and were available throughout the 1920s. Fulper also produced several ceramic figures for Frankart, including a Nude candlestick, Spirit of Modernism lamp, and Clown ashtray. These were available in the Fulper Fayence glaze colors of Silver Green, Persian Yellow, Chinese Ivory, or Rose. The ashtray inserts were produced in Black, Silver Green, and Persian Yellow glazes, except for the insert for the #T330 smoking stand which came in Multi-Color glaze only. Several candy dish inserts were made of Fulper Pottery stoneware body and were glazed in Jade Green, Yellow Flambé, Moss Rose, or Green.

Frankart smoking stand supporting a Fulper Pottery bowl. The bowl was available in Fulper's Yellow Flambé glaze. Courtesy of the Negley collection.

By the mid 1920s, the popularity of Frankart's novelty cast metal statuary sparked a bevy of competitors to produce their own versions of white metal artware. Some of those companies brashly copied Frankart designs, causing many design patent lawsuits, and even contracted with Fulper Pottery Company to produce ceramic inserts for their products. Some of the Frankart competitors using Fulper inserts were A.P.T., N.Y.; Nuart Metal Creations; Bronzeart, Inc.; and L.V. Aronson/Art Metal Works (ultimately Ronson, Inc.). Each of these companies had their own exclusive ashtray or smoking accessory designs produced by Fulper. By the early 1930s, cast metal novelties were losing favor, and most of the inserts were discontinued by 1934.

Frankart ashtray inserts #1015 3½", $60.00 – 75.00 (left), and #1006 4½", $100.00 – 125.00 (right), both in Silver Green. Courtesy of the Negley collection.

During the 1980s and 1990s, interest was renewed in Frankart and similar cast metal products. By 2000, a collecting craze was in full swing, in turn creating a demand for the Fulper Pottery Company ceramic inserts. Value of the inserts is based on the need of Frankart collectors to complete a figure with original Fulper ceramic components. Values shown are for the ceramic inserts only and do not include the metal figures.

Not Shown:

#1006 ashtray, 4½", for Frankart, Silver Green, Persian Yellow or Black, 1925 – 1934. $100.00 – 125.00.

#1015 ashtray, 3½", for Frankart, Silver Green, Persian Yellow or Black, 1925 – 1934. $60.00 – 75.00.

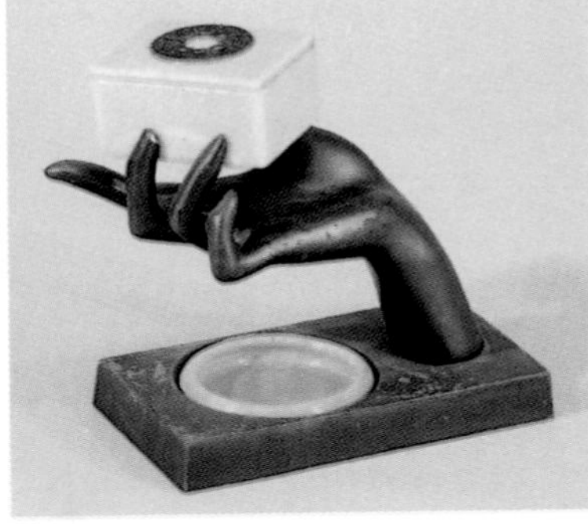

Frankart Gunmetal finish #T336 Smoker's Set, 7", Frankart's Gunmetal finish with Silver Green ashtray insert #1015, 3½". The cigarette box is Jadeite glass. Ashtray only, $60.00 – 75.00. Courtesy of the Negley collection.

Frankart Jap finish #T301 Renowned Tray, 9½", with Persian Yellow ashtray insert #1015, 3½". Ashtray only, $60.00 – 75.00. Courtesy of the Negley collection.

Frankart Roman Green finish #T301 re-styled Renowned Tray, 9½", with ashtray insert #1015, 3½" in Black glaze. Ashtray only, $60.00 – 75.00. Courtesy of the Negley collection.

Frankart Roman Green #T316 Aesthetic Dancing Figure Ashtray, 10", with Silver Green ashtray insert #1015, 3½". Ashtray only, $60.00 – 75.00. Courtesy of the Negley collection.

Frankart Roman Green finish #T313 Kneeling Figure Ashtray, 6", with Silver Green ashtray insert #1015, 3½". Ashtray only, $60.00 – 75.00. Courtesy of the Negley collection.

Frankart Gunmetal finish Aesthetic Dancing Figure Smoker's Set, 10", with Silver Green ashtray insert #1015, 3½", and Jadeite glass cigarette box. Ashtray only, $60.00 – 75.00. Courtesy of the Negley collection.

Frankart Gunmetal finish Renowned Smoker's Set, 9½", with Silver Green ashtray insert #1015, 3½". The cigarette box is Jadeite glass. Ashtray only, $60.00 – 75.00. Courtesy of the Negley collection.

Frankart Roman Green finish #T311 Exotic Nude Ashtray, 11", with Silver Green ashtray insert #1006, 4½". Ashtray only, $60.00 – 75.00. Courtesy of the Negley collection.

1926 Introductions

Light Rose glaze #1087 Nude Candlestick, 5" Fulper Fayence. Also made in Persian Yellow, Silver Green, Black, for Frankart 1926 – 1927. $300.00 – 400.00 pair. Courtesy of the Negley collection.

Persian Yellow #1088 Ball Ashtray (base, inset), 3" tall, for Frankart, 1926 – 1927. Also glazed in Silver Green and Black, $175.00 – 200.00. Frankart discontinued the #1088 pottery ashtray insert in 1927 and replaced the shape with a similar glass ball ashtray in Jadeite or black.

Frankart Roman Green finish #T322 Gaucho on Horseback with Mexican Hat ashtray #1089, 4", 1926 – 1931. Ashtray only, Silver Green (shown below), also glazed in Persian Yellow, $175.00– 200.00. Courtesy of the Hill-Fulper-Stangl Museum.

Persian Yellow #1107 6" bowl and Silver Green #1107A 6" ashtray, $120.00 – 150.00 each. These were sold to Frankart for 25¢ each in 1926; by 1934, the price was 30¢ each. Courtesy of the Negley collection.

Frankart Gunmetal finish #T332 Whimsical Ape Ashtray, 8¾", with Silver Green ashtray insert #1107A, 6". Ashtray only, $120.00 – 150.00. Courtesy of the Negley collection.

Frankart Jap finish #T315 Tray, 13", with Persian Yellow bowl insert #1107, 6". Bowl, $120.00 – 150.00. Courtesy of the Negley collection.

#1107 bowl, 6", for Frankart, Silver Green, Persian Yellow, or Black, 1926 – 1934. $125.00 – 155.00.

#1107A ashtray, 6", for Frankart, Silver Green, Persian Yellow, or Black, 1926 – 1934. $125.00 – 155.00.

Frankart Roman Green finish #T330 Smoking Stand, 25½", with #1148 6" Multi-Color glaze ashtray. Ashtray only (inset), 1927 – 1934. $190.00 – 225.00. Courtesy of the Negley collection.

1927 introductions:

Not Shown:

#393 Angular ashtray, Fulper Decorated (same as #1142), 1927 – 1929. $200.00 – 250.00.

#1142 Angular ashtray, Fulper-Stangl solid-color glazes (same as #393), 1927 – 1929. $100.00 – 125.00.

#395 Angular ashtray, Fulper Decorated (same as #1143), 1927 – 1929. $200.00 – 250.00.

#1143 Angular ashtray, Fulper-Stangl solid-color glazes (same as #395), 1927 – 1929. $100.00 – 125.00.

Fulper Decorated #392 Angular cigarette box, Silver Green with black (same as #1168), 1927 – 1929. $400.00 – 450.00. Courtesy of the Hill-Fulper-Stangl Museum.

#394 Square cigarette box, Fulper Decorated (same as #1163), 1927 – 1929. $450.00 – 500.00.

#1163 Square cigarette box, Fulper-Stangl solid-color glazes (same as #394), 1927 – 1929. $290.00 – 325.00.

#1164 Bridge Ashtray, small, 1927 – 1929. $35.00 – 45.00.

#1165 Round Ring Jar, Fulper Decorated, 1927 – 1929. $200.00 – 250.00.

#1168 Angular cigarette box, Fulper-Stangl solid-color glazes (same as #392), 1927 – 1929. $290.00 – 325.00.

Wrought-iron 31" smoking stand with Silver Green 5½" #966 Fish powder jar base used as an ash bowl. Fulper Pottery sold a number of bowl shapes to several wrought iron companies during the late 1920s. $130.00 – 175.00 with stand.

1928 Introductions

Nuart Metal Creations

Nuart Metal Creations was a brand of cast metal novelty lamps and ashtrays competing with Frankart, Inc. during the late 1920s and early 1930s. Nuart Metal Creations statuary was produced for The Gift House Inc., a division of the L.D. Bloch Company, a New York gift importer and wholesaler. Beginning in 1928, Fulper Pottery Company began producing ceramic ashtray inserts for the L.D. Bloch Company for their Nuart line of figures. These inserts were sometimes, but not always, marked with the in-mold name "NUART." The Nuart ashtray inserts were occasionally produced in Silver Green, Per-

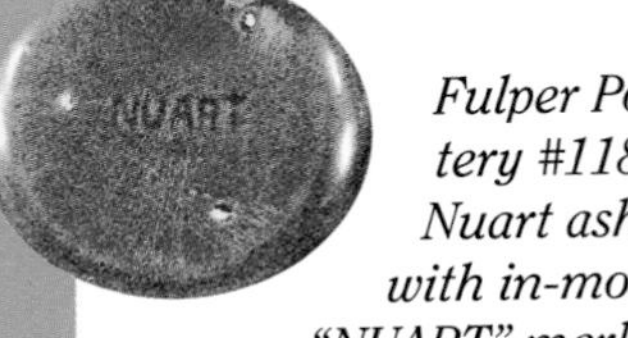

Fulper Pottery #1186 Nuart ashtray with in-mold "NUART" mark.

sian Yellow, and Black glazes. However, the primary glaze used on Nuart inserts was specially developed and was known as "Bloch Fayence." This was a gold, brown, and ivory dripping/blending glaze. Martin Stangl developed this glaze in November 1927 and had refined the formula by March 20, 1928. The Bloch Fayence glaze somewhat resembled Nelson McCoy's Onyx glaze of the 1930s but was much more golden in color with deep ivory highlights over a golden-brown ground. The Nelson McCoy Onyx glaze featured black, white, and copper green striations over a warm brown ground much darker than the Bloch Fayence glaze

Comparisons of Fulper Pottery #1186 Nuart ashtray (right) and Nelson McCoy #037 ashtray (left).

As with Frankart, value of the Nuart inserts is based on the need of collectors to complete a figure with original Fulper ceramic components. Values shown are for the ceramic inserts only and do not include the metal figures.

From 1932 through 1937, Nelson McCoy produced a 3½" Onyx glazed ashtray very similar to the #1186 3½" Nuart ashtray with Bloch Fayence glaze. The base of the Fulper Pottery #1186 Nuart ashtray is flat and, in typical Fulper fashion, excess glaze drips were ground smooth; also the base is sometimes marked "NUART." The base of the Nelson McCoy ashtray is dark brown, has three raised feet, is never ground, and is usually marked with #037.

Not Shown:

#1186 ashtray, 3 grooved, 3½", for Nuart with Bloch Fayence glaze, 1928 – early 1930s. $80.00 – 100.00.

#1188 round Ringed bowl, 6", for Levin, solid-color glazes, 1928 – 1932. $25.00 – 35.00.

#1197 bowl, 6", for Nuart with Bloch Fayence glaze, 1928 – early 1930s. $80.00 – 100.00.

#1198 Scallop ashtray, 6", for Nuart with Bloch Fayence glaze, 1928 – early 1930s. $80.00 – 100.00.

cigarette jar, 2½"x 1⅝", for Nuart with Bloch Fayence glaze, 1928 – early 1930s. $80.00 – 100.00.

Original 1930 Nuart Metal Creations catalog photo showing three different nude figure ash stands, all holding the #1198 Scallop ashtray.

Tangerine with green lining #1188 round Ringed bowl mounted on metal stand with nude figures. Bowl, $25.00 – 35.00.

Nuart #K743 Offering Girl cigarette holder and ashtray with #1186 3½" ashtray and #1199 cigarette jar. $80.00 – 100.00 each. Courtesy of the Hill-Fulper-Stangl Museum.

L.V. Aronson's Art Metal Works

Beginning in the nineteenth century, Louis V. Aronson's Art Metal Works of Newark, New Jersey, produced a wide variety of high quality metal sculptures, castings, novelties, and toys. Known now as Ronson, Inc. and famous for cigarette lighters, the company also purchased ceramic ashtray inserts from Fulper Pottery Company during the 1920s and 1930s. The ashtray inserts for Art Metal Works were usually glazed in Persian Yellow, Silver Green, or Black.

Not Shown:

#1194A ashtray with rests, 2½", for Art Metal Works, Persian Yellow, Silver Green or Black, 1928 – early 1930s. $65.00 – 80.00.

#1195 ashtray, 3¼", for Art Metal Works, Persian Yellow, Silver Green or Black, 1928 – early 1930s. $70.00 – 85.00.

Silver Green #1194 ashtray, 2½", for Art Metal Works, also glazed in Persian Yellow or Black, 1928-early 1930s. $65.00 – 95.00.

#1195A ashtray with 3 rests, 3¼", for Art Metal Works, Persian Yellow, Silver Green or Black, 1928 – early 1930s. $70.00 – 85.00.

#1196 ashtray 4¾", for Art Metal Works, Persian Yellow, Silver Green or Black, 1928 – early 1930s. $80.00 – 90.00.

#1197 bowl, 6", for Art Metal Works, Persian Yellow, Silver Green or Black, 1928 – early 1930s. $80.00 – 100.00.

#1207 ashtray, 4½", like #1006 but no foot, for Art Metal Works, Persian Yellow, Silver Green or Black, 1928 – early 1930s. $80.00 – 90.00.

Silver Green #1259 Bird ashtray & match holder 5¾"x 3¾", with ridged match striker along bird's head, 1929 – 1932. $200.00 – 250.00.

#1207A ashtray with 3 rests, 4½", for Art Metal Works, Persian Yellow, Silver Green or Black, 1928 – early 1930s. $80.00 – 90.00.

#1208 square cigarette box, for Rena Rosenthal, 1928 – 1930. $130.00 – 150.00.

#1209 cigarette & match box, for Rena Rosenthal, 1928 – 1931. $150.00 – 165.00.

Bronzeart elephant ashtray stand with original #1300 4½" bowl ashtray in Oxblood glaze (base, inset). $65.00 – 80.00.

1929 Introduction

1930 Introductions

Not Shown:

#1262 cigar cup/vase, 4"x3¾", for Art Metal Works, Silver Green, Persian Yellow, Black, 1930 – 1931. $55.00 – 65.00.

#1262 cigar cup/vase, 4"x3¾", for Art Metal Works, Multi-Color, 1930. $60.00 – 75.00.

#1280 ball ashtray, 6½", for Frankart, Silver Green, Rose, Persian Yellow or Black, 1930 – 1934. $130.00 – 180.00.

#1281 cup ashtray, 2½"x2", for Frankart, Silver Green, Persian Yellow or Black, 1930 – 1934. $120.00 – 150.00.

#1282 square ashtray, 4½", for Frankart, Silver Green, Persian Yellow or Black, 1930 – 1934. $120.00 – 150.00.

#1300 bowl ashtray, 4½", 3 cigar rests (same as Fulper #828), made for Bronzeart, solid-color glazes, 1930 – 1935. $65.00 – 80.00.

#1308 nest ashtray, 3" square, for Frankart, Silver Green or Black, 1930 – 1934. This was the last ashtray shape introduced by Fulper Pottery for Frankart, Inc. $55.00 – 65.00.

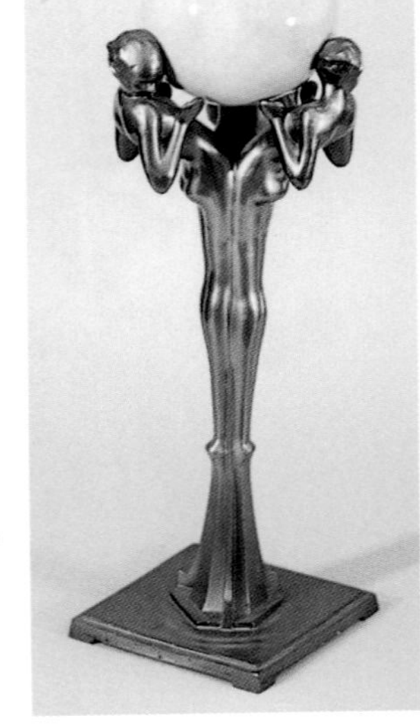

Frankart Gunmetal finish #T335 Three Nudes Smoker's Stand with #1280 6½" ball ashtray insert. Ashtray only, $130.00 – 180.00. Courtesy of the Negley collection.

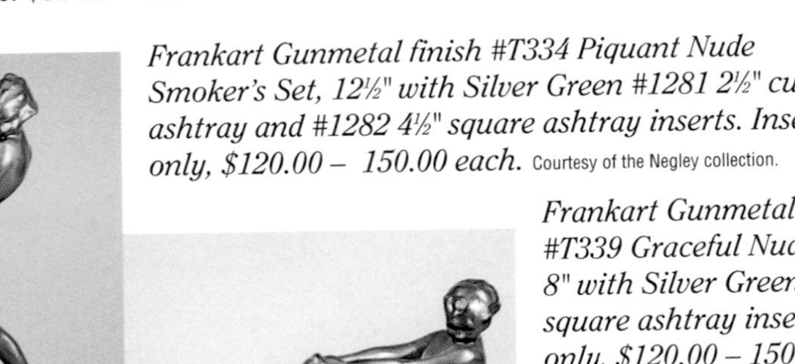

Frankart Gunmetal finish #T334 Piquant Nude Smoker's Set, 12½" with Silver Green #1281 2½" cup ashtray and #1282 4½" square ashtray inserts. Inserts only, $120.00 – 150.00 each. Courtesy of the Negley collection.

Frankart Gunmetal finish #T339 Graceful Nude Ashtray, 8" with Silver Green #1282 4½" square ashtray insert. Ashtray only, $120.00 – 150.00. Courtesy of the Negley collection.

Frankart Gunmetal #T337 Seated Nude Smoker's Set, 7½" with two Silver Green #1308 3" square ashtray inserts and Jadeite glass cigarette box. Ashtray only, $55.00 – 65.00. Courtesy of the Negley collection.

The #1315 – 1317 Jazz Musician ashtrays were only made for approximately one year. The 1930 "Stangl Pottery made by Fulper Pottery Company" catalog stated that these ashtrays were available in the Apple Green, Oxblood, and Lavender glazes, but they were also produced in Silver Green, Persian Yellow, Tangerine, and Colonial Blue.

Not Shown:

#1316 Saxophone ashtray, 10" jazz musician, Stangl 1930 – 1931. $350.00 – 400.00.

#1318 Horse ashtray and match holder, 5½" diameter, 1930 – 1931. $130.00 – 150.00.

#1322 Elephant ashtray, 6" diameter, solid-color glazes, 1930 – 1934. $130.00 – 150.00.

#1322 Elephant ashtray, 6" diameter, Sunburst glaze, 1930 – 1934. $400.00 – 450.00.

#1323 Bird ashtray, 5½" diameter, Sunburst glaze, 1930 – 1934. $200.00 – 250.00.

#1324 Monkey ashtray, 5" diameter, solid-color glazes, 1930 – 1931. $190.00 – 225.00.

#1324 Monkey & Dog ashtray, 5" diameter, solid-color glazes, 1930 – 1931. $190.00 – 225.00.

Oxblood glaze #1315 Mandolin ashtray (left) and #1317 Accordion ashtray (right), 10" jazz musicians, Stangl 1930 – 1931. $350.00 – 400.00 each. From the Stangl and Fulper archival collection, courtesy the Wheaton Village Museum of American Glass.

Tangerine #1323 Bird ashtray, 5½" diameter, color glazes, 1930 – 1934. $130.00 – 150.00. Courtesy of the Brian and Cristi Hahn collection.

Back of a typical APT, NY ashtray insert.

APT, NY

Beginning in 1930, Fulper Pottery Company produced ashtray inserts for APT, NY, yet another manufacturer of novelty cast metal lamps and smoking sets. The inserts were usually identified with the shape number and "APT NY" in-mold marks. The APT, NY metal castings and figures were sometimes, but not always, marked with "APT, NY" or "APT, NY; Pat Applied For."

Not Shown:

#1333 ashtray, 5½", for APT, NY, 1930 – 1932. $60.00 – 75.00.

#1337 round ashtray, 4", for APT, NY, solid-color glazes, 1930 – 1932. $50.00 – 65.00.

#1338 oblong cigarette box, for APT, NY, solid-color glazes, 1930 – 1931. $150.00 – 175.00.

#1339 oblong ashtray, for APT, NY, solid-color glazes, 1930 – 1931. $45.00 – 55.00.

#1375 large ashtray, for APT, NY, solid-color glazes, 1930 – 1931. $75.00 – 95.00.

APT, NY nude figure ashtray stand with #1337 Multi-Color 4" round ashtray. Ashtray only, 1930 – 1931. $80.00 – 95.00. Courtesy of the Hill-Fulper-Stangl Museum.

1931 Introductions

Not Shown:

#1384-A 6-sided ashtray with bird handle, 4", for APT, NY, solid-color glazes, 1931 – 1932. $40.00 – 50.00.

#1384-A 6-sided ashtray with bird handle, 4", for APT, NY, Sunburst glaze, 1931 – 1932. $85.00 – 95.00.

1933 Introductions

During the early 1930s, the following ashtray shapes were produced in the solid-color glazes Colonial Blue, Persian Yellow, Silver Green, Blue-of-the-Sky, Rust, Tangerine, Apple Green, and Surf White. By 1938, the Satin glazes Satin Blue, Satin Green, Satin Yellow, and Satin White were added to the assortment.

Not Shown:

#1656 ashtray with bird and rests, 4", 1933 – 1934. $70.00 – 85.00.

#1657 ashtray bowl, 2 rests, 3½", 1933 – 1940. $20.00 – 25.00.

#1658 ashtray square, triple rests, 1933 – 1940. $20.00 – 25.00.

Small ashtrays #1657 in Silver Green, #1957 in Satin White, and #1658 in Persian Yellow. $20.00 – 25.00 each.

#1659 ashtray round, flat rim, 1933 – 1940. $20.00 – 25.00.
#1660 ashtray round, double rests, 1933 – 1940. $20.00 – 25.00.
#1661 ashtray, six sided, 2 rests, 1933 – 1936. $25.00 – 30.00.

The #1744 Wolf cigarette holder, #1745 Small Pig ashtrays, and #1746 Large Pig ashtrays were intended to be used together as smoking sets. The #1745 Small Pigs were ideal for bridge parties, while the #1746 Large Pig ashtrays were better suited to poker games where most participants smoked cigars.

See page 198 for a comparison of Stangl's #1745 Small Pig ashtray and knock-offs.

Apple Green #1746 Large Pig ashtray, 5½", 1933 – 1934. $150.00 – 175.00. Courtesy of the Cruser collection.

Silver Green #1744 Wolf cigarette holder, 9", Silver Green, made during 1933 only. $2,000.00 – 2,500.00. Courtesy of the Hill-Fulper-Stangl Museum.

Group of #1745 Small Pig ashtray, 3", 1933 – 1944. $35.00 – 45.00 each. Glazed in Green Matte, Persian Yellow, Rust, Silver Green, and Colonial Blue. Courtesy of the Cruser collection.

1935 Introductions

Rust glaze #1388 cigarette box (right), 4½"x3½", matches #1388 Colonial dinnerware, 1935 – 1943. $85.00 – 95.00. #1388 4" ashtray (left), Silver Green. $20.00 – 25.00.

Three #1388 4" coaster ashtrays in Rose, Silver Green, and Cobalt Blue glazes. These were also part of the Colonial dinnerware pattern, 1933 – 1935. $25.00 – 30.00 each.

Not Shown:
#1939 No-Smoke ashtray & cover, 1935 – 1936. $55.00 – 65.00.
#1952 No-Smoke cylinder ashtray, 1935 – 1936. $55.00 – 65.00.
#1953 ashtray oblong, 4¼" 1935 – 1938. $20.00 – 25.00.
#1954 ashtray double ovals, 4¼" 1935 – 1938. $20.00 – 25.00.
#1955 ashtray round snuffer, 1935 – 1936. $25.00 – 35.00.
#1956 round double rest, 4½", 1935 – 1938. $20.00 – 25.00.

Satin Brown #1388 baking shell, also marketed as an ashtray, 1936 – 1942. $12.00 – 18.00.

Satin White #1957 round modern rest, 5", 1935 – 1940. $20.00 – 25.00.

Leaf Green #1958 ashtray boat shape, 5½", 1935 – 1940. $25.00 – 30.00. Courtesy of the Marcena North collection.

See page 241 for special-order ashtray for Restaurant Mayan, New York.

#2022 shell ashtray, 3", 1935 – 1942. $20.00 – 25.00.

#2030 ashtray 4-sided modern, 5½", 1935 – 1936. $35.00 – 45.00.

#2031 ashtray round modern, large, 6", 1935 – 1936. $35.00 – 45.00.

#2032 ashtray round modern, small, 4½", 1935 – 1936. $35.00 – 45.00.

#2074 round ashtray, 6", 1935 – 1938. $20.00 – 25.00.

#2083 Pelican ashtray round, made for B&A Co. solid-color glazes, 1935 – 1936. $275.00 – 350.00.

#2084 Pelican ashtray oval, made for B&A Co. solid-color glazes, 1935 – 1936. $275.00 – 350.00.

#2089 Scotty Dog ashtray, 4½", made for B&A Co. solid-color glazes, 1935 – 1936. $275.00 – 350.00.

Colonial Blue #2000 ashtray 4", matches #2000 Americana dinnerware, 1935 – 1944. $20.00 – 25.00. During the early 1940s, the #2000 ashtray was also sold in sets of three with a wrought aluminum or chrome stand for $1.20 per set.

1937 Introductions

Not Shown:

#3041 Spiral ashtray, 5", 1937 – 1945. $20.00 – 25.00.

#3044 Scroll ashtray, 5"x4", 1937 – 1937. $25.00 – 35.00.

#3049 No-Smoke cylinder ashtray, 1937 – 1938. $55.00 – 65.00.

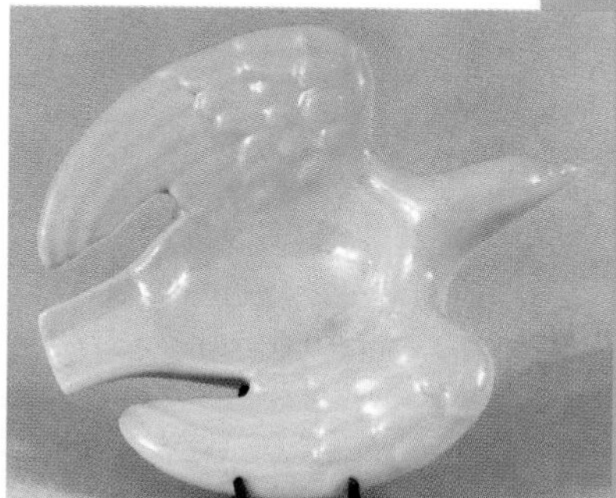

Persian Yellow #3210 Bird ashtray, 4", 1938 – 1942. $50.00 – 60.00.

1938 Introductions

Not Shown:

#3239 ashtray Leaf, 8"x7¾", Satin glazes, 1938 – 1942. $25.00 – 35.00.

#3240 ashtray Shell, 8"x7½", Satin glazes, 1938 – 1942. $25.00 – 35.00.

#3241 ashtray Rectangle, 7"x6", Satin glazes, 1938 – 1942. $25.00 – 30.00.

#3242 ashtray Three Arm, 9" diameter, Satin glazes, 1938 – 1942. $30.00 – 40.00.

Cigarette Boxes and Smokers Giftware, 1940s – 1970s

By the late 1930s, hand-painted peasant-style ceramics had become especially trendy. Martin Stangl's hand-painted Terra Rose art finish and Pennsylvania Dutch-inspired hand-carved, hand-painted dinnerware patterns were the Fulper Pottery Company's answer to these style demands. Even though these two styles of decoration were vastly different, Stangl classified both in the Terra Rose category because of the red color base clay showing through the finish. During the 1940s, the solid-color and satin glazes were gradually giving way to the increasingly popular Terra Rose and hand-carved, hand-painted finishes.

Throughout the 1950s, 1960s, and 1970s, Stangl applied a great assortment of fashionable decorative finishes to the most popular smoking accessory shapes. However, it was Stangl's cigarette box sets and large ashtrays with vibrant hand-carved, hand-painted floral, abstract, and game bird motifs that were most popular and that continue to be the most widely collected of Stangl's smoking memorabilia.

The following lists include primarily cigarette boxes and matching ashtrays. For complete listings of all items, including all ashtrays and smoking items produced in these finishes, please see the sections for the individual artware finishes.

1941 Introductions

Terra Rose

These items were produced in the Terra Rose colors Blue, Green or Mauve. During the later 1940s, a very few of the pieces were also produced in Terra Rose Yellow, a hard-to-find color. Terra Rose Blue is the most desirable of the Terra Rose colors. Green was produced in the greatest quantities so is easiest to find. Mauve is the least desirable of the Terra Rose colors so usually sells for much less than Blue. The Mauve color can vary from rich purplish-brown to a subtle dark brown. Mauve is *not* the pale pinky gray-brown color of undecorated portions of Terra Rose pieces. These undecorated portions show the true color of the red-clay body reacting with the Silk glaze.

Terra Rose Green #3241 ashtray, rectangle, 7"x6", 1942 – 1944. $25.00 – 30.00.

Terra Rose Blue #3242 ashtray, three arm, 9" diameter, 1942 – 1944. $25.00 – 35.00.

Terra Rose Mauve #3520 cigarette box, ashtray cover, flower, 4½"x4", 1941 – 1943. $85.00 – 95.00. Courtesy of the Robert Sherman collection.

Terra Rose Blue #3524 ashtray, Ivy leaf 5¼"x4¼", 1941 – 1943. $15.00 – 20.00.

Terra Rose Mauve #3549 match holder Horse, 4¼" x 3½", 1941 only. $450.00 – 550.00. Courtesy of the Robert and Shirley Bond collection.

Terra Rose Green #3602 cigarette cup, 3 corner, 2¾", for Frederik Lunning. $25.00 – 35.00.

Terra Rose Green #3817 ashtray, windproof, 6", 1949 – 1960 (Kay Hackett design). $12.00 – 18.00.

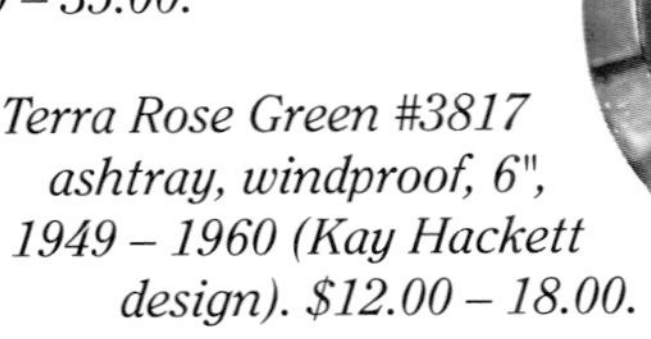

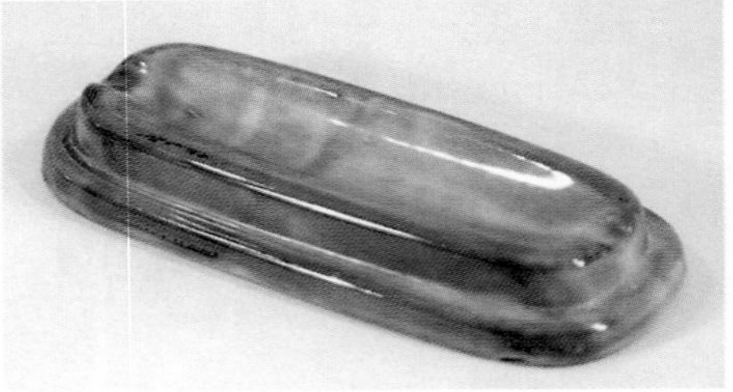

Terra Rose Green #3846 long ashtray, 6¼"x2⅝", 1953 – 1960. $15.00 – 20.00.

#2022 shell ashtray, 3", 1941 – 1942. $20.00 – 25.00.
#3239 leaf server or ashtray 8", 1942 – 1944. $20.00 – 25.00.
#3240 shell candy dish or ashtray, 8", 1942 – 1944. $25.00 – 35.00.
#3521 cigarette box, ashtray cover, square leaf, 5½"x4", 1941 – 1943. $85.00 – 95.00.
#3434 coaster ashtray, 5", Blue, Green, Mauve or Yellow, 1942 – 1960. $18.00 – 22.00.
#3522 ashtray, shell 5"x4½", 1941 – 1943. $20.00 – 25.00.
#3523 ashtray, triangle leaf 6¼" x4", 1941 – 1943. $20.00 – 25.00.
#3525 ashtray, Oak leaf 5½"x5", 1941 – 1943. $20.00 – 25.00.
#3526 ashtray, Cosmos 5½"x5", 1941 – 1943. $20.00 – 25.00.
#3527 ashtray, triangle leaf, 4¼"x3", 1941 – 1943. $15.00 – 20.00.
#3528 ashtray, square leaf, 3¼"x3", 1941 – 1943. $15.00 – 20.00.
#3529 ashtray, Ivy leaf, 4"x3½", 1941 – 1943. $15.00 – 20.00.
#3530 ashtray, Oak leaf, 4"x2¾", 1941 – 1943. $15.00 – 20.00.
#3531 ashtray, square Cosmos, 3½", 1941 – 1943. $15.00 – 20.00.
#3532 ashtray, square leaf, 5¾"x4½", 1941 – 1943. $15.00 – 20.00.
#3533 match holder, Rabbit, 4¼" x 3", 1941 only. $550.00 – 600.00.
#3534 match holder, Dog, 4¼" x 4", 1941 only. $450.00 – 550.00.
#3601 ashtray, 3 corner, 3¾", for Frederik Lunning. $25.00 – 30.00.
#3603 cigarette holder, 2⅝", for Frederik Lunning. $25.00 – 35.00.
#3604 cigarette box, 3¾" high, for Frederik Lunning. $85.00 – 95.00.
#3610 ashtray, 3 corner, 5½", for Frederik Lunning. $25.00 – 35.00.
#3636 cigarette box 4"x3½", flat top, Blue, Green, Mauve or Yellow, 1942 – 1946
#3636 coaster ashtray, 4", Blue, Green, Mauve or Yellow, 1942 – 1960. $18.00 – 22.00.
#3816 ashtray, windproof, 8", 1949 – 1960 (Kay Hackett design). $18.00 – 22.00.

Terra Rose Green #3897S Pond ashtray, square, 4"x4", with green crystals (Ed Pettingil design), 1954 – 1956. $20.00 – 25.00. Courtesy of the Ben and Floss Avila collection.

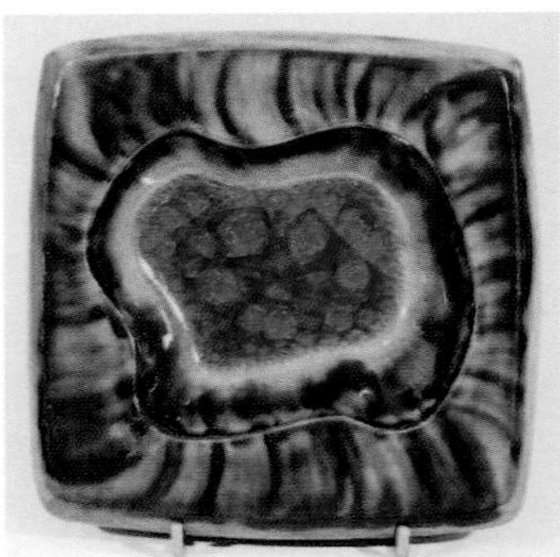

Terra Rose Green #3897M Pond ashtray, 5" square, with blue crystals (Ed Pettingil design), 1954 – 1956. $22.00 – 28.00. Courtesy of the Luke and Nancy Ruepp collection.

#3897L Pond ashtray, square 6½"x6½" (Ed Pettingil design), 1954 – 1956. $25.00 – 35.00.
#3904 ashtray, free form 7"x4½" (Ed Pettingil design), 1954 – 1956. $20.00 – 25.00.
#3905 ashtray, free form (same as #3904), 5"x3½" (Ed Pettingil design), 1954 – 1956. $15.00 – 20.00.
#3906 ashtray, notched, free form 5½" (Ed Pettingil design), 1954 – 1956. $12.00 – 18.00.
#3914 ashtray, square with square well 9" (Kay Hackett design), 1954 – 1956. $20.00 – 25.00.
#3915 ashtray, square with round well 9" (Kay Hackett design), 1954 – 1956. $20.00 – 25.00.
#3926 ashtray, oval, plain, 10¾"x8" (Kay Hackett design), 1955 – 1956. $15.00 – 20.00.
#3927 ashtray, casual, 10½"x 7½" (Kay Hackett design), 1955 – 1956. $25.00 – 30.00.
#3937 ashtray, 7" diameter, 1955 – 1956. $25.00 – 30.00.
#3938 ashtray, free form 7¼"x5⅝" (Ed Pettingil design), 1955 – 1956. $20.00 – 25.00.
#3939 ashtray, rectangular, 9⅛"x9⅛" (Ed Pettingil design), 1955 – 1956. $20.00 – 25.00.
#3940 ashtray, irregular shape 6½"x5"x8" (Ed Pettingil design), 1955 – 1956. $20.00 – 25.00.
#3941 ashtray, Safety, free form 5⅜"x6¼"x7 (Ed Pettingil design), 1955 – 1956. $20.00 – 25.00.
#3942 ashtray, Safety, oval 8½"x7" (Ed Pettingil design), 1955 – 1956. $15.00 – 20.00.
#4032 ashtray, Oak leaf 5½"x4" (orig. #3525), 1958 – 1960. $10.00 – 15.00.
#4033 ashtray, Cosmos 5½" (orig. #3526), 1958 – 1960. $10.00 – 15.00.
#4034 ashtray, triangle leaf 6½"x4" (orig. #3523), 1958 – 1960. $10.00 – 15.00.
#4035 ashtray, Ivy leaf 5¼"x4¼" (orig. #3524), 1958 – 1960. $10.00 – 15.00.
#4036 ashtray, leaf 6"x4½", 1958 – 1960. $10.00 – 15.00.
#4037 ashtray, shell dish, 5"x5½" (orig. #3522), 1958 – 1960. $10.00 – 15.00.

Hand-Carved, Hand-Painted Cigarette Box Sets

Kay Hackett designed the first hand-carved, hand-painted cigarette box motifs. Directly influenced by antique Pennsylvania Dutch redware, these cigarette boxes were instantly popular. Several of the motifs went on to become even more popular as dinnerware patterns than they had as cigarette box sets. The Tulip, Single Bird, and Double Bird motifs each began on cigarette boxes but attained much greater recognition as dinnerware patterns.

During the 1940s, the engobe was hand-brushed on all the cigarette box and coaster ashtray shapes, so each exhibits an authentic hand-crafted appearance. These items were usually marked with a "Terra Rose" underglaze stamp, and the pattern number, pattern name, or both. Sometimes they were simply not marked at all.

All names used are original Stangl Pottery names for these items. Shape numbers (usually also a pattern number) used for each motif are in parentheses. Following are basic box and ashtray shapes used for Stangl's hand-carved, hand-painted smoking item motifs with sizes.

Early 1940s sample of a Pennsylvania Dutch styled smoking set on experimental cigarette box and ashtray shapes. From the Stangl and Fulper archival collection, courtesy the Wheaton Village Museum of American Glass.

Not Shown:
#3630 cigarette box 5½"x4½", straight sides, introduced 1942.
#3630 coaster ashtray 5" round (also called #3434), introduced 1942.
#3636 cigarette box 4½"x3¾", straight sides, introduced 1942.
#3636 coaster ashtray 4½" round, introduced 1942.
#3665 cigarette box 5½"x4½", fluted sides, introduced 1942.
#3665 coaster ashtray 4½" square, fluted edge, introduced 1942.
#3772 cigarette box 5"x4", pagoda top, introduced 1947.
#3773 coaster ashtray 5¼" squared-round, introduced 1947.
#3791 cigarette box 7¾"x3½" double compartment, oblong, introduced 1948.
#3816 ashtray 8" windproof, introduced 1949.
#3817 ashtray 6" windproof, introduced 1949.
#3876 ashtray 8⅞"x3½" double compartment, oblong, introduced 1952.
#3898 cigarette box 5½"x4¼" fluted, introduced 1954.
#3898-5 ashtray 5" fluted, introduced 1954.

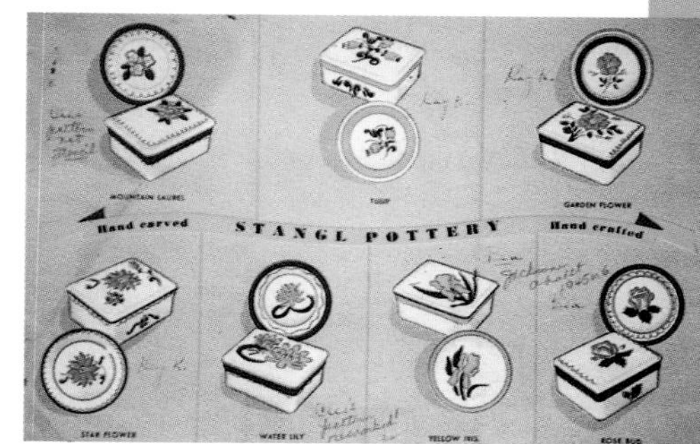

Stangl Pottery cigarette set brochure from 1946 showing the six cigarette set patterns promoted that year. Courtesy of Cleo Salerno.

#3898-7 ashtray 7" fluted, introduced 1954.
#3902 cigarette box 5¼"x5¼" modern square, introduced 1954.
#3902 coaster ashtray 5¼" modern round, introduced 1954.
#3903 cigarette box 5¾"x4½" high-edged cover, introduced 1954.
#3903A cigarette box 5¾"x4½" high-edged ashtray cover, introduced 1954.
#3914 ashtray 9¼" square with square well, introduced 1954.
#3915 ashtray 9¼" square with round well, introduced 1954.
#3926 ashtray 10¾"x8" oval, introduced 1955.
#3926-9 ashtray 9"x7" oval, introduced 1955.
#3927 ashtray 10½"x7" casual, introduced 1955.

1942 Introductions

Pennsylvania Dutch styles predominate this assortment of patterns.

Tulip #3630 cigarette box (shape #3630), yellow (Kay Hackett design), 1942 – 1960. $50.00 – 60.00.

Tulip #3630 coaster ashtray (shape #3630), yellow (Kay Hackett design), 1942 – 1960. $20.00 – 25.00.

Tulip #3630 cigarette box (shape #3630), blue for Marshall, Field & Co. (Kay Hackett design), 1942 – 1955. $180.00 – 225.00.

Tulip #3630 coaster ashtray (shape #3630), blue for Marshall, Field & Co. (Kay Hackett design), 1942 – 1955. $25.00 – 35.00.

Pink Star Flower #3631 cigarette box (shape #3630, Kay Hackett design), 1942 – 1948. $55.00 – 65.00.

Pink Star Flower #3631 coaster ashtray (shape #3630, Kay Hackett design), 1942 – 1948. $25.00 – 30.00.

Single Bird #3632 coaster ashtray (shape #3630) for Lunning (Kay Hackett design), 1942 – 1952. $65.00 – 75.00.

Double Bird #3633 cigarette box (shape #3630) for Lunning (Kay Hackett design), 1942 – 1948. $400.00 – 500.00.

Floral Design #3636 cigarette box (shape #3636, Kay Hackett design), 1942 – 1945. $55.00 – 65.00.

Floral Design #3636 coaster ashtray (shape #3636, Kay Hackett design), 1942 – 1945. $20.00 – 25.00.

Hearts Design #3638 cigarette box (shape #3636, Kay Hackett design), 1942 – 1945. $60.00 – 75.00.

Hearts Design #3638 coaster ashtray (shape #3636, Kay Hackett design), 1942 – 1945. $25.00 – 35.00.

Yellow Tulip #3630 cigarette box, $50.00 – 60.00, and coaster ashtrays, $20.00 – 25.00 each, 1942 – 1960. Courtesy of the Luke and Nancy Ruepp collection.

Pink Star Flower #3631 cigarette box, $55.00 – 65.00, and coaster ashtray, $25.00 – 30.00, 1942 – 1948. Courtesy of the Marcena North collection.

Single Bird #3632 cigarette box (shape #3630) for Lunning (Kay Hackett design), 1942 – 1952. $200.00 – 250.00. Courtesy of the Marcena North collection.

Double Bird #3633 coaster ashtray (shape #3630) for Lunning (Kay Hackett design), 1942 – 1948. $85.00 – 125.00. Courtesy of the Luke and Nancy Ruepp collection.

Floral Design #3636 cigarette box, $55.00 – 65.00, and coaster ashtray, 1942 – 1945, $20.00 – 25.00 each. Courtesy of the Luke and Nancy Ruepp collection.

Hearts Design #3638 cigarette box, $60.00 – 75.00, and coaster ashtray, $25.00 – 35.00, 1942 – 1945. Courtesy of the Marcena North collection.

Pink Tulip & Buds #3665 cigarette box, $55.00 – 70.00, and coaster ashtray, $25.00 – 35.00, 1942 – 1945. Courtesy of the Marcena North collection.

Daisy Design #3666 cigarette box, $60.00 – 75.00, and coaster ashtrays, $25.00 – 35.00 each, 1942 – 1945. Courtesy of the Luke and Nancy Ruepp collection.

Garden Flower #3698 cigarette box, $55.00 – 70.00, and coaster ashtray, $25.00 – 35.00, 1942 – 1948. Courtesy of the Luke and Nancy Ruepp collection.

Pink Tulip & Buds #3665 cigarette box (shape #3666, Kay Hackett design), 1942 – 1945. $55.00 – 70.00.

Pink Tulip & Buds #3665 coaster ashtray (shape #3666, Kay Hackett design), 1942 – 1945. $25.00 – 35.00.

Daisy Design #3666 cigarette box (shape #3666, Kay Hackett design), 1942 – 1945. $60.00 – 75.00.

Daisy Design #3666 coaster ashtray (shape #3666, Kay Hackett design), 1942 – 1945. $25.00 – 35.00.

Garden Flower #3698 cigarette box (shape #3630, Kay Hackett design), 1942 – 1948. $55.00 – 70.00.

Garden Flower #3698 coaster ashtray (shape #3630, Kay Hackett design), 1942 – 1948. $25.00 – 35.00.

1944 Introductions

By the mid 1940s, the Pennsylvania Dutch styles were giving way to more modern floral motifs.

Jonquil #3744 cigarette box (shape #3630) for Lunning (Betty Stangl Thomas design), 1944 – 1948. $185.00 – 225.00.

Jonquil #3744 coaster ashtray (shape #3630) for Lunning (Betty Stangl Thomas design), 1944 – 1948. $60.00 – 75.00.

Jonquil #3744 coaster ashtray (experimental coupe shape) for Lunning, 1947 only. $130.00 – 150.00.

Doylestown Rotary cigarette box (shape #3630), commemorative for Doylestown Rotary Club, Doylestown, PA, 1944 only. $175.00 – 200.00.

Doylestown Rotary coaster ashtray (shape #3630), commemorative for Doylestown Rotary Club, Doylestown, PA, 1944 only. $85.00 – 95.00.

1945 Introductions

Morrisville Rotary #3630 coaster ashtray with blue balloon flower, made for Morrisville Rotary Club, Morrisville, PA, 1945 – 1946. $85.00 – 95.00.

1946 Introductions

Mountain Laurel #3759 cigarette box (shape #3630, Cleo Salerno design), 1946 – 1948. $65.00 – 80.00. Courtesy of the Robert Sherman collection.

Mountain Laurel #3759 coaster ashtray (shape #3630, Cleo Salerno design), 1946 – 1948. $25.00 – 30.00. Courtesy of the Jim and Barbara Nelson collection.

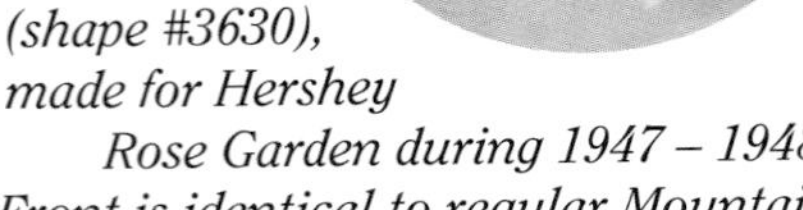

Back of Mountain Laurel #3759 coaster ashtray (shape #3630), made for Hershey Rose Garden during 1947 – 1948. Front is identical to regular Mountain Laurel coaster ashtrays. $50.00 – 60.00. Courtesy of the Jim and Barbara Nelson collection.

Rose Bud #3760 cigarette box, $65.00 – 80.00, and coaster ashtray, $25.00 – 35.00, 1946 – 1948. Courtesy of the Marcena North collection.

Yellow Iris #3761 cigarette box, $60.00 – 75.00, and coaster ashtray, $25.00 – 30.00, 1946 – 1948. Courtesy of the Marcena North collection.

Not Shown:

Rose Bud #3760 cigarette box (shape #3630, Bea Jackson design), 1946 – 1948. $65.00 – 80.00.

Rose Bud #3760 coaster ashtray (shape #3630, Bea Jackson design), 1946 – 1948. $25.00 – 35.00.

Yellow Iris #3761 cigarette box (shape #3630, Bea Jackson design), 1946 – 1948. $60.00 – 75.00.

Yellow Iris #3761 coaster ashtray (shape #3630, Bea Jackson design), 1946 – 1948. $25.00 – 30.00.

Water Lily #3762 cigarette box (shape #3630, Cleo Salerno design), 1946 – 1948. $65.00 – 80.00.

Water Lily #3762 coaster ashtray (shape #3630, Cleo Salerno design), 1946 – 1948. $25.00 – 30.00.

American Garden #3763 cigarette box (shape #3630) for Lunning (Martin Stangl design), 1946 – 1948. $200.00 – 250.00.

American Garden #3763 coaster ashtray (shape #3630) for Lunning (Martin Stangl design), 1946 – 1948. $60.00 – 75.00.

1947 Introductions

Water Lily #3762 cigarette box, $65.00 – 80.00, and coaster ashtray, $25.00 – 30.00, 1946 – 1948. Courtesy of the Marcena North collection.

American Garden #3763 cigarette box, $200.00 – 250.00, and coaster ashtray, $60.00 – 75.00, 1946 – 1948. Courtesy of the Luke and Nancy Ruepp collection.

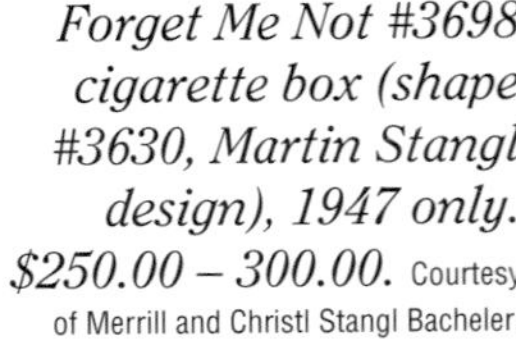

Alfred University Summer Picnic 1947 #3630 coaster ashtray, commemorative. 1947 only. $130.00 – 150.00. Courtesy of the Hill-Fulper-Stangl Museum.

Prelude #3769 coaster ashtray (shape #3630), 1947 – 1950. $20.00 – 25.00.

Forget Me Not #3698 cigarette box (shape #3630, Martin Stangl design), 1947 only. $250.00 – 300.00. Courtesy of Merrill and Christl Stangl Bacheler.

Forget Me Not #3698 coaster ashtray (experimental coupe shape, Martin Stangl design), 1947 only. $130.00 – 150.00. Courtesy of Merrill and Christl Stangl Bacheler.

1948 Introductions

Kay Hackett was inspired to create several tropical flower motifs after a friend presented her with a book of Hawaiian flora. Other motifs were simply adaptations of popular New Jersey garden and landscape plants.

The shapes of the oblong and pagoda top cigarette boxes challenged designers to develop design motifs beyond the established horizons. The pagoda top box was a particular test. Kay Hackett sought to design motifs for that shape that would be accentuated by the contour of the lid and appear three-dimensional. The Grape and Marsh Rose motifs are particularly good examples of this illusion.

In 1952, the #3772 pagoda top box and #3773 squared-round coaster ashtray shapes were discontinued. Many of the motifs on those shapes were then adapted to the #3630 cigarette box shape and produced for several more years. Look under the 1952 Introductions heading for these motifs on the #3630 box shape.

Tropic Flower (originally Hibiscus) #3791 cigarette box, $80.00 – 90.00, and coaster ashtrays, $20.00 – 25.00, 1948 – 1952. Courtesy of the Luke and Nancy Ruepp collection.

Tropic Flower (originally Hibiscus) #3791 cigarette box (shape #3791, Kay Hackett design), 1948 – 1952. $80.00 – 90.00.

Tropic Flower (originally Hibiscus) #3791 coaster ashtray (shape #3773, Kay Hackett design), 1948 – 1952. $20.00 – 25.00.

Flower Buds (originally Shell Ginger) #3792 cigarette box (shape #3791, Kay Hackett design), 1948 – 1952. $80.00 – 90.00.

Flower Buds (originally Shell Ginger) #3792 coaster ashtray (shape #3773, Kay Hackett design), 1948 – 1952. $20.00 – 25.00.

Flower Buds (originally Shell Ginger) #3792 cigarette box, $80.00 – 90.00, and coaster ashtray, $20.00 – 25.00, 1948 – 1952. Courtesy of the Marcena North collection.

Trillium #3793 cigarette box (shape #3791, Kay Hackett design), 1948 – 1952. $70.00 – 85.00. Courtesy of the Luke and Nancy Ruepp collection.

Gladiola #3794 cigarette box, $70.00 – 85.00, and coaster ashtrays, $22.00 – 28.00 each, 1948 – 1952. Courtesy of the Marcena North collection.

Trillium #3793 coaster ashtray (shape #3773, Kay Hackett design), 1948 – 1952. $25.00 – 30.00.

Gladiola #3794 cigarette box (shape #3791, Kay Hackett design), 1948 – 1952. $70.00 – 85.00.

Gladiola #3794 coaster ashtray (shape #3773, Kay Hackett design), 1948 – 1952. $22.00 – 28.00.

Trumpet Flower (originally Honeysuckle) #3795 cigarette box (shape #3791, Kay Hackett design), 1948 – 1952. $85.00 – 95.00.

Trumpet Flower (originally Honeysuckle) #3795 coaster ashtray (shape #3773, Kay Hackett design), 1948 – 1952. $25.00 – 30.00.

Dogwood #3796 coaster ashtray (shape #3773, Kay Hackett design), 1948 – 1952. $25.00 – 30.00.

Dogwood #3796 cigarette box (shape #3791, Kay Hackett design), 1948 – 1952. $80.00 – 90.00. Courtesy of the Luke and Nancy Ruepp collection.

Trumpet Flower (originally Honeysuckle) #3795 cigarette box, $85.00 – 95.00, and coaster ashtray, $25.00 – 30.00, 1948 – 1952. Courtesy of the Brian and Cristi Hahn collection.

Variety of Ivy #3797 cigarette boxes, $45.00 – 60.00 each, and coaster ashtrays, $20.00 – 25.00 each, 1948 – 1952. Courtesy of the Marcena North collection.

Citrus Fruit #3798 cigarette box, $55.00 – 65.00, and coaster ashtrays, $25.00 – 30.00 each, 1948 – 1952. Courtesy of the Luke and Nancy Ruepp collection.

Marsh Rose (originally Apple Blossom) #3799 cigarette box, $70.00 – 85.00, and coaster ashtrays, $25.00 – 30.00 each, 1948 – 1952. Courtesy of the Brian and Cristi Hahn collection.

Grape #3800 cigarette box, $80.00 – 90.00, and coaster ashtrays, $25.00 – 35.00 each, 1948 – 1950. Courtesy of the Brian and Cristi Hahn collection.

Blue Butterfly #3802 cigarette box, $65.00 – 80.00, and coaster ashtrays, $25.00 – 30.00 each. 1948 – 1950. Courtesy of the Luke and Nancy Ruepp collection.

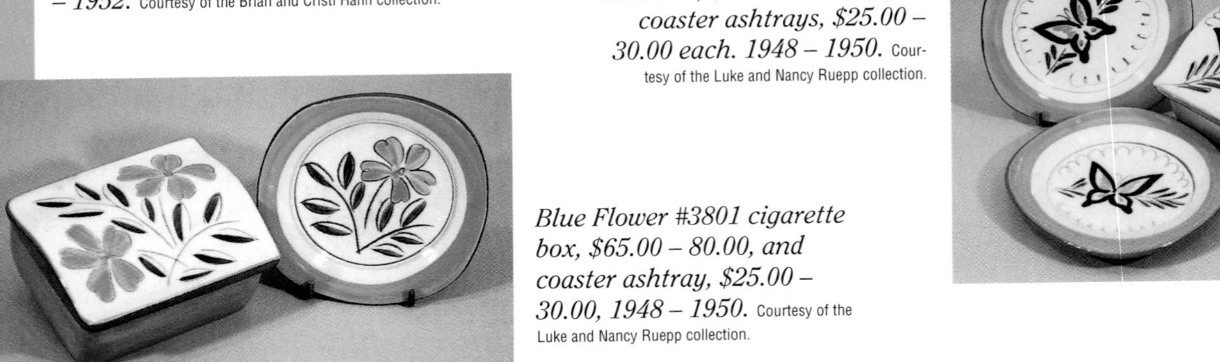

Blue Flower #3801 cigarette box, $65.00 – 80.00, and coaster ashtray, $25.00 – 30.00, 1948 – 1950. Courtesy of the Luke and Nancy Ruepp collection.

Ivy #3797 cigarette box (shape #3791, Kay Hackett design), 1948 – 1952. $45.00 – 60.00.
Ivy #3797 coaster ashtray (shape #3773, Kay Hackett design), 1948 – 1952. $20.00 – 25.00.
Ivy #3797 cigarette box (shape #3772, Kay Hackett design), 1948 – 1952. $45.00 – 60.00.
Citrus Fruit #3798 cigarette box (shape #3772, Kay Hackett design), 1948 – 1952. $55.00 – 65.00.
Citrus Fruit #3798 coaster ashtray (shape #3773, Kay Hackett design), 1948 – 1952. $25.00 – 30.00.
Marsh Rose (originally Apple Blossom) #3799 cigarette box (shape #3772, Kay Hackett design), 1948 – 1952. $70.00 – 85.00.
Marsh Rose (originally Apple Blossom) #3799 coaster ashtray (shape #3773, Kay Hackett design), 1948 – 1952. $25.00 – 30.00.
Grape #3800 cigarette box (shape #3772, Kay Hackett design), 1948 – 1950. $80.00 – 90.00.
Grape #3800 coaster ashtray (shape #3773, Kay Hackett design), 1948 – 1950. $25.00 – 35.00.
Blue Flower #3801 cigarette box (shape #3772, Kay Hackett design), 1948 – 1950. $65.00 – 80.00.
Blue Flower #3801 coaster ashtray (shape #3773, Kay Hackett design), 1948 – 1950. $25.00 – 30.00.
Blue Butterfly #3802 cigarette box (shape #3772, Kay Hackett design), 1948 – 1950. $65.00 – 80.00.
Blue Butterfly #3802 coaster ashtray (shape #3773, Kay Hackett design), 1948 – 1950. $25.00 – 30.00.

The following motifs were in very limited production during 1948 only.

Pink Butterfly #3802 cigarette box (shape #3772, Kay Hackett design), 1948 only. $275.00 – 325.00.

Calla Lily coaster ashtray (shape #3773, Kay Hackett design), 1948 only. $100.00 – 125.00.

Fruit (#3697 dinnerware motif) coaster ashtray, carved motif (shape #3773, Kay Hackett design), 1948 only. $100.00 – 125.00.

Shore Birds coaster ashtray (shape #3773), 1948 only. $100.00 – 125.00.

Tropic Birds coaster ashtray (shape #3773), 1948 only. $100.00 – 125.00.

Pink Butterfly #3802 coaster ashtray (shape #3773, Kay Hackett design), 1948 only. $100.00 – 125.00. Courtesy of the Luke and Nancy Ruepp collection.

Calla Lily cigarette box (shape #3791, Kay Hackett design), 1948 only. $375.00 – 400.00.

Fruit (#3697 dinnerware motif) cigarette box (shape #3791, Kay Hackett design), 1948 only. $450.00 – 500.00.

Shore Birds cigarette box (shape #3791), 1948 only. $500.00 – 600.00.

On The Line In '49 #3630 coaster ashtray, commemorative, 1948 only. $85.00 – 95.00. Courtesy of the Hill-Fulper-Stangl Museum.

Tropic Birds cigarette box (shape #3791), 1948 only. $500.00 – 600.00.

1949 Introductions

Not Shown:

Willow #3806 cigarette box (shape #3630, Kay Hackett design), 1949 only. $175.00 – 200.00.

Willow #3806 coaster ashtray (shape #3630, Kay Hackett design), 1949 only. $40.00 – 50.00.

Chicory #3809 cigarette box, brushed engobe (shape #3630, Kay Hackett design), 1949 only. $175.00 – 225.00.

Chicory #3809 coaster ashtray, brushed engobe (shape #3630, Kay Hackett design), 1949 only. $35.00 – 45.00.

Egret #3823 ashtray 8" windproof (Kay Hackett design), 1949 – 1950. $225.00 – 275.00.

Kay Hackett's original rendering for the #3820 Duck ashtray motif. Courtesy of Kay Hackett.

The trend for large decorated ashtrays was just beginning in the late 1940s, so Kay Hackett designed the windproof ashtray shapes and a series of motifs for them in 1949. The decorative theme of the ashtray motifs was geared toward patio entertaining and featured outdoor themes. By the end of the 1950s, these motifs evolved into Stangl's popular Sportsman's Giftware. The interiors of the windproof ashtrays were brushed with engobe for the motif, and the rim was left red clay. The exteriors of the ashtrays were glazed with Silk glaze.

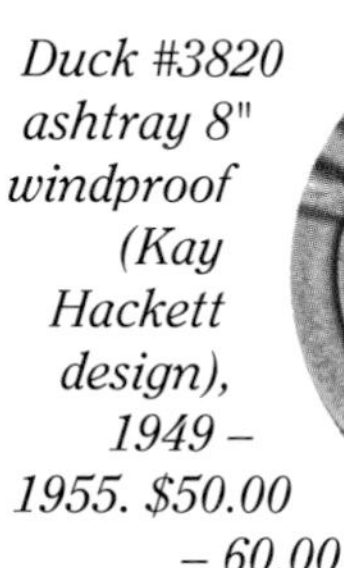

Duck #3820 ashtray 8" windproof (Kay Hackett design), 1949 – 1955. $50.00 – 60.00.

Horse #3821 ashtray 8" windproof (Kay Hackett design), 1949 – 1950. $200.00 – 250.00. Courtesy of Elaine Martin.

Buck #3822 ashtray 8" windproof, facing right (Kay Hackett design), 1949 – 1950. $200.00 – 250.00. Courtesy of the Hill-Fulper-Stangl Museum.

Hunting Dog #3824 ashtray 8" windproof (Kay Hackett design), 1949 – 1955. $50.00 – 60.00.

Fish #3824 ashtray 8" windproof (Kay Hackett design), 1949 – 1955. $65.00 – 80.00.

"Bird Dog" ashtray 8" windproof, novelty motif - dog's head with pheasant's tail, 1949 only. $500.00 – 600.00.

1950 Windproof Ashtray Introductions

Thatcher Furnace 100th Anniversary 6" windproof ashtray commemorative 1950 only. $35.00 – 45.00. Courtesy of the Brian and Cristi Hahn collection.

Wind Swept 8" windproof ashtray, designed by Martin Stangl, executed by Kay Hackett. Courtesy of Merrill and Christl Stangl Bacheler.

Wind Swept 6" windproof ashtray with Tern, designed by Kay Hackett, another gift from Martin Stangl. Courtesy of Merrill and Christl Stangl Bacheler.

Martin Stangl presented the "Wind Swept" ashtrays to his son-in-law and daughter Merrill and Christl Bacheler on the purchase of their beach house in 1950. Martin Stangl's sense of humor is shown by his having the house seem to be a tar-paper beach shack, complete with overgrown weeds and litter! He also gave them at the same time an ashtray showing the house as it really appeared. This ashtray has been treasured by the Bacheler family for over 50 years.

1951 Windproof Ashtray Introductions

By the end of 1950, the Horse, Buck, and Egret windproof ashtrays were discontinued and replaced with three newly designed motifs, Sword Fish, Deer, and Pheasant. These remaining six windproof ashtray designs were then produced through 1955.

Sword Fish #3861 ashtray 8" windproof (Kay Hackett design), 1951 – 1955. $50.00 – 60.00.

Deer #3862 ashtray 8" windproof, facing left (Kay Hackett design), 1951 – 1955. $50.00 – 60.00.

Pheasant #3863 ashtray 8" windproof (Kay Hackett design), 1951 – 1955. $60.00 – 75.00.

1954 Windproof Ashtray Introductions

D.V.T.G.A 8" windproof ashtray, made to commemorate the 35th tournament of the Delaware Valley Golf Association. One ashtray was made for each participant and inscribed with his name. 1954 only. $95.00 – 130.00. Courtesy of the Bill Servis, Susan Lewis collection.

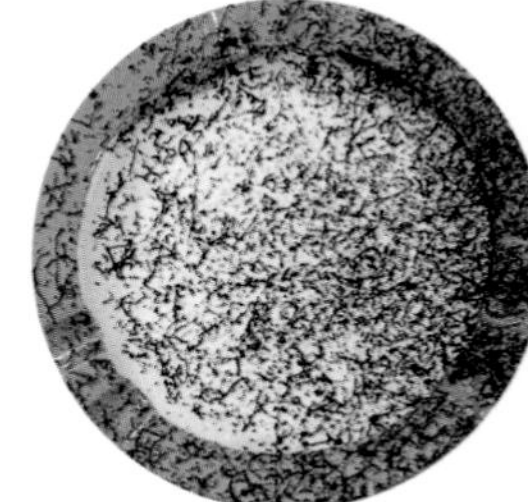

Veiled #3816 ashtray, windproof, 8", 1954 only (Kay Hackett design). $40.00 – 50.00. Courtesy of the Hill-Fulper-Stangl Museum.

Veiled #3817 ashtray, windproof, 6", 1954 only (Kay Hackett design). $25.00 – 35.00.

1957 Windproof Ashtray Introductions

Holly Wreath 8" windproof ashtray (Kay Hackett design), 1957 – 1962. $55.00 – 65.00. Courtesy of the Luke and Nancy Ruepp collection.

1972 Windproof Ashtray Introductions

Several game bird and Christmas motif decals were applied to the windproof ashtray shapes during 1972 and 1973.

Not Shown:

Game bird decal #3816, windproof 8" ashtray, 1972 – 1973. $45.00 – 55.00.

Father Christmas decal ashtray #3816, windproof 8", 1972 – 1973. $35.00 – 45.00. Courtesy of the Marcena North collection.

Cigarette Box and Coaster Ashtray Seconds, late 1940s:

During the late 1940s and early 1950s, many flawed cigarette boxes and coaster ashtrays were decorated with the pattern wholly painted French Green, Yellow, or very rarely Blue #95. In most cases the value of a French Green second cigarette box or coaster ashtray is less than that of the same pattern decorated in full-color.

French Green seconds Rhododendron cigarette box and coaster ashtray. Courtesy of the Luke and Nancy Ruepp collection.

French Green seconds Blue Flower and Dogwood cigarette boxes. Courtesy of the Brian and Cristi Hahn collection.

French Green seconds Calla Lily cigarette box. Courtesy of the Robert Sherman collection.

1950 Introductions

In 1950, the following motifs were all produced with hand-brushed engobe. By 1952, these motifs were applied to bright, smooth sprayed engobe so can be found on either finish. Most of these cigarette sets were so popular they enjoyed continual production for nearly 10 years.

Not Shown:

Brown Wren #3840 cigarette box (shape #3630, Kay Hackett design), 1950 – 1960. $65.00 – 85.00.

Brown Wren #3840 coaster ashtray (shape #3630, Kay Hackett design), 1950 – 1960. $25.00 – 30.00.

Rhododendron #3841 cigarette box (shape #3630, Kay Hackett design), 1950 – 1960. $60.00 – 75.00.

Rhododendron #3841 coaster ashtray (shape #3630, Kay Hackett design), 1950 – 1960. $22.00 – 28.00.

Humming Bird #3842 cigarette box (shape #3630, Kay Hackett design), 1950 – 1955. $85.00 – 95.00.

Humming Bird #3842 coaster ashtray (shape #3630, Kay Hackett design), 1950 – 1955. $25.00 – 35.00.

Brown Wren #3840 cigarette box, $65.00 – 85.00, and coaster ashtray, $25.00 – 30.00, 1950 – 1960. Courtesy of the Luke and Nancy Ruepp collection.

Rhododendron #3841 cigarette box, $60.00 – 75.00, and coaster ashtray, $22.00 – 28.00, 1950 – 1960. Courtesy of the Marcena North collection.

Humming Bird #3842 cigarette box, $85.00 – 95.00, and coaster ashtray, $25.00 – 35.00, 1950 – 1955. Courtesy of the Marcena North collection.

Goldfinch #3843 cigarette box (shape #3630, Kay Hackett design), 1950 – 1957. $65.00 – 80.00.

Goldfinch #3843 coaster ashtray, sunflower motif (shape #3630, Kay Hackett design), 1950 – 1957. $25.00 – 30.00.

Goldfinch #3843 cigarette box, $65.00 – 80.00, and coaster ashtray, $25.00 – 30.00, 1950 – 1957. Courtesy of the Marcena North collection.

The Thistle cigarette box set design was such an instant hit that Ed Hawley and Dave Thomas, Stangl's sales manager and plant manager at the time, decided to put the motif into dinnerware production in Mr. Stangl's absence. They instructed Kay Hackett to create the stencils necessary and soon had the Thistle dinnerware pattern in production with standing orders from department stores. When Martin Stangl returned from vacation, he remarked, "Thistles?! Who would want dinnerware with weeds on it? Only *cows* like thistles!" Ironically, the Thistle dinnerware pattern went on to become one of the bestselling patterns of the 1950s.

Not Shown:

Thistle #3844 cigarette box (shape #3630, Kay Hackett design), 1950 – 1963. $60.00 – 85.00.

Thistle #3844 coaster ashtray (shape #3630, Kay Hackett design), 1950 – 1963. $25.00 – 30.00.

Apple Tree #3845 cigarette box (shape #3630, Kay Hackett design), 1950 – 1960. $50.00 – 75.00.

Apple Tree #3845 coaster ashtray (shape #3630, Kay Hackett design), 1950 – 1960. $25.00 – 30.00.

"Stangl Farm" Apple Tree #3845 cigarette box made specifically for Martin Stangl's farm near Stockton, NJ (shape #3630), 1950 only. $900.00 – 1,000.00.

New Yorker magazine cartoon cigarette box, various cartoon motifs (shape #3630,), 1950 only (see page 248 for photo). $900.00 – 1,000.00.

New Yorker magazine cartoon coaster ashtray, various cartoon motifs (shape #3630), 1950 only. $200.00 – 250.00.

Thistle #3844 cigarette box, $60.00 – 85.00, and coaster ashtrays, $25.00 – 30.00 each, 1950 – 1963. Courtesy of the Luke and Nancy Ruepp collection.

Apple Tree #3845 cigarette box, $50.00 – 75.00, and coaster ashtray, $25.00 – 30.00, 1950 – 1960. Courtesy of the Marcena North collection.

"Stangl Farm" Apple Tree #3845 coaster ashtray, made specifically for Martin Stangl's farm near Stockton, NJ (shape #3630), 1950 only. $450.00 – 500.00.

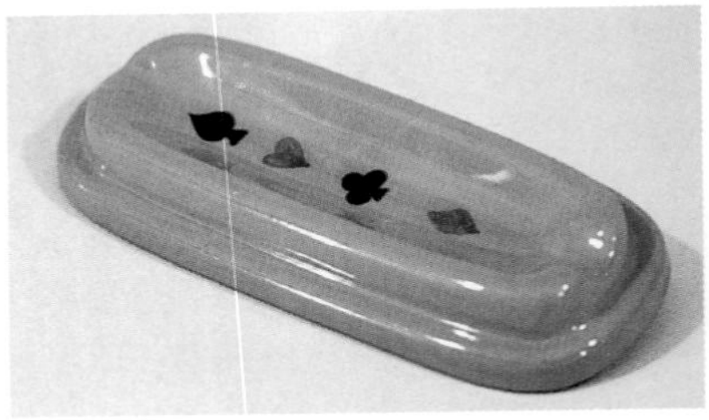

#3846 long ashtray, 6¼"x2⅝", Bridge decoration 1950 – 1960. $30.00 – 40.00. Courtesy of the Ben and Floss Avila collection.

D.W.T. monogram #3630 coaster ashtray, made for David W. Thomas, only 24 made, 1950. $180.00 – 225.00. Courtesy of Dave and Betty Stangl Thomas.

E.S.T. monogram #3630 coaster ashtray, made for Elizabeth (Betty) Stangl Thomas, only 24 made, 1950. $180.00 – 225.00. Courtesy of Dave and Betty Stangl Thomas.

Clayworker's Assoc. of New Jersey #3630 coaster ashtray, Fall Meeting commemorative. 1950 only. $100.00 – 125.00. Courtesy of the Hill-Fulper-Stangl Museum.

Gateway #3630 coaster ashtray commemorative made for Steiger's Department Store, Hartford, Conn. 1950 – 1951. $45.00 – 55.00. Courtesy of the Hill-Fulper-Stangl Museum.

Back of Gateway coaster ashtray showing the "Made for Steiger's" backstamp.

Camel cigarette holder, 5", made briefly during 1950. $400.00 – 450.00. From the Stangl and Fulper archival collection, courtesy the Wheaton Village Museum of American Glass.

Thatcher Furnace 100th Anniversary 6" windproof ashtray commemorative, 1950 only. $35.00 – 45.00.

Thatcher Furnace 100th Anniversary #3630 coaster ashtray commemorative, 1950 only. $55.00 – 65.00.

1951 Introductions

Not Shown:

Fruit and Butterflies #3854 cigarette box (shape #3630) for Lunning (Kay Hackett design), 1951 – 1952. $250.00 – 275.00.

Fruit and Butterflies #3854 coaster ashtray (shape #3630) for Lunning (Kay Hackett design), 1951 – 1952. $50.00 – 60.00.

Blueberry #3770 cigarette box (shape #3630, Kay Hackett design), 1951 – 1960. $200.00 – 250.00. Courtesy of the Marcena North collection.

Blueberry #3770 coaster ashtray (shape #3630, Kay Hackett design), 1951 – 1960. $35.00 – 45.00.

1952 Introductions

In 1952, Stangl's new colored engobe was perfected and became the background for several dinnerware and cigarette box motifs.

Not Shown:

Star Flower #3866 cigarette box (shape #3630, Kay Hackett design), 1952 – 1960. $40.00 – 50.00.

Star Flower #3866 coaster ashtray (shape #3630, Kay Hackett design), 1952 – 1960. $18.00 – 22.00.

Holly #3869 cigarette box (shape #3630, Kay Hackett design), 1952 – 1960. $250.00 – 275.00.

Star Flower #3866 cigarette box, $40.00 – 50.00, and coaster ashtrays, $18.00 – 22.00 each, 1952 – 1960. Courtesy of the Luke and Nancy Ruepp collection.

Holly #3869 coaster ashtray (shape #3630, Kay Hackett design), 1952 – 19670. $30.00 – 40.00. Courtesy of the Luke and Nancy Ruepp collection.

Two Holly #3869 5" fluted ashtrays showing the two motif variations (shape #3898, Kay Hackett design), 1965 – 1970. $25.00 – 35.00 each.

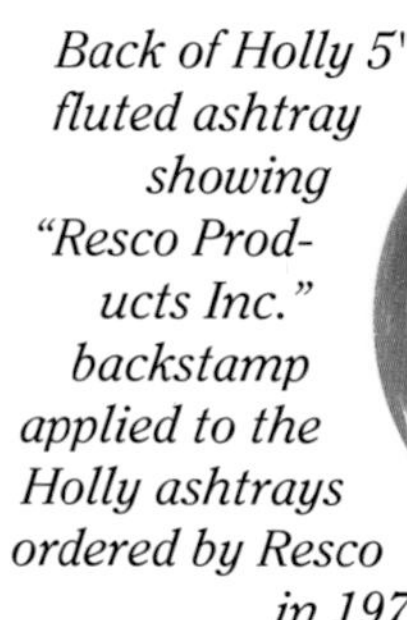

Back of Holly 5" fluted ashtray showing "Resco Products Inc." backstamp applied to the Holly ashtrays ordered by Resco in 1970.

Magnolia #3872 cigarette box, $45.00 – 55.00, and coaster ashtray, $22.00 – 28.00, 1952 – 1960. Courtesy of the Luke and Nancy Ruepp collection.

Holly #3881 double ashtray (#3876, Kay Hackett design), 1952 – 1955. $55.00 – 65.00. Courtesy of the Luke and Nancy Ruepp collection.

Magnolia #3872 cigarette box (shape #3630, Kay Hackett design), 1952 – 1960. $45.00 – 55.00.
Magnolia #3872 coaster ashtray (shape #3630, Kay Hackett design), 1952 – 1960. $22.00 – 28.00.
Magnolia (white engobe) #3872 cigarette box (shape #3630, Kay Hackett design), 1952 – 1955. $175.00 – 200.00.
Magnolia (white engobe) #3872 coaster ashtray (shape #3630, Kay Hackett design), 1952 – 1955. $50.00 – 60.00.
Star Flower #3877 double ashtray (#3876, Kay Hackett design), 1952 – 1955. $25.00 – 35.00.
Blueberry #3878 double ashtray (#3876, Kay Hackett design), 1952 – 1955. $50.00 – 60.00.
Magnolia #3878 double ashtray (#3876, Kay Hackett design), 1952 – 1955. $25.00 – 35.00.
Thistle #3880 double ashtray (#3876, Kay Hackett design), 1952 – 1955. $50.00 – 60.00.

Restyled motifs originally introduced in 1948.
Tropic Flower #3791 coaster ashtray (shape #3630, Kay Hackett design), 1952 – 1960. $20.00 – 25.00.
Flower Buds #3792 coaster ashtray (shape #3630, Kay Hackett design), 1952 – 1960. $20.00 – 25.00.
Trillium #3793 coaster ashtray (shape #3630, Kay Hackett design), 1952 – 1960. $25.00 – 30.00.
Gladiola #3794 coaster ashtray (shape #3630, Kay Hackett design), 1952 – 1960. $22.00 – 28.00.
Trumpet Flower #3795 coaster ashtray (shape #3630, Kay Hackett design), 1952 – 1960. $25.00 – 30.00.
Dogwood #3796 coaster ashtray (shape #3630, Kay Hackett design), 1952 – 1960. $25.00 – 30.00.
Ivy #3797 cigarette box (shape #3630, Kay Hackett design), 1952 – 1960. $45.00 – 55.00.
Ivy #3797 coaster ashtray (shape #3630, Kay Hackett design), 1952 – 1960. $20.00 – 25.00.
Citrus Fruit #3798 cigarette box (shape #3630, Kay Hackett design), 1952 – 1960. $55.00 – 65.00.
Marsh Rose #3799 cigarette box (shape #3630, Kay Hackett design), 1952 – 1960. $70.00 – 85.00.
Marsh Rose #3799 coaster ashtray (shape #3630, Kay Hackett design), 1952 – 1960. $25.00 – 30.00.
Blue Flower #3801 cigarette box (shape #3630, Kay Hackett design), 1952 only. $85.00 – 95.00.
Blue Flower #3801 coaster ashtray (shape #3630, Kay Hackett design), 1952 only. $25.00 – 30.00.
Blue Butterfly #3802 cigarette box (shape #3630, Kay Hackett design), 1952 only. $85.00 – 95.00.
Blue Butterfly #3802 coaster ashtray (shape #3630, Kay Hackett design), 1952 only. $25.00 – 30.00.

Citrus Fruit #3798 coaster ashtray (shape #3630, Kay Hackett design), 1952 – 1960. $25.00 – 30.00.

Citrus Fruit #3798 coaster ashtray (shape #3630) made for New Jersey Banker's Association, April 1956 only. $85.00 – 95.00. Courtesy of the Luke and Nancy Ruepp collection.

Backstamp of Citrus Fruit #3798 coaster ashtray (shape #3630) made for Somerville Kiwanis Club, Somerville, NJ, 1958. $45.00 – 55.00.

Marsh Rose #3799 cigarette box, $70.00 – 85.00, and coaster ashtray, $25.00 – 30.00. Courtesy of the Marcena North collection.

1953 Introductions

Not Shown:

Garland (pink) #3884 coaster ashtray (shape #3630, Kay Hackett design), 1953 – 1960. $22.00 – 28.00.

Garland (yellow) #3884 coaster ashtray (shape #3630, Kay Hackett design), 1953 – 1955. $45.00 – 55.00.

Garland (blue) #3884 coaster ashtray (shape #3630, Kay Hackett design), 1953 – 1955. $45.00 – 55.00.

Garland (pink) #3884 cigarette box, $60.00 – 75.00, and coaster ashtrays, $22.00 – 28.00 each, 1953 – 1960. Courtesy of the Luke and Nancy Ruepp collection.

Poppies #3885 cigarette box (shape #3630, Kay Hackett design), 1953 – 1960. $60.00 – 75.00.

Poppies #3885 coaster ashtray (shape #3630, Kay Hackett design), 1953 – 1960. $25.00 – 30.00.

Garland (yellow) #3884 cigarette box (shape #3630, Kay Hackett design), 1953 – 1955. $175.00 – 200.00. Courtesy of the Robert Sherman collection.

Garland (blue) #3884 cigarette box (shape #3630, Kay Hackett design), 1953 – 1955. $175.00 – 200.00. Courtesy of the Robert Sherman collection.

Poppies #3885 cigarette box, $60.00 – 75.00, and coaster ashtray, $25.00 – 30.00, 1953 – 1960. Courtesy of the Luke and Nancy Ruepp collection.

Blossom Time #3886 cigarette box (shape #3630, Kay Hackett design), 1953 – 1960. $70.00 – 95.00.
Blossom Time #3886 coaster ashtray (shape #3630, Kay Hackett design), 1953 – 1960. $25.00 – 35.00.
Golden Harvest #3887 cigarette box (shape #3630, Kay Hackett design), 1953 – 1960. $30.00 – 40.00.
Golden Harvest #3887 coaster ashtray (shape #3630, Kay Hackett design), 1953 – 1960. $10.00 – 12.00.
Pink Lily #3888 cigarette box (shape #3630, Kay Hackett design), 1953 – 1960. $55.00 – 65.00.
Pink Lily #3888 coaster ashtray (shape #3630, Kay Hackett design), 1953 – 1960. $25.00 – 35.00.

Blossom Time #3886 cigarette box, $70.00 – 95.00, and coaster ashtray, $25.00 – 35.00, 1953 – 1960. Courtesy of the Marcena North collection.

Kay Hackett's sample for Strawberry cigarette box, very few produced. $400.00 – 500.00. Courtesy of the Luke and Nancy Ruepp collection.

Golden Harvest #3887 cigarette box, $30.00 – 40.00, and coaster ashtrays, $10.00 – 12.00 each, 1953 – 1960. Courtesy of the Luke and Nancy Ruepp collection.

Poppies coaster ashtray with attached spun brass rim, mid 1950s. $30.00 – 40.00. Courtesy of the Luke and Nancy Ruepp collection.

During the mid 1950s, several metalwork companies affixed spun aluminum or brass rims to Stangl coaster ashtrays. These are interesting and usually increase the value of the attached coaster ashtray by several dollars.

1954 Introductions

Not Shown:

Lyric #3896 cigarette box (shape #3630, Kay Hackett design), 1954 – 1960. $175.00 – 200.00.

Lyric #3896 coaster ashtray (shape #3630, Kay Hackett design), 1954 – 1960. $55.00 – 65.00.

White Embroidery Edge #3898-A fluted cigarette box, white engobe, blue and yellow motif, yellow band (Kay Hackett design), 1954 – 1956. $85.00 – 125.00.

White Embroidery Edge #3898-A, 5" fluted coaster ashtray, white engobe, blue and yellow motif, yellow band (Kay Hackett design), 1954 – 1956. $25.00 – 35.00.

Lyric #3896 cigarette box, $175.00 – 200.00, and coaster ashtray, $55.00 – 65.00. Courtesy of the Luke and Nancy Ruepp collection.

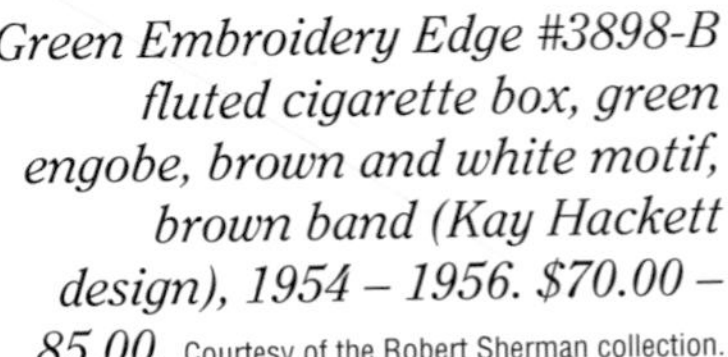

White Embroidery Edge #3898-A, 7" fluted coaster ashtray, white engobe, blue and yellow motif, yellow band (Kay Hackett design), 1954 – 1956. $35.00 – 45.00.

White Embroidery Edge cigarette box, $85.00 – 125.00, and 5" coaster ashtray, $25.00 – 35.00, 1954 – 1956. Courtesy of the Luke and Nancy Ruepp collection.

Green Embroidery Edge #3898-B fluted cigarette box, green engobe, brown and white motif, brown band (Kay Hackett design), 1954 – 1956. $70.00 – 85.00. Courtesy of the Robert Sherman collection.

Green Embroidery Edge #3898-B 5" fluted coaster ashtray, green engobe, brown and white motif, brown band (Kay Hackett design), 1954 – 1956. $25.00 – 30.00.

Green Embroidery Edge #3898-B 7" fluted coaster ashtray, green engobe, brown and white motif, brown band (Kay Hackett design), 1954 – 1956. $25.00 – 35.00.

Gray Embroidery Edge #3898-C fluted cigarette box, gray engobe, red and white motif, black band (Kay Hackett design), 1954 – 1956. $80.00 – 95.00.

Gray Embroidery Edge #3898-C 5" fluted coaster ashtray, gray engobe, red and white motif, black band (Kay Hackett design), 1954 – 1956. $25.00 – 35.00.

Embroidery Edge #3898-C fluted cigarette box, second, no color, 1954 – 1956. $55.00 – 70.00.

Embroidery Edge #3898-C 7" fluted coaster ashtray, second, no color, 1954 – 1956. $22.00 – 28.00.

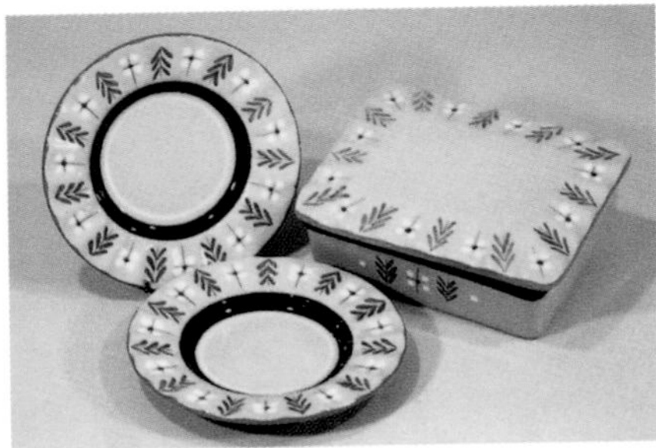

Gray Embroidery Edge cigarette box, $80.00 – 95.00, and 5" coaster ashtrays, $25.00 – 35.00 each, 1954 – 1956. Courtesy of the Robert Sherman collection.

Gray Embroidery Edge #3898-C 7" fluted coaster ashtray, gray engobe, red and white motif, black band (Kay Hackett design), 1954 – 1956. $30.00 – 40.00.

Embroidery Edge #3898-C 5" fluted coaster ashtray, second, no color, 1954 – 1956. $18.00 – 22.00.

Amber-Glo #3899 cigarette box (shape #3630, Kay Hackett design), 1954 – 1960. $55.00 – 70.00.
Amber-Glo #3899 coaster ashtray (shape #3630, Kay Hackett design), 1954 – 1960. $20.00 – 25.00.
Carnival #3900 cigarette box (shape #3630, Kay Hackett design), 1954 – 1960. $50.00 – 60.00.
Carnival #3900 coaster ashtray (shape #3630, Kay Hackett design), 1954 – 1960. $25.00 – 30.00.

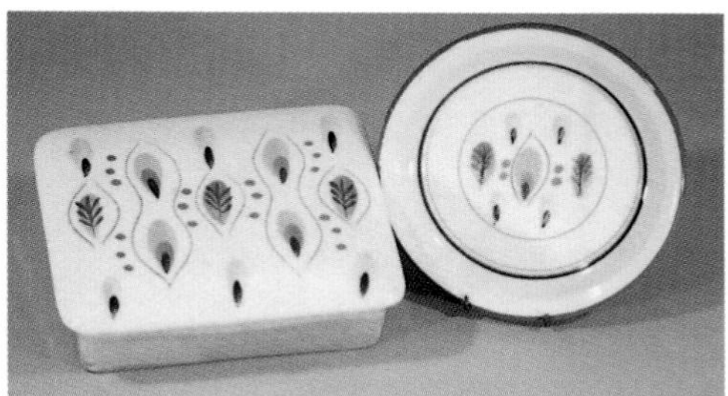

Amber-Glo #3899 cigarette box, $55.00 – 70.00, and coaster ashtray, $20.00 – 25.00, 1954 – 1960. Courtesy of the Robert Sherman collection.

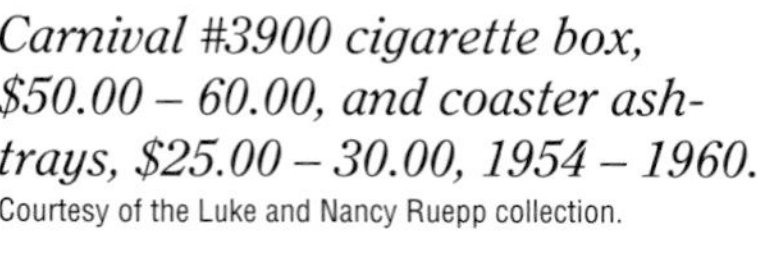

Carnival #3900 cigarette box, $50.00 – 60.00, and coaster ashtrays, $25.00 – 30.00, 1954 – 1960. Courtesy of the Luke and Nancy Ruepp collection.

Kay Hackett's Sample #3903 high-edged cigarette box, decorated with unproduced "Radiation" pattern, 1954. Courtesy of the Hill-Fulper-Stangl Museum.

Quasar #3903 cigarette box, ashtray cover (shape #3903), 1954 only. $200.00 – 250.00.

Harlequin #3907 cigarette box (shape #3630), 1954 – 1955. $175.00 – 200.00.

Harlequin #3907 coaster ashtray (shape #3630), 1954 – 1955. $45.00 – 55.00.

Harlequin #3907 cigarette box, $175.00 – 200.00, and coaster ashtrays, $45.00 – 55.00 each, 1954 – 1955. Courtesy of the Luke and Nancy Ruepp collection.

Aztec-A cigarette box, $450.00 – 500.00, and coaster ashtrays A and B, $100.00 – 125.00 each. Courtesy of Dave and Betty Stangl Thomas.

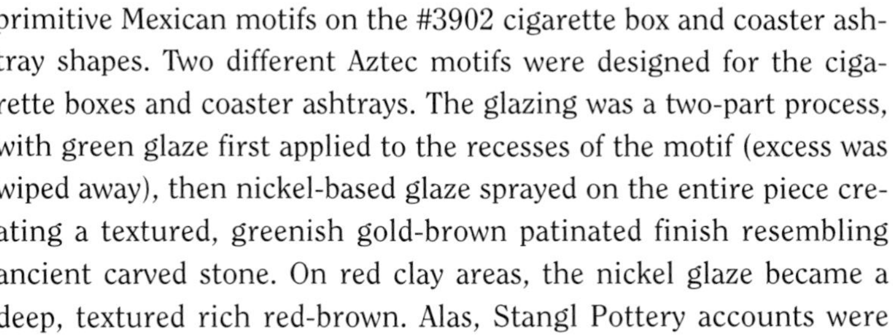

Aztec Cigarette Box Sets

In 1954, Dave Thomas developed Aztec, a combination of molded design and antiquing glaze. The Aztec decorations were molded primitive Mexican motifs on the #3902 cigarette box and coaster ashtray shapes. Two different Aztec motifs were designed for the cigarette boxes and coaster ashtrays. The glazing was a two-part process, with green glaze first applied to the recesses of the motif (excess was wiped away), then nickel-based glaze sprayed on the entire piece creating a textured, greenish gold-brown patinated finish resembling ancient carved stone. On red clay areas, the nickel glaze became a deep, textured rich red-brown. Alas, Stangl Pottery accounts were reluctant to carry Aztec, feeling it did not look "Stangl" enough. Aztec never did go into full production, thereby causing its rarity today.

Interior of Aztec cigarette box showing the effect of the nickel glaze.

Not Shown:

Aztec-A cigarette box (shape #3902, Dave Thomas design), very briefly during 1954 only. $450.00 – 500.00.

Aztec-A coaster ashtray (shape #3902, Dave Thomas design), very briefly during 1954 only. $100.00 – 125.00.

Aztec-B cigarette box (shape #3902, Dave Thomas design), very briefly during 1954 only. $450.00 – 500.00.

Aztec-B coaster ashtray (shape #3902, Dave Thomas design), very briefly during 1954 only. $100.00 – 125.00.

High-Relief Cigarette Boxes

Other molded motif cigarette boxes in a more traditional "Stangl-esque" style were developed during 1954 as well. These featured exaggerated molded motifs of foliage and flowers. Several variations of each were tried with underglaze color decoration; colored, textured and satin glazes and various engobe colors. Nevertheless, at that time, no other Stangl creation could ever compare to Stangl's famous "Hand-Carved, Hand-Painted" designs. So, the High-Relief cigarette boxes were abandoned after a very short run.

High-Relief Daisies cigarette box (shape #3630), very briefly during 1954 only. $200.00 – 250.00.

High-Relief Aster cigarette box (shape #3630), very briefly during 1954 only. $200.00 – 250.00.

Trailer Cigarette Box Sets

In 1954, Kay Hackett developed the abstract "Trailer" decorations for the modern-styled #3902 square cigarette box shape. These motifs incorporated a combination of carving, hand-painting, and applied "trailing" to create a modern effect. The "trailing" was very similar to the slip-trail style of decoration but utilized a colored glaze material instead of the engobes usually used in traditional slip-trailing. This glaze material was formulated in several trendy colors and was applied to the boxes with a rubber syringe. Upon firing, the glaze material frothed, foamed, and blended with the surrounding clear glaze, creating a raised textured effect.

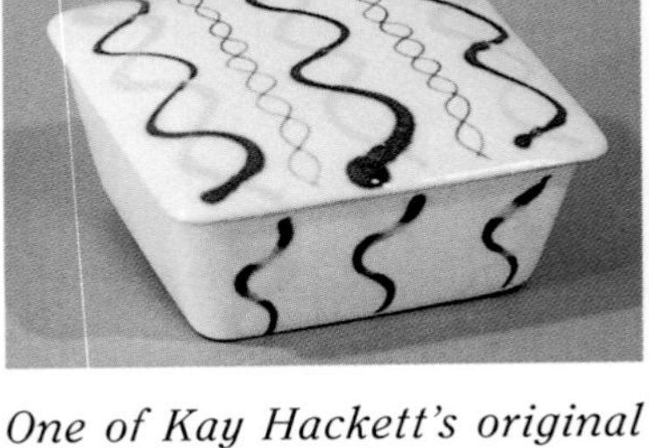

One of Kay Hackett's original sample "Trailer" cigarette boxes with a motif of interlacing yellow and green trailers and carving. Courtesy of the Hill-Fulper-Stangl Museum.

What Kay Hackett could successfully produce in her design studio could not always be replicated by the decorating department. Such was the case with the Trailer boxes. Because the colored glaze material would float and move during firing, it needed to be meticulously applied in order to finish correctly. This could not always be done. The glaze material often floated away from where it should have been, and being glaze itself, usually caused the clear glaze surrounding it to craze. Shortly after introduction, the trailing on most of these boxes was replaced with simple hand-painted underglaze color. The effect was not as originally designed, but these cigarette sets could now be produced more quickly with fewer failures.

Unglazed interior of the Trailer sample box.

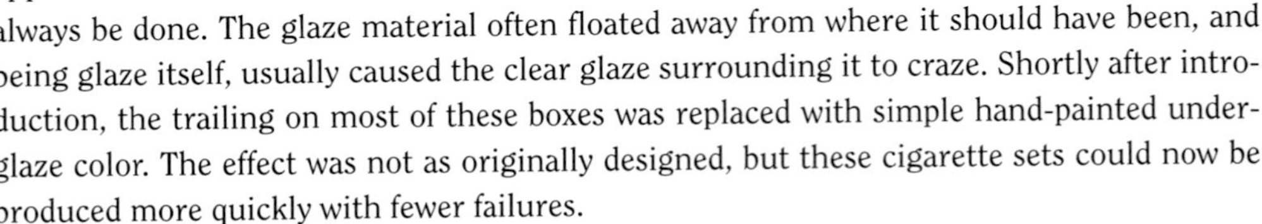

Another change in these motifs was the colors used. Originally, decorations #3910 and #3911 used Lily Pink, Lily Yellow, and Orchid on the blossoms. Lily Pink and Lily Yellow (Golden Harvest Yellow) were heavy, opaque colors used on the gray background of the Pink Lily and Golden Harvest dinnerware patterns and lacked the brilliance of Stangl's other underglaze colors. They were replaced with Dark Yellow and Pink #160, colors that could stand out against the gray or green backgrounds. The original color Orchid was replaced for the same reason: it was lost against the dark gray and green so was replaced with the stronger Purple underglaze color. Unfortunately, the delicacy and artistic merit of the original motifs were lost with the modifications, but the original designs could not be carried out in production.

Cigarette box lid #3911 with original motif of white froth glaze material interlacing and Lily Pink, Lily Yellow, and Orchid blossoms. #3911 coaster ashtray with modified motif of White #10 interlacing and Dark Yellow, Purple, and Pink #160 blossoms.

Trailer Design #3908 cigarette box (left), $70.00 – 85.00, and coaster ashtray (right), $25.00 – 30.00, green engobe, yellow and green trailer stripes (shape #3902, Kay Hackett design), 1954 – 1960. Courtesy of the Robert Sherman collection and the Luke and Nancy Ruepp collection.

Trailer Design #3909 coaster ashtray, coral engobe, brown and white trailer stripes (shape #3902, Kay Hackett design), 1954 – 1960. $25.00 – 30.00.

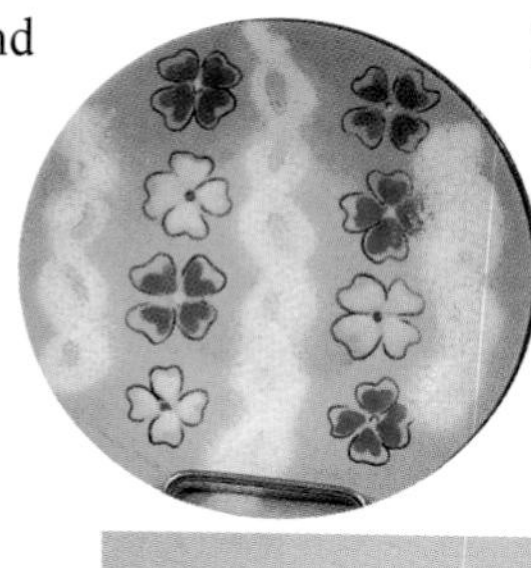

Trailer Design #3910 coaster ashtray, green engobe, pink, yellow, orchid flowers with yellow trailer interlacing (shape #3902, Kay Hackett design), 1954 – 1960. $25.00 – 30.00. Courtesy of the Jim and Barbara Nelson collection.

Trailer Design #3909 cigarette box, coral engobe, brown, and white trailer stripes (shape #3902, Kay Hackett design), 1954 – 1960. $70.00 – 85.00. Courtesy of the Robert Sherman collection.

Trailer Design #3910 cigarette box, green engobe, pink, yellow, orchid flowers with yellow trailer interlacing (shape #3902, Kay Hackett design), 1954 – 1960. $85.00 – 95.00. Courtesy of the Robert Sherman collection.

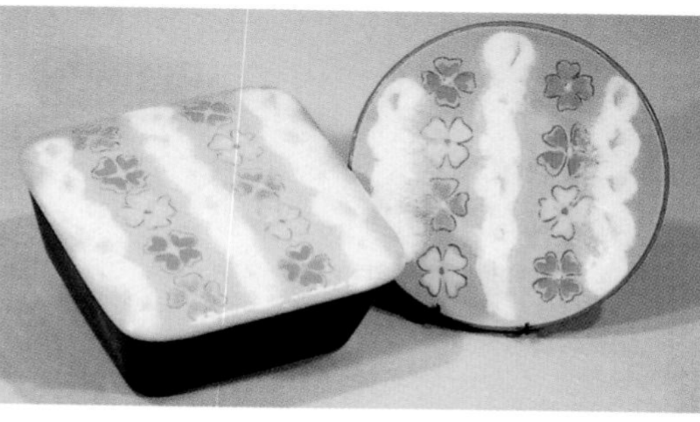

Trailer Design #3911 cigarette box, $85.00 – 95.00, and coaster ashtray, $25.00 – 30.00, gray engobe, pink, yellow, orchid flowers with white froth glaze trailer interlacing (shape #3902, Kay Hackett design), 1954 – 1960. Courtesy of the Robert Sherman collection.

Trailer Design #3912 cigarette box, green engobe, white #10 underglaze color trailer stripes with Lily Yellow decoration in the carved interlacing (shape #3902, Kay Hackett design), 1954 – 1960. $70.00 – 85.00. Courtesy of the Robert Sherman collection.

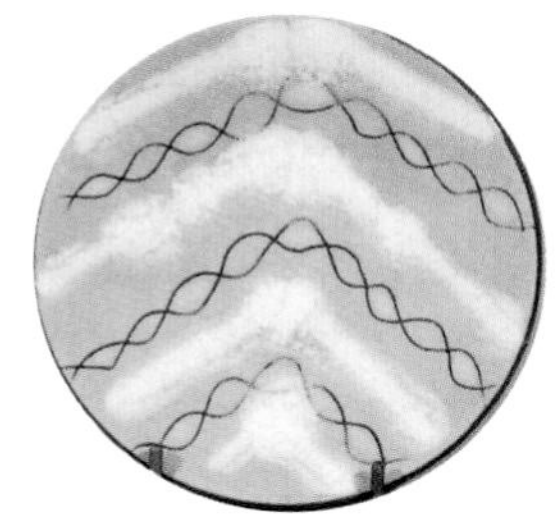

Trailer Design #3912 coaster ashtray, green engobe, white froth glaze trailer stripes with Lily Yellow decoration in the carved interlacing (shape #3902, Kay Hackett design), 1954 – 1960. $25.00 – 30.00. Courtesy of the Luke and Nancy Ruepp collection.

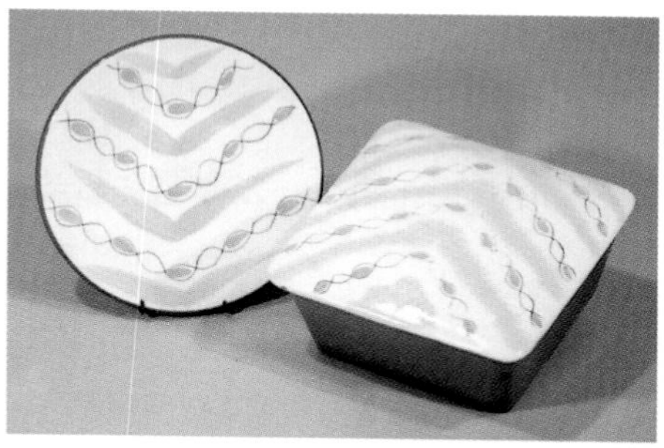

Trailer Design #3913 cigarette box, $85.00 – 95.00, and coaster ashtray, $25.00 – 35.00, white engobe, yellow trailer stripes with orange decoration in the carved interlacing (shape #3902, Kay Hackett design), 1954 – 1960. Courtesy of the Robert Sherman collection.

Marbled Ashtrays

The Marbled products were developed by Dave Thomas in 1954 primarily as a line of ashtrays and were produced in limited quantities from 1954 through 1956. Marbled items were cast of colored slips poured into the mold at the same time while the mold was spun on a turntable. The colored slips then swirled together, creating a vibrant marbled effect. The two primary Marbled color combinations were light and dark green with cream, and pink and black with cream. The letter designation on the Marbled ashtrays indicated the color; "A" was pink Marbled, "B" was green. Marbled was a premium ashtray finish and retailed for twice the retail of the same shapes in Terra Rose finishes. In 1956, the #3939 square ashtray retailed at $2.50 in Terra Rose and $5.00 in Marbled, ashtray #3905 was 50¢ in Terra Rose and $1.00 in Marbled.

Not Shown:

Marbled #3904 ashtray, free form 7"x4½" (Ed Pettingil design), 1954 – 1956. $20.00 – 25.00.

Marbled #3905 ashtray, free form (same as #3904), 5"x3½" (Ed Pettingil design), 1954 – 1956. $15.00 – 20.00.

Marbled #3906 ashtray, notched, free form 5½" (Ed Pettingil design), 1954 – 1956. $12.00 – 18.00.

Marbled #3914 ashtray, square with square well 9" (Kay Hackett design), 1954 – 1956. $20.00 – 25.00.

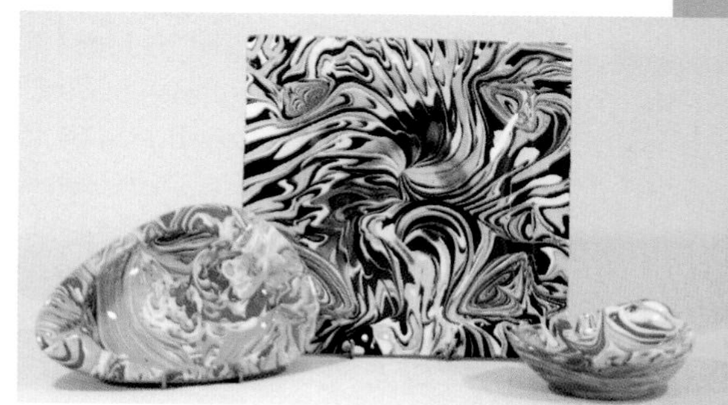

Group of Marbled ashtrays.

Marbled #3915 ashtray, square with round well 9" (Kay Hackett design), 1954 – 1956. $20.00 – 25.00.
Marbled #3926 ashtray, oval, plain, 10¾"x8" (Kay Hackett design), 1955 – 1956. $15.00 – 20.00.
Marbled #3927 ashtray, casual, 10½"x 7½" (Kay Hackett design), 1955 – 1956. $25.00 – 30.00.
Marbled #3937 ashtray, 7" diameter, 1955 – 1956. $25.00 – 30.00.
Marbled #3938 ashtray, free form 7¼"x5⅞" (Ed Pettingil design), 1955 – 1956. $20.00 – 25.00.
Marbled #3939 ashtray, rectangular, 9⅛"x9⅛" (Ed Pettingil design), 1955 – 1956. $20.00 – 25.00.
Marbled #3940 ashtray, irregular shape 6½"x5"x8" (Ed Pettingil design), 1955 – 1956. $20.00 – 25.00.
Marbled #3941 ashtray, Safety, free form 5⅜"x6¼"x7 (Ed Pettingil design), 1955 – 1956. $20.00 – 25.00.
Marbled #3942 ashtray, Safety, oval 8½"x7" (Ed Pettingil design), 1955 – 1956. $15.00 – 20.00.

Veiled

The Veiled finish used on several smokers' accessories during 1954 was a smooth, even, white veiling over black satin glaze, not the gloppy, uneven veiling used as a dinnerware seconds treatment during the same year. However, several smoking items did end up with the seconds treatment applied to them. The more refined Veiled finish did not last very long, and few Veiled items were produced. Both finishes are valued about the same.

Not Shown:

Veiled #3630 coaster ashtray, 5" (same as #3434), 1954 only. $25.00 – 35.00.
Veiled #3630 cigarette box flat top 1954 only. $85.00 – 95.00.
Veiled #3817 ashtray, windproof, 6", 1954 only (Kay Hackett design). $25.00 – 35.00.
Veiled #3816 ashtray, windproof, 8", 1954 only (Kay Hackett design). $40.00 – 50.00.
Veiled #3897M ashtray, square 5"x5" (Ed Pettingil design), 1954 only. $25.00 – 30.00.
Veiled #3897L ashtray, square 6½"x6½" (Ed Pettingil design), 1954 only. $25.00 – 35.00.
Veiled #3902 cigarette box, square, 1954 only. $120.00 – 140.00.
Veiled #3902-5 coaster ashtray, 5", 1954 only. $30.00 – 40.00.
Veiled #3903-A cigarette box, ashtray cover, 1954 only. $130.00 – 150.00.
Veiled #3904 ashtray, free form 7"x4½" (Ed Pettingil design), 1954 only. $20.00 – 25.00.
Veiled #3905 ashtray, free form (same as #3904), 5"x3½" (Ed Pettingil design), 1954 only. $20.00 – 25.00.
Veiled #3906 ashtray, notched, free form 5½" (Ed Pettingil design), 1954 only. $20.00 – 25.00.
Veiled #3914 ashtray, square with square well 9" (Kay Hackett design), 1954 only. $35.00 – 45.00.
Veiled #3915 ashtray, square with round well 9" (Kay Hackett design), 1954 only. $35.00 – 45.00.

Veiled #3897S ashtray, square 4"x4" (Ed Pettingil design), 1954 only. $20.00 – 25.00. Courtesy of the Hill-Fulper-Stangl Museum.

Veiled #3903 cigarette box, high-edged cover, 1954 only. $130.00 – 150.00. Courtesy of the Sherman collection.

Nature Embossed

Nature Embossed was a small series of ashtrays with stylized raised decoration in the wells. These were primarily wildlife motifs, but other abstracts and arabesques were also produced. The shapes included Stangl's first large-sized conference table ashtrays, designed by Kay Hackett. These were glazed with solid-color glazes created specifically for this line. The glaze palette included matte and gloss textures as well as some speckling. They were typical fashion colors and included Fern Green (gloss), Moss Green (matte), Pine Brown (matte), Manganese Brown (gloss), Marine Blue (gloss), and Fawn Taupe (specked). The Nature Embossed ashtrays were discontinued by 1955 in favor of the more popular hand-carved, hand-painted ashtray motifs.

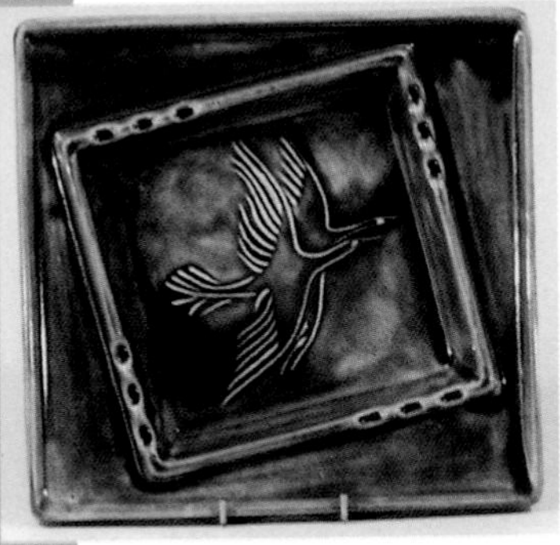

Gulls #3914 ashtray, square with square well 9" (Kay Hackett design), 1954 only. Marine Blue glaze, $130.00 – 150.00.

Not Shown:

Stag #3914 ashtray, square with square well 9" (Kay Hackett design), 1954 only. $130.00 – 150.00.
Waves #3914 ashtray, square with square well 9" (Kay Hackett design), 1954 only. $130.00 – 150.00.
Cactus #3915 ashtray, square with round well 9" (Kay Hackett design), 1954 only. $130.00 – 150.00.
Birds #3915 ashtray, square with round well 9" (Kay Hackett design), 1954 only. $130.00 – 150.00.
Arabesque #3915 ashtray, square with round well 9" (Kay Hackett design), 1954 only. $130.00 – 150.00.

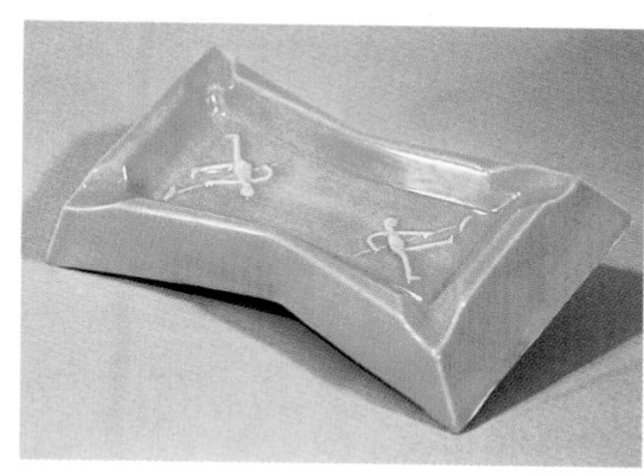

Sweeper ashtray, 6½"x3¾", six-sided (Ed Pettingil design), 1954 only. Fawn Taupe glaze, $85.00 – 95.00.

1955 Introductions

Modern and abstract styles were still predominant in 1955; consequently Kay Hackett developed several modern motifs for her newly designed large ashtray shapes. This was also the year Stangl introduced the beginnings of the Sportsmen's Giftware line of ashtrays. For the complete list of Sportsmen's items, please see the Sportsmen's Giftware section.

Not Shown:

Coral #3914 square ashtray, based on Amber-Glo motif (Kay Hackett design), 1955 – 1962. $35.00 – 45.00.

Radiant #3926 oval ashtray (Kay Hackett design), 1955 – 1957. $35.00 – 45.00.

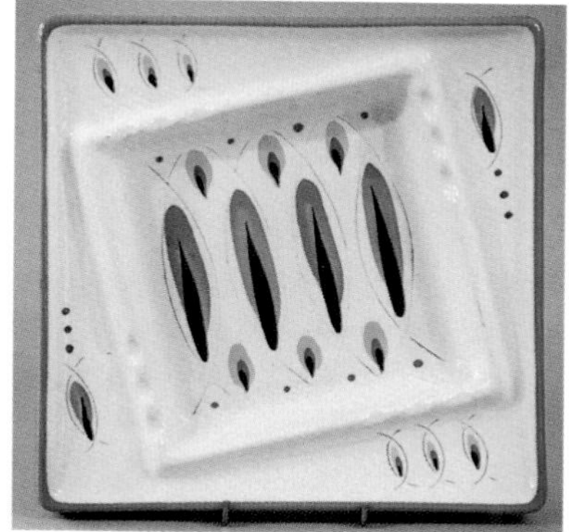

White #3914 square ashtray, based on Amber-Glo motif (Kay Hackett design), 1955 – 1962. $40.00 – 50.00. Courtesy of the Robert Sherman collection.

Gray #3914 square ashtray, based on Amber-Glo motif (Kay Hackett design), 1955 – 1962. $30.00 – 40.00.

Pink Elephant #3915 square ashtray intended for New Year's Eve entertaining (Kay Hackett design), 1955 – 1957. $225.00 – 275.00.

Pink Elephant #3914 square ashtray in gold on Satin Black glaze, a very few ashtrays of similar motif were tried briefly during 1967. $290.00 – 325.00.

Big Top #3915 square ashtray (Kay Hackett design), 1955 – 1957. $225.00 – 275.00. Courtesy of the Bill Servis, Susan Lewis collection.

Abstract Fish #3926 oval ashtray (Kay Hackett design), 1955 only. $290.00 – 325.00. Courtesy of the Robert and Shirley Bond collection.

Spectrum #3926 oval ashtray (Kay Hackett design), 1955 – 1957. $35.00 – 45.00. Courtesy of the Bill Servis, Susan Lewis collection.

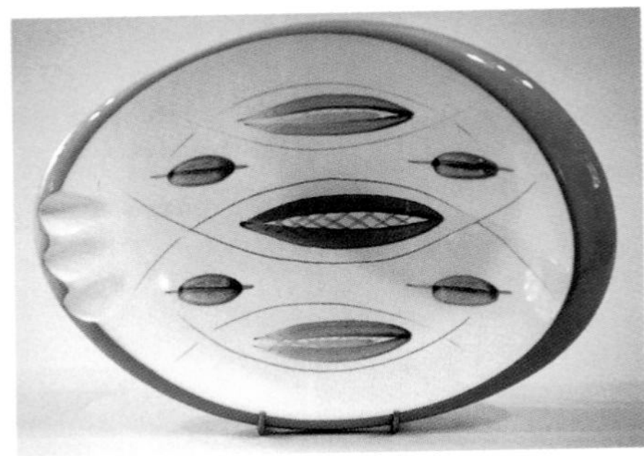

Fantasy #3926 oval ashtray (Kay Hackett design), 1955 – 1957. $35.00 – 45.00.

Pine #3927 casual ashtray (Kay Hackett design), 1955 – 1957. $45.00 – 60.00. Courtesy of the Bill Servis, Susan Lewis collection.

Brook's Brother's #3928 ashtray, 10"x10", Manganese Brown glaze with black drip, made for Brook's Brothers Men's Store, and was originally sold with a #3902 cigarette box in the center well. 1955 only. $60.00 – 75.00. Courtesy of Marion Farrell Antiques.

Wild Rose #3929 cigarette box (shape #3630, Kay Hackett design), 1955 – 1960. $70.00 – 85.00. Courtesy of the Luke and Nancy Ruepp collection.

Windfall 150th Anniversary of Stangl Pottery #3930 coaster ashtray commemorative (shape #3630, Kay Hackett design), 1955 only. $40.00 – 50.00.

Backstamp on the 150th Anniversary commemorative coaster ashtrays. This mark was only used on the Wild Rose and Windfall patterns, both new introductions for 1955.

Goldfinch #3931 cigarette box, $150.00 – 175.00, and coaster ashtrays, $45.00 – 55.00 each, 1955 – 1960. Courtesy of the Robert Sherman collection.

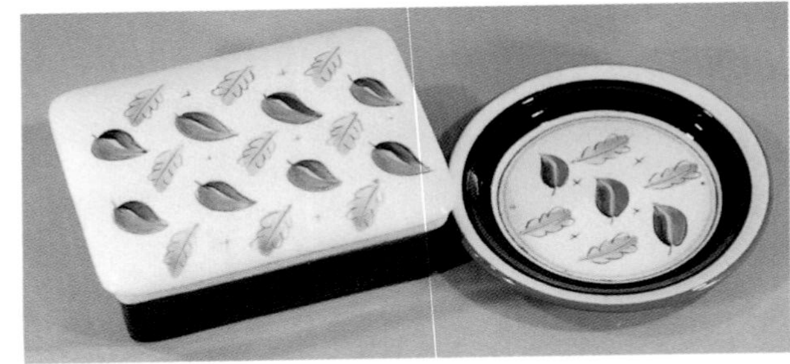

Windfall #3930 cigarette box, $70.00 – 85.00, and coaster ashtray, $22.00 – 28.00, 1955 – 1960. Courtesy of the Robert Sherman collection.

Wild Rose #3929 coaster ashtray (shape #3630, Kay Hackett design), 1955 – 1960. $25.00 – 30.00.

Wild Rose 150th Anniversary of Stangl Pottery #3929 coaster ashtray commemorative (shape #3630, Kay Hackett design), 1955 only. $40.00 – 50.00.

Windfall #3930 cigarette box (shape #3630, Kay Hackett design), 1955 – 1960. $70.00 – 85.00.

Windfall #3930coaster ashtray (shape #3630, Kay Hackett design), 1955 – 1960. $22.00 – 28.00.

Goldfinch #3931 cigarette box (shape #3630, Kay Hackett design), 1955 – 1960. $150.00 – 175.00.

Goldfinch #3931 coaster ashtray (shape #3630, Kay Hackett design), 1955 – 1960. $45.00 – 55.00.

Prothonotary Warbler #3932 coaster ashtray (shape #3630, Kay Hackett design), 1955 – 1960. $45.00 – 55.00.

Purple Finch #3933 cigarette box (shape #3630, Kay Hackett design), 1955 – 1960. $130.00 – 160.00.

Purple Finch #3933 coaster ashtray (shape #3630, Kay Hackett design), 1955 – 1960. $40.00 – 50.00.

Prothonotary Warbler #3932 cigarette box (shape #3630, Kay Hackett design), 1955 – 1960. $150.00 – 175.00.

Purple Finch #3933 cigarette box, $130.00 – 160.00, and coaster ashtray, $40.00 – 50.00, 1955 – 1960. Courtesy of the Robert Sherman collection.

Baltimore Oriole #3934 cigarette box, $130.00 – 160.00, and coaster ashtray, $40.00 – 50.00, 1955 – 1960. Courtesy of the Marcena North collection.

Blue Bird #3936 cigarette box, $160.00 – 180.00, and coaster ashtray, $45.00 – 55.00, 1955 – 1960.

Scarlet Tanager #3935 cigarette box (shape #3630, Kay Hackett design), 1955 – 1960. $130.00 – 150.00.

Merry Andrew #3938 free-form ashtray, 7½"x6½" (Ed Pettingil design), 1955 only. $275.00 – 300.00.

Baltimore Oriole #3934 cigarette box (shape #3630, Kay Hackett design), 1955 – 1960. $130.00 – 160.00.
Baltimore Oriole #3934 coaster ashtray (shape #3630, Kay Hackett design), 1955 – 1960. $40.00 – 50.00.
Scarlet Tanager #3935 coaster ashtray (shape #3630, Kay Hackett design), 1955 – 1960. $40.00 – 50.00.
Blue Bird #3936 cigarette box (shape #3630, Kay Hackett design), 1955 – 1960. $160.00 – 180.00.
Blue Bird #3936 coaster ashtray (shape #3630, Kay Hackett design), 1955 – 1960. $45.00 – 55.00.

1956 Introductions

Not Shown:

Country Garden #3943 fluted ashtray 5" no carving, made for Flemington Outlet (shape #3898, Kay Hackett design), 1963 – 1974. $6.00 – 10.00.

Country Garden #3943 coaster ashtray with carved decoration (shape #3630, Kay Hackett design), 1956 – 1959. $25.00 – 35.00.

Country Garden #3943 coaster ashtray, no carving, made for Flemington Outlet (shape #3630, Kay Hackett design), 1960 – 1974. $8.00 – 12.00.

Country Garden #3943 cigarette box (shape #3630, Kay Hackett design), 1956 – 1959. $120.00 – 145.00.

Country Garden #3943 fluted ashtray 5" with carved decoration (shape #3898, Kay Hackett design), 1965 – 1968. $25.00 – 30.00. Courtesy of the Luke and Nancy Ruepp collection.

Country Life #3943 coaster ashtray with (shape #3630, Kay Hackett design), 1956 – 1959. $40.00 – 50.00.

Christmas Tree #3957 cigarette box with edge decoration (shape #3630, Kay Hackett design), 1956 – 1974. $95.00 – 130.00.

Christmas Tree #3957 cigarette box without edge decoration (shape #3630, Kay Hackett design), 1956 – 1974. $95.00 – 130.00.

Christmas Tree #3957 stamped "Merry Christmas" coaster ashtray (shape #3630, Kay Hackett design), 1956 – 1974. $50.00 – 60.00.

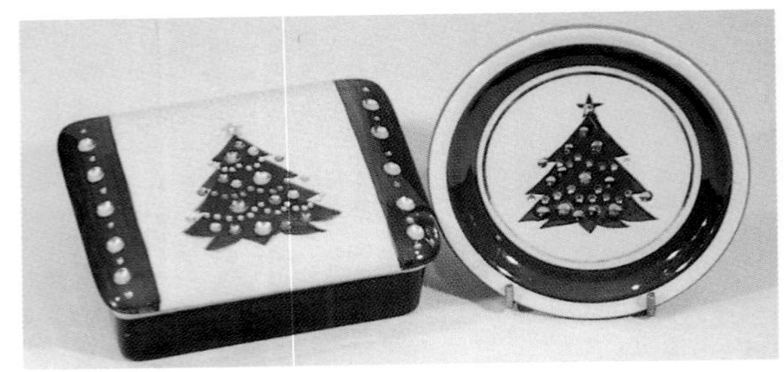

Christmas Tree #3957 cigarette box (with edge decoration), 1956 – 1974, $95.00 – 130.00; and coaster ashtray (shape #3630, Kay Hackett design), 1956 – 1974, $25.00 – 35.00. Courtesy of the Luke and Nancy Ruepp collection.

Trenton Rotary Christmas Tree #3957 coaster ashtray (shape #3630, Kay Hackett design) made for Trenton Rotary Club, 1956 – 1960. $40.00 – 50.00. Courtesy of the Jim and Barbara Nelson collection.

In 1956, Kay Hackett conducted extensive experimentation with metallic lusters and their application to cigarette box motifs. Following is a partial list of some of her experimental patterns. Some of these were actually produced in very limited quantities.

Not Shown:

"Amber Glo" cigarette box, Terra Rose Blue, Satin White glaze and gold lusters (shape #3630, Kay Hackett design), limited production 1956 only. $450.00 – 500.00.

"Amber Glo" coaster ashtray, Satin White glaze and metallic lusters (shape #3630, Kay Hackett design), limited production 1956 only. $85.00 – 95.00.

"Blu Feather" coaster ashtray, Satin White glaze and metallic lusters (shape #3630, Kay Hackett design), limited production 1956 only. $85.00 – 95.00.

Kay Hackett's design sample for "Fern" cigarette box in pink luster. Courtesy of the North collection.

"Fern" coaster ashtray, Satin White glaze and metallic lusters (shape #3898, Kay Hackett design), limited production 1956 only. $85.00 – 95.00.

"Golden Fruit" cigarette box, Satin White glaze and metallic lusters (shape #3630, Kay Hackett design), limited production 1956 only. $450.00 – 500.00.

"Golden Fruit" coaster ashtray, Satin White glaze and metallic lusters (shape #3630, Kay Hackett design), limited production 1956 only. $85.00 – 95.00.

"Grape" cigarette box, Satin White glaze and metallic lusters (shape #3630, Kay Hackett design), limited production 1956 only. $450.00 – 500.00.

"Grape" coaster ashtray, Satin White glaze and metallic lusters (shape #3630, Kay Hackett design), limited production 1956 only. $85.00 – 95.00.

"Blu Feather" cigarette box, Terra Rose Blue, Satin White glaze and gold lusters (shape #3630, Kay Hackett design), limited production 1956 only. $450.00 – 500.00. Courtesy of the Robert Sherman collection.

"Fern" cigarette box, metallic lusters (shape #3898, Kay Hackett design), limited production 1956 only. $450.00 – 500.00. Courtesy of the Robert Sherman collection.

"Holly" cigarette box, Satin White glaze and metallic lusters (shape #3630, Kay Hackett design), limited production 1956 only. $450.00 – 500.00.

"Holly" coaster ashtray, Satin White glaze and metallic lusters (shape #3630, Kay Hackett design), limited production 1956 only. $85.00 – 95.00.

"Midnite Sky" cigarette box, Satin White glaze and metallic lusters (shape #3630, Kay Hackett design), limited production 1956 only. $450.00 – 500.00.

"Midnite Sky" coaster ashtray, Satin White glaze and metallic lusters (shape #3630, Kay Hackett design), limited production 1956 only. $85.00 – 95.00.

"Queen Anne's Lace" cigarette box, metallic lusters (shape #3630, Kay Hackett design), limited production 1956 only. $450.00 – 500.00.

"Queen Anne's Lace" coaster ashtray, metallic lusters (shape #3630, Kay Hackett design), limited production 1956 only. $85.00 – 95.00.

"Undersea" cigarette box, metallic lusters (shape #3630, Kay Hackett design), limited production 1956 only. $450.00 – 500.00.

"Undersea" coaster ashtray, Satin White glaze and metallic lusters (shape #3630, Kay Hackett design), limited production 1956 only. $85.00 – 95.00.

"Wheat" cigarette box, Satin White glaze and metallic lusters (shape #3630, Kay Hackett design), limited production 1956 only. $450.00 – 500.00.

"Wheat" coaster ashtray, Satin White glaze and metallic lusters (shape #3630, Kay Hackett design), limited production 1956 only. $85.00 – 95.00.

Lady Luck #3926 oval ashtray (Kay Hackett design), limited production 1955 only. $290.00 – 325.00.

Stitch in Time #3926 oval ashtray (Kay Hackett design), limited production 1955 only. $290.00 – 325.00.

Citrus Fruit coaster ashtray (shape #3630) made for New Jersey Banker's Association, April 1956 only. $85.00 – 95.00.

Governor Clement ashtray, made for Governor Clement of Tennessee, only 25 made by Kay Hackett in April 1956. $150.00 – 175.00.

Kay Hackett's original sample for Undersea cigarette box and coaster ashtray. Courtesy of Merrill and Christl Stangl Bacheler.

1957 Introductions

Hedera cigarette box, metallic lusters, green version of Red Ivy #3961 (shape #3630, Kay Hackett design), 1957 only. $190.00 – 225.00. Courtesy of the Robert Sherman collection.

Wildwood #3962 cigarette box, metallic lusters (shape #3630, Kay Hackett design), 1957 only. $175.00 – 200.00. Courtesy of the Luke and Nancy Ruepp collection.

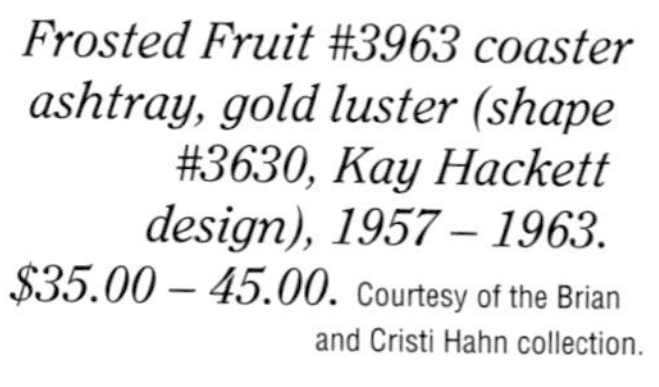

Frosted Fruit #3963 coaster ashtray, gold luster (shape #3630, Kay Hackett design), 1957 – 1963. $35.00 – 45.00. Courtesy of the Brian and Cristi Hahn collection.

Frosted Fruit #3963 cigarette box, gold luster (shape #3630, Kay Hackett design), 1957 – 1963. $130.00 – 150.00. Courtesy of the Luke and Nancy Ruepp collection.

Concord #3964 cigarette box, gold luster (shape #3630, Kay Hackett design), 1957 – 1959. $170.00 – 195.00.

Tiger Lily #3965 coaster ashtray (shape #3630, Kay Hackett design), 1957 – 1962. $35.00 – 45.00.

Provincial #3966 coaster ashtray (shape #3630, Kay Hackett design), 1957 – 1965. $25.00 – 30.00.

Not Shown:

Red Ivy #3961 cigarette box, gold luster (shape #3630, Kay Hackett design), 1957 – 1959. $175.00 – 200.00.

Red Ivy #3961 coaster ashtray, gold luster (shape #3630, Kay Hackett design), 1957 – 1959. $50.00 – 60.00.

Hedera coaster ashtray, metallic lusters, green version of Red Ivy #3961 (shape #3630, Kay Hackett design), 1957 only. $60.00 – 75.00.

Wildwood #3962 coaster ashtray, metallic lusters (shape #3630, Kay Hackett design), 1957 only. $60.00 – 75.00.

Concord #3964 coaster ashtray, gold luster (shape #3630, Kay Hackett design), 1957 – 1959. $40.00 – 50.00.

Tiger Lily #3965 cigarette box (shape #3630, Kay Hackett design), 1957 only. $150.00 – 175.00.

Provincial #3966 cigarette box (shape #3630, Kay Hackett design), 1957 only. $130.00 – 150.00.

Haarlem #3966 cigarette box, colorful version of Provincial #3966 (shape #3630, Kay Hackett design) made for Flemington Outlet, 1957 only. $275.00 – 300.00.

Haarlem #3966 coaster ashtray, colorful version of Provincial #3966 (shape #3630, Kay Hackett design) made for Flemington Outlet, 1957 only. $60.00 – 75.00.

Woodmere #3967 coaster ashtray, gold luster (shape #3630, Kay Hackett design), 1957 – 1958. $35.00 – 45.00.

Wakefield #3967 cigarette box, platinum luster (shape #3630, Kay Hackett design), 1957 – 1958. $150.00 – 175.00.

Wakefield #3967 coaster ashtray, platinum luster (shape #3630, Kay Hackett design), 1957 – 1958. $40.00 – 50.00.

Holly Wreath 8" windproof ashtray (Kay Hackett design), 1957 – 1962. $55.00 – 65.00.

Woodmere #3967 cigarette box, gold luster (shape #3630, Kay Hackett design), 1957 – 1958. $110.00 – 135.00. Courtesy of the Jim and Barbara Nelson collection.

Group of Antique Gold conference table ashtrays. See the Brushed Gold chapter for information and values of these items.

Antique Gold Cigarette Boxes and Coaster Ashtrays

Stangl's Antique Gold finish was introduced in 1957 and was applied to many cigarette box and ashtray shapes through 1978. Several other brushed gold finishes were applied to smoking accessories during that time as well. Values for the other gold finishes are usually about the same or a little less than for Antique Gold. For many other Antique Gold ashtrays and smoking items and artware, please see the chapter on Brushed Gold Artware.

Antique Gold #3434 coaster ashtray, 5", 1957 – 1963. $18.00 – 22.00.

Antique Gold, #3630 cigarette box, flat top or quilt top, 1965 – 1978. $50.00 – 60.00. Courtesy of the Robert Sherman collection.

Antique Gold #3898-7 ashtray, fluted 7", 1965 – 1978. $20.00 – 25.00.

Antique Gold, #3898 cigarette box fluted, $50.00 – 60.00, and 5" coaster ashtrays, $15.00 – 20.00 each. 1965 – 1978. Courtesy of the Luke and Nancy Ruepp collection.

Antique Gold #3898-5 ashtray, fluted 5", "Stangl Pottery 1805" 1965 only. $80.00 – 110.00. Courtesy of the Luke and Nancy Ruepp collection.

Not Shown:

Antique Gold #3630 coaster ashtray, 5" (same as #3434), 1957 – 1963. $20.00 – 25.00.

Antique Gold #3898-5 ashtray, fluted 5", 1965 – 1978. $15.00 – 20.00.

Antique Gold #3898-7 ashtray, fluted 7", "Stangl Pottery 1805," 1965 only. $95.00 – 130.00.

Antique Gold #3902 cigarette box square, 1959 only. $100.00 – 125.00.

Antique Gold #3902-5 coaster ashtray, 5", 1959 only. $25.00 – 30.00.

Antique Gold #3903 cigarette box high-edged cover, 1959 only. $100.00 – 125.00.

Antique Gold #4070 coaster ashtray with center medallion 5", lavender, green, ivory and blue centers, sold as sets of four 1958 – 1963. $18.00 – 20.00 each.

Antique Gold #4085 cigarette box flat cover, Lion 1959 – 1960. $100.00 – 125.00.

Antique Gold #4085, 5¾", ashtray, embossed border Lion 1959 – 1960. $20.00 – 25.00.

Antique Gold #4086 cigarette box, flat cover, hinge, 1959 – 1960. $100.00 – 125.00. Courtesy of the Robert Sherman collection.

Antique Gold #4086, 5¾", ashtray, embossed border Hinge 1959 – 1960. $20.00 – 25.00.

Antique Gold #4087 cigarette box, hump cover, Diamond 1959 – 1960. $100.00 – 125.00.

Antique Gold #4087, 5¾", ashtray, embossed border Diamond 1959 – 1960. $20.00 – 25.00.

Antique Gold #4088, 53/4", ashtray, embossed border Basket Weave 1959 – 1960. $20.00 – 25.00.

Antique Gold #4089 cigarette box, curved cover, Stag 1959 – 1960. $100.00 – 125.00. Courtesy of the

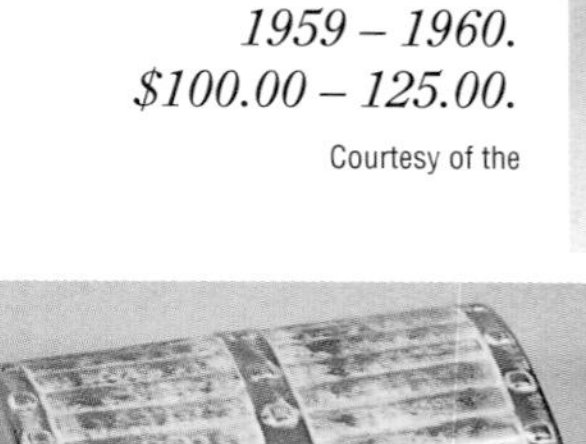

Antique Gold #4090 cigarette box, curved cover, Corduroy 1959 – 1960. $100.00 – 125.00. Courtesy of the Robert Sherman collection.

Antique Gold #4088 cigarette box hump cover, Basket Weave 1959 – 1960. $100.00 – 125.00.

Antique Gold #4089, 5¾", ashtray, embossed border Stag 1959 – 1960. $10.00 – 15.00.

Antique Gold #4090, 5¾", ashtray, embossed border Corduroy 1959 – 1960. $10.00 – 15.00.

Antique Gold #5154 ashtray, 7" fluted with Appliqué motif (orig. #3898), 1964 only. $20.00 – 25.00.

1958 Introductions

Not Shown:

Fruit and Flowers #4030 cigarette box (shape #3630, Kay Hackett design), 1958 only. $175.00 – 200.00.

Florentine (originally called Heritage) #4031 cigarette box (shape #3630, Kay Hackett design), 1958 – 1959. $130.00 – 150.00.

Florentine (originally called Heritage) #4031 coaster ashtray (shape #3630, Kay Hackett design), 1958 – 1959. $35.00 – 45.00.

Citrus Fruit #3798 coaster ashtray (shape #3630) made for Somerville Kiwanis Club, Somerville, NJ, 1958. $45.00 – 55.00.

Florentine (originally Heritage) #4031 cigarette box, $130.00 – 150.00, and coaster ashtray, $35.00 – 45.00, 1958 – 1959. Courtesy of the Robert Sherman collection.

Fruit and Flowers #4030 coaster ashtray (shape #3630, Kay Hackett design), 1958 – 1960. $40.00 – 50.00.

1959 Introductions

Not Shown:

Garland #4067 cigarette box (shape #3630, Kay Hackett design), 1959 only. $170.00 – 195.00.

Garland #4067 coaster ashtray (shape #3630, Kay Hackett design), 1959 – 1963. $35.00 – 45.00.

Fairlawn #4068 cigarette box (shape #3630, Kay Hackett design), 1959 only. $175.00 – 200.00.

Fairlawn #4068 coaster ashtray (shape #3630, Kay Hackett design), 1959 – 1960. $40.00 – 50.00.

1960 Introductions

Not Shown:

Chicory #5046 cigarette box, sprayed engobe (shape #3630, Kay Hackett design), 1960 only. $175.00 – 200.00.

Chicory #3809 coaster ashtray, sprayed engobe (shape #3630, Kay Hackett design), 1960 only. $35.00 – 45.00.

Bella Rosa #5047 cigarette box (shape #3630, Kay Hackett design), 1960 only. $170.00 – 195.00.

Bella Rosa #5047 coaster ashtray (shape #3630, Kay Hackett design), 1960 – 1961. $25.00 – 35.00.

1961 Introductions

Not Shown:

Festival #5072 cigarette box (shape #3630), 1961 only. $170.00 – 195.00.

Festival #5072 coaster ashtray (shape #3630), 1961 only. $50.00 – 60.00.

Florette #5073 cigarette box (shape #3630, Betty Powell design), 1961 only. $170.00 – 195.00.

Florette #5073 coaster ashtray (shape #3630, Betty Powell design), 1961 – 1963. $35.00 – 45.00.

Platina

For many other Platina ashtrays and smoking items, please see the chapter on Brushed Gold Artware.

Platina #3630 coaster ashtray, 5", 1961 – 1963. $20.00 – 25.00.

Platina, #3630 cigarette box, flat top, 1961 – 1963. $50.00 – 60.00.

Platina, #3898 cigarette box, fluted, 1961 – 1963. $50.00 – 60.00.

Platina #3898-5 ashtray, fluted 5", 1961 – 1963. $15.00 – 20.00.

Platina #3898-7 ashtray, fluted 7", 1961 – 1963. $20.00 – 25.00.

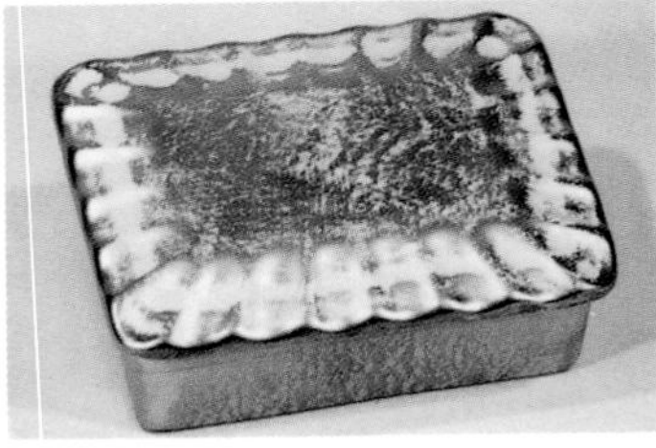

Platina, #3898 cigarette box, fluted, $50.00 – 60.00. Courtesy of the Robert Sherman collection.

1962 Introductions

Not Shown:

Orchard Song #5110 fluted ashtray 5"(shape #3898, Irene Sarnecki design), 1962 – 1974. $6.00 – 8.00.

Orchard Song #5110 coaster ashtray (shape #3630, Irene Sarnecki design), 1962 – 1974. $6.00 – 8.00.

Bittersweet #5111 coaster ashtray, carved decoration (shape #3630, Irene Sarnecki design), 1962 – 1974. $8.00 – 12.00.

Bittersweet #5111 fluted ashtray 5"(shape #3898, Irene Sarnecki design), 1965 – 1974. $6.00 – 8.00.

Fathom Green #5127 coaster ashtray (shape #3630) made for Jordan Marsh, 1962 only. $25.00 – 30.00.

Bittersweet #5111 coaster ashtray, no carving (shape #3630, Irene Sarnecki design), 1966 – 1974. $6.00 – 8.00.

Golden Glo

For many other Golden Glo artware items, please see the chapter on Brushed Gold Artware.

Golden Glo #3630 coaster ashtray, 5", 1962 – 1963. $20.00 – 25.00.

Golden Glo #3898-5 ashtray, fluted 5", 1962 – 1963. $15.00 – 20.00.

Golden Glo #3898-7 ashtray, fluted 7", 1962 – 1963. $20.00 – 25.00.

Golden Glo #4070 coaster ashtray with center medallion 5", 1962 only. $20.00 – 25.00.

Golden Glo, #3630 cigarette box, flat top, 1962 – 1963. $60.00 – 75.00.

Golden Glo, #3898 cigarette box, fluted, 1962 – 1963. $60.00 – 75.00.

1963 Introductions

Blue Daisy #5131 fluted ashtray 5" (shape #3898, Irene Sarnecki design), 1963 – 1972. $8.00 – 12.00. Courtesy of the Luke and Nancy Ruepp collection.

Golden Grape #5129 coaster ashtray (shape #3630, Irene Sarnecki design), 1963 – 1970. $8.00 – 12.00.

Golden Grape #5129 fluted ashtray 5"(shape #3898, Irene Sarnecki design), 1963 – 1970. $6.00 – 8.00.

Paisley #5130 coaster ashtray (shape #3630, Irene Sarnecki design), 1963 – 1965. $20.00 – 25.00.

Paisley #5130 fluted ashtray 5"(shape #3898, Irene Sarnecki design), 1963 – 1965. $10.00 – 15.00.

Blue Daisy #5131 coaster ashtray (shape #3630, Irene Sarnecki design), 1963 – 1965. $15.00 – 20.00.

Aztec

Aztec #A-3630 cigarette box flat top, 1963 – 1965. $75.00 – 95.00.

Aztec #A-3898 cigarette box fluted, 1963 – 1965. $75.00 – 95.00.

Aztec #A-3898-5 ashtray, fluted 5", 1963 – 1965. $15.00 – 20.00.

Aztec #A-3630 coaster ashtray, 5", 1963 – 1965. $20.00 – 25.00.

Aztec #A-3898-7 ashtray, fluted 7", 1963 – 1965. $20.00 – 25.00.

1964 Introductions

Not Shown:

Golden Blossom #5155 coaster ashtray (shape #3630, Irene Sarnecki design), 1964 – 1965. $10.00 – 15.00.

Caughley #5150 cigarette box, flat top or quilt top (shape #3630), 1967 – 1978. $100.00 – 125.00.

Caughley #5150 cigarette box, fluted (shape #3898), 1964 – 1978. $100.00 – 125.00.

Caughley #5150 coaster ashtray (shape #3630), 1964 – 1978. $20.00 – 25.00.

Caughley #5150 ashtray, fluted 5" (shape #3898), 1964 – 1978. $20.00 – 25.00.

Caughley #5150 ashtray, fluted 7" (shape #3898), 1964 – 1978. $25.00 – 35.00.

Antique Rose cigarette box (shape #3630), 1964 – 1965. $150.00 – 175.00.

Antique Rose coaster ashtray (shape #3630), 1964 – 1965. $40.00 – 50.00.

Golden Blossom #5155 fluted ashtray 5" (shape #3898, Irene Sarnecki design), 1964 – 1972. $8.00 – 10.00.

Appliqué

Appliqué featured a sprigged floral motif in white on a colored background. Jade green, dark green, and blue colored clays were used to cast the shapes of the Appliqué line.

Appliqué cigarette box in Jade Green, $65.00 – 80.00, square ashtray in Blue, $15.00 – 20.00, and oval ashtray in Dark Green, $15.00 – 20.00. Courtesy of the Robert Sherman collection.

Appliqué #3666 ashtray, square 4½", 1964 – 1965. $15.00 – 20.00.

Appliqué, #3996 cigarette holder, oval, 2½". $20.00 – 25.00.

Appliqué, #3997 ashtray, oval 3½". $15.00 – 20.00.

Appliqué, #5058 ashtray, round 7¼". $20.00 – 25.00.

Appliqué, #5153 cigarette lighter, 4". $25.00 – 35.00.

Appliqué #5154 ashtray, fluted, 7", 1964 – 1965. $15.00 – 20.00.

Appliqué Dark Green, #3898 cigarette box, flat top, 1964 – 1965. $65.00 – 80.00. Courtesy of the Robert Sherman collection.

Granada Gold Cigarette Boxes and Coaster Ashtrays

For many other Granada Gold ashtrays and smoking items, please see the chapter on Brushed Gold Artware.

Granada Gold #3630 cigarette box, flat top or quilt top, 1964 – 1978. $45.00 – 55.00.

Granada Gold #3630 coaster ashtray, 5", 1964 – 1978. $15.00 – 20.00.

Granada Gold #3898 cigarette box, fluted, 1964 – 1978. $45.00 – 55.00.

Granada Gold #3898-5 ashtray, fluted 5", 1964 – 1970. $10.00 – 15.00.

Granada Gold #3898-7 ashtray, fluted 7", 1964 – 1970. $20.00 – 25.00.

Silver Haze Cigarette Boxes and Coaster Ashtrays

Silver Haze #3898-5 ashtray, fluted 5", 1964 only. $12.00 – 18.00.

Silver Haze, #3898 cigarette box, fluted, 1964 only. $65.00 – 80.00.

Silver Haze, #3898 cigarette box, fluted, $65.00 – 80.00, and coaster ashtrays, $12.00 – 18.00 each, 1964 only. Courtesy of the Robert Sherman collection.

1965 Introductions

Not Shown:

Apple Delight #5161 coaster ashtray (shape #3630, Kay Hackett design), 1965 – 1970. $20.00 – 25.00.

Apple Delight #5161 fluted ashtray 5" (shape #3898, Kay Hackett design), 1965 – 1974. $8.00 – 12.00.

Fruit #3697 coaster ashtray (shape #3630), no carving, made for Flemington Outlet (Kay Hackett design), 1965 – 1970. $20.00 – 25.00.

Fruit #5174 ashtray, square, no rests, 7" made for Flemington Outlet and Nelson Lebo Lamp Co., 1965 – 1978. $55.00 – 65.00.

Bachelor's Button #5177 coaster ashtray (shape #3630, Irene Sarnecki design), 1965 – 1973. $8.00 – 12.00.

Bachelor's Button #5177 fluted ashtray 5" (shape #3898, Irene Sarnecki design), 1965 – 1973. $6.00 – 8.00.

Fruit #3697 fluted ashtray 5" (shape #3898), no carving, made for Flemington Outlet (Kay Hackett design), 1965 – 1974. $12.00 – 18.00.

Mediterranean

For many other Mediterranean ashtrays and smoking items, please see the Mediterranean section in the chapter on Hand Decorated Artware.

Mediterranean #3630 coaster ashtray, 5", 1965 – 1972. $20.00 – 25.00.

Mediterranean, #3898 cigarette box, fluted, 1965 – 1972. $85.00 – 95.00.

Mediterranean #3898-5 ashtray, fluted 5", 1965 – 1972. $15.00 – 20.00.

Mediterranean #3898-7 ashtray, fluted 7", 1965 – 1972. $20.00 – 25.00.

Mediterranean, #3630 cigarette box, flat top or quilt top, 1965 – 1972. $75.00 – 95.00. Courtesy of the Luke and Nancy Ruepp collection.

Scandinavia #2074 ashtray, 6", 1965 only. $25.00 – 35.00.

Scandinavia

Scandinavia #2089 ashtray, Scotty dog 4½"x5", 1965 only. $60.00 – 80.00.

Scandinavia #3044 ashtray Scroll, 4"x5". $20.00 – 25.00.

Scandinavia #3630 coaster ashtray, 5", 1965 only. $20.00 – 25.00.

Scandinavia, #3630 cigarette box, flat top, 1965 only. $95.00 – 110.00.

Scandinavia #3898-5 ashtray, fluted 5", 1965 only. $15.00 – 20.00.

Scandinavia #3898-7 ashtray, fluted 7", 1965 only. $20.00 – 25.00.

Scandinavia, #3898 cigarette box, fluted, 1965 only. $95.00 – 110.00. Courtesy of the Luke and Nancy Ruepp collection.

1967 Introductions: White Grape

White Grape #5187 ashtray, 7" (Rose Herbeck design), 1967 only. $25.00 – 35.00.

White Grape #5187 coaster ashtray, 5" (Rose Herbeck design), 1967 only. $40.00 – 50.00.

Black Gold Cigarette Boxes and Coaster Ashtrays

For many other Black Gold ashtrays and smoking items, please see the chapter on Brushed Gold Artware.

Black Gold #3630 coaster ashtray, 5", 1967 – 1976. $20.00 – 25.00.

Black Gold #3898-5 ashtray, fluted 5", 1967 – 1970. $15.00 – 20.00.

Black Gold #3898-7 ashtray, fluted 7", 1967 – 1970. $20.00 – 25.00.

White Grape #5187 cigarette box (shape #3630, Rose Herbeck design), 1967 only. $110.00 – 160.00. Courtesy of the Robert Sherman collection.

Black Gold, #3630 cigarette box, flat top or quilt top, 1967 – 1976. $45.00 – 55.00.

Black Gold, #3898 cigarette box, fluted, 1967 – 1976. $45.00 – 55.00.

1968 Introductions

Not Shown:

Stardust #5202 coaster ashtray (shape #3630, Irene Sarnecki design), 1968 – 1970. $15.00 – 20.00.

Stardust #5202 fluted ashtray 5"(shape #3898, Irene Sarnecki design), 1968 – 1970. $6.00 – 8.00.

First Love #5203 coaster ashtray (shape #3630, Irene Sarnecki design), 1968 – 1970. $12.00 – 18.00.

First Love #5203 fluted ashtray 5"(shape #3898, Irene Sarnecki design), 1968 – 1970. $6.00 – 8.00.

Caribbean

For many other Caribbean ashtrays and smoking items, please see the Caribbean section in the chapter on Hand Decorated Artware.

Caribbean #3630 coaster ashtray, 5", 1968 – 1970. $20.00 – 25.00.

Caribbean #3898-5 ashtray, fluted 5", 1968 – 1970. $15.00 – 20.00.

Caribbean #3898-7 ashtray, fluted 7", 1968 – 1970. $20.00 – 25.00.

Caribbean, #3630 cigarette box, flat top or quilt top, 1968 – 1970, $85.00 – 95.00.

Caribbean, #3898 cigarette box, fluted, 1968 – 1970, $85.00 – 95.00.

Caribbean #5174 square ashtray 7", 1968 – 1970. Courtesy of the Ben and Floss Avila collection.

1969 Introductions

Not Shown:

Colonial Silver Cigarette Boxes and Coaster Ashtrays

For many other Colonial Silver ashtrays and smoking items, please see the chapter on Brushed Gold Artware.

Colonial Silver #3630 coaster ashtray, 5", 1969-71. $20.00 – 25.00.

Colonial Silver #3898 cigarette box, fluted, 1969 – 1971. $50.00 – 60.00.

Colonial Silver #3898-5 ashtray, fluted 5", 1969 – 1970. $15.00 – 20.00.

Colonial Silver #3898-7 ashtray, fluted 7", 1969 – 1970. $20.00 – 25.00.

Colonial Silver, #3630 cigarette box, flat top or quilt top, 1969 – 1971. $50.00 – 60.00. Courtesy of the Bill Servis, Susan Lewis collection.

1970 Introductions

Not Shown:

Star Flite cigarette box, gold luster (shape #3630, Martin Stangl design), 1971 only. $200.00 – 250.00.

Star Flite coaster ashtray, gold luster (shape #3630, Martin Stangl design), 1971 only. $50.00 – 60.00.

Star Flite cigarette box, $200.00 – 250.00, and coaster ashtray, $50.00 – 60.00, 1971 only. Courtesy of the Robert Sherman collection.

Antique French Crackle

Antique French Crackle, #3630 coaster ashtray, 5", 1970 – 1971. $20.00 – 25.00.

Antique French Crackle, #3630 cigarette box, flat top or quilt top, 1970 – 1971. $100.00 – 125.00.

Antique French Crackle, #3898 cigarette box, fluted, 1970 – 1971. $100.00 – 125.00.

Tangerine

For a short time during 1970, the following series of smoking items was produced in a new glaze called Tangerine. Many of the same ashtray shapes were also produced in the vibrant blue-green Mediterranean finish during 1970 to complement the Tangerine glaze. Tangerine was an energetic orange/red glaze color and does not remotely resemble Stangl's original uranium-based Tangerine glaze from the 1930s. These smoking items were discontinued by the end of 1970.

Tangerine #3630 cigarette box 4½"x5½", flat top, 1970 only. $70.00 – 85.00.

Tangerine #3630 cigarette box 4½"x5½", quilt top, 1970 only. $70.00 – 85.00.

Tangerine #3897S ashtray, square 4"x4" (Ed Pettingil design), 1970 only. $20.00 – 25.00.

Tangerine #3897M ashtray, square 5"x5" (Ed Pettingil design), 1970 only. $22.00 – 28.00.

Tangerine #3897L ashtray, square 6½"x6½" (Ed Pettingil design), 1970 only. $25.00 – 35.00.

Tangerine ashtray #3897L, 6½"x6½", 1970 only. $25.00 – 35.00.

Tangerine #3914 ashtray, square with square well 9", 1970 only (Kay Hackett design). $25.00 – 30.00.
Tangerine #3915 ashtray, square with round well 9", 1970 only (Kay Hackett design). $25.00 – 30.00.
Tangerine #3926 ashtray, oval, plain, 10¾"x8", 1970 only (Kay Hackett design). $20.00 – 25.00.
Tangerine #3942 ashtray, Safety, oval 8½"x7", 1970 only (Ed Pettingil design). $20.00 – 25.00.
Tangerine #3972 ashtray, Flying Saucer 10", 1970 only (Kay Hackett design). $25.00 – 35.00.
Tangerine #4026 ashtray, conference table 11¼", 1970 only (Kay Hackett design). $25.00 – 30.00.
Tangerine #5004 ashtray, rectangular, 12½"x6½", 1970 only (Kay Hackett design). $25.00 – 35.00.
Tangerine #5060 ashtray, round 8¼", 1970 only. $18.00 – 22.00.
Tangerine #5174 ashtray, square, no rests, 7", 1970 only. $20.00 – 25.00.

1971 Introductions

Not Shown:

Pompeii

The entire Pompeii line was discontinued by November 1971, less than one year after introduction. For many other Pompeii ashtrays and artware items, please see the Pompeii section in the chapter on Hand Decorated Artware.

Blue Pompeii #5232 6" jiggered ashtray and Yellow Pompeii #5231 4" jiggered ashtray, 1971 only. $20.00 – 25.00 each.

Pompeii #3630 cigarette box flat top, 1971 only. $95.00 – 110.00.
Pompeii #3630 coaster ashtray, 5", 1971 only. $20.00 – 25.00.
Pompeii #3898 cigarette box fluted, 1971 only. $95.00 – 110.00.
Pompeii #3898-5 ashtray, fluted 5", 1971 only. $15.00 – 20.00.
Pompeii #3915 ashtray, square, 9" 1971 only. $20.00 – 25.00.
Pompeii #3942 ashtray, oval, 8½"x 7" 1971 only. $15.00 – 20.00.
Pompeii #3972 ashtray, round, 10" 1971 only. $20.00 – 25.00.
Pompeii #4018 dish, shell, 7½" 1971 only. $20.00 – 25.00.
Pompeii #4026 ashtray, round, 11½" 1971 only. $20.00 – 25.00.
Pompeii #4033 ashtray, flower, 5½" 1971 only. $15.00 – 20.00.
Pompeii #4034 ashtray, leaf, 6½" 1971 only. $15.00 – 20.00.
Pompeii #4036 ashtray, leaf, 6". $15.00 – 20.00.
Pompeii #4037 ashtray, shell, 5"x 5½" 1971 only. $15.00 – 20.00.
Pompeii #5004 ashtray, 12½"x 6½" 1971 only. $20.00 – 25.00.
Pompeii #5060 ashtray, round, 8" 1971 only. $20.00 – 25.00.
Pompeii #5075 ashtray, prism, 6"x 4" 1971 only. $20.00 – 25.00.
Pompeii #5097 ashtray, apple, 6½"x 4½" 1971 only. $15.00 – 20.00.
Pompeii #5174 ashtray, square, 7" 1971 only. $15.00 – 20.00.
Pompeii #5231 jiggered ashtray, 4" 1971 only. $20.00 – 25.00.
Pompeii #5232 jiggered ashtray, 6" 1971 only. $20.00 – 25.00.
Pompeii #5233 pipe knockout ashtray, 8" 1971 only. $25.00 – 35.00.

Ashtray with Bird and Solebury National Bank Ashtray

After Pennsbury Pottery of Morrisville, Pennsylvania closed in 1970, two of Pennsbury's former accounts contacted Stangl Pottery to manufacture items similar to products previously produced by Pennsbury. One account was Zephanelli Gift Importers, Inc., who wanted Stangl Pottery to make a small "bird on a gourd" ashtray similar to Pennsbury's "Slick Chick" ashtray. Stangl accommodated by perching one of the small birds from the #3635 Goldfinch Group on gourd-shaped #3896 Casual Ashtray shape and called it #5253 Ashtray with Bird. The "gourd" ashtray shapes were either plain white or hand-painted Pomona Green. The birds were usually decorated yellow and brown, but other colors were used also. The #5253 Ashtray with Bird was produced during 1971 and 1972 only.

Not Shown:

#5253 Ashtray with Bird, 6", green with blue and yellow bird, 1971 – 1972. $250.00 – 300.00.
#5253 Ashtray with Bird, 6", white with yellow and brown bird, 1971 – 1972. $200.00 – 250.00.

#5253 Ashtray with Bird, 6", white with yellow and brown bird, 1971 – 1972. $200.00 – 250.00.

The other Pennsbury account that also contracted with Stangl was the Solebury National Bank of Lahaska, Pennsylvania. During the 1960s, Pennsbury Pottery had produced a small promotional ashtray for the Solebury National Bank depicting a local canal scene with a bridge, canal boat, and mules. The Pennsbury ashtrays were molded with the decoration and hand-painted. Stangl began producing a similar ashtray for the Solebury National Bank in 1971. The Stangl version of the Solebury ashtray was on a #5242 Croyden 6" plate that was spun with Tan underglaze color. The motifs on the Stangl pieces were hand-carved, not molded, as on the Pennsbury ashtrays. The hand-carved motifs add an ingenuous quality that is absent from the Pennsbury Solebury National Bank ashtrays. Stangl Pottery discontinued these items by 1972.

Solebury National Bank 6" plate, 1971 only. $25.00 – 35.00. Courtesy of the Brian and Cristi Hahn collection.

1972 Introductions

Not Shown:

Decal Decorated Ashtrays

Produced on items cast of red clay with engobe from 1972 through 1974. Items were cast entirely of white clay from 1974 until 1978.

Decal ashtray #5058, round 7¼". $20.00 – 25.00.

Decal ashtray #3942, oval 8½"x7". $25.00 – 35.00.

Father Christmas Decal ashtray #3816, windproof 8", 1972 – 1973. $35.00 – 45.00.

Decal ashtray #3816, windproof 8", 1972 – 1973. $25.00 – 35.00.

Decal decorated #3630 quilt top cigarette box with Butterfly on Harvest Yellow glaze, 1977 – 1978. $100.00 – 125.00. Courtesy of the Luke and Nancy Ruepp collection.

Rotary Decal ashtray #5058, round 7¼". $30.00 – 40.00.

Christmas Decal ashtray #3942, oval 8½"x7". $40.00 – 50.00.

Decal ashtray, #5174 square 7" made for Nelson Lebo Lamp Co., 1965 – 1978. $30.00 – 40.00.

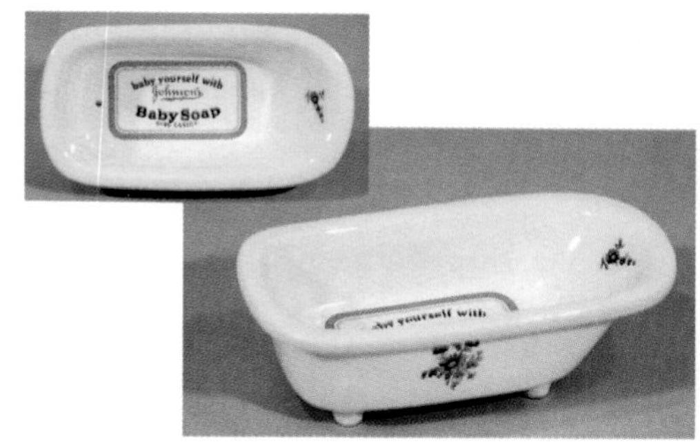

Johnson & Johnson's Baby Soap bathtub ashtray (interior, inset). $60.00 – 75.00. Courtesy of the Ruepp collection.

Green Lustre Cigarette Boxes and Coaster Ashtrays

For many other Green Lustre artware items, please see the chapter on Brushed Gold Artware.

Green Lustre #3630 cigarette box flat top or quilt top, 1972 – 1974. $50.00 – 60.00.

Green Lustre #3630 coaster ashtray, 5", 1972 – 1974. $20.00 – 25.00.

Green Lustre #3898 cigarette box fluted, 1972 – 1974. $50.00 – 60.00.

Green Lustre #3898-5 ashtray, fluted 5", 1972 – 1974. $15.00 – 20.00.

Green Lustre #3898-7 ashtray, fluted 7", 1972 – 1974. $20.00 – 25.00.

Green Lustre #5259 ashtray, triangular 6¾", 1972 – 1973. $25.00 – 35.00. Courtesy of the Hill-Fulper-Stangl Museum.

1973 Introductions

Porch & Patio ashtray, 8" round, gray glaze interior, unglazed bisque exterior 1973 – 1974. $25.00 – 35.00.

Terra White

Terra White was a marbled technique similar to Dave Thomas' Marbled products of 1954. Terra White items had a bolder, less swirling figure than the Marbled. Usually, Terra White was made of red and white clays, but occasionally green or blue clays were added to the mix. Terra White was primarily used for flowerpot and patio items during 1975, but ashtrays made of Terra White were available as early as 1973.

Not Shown:

#5074 ashtray, square 5⅞"x5⅞", 1973 – 1975. $25.00 – 30.00.
#5075 ashtray, Prism 6"x4", 1973 – 1975. $25.00 – 30.00.
#5076 ashtray, 8½"x4", 1973 – 1975. $30.00 – 40.00.
#5077 ashtray 8½"x5¼", 1973 – 1975. $30.00 – 40.00.

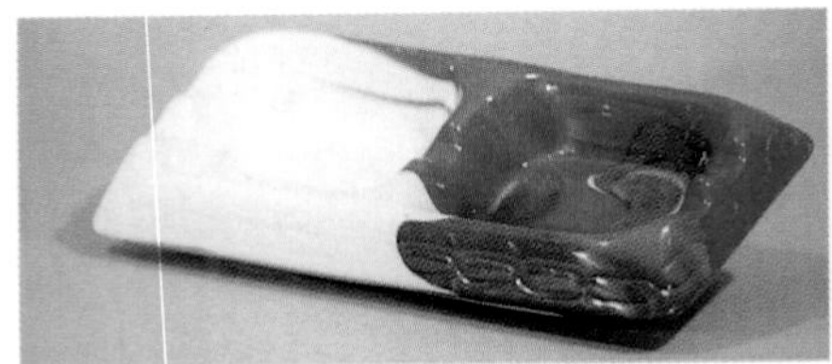

Terra White #5076 ashtray, 8½"x4", 1973 – 1975. $30.00 – 40.00.

1974 Introduction: Town & Country

Not Shown:

Town & Country blue #1953 ashtray, 4¼", 1974 – 1978. $25.00 – 35.00.
Town & Country other colors #1953 ashtray, 4¼", 1974 – 1978. $15.00 – 20.00.
Town & Country blue #3942 ashtray, 8½", 1974 – 1978. $35.00 – 45.00.
Town & Country other colors #3942 ashtray, 8½", 1974 – 1978. $20.00 – 25.00.
Town & Country blue bathtub ashtray, 1977 – 1978. $50.00 – 60.00.
Town & Country other colors bathtub ashtray, 1977 – 1978. $40.00 – 50.00.

Town & Country Blue bathtub ashtray, 1977 – 1978. $50.00 – 60.00. Courtesy of the Luke and Nancy Ruepp collection.

1977 Introduction: Solid-Color

During 1977 and 1978, several smoking items were produced in solid-color glazes for the Flemington Outlet. Occasionally, these items were also embellished with fired-on decals. Some of the glazes used were Summer-Green, Pioneer-Brown, Harvest-Yellow, Winter-Tan, Canary Yellow, Chartreuse Green, Dark Green, Peach, and White.

Not Shown:

#3630 flat top or quilt top, 1977 – 1978. $60.00 – 75.00.
#3926 ashtray, oval, 10¾"x8", 1977 – 1978 (Kay Hackett design). $20.00 – 25.00.

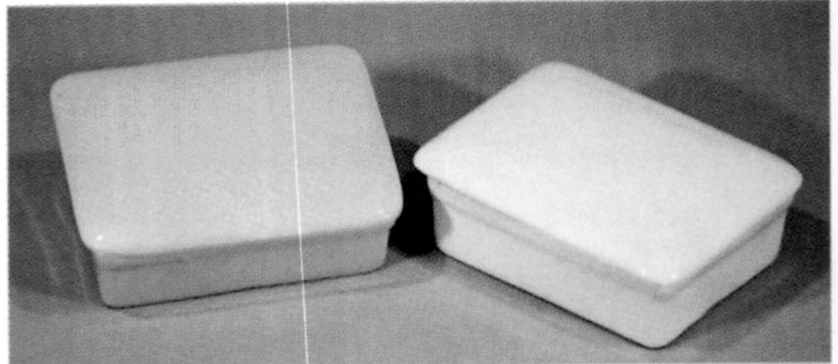

Two #3630 quilt top cigarette boxes in Harvest-Yellow and White glazes, $60.00 – 75.00 each. Courtesy of the Robert Sherman collection.

Martin Stangl's Christmas Cards, 1955 – 1971

Beginning in 1955, Martin Stangl sent coaster ashtray "Christmas cards" to business associates, friends, and family. On average, between 200 and 300 Christmas cards were produced each year. The "cards" were embellished with gold and platinum lusters and stamped "Merry Christmas."

"Mr. and Mrs. J.M. Stangl" Christmas card stamp.

"Betty and Martin Stangl" Christmas card stamp.

The signet "Mr. and Mrs. J.M. Stangl" was stamped on the cards sent to business associates and professionals. Family members and close friends received cards stamped with "Betty and Martin Stangl" until 1960, when Betty passed away. That same year, Martin Stangl married Natalie, but she left him after six weeks. Martin Stangl then married Vera in 1962. His daughter, Betty Stangl Thomas, suggested that he stamp all the cards with "Mr. and Mrs. J.M. Stangl," so he wouldn't have to make a new stamp every time he remarried. He followed this practice for the next two years, then began having the personal cards stamped "Vera and Martin Stangl," while the business cards continued to be stamped "Mr. and Mrs. J.M. Stangl."

Each year, an assortment of several cards would be produced, which is why cards bearing the same motif can be found stamped with different wives' names. The last Christmas card in 1971 was the one bearing the Father Christmas decal. Martin Stangl was hospitalized with a heart attack in October 1971, so he approved the hastily produced decal coaster for his Christmas greeting that year. Normally, designs, sketches, and samples would be created before a card was put into production. Many of the motifs were designed by Irene Sarnecki, but a few were Kay Hackett adaptations.

Fewer personal Christmas cards stamped with "Betty and Martin Stangl" or "Vera and Martin Stangl" were made than business cards stamped "Mr. and Mrs. J.M. Stangl." In addition, the personal cards are more desirable and usually sell for more than the same card with the "Mr. and Mrs. J.M. Stangl" signet.

Values represented here are for cards in pristine condition. Christmas cards that have been used as ashtrays usually show signs of wear. The "Merry Christmas" stamp is most vulnerable, as is the bright red overglaze color. Evidence of wear in these areas can reduce the value by up to 50 percent.

Blue Bells and Pine Christmas card. Courtesy of the Bill Servis, Susan Lewis collection.

Blue Bells and Pine business Christmas card. $150.00 – 175.00.
Blue Bells and Pine personal Christmas card. $190.00 – 225.00.
Candle and Pine business Christmas card. $130.00 – 150.00.
Candle and Pine personal Christmas card. $170.00 – 190.00.
Carolers business Christmas card. $170.00 – 195.00.
Carolers personal Christmas card. $200.00 – 250.00.
Christmas Tree business Christmas card. $100.00 – 125.00.
Christmas Tree personal Christmas card. $130.00 – 150.00.
Della Robbia Wreath business Christmas card. $150.00 – 175.00.
Della Robbia Wreath personal Christmas card. $175.00 – 200.00.
Evergreen Star business Christmas card. $130.00 – 150.00.
Evergreen Star personal Christmas card. $170.00 – 195.00.

Candle and Pine Christmas card. Courtesy of the Bill Servis, Susan Lewis collection.

Carolers Christmas card. Courtesy of the Luke and Nancy Ruepp collection.

Christmas Tree personal card with signet on front instead of back. $190.00 – 225.00.

Della Robbia Wreath Christmas card. Courtesy of the Bill Servis, Susan Lewis collection.

Evergreen Star Christmas card. Courtesy of the Bill Servis, Susan Lewis collection.

Evergreen Wreath business Christmas card. $130.00 – 150.00.
Evergreen Wreath personal Christmas card. $170.00 – 190.00.
Father Christmas business Christmas card. $130.00 – 150.00.
Father Christmas personal Christmas card. $150.00 – 175.00.
Gold Bells and Holly business Christmas card. $150.00 – 175.00.
Gold Bells and Holly personal Christmas card. $190.00 – 225.00.
Holly Nosegay business Christmas card. $150.00 – 175.00.
Holly Nosegay personal Christmas card. $170.00 – 195.00.

Evergreen Wreath Christmas card. Courtesy of the Bill Servis, Susan Lewis collection.

Father Christmas Christmas card. Courtesy of the Bill Servis, Susan Lewis collection.

Gold Bells and Holly Christmas card. Courtesy of the Bill Servis, Susan Lewis collection.

Holly Nosegay Christmas card. Courtesy of the Bill Servis, Susan Lewis collection.

Holly Sprig Christmas card. Courtesy of the Bill Servis, Susan Lewis collection.

Holly Scroll business Christmas card. $170.00 – 190.00.
Holly Scroll personal Christmas card. $190.00 – 225.00.
Holly Sprig business Christmas card. $150.00 – 175.00.
Holly Sprig personal Christmas card. $175.00 – 200.00.
Poinsettia business Christmas card. $150.00 – 175.00.
Poinsettia personal Christmas card. $170.00 – 195.00.
Snow Elf business Christmas card. $150.00 – 175.00.
Snow Elf personal Christmas card. $170.00 – 195.00.
Snowman business Christmas card. $150.00 – 175.00.
Snowman personal Christmas card. $175.00 – 200.00.
Spaniel business Christmas card. $170.00 – 190.00.
Spaniel personal Christmas card. $190.00 – 225.00.
Three Trees business Christmas card. $130.00 – 150.00.
Three Trees personal Christmas card. $150.00 – 175.00.

Poinsettia Christmas card. Courtesy of the Bill Servis, Susan Lewis collection.

Snow Elf Christmas card. Courtesy of the Bill Servis, Susan Lewis collection.

Snowman Christmas card. Courtesy of the Bill Servis, Susan Lewis collection.

Three Trees Christmas card. Courtesy of the Bill Servis, Susan Lewis collection.

Golf Ball Ashtrays

This series of Antique Gold ashtrays with attached ceramic golf ball decoration was introduced in 1958 and produced only until 1959. The Golfer #3915GBDC (Golf Ball DeCorated) was the most popular of this series and was produced from 1958 until August 1965. Based on the popularity of the Golfer #3915GBDC, the oval Golfer #3926 was introduced in 1960. For a very brief time, this ashtray also bore an attached golf ball, a practice almost immediately discontinued, making them exceedingly rare. The ceramic golf balls were also produced as salt and pepper shakers for the Flemington Outlet.

Not Shown:

Antique Gold #3914GB ashtray, square with square well and golf ball center, 1958 – 1959. $75.00 – 95.00.
Antique Gold #3976GB ashtray, oval 11¼"x7¾" with golf ball center, 1958 – 1959. $75.00 – 95.00.
Antique Gold #3926GB ashtray, oval with golf ball center, 1958 – 1959. $75.00 – 95.00.
Golfer #3926 ashtray, oval with Golf Course landscape decoration and golf ball center, 1960 only. $275.00 – 300.00.
Antique Gold #4026GB ashtray, conference table 11¼" with golf ball center, 1958 – 1959. $75.00 – 95.00.
Antique Gold #3972GB ashtray, Flying Saucer, 10" with golf ball center, 1958 – 1959. $75.00 – 95.00.

Golfer #3915GBDC, square with round well and Golf Course landscape decoration, 1958 – 1965. $150.00 – 195.00.

Golfer #3926 ashtray, oval with Golf Course landscape decoration, no golf ball center, 1960 – 1965. $120.00 – 140.00.

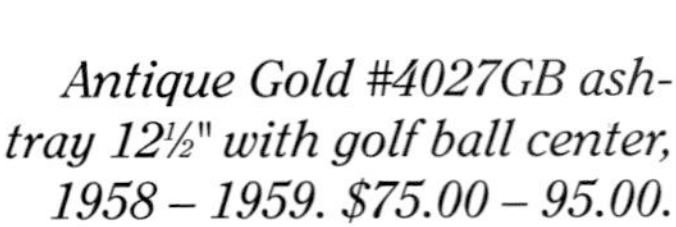

Antique Gold #4027GB ashtray 12½" with golf ball center, 1958 – 1959. $75.00 – 95.00.

Miniature Cigarette Urns, Ashtrays, and Cigarette Lighters

Miniature Cigarette Urns and Ashtrays

For many other Antique Gold ashtrays and smoking items, please see the chapter on Brushed Gold Artware.

Not Shown:

Antique Gold #3992 cigarette holder, urn, 3¼" 1957 – 1960. $20.00 – 25.00.

Antique Gold #3994 cigarette holder, cylinder, 2"x2½" 1957 – 1960. $20.00 – 25.00.

Antique Gold #3995 ashtray for #3994 cigarette holder 3½", 1957 – 1960. $15.00 – 20.00.

Antique Gold #3996 cigarette holder, oval, 2½", 1957 – 1960. $20.00 – 25.00.

Antique Gold #3997 ashtray for #3996 cigarette holder, oval 3½", 1957 – 1960. $15.00 – 20.00.

Antique Gold #3998 ashtray for #3992 cigarette holder, 3", 1957 – 1960. $15.00 – 20.00.

Appliqué #3996 cigarette holder, oval, 2½", 1964 – 1965. $20.00 – 25.00.

Antique Gold #3992 cigarette holder and #3998 ashtray.

Antique Gold #3996 oval cigarette holder and #3997 oval ashtray.

Cigarette Lighters

Not Shown:

Antique Gold #5007 lighter, urn shape, large, 1959 – 1960. $50.00 – 60.00.

Antique Gold #5153 lighter, 4" (Kay Hackett design), 1964 – 1971. $25.00 – 35.00.

Black Gold #5153 lighter, 4" (Kay Hackett design), 1967 – 1971. $25.00 – 35.00.

Antique Gold #5153 lighter, 4" with Appliqué motif 1964 only. $30.00 – 40.00.

Pompeii #5153 lighter, 4", 1971 only. $35.00 – 45.00.

Ronson Sunrise #5122 lighter, 7", 1962 – 1965. $25.00 – 35.00.

Ronson Fantasy #5123 lighter, 8" long, 1962 – 1970. $25.00 – 35.00.

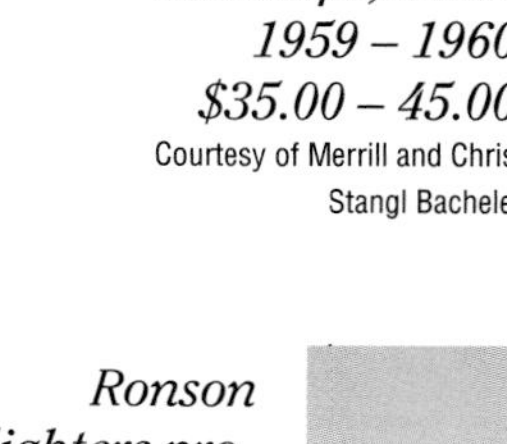

Antique Gold #5006 lighter, urn shape, small, 1959 – 1960. $35.00 – 45.00. Courtesy of Merrill and Christl Stangl Bacheler.

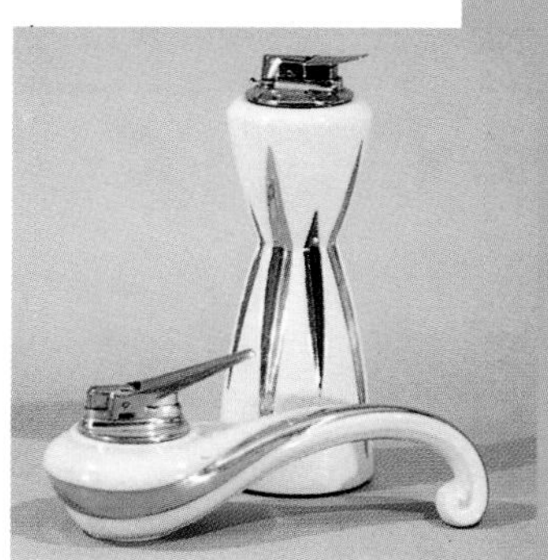

Ronson lighters produced by Stangl, Fantasy (long) and Sunrise (tall). $25.00 – 35.00 each. Courtesy of the Hill-Fulper-Stangl Museum.

Granada Gold #5153 lighter, 4" (Kay Hackett design), 1964 – 1971. $25.00 – 35.00.

Appliqué #5153 lighter, 4" (with square ashtray), 1964 – 1965. $25.00 – 35.00.

Small Flower, Leaf, and Pansy Ashtrays

Stangl's first small flower and leaf ashtrays were introduced in 1941 with the Terra Rose finishes of Blue, Green, or Mauve. These were produced only during the early 1940s; most were discontinued by 1945. Several of these shapes were reintroduced in 1958 and produced in Terra Rose colors until 1960. The reintroduced leaf and flower ashtray shapes were also produced in the Antique Gold and brushed gold finishes during most of the 1960s. Some of them continued in production well into the 1970s.

Terra Rose Flower and Leaf Ashtrays

Produced in the Terra Rose colors Blue, Green or Mauve.

Not Shown:

#2022 shell ashtray, 3", 1941 – 1942. $20.00 – 25.00.
#3520 flower cigarette box, ashtray cover, 4½"x4", 1941 – 1943. $85.00 – 95.00.
#3521 square leaf cigarette box, ashtray cover, 5½"x4", 1941 – 1943. $85.00 – 95.00.
#3522 ashtray, shell 5"x4½", 1941 – 1943. $20.00 – 25.00.
#3523 ashtray, triangle leaf 6¼" x4", 1941 – 1943. $20.00 – 25.00.
#3525 ashtray, Oak leaf 5½"x5", 1941 – 1943. $20.00 – 25.00.
#3526 ashtray, Cosmos 5½"x5", 1941 – 1943. $20.00 – 25.00.
#3527 ashtray, triangle leaf, 4¼"x3", 1941 – 1943. $15.00 – 20.00.
#3528 ashtray, square leaf, 3¼"x3", 1941 – 1943. $15.00 – 20.00.
#3529 ashtray, Ivy leaf, 4"x3½", 1941 – 1943. $15.00 – 20.00.
#3530 ashtray, Oak leaf, 4"x2¾", 1941 – 1943. $15.00 – 20.00.
#3531 ashtray, Cosmos, 3½"x3½", 1941 – 1943. $15.00 – 20.00.
#3532 ashtray, square leaf, 5¾"x4½", 1941 – 1943. $15.00 – 20.00.

Terra Rose Blue #3524 ashtray, Ivy leaf 5¼"x4¼", 1941 – 1943. $15.00 – 20.00.

#4032 ashtray, Oak leaf 5½"x4" (orig. #3525), 1958 – 1960. $10.00 – 15.00.
#4033 ashtray, Cosmos 5½"x5" (orig. #3526), 1958 – 1960. $10.00 – 15.00.
#4034 ashtray, triangle leaf 6½"x4" (orig. #3523), 1958 – 1960. $10.00 – 15.00.
#4035 ashtray, Ivy leaf 5¼"x4¼" (orig. #3524), 1958 – 1960. $10.00 – 15.00.
#4036 ashtray, square leaf 6"x4½" (orig. #3532), 1958 – 1960. $10.00 – 15.00.
#4037 ashtray, shell dish, 5"x5½" (orig. #3522), 1958 – 1960. $10.00 – 15.00.

Group of flower ashtrays in Brushed Gold finishes $10.00 – 15.00 each. Courtesy of the Luke and Nancy Ruepp collection.

Antique Gold Flower and Leaf Ashtrays

Not Shown:

#4032 ashtray, leaf 5½"x4", 1958 – 1962. $10.00 – 15.00.
#4033 ashtray, Cosmos 5½", 1958 – 1978. $10.00 – 15.00.
#4034 ashtray, leaf 6½"x4", 1958 – 1968. $10.00 – 15.00.
#4035 ashtray, leaf, Ivy 5¼"x4¼", 1958 – 1962. $10.00 – 15.00.
#4036 ashtray, leaf 6"x4½", 1958 – 1965. $10.00 – 15.00.
#4037 ashtray, shell dish, 5"x5½", 1958 – 1977. $10.00 – 15.00.

Hand-Painted Flower and Pansy Ashtrays

Beginning in 1960, Stangl started having these small ashtray shapes hand-painted with bright underglaze colors at decorating demonstrations in the Flemington Outlet Workshop. The demonstrations were very popular and continued throughout the 1960s. The Pansy ashtray shape was introduced in 1960 and because it could be decorated in a wide variety of eye-catching colors, it quickly became the most popular small ashtray shape produced at the Flemington Outlet workshop.

Original demonstration items used at the Flemington Outlet Workshop to illustrate Stangl's pansy production. Shown are the pansy mold, the cast clay shape, then cleaned and fired to bisque, then hand-painted with Stangl's bright underglaze colors, glazed and fired again. From the Stangl and Fulper archival collection, courtesy the Wheaton Village Museum of American Glass.

One of the Flemington Outlet workshop demonstrators, Shirley Thatcher Spaciano, remembers: "I had been a salesgirl in Flemington during high school and painted birds during the war, so Christl Stangl Bacheler asked me to come back in 1960 to demonstrate decorating at the new workshop. We had a big kiln where we did the firing that had originally been a gold kiln in Trenton. I painted flower ashtrays and the little flower buttons. I could paint 150 pansies per day in colors to match the dinnerware patterns. Rae Killinger was still there then, she had been the bird decorating supervisor during the war, and she took

Brightly colored cosmos ashtray and sponged leaf ashtray, both decorated and signed by Anné Fritsche Martin $40.00 – 75.00 – each. Courtesy of the Luke and Nancy Ruepp collection.

One of Anné Fritsche Martin's "Anné" signatures. Courtesy of the Luke and Nancy Ruepp collection.

over demonstrating for me when I left in 1962."

Occasionally, colors and motifs on these ashtrays were determined by the caprice of the Flemington Outlet workshop decorators. One of the Flemington Outlet demonstrators during the summer of 1965 was Anné Fritsche Martin. During an interview she stated: "When I wasn't turning pots in the Log Cabin, we were painting all those pansies and flowers. That was interesting because we could almost decorate them any way we liked. It was fun to use the bright colors, which sold better anyway. I came up with a way to sponge the colors on the ashtrays; wrong! *And* I was signing my full first name "Anné" on the back instead of just initials; wrong! I was reprimanded for the sponged colors, but Mr. Stangl *himself* told me not to sign the ashtrays that way. He said 'As long as it is my company, I only want *my* name on the back!'"

#953 Diamond ashtray with Fruit cherries motif, produced and sold at the Flemington Outlet. $55.00 – 70.00.

Many of the flower ashtrays produced at the Flemington Outlet workshop were vibrantly hued in bright or pastel colors. These are the ashtrays most popular with collectors today. All the small ashtrays produced in the workshop were sold at the Flemington Outlet as inexpensive souvenirs. Also produced at the Flemington Outlet workshop during the early 1960s were #953 Card Suit ashtrays. They were done either in tinted solid-color glazes or with hand-painted dinnerware motifs. Card Suit ashtrays or leaf or flower ashtrays with dinnerware motifs were not made in great quantities, so are hard to find and very desirable today.

In 1964, Stangl began producing pansy ashtrays for department store accounts. The ashtrays made for department stores were decorated only at the Trenton factory with a predetermined arrangement of colors. Many of the colors used on the Trenton ashtrays were combinations of the muddy shades of green, gold, and brown, popular in dinnerware motifs at that time. The Trenton-made Pansies were decorated with several color combinations of the fashion colors Old Gold, Pomona Brown, Yellow, Saddle Brown, Pomona Green, and Walnut Brown. Some of the more lively Trenton Pansy color combos were Old Gold with Dark Purple (but usually overstroked with brown), Pink #167 or Pink #160 with Pink #193, Yellow with Pink #160, and Pink #167 with Light Purple.

The Trenton factory Pansy ashtrays were distributed to department stores by the piece. Pansies were also put together in boxed sets of four as "Stangl Pansy Pak" ashtray sets. Each Pansy Pak set retailed for $3.95 in 1964. Pansy Paks at that time could be had with pansies all the same or with different decorations. The Pansy Pak sets were sold in pasteboard display boxes with a clear cellophane cover and "Stangl Pansy Pak" gold-foil paper label on the upper corner. The Pansy Pak ashtray sets were discontinued after the fire at the Trenton factory in August 1965, but were brought back in 1970. The Pansy Pak box was redesigned at that time and only showed one of the pansy ashtrays contained within. These were offered from June 1970 through 1974. In 1973 the Pansy Pak retailed for $5.50, and by 1974 it had increased to $6.00.

Two Stangl Pansy Pak boxed ashtray sets, original 1964 set with cellophane cover, $135.00 – 165.00 (right); and redesigned 1970 set, $95.00 – 110.00 (left). Courtesy of the Ruepp collection.

In August 1965, other flower shapes were added to the assortment. These too were produced both at the Flemington Outlet and at the Trenton factory. The shapes added at that time were Rose, Single Rose, Tulip, and Poppy. Most of these shapes were made in two styles, one rather flat, the other deeper, almost a bowl. The flat Poppy ashtray shape is a side view of the flower while the deep Poppy ashtray is a fully open blossom.

Group of deep and flat Poppy ashtrays. Courtesy of the Luke and Nancy Ruepp collection.

Group of large and small Cosmos ashtrays. Courtesy of the Luke and Nancy Ruepp collection.

Group of deep and flat Rose ashtrays. Courtesy of the Luke and Nancy Ruepp collection.

Group of deep and flat Tulip ashtrays. Courtesy of the Luke and Nancy Ruepp collection.

Single Rose deep ashtray. Courtesy of the Luke and Nancy Ruepp collection.

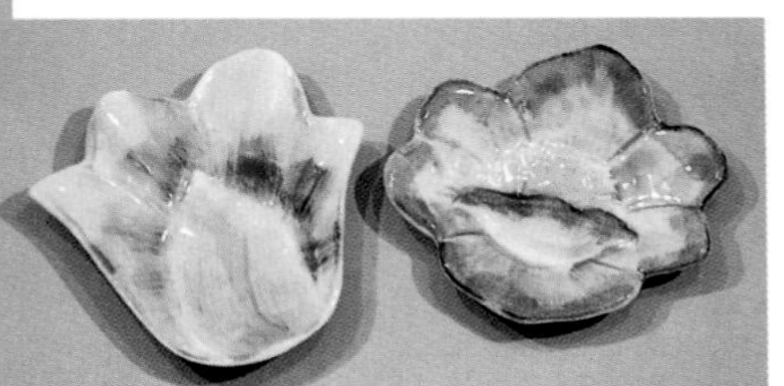

Flemington Outlet Victoria Green tulip and Light Purple poppy ashtrays.

As before, the ashtrays produced in Flemington could be nearly any color, while those from Trenton were decorated in predetermined colors. The Trenton Roses were decorated in Yellow with Orange, Pink #193 with Pink #160, and Light Purple with Dark Purple. Tulips were Yellow with Orange, and Light Purple with Dark Purple. The Poppy ashtrays were Yellow with Orange, Pink #160, and Tan (the orange color on the Bittersweet pattern). The Single Roses were either Orange with Pink #193 or Pink #160 with Pink #193 and Yellow.

Pansy 6" ashtrays, two 6" flat ashtrays on left, 6" deep ashtray on right. Courtesy of the Luke and Nancy Ruepp collection.

Other pansy shapes were developed at that time as well. Large 6" pansy deep and flat ashtrays were introduced, as were nearly round pansy 5" flat ashtrays. The larger 5" and 6" pansy ashtrays were produced in Trenton only so were usually available only in sedate colors.

Vibrant bright or pastel combinations
Cosmos, large 5½". $25.00 – 30.00
Cosmos, small 3½", flat. $22.00 – 28.00
Cosmos, small 3½", deep. $22.00 – 28.00
Pansy, large 6", flat. $55.00 – 65.00
Pansy, large 6", deep. $50.00 – 60.00
Pansy, medium, 5", flat . $60.00 – 75.00
Pansy, small, 4", flat . $22.00 – 28.00
Poppy, 4", flat. $22.00 – 28.00
Poppy, 4", deep. $20.00 – 25.00
Rose, 4", flat. $20.00 – 25.00
Rose, 4", deep. $20.00 – 25.00
Single Rose, 4", deep. $35.00 – 45.00
Tulip, 4", flat. $20.00 – 25.00
Tulip, 4", deep. $20.00 – 25.00
Tulip, 6½" (actually Wheatonware Exclusive soap dish produced only in red or yellow). $25.00 – 35.00.

Monochrome golds and browns
Cosmos, large 5½", deep. $15.00 – 20.00
Cosmos, small 3½", flat. $10.00 – 15.00
Cosmos, small 3½", deep. $10.00 – 15.00
Pansy, large 6", flat. $35.00 – 45.00
Pansy, large 6", deep. $30.00 – 40.00
Pansy, medium, 5", flat . $45.00 – 55.00
Pansy, small, 4", flat . $8.00 – 12.00
Poppy, 4", flat. $12.00 – 18.00
Poppy, 4", deep. $12.00 – 18.00
Rose, 4", flat. $12.00 – 18.00
Rose, 4", deep. $12.00 – 18.00
Single Rose, 4", deep. $22.00 – 28.00
Tulip, 4", flat. $12.00 – 18.00
Tulip, 4", deep. $12.00 – 18.00

Hand-Painted Leaf Ashtrays

Vibrant Autumn colors
Ivy leaf, large, 5¼"x4¼". $22.00 – 28.00
Ivy leaf, small, 4"x3½". $20.00 – 25.00
Oak leaf, large, 5½"x4". $25.00 – 30.00
Oak leaf, small, 4"x2¾". $22.00 – 28.00
Square leaf, large, 5¾". $20.00 – 25.00
Square leaf, small, 3¼". $18.00 – 22.00
Triangle leaf, large, 6½". $25.00 – 30.00
Triangle leaf, small, 4¼". $22.00 – 28.00

Monochrome golds and browns
Ivy leaf, large, 5¼"x4¼". $12.00 – 18.00
Ivy leaf, small, 4"x3½". $10.00 – 15.00
Oak leaf, large, 5½"x4". $12.00 – 18.00
Oak leaf, small, 4"x2¾". $10.00 – 15.00
Square leaf, large, 5¾". $12.00 – 18.00
Square leaf, small, 3¼". $10.00 – 15.00
Triangle leaf, large, 6½". $15.00 – 20.00
Triangle leaf, small, 4¼". $12.00 – 18.00

Assortment of hand-painted leaf ashtrays. Courtesy of the Luke and Nancy Ruepp collection.

Very rare Engobe Decorated "Gingerbread" small cosmos ashtray signed by Rose Herbeck. $60.00 – 75.00. Courtesy of the Luke and Nancy Ruepp collection.

Group of very desirable sponged square leaf ashtrays by Anné Fritsche Martin and a Thistle ashtray decorated by Shirley Thatcher Spaciano. Flower and leaf ashtrays signed "Anné," especially those with aberrant decorations, and ashtrays with popular dinnerware motifs have been selling for $40.00 – 75.00 each.

Sportsmen's Giftware, 1955 – 1976

The success of the wildlife-decorated windproof ashtrays and Mutual Sunset lamps of the early 1950s prompted Martin Stangl to develop a line of smoking accessories with wildlife motifs. In 1955, Stangl introduced a selection of large decorative ashtrays that would ultimately become the celebrated Sportsmen's Giftware line. This assortment was advertised as "a most interesting collection of hand-crafted ashtrays by Stangl. These trays have been specially designed to meet the increasing demand for large and decorated ashtrays. They are practical and ample in size for all purposes. Shapes are both conventional and casual. The square or conventional trays measure 9" in diameter. The casual shapes are 10½" long by 7¼" wide. Decorations are colored and varied. Special attention has been given to outdoor subjects for the sportsman."

That humble beginning was the only reference to sportsmen in the original 1955 ad copy. The line would not become known as "Sportsmen's Giftware" until 1960. Throughout the late 1950s, the large ashtray line was finessed and promoted and by the mid 1960s had reached its peak of popularity as the perfect line of ceramic gift items for men.

Kay Hackett adapted several of the Sportsmen's motifs from designs she had done for the Mutual Sunset lamps in 1950. She also developed new motifs in 1955 and many subsequent additions throughout the 1950s. A number of the designs of the 1960s were adaptations of Kay Hackett's original motifs.

New Sportsmen's motifs and treatments were always in development during the 1950s. When gold and metallic lusters were very popular in 1956, Kay Hackett decorated several Canvasback and Wood Duck ashtrays with metallic and gold lusters. However few, if any, of these were put into production.

The Stangl Sportsmen's Giftware motifs are known for their background of gray engobe, usually with a dark brown border. Some of the motifs, however, were on white engobe, while still others can be found on either.

Production of Sportsmen's Giftware waned a bit during the late 1960s due to the August 1965 fire, but by the early 1970s, a limited assortment of the Sportsmen's line was again showing healthy sales.

When the red clay body and hand-carving were phased out in 1974 – 75, so went Stangl's Sportsmen's Giftware. Because there was still a demand for masculine ceramic accessories and gift items, a group of white-bodied ashtrays and mugs with fired-on decals were produced. The decals featured hunting scenes with dogs and game birds, but these decals were not exclusive to Stangl. Many other pottery companies, such as Hall China, and hobby ceramists were also using the same decals at that time.

During the 1960s and 1970s, Stangl produced many Sportsmen's items for Resco Products, a refractory and ceramics materials company in Norristown, Pennsylvania. Resco used the Sportsmen's items as corporate and holiday gifts. Items made for Resco were marked with a "Resco Products" underglaze stamp in addition to the usual Stangl Pottery stamp.

Resco Products backstamp.

Stangl identified many of the Sportsmen's ashtrays by their shape number and name of the decoration. There were usually no new numbers assigned to the Sportsmen's designs. The primary shapes used were:

#3914 ashtray 9¼" square with square well
#3915 ashtray 9¼" square with round well
#3926 ashtray 10¾"x8" oval
#3926-9 ashtray 9½"x6½" oval
#3927 ashtray 10½"x7" casual
#3972 ashtray 10" Flying Saucer

Many of the Sportsmen's designs were produced throughout the 1950s but in such limited quantities to cause them to be very hard to find today. The length of active productive time is not always an indication of the quantity produced. See also the Lamp chapter for Sportsmen's lamp listings.

Square Ashtray shape #39114

Canvasback, gray engobe #3915 square ashtray (Kay Hackett design), 1955 – 1965. $70.00 – 85.00. Courtesy of the Bill Servis, Susan Lewis collection.

Canvasback white engobe #3915 square ashtray (Kay Hackett design), 1955 – 1965. $110.00 – 135.00. Courtesy of the Brian and Cristi Hahn collection.

Caribbean #3915 square ashtray (Kay Hackett design), 1955 – 1962. $85.00 – 95.00. Courtesy of the Bill Servis, Susan Lewis collection.

Golfer #3915GBDC, square ashtray Golf Course landscape and Golf Ball, 1958 – 1965. $150.00 – 195.00. Courtesy of the Bill Servis, Susan Lewis collection.

Mallard #3915 square ashtray (Kay Hackett design), 1955 – 1965. $60.00 – 75.00. Courtesy of the Bill Servis, Susan Lewis collection.

Porpoise #3915 square ashtray (Kay Hackett design), 1955 – 1957. $100.00 – 125.00. Courtesy of the Bill Servis, Susan Lewis collection.

Rainbow Trout #3915 square ashtray (Kay Hackett design), 1955 – 1957. $125.00 – 160.00. Courtesy of the Bill Servis, Susan Lewis collection.

Redhead #3915 square ashtray (Kay Hackett design), 1958 – 1965. $100.00 – 125.00. Courtesy of the Bill Servis, Susan Lewis collection.

Oval Ashtray shape #3926

Not Shown:

Antelope #3926 oval ashtray 1955 only. $290.00 – 325.00.

Golfer #3926 ashtray, oval with Golf Course landscape decoration and golf ball center, 1960 only. $275.00 – 300.00.

Goose (also Canada Goose) #3926 oval ashtray (Kay Hackett design), 1955 – 1974. $25.00 – 35.00.

Blue Wing Teal #3926 oval ashtray, 1960 – 1965. $140.00 – 185.00. Courtesy of the Jim Horner collection.

California Quail #3926 oval ashtray (Kay Hackett design), 1958 – 1962. $130.00 – 150.00. Courtesy of the Brian and Cristi Hahn collection.

Canada Goose (also Goose) #3926 oval ashtray (Kay Hackett design), 1955 – 1974. $25.00 – 35.00. Courtesy of the Bill Servis, Susan Lewis collection.

Deer #3926 oval ashtray, 1960 – 1974. $45.00 – 55.00. Courtesy of the Bill Servis, Susan Lewis collection.

Duck #3926 10¾"x8" oval ashtray (Kay Hackett design), 1955 – 1974. $25.00 – 35.00. Courtesy of the Bill Servis, Susan Lewis collection.

Duck #3926-9 9½"x6½" oval ashtray (Kay Hackett design), 1958 only. $150.00 – 175.00. Courtesy of the Bill Servis, Susan Lewis collection.

Golfer #3926 ashtray, oval with Golf Course landscape decoration, no golf ball center, 1960 – 1965. $120.00 – 140.00. Courtesy of the Bill Servis, Susan Lewis collection.

Green Wing Teal #3926 oval ashtray, 1960 – 1965. $140.00 – 185.00. Courtesy of the Bill Servis, Susan Lewis collection.

Partridge #3926 oval ashtray (Kay Hackett design), 1958 – 1962. $130.00 – 150.00. Courtesy of the Bill Servis, Susan Lewis collection.

Pheasant #3926 oval ashtray (Kay Hackett design), 1955 – 1974. $30.00 – 40.00. Courtesy of the Bill Servis, Susan Lewis collection.

Pintail #3926 oval ashtray (Kay Hackett design), 1955 – 1965. $60.00 – 75.00. Courtesy of the Bill Servis, Susan Lewis collection.

Quail #3926 oval ashtray (Kay Hackett design), 1955 – 1974. $35.00 – 45.00. Courtesy of the Bill Servis, Susan Lewis collection.

Ruffed Grouse #3926 oval ashtray (Kay Hackett design), 1958 – 1962. $130.00 – 150.00. Courtesy of the Bill Servis, Susan Lewis collection.

Sailfish #3926 white engobe oval ashtray (Kay Hackett design), 1960 – 1965. $65.00 – 80.00. Courtesy of the Bill Servis, Susan Lewis collection.

Snow Goose #3926 oval ashtray, 1955 only. $290.00 – 325.00. Courtesy of the Frank and Elizabeth Kramar collection.

Striped Bass #3926 oval ashtray, 1960 – 1965. $140.00 – 170.00. Courtesy of the Bill Servis, Susan Lewis collection.

Swordfish #3926 gray engobe oval ashtray (Kay Hackett design), 1970 – 1974. $70.00 – 85.00. Courtesy of the Bill Servis, Susan Lewis collection.

Wood Duck #3926 oval ashtray (Kay Hackett design), 1955 – 1965. $60.00 – 75.00. Courtesy of the Bill Servis, Susan Lewis collection.

Woodcock #3926 oval ashtray (Kay Hackett design), 1958 – 1962. $130.00 – 150.00.

Casual Ashtray shape #3927

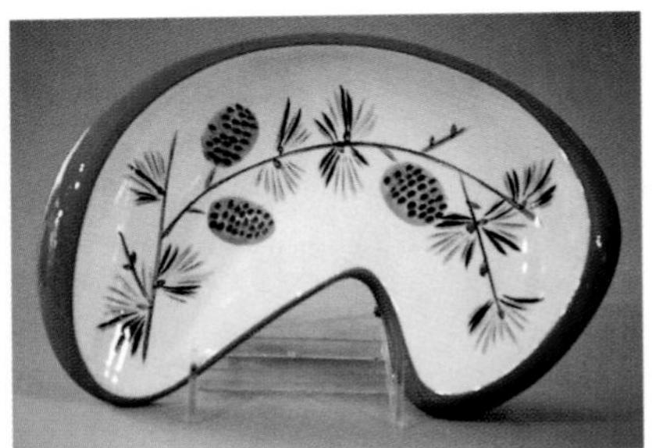

Pine #3927 casual ashtray (Kay Hackett design), 1955 – 1957. $45.00 – 60.00. Courtesy of the Bill Servis, Susan Lewis collection.

Sailfish #3927 casual ashtray (Kay Hackett design), 1955 – 1962. $80.00 – 90.00. Courtesy of the Bill Servis, Susan Lewis collection.

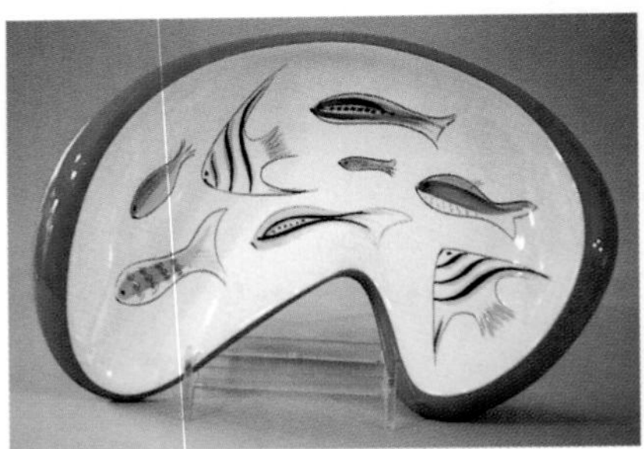

Tropical #3927 casual ashtray (Kay Hackett design), 1955 – 1962. $80.00 – 90.00. Courtesy of the Bill Servis, Susan Lewis collection.

Flying Saucer Ashtray shape #3972

Not Shown:

Canvasback #3972 Flying Saucer ashtray (Kay Hackett design), 1957 only. $160.00 – 180.00.

Mallard #3972 Flying Saucer ashtray (Kay Hackett design), 1957 only. $160.00 – 180.00.

Pheasant #3972 Flying Saucer ashtray (Kay Hackett design), 1957 only. $160.00 – 180.00.

Seagull #3972 Flying Saucer ashtray (Kay Hackett design), 1957 only. $180.00 – 220.00.

Sailboat #3972 Flying Saucer ashtray (Kay Hackett design), 1957 only. $180.00 – 220.00.

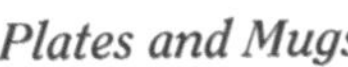

Marlin #3972 Flying Saucer ashtray (Kay Hackett design), 1957 only. $180.00 – 220.00. Courtesy of Merrill and Christl Stangl Bacheler.

Plates and Mugs

The Sportsmen's decorative plates were tried as a short salad set in 1960, but were primarily produced as decorative objects. The plates featured Kay Hackett's original ashtray motifs adapted to the plate shapes by Irene Sarnecki. The Sportsmen's plates were produced in gray engobe from 1960 until the fire at the Trenton factory in August 1965.

Sportsmen's plates were not produced again until 1973 when they were reintroduced on white engobe. They were produced with white engobe on the original 11" #3774 Coupe shape during 1973 and 1974. The Sportsmen's motifs were also produced on 10" #3434 Rim and #5129 Tiara shape plates during that time, but the 10" plates were sold only at the Flemington Outlet, and few were produced. The white background Sportsmen's plates are more scarce and much more vibrant than the original gray plates, so sell for a bit more than the gray.

Plates, Coupe shape #3774, Gray Engobe, 1960 – 1965

Canvasback 11" plate, 1960 – 1965. $60.00 – 75.00. Courtesy of the Bill Servis, Susan Lewis collection.

Mallard 11" plate, 1960 – 1965. $60.00 – 75.00. Courtesy of the Bill Servis, Susan Lewis collection.

Wood Duck 11" plate, 1960 – 1965. $70.00 – 85.00. Courtesy of the Bill Servis, Susan Lewis collection.

Pheasant 8" plate with cup and saucer, produced during 1960 only. $45.00 – 55.00.

Not Shown:

Canada Goose 11" plate, 1960 – 1965. $60.00 – 75.00.
Pheasant 11" plate, 1960 – 1965. $60.00 – 75.00.
Pheasant 14" plate, 1960 – 1965. $150.00 – 175.00.
Pheasant 8" plate, 1960 only. $60.00 – 75.00.
Pheasant cup & saucer, 1960 only. $45.00 – 55.00.
Pheasant 10" salad bowl, 1960 only. $95.00 – 110.00.
Quail 11" plate, 1960 – 1965. $60.00 – 75.00.

Plates, Coupe shape #3774, White Engobe, 1973 – 1974

Pheasant 14" plate, 1973 – 1974. $175.00 – 200.00.
Pheasant 11" plate, 1973 – 1974. $100.00 – 125.00.

Canada Goose 11" plate, 1973 – 1974. $100.00 – 125.00. Courtesy of the Bill Servis, Susan Lewis collection.

Canvasback 11" plate, 1973 – 1974. $100.00 – 125.00. Courtesy of the Brian and Cristi Hahn collection.

Mallard 11" plate, 1973 – 1974. $100.00 – 125.00. Courtesy of the Bill Servis, Susan Lewis collection.

Quail 11" plate, 1973 – 1974. $100.00 – 125.00. Courtesy of the Bill Servis, Susan Lewis collection.

Wood Duck 11" plate, 1960 – 1965. $100.00 – 125.00. Courtesy of the Bill Servis, Susan Lewis collection.

Plates, Tiara #5129 or Rim #3434, White Engobe, 1973 – 1974

Canada Goose 10" plate, 1973 – 1974. $60.00 – 75.00.
Canvasback 10" plate, 1973 – 1974. $60.00 – 75.00.
Flying Duck 10" plate, 1973 – 1974. $60.00 – 75.00.
Mallard 10" plate, 1973 – 1974. $60.00 – 75.00.
Pheasant 14" plate, 1973 – 1974. $175.00 – 200.00.
Pheasant 10" plate, 1973 – 1974. $60.00 – 75.00.
Quail 10" plate, 1973 – 1974. $60.00 – 75.00.

Clocks

During 1973 and 1974, Sportsman motif clock faces were made for Verichron Clock. Numerals and the name Verichron were fired on the face of 11" Sportsmen's plates with holes drilled in the center to accommodate battery clock works. Clock faces bearing some of Stangl's regular dinnerware patterns were produced at that time also.

Clock face made for Verichron, 11" Sportsmen's plate, 1973 – 1974. $85.00 – 95.00.

Mugs

Kay Hackett designed the Hunter mug motif in 1956. It was produced on the #3898 coffee mug shape from 1957 until the 1965 fire, when it was discontinued.

Front and back of the #3898 Hunter mug, 1957 – 1965. $30.00 – 40.00 each.

Hunter #3896 coffee mug (white engobe, Kay Hackett design), 1957 only. $50.00 – 60.00.

In 1961, the Sportsmen's decorated #5092 two-cup mugs were introduced. These mugs were cast entirely of white clay with hand-painted motifs and were produced until the August 1965 fire.

Canada Goose #5092 2-cup mug, 1961 – 1965. $40.00 – 50.00.
Flying Duck #5092 2-cup mug, 1961 – 1965. $40.00 – 50.00.
Mallard #5092 2-cup mug, 1961 – 1965. $40.00 – 50.00.
Pheasant #5092 2-cup mug, 1961 – 1965. $40.00 – 50.00.

Group of Sportsmen's #5092 2-cup mugs. $40.00 – 50.00 each. Courtesy of the Bill Servis, Susan Lewis collection.

From 1972 through 1978, ashtrays and mugs were produced with Sportsman-like decals featuring game bird motifs. The decal-decorated mug shape most often used was the #5129 Tiara, and the ashtrays were usually the #5058 round and #3942 oval ashtrays.

Sportsmen's decal decorated #5129 mug, late 1970s, $35.00 – 45.00 each.

Sportsmen's Cigarette Boxes, Coaster Ashtrays, Fluted Ashtrays

During 1959, shape #3630 5" coaster ashtrays with Sportsmen's motifs were developed and introduced. All motifs were designated with the number 5011. In 1960, Sportsmen's #3630 cigarette boxes and 7" #3898 fluted ashtrays were added to the line. During the early 1960s, cigarette box and ashtray items were sold individually or as boxed gift sets. Cigarette box gift sets originally included a cigarette box with four ashtrays, which was reduced to a box with two ashtrays by 1961. Coaster ashtray gift sets were comprised of one each of Pheasant, Canada Goose, Mallard, and Flying Duck #5011 coaster ashtrays.These items were all discontinued following the 1965 fire.

Canada Goose #5011 coaster ashtray (shape #3630, Kay Hackett design), 1959 – 1965. $30.00 – 40.00. Courtesy of the Jim and Barbara Nelson collection.

Canvasback #5011 coaster ashtray (shape #3630, Kay Hackett design), 1959 – 1960. $85.00 – 95.00. Courtesy of the Jim and Barbara Nelson collection.

Flying Duck #5011 coaster ashtray (shape #3630, Kay Hackett design), 1959 – 1965. $30.00 – 40.00. Courtesy of the Jim and Barbara Nelson collection.

Mallard #5011 left-facing coaster ashtray (shape #3630, Kay Hackett design), 1959 – 1965. $30.00 – 40.00. Courtesy of the Jim and Barbara Nelson collection.

Mallard #5011 right-facing coaster ashtray, unusual (shape #3630, Kay Hackett design), 1959 – 1965. $45.00 – 55.00. Courtesy of the Jim and Barbara Nelson collection.

Pheasant #5011 coaster ashtray (shape #3630, Kay Hackett design), 1959 – 1965. $30.00 – 40.00. Courtesy of the Jim and Barbara Nelson collection.

Sailboat #5011 coaster ashtray (shape #3630, Kay Hackett design), 1959 – 1960. $95.00 – 110.00. Courtesy of the Jim and Barbara Nelson collection.

Porpoise #5011 coaster ashtray (shape #3630, Kay Hackett design), 1959 – 1960. $95.00 – 110.00. Courtesy of the Jim and Barbara Nelson collection.

Quail #5011 coaster ashtray (shape #3630, Kay Hackett design), 1960 only. $95.00 – 110.00. Courtesy of the Jim and Barbara Nelson collection.

Pheasant #5051 cigarette box (shape #3630), 1960 – 1963. $65.00 – 80.00. Courtesy of the Luke and Nancy Ruepp collection.

Ashtray gift box set #5067, which included four 7" #3898 fluted ashtrays in Canada Goose, Pheasant, Flying Duck, and Mallard. $40.00 – 50.00 each. Courtesy of the Jim and Barbara Nelson collection.

Flying Duck #5053 cigarette box (shape #3630), 1960 – 1963. $65.00 – 80.00. Courtesy of the Brian and Cristi Hahn collection.

Sailfish #5011 coaster ashtray (shape #3630, Kay Hackett design), 1959 – 1960. $95.00 – 110.00.
Wood Duck #5011 coaster ashtray (shape #3630, Kay Hackett design), 1960 only. $95.00 – 110.00.
Mallard #5052 cigarette box (shape #3630), 1960 – 1963. $65.00 – 80.00.
Canada Goose #5054 cigarette box (shape #3630), 1960 – 1963. $65.00 – 80.00.
Canada Goose #5067 7" fluted ashtray (shape #3898-7), 1960 – 1965. $40.00 – 50.00.
Flying Duck #5067 7" fluted ashtray (shape #3898-7), 1960 – 1965. $40.00 – 50.00.
Mallard #5067 7" fluted ashtray (shape #3898-7), 1960 – 1965. $40.00 – 50.00.
Pheasant #5067 7" fluted ashtray (shape #3898-7), 1960 – 1965. $40.00 – 50.00.
Quail #5067 7" fluted ashtray (shape #3898-7), 1960 only. $95.00 – 110.00.
Wood Duck #5067 7" fluted ashtray (shape #3898-7), 1960 only. $95.00 – 110.00.

Decal "Sportsman," various motifs, 1972 – 1978

Produced on items cast of red clay with engobe or cast entirely of white or gray clay.
Decal ashtray #5058, round 7¼". $30.00 – 40.00.
Decal ashtray #3942, oval 8½"x7". $30.00 – 40.00.
Decal ashtray #3816, windproof 8". $30.00 – 40.00.
Decal mug #5092 2-cup. $25.00 – 35.00.
Decal mug #5129 Tiara. $25.00 – 35.00.
Decal tankard #5219. $25.00 – 35.00.

Platinum or Gold Decorated Modern Vases, 1933

During 1933 only, the following shapes were produced in Ivory or Black glaze with the handles highlighted with platinum or gold luster. Occasionally, these shapes were also decorated entirely with platinum or gold. This was a very dramatic "Art Deco" finish, exceedingly rare today. During 1934, the #1076 Pig bank was also decorated with platinum or gold luster over solid-color glazes and retailed for $9.00 each, which was quite a price for the time. See also the Solid-Color Artware, Giftware, and Novelties chapter for photos of some of these hard-to-find shapes.

Not Shown:

#1733 cylinder vase, 2 flat handles, 12" 1933 only. $175.00 – 200.00.
#1733 cylinder vase, 2 flat handles, 10" 1933 only. $150.00 – 175.00.
#1733 cylinder vase, 2 flat handles, 6" 1933 only. $95.00 – 130.00.
#1734 cylinder vase, 2 flat handles, 8" 1933 only. $120.00 – 140.00.
#1735 vase, 3 step-handles, 12" 1933 only. $190.00 – 225.00.
#1735 vase, 3 step-handles, 9" 1933 only. $170.00 – 195.00.
#1736 vase, cone, 3 step-handles, 12" 1933 only. $190.00 – 225.00.
#1736 vase, cone, 3 step-handles, 10" 1933 only. $170.00 – 195.00.
#1736 vase, cone, 3 step-handles, 8" 1933 only. $130.00 – 150.00.
#1737 ball bowl, 3 handles, 6½" 1933 only. $150.00 – 175.00.
#1738 bowl, 3-groove foot, 9" diameter 1933 only. $175.00 – 200.00.
#1739L vase, 3-groove foot, 9¼" high 1933 only. $200.00 – 250.00.
#1739S vase, 3-groove foot, 8" high 1933 only. $175.00 – 200.00.
#1740 bowl, 3 step-feet, 9" diameter 1933 only. $175.00 – 200.00.
#1741 bowl, pie crust rim, 8" diameter 1933 only. $120.00 – 145.00.
#1742 bowl, pie crust rim, 12" diameter 1933 only. $150.00 – 175.00.
#1743 bowl, oblong, 2 handles, 6¼"x4" 1933 only. $130.00 – 150.00.
#1076 Pig bank, 4" gold luster over solid-color glazes, 1934 only. $190.00 – 225.00.

Black glaze with gold luster dealer sign, 1933 only. $500.00 – 600.00. Courtesy of the Avila collection.

American Bone China, 1954 – 1956

Martin Stangl's crusade to prove to the world that America could produced china of comparable quality to Europe or the Orient became evident again in 1953 when he began developing his American Bone China line of giftware. Stangl's first American china was the Fulper Porcelaine dolls and novelties produced from 1918 through 1929, and the second was the Stangl Porcelain Birds series of figurines made during 1944. American Bone China was true china, cream-colored and translucent. It was developed to make the most of the popularity of gold-decorated ceramics during the 1950s. The American Bone China formula followed closely Stangl's porcelain formula he used for Fulper's doll heads and the Porcelain Birds of America figurines but used the component nepheline syenite instead of feldspar. Being a pre-fired and ground material, nepheline syenite did not require the 100 hours of milling required to use feldspar.

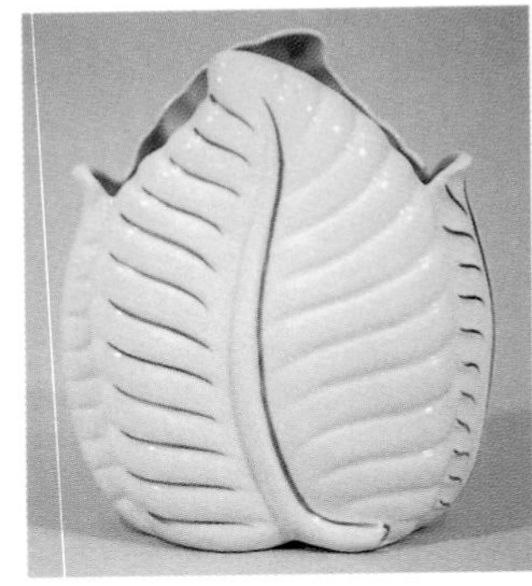
Stangl American Bone China #3441 8" vase. $65.00 – 75.00.

Stangl's initial American Bone China products were popular vase shapes delicately trimmed in satin gold. Several small- to medium-sized vase and bird figurine shapes were produced in American Bone China, such as #1878 tulip, #3612 lily, and #3456 Cerulean warbler. Also cast in American Bone China at that time were novelty coffee and tea sets in older Stangl shapes such as #3636 and #1800. Very little American Bone China was produced on the #3636 shape, so these pieces are quite rare.

American Bone China sugar bowl in pattern #1800. $30.00 – 40.00.

To augment the line, Martin Stangl instructed Kay Hackett to develop decorative motifs to be used on coffee sets, based on the #3434 shape. Kay Hackett tried floral and abstract motifs incorporating such things as carved detail, underglaze colors, and even overglaze china colors. The American Bone China motifs that finally went into production were simple florals and abstract leaves in satin gold or overglaze colors.

Kay Hackett's sample American Bone China coffee pot, sugar and creamer with a carved Queen Anne's Lace floral motif accented in satin gold. This motif was produced only in a few samples. Courtesy of Kay Hackett.

Martin Stangl abandoned the American Bone China line by the end of 1955. He felt the "fussy" appearance of the American Bone China products was too unlike the bold, earthy style for which Stangl Ware had come to be known. He redirected his energies to develop gold-decorated earthenware products that would be more "Stangl-like." Also, Martin Stangl did not wish to directly compete with Lenox China, also of Trenton, and their line of gold-trimmed cream-colored china giftware very much like American Bone China. The Lenox product is still popular today.

American Bone China products were back-stamped with "Stangl American Bone China" gold or the Stangl "seconds" marks in gold. Many vases were not stamped if the shape already possessed Stangl in-mold markings.

Not Shown:

bird figurines, each. $200.00 – 250.00.
coffee pot. $80.00 – 95.00.
creamer. $25.00 – 35.00.
cup. $10.00 – 15.00.
plate. $40.00 – 50.00.
saucer. $10.00 – 12.00.
sauce tureen, covered. $90.00 – 110.00.
sauce under plate. $15.00 – 20.00.
sauce ladle. $25.00 – 35.00.
sugar. $30.00 – 40.00.
teapot. $95.00 – 120.00.
vase, various shapes or sizes. $60.00 – 95.00.

American Bone China coffee set with hand-painted Honeysuckle motif in fired-on china colors. $135.00 – 170.00 per set. Courtesy of Barbara Miller.

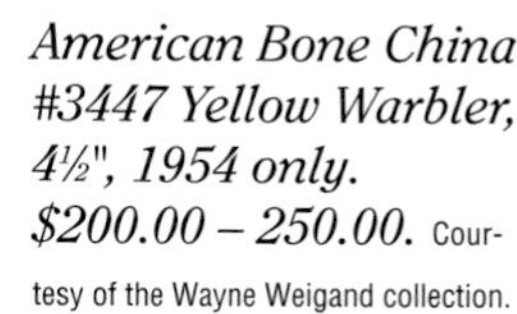

American Bone China #3447 Yellow Warbler, 4½", 1954 only. $200.00 – 250.00. Courtesy of the Wayne Weigand collection.

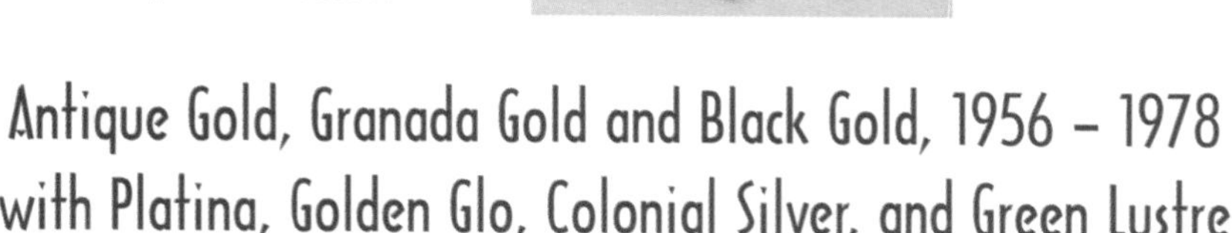

Antique Gold, Granada Gold and Black Gold, 1956 – 1978 with Platina, Golden Glo, Colonial Silver, and Green Lustre

Because gold-decorated artware continued to increase in popularity throughout the 1950s, Martin Stangl persevered in developing a gold-decorated artware line that truly characterized Stangl pottery. During 1956, Martin Stangl directed Kay Hackett to work up glaze treatments with metallic luster finishes on hand-thrown earthenware vase shapes. Kay Hackett experimented with cobalt oxide, manganese oxide, and copper oxide stains under a matte-white titanium, tin, and zinc oxide glaze called Satin White. The metallic oxide stains would "float" to the surface of the matte glaze, coloring it blue if cobalt were used, blue-green with copper, and purple-brown with manganese. Over the Satin White glaze, metallic lusters were thinly dry-brushed, allowing the cobalt, copper, or manganese colors to show through and create an "antique" appearance. Kay Hackett experimented with dry-brushed copper luster, satin gold, and liquid bright gold on the hand-thrown shapes.

Three of Kay Hackett's brushed gold samples; the left is brushed gold over cobalt stain on a hand-thrown bottle shape, hand-thrown jug with brushed gold over heavily dripped copper stain, and another hand-thrown bottle sample with brushed copper luster over manganese. Courtesy of Kay Hackett.

Martin Stangl was looking for a way to create a dull, "antiqued" gold appearance by using liquid bright gold. Satin gold luster was 24 carat and required burnishing after being fired to bring up the color. Liquid bright gold was only 22 carat and required no further labor after firing so was less costly. Martin Stangl discovered that by increasing the matte properties of the Satin

White glaze and strengthening the metallic stains under the glaze, dry-brushed liquid bright gold would take on the appearance of satin gold at a fraction of the cost. Martin Stangl filed for a patent on this process in February 1958 and again in January 1959. A patent was granted or his Antique Gold decorating process on October 30, 1962.

It was decided that cobalt and copper oxide stains would be used under the Satin White glaze as the blue and green provided more contrast to the gold than the purple-brown manganese. These were in fact the same Art Ware Blue and Art Ware Green colors that had been used to decorate the Terra Rose lines since 1941. Heavy applications of concentrated Art Ware Green created deep black-green streaks that further enhanced the "antique" of Antique Gold artware. Great depth of finish was achieved by the interplay of the dark black-green copper oxide of the Art Ware Green and the brushed gold highlights.

Several early handmade Antique Gold artware shapes. Many of the Antique Gold shapes were indeed hand-thrown during the late 1950s.

During this time, large, conference table-sized ashtrays were becoming increasingly popular, so Kay Hackett was designing several large ashtray shapes as well. The first shape approved for production that was designed specifically for the Antique Gold finish was Kay Hackett's #3972 Flying Saucer ashtray on May 9, 1957.

Kay Hackett's original sample for the #3972 Flying Saucer ashtray. Courtesy of Kay Hackett.

The original Antique Gold finish featured heavily-brushed Art Ware Green under the Satin White glaze. This created rich, deep greenish-black striations of oxidized copper under the dry brushed gold. The heavy brushing of Art Ware Green was minimized by 1959 because it was found that the heavy black striations were bleached to pale green by dishwasher detergents.

Martin Stangl combined the popular Antique Gold conference table ashtrays with his love of golf in 1958 with the introduction of seven golf ball ashtrays. Six of the ashtrays were finished in Antique Gold and had a life-sized ceramic golf ball in the center. The seventh ashtray was hand-painted with "a reproduction of a golf course landscape in natural colors. The newest idea in tournament prizes and gifts for golfers," as the brochure stated. The golf ball ashtrays were very short-lived and were discontinued during 1959.

As the popularity of Antique Gold increased during the 1950s, many more ashtray and artware shapes were designed for this finish. Modern streamlined forms were introduced, as were classically-styled shapes featuring carved decorative bands, all designed to accentuate the brushed-gold finish.

Three of Kay Hackett's classically styled shapes. Courtesy of the Marcena North collection.

Many Antique Gold shapes were also decorated with brushed cobalt Art Ware Blue under the Satin White glaze and gold luster. Usually the Art Ware Blue was simply spun on certain areas of the pieces, such as a carved decorative band, to provide contrast to the green. Some pieces were wholly decorated with Art Ware Blue, so are a vibrant deep blue under the brushed gold. Although blue instead of green, Stangl considered these pieces part of the Antique Gold line, so all were marked with the Antique Gold backstamp. The use of Art Ware Blue on Antique Gold pieces was discontinued by 1963.

Antique Gold #4028 footed bowl and #4017 handled candleholder decorated with Art Ware Blue. Because pieces decorated with cobalt Art Ware Blue are now much more elusive than those decorated with green, the cobalt blue Antique Gold pieces usually command a higher value than the same piece in Art Ware Green.

By the late 1950s, as Stangl's aging skilled potters were retiring, many of the original hand-thrown Antique Gold shapes were converted to mold-formed slip-cast production. In addition, the "handmade" look was falling from favor as decorators were promoting sleek Mediterranean- and Italian-styled shapes with greatly embellished decorative adornments. Stangl then began to resurrect old shapes from the 1930s and 1940s for the Antique Gold line. Shapes with fluted decoration or ornamental handles were the best candidates for the Antique Gold finish.

Elaborate designs were becoming popular by the late 1950s and early 1960s, so many old ornate shapes, like the #1806 tall rope candleholders, were resurrected and paired with highly wrought new designs such as the #5105 fruit bowl. Like many old shapes, the #1806 candles were renumbered to #4016.

By 1960, all Antique Gold shapes were mold-cast. Earlier hand-thrown Antique Gold shapes have a perfectly flat bottom and no evidence of mold seams. Mold-cast versions of the hand-thrown shapes have a slightly concave base and mold seams that are very evident and accentuated by a vertical solid stripe of gold. Original hand-thrown pieces usually sell for a bit more.

To illustrate the wear-resistance and durability of Stangl's Antique Gold finish, Martin Stangl placed an Antique Gold covered ginger jar that had served as an outdoor flagpole finial on display at the Flemington Outlet. A typed card was displayed with the jar, stating that after four years of enduring adverse conditions, the jar "was as good when taken down as when first put up."

Antique Gold ginger jar that served as a flagpole finial at the Stangl Flemington Outlet during the 1960s. From the Stangl and Fulper archival collection, courtesy the Wheaton Village Museum of American Glass.

As the popularity of Stangl's Antique Gold grew, James Paul, Stangl's general manager, initiated experiments to develop more hand-brushed metallic luster finishes to keep the brushed gold lines exciting and fresh. Some of James Paul's trials included brushed platinum luster, as well as gold or platinum brushed over a variety of colored satin glazes.

A 1960 sample #1878 tulip vase with brushed gold over an experimental light satin yellow glaze.

These experiments resulted in the introduction of the Platina finish in 1961, Golden Glo in 1962, and the Granada Gold finish in 1964. Platina featured satin platinum luster dry-brushed over a dark gray satin glaze. Golden Glo pieces were glazed with a satin flesh-pink glaze and gold luster was dry-brushed over specific areas of the pieces, usually the edges or bands of carving. Because Platina and Golden Glo were never able to compete with the popularity of Antique Gold, both were discontinued by 1963.

Interesting sample #4004 vase with satin platinum brushed over an experimental dark turquoise satin glaze.

Platina #4004 vase (backstamp, inset). Courtesy of the Ben and Pauline Jensen collection.

James Paul's 1964 Granada Gold, with dry-brushed gold over a satin orange-tan glaze, proved to be much more popular. Rivaling Antique Gold in gross sales, it was produced continually until 1978. By 1967, James Paul had developed the Black Gold finish, gold luster dry-brushed over a satin black glaze. The dramatic contrasts of the Black Gold finish propelled it to popularity, and it was in production until 1976.

A group of Golden Glo pieces, #5023 Phoenician vase, #4028 pedestal bowl, and #5005 ashtray. Golden Glo items usually sell for a bit less than Antique Gold. Courtesy of the Marcena North collection.

Colonial Silver #1800-T triple relish and vase #3264. Courtesy of the Ben and Pauline Jensen collection.

In 1969, Colonial Silver was introduced as a brushed dinnerware and artware finish. This finish was bright platinum dry-brushed over a light satin gray glaze. Even though the name is Colonial Silver and platinum luster is much more costly than silver, platinum was used because it provides a much more durable silvery finish and does not tarnish, as would silver. Because this finish was guaranteed not to tarnish, Colonial Silver pieces were affixed with labels stating, "Will not tarnish." Colonial Silver was only slightly more popular than its platinum predecessor, Platina, and was produced only until 1971. Colonial Silver usually sells for a bit less than Antique Gold.

Three "weeping gold" style experimental finishes in Black Gold, Antique Gold, and Granada Gold, early 1970s. Courtesy of the Wayne Weigand collection.

Experimental finish on #5180 Fruit candy dish, gloss Canary Yellow glaze under dry-brushed liquid bright gold.

During the early 1970s, more brushed gold finishes were tested. Some tests were dry-brushed gold over various textured finishes. Other dry-brushed gold tests were on brightly colored gloss glazes instead of the satin glazes normally used under the gold luster.

In 1972, the bright Green Lustre finish was introduced. Green Lustre featured dry-brushed liquid bright gold over glossy Chartreuse glaze. Green Lustre was produced sporadically through 1974 on many of the Antique Gold shapes. A Green Lustre backstamp was never made; so many items are simply marked "Stangl." Green Lustre pieces can also be found that were stamped with the Antique Gold, Granada Gold, or Black Gold name, but an incorrect name does not affect the value of Green Lustre. The Green Lustre finish was discontinued during 1974 and is difficult to find now. It is valued slightly less than Antique Gold.

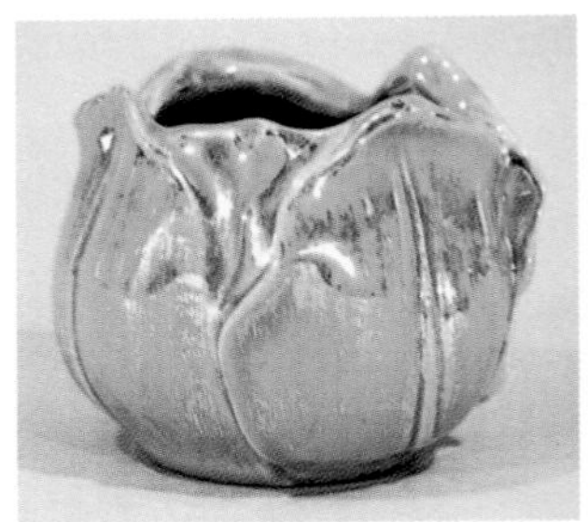

Green Lustre #5144 tulip bowl, 4", 1972 – 1974. $20.00 – 25.00.

Values for all the brushed-gold finishes are approximately the same. Antique Gold is more popular and sells higher than the other finishes. Antique Gold with cobalt decoration sells at the high end of the range or a bit more. This list encompasses nearly all known brushed-gold finished shapes, but not all shapes were produced in all finishes. Because Stangl Pottery was always trying old finishes on new shapes and new finishes on old shapes, many more items can be found than are included here. Unless marked "SAMPLE," the values of items not listed here are equivalent to items of similar size, style, and finish.

The dates listed refer to the years the shapes were actively produced and do not necessarily coincide with the production years of the finishes shown.

Stangl Pottery individual display letters, Cobalt Antique Gold, 1957. $850.00 – 1,200.00 per complete set. From the Stangl and Fulper archival collection, courtesy the Wheaton Village Museum of American Glass.

Original Antique Gold dealer sign with crisp crosshatching, 1958 – 1965. $120.00 – 145.00. Courtesy of Ed Alvater.

Re-styled Antique Gold dealer sign, 1965 – 1977. $85.00 – 95.00.

Re-styled Granada Gold dealer sign, 1965 – 1977. $70.00 – 85.00.

Three #1076 Pig Banks in Black Gold, Antique Gold, and Granada Gold, 1960 – 1978. $95.00 – 130.00 each. Courtesy of the Wayne Weigand collection.

Not Shown:
#1574 vase, twirl 8½", 1967 – 1969. $30.00 – 40.00.
#1647 beer pitcher, 1961 only. $60.00 – 80.00.
#1647 beer mug, 1961 only. $20.00 – 25.00.
#1800D double Cabbage leaf tray 6"x9½", pottery handle, 1969 – 1978. $10.00 – 15.00.
#1800D double Cabbage leaf tray 6"x9½", metal handle, 1969 – 1978. $8.00 – 10.00.
#1800T triple Cabbage leaf tray 12" diameter, pottery handle, 1969 – 1972. $20.00 – 25.00.
#1800T triple Cabbage leaf tray 12" diameter, metal handle, 1969 – 1972. $10.00 – 15.00.

Cobalt Antique Gold #1806 tall rope candleholders, 7½", 1962 – 1963. $100.00 – 125.00 pair.

Green Lustre #1905 bud vase 7½", 1967 – 1978. $25.00 – 35.00.

Granada Gold #1872 bowl, Zinnia 10" diameter, 1962 – 1970. $45.00 – 55.00. Courtesy of the Ben and Pauline Jensen collection.

#1869 bowl, Cosmos, 12" diameter, 1962 – 1977. $45.00 – 55.00.
#1874 bowl, Rose 10" diameter, 1962 – 1965. $30.00 – 40.00.
#1875 candleholders, Rose 2½", 1960 – 1963 $20.00 – 25.00 pair.
#1878 Tulip, large, 8", 1959 only. $50.00 – 60.00.
#1878 Tulip, medium, 5½", 1959 – 1978. $25.00 – 30.00.
#1878 Tulip, small, 4", 1959 – 1978. $20.00 – 25.00.
#1906 urn vase 7¾", 1968 – 1978. $30.00 – 40.00.
#1907 ball vase 4¾", 1968 – 1970. $25.00 – 35.00.
#1919 bowl 7", 1959 – 1960. $30.00 – 40.00.
#1940 plate, 9", 1965 only. $25.00 – 35.00.
#1940 chop plate, 14", 1965 only. $80.00 – 100.00.
#1940 bowl, 9", 1965 only. $80.00 – 100.00.
#1950-10 floral ring, 10" diameter, 1965 only. $40.00 – 50.00.
#1950-8 floral ring, 8" diameter, 1965 only. $35.00 – 45.00.
#1950-6 floral ring, 6" diameter, 1965 only. $25.00 – 35.00.
#1950-10 floral semi-ring, 10" diameter, 1965 only. $15.00 – 20.00 pair.
#1950-8 floral semi-ring, 8" diameter, 1965 only. $15.00 – 20.00 each.
#1950-6 floral semi-ring, straight add on, 6", 1965 only. $15.00 – 20.00 pair.
#1950-C candle cups for floral rings, 1965 only. $6.00 – 8.00 each.
#1953 ashtray, oblong 4¼", 1965 – 1978. $15.00 – 20.00.
#1954 two compartment ashtray 4"x6", 1965 – 1976. $15.00 – 20.00.
#1956 ashtray, round 4¼", 1965 only. $20.00 – 25.00.
#1999 vase 7", 1959 – 1960. $40.00 – 50.00.
#2000 ashtray 4", 1968 – 1970. $12.00 – 18.00.
#2016 vase, 3¾", 1965 – 1970. $25.00 – 30.00.
#2048 urn, 3", 1965 – 1970. $25.00 – 30.00.
#2050 scalloped bowl 8" diameter, 1965 only. $25.00 – 35.00.
#2052 scalloped vase 9½", 1965 only. $30.00 – 40.00.
#2064 scalloped oval bowl 5"x9", 1965 – 1976. $20.00 – 25.00.
#2067 scallop Vase 7", 1965 – 1968. $35.00 – 45.00.
#2071 vase, tall footed 10½", 1967 – 1968. $75.00 – 95.00.
#2074 ashtray, 6", 1965 only. $25.00 – 35.00.
#2091 vase Cosmos 7½", 1959 – 1965. $30.00 – 40.00.
#2092 vase Rhythmic 11", 1959 – 1961. $50.00 – 60.00.
#2092 vase Rhythmic 4", 1959 – 1961. $25.00 – 30.00.
#2092 bowl Rhythmic 10¼"x5½", 1974 – 1977. $35.00 – 45.00.
#3034 vase Spiral 7", 1959 – 1961. $30.00 – 40.00.
#3036 bowl Spiral 4"x9", 1959 – 1961. $25.00 – 35.00.
#3044 ashtray Scroll 4"x5", 1965 only. $25.00 – 30.00.

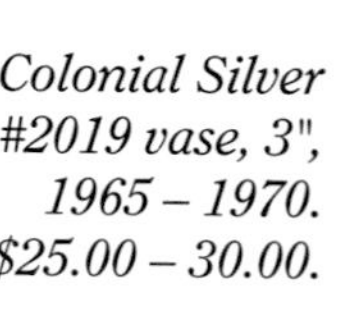

Colonial Silver #2019 vase, 3", 1965 – 1970. $25.00 – 30.00.

Black Gold #2041 urn, footed Grecian 8", 1967 – 1970. $35.00 – 45.00.

Antique Gold #2089 ashtray, Scotty dog 4½"x5", 1965 – 1967. $85.00 – 95.00.

Granada Gold #2091 vase Cosmos 10½", 1959 – 1965. $50.00 – 60.00. Courtesy of the Ben and Pauline Jensen collection.

#3103 vase with handles 7½", 1959 – 1965, and 1972 – 1978. $40.00 – 50.00.
#3111 vase with handles, 7", 1968 – 1969. $40.00 – 50.00.
#3112 vase, 5½", 1968 – 1970. $35.00 – 45.00.
#3113 vase, 5½", 1968 – 1970. $35.00 – 45.00.
#3117 vase, 5½", 1968 – 1970. $35.00 – 45.00.
#3211 vase pitcher, 6", 1959 – 1962. $35.00 – 45.00.
#3214 vase pitcher, 8", 1959 – 1962. $35.00 – 45.00.
#3217 flared vase 7½", 1959 – 1977. $35.00 – 45.00.
#3218 vase 7½", 1959 – 1965 and 1972 – 1976. $45.00 – 55.00.
#3220 oval vase, 7½", 1972 – 1976. $40.00 – 50.00.
#3222 vase 5½", 1965 only. $30.00 – 40.00.
#3224 vase, petal 5½", 1967 – 1968. $25.00 – 35.00.
#3228 bowl, leaves 7½"x4", 1959 – 1960. $25.00 – 35.00.
#3229S bowl 6", 1957 – 1962. $15.00 – 20.00.
#3229M bowl 9" 1957 – 1962. $25.00 – 30.00.
#3229L bowl 12", 1957 – 1962. $25.00 – 35.00.
#3239 leaf server 8", 1961 – 1969. $25.00 – 30.00.
#3240 shell candy dish, 8" 1957 – 1958. $40.00 – 50.00.
#3241 ashtray, 6"x7", 1957 – 1958. $25.00 – 35.00.
#3242 ashtray, round, 9", 1957 – 1958. $35.00 – 45.00.
#3265 ribbed vase, 9", 1972 – 1976. $45.00 – 55.00.
#3268 vase, scroll top, 10", 1959 – 1965. $60.00 – 75.00.
#3283-9 scallop bowl 9", 1965 only. $25.00 – 30.00.
#3283-7 scallop bowl 7", 1965 only. $25.00 – 30.00.
#3410 bowl, Rose 10", 1965 only. $35.00 – 45.00.
#3410-9 bowl, Rose 9", 1965 – 1976. $25.00 – 35.00.
#3410-7 bowl, Rose 7", 1965 – 1976. $25.00 – 30.00.
#3412 square candle warmer, 1961 only. $25.00 – 35.00.
#3413 Cosmos vase, oval, 7", 1959 – 1965. $40.00 – 50.00.
#3416 vase, fleur-de-lis 9", 1965 only. $45.00 – 55.00.
#3417 vase, fleur-de-lis 6½", 1965 only. $40.00 – 50.00.
#3434 coaster ashtray, 5", 1957 – 1963. $18.00 – 22.00.
#3441 vase, standing leaf, 8", 1959 – 1965. $40.00 – 50.00.
#3442 vase, standing leaf, 6", 1959 – 1965. $25.00 – 35.00.
#3527 ashtray, leaf, 4¼"x3", 1959 – 1965. $20.00 – 25.00.
#3528 ashtray, leaf, 3¼"x3", 1959 – 1965. $20.00 – 25.00.
#3529 ashtray, Ivy leaf, 4"x3½", 1959 – 1965. $20.00 – 25.00.
#3530 ashtray, Oak leaf, 4"x2¼", 1959 – 1965. $20.00 – 25.00.
#3531 ashtray, leaf, 3½" square, 1959 – 1965. $20.00 – 25.00.
#3546 apple tray 13" diameter, 1969 – 1970. $45.00 – 55.00.
#3563 vase, Lily, 7", 1959 – 1962. $30.00 – 40.00.
#3612 vase, Lily, 8", 1959 – 1962. $25.00 – 35.00.
#3613 vase, basket with fish, 5", 1960 only. $45.00 – 55.00.
#3617 horn of plenty 10½"x16", 1960 – 1964. $100.00 – 125.00.
#3630 cigarette box 4½"x5½", quilt top, 1968 – 1977. $50.00 – 60.00 (see page 306 for photo).
#3630 coaster ashtray, 5", (same as #3434), 1959 – 1961. $18.00 – 22.00 (see page 306 for photo).
#3666 ashtray, 4½" square, 1962 – 1965. $20.00 – 25.00.
#3675 oval vase, Morning Glory, 9½", 1960 only. $75.00 – 95.00.

Antique Gold #3264 oval vase, 9", 1971 – 1976. $65.00 – 80.00.

Colonial Silver #3264 oval vase, 9", 1971 only. $50.00 – 65.00.

Antique Gold #3440 vase, standing leaf, 12", 1959 – 1960. $70.00 – 85.00. Courtesy of the Marcena North collection.

Antique Gold #3611 Horse head vase, 13", 1959 – 1962. $350.00 – 400.00.

Black Gold #3621 small basket with handle 5½", 1965 – 1977. $25.00 – 30.00.

Colonial Silver #3630 cigarette box 4½"x5½", flat top, 1959 – 1977. $50.00 – 60.00. Courtesy of the Robert Sherman collection.

Granada Gold #3672 double shell vase, 7½"x11", 1969 – 1971. $100.00 – 125.00. Courtesy of the Marcena North collection.

#3685 ovoid vase 7", 1969 – 1970. $30.00 – 40.00.
#3688 vase, milk can, 7", 1969 – 1977. $35.00 – 45.00.
#3689 ovoid vase 4½", 1969 – 1970. $30.00 – 40.00.
#3691 ovoid vase 5", 1969 – 1970. $30.00 – 40.00.
#3694 round vase 5", 1969 – 1970. $30.00 – 40.00.
#3705 vase, large scroll horn, 10", 1959 – 1960. $75.00 – 95.00.
#3774 tray, fruit 15"x6", 1962 – 1964 and 1972 – 1976. $25.00 – 30.00.

Antique Gold #3676 covered candy dish, square, 4½"x5½", 1965 – 1971. $30.00 – 40.00.

Kay Hackett designed several decorative 14½" chop plates in 1957. Many of the designs were too intricate for production, but Martin Stangl directed Kay Hackett to produce 12 each of the Persian and Compass patterns to sell at the Flemington Outlet.

The Peacock chop plate was produced for two years, and the Bands pattern was produced for three. In 1958, Chicago jeweler C.D. Peacock had seen one of Stangl's 14½" Peacock plates and asked Stangl if he could order the same motif on a smaller plate for Christmas promotions. Each Christmas throughout the 1960s, Stangl produced a quantity of 11" Peacock plates for C.D. Peacock. Irene Sarnecki, head of decorating, applied the C.D. Peacock "signature" to each of the 11" Peacock plates.

#3774 Compass chop plate (left) and Persian (right), 14½" (Kay Hackett design), only twelve made. $550.00 – 650.00 each. Courtesy of Kay Hackett and the Jim Horner collection.

Bands #3774 chop plate, 14½" (Kay Hackett design), 1957 – 1960. $75.00 – 95.00. Courtesy of Kay Hackett.

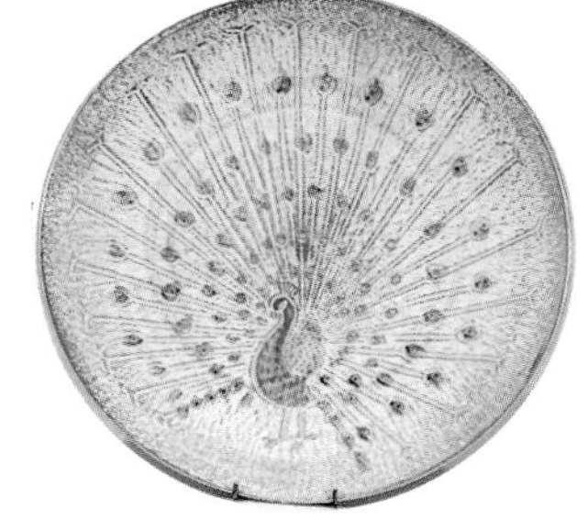

Peacock #3774 chop plate, 14½" (Kay Hackett design), 1957 – 1959. $275.00 – 300.00. Courtesy of Kay Hackett.

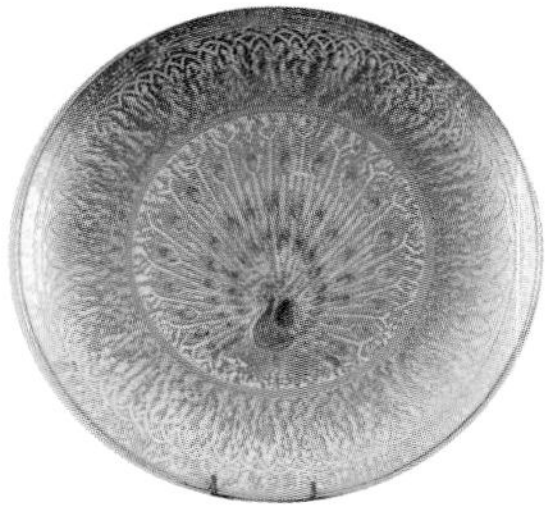

Peacock #3774 plate, 11", made for C.D. Peacock, jeweler, during 1960s. $130.00 – 150.00. Courtesy of the Ben and Floss Avila collection.

Antique Gold #3774 plate, 10", "S.A.G. 1957, Martin Stangl" (Stangl Antique Gold), 1957 only. $200.00 – 250.00. Courtesy of Merrill and Christl Stangl Bacheler.

Not Shown:
#3779 leaf server, 7"x14½", 1969 – 1970. $30.00 – 40.00.
#3781 triple Shell tray, 12" diameter, 1969 – 1970. $35.00 – 45.00.
#3782 double Pear dish, 7½"x7½", 1959 – 1971. $20.00 – 25.00.
#3783 single Pear dish, 7½"x4", 1959 – 1971. $15.00 – 20.00.
#3784 double Apple dish, 10"x5½", 1959 – 1978. $20.00 – 25.00.
#3785 single Apple dish, 6", 1959 – 1978. $15.00 – 20.00.
#3786 square snack dish, 4½", 1959 – 1961. $15.00 – 20.00.
#3787 heart dish, 6", 1959 – 1970. $15.00 – 20.00.
#3788 heart dish 8", 1969 – 1970. $20.00 – 25.00.

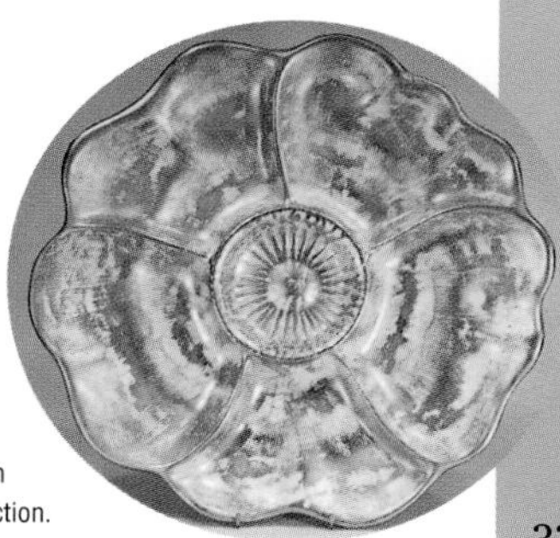

Antique Gold #3766 hors d'oeuvre, Rose, 14" round, 1959 – 1962. $120.00 – 145.00. Courtesy of the Ben and Pauline Jensen collection.

#3816S ashtray, windproof, 6" (Kay Hackett design), 1959 – 1962. $20.00 – 25.00.

#3816L ashtray, windproof, 8" (Kay Hackett design), 1959 – 1962. $25.00 – 30.00.

#3855 leaf server, 9¼"x5" (Kay Hackett design), 1959 only. $25.00 – 35.00.

#3856 apple server, 7¼"x8", 1959 only. $20.00 – 25.00.

#3857 clover server, 7"x7½", 1959 – 1978. $20.00 – 25.00.

#3858 comport, 8"x4", 1959 only. $25.00 – 35.00.

#3859 leaf server, 8"x7", 1959 – 1971. $20.00 – 25.00.

#3860 relish dish, footed, 11½"x4½" (Kay Hackett design), 1957 only. $25.00 – 35.00.

#3873 round candle warmer, 1961 only. $25.00 – 30.00.

#3871 gladiola vase, 13" high, 17" long, 1964 only. $150.00 – 175.00.

#3889 large candle holder, 6", 1958 only. $25.00 – 35.00.

#3889 large candle holder, 3", 1958 only. $20.00 – 25.00.

Antique Gold #3889 large candle holder, 9", 1958 only. $35.00 – 45.00.

#3897S ashtray, square 4"x4" (Ed Pettingil design), 1959 only. $20.00 – 25.00.

#3897M ashtray, square 5"x5" (Ed Pettingil design), 1959 – 1970. $15.00 – 20.00.

#3897L ashtray, square 6½"x6½" (Ed Pettingil design), 1959 – 1970. $20.00 – 25.00.

#3898 cigarette box, fluted, 1957 – 1968. $50.00 – 60.00 (see page 306 for photo).

#3898-5 ashtray, fluted 5", 1957 – 1968. $15.00 – 20.00.

#3898-7 ashtray, fluted 7", 1957 – 1965. $20.00 – 25.00.

#3898-5 ashtray, fluted 5", "Stangl Pottery 1805," 1965 only. $80.00 – 110.00 (See page 306 for photo).

#3898-7 ashtray, fluted 7", "Stangl Pottery 1805" 1965 only. $95.00 – 130.00.

The fluted ashtrays bearing the phrase "Stangl Pottery 1805" were made only for the "Fifty Years of Progress in Pottery" celebration in the summer of 1965.

#3902 cigarette box, square, 1959 only. $100.00 – 125.00.

#3902-5 coaster ashtray, 5", 1959 only. $25.00 – 30.00.

#3903 cigarette box, high cover, 1959 only. $100.00 – 125.00.

#3903-A cigarette box, ashtray cover, 1959 only. $100.00 – 125.00.

#3904 ashtray, free form 7"x4½" (Ed Pettingil design), 1959 – 1965. $20.00 – 25.00.

#3904S ashtray, Safety, free form 7"x4½" (Ed Pettingil design), 1962 – 1965. $20.00 – 25.00.

#3904M ashtray, Safety, 8"x5" (Ed Pettingil design), 1962 – 1965. $20.00 – 25.00.

#3904L ashtray, Safety, 9¼"x5" (Ed Pettingil design), 1962 – 1965. $25.00 – 30.00.

#3905 ashtray, free form (same as #3904), 5"x3½" (Ed Pettingil design), 1957 – 1965. $15.00 – 20.00.

#3906 ashtray, notched, free form 5½" (Ed Pettingil design), 1957 – 1965. $12.00 – 18.00.

#3914 ashtray, square with square well, 9" (Kay Hackett design), 1958 – 1965. $20.00 – 25.00.

#3914GB ashtray, square with square well and golf ball center, 1958 – 1959. $75.00 – 95.00.

Green Lustre #3915 ashtray, square with round well, 9" (Kay Hackett design), 1958 – 1978. $20.00 – 25.00.

#3926 ashtray, oval, plain, 10¾"x8" (Kay Hackett design), 1972 – 1976. $15.00 – 20.00.

#3926GB ashtray, oval with golf ball center, 1958 – 1959. $75.00 – 95.00.

#3927A ashtray, casual, 10½"x 7½" (Kay Hackett design), 1958 – 1960. $25.00 – 30.00.

#3937 ashtray, 7" diameter, 1958 – 1960. $25.00 – 30.00.

#3938 ashtray, free form 7¼"x5⅞" (Ed Pettingil design), 1957 – 1962. $20.00 – 25.00.

#3938S ashtray, Safety, free form 6½" (Ed Pettingil design), 1962 – 1965. $15.00 – 20.00.

#3938M ashtray, Safety, free form 7½" (Ed Pettingil design), 1962 – 1964. $20.00 – 25.00.

#3938L ashtray, Safety, free form 8" (Ed Pettingil design), 1962 – 1964. $20.00 – 25.00.

#3939 ashtray, rectangular, 9⅛"x9⅛" (Ed Pettingil design), 1958 – 1960. $20.00 – 25.00.

#3940 ashtray, irregular shape 6½"x5"x8" (Ed Pettingil design), 1958 – 1960. $20.00 – 25.00.

#3941 ashtray, Safety, free form 5⅜"x6¼"x7" (Ed Pettingil design), 1958 – 1960. $20.00 – 25.00.

#3942 ashtray, Safety, oval 8½"x7" (Ed Pettingil design), 1959 – 1978. $15.00 – 20.00.

#3944 bowl, low footed 3-corner 2½" high x 10" diameter (Ed Pettingil design), 1958 – 1960. $45.00 – 55.00.

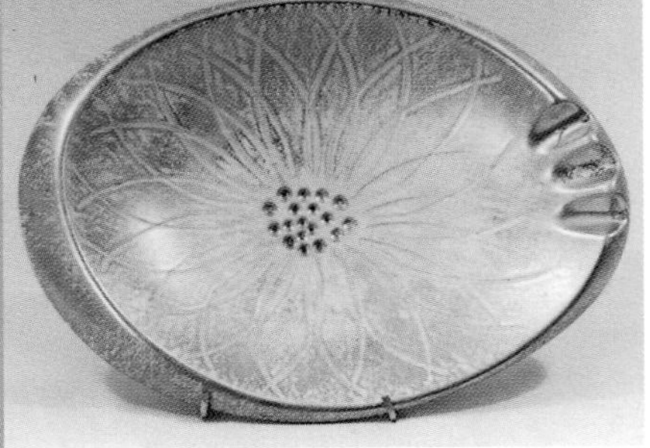

#3926 ashtray, oval, carved decoration, 10¾"x8" (Kay Hackett design), 1958 – 1962. $25.00 – 30.00.

Antique Gold #3973 ashtray, 8½"x2⅛" (Kay Hackett design), 1957 – 1963. $35.00 – 45.00.

Antique Gold #3974 salt and pepper, 6" high, handmade, 1957 – 1962. $50.00 – 60.00 pair. Courtesy of the Robert Sherman collection.

Cobalt Antique Gold #3975M pitcher, strap handle, 5¾", 1½-pint, handmade, 1957 – 1962. $25.00 – 35.00. Courtesy of the Ben and Pauline Jensen collection.

#3975L pitcher, strap handle, 7¼", 1½-quart, handmade, 1957 – 1962. $30.00 – 40.00. Courtesy of the Ben and Pauline Jensen collection.

#3945 bowl, semi-round 2½"x 6¼" (Ed Pettingil design), 1958 – 1960. $45.00 – 55.00.

#3945 bowl, semi-round 3¼"x 8¼" (Ed Pettingil design), 1958 – 1960. $25.00 – 30.00.

#3945 bowl, semi-round 4"x10⅜" (Ed Pettingil design), 1958 – 1960. $30.00 – 40.00.

#3952 cylinder vase, 10" (Kay Hackett design), 1961 – 1962. $40.00 – 50.00.

#3952 cylinder vase, 8" (Kay Hackett design), 1961 – 1962. $30.00 – 40.00.

#3952 cylinder vase, 6" (Kay Hackett design), 1961 – 1962. $25.00 – 30.00.

#3952 cylinder vase, 4" (Kay Hackett design), 1961 – 1962. $25.00 – 30.00.

#3953 pencil holder, made for Tri-Rex pencils, 1958 – 1961. $85.00 – 95.00.

#3954 square tray 10¾"x2½" (Ed Pettingil design), 1958 – 1960. $45.00 – 55.00.

#3955 vase, square 2" high 8"x9", 1961 only. $25.00 – 35.00.

#3955 vase, square 4" high 6"x7", 1961 only. $25.00 – 35.00.

#3955 vase, square 6" high 4"x5", 1961 only. $25.00 – 35.00.

#3955 vase, square 8" high 2"x3", 1961 only. $25.00 – 35.00.

#3972 ashtray, Flying Saucer, 10" (Kay Hackett design), 1957 – 1977. $40.00 – 50.00 (see page 330 for photo).

#3972GB ashtray, Flying Saucer, 10" with golf ball center, 1958 – 1959. $75.00 – 95.00.

#3975XL pitcher, strap handle, 9½", 2½-quart, handmade 1957 – 1962. $50.00 – 60.00.

#3976 ashtray, oval 11¼"x7¾" (Kay Hackett design), 1957 – 1965. $45.00 – 55.00.

#3976GB ashtray, oval 11¼"x7¾" with golf ball center, 1958 – 1959. $75.00 – 95.00.

#3977S ashtray, Safety, semi-oval 6"x4½" (Kay Hackett design), 1962 – 1959. $15.00 – 20.00.

#3977M ashtray, Safety, semi-oval 7½"x6¼" (Kay Hackett design), 1962 – 1965. $20.00 – 25.00.

#3977L ashtray, Safety, semi-oval 8½"x7" (Kay Hackett design), 1962 – 1964. $25.00 – 30.00.

#3978 vase 10", handmade 1957 – 1962. $50.00 – 60.00.

#3979 vase 9", handmade 1957 – 1962. $50.00 – 60.00.

#3980 bowl, 8¼" diameter, handmade 1957 – 1969. $25.00 – 30.00.

#3981 vase, bud 6¾", handmade 1957 – 1964. $35.00 – 45.00.

#3982 vase 8¼", handmade 1957 – 1960. $50.00 – 60.00.

#3983 bowl, 9" diameter, handmade 1957 – 1964. $25.00 – 30.00.

#3984 vase 7", handmade 1957 – 1960. $45.00 – 55.00.

#3986 vase 6", handmade 1957 – 1960. $45.00 – 55.00.

#3988 vase 6¾", handmade 1957 – 1960. $45.00 – 55.00.

#3989 vase 7¼", handmade 1957 – 1965. $45.00 – 55.00.

Antique Gold #3977 ashtray, semi-oval 7½"x6¼", hand-carved decoration (Kay Hackett design), 1957 – 1962. $30.00 – 40.00. Courtesy of the Ben and Pauline Jensen collection.

Antique Gold Geigy #3977 ashtray, semi-oval 7½"x6¼", made for Ceba Geigy Pharmaceuticals, 1958 only. $45.00 – 55.00.

Antique Gold #3985 vase 7¾", handmade 1957 – 1960. $40.00 – 50.00.

Cobalt Antique Gold #3987 vase, urn 6", handmade, 1957 – 1969. $40.00 – 50.00.

#3990 vase 6⅜", handmade, 1957 – 1960. $40.00 – 50.00.

Antique Gold #3993 vase, urn 12", handmade 1957 – 1965 and 1972 – 1976. $110.00 – 135.00.

Antique Gold bud vase, 5½", handmade, 1957 only. $30.00 – 40.00. Courtesy of the Robert and Tammie Cruser collection.

Antique Gold ewer, 10", handmade, 1957 only. $70.00 – 95.00. Courtesy of the Robert and Tammie Cruser collection.

Antique Gold #4002 vase 6"x5", handmade, 1958 – 1964. $35.00 – 45.00.

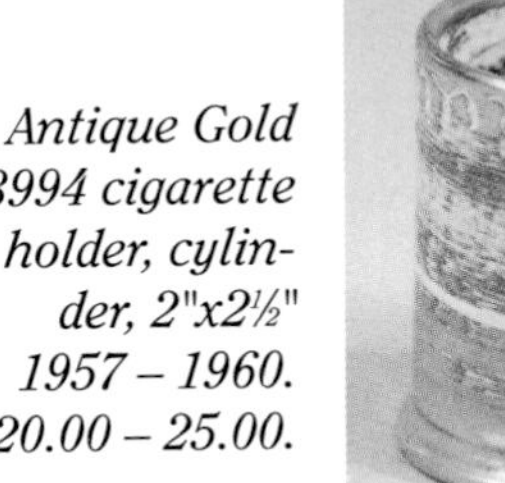

Antique Gold #3994 cigarette holder, cylinder, 2"x2½" 1957 – 1960. $20.00 – 25.00.

#3991 vase 6⅝", handmade 1957 – 1960. $45.00 – 55.00.

#3992 cigarette holder, urn, 3¼", $20.00 – 25.00, and #3998 3" ashtray for #3992 cigarette holder, 1957 – 1960, $15.00 – 20.00 (see page 317 for photo).

#3992 cigarette holder, urn, 3¼", 1957 – 1960. $20.00 – 25.00.

#3995 ashtray for #3994 cigarette holder 3½", 1957 – 1960. $15.00 – 20.00.

#3996 cigarette holder, oval, 2½", 1957 – 1960. $20.00 – 25.00 (see page 317 for photo).

#3997 ashtray for #3996 cigarette holder, oval 3½", 1957 – 1960. $15.00 – 20.00 (see page 317 for photo).

#3998 ashtray for #3992 cigarette holder, 3", 1957 – 1960. $15.00 – 20.00.

#3999 vase, bottle shape 15x4¾", handmade 1957 – 1960. $75.00 – 95.00.

#4000 bowl 13"x7", handmade 1957 – 1960. $35.00 – 45.00.

#4001 vase 9"x8", handmade 1958 – 1960. $35.00 – 45.00.

#4003 vase 12"x8", handmade 1958 – 1960. $50.00 – 60.00.

#4004 vase 5½"x4½", handmade 1958 – 1964. $35.00 – 45.00.

#4006 bowl 11"x9", handmade 1958 – 1960. $35.00 – 45.00.

#4007 vase 6¾"x4¼", handmade 1958 – 1964. $30.00 – 40.00.

#4008 vase 9"x5¾", handmade 1958 – 1960. $45.00 – 55.00.

#4009 vase 8¾"x4¼", handmade 1958 – 1960. $$45.00 – 55.00.

#4010 vase 6½"x5¼", handmade 1958 – 1960. $30.00 – 40.00.

#4015 candleholder, small 3½" (orig. #1388), 1958 – 1961 and 1967 – 1977. $15.00 – 20.00 pair.

#4016 candleholder, tall, 7½" (orig. #1806), 1958 – 1960. $100.00 – 125.00 pair (see page 331 for photo).

Antique Gold #4005 vase 8½"x6½", handmade, 1958 – 1960. $45.00 – 55.00 Courtesy of the Ben and Pauline Jensen collection.

Antique Gold #4011 bell, 3½", 1958 – 1960. $75.00 – 95.00. Courtesy of the Frank and Elizabeth Kramar collection.

Antique Gold #4017 candleholder, handled, 8½" (orig. #1388), 1958 – 1960. $65.00 – 80.00 each.

Antique Gold #4018 shell dish, small, 7½", 1958 – 1977. $15.00 – 20.00.

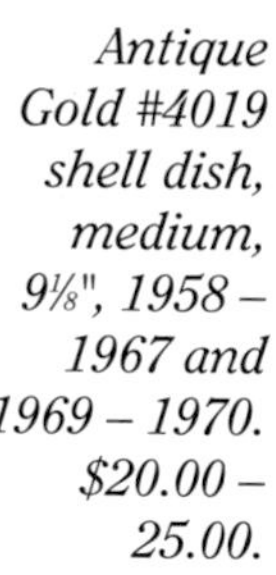

Antique Gold #4019 shell dish, medium, 9⅞", 1958 – 1967 and 1969 – 1970. $20.00 – 25.00.

Cobalt Antique Gold #4020 shell dish, large, 10½", 1958 – 1963 and 1969 – 1970. $30.00 – 40.00. Courtesy of the Marcena North collection.

#4021 compote 3½"x6½" (orig. #1388), 1958 – 1977. $15.00 – 20.00.
#4022 bowl, oval 13½"x7½"x3¾" (orig. #1388), 1958 – 1962. $25.00 – 30.00.
#4025 vase, urn 7½", 1958 – 1965. $35.00 – 45.00.
#4026 ashtray, conference table 11¼" (Kay Hackett design), 1958 – 1976. $40.00 – 50.00.
#4026GB ashtray, conference table 11¼" with golf ball center, 1958 – 1959. $75.00 – 95.00.
#4027 ashtray, 12½" (Kay Hackett design), 1958 – 1964. $45.00 – 55.00.
#4027GB ashtray, 12½" with golf ball center, 1958 – 1959. $75.00 – 95.00.
#4028 bowl, 9", pedestal (orig. #3434 bowl, Kay Hackett design), 1958 – 1965. $25.00 – 30.00.
#4029 bowl, 10", pedestal (orig. #3774 bowl, Kay Hackett design), 1958 – 1964. $25.00 – 30.00.
#4032 ashtray, leaf, 5½"x4", 1958 – 1962. $10.00 – 15.00.
#4033 ashtray, Cosmos, 5½", 1958 – 1978. $10.00 – 15.00.
#4034 ashtray, leaf, 6½"x4", 1958 – 1968. $10.00 – 15.00.
#4035 ashtray, leaf, Ivy, 5¼"x4¼", 1958 – 1962. $10.00 – 15.00.
#4036 ashtray, leaf, 6"x4½", 1958 – 1965. $10.00 – 15.00.
#4037 ashtray, shell dish, 5"x5½", 1958 – 1977. $10.00 – 15.00.
#4038 leaf server, Oak, 13½"x9", 1958 – 1965 and 1969 – 1977. $25.00 – 35.00.
#4039 leaf server, 12"x8½", 1958 – 1963 and 1969 – 1970. $20.00 – 25.00.
#4040 candleholder, flower, 4¼", 1958 – 1965. $25.00 – 35.00 pair.
#4041 leaf server, 18½"x13", 1958 – 1965 and 1969 – 1970. $40.00 – 50.00.
#4042 leaf server, 16½"x10", 1958 – 1965 and 1969 – 1970. $40.00 – 50.00.
#4043 candleholder, Calla Lily, 3¼", 1958 – 1962. $25.00 – 30.00 pair.
#4049 vase, bud 9¼" (Kay Hackett design), 1958 – 1964. $30.00 – 40.00.
#4050 vase, bud 8" (Kay Hackett design), 1958 – 1978. $20.00 – 25.00.

Antique Gold #4026 Dancing Elephant Ashtray (also #5281), 11¼", 1973 – 1975. $150.00 – 200.00.

Group of Antique Gold vases, handmade #3984 7" vase, $45.00 – 55.00; #4051 8¾" vase, $30.00 – 40.00; #4052 14½" pitcher, $45.00 – 55.00; and #4049 9¼" bud vase, $30.00 – 40.00. Courtesy of the Marcena North collection.

Colonial Silver #4050 bud vase, 8", commemorative "President's Week Winner 1970," 1970 only, Colonial Silver only (backstamp, inset). $20.00 – 25.00.

#4051 vase, bud, 8¾" (Kay Hackett design), 1958 – 1963. $30.00 – 40.00.
#4052 pitcher, 14½" (Kay Hackett design), 1958 – 1965. $45.00 – 55.00.
#4053 pitcher, 12" (Kay Hackett design), 1958 – 1970. $35.00 – 45.00.
#4054 pitcher, 16" (Kay Hackett design), 1958 – 1978. $50.00 – 60.00.
#4055 pitcher, 11¼" (Kay Hackett design), 1958 – 1978. $25.00 – 35.00.
#4056 pitcher, 8¼" (Kay Hackett design), 1958 – 1978. $20.00 – 25.00.
#4057 pitcher, 12¾" (Kay Hackett design), 1958 – 1962. $40.00 – 50.00.
#4058 pitcher, 7½" (Kay Hackett design), 1958 – 1965. $25.00 – 35.00.
#4059 pitcher, 6¼" (Kay Hackett design), 1958 – 1973. $25.00 – 30.00.

Antique Gold #4054 pitcher 16", $50.00 – 60.00, and Granada Gold #4055 pitcher 11¼", $25.00 – 35.00.

Antique Gold #4059 pitcher 6¼", $25.00 – 30.00, and #4060 pitcher 5¼", $20.00 – 25.00. Courtesy of the Ben and Pauline Jensen collection.

#4061 bowl, scalloped-ruffled, 8" (Kay Hackett design), 1958 – 1970. $25.00 – 30.00.

#4062 bowl, scalloped-ruffled, 10¼" (Kay Hackett design), 1958 – 1970. $25.00 – 35.00.

Golden Glo #4060 pitcher 5¼" (Kay Hackett design), 1962 – 1963. $20.00 – 25.00.

Antique Gold #4064 candleholders, pedestal, 4" (Kay Hackett design), 1958 – 1962. $35.00 – 45.00 pair. Courtesy of the Marcena North collection.

#4063 sherbet with Florentine decoration, 5¾", 1958 only. $20.00 – 25.00.

#4065 bowl, 11¼"x10¾" (Kay Hackett design), 1958 – 1964 and 1969 – 1970. $35.00 – 45.00.

#4066 urn, 16" (orig. #1758 without handles), 1958 – 1965. $55.00 – 65.00.

#4070 coaster ashtray with center medallion 5", lavender, green, ivory, and blue centers, sold as sets of four, 1958 – 1963. $12.00 – 18.00 each.

#4070 coaster ashtray with center medallion 5", Golden Glo, 1962 only. $20.00 – 25.00.

#4071 fluted flowerpot, 4" (orig. #3662), 1959 – 1963. $20.00 – 25.00.
#4071 fluted flowerpot, 5" (orig. #3662), 1959 – 1963. $20.00 – 25.00.
#4071 fluted flowerpot, 7" (orig. #3662), 1959 – 1963. $25.00 – 35.00.
#4072 candy dish, flared, 5"x1½", 1959 – 1965. $20.00 – 25.00.
#4073 candy dish, flared, footed, 5"x3¼", 1959 – 1965. $20.00 – 25.00.
#4074 candy dish, flared, footed, 5"x2¼", 1959 – 1965. $20.00 – 25.00.
#4075 candy dish, flared, footed, 5"x3¾", 1959 – 1965. $20.00 – 25.00.
#4076 candy dish, flared, footed, 8"x3¼", 1959 – 1965. $25.00 – 35.00.

Antique Gold #4069 candy dish with cover, 11" x 6¾", 1958 – 1965. $100.00 – 125.00.

Group of Antique Gold flared vases and dishes, #4080 5¾" vase, $40.00 – 50.00; #4081 8¼", vase, $35.00 – 45.00; #4075 5"x3¾" candy dish, $20.00 – 25.00; and #4077 7"x4⅛" candy dish, $25.00 – 35.00. Courtesy of the Marcena North collection.

Antique Gold #4069 candy dish with cover, 11" high x 6¾", pierced, 1959 only. $190.00 – 225.00. Courtesy of Merrill and Christl Stangl Bacheler.

#4077 candy dish, flared, footed, 7"x4⅛", 1959 – 1963. $25.00 – 35.00.
#4078 candy dish, flared, footed, 8" x3¼", 1959 – 1962. $25.00 – 35.00.
#4079 vase, large flared, 5¾", 1959 – 1965. $30.00 – 40.00.
#4080 vase, flared, 5¾", 1959 – 1963. $40.00 – 50.00.
#4081 vase, flared, 8¼", 1959 – 1965. $35.00 – 45.00.
#4082 vase, flared, 8¼", 1959 – 1965. $35.00 – 45.00.
#4083 candleholders, flared, 3⅞", 1959 – 1963. $25.00 – 35.00 pair.
#4084 bowl, flared, footed, 10"x4", 1959 – 1963. $35.00 – 45.00.
#4085 cigarette box, flat cover, Lion, 1959 – 196. $100.00 – 125.00.
#4085 ashtray, 5¾", embossed border, Lion, 1959 – 1960. $10.00 – 15.00.
#4086 cigarette box, flat cover, Hinge, 1959 – 1960. $100.00 – 125.00 (see page 307 for photo).
#4086 ashtray, 5¾", embossed border, Hinge, 1959 – 1960. $10.00 – 15.00.
#4087 cigarette box, hump cover, Diamond, 1959 – 1960. $100.00 – 125.00 (see page 307 for photo).
#4087 ashtray, 5¾", embossed border, Diamond, 1959 – 1960. $10.00 – 15.00.
#4088 cigarette box, hump cover, Basket Weave, 1959 – 1960. $100.00 – 125.00.
#4088 ashtray, 5¾", embossed border, Basket Weave, 1959 – 1960. $10.00 – 15.00.
#4089 cigarette box, curved cover, Stag, 1959 – 1960. $100.00 – 125.00 (see page 307 for photo).
#4089 ashtray, 5¾", embossed border, Stag, 1959 – 1960. $10.00 – 15.00.
#4090 cigarette box, curved cover, Corduroy, 1959 – 1960. $100.00 – 125.00 (see page 307 for photo).
#4090 ashtray, 5¾", embossed border, Corduroy, 1959 – 1960. $10.00 – 15.00.
#4091 candy dish with cover, 8", same as #4069, 1959 – 1963. $65.00 – 80.00.
#4091 candy dish with cover, 8", pierced, 1959 only. $70.00 – 85.00.
#4093 deep salad bowl, 12½" (orig. #3608), 1959 only. $100.00 – 125.00.
#4094 plate, 8" (orig. #3434), 1959 only. $20.00 – 25.00.
#4095 bowl, flared and footed, 10"x7¼" (orig. #4084), 1959 – 1963. $35.00 – 45.00.
#4096 bowl, flared and footed, 8" (orig. #4078), 1959 – 1963. $25.00 – 35.00.
#4097 ashtray with island, 9", made for McDonald, 1959 – 1962. $25.00 – 35.00.
#4098 ashtray only, 9", made for McDonald, 1959 – 1962 . $25.00 – 35.00.
#5000 ashtray, deep, 7", made for McDonald, 1959 – 1962. $25.00 – 35.00.
#5002 ashtray, round 9¼" (Kay Hackett design), 1959 – 1962. $25.00 – 35.00.
#5003 ashtray, triangular 7½"x6½" (Kay Hackett design), 1959 – 1960. $25.00 – 35.00.
#5004 ashtray, rectangular, 12½"x6½" (Kay Hackett design), 1959 – 1971. $20.00 – 25.00.
#5005 ashtray, square 7½"x7½" (Kay Hackett design), 1959 – 1964. $20.00 – 25.00.
#5006 cigarette lighter, urn shape, small, 1959 – 1960. $35.00 – 45.00 (see page 317 for photo).
#5007 cigarette lighter, urn shape, large, 1959 – 1960. $50.00 – 60.00.
#5012 vase, bud, 5¼" (Kay Hackett design), 1959 – 1960. $25.00 – 30.00.
#5013 vase, bud, medium, 7¼" (Kay Hackett design), 1959 – 1960. $30.00 – 40.00.
#5015 ginger jar, 5½" with cover (Kay Hackett design), 1959 – 1960. $55.00 – 65.00.
#5017 ashtray, triangular, 7½"x6⅜"(orig. #3906), 1959 – 1965. $12.00 – 18.00.
#5021 vase, 6⅞" (Kay Hackett design), 1959 – 1964. $45.00 – 55.00.
#5022 vase, 7¾" (Kay Hackett design), 1959 – 1965. $50.00 – 60.00.
#5023 vase, Phoenician, 9¾" (Kay Hackett design), 1959 – 1978. $40.00 – 50.00.
#5024 vase, 9¾" (Kay Hackett design), 1959 – 1964. $55.00 – 65.00.
#5026-1 Strawberry chop plate, 14½" 1972 – 1975. $160.00 – 180.00.

Antique Gold #4092 candy dish with tureen cover, octagonal, 6½", 1959 – 1968. $35.00 – 45.00. Courtesy of the Marcena North collection.

Cobalt Antique Gold #5014 vase, bud, large 8¾" (Kay Hackett design), 1959 – 1960. $45.00 – 55.00. Courtesy of the Marcena North collection.

Antique Gold #5016 ginger jar, 7¼", with cover (Kay Hackett design), 1959 – 1960. $80.00 – 90.00. Courtesy of the Ben and Pauline Jensen collection.

Antique Gold Grape #5026 chop plate, 14½", 1960 – 1965 and 1972 – 1975. $120.00 – 135.00. Courtesy of the Marcena North collection.

Antique Gold Sailboat #5027 chop plate, 14½", 1960 – 1962 and 1972 – 1975. $120.00 – 135.00. Courtesy of the Marcena North collection.

Antique Gold Butterfly #5028 chop plate, 14½", 1960 – 1962 and 1972 – 1975. $120.00 – 135.00. Courtesy of the Marcena North collection.

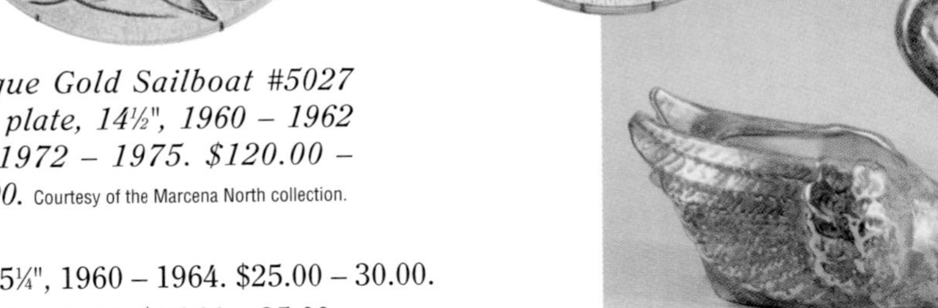

Cobalt Antique Gold #5032 swan planter EL, 9¾"x 12½" (orig. #1771), 1960 – 1962. $100.00 – 125.00.

#5029 bowl, footed, round, pierced, 5¼", 1960 – 1964. $25.00 – 30.00.
#5030 bowl, footed, pierced, 6¼", 1960 – 1964. $25.00 – 35.00.
#5031 bowl, footed, pierced, 8¼", 1960 – 1964. $30.00 – 40.00.
#5033 swan planter L, 6¾"x8½" (orig. #1394), 1960 – 1962. $35.00 – 45.00.
#5034 swan planter M, 5" high (orig. #1394), 1960 – 1978. $25.00 – 30.00.
#5035 swan planter, SM, 3½" high (orig. #1394), 1960 – 1963 and 1968 – 1970. $20.00 – 25.00.
#5036 vase, pierced 10" (same as #5023), 1960 – 1963. $85.00 – 95.00.
#5038 bowl, footed, pierced, 6", 1960 – 1964. $25.00 – 35.00.
#5039 bowl, pierced, 8"x4", 1960 – 1964. $40.00 – 50.00.
#5040 bowl, pierced, 6¾", 1960 – 1964. $30.00 – 40.00.
#5041 bowl, pierced, 10½", 1960 – 1964. $50.00 – 60.00.
#5042 urn, 2 handles, 10", 1960 – 1961. $45.00 – 55.00.
#5044 ashtray, oval 7½"x5", 1960 – 1962. $20.00 – 25.00.
#5045 bowl, footed, 6"x4", 1960 – 1962. $25.00 – 35.00.
#5046 bowl, oval pierced, 8"x5½", 1960 – 1962. $25.00 – 35.00.
#5047 bowl, oval pierced, 9"x6" , 1960 – 1962. $35.00 – 45.00.
#5055 ashtray, 5 slots, 5"x1⅝", 1960 – 1962. $20.00 – 25.00.
#5056 ashtray, round, 4⅝" (orig. #1955), 1960 – 1965. $20.00 – 25.00.
#5057 ashtray, 5⅜" (orig. #1957), 1960 – 1965. $20.00 – 25.00.
#5058 ashtray, round, 7¼", plain, 1960 – 1970. $20.00 – 25.00.
#5058 ashtray, round, 7¼", "Stangl Pottery, Flemington NJ" only two dozen made in 1960. $130.00 – 150.00.
#5059 ashtray, 11½"x7½", 1960 – 1961. $25.00 – 30.00.

Antique Gold #5037 pierced vase, 9¼" (same as #5024), 1960 – 1962. $100.00 – 125.00. Courtesy of Merrill and Christl Stangl Bacheler.

Antique Gold #5043 ashtray, round, 6¼"x6¼", 1960 – 1962. $20.00 – 25.00.

Antique Gold #5058 ashtray, round, 7¼", "John Martin Stangl," only six made for Martin Stangl's personal use in 1960. $300.00 – 350.00.

Three Antique Gold pierced bowls, #5038, 6", $25.00 – 35.00; #5061, 7", $25.00 – 30.00; and #5045, 6"x4" oval, $25.00 – 35.00. Courtesy of the Marcena North collection.

Antique Gold #5058 ashtray, round, 7¼", "Nevius Brothers, Flemington NJ," only four made for Howard Nevius in 1960, owner of Nevius Brothers' Dept. Store, a personal friend of Martin Stangl. $275.00 – 300.00.

Black Gold #5065 small horn of plenty, $20.00 – 25.00; and Antique Gold #3617 extra large horn of plenty, 10½"x16", $100.00 – 125.00.

Antique Gold #5098 11½" large Moderne pitcher, $55.00 – 65.00; #4064 4" pedestal candleholder, $35.00 – 45.00 pair; and #5096 5¾" bud vase, $20.00 – 25.00. Courtesy of the Marcena North collection.

#5060 ashtray, round, 8¼", 1960 – 1964 and 1967 – 1977. $20.00 – 25.00.
#5061 bowl, pierced, 7", 1960 – 1964. $25.00 – 30.00.
#5062 bowl, pierced, 9½", 1960 – 1964. $25.00 – 35.00.
#5063 bowl, footed (#5061), pierced, 7", 1960 – 1965. $25.00 – 35.00.
#5064 bowl, footed, pierced, 9½"x4", 1960 – 1965. $35.00 – 45.00.
#5065 horn of plenty, small, 4½"x7¼" (orig. #3617), 1960 – 1978. $20.00 – 25.00.
#5066 horn of plenty, large, 6½"x10" (orig. #3617), 1960 – 1977. $30.00 – 40.00.
#5068 candleholder, ruffled, 3½"x1¼", 1960 only. $25.00 – 30.00 pair.
#5069 candleholders, ruffled, footed, 3½"x 2", 1960 – 1978. $20.00 – 25.00 pair.
#5070 candleholders, 3" x 2½" (orig. #3687), 1960 – 1965. $25.00 – 35.00 pair.
#5074 ashtray, square, 5⅞"x5⅞", 1961 – 1963 and 1968 – 1969. $15.00 – 20.00.
#5075 ashtray, Prism, 6"x4", 1961 – 1963 and 1968 – 1971. $15.00 – 20.00.
#5076 ashtray, 8½"x4", 1961 – 1963 and 1968 – 1970. $15.00 – 20.00.
#5077 ashtray, 8½"x5¼", 1961 – 1963 and 1968 – 1970. $15.00 – 20.00.
#5078 bowl, side strap handle, 5¼"x2", 1961 – 1963. $20.00 – 25.00.
#5079 bowl, side strap handle, 7"x2⅝", 1961 – 1963. $20.00 – 25.00.
#5080 bowl, side strap handle, 8⅞"x3⅜", 1961 – 1963. $25.00 – 30.00.
#5081 jar, side strap handle, 2¾"x3?", 1961 – 1962. $20.00 – 25.00.
#5082 jar, side strap handle, 4¼"x5¼", 1961 – 1963. $20.00 – 25.00.
#5083 jar, side strap handle, 5½"x5½", 1961 – 1963. $25.00 – 30.00.
#5084 candleholders, side strap handle, 2¾"x4⅛", 1961 – 1963. $25.00 – 35.00 pair.
#5094 vase, bud, 7½", 1961 – 1964. $25.00 – 30.00.
#5095 vase, bud, 7½", 1961 – 1963. $25.00 – 30.00.
#5096 vase, bud, 5¾", 1961 – 1963. $20.00 – 25.00.
#5097 ashtray, 6½"x4½", 1961 – 1971. $15.00 – 20.00.
#5098 Moderne pitcher, large, 11½", 1961 – 1965. $55.00 – 65.00.
#5099 Moderne pitcher, medium, 9½", 1961 – 1964. $45.00 – 55.00.
#5100 Moderne pitcher, small, 7½", 1961 – 1964. $35.00 – 45.00.
#5103 vase, medium, 6", 1962 – 1963. $25.00 – 30.00.
#5104 vase, large 9", 1962 – 1963. $35.00 – 45.00.
#5105 fruit bowl, footed, 10", without cover, 1962 – 1965. $60.00 – 75.00.

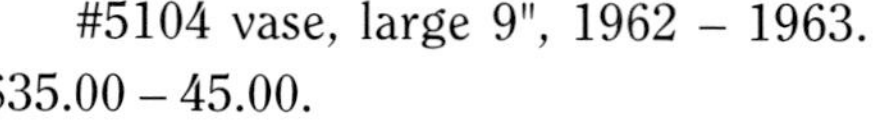

Experimental brushed gold finish #5092 coffee mug, 1961 only. $25.00 – 30.00.

Antique Gold #5093 vase, bud, 5¾", 1961 – 1978. $15.00 – 20.00.

Antique Gold #5101 ashtray, round, 4", 1962 only. $20.00 – 25.00.

Golden Glo #5102 vase, small, 4", 1962 – 1963. $20.00 – 25.00.

Granada Gold #5105 Fruit bowl, footed, 10" with open work cover, 1962 – 1964. $120.00 – 135.00.

Two #5115 oval footed bowls, 11¼" small in Colonial Silver, $20.00 – 25.00, and 14" medium in Green Lustre. $25.00 – 30.00 Courtesy of the Marcena North collection.

Antique Gold #5121 picture frame, square, round opening, 1962 – 1965. $50.00 – 60.00. Courtesy of the Marcena North collection.

Granada Gold #5132 vase, flared, 10½" (orig. #2091), 1963 – 1965. $50.00 – 60.00. Courtesy of the Ben and Pauline Jensen collection.

#5106 vase, cylinder, 10", Antique Gold or Golden Glo, 1962 only. $35.00 – 45.00.
#5106 triple cylinder vase, 10"x5", 1970 – 1977. $35.00 – 45.00.
#5107 vase, cylinder 8", Golden Glo, 1962 only. $25.00 – 35.00.
#5108 vase, cylinder 6", Golden Glo, 1962 only. $20.00 – 25.00.
#5109 vase, cylinder 4", Golden Glo, 1962 only. $20.00 – 25.00.
#5112 chop plate, 14½", Fish (Kay Hackett design), Golden Glo, 1962 only. $100.00 – 125.00.
#5113 chop plate, 14½", Leaves (Kay Hackett design), Golden Glo, 1962 only. $100.00 – 125.00.
#5114 chop plate, 14½", Florentine (Kay Hackett design), Golden Glo, 1962 only. $100.00 – 125.00.
#5115S bowl, oval footed, 11¼", 1962 – 1964 and 1969 – 1977. $20.00 – 25.00.
#5115M bowl, oval footed, 14", 1962 – 1964 and 1969 – 1971. $25.00 – 30.00.
#5115L bowl, oval footed, 17½", 1962 – 1964 and 1969 – 1970. $25.00 – 35.00.

Antique Gold #4038 13½"x9" leaf server, $25.00 – 35.00; and #5137 13"x5" elongated bowl, $30.00 – 40.00. Courtesy of the Ben and Pauline Jensen collection.

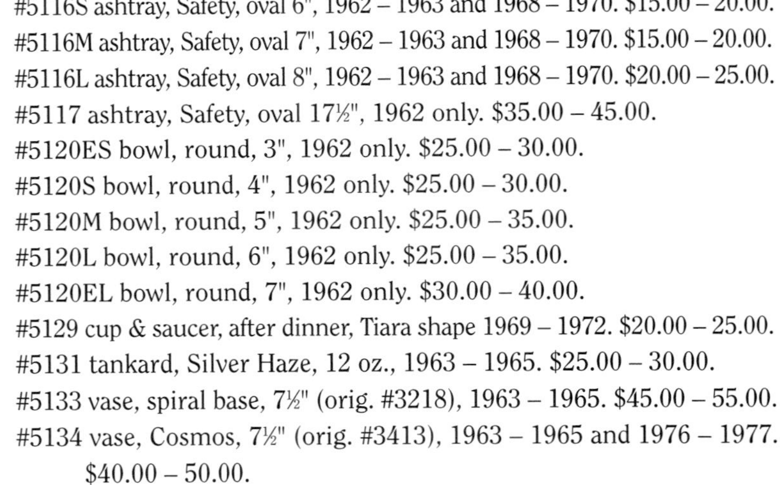

#5116ES ashtray, Safety, square 4½", 1962 only. $20.00 – 25.00.
#5116S ashtray, Safety, oval 6", 1962 – 1963 and 1968 – 1970. $15.00 – 20.00.
#5116M ashtray, Safety, oval 7", 1962 – 1963 and 1968 – 1970. $15.00 – 20.00.
#5116L ashtray, Safety, oval 8", 1962 – 1963 and 1968 – 1970. $20.00 – 25.00.
#5117 ashtray, Safety, oval 17½", 1962 only. $35.00 – 45.00.
#5120ES bowl, round, 3", 1962 only. $25.00 – 30.00.
#5120S bowl, round, 4", 1962 only. $25.00 – 30.00.
#5120M bowl, round, 5", 1962 only. $25.00 – 35.00.
#5120L bowl, round, 6", 1962 only. $25.00 – 35.00.
#5120EL bowl, round, 7", 1962 only. $30.00 – 40.00.
#5129 cup & saucer, after dinner, Tiara shape 1969 – 1972. $20.00 – 25.00.
#5131 tankard, Silver Haze, 12 oz., 1963 – 1965. $25.00 – 30.00.
#5133 vase, spiral base, 7½" (orig. #3218), 1963 – 1965. $45.00 – 55.00.
#5134 vase, Cosmos, 7½" (orig. #3413), 1963 – 1965 and 1976 – 1977. $40.00 – 50.00.

Granada Gold #5144 vase, Tulip, small, 4" (orig. #1878S), 1964 – 1978. $20.00 – 25.00.

#5135 vase, flared, 7½" (orig. # 2091), 1963 – 1971. $30.00 – 40.00.
#5136 vase, Lily, 7½" (orig. #3612), 1963 – 1965. $25.00 – 35.00.
#5137 bowl, elongated base, 13"x5" (orig. #3438), 1963 – 1965. $30.00 – 40.00.
#5138 candleholders, Rose, 2½" (orig. #1875), 1963 – 1978. $20.00 – 25.00 pair.
#5139 bowl, Cosmos, 12" diameter (orig. #1869), 1963 – 1977. $35.00 – 45.00.
#5145 vase, Tulip, large 5½" (orig. #1878M), 1964 – 1971. $25.00 – 30.00.
#5146 leaf dish, ivy 8"x7¾"(orig. #3239), 1964 – 1971. $20.00 – 25.00.
#5147 basket, bow 12"x6½"(orig. #3252), 1964 – 1968. $50.00 – 60.00.
#5148 basket, leaf 11"x6½" (orig. #3253), 1964 – 1965. $50.00 – 60.00.
#5149 basket, braided handle 11"x6½" (orig. #3251), 1964 – 1965. $45.00 – 55.00.

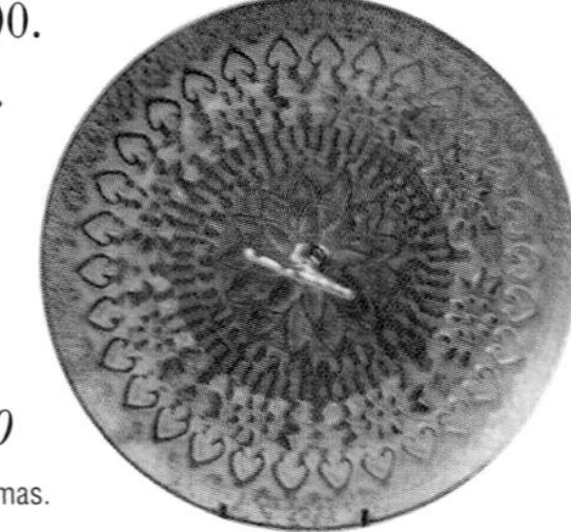

Cobalt Antique Gold #5151 Hearts & Flowers tidbit, 10", 1964 only. $20.00 – 25.00. Courtesy of Dave and Betty Stangl Thomas.

#5151 Hearts & Flowers tidbit, 10", 1964 – 1978. $12.00 – 18.00.
#5152-7 vase, jug, small 7", 1964 – 1965. $25.00 – 35.00.
#5152-9 vase, jug, medium 9", 1964 – 1965. $30.00 – 40.00.
#5152-11 vase, jug, large 11", 1964 – 1965. $45.00 – 55.00.
#5153 cigarette lighter, 4" (Kay Hackett design), 1964 – 1971. $25.00 – 35.00 (see page 317 for photo).
#5153 cigarette lighter, 4" with Appliqué motif, 1964 only. $30.00 – 40.00.
#5154 ashtray, 7" fluted with Appliqué motif (orig. #3898), 1964 only. $20.00 – 25.00.
#5156 Hearts & Flowers two-tier tidbit, 10"x6", 1964 – 1978. $22.00 – 28.00.
#5157, #5158 pitcher & bowl set, large 11"x15", 1965 only. $250.00 – 300.00.
#5157, #5158 pitcher & bowl set, small 9"x12", 1972 – 1974. $250.00 – 300.00.
#5160 tumbler 1965 only. $25.00 – 30.00.
#5162 dish, scalloped 5", 1965 – 1967. $25.00 – 30.00.
#5163 dish, scalloped 7", 1965 – 1967. $25.00 – 35.00.
#5169 Boy & Fish wall console set — boy 15"x6", bowl 8¼"x6½", 1965 only. $275.00 – 300.00.
#5169 boy only, 15"x6", $150.00 – 175.00.
#5169 bowl only, 8¼"x6½", $60.00 – 75.00.
#5170 Ram's Head wall console set: ram's head, 12¾"x11½", bowl, 7¼"x5½", 1965 only. $275.00 – 300.00.
#5170 ram's head only, 12¾"x11½". $150.00 – 175.00.
#5170 bowl only, 7¼"x5½". $60.00 – 75.00.
#5171 Aladdin's Lamp, 5½"x3", 1965 only. $35.00 – 45.00.
#5172 ashtray, pipe and cigar, 7"x9", 1965 – 1969. $25.00 – 30.00.
#5173 ashtray, square, 4½", 1965 – 1970. $15.00 – 20.00.
#5174 ashtray, square, 7", 1965 – 1976. $20.00 – 25.00.
#5174 ashtray, square, no rests, 7", made for Nelson Lebo Lamp Co., 1965 – 1978. $20.00 – 25.00.
#5188 candy dish, round, rosebud knob, 7" (orig. #3684), 1967 – 1971. $20.00 – 30.00.
#5190 vase, Chalice, 6¼", 1967 – 1971. $25.00 – 30.00.
#5194 candleholders, 3½" (originally #1388), 1967 – 1976. $15.00 – 20.00 pair.
#5195 switch plate, single, 1967 – 1968. $50.00 – 60.00.
#5196 switch plate, double, 1967 – 1968. $60.00 – 75.00.
#5207 footed server, 12½", 1968 only. $45.00 – 55.00.
#5211 compote, footed shell, 6"x8½"x8", 1968 – 1970. $35.00 – 45.00.
#5212 candleholders, footed shell, 3", 1968 – 1970. $25.00 – 30.00 pair.
#5231 jiggered ashtray, 4", 1971 – 1972. $20.00 – 25.00.
#5232 jiggered ashtray, 6", 1971 – 1972. $20.00 – 25.00.
#5233 ashtray, pipe knockout, 1971 only. $25.00 – 35.00.

Colonial Silver #5180 candy dish, Raised Fruit, 7", 1966 – 1977. $35.00 – 45.00.

Two #5195 single switch plates in Granada Gold and Antique Gold, $50.00 – 60.00 each. Courtesy of the Frank and Elizabeth Kramar collection.

Back of Antique Gold switch plate showing the bisque vitreous china of these items. A few were cast of Stangl's own red clay, but many switch plate blanks were purchased from Stangl's neighbors Star Porcelain and Wenczel Tile, then decorated at Stangl Pottery.

Green Lustre #5213 dish, footed shell, 3", 1968 – 1978. $15.00 – 20.00.

Green Lustre #5214 bowl, Conch shell, 7"x10", 1968 – 1977. $35.00 – 45.00. Courtesy of the Ben and Pauline Jensen collection.

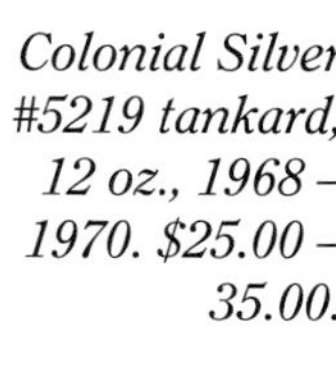

Colonial Silver #5219 tankard, 12 oz., 1968 – 1970. $25.00 – 35.00.

Colonial Silver #5243 scoop server, 18", 1971 only. $120.00 – 145.00. Courtesy of the Marcena North collection.

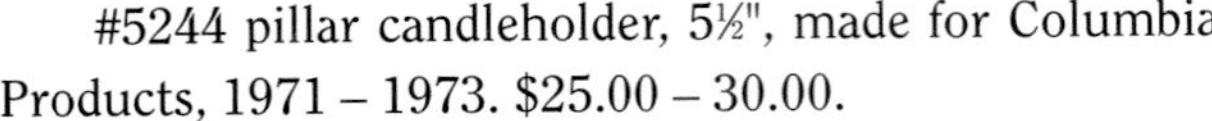

Antique Gold #5303 planter, French Phone, square base with dial, 1976 only. $175.00 – 200.00. Courtesy of the Marcena North collection.

#5244 pillar candleholder, 5½", made for Columbia Products, 1971 – 1973. $25.00 – 30.00.

#5254 Dollar Sign ashtray, 1971 only. $45.00 – 55.00.

#5259 ashtray, triangular, 6¾", 1971 – 1973. $25.00 – 35.00 (see page 313 for photo).

#5260 ashtray, Camper Windproof, 5¾", 1971 – 1973. $25.00 – 30.00.

#5270 candy dish, round knob, 7" (orig. #3684), 1972 – 1974. $25.00 – 35.00.

#5271 ashtray, 7¼", 1972 – 1974. $25.00 – 30.00.

#5272 candleholder, multi-tapers, 7½", 1972 – 1974. $25.00 – 35.00.

#5273 candleholder, pillar, 5", 1972 – 1974. $20.00 – 25.00.

#5274 bottle vase, 8½" (Rose Herbeck design), 1972 – 1974. $45.00 – 55.00.

#5287 candleholder, with globe, 6"x9", 1974 – 1977. $30.00 – 40.00.

#5299 candleholders, 7½", Town & Country shape, 1974 – 1977. $30.00 – 40.00 pair.

#5300 bowl, flower, 10½" (orig. #3410), 1976 – 1978. $35.00 – 45.00.

#5301 bowl, flower, 8½" (orig. #3410), 1976 – 1978. $25.00 – 35.00.

#5302 bowl, flower, 6" (orig. #3410), 1976 – 1978. $25.00 – 30.00.

#5323 ginger jar, 12", 1977 – 1978. $75.00 – 95.00.

#5324 candleholder, hurricane base, 1977 – 1978. $35.00 – 45.00.

strawberry planter, 8½"x9½", 6 pockets, 1973 – 1975. $45.00 – 55.00.

strawberry planter, 10"x10½", 8 pockets, 1973 – 1975. $60.00 – 75.00.

cactus planter, 8"x 5½", 3 pockets, 1975 only. $30.00 – 40.00.

cactus planter, 10¾"x7½", 4 pockets, 1975 only. $40.00 – 50.00.

Antique Gold #5303 planter, French Phone 8½"x6½", 1976 – 1978. $150.00 – 175.00. Courtesy of the Wayne Weigand collection.

Granada Gold #5303 French Phone planter, "It's for you, Dear…" $150.00 – 175.00

Antique Gold strawberry planter, 12", 10 pockets, 1973 only. $100.00 – 125.00. Courtesy of the David and Laura Solomon collection.

Granada Gold Seahorse wall plaque, 8", 1966 – 1968. $70.00 – 85.00. From the Stangl and Fulper archival collection, courtesy the Wheaton Village Museum of American Glass.

Granada Gold and Black Gold 6", round tiles, 1968 – 1974, $18.00 – 22.00 each.

Ten-inch tidbits with a variety of embossed patterns were produced with the Antique Gold finish. Also produced were 10" tidbits with carved dinnerware motifs and entirely covered in Antique Gold. These were seconds, and the Antique Gold was simply spun on to create an inexpensive seconds treatment. Such tidbits were sold at the Flemington Outlet and continue to turn up frequently.

Antique Gold tidbit, 10", with brass handle, 1959 – 1970. $15.00 – 20.00.

Brushed Gold finished Bird and Animal figurines

Not Shown:

#3244 Draft Horse, 3", 1973 only. $300.00 – 400.00.
#3245 Rabbit, 2", 1973 only. $350.00 – 450.00.
#3246 Bison, 2½", 1973 only. $350.00 – 450.00.
#3247 Giraffe, 3½", 1973 only. $500.00 – 600.00.
#3249 Elephant, 3", 1973 only. $350.00 – 450.00.
#3280 Dog, 5¼", 1973 only. $450.00 – 550.00.
#5281 Dancing Elephant Ashtray, 1973 – 1975. $175.00 – 200.00.
#3250A Standing Duck, 3½", 1965 – 1975. $45.00 – 60.00.
#3250B Preening Duck, 2¾", 1965 – 1975. $45.00 – 60.00.
#3250C Feeding Duck, 1¾", 1965 – 1975. $45.00 – 60.00.
#3250D Gazing Duck, 3¾", 1965 – 1975. $45.00 – 60.00.
#3250E Drinking Duck, 2¼", 1965 – 1975. $45.00 – 60.00.
#3250F Quacking Duck, 3¾", 1965 – 1975. $45.00 – 60.00.
#3401 Wren, 3½", 1968 – 1975. $50.00 – 75.00.
#3402 Oriole, 3¼", 1965 – 1975. $50.00 – 75.00.
#3443 Flying Duck, 9", Antique Gold only, 1959 – 1962. $350.00 – 400.00.
#3445 Medium Rooster, 9", Antique Gold only, 1959 – 1962. $250.00 – 300.00.
#3456 Medium Hen, 7", Antique Gold only, 1959 – 1962. $250.00 – 300.00.
#3491 Hen Pheasant, 6¼"x11", Antique Gold only, 1959 – 1963. $200.00 – 225.00.
#3492 Cock Pheasant, 6¼"x11", Antique Gold only, 1959 – 1963. $225.00 – 250.00.
#3584 Large Cockatoo, 11?", Antique Gold only, 1959 – 1962. $200.00 – 250.00.
#3585 Humming Bird, 3", 1968 – 1975. $60.00 – 80.00.
#3597 Wilson Warbler 3½", 1968 – 1975. $65.00 – 80.00.
#3598 Kentucky Warbler, 3", 1968 – 1975. $65.00 – 80.00.
#3715 Feeding Blue Jay, with peanut, 10¼", Antique Gold only, 1959 – 1963. $500.00 – 600.00.
#3716 Flying Blue Jay, with leaf, 10¼", Antique Gold only, 1959 – 1963. $500.00 – 600.00.

Group of Sitting Cats, 9", in Granada Gold, Antique Gold, and Black Gold. $250.00 – 350.00 each. Courtesy of the Wayne Weigand collection.

Granada Gold #5281 Elephant, 5", 1973 – 1975. $75.00 – 125.00.

Group of Black Gold, Antique Gold, and Granada Gold bird figurines. $45.00 – 80.00 each.

Silver Haze, 1964

Silver Haze was a small group of artware and novelty dinnerware shapes produced briefly during 1964. The shapes were covered with gray engobe and clear gloss glaze. Platinum luster was banded on the rims and entirely covered handles and spouts. The #5093 bud vase and after-dinner cup and saucer were entirely covered in platinum. Silver Haze was discontinued before the end of 1964. Difficult to find, Silver Haze is one of Stangl's more challenging brushed-luster finishes to collect.

Not Shown:

#1388 cup & saucer, after-dinner. $25.00 – 30.00.
#1388 coffee pot, after-dinner. $75.00 – 95.00.
#1388 creamer, after-dinner. $20.00 – 25.00.
#1388 creamer. $25.00 – 30.00.
#1388 sugar, after-dinner. $20.00 – 25.00.
#1388 sugar. $20.00 – 25.00.
#1388 teapot. $75.00 – 95.00.
#3898 cigarette box, fluted. $65.00 – 80.00.
#3898-5 ashtray, fluted 5". $12.00 – 18.00.
#5093 vase, bud, 5¾". $15.00 – 20.00.
#5126 picture frame, square, round opening. $50.00 – 60.00.
#5131 tankard, 12 oz. $20.00 – 25.00.
#5140 creamer. $25.00 – 30.00.

Group of Silver Haze items, #5131 tankard $20.00 – 25.00, with #5140 after-dinner cup, $10.00 – 15.00, coffee pot, $100.00 – 125.00, creamer, and sugar, $25.00 – 30.00 each.

#5140 cup & saucer, after-dinner. $25.00 – 30.00.
#5140 cup & saucer, tea. $25.00 – 30.00.
#5140 coffee pot, 8½". $100.00 – 125.00.
#5140 porringer, 5". $25.00 – 30.00.
#5140 porringer, 3½". $25.00 – 35.00.
#5140 sugar. $25.00 – 30.00.
#5140 tidbit, 10". $10.00 – 15.00.

Golden Guernsey Milk Jugs, 1967 – 1968

In 1967, Stangl Pottery introduced replicas of the Isle of Guernsey milk jugs in two sizes, 12 ounce and 24 ounce. They were cast of white clay and decorated with 22 karat gold pinstripes. The Guernsey jugs were sold in Stangl's national catalogs and the Flemington Outlet. Each jug was sold with a pamphlet explaining the history of the Guernsey jugs, how they were brought to the Isle of Guernsey in 980 A.D. with cattle from Normandy, and to this day represent quality and thriftiness. Seconds without the gold pinstriping were sold at the Flemington Outlet only and are now valued less than those with gold pinstripes. A limited number of Guernsey jugs were decorated with all-over gold luster as a special order and are quite rare. By the end of 1968, the Guernsey jugs were discontinued.

Not Shown:
#5191 Guernsey jug, 12 oz., 6", all-over gold. $45.00 – 55.00.
#5192 Guernsey jug, 24 oz., 7½", pinstripe. $45.00 – 55.00.
#5192 Guernsey jug, 24 oz., 7½", all-over gold. $70.00 – 85.00.

Guernsey jug #5191, 12 oz., 6", pinstripe. $25.00 – 35.00.

Golden Guernsey pamphlet. $5.00 – 7.00.

The increased popularity of Italian and Spanish faience pottery during the 1930s, and its subsequent unavailability in America as war in Europe became imminent prompted Martin Stangl to develop his Terra Rose artware finish. The following is Martin Stangl's description of the Terra Rose finish as stated in his application to the U.S. Patent Office in 1940: "My invention relates to decorated pottery ware and methods of producing the same and particularly to pottery ware which has a novel appearance generally similar to that of Italian pottery. In accordance with my invention, a colored or decorated body is provided with a semi-opaque or 'milk glaze' which produces a subdued or modified effect on the color or design of the body. In the practice of my invention, the body preferably contains a small amount of pyrophyllite and the glaze contains tin oxide. It is my belief that these two substances react to produce a precipitate, which gives the desired milky cast to the glaze of the finished product. A typical glaze may be formed of china clay, lead oxide, and tin oxide, with the tin oxide comprising from about 2 to 10% of the total weight of the glaze. When fired, the glaze contains a limited precipitate of tin oxide, which serves to render it semi-opaque or slightly clouded. The design remains clear-cut in its outline and features, but its colors are so modified that they blend harmoniously with each other and with the background color of the base. There frequently is a slight and inconspicuous mottled effect in the glaze which is more noticeable on the undecorated areas and adds to the pleasing effect produced by the process." Actual production of Terra Rose Artware began on July 29, 1940. The United States Patent Office published the registration of Stangl's Terra Rose trademarks on February 11, 1941, and finally granted the patent for the glazing process on August 17, 1943, over three years after the Terra Rose finish was introduced. The name for Stangl's Terra Rose finish was an Americanized version of an ancient name for the color Venetian Red, Terra Rosa. Both the artist's color Venetian Red and Stangl's Terra Rose glaze relied on red iron oxide for their unique coloring.

Stangl's Terra Rose Artware was introduced in three primary colors: Terra Rose Blue, Terra Rose Mauve, and Terra Rose Green. The colors were applied as mineral oxide stains with broad brushstrokes under the tin oxide Silk glaze, creating a bold effect: Terra Rose Blue was cobalt oxide, Terra Rose Green was copper oxide, and Terra Rose Mauve was manganese oxide. Earlier pieces of Terra Rose Green with a proper, heavy application of copper oxide usually have pools or streaks of lustrous black copper oxide on the surface of the glaze. Later pieces of Terra Rose Green, particularly those produced during the 1950s, exhibit a weak, washed-out green finish. Terra Rose Mauve can sometimes appear purplish but is usually a warm milky brown. A color called Terra Rose Amethyst was applied to dinnerware shapes for Russel Wright's American Way program during 1940, but Terra Rose Amethyst was a deep, dusky violet and seldom appeared on artware shapes.

During 1940 and most of 1941, the Terra Rose shapes were all cast of white clay and airbrushed with a light, uneven spritzing of red iron oxide. The red iron oxide imparted an earthy quality to the finish and provided a pink tint to the tin oxide glaze. Undecorated areas where there was no red iron oxide usually had a yellow tone caused by the tin oxide of the glaze.

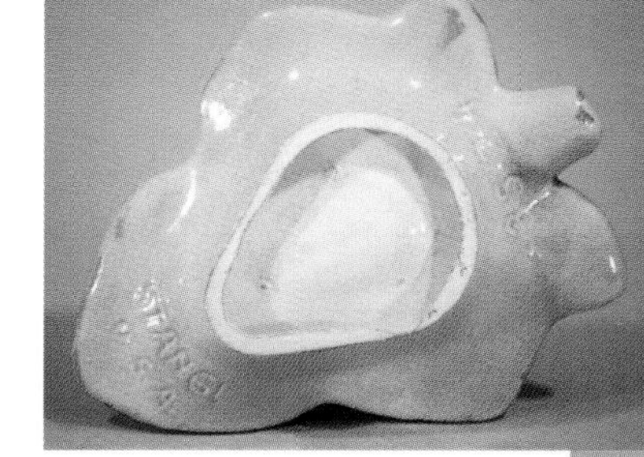

Back of a Terra Rose #3524 ivy leaf ashtray showing the airbrushed red iron oxide. The white body of the piece is evident on the ground foot, while the glazed interior is tinted yellow where there is no red iron oxide.

By late 1941, Stangl began casting Terra Rose Artware from red clay, thereby eliminating the spraying of red iron oxide. Since nearly all bird figurines decorated with Terra Rose colors were discontinued during 1941, they are usually white clay with a red iron oxide spritz under the Terra Rose color.

Many of the shapes designed specifically for the Terra Rose art finish were bold forms inspired by large tropical leaves and blossoms. Vases, bowls, and baskets emulating stylized vegetation remained popular throughout most of the 1940s. Shapes mimicking oversized shells and waves were introduced by the mid-1940s. Stangl's sculptor John Tierney designed and sculpted many of the Terra Rose shapes. There was such an urgent need for artware shapes during the late 1930s and early 1940s that freelance sculptor August Jacob was hired to sculpt the items that John Tierney was unable to fit into his busy schedule. Assistant sculptor Herman Eichorn aided both Tierney and Jacob in the sculpting of many of the artware shapes. August Jacob's most notable Terra Rose shape was the #3611 Horse Head vase.

Stangl's Terra Rose Artware became immediately popular. So popular that, by 1943, the Terra Rose finish was being applied to many of Stangl's better-selling older shapes in addition to the newly designed leaf and shell Terra Rose shapes. Several shapes became staples of the Terra Rose line and were in continual production during the 1940s and 1950s. Terra Rose Green remained the bestselling Terra Rose color. Terra Rose Mauve and Terra Rose Blue were gradually phased out during the late 1940s and were produced very sporadically during the 1950s. Terra Rose Green was in continual production throughout the 1950s and into the early 1960s. During the late 1950s, Antique Gold supplanted Terra Rose Green as the artware finish of choice, but Terra Rose Green continued as a popular serve-ware finish and seconds treatment into the early 1960s. At this time, Terra Rose Blue is the most coveted of the Terra

Rose colors, but Terra Rose Green still enjoys mass appeal and usually sells as well as Terra Rose Blue. Terra Rose Mauve is the least desired of the Terra Rose colors and nearly always sells at the low end of the price range.

Two-tone Terra Rose Blue #3675 Morning Glory vase. Note the cobalt stain is applied to the interior as well as the leaves at the base.

In 1942, Martin Stangl introduced a Terra Rose line called Two-tone Terra Rose. Most Terra Rose shapes were covered with color coarsely applied with very wide brushes. The Two-tone items were carefully decorated in certain areas with a single color to accentuate the design, such as specific leaves or waves. Once glazed and fired, the undecorated portions took on the milky-pink color of the tin oxide glaze reacting with the red iron oxide of the clay body. Inexperienced collectors have mistakenly referred to the undecorated portions of Two-tone Terra Rose as "mauve," but the undecorated portions are simply that, undecorated. Whether blue, green, or mauve, only one mineral oxide stain at a time was ever applied to Terra Rose artware shapes. The only time two Terra Rose colors were used on the same piece was the banding of Terra Rose Green and Terra Rose Amethyst on the Ivy Leaf pattern of American Way dinnerware. Occasionally yellow underglaze color was used as an accent color, such as the yellow flower on the Saks Fifth Avenue #3467 scallop bowl or the yellow center of the #3420 Daisy plaque. Even though the Two-tone items used less mineral oxide stains than solid-color items, they were more costly because of the added time it took to carefully paint the decorated portion. The mineral oxide color could be slap-dashed onto the solid Terra Rose shapes very quickly. By the end of 1944, the Two-tone Terra Rose finish was discontinued. Many of the Two-tone shapes continued to be produced but were painted solid. In 1951, several old Two-tone shapes were produced in solid Terra Rose colors for the Flemington Outlet. At this time, Two-tone Terra Rose items usually sell for 25% to 50% more than a comparable solid Terra Rose piece.

Solid Terra Rose Blue #3554 petals with shells vase, produced for the Flemington Outlet during 1951.

Translated from Latin, the name Terra Rose literally means "pink earth." For that reason, when Martin Stangl introduced the hand-carved, hand-painted Early Pennsylvania dinnerware and artware items in 1942, he classified that finish as Terra Rose also, due to the "pink earth" of the red body showing through the thinly brushed engobe. Terra Rose was the name of the "earthy" finish on these items, not the name of the pattern or decoration. During the late 1940s, Martin Stangl stopped using the Terra Rose designation on hand-carved, hand-painted dinnerware and artware. From that time forward, the name Terra Rose was used exclusively on items decorated with cobalt, copper, and manganese metallic stains glazed with tin oxide Silk glaze.

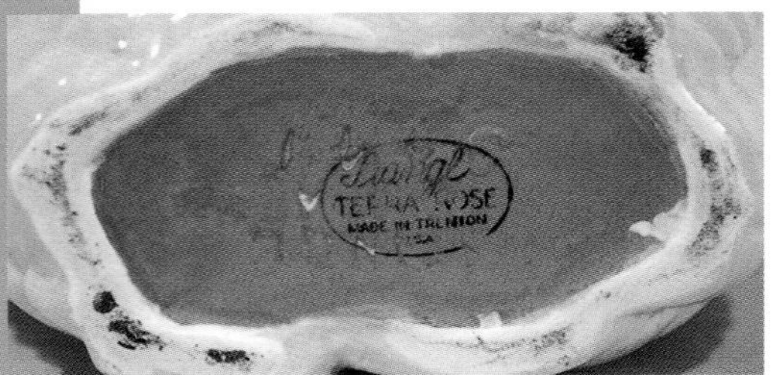

Base of a #3441 Terra Rose Yellow vase showing the white engobe under the yellow underglaze color.

Martin Stangl introduced the Terra Rose Yellow finish in 1952. This finish was yellow underglaze color brushed under the milky tin oxide glaze. So that the yellow would stay vibrant, the red-bodied shapes were first sprayed with white engobe before the yellow was applied. No engobe was used on the Terra Rose Blue, Green, or Mauve items as the metallic oxides used to color those finishes actually would "float" to the surface of the glaze during firing and essentially color the glaze. Without the white engobe, the yellow underglaze color would simply bond to the red clay body and be unnoticed under the tin oxide glaze. Very few Terra Rose Yellow art pieces were produced. The finish was primarily used on serve-ware items. Terra Rose Yellow artware pieces usually sell a bit higher than the high end of the price range, while Terra Rose Yellow serve-ware pieces are no more valuable than blue, green, or mauve serve-ware.

See also the chapter on Cigarette Boxes and Smoking items for Terra Rose ashtrays and the chapter on Bird and Animal Figurines for Terra Rose bird figurines and animal-shape match holders.

Two-tone Terra Rose items usually sell for 25% to 50% more than the same shape decorated entirely in solid Terra Rose.

Terra Rose Mauve dealer sign, Rose shape, 1940 – 1945. $300.00 – 350.00. Courtesy of Ed Alvater.

Terra Rose Blue dealer sign, oval, late 1940s – 1950s. $375.00 – 400.00. Courtesy of Ed Alvater.

Terra Rose Green #1076 Pig Bank, 4", 1940 – 1961. $150.00 – 200.00.

Not Shown:

#1388 candy jar, 5"x5", early 1940s. $80.00 – 100.00.

#1388 candleholder, 3½", early 1940s – 1950s. $30.00 – 40.00 pair.

#1388 cigarette box, 4½"x3½", early 1940s. $100.00 – 125.00.

#1388 ashtray, 4", early 1940s. $25.00 – 35.00.

#1388 oval console bowl, 12"x8", early 1940s – 1950s. $35.00 – 45.00.

#1574 vase, twirl, 9", late 1940s – 1950s. $55.00 – 65.00.

#1800 Cabbage Leaf oblong triple relish, 14", marked Della-Ware, made for Fisher, Bruce & Co., 1941 – 1952. $35.00 – 45.00.

#1800 Cabbage Leaf round triple relish, 9½", marked Della-Ware, made for Fisher, Bruce & Co., 1941 – 1952. $35.00 – 45.00.

#1800 Cabbage Leaf double relish, 9½", marked Della-Ware, made for Fisher, Bruce & Co., 1941 – 1952. $20.00 – 25.00.

#1800 Cabbage Leaf single relish, 13", marked Della-Ware, made for Fisher, Bruce & Co., 1941 – 1952. $25.00 – 35.00.

#1800 Cabbage Leaf cake stand, 10", marked Della-Ware, made for Fisher, Bruce & Co., 1941 – 1952s. $30.00 – 40.00.

#1869 bowl, Cosmos, 12" diameter, 1940s. $50.00 – 60.00.

#1872 bowl, Zinnia, 10" diameter, 1940s. $35.00 – 45.00.

#1874 bowl, Rose, 10" diameter, 1940s. $35.00 – 45.00.

#1878 Tulip, large, 8", late 1940s – 1950s. $70.00 – 85.00.

#1878 Tulip, medium, 5½", late 1940s – 1950s. $40.00 – 50.00.

#1905 Twist bud vase, 7½", 1940s. $30.00 – 40.00.

#1906 urn vase, 7¾", 1940s. $55.00 – 65.00.

#1907 ball vase, medium, 7½", 1940s. $35.00 – 45.00.

#1907 ball vase, small, 5", 1940s. $25.00 – 35.00.

#1908 ball vase, large, 9", 1940s. $60.00 – 75.00.

#1940 chop plate, 14", made for Frederik Lunning, Inc., 1941 – 1953. $100.00 – 125.00.

#1940 plate, 9", made for Frederik Lunning, Inc., 1941 – 1953. $22.00 – 28.00.

#1940 bowl, 9", made for Frederik Lunning, Inc., 1941 – 1953. $70.00 – 85.00.

#1950 – 10 floral ring, 10" diameter, 1950s – 1960s. $30.00 – 40.00.

#1950-8 floral ring, 8" diameter, 1950s – 1960s. $25.00 – 30.00.

#1950-6 floral ring, 6" diameter, 1950s – 1960s. $15.00 – 20.00.

#1950-C candle cups for floral rings, 1950s – 1960s. $8.00 – 10.00 each.

#1953 ashtray, oblong, 4¼", 1950s. $20.00 – 25.00.

#1954 two compartment ashtray, 4"x6", 1950s. $20.00 – 25.00.

#1956 ashtray, round, 4¼", 1950s. $20.00 – 25.00.

Della-Ware Terra Rose Green #1800 single relish, $25.00 – 35.00, and double relish, $20.00 – 25.00, made for Fisher, Bruce & Co.

Two-tone Terra Rose Blue #1878 Tulip, small, 4", late 1940s – 1950s. $35.00 – 45.00.

Terra Rose Green #1919 bowl 7", late 1940s – 1950s. $20.00 – 25.00.

Terra Rose Green #1999 vase, 7", late 1940s – 1950s. $45.00 – 55.00.

#2016 vase, 3¾", late 1940s. $60.00 – 75.00.
#2019 vase, 3", late 1940s. $60.00 – 75.00.
#2022 shell ashtray, 3", 1941 – 1942. $20.00 – 25.00.
#2041 urn, footed Grecian 8", late 1940s – early 1950s. $55.00 – 70.00.
#2048 urn, 3", late 1940s. $60.00 – 75.00.
#2049 vase, tall tulip, 12", late 1940s – 1950s. $80.00 – 90.00.
#2050 Round Scallop bowl, 8" diameter, late 1940s – 1950s. $35.00 – 45.00.
#2052 Round Scallop vase, 9½", late 1940s – 1950s. $50.00 – 60.00.
#2051 Round Scallop candleholder, 2½", late 1940s – 1950s. $25.00 – 35.00 pair.
#2056 vase, horn, 7", late 1940s – 1950s. $25.00 – 30.00.
#2057 Shell oblong flower jar, 10"x4", late 1940s. $55.00 – 65.00.
#2058 Shell candleholder, 4"x2", late 1940s. $55.00 – 65.00 pair.
#2059 Scallop Oval candleholder, 4"x2", late 1940s – 1950s. $25.00 – 30.00 pair.
#2060 Cradle bowl, 7"x4", late 1940s. $55.00 – 65.00.
#2061 Cradle candleholder, 3"x2", late 1940s. $55.00 – 65.00 pair.
#2064 Scallop Oval bowl, 5"x9½", late 1940s – 1950s. $20.00 – 25.00.
#2067 Scallop Vase, 7", late 1940s – 1950s. $30.00 – 40.00.
#2071 vase, tall footed, 10½", late 1940s. $100.00 – 125.00.
#2074 ashtray, 6", late 1940s – 1950s. $25.00 – 35.00.
#2089 ashtray, Scotty dog, 4½"x5", late 1940s – 1950s. $70.00 – 85.00.
#2091 Cosmos vase, 10½", late 1940s – 1950s. $60.00 – 75.00.
#2091 Cosmos jardiniere, large, 7", late 1940s – 1950s. $35.00 – 45.00.
#2091 Cosmos bud vase, 7½", late 1940s – 1950s. $55.00 – 65.00.
#2092 Rhythmic bowl, 10¼"x5½", late 1940s – 1950s. $45.00 – 55.00.
#2092 Rhythmic low bowl, 10"x4", 1942 – 1950s. $30.00 – 40.00.
#2092 Rhythmic candleholder, 3½", 1942 – 1950s. $35.00 – 45.00 pair.
#2092 Rhythmic miniature vase, 3½", 1942 – 1950s. $25.00 – 30.00.
#2092 Rhythmic tall vase, 11", 1940s – 1950s. $65.00 – 80.00.
#2092 Rhythmic tall vase, 7", late 1940s – 1950s. $55.00 – 65.00.
#2092 Rhythmic large jar, 9", late 1940s – 1950s. $65.00 – 80.00.
#2092 Rhythmic small jar, 6" late 1940s – 1950s. $45.00 – 55.00.
#2092 Rhythmic wall pocket, 6"x9", 1936 – 1937. $120.00 – 145.00.
#3034 Spiral vase, 7", late 1940s – 1950s. $45.00 – 55.00.
#3036 Spiral bowl, 4"x9", late 1940s – 1950s. $30.00 – 40.00.
#3041 Scroll ashtray, 4"x5", late 1940s – 1950s. $20.00 – 25.00.
#3042 Scroll oval bowl, 10"x7", late 1940s – 1950s. $45.00 – 55.00.
#3046 Scroll candleholder, 3¾", late 1940s – 1950s. $35.00 – 45.00 pair.
#3047 Scroll 4-sided bowl, 10", late 1940s – 1950s. $45.00 – 55.00.
#3056 basket with handle, 5", 1942 – 1945. $45.00 – 55.00.
#3101 Lily vase, 7", 1940s. $55.00 – 65.00.
#3103 vase, long neck and handles, 7¼", 1945 – 1952. $40.00 – 50.00.
#3111 vase with handles, 7", 1946 – 1952. $55.00 – 65.00.

Terra Rose Mauve #2001 raised leaf design, 5½". $45.00 – 55.00.

Two-tone Terra Rose Blue #2091 Cosmos wall pocket, 7½", 1942 – 1950s. $60.00 – 75.00. Courtesy of the Robert and Tammie Cruser collection.

Terra Rose Blue #3103 vase with handles, 7½", 1943 – 1950s. $40.00 – 50.00.

#3112 vase, 5½", 1946 – 1952. $50.00 – 60.00.
#3113 vase, 5½", 1946 – 1952. $50.00 – 60.00.
#3116 vase, scroll handles, 5½", 1946 – 1952. $55.00 – 65.00.
#3117 vase, 5½", 1946 – 1952. $50.00 – 60.00.

Terra Rose Blue, Green, and Mauve #2092 Rhythmic 3½" miniature vase (Green), $25.00 – 30.00; 10"x4" bowl (Blue), $30.00 – 40.00; and 6" small jar (mauve), $45.00 – 55.00. Courtesy of the Marcena North collection.

Terra Rose Green #3153 vase with handles, 13½". 1942 – 1946. $100.00 – 125.00.

Terra Rose Green and Terra Rose Mauve #3212 pitcher vases, 6" tall, late 1943 – 1952. $35.00 – 45.00 each.

Two-tone Terra Rose Mauve #3218 flare vase, 7", 1946 – 1952. $55.00 – 65.00.

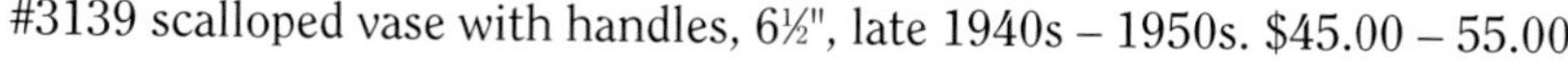

#3139 scalloped vase with handles, 6½", late 1940s – 1950s. $45.00 – 55.00.
#3140 scalloped vase with handles, 7", late 1940s – 1950s. $45.00 – 55.00.
#3212 flat pitcher, 4"x7½", 1943 – 1958. $22.00 – 28.00.
#3214 streamlined pitcher, 8", 1943 – 1955. $25.00 – 35.00.
#3215 oval vase, 7", 1940s. $55.00 – 65.00.
#3216 horn vase, 8", 1940s. $55.00 – 65.00.
#3217 scallop vase, 7", 1940s. $35.00 – 45.00.
#3219 oval vase, 7", 1940s. $40.00 – 50.00.
#3220 oval leaves vase, 7½", 1940s. $50.00 – 60.00.
#3221 footed vase, 5½", 1940s. $40.00 – 50.00.
#3222 points vase, 5½", 1940s. $35.00 – 45.00.
#3223 drape vase, 5½", 1940s. $25.00 – 35.00.
#3224 leaves vase, 5½", 1940s. $25.00 – 35.00.
#3226 basket, 9"x4½", 1941 – 1943. $35.00 – 45.00.
#3227 bowl, 9"x4", 1940s. $30.00 – 40.00.
#3228 leaf bowl, 7½"x4", 1940s. $35.00 – 45.00.
#3229L bowl, 12", 1940s. $35.00 – 45.00.
#3229M bowl 9", 1940s. $25.00 – 35.00.
#3229S bowl 6", 1940s. $20.00 – 25.00.
#3229 candleholder, 3¼", 1940s. $40.00 – 50.00 pair.
#3236 wall pocket, leaves, 7", 1941 – 1943. $70.00 – 85.00.
#3237 wall pocket, scallop, 8"x5½", 1940s. $60.00 – 75.00.
#3238 wall pocket, snail, 9"x7", 1940s. $85.00 – 95.00.
#3239 leaf candy dish/ashtray, 8"x7¾", 1938 – 1942. $25.00 – 35.00.
#3240 shell candy dish/ashtray, 8"x7½", 1942 – 1944. $25.00 – 35.00.
#3241 rectangle ashtray, 7"x6", 1942 – 1944. $25.00 – 30.00.
#3242 three arm candy dish/ashtray, 9" diameter, 1942 – 1944. $30.00 – 40.00 (see page 282 for photo).

Terra Rose Blue #3225 basket, 7"x7", 1940s. $35.00 – 45.00.

Terra Rose Blue #3251 basket, twist handle, 8½"x11", 1941 – 1948. $35.00 – 50.00.

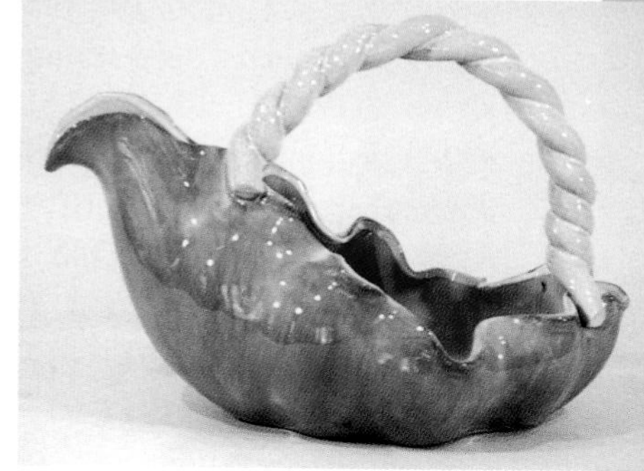

Terra Rose Mauve #3139 scalloped vase, $45.00 – 55.00. Terra Rose Blue #3220 oval leaves vase, $50.00 – 60.00, and Terra Rose Green #3222 points vase, $35.00 – 45.00. Courtesy of the Marcena North collection.

Terra Rose Green #3252 basket, Hat, 12"x7", 1941 – 1944. $80.00 – 90.00. Courtesy of the Marcena North collection.

Terra Rose Blue #3253 basket, leaf, and handle, 11"x6½", 1941 – 1944. $60.00 – 75.00. Courtesy of the Marcena North collection.

Terra Rose Blue #3257 bowl, horn, 2¾"x5", 1940s. $20.00 – 25.00.

Terra Rose Green, Blue, and Mauve #3256 bowl, 3-sided scallop, 2¼"x5", 1940s. $18.00 – 22.00 each.

Terra Rose Green #3259 Lady slipper, 3½"x5", 1940s. $55.00 – 65.00. Courtesy of the Frank and Elizabeth Kramar collection.

#3254 bowl, deep shell, 2"x5", 1940s. $20.00 – 25.00.
#3255 bowl, horn shell, 2¼"x6½", 1940s. $25.00 – 35.00.
#3258 Dutch slipper, 2¼"x5", 1939 – 1942. $45.00 – 55.00.
#3260 vase, round, 2 curl handles, 7", 1940s. $60.00 – 75.00.
#3261 vase, ovoid, 2 small handles, 1940s. $60.00 – 75.00.
#3262 vase, petals and base, 7", 1940s. $40.00 – 50.00.
#3263 vase, flared cup, 7", 1940s. $35.00 – 45.00.
#3264 vase, modern, 9", 1941 – 1943. $70.00 – 85.00.
#3265 vase, round ribbed, rope base, 9", 1941 – 1943. $60.00 – 75.00.
#3266 vase, ovoid, small handles, 5½", 1940s. $30.00 – 40.00.
#3267 vase, cup, ovoid, 5½", 1940s. $25.00 – 35.00.
#3268 vase, scroll top, 10", 1940s. $85.00 – 95.00.
#3269 vase, petals, deep scallop top, 10", 1941 – 1943. $60.00 – 75.00.
#3283 scalloped bowl, 11", 1940s. $30.00 – 40.00.
#3283 scalloped bowl, 9", 1940s. $20.00 – 25.00.
#3283 scalloped bowl, 7", 1940s. $15.00 – 20.00.
#3284 pie crust bowl, 7", 1940s. $25.00 – 35.00.
#3410 rose bowl, 10", 1942 – 1943. $30.00 – 40.00.
#3410 rose bowl, 9", 1942 – 1945. $25.00 – 30.00.
#3410 rose bowl, 7", 1942 – 1945. $25.00 – 30.00.
#3410 rose candleholder, 3", 1940 – 1945. $25.00 – 30.00 pair.
#3414A basket, scalloped leaves, no handle, 12½", 1940 – 1945. $30.00 – 40.00.
#3416 vase, fleur-de-lis 9", 1940 – 1942. $70.00 – 85.00.

Terra Rose Blue #3411 rose vase, 6½", 1940 – 1942. $60.00 – 75.00.

Terra Rose Green #3412 stove candle warmer, 4½"x4½"x3¼", 1940 – 1960. $8.00 – 12.00.

Terra Rose Mauve #3414 basket, scalloped leaves with handle, 12½", 1940 – 1947. $50.00 – 60.00.

Terra Rose Mauve #3413 Cosmos vase, oval, 7", 1940 – 1950s. $30.00 – 40.00.

Terra Rose Mauve #3415 vase, arum berries, 9", 1940 – 1942. $60.00 – 75.00.

Terra Rose Mauve #3417 vase, fleur-de-lis, 6½", 1940 – 1948. $45.00 – 55.00.

Terra Rose #3420 Daisy plaque, 10"x6¾", 1940 only, and sporadically throughout the 1940s – 1950s as special-order items (back, inset). $190.00 – 225.00.

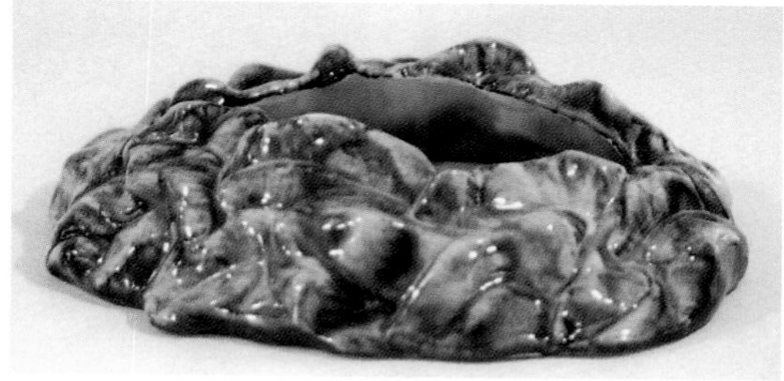

Terra Rose Mauve #3426 bowl, low, leaves, 10"x7½", 1940 – 1941. $60.00 – 75.00.

Terra Rose Mauve #3427 basket, acanthus leaf, 14"x7", 1940 – 1943. $70.00 – 85.00.

#3421 tropical leaves vase, 10", 1940 – 1942. $70.00 – 85.00.
#3423 oblong leaf bowl, 11"x6", 1940 – 1941. $40.00 – 50.00.
#3424 round leaf bowl, 7", 1940 – 1941. $30.00 – 40.00.
#3425 square leaf bowl, 7½"x7½", 1940 – 1941. $30.00 – 40.00.
#3429 bowl, Calla lily, 16"x10", 1940 – 1942. $50.00 – 60.00.
#3434 coaster ashtray, 5", 1942 – 1960. $18.00 – 22.00.
#3435 vase, feather, 8½", 1940 only. $55.00 – 65.00.
#3437 vase, scroll bud leaf, 9½", 1940 – 1941. $100.00 – 125.00.
#3438 basket, scalloped shell, 12"x5", 1940 – 1943. $30.00 – 40.00.
#3440 vase, standing leaf, 12", 1940 – 1945. $50.00 – 60.00.
#3441 vase, standing leaf, 8", 1940 – 1950. $35.00 – 45.00.
#3442 vase, standing leaf, 6", 1940 – 1960. $20.00 – 25.00.

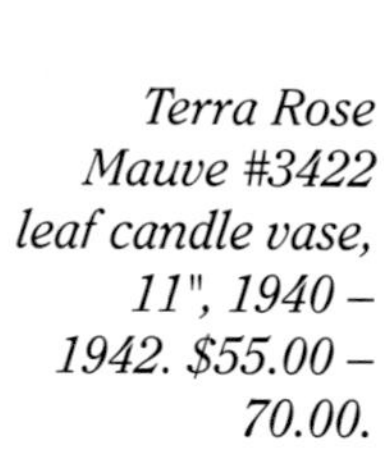

Terra Rose Mauve #3422 leaf candle vase, 11", 1940 – 1942. $55.00 – 70.00.

Terra Rose Mauve and Green #3428 candleholder, Calla lily, 3½", 1940 – 1950s. $45.00 – 60.00 pair. Courtesy of the Marcena North collection.

Terra Rose Green #3439 basket, scroll leaves, 12"x5", 1940 – 1944. $65.00 – 80.00.

Terra Rose Mauve #3436 vase, feather, 9", 1940 only. $60.00 – 75.00.

Terra Rose #3440 vase, 12" Mauve, $50.00 – 60.00; vase #3441, 8" Blue, $35.00 – 45.00; and vase #3442, 6" Green, $20.00 – 25.00. Courtesy of the Marcena North collection.

Terra Rose vase #3442, 6", Mauve, $20.00 – 25.00, and #3441, 8" Yellow, $70.00 – 85.00.

Saks Fifth Avenue Serve Ware

The following items were handmade exclusively for Saks Fifth Avenue department store during 1940 and 1941. Another group of Saks Fifth Avenue handmade items was introduced in 1942, which replaced many of these shapes. The Saks items were usually marked with "Made for Saks 5th Ave" in blue underglaze crayon.

Saks Fifth Avenue back

Saks Fifth Avenue handmade #3462 double bowl, $40.00 – 50.00; #3466 8" plate, $40.00 – 50.00; and #3460 square bowl, $25.00 – 30.00.

Terra Rose Mauve #3467 bowl, scallop with flower, 7", handmade for Saks Fifth Avenue, 1940 – 1941. $25.00 – 35.00.

Not Shown:

#3460 bowl, 4" square, handmade for Saks Fifth Avenue, 1940 – 1941. $25.00 – 30.00.
#3461 bowl, 8" heart, handmade for Saks Fifth Avenue, 1940 – 1941. $25.00 – 35.00.
#3461 bowl, 6" heart, handmade for Saks Fifth Avenue, 1940 – 1941. $25.00 – 30.00.
#3462 bowl, double 10"x8", ribbon handles, handmade for Saks Fifth Avenue, 1940 – 1941. $40.00 – 50.00.
#3464 tray, 2-part 8½", handmade for Saks Fifth Avenue, 1940 – 1941. $30.00 – 40.00.
#3465 tray, 2-part 10½", handmade for Saks Fifth Avenue, 1940 – 1941. $35.00 – 45.00.
#3466 plate, 8", handmade for Saks Fifth Avenue, 1940 – 1941. $40.00 – 50.00.
#3472 relish, 3-part, 16½"x9¾", handmade for Saks Fifth Avenue, 1940 – 1941. $50.00 – 60.00.
#3473 bowl, double, 10"x9", with ribbon handles, handmade for Saks Fifth Avenue, 1940 – 1941. $40.00 – 50.00.
#3476 tray, high handle, 2-part, 10½"x6½", handmade for Saks Fifth Avenue, 1940 – 1941. $50.00 – 60.00.
#3477 tray, high handle, 2-part, 15½"x7½", handmade for Saks Fifth Avenue, 1940 – 1941. $60.00 – 75.00.
#3478 tray, side handle, 2-part, 11"x7", handmade for Saks Fifth Avenue, 1940 – 1941. $50.00 – 60.00.
#3479 tray, side handle, 2-part, 13"x8", handmade for Saks Fifth Avenue, 1940 – 1941. $55.00 – 65.00.
#3480 platter, 15"x9", handmade for Saks Fifth Avenue, 1940 – 1941. $60.00 – 75.00.
#3481 dish, 15"x6" & centerpiece, handmade for Saks Fifth Avenue, 1940 – 1941. $85.00 – 95.00.
#3482 cocktail dish, handmade for Saks Fifth Avenue, 1940 – 1941. $40.00 – 50.00.
#3483 shell dish, handmade for Saks Fifth Avenue, 1940 – 1941. $25.00 – 30.00.
#3484 vegetable dish, 15"x7½", handmade for Saks Fifth Avenue, 1940 – 1941. $40.00 – 50.00.
#3485 bread basket, 11½"x7½", handmade for Saks Fifth Avenue, 1940 – 1941. $50.00 – 60.00.
#3486 double shell, handmade for Saks Fifth Avenue, 1940 – 1941. $40.00 – 50.00.
#3487 shell, 10"x10", handmade for Saks Fifth Avenue, 1940 – 1941. $40.00 – 50.00.

Two Saks Fifth Avenue decorated pie crust 11" trays with Horse motif, Terra Rose Mauve, and Terra Rose Blue.

Terra Rose Green #3497 candleholder, fluted leaves, 4", 1941 – 1943. $45.00 – 55.00 pair.

Terra Rose Green #3499 candleholder, curl petals & leaves, 4", 1941 – 1943. $50.00 – 60.00 pair.

#3488 decorated tray, pie crust, 11", handmade for Saks Fifth Avenue, 1940 – 1941. $290.00 – 325.00.

#3495 basket, scalloped leaves with handle (same as #3414), 8", 1941 – 1943. $40.00 – 50.00.

#3495A basket, scalloped leaves, no handle (same as #3414A), 8", 1941 – 1943. $25.00 – 35.00.

#3496 bowl, fluted leaf, 12"x8", 1941 – 1943. $55.00 – 65.00.

#3498 bowl, curl petals & leaves, 9"x6", 1941 – 1943. $45.00 – 55.00.

#3501 Bonnet candleholders, 1941 only. $130.00 – 150.00 pair.

#3503 vase, flower petals with leaf, 6¾", 1941 – 1947. $40.00 – 50.00.

#3510 round water sprinkler, 7¼", 1941 – 1952. $70.00 – 85.00.

#3511 tall water sprinkler, cylinder, 10", 1941 – 1942. $150.00 – 175.00.

#3512 bowl, medium clam shell, 10"x5", 1941 – 1942. $60.00 – 75.00.

#3513 bowl, large clam shell, 14"x8", 1941 only. $100.00 – 125.00.

#3517 Chinese shoe, 2"x5", 1941 – 1945. $35.00 – 45.00.

Terra Rose Mauve #3500 Bonnet basket, no handle, 8"x9", 1941 only. $150.00 – 175.00. Courtesy of the Hill-Fulper-Stangl Museum.

Two Terra Rose Blue #3503 flower petals with leaf vases showing red-bodied ware on left, produced after 1942, and white-bodied on right, made from 1941 – 1942, $40.00 – 50.00 each.

Terra Rose Mauve #3514 vase, tropical leaves, 6½", 1941 – 1943. $40.00 – 50.00.

Terra Rose Green #3502 Daisy vase, large, 11", 1941 only. $100.00 – 125.00.

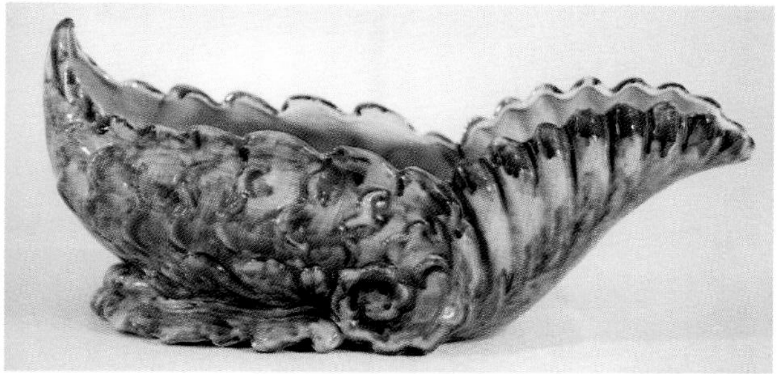

Terra Rose Mauve #3516 bowl, ruffled leaves, 13"x6", 1941 only. $85.00 – 95.00.

Terra Rose Blue #3515 vase, oval pointed leaves, 7½", 1941 – 1943. $40.00 – 50.00.

Terra Rose Green #3542 leaf bowl, 12"x9", 1941 – 1942. $55.00 – 65.00.

Terra Rose Mauve large 16" Apple tray #3543, $55.00 – 70.00; Green small 12" Apple tray #3546, $45.00 – 55.00; and Green Apple triple relish #3587, $40.00 – 50.00.

#3521 cigarette box, ashtray cover, square leaf, 5½"x4", 1941 – 1943. $85.00 – 95.00.

#3522 ashtray, shell, 5"x4½", 1941 – 1943. $20.00 – 25.00.

#3523 ashtray, leaf, 6¼" x4" , 1941 – 1943. $20.00 – 25.00.

#3524 ashtray, ivy leaf, 5¼"x4¼", 1941 – 1943. $15.00 – 20.00.

#3525 ashtray, oak leaf, 5½"x5", 1941 – 1943. $20.00 – 25.00.

#3526 ashtray, cosmos, 5½"x5", 1941 – 1943. $20.00 – 25.00.

#3527 ashtray, leaf, 4¼"x3", 1941 – 1943. $15.00 – 20.00.

#3528 ashtray, square leaf, 3¼"x3", 1941 – 1943. $15.00 – 20.00.

#3529 ashtray, Ivy leaf, 4"x3½", 1941 – 1943. $15.00 – 20.00.

#3530 ashtray, Oak leaf, 4"x2¾", 1941 – 1943. $15.00 – 20.00.

#3531 ashtray, leaf, 3½" square, 1941 – 1943. $15.00 – 20.00.

#3532 ashtray, square leaf, 5¾"x4½", 1941 – 1943. $15.00 – 20.00.

#3533 match holder, Rabbit, 4¼"x3", 1941 only. $550.00 – 600.00.

#3534 match holder, Dog, 4¼"x4", 1941 only. $450.00 – 550.00.

#3535 bowl, leaf, 16"x13", 1941 – 1943. $55.00 – 65.00.

#3536 bowl, leaf, 18"x13", 1941 – 1942. $70.00 – 85.00.

#3537 bowl, leaf, 18"x11", 1941 – 1942. $65.00 – 80.00.

#3538 bowl, oak leaf, 17"x13", 1941 – 1943. $60.00 – 75.00.

#3539 bowl, leaf, 12"x9", 1941 – 1942. $25.00 – 35.00.

#3540 bowl, leaf, 13"x8", 1941 – 1942. $40.00 – 50.00.

#3541 bowl, leaf ,12¾"x7½", 1941 – 1942. $45.00 – 55.00.

#3543 tray, large apple, 16½"x16", 1941 – 1942. $55.00 – 70.00.

#3544 tray, large pear, 18"x13", 1941 – 1942. $60.00 – 75.00.

#3545 tray, large fish, 18"x13", 1941 – 1942. $110.00 – 135.00.

#3546 tray, small apple, 12½"x12", 1941 – 1942. $45.00 – 55.00.

#3547 tray, small pear, 14"x10½", 1941 – 1942. $45.00 – 55.00.

#3548 tray, small fish, 14"x11¼", 1941 – 1942. $95.00 – 110.00.

#3549 match holder, Horse, 4¼" x 3½", 1941 only. $450.00 – 550.00.

#3550 bowl, apple double, 12", 1941 – 1942. $25.00 – 35.00.

#3551 bowl, pear double, 11", 1941 – 1942. $25.00 – 35.00.

#3552 bowl, apple single, 6½", 1941 – 1942. $18.00 – 22.00.

#3553 bowl, pear single, 8", 1941 – 1942. $18.00 – 22.00.

#3555 basket, 13"x8½", 1941 only, and again during 1951 for Flemington Outlet. $110.00 – 135.00.

#3556 vase, scalloped leaves, 8½", 1941 – 1942. $60.00 – 75.00.

No. 3555
13" x 8½"

#3555 basket as shown in original 1941 Stangl Terra Rose Artware catalog, $100.00 – 135.00.

Terra Rose Mauve #3520 cigarette box, ashtray cover, flower, 4½"x4", 1941 – 1943. $85.00 – 95.00. Courtesy of the Luke and Nancy Ruepp collection.

Terra Rose Mauve #3554 vase, petals with shells, 12"x8", 1941 – 1942 and again during 1951 for Flemington Outlet. $80.00 – 90.00.

Terra Rose Blue #3557 basket, 13½"x10", deep flutes, 1941 – 1943. $70.00 – 85.00.

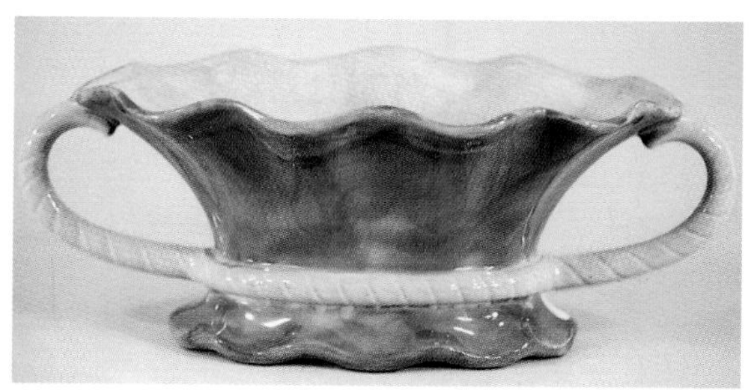

Terra Rose Blue #3558 bowl, rope handles, 11"x4½", 1941 – 1943. $65.00 – 85.00.

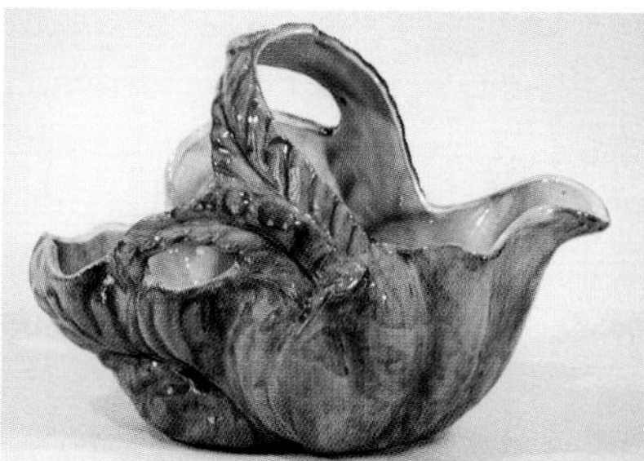

Terra Rose Blue #3561 basket, leaf handles, 11", 1941 – 1942. $85.00 – 95.00.

Terra Rose Green #3569 Dolphin bowl, 11"x7½", 1941 – 1942. $275.00 – 350.00. Courtesy of the Jim and Barbara Nelson collection.

Terra Rose Blue and Terra Rose Green #3563 Lily vases, 7", 1941 – 1952. $22.00 – 28.00 each.

#3559 bowl, rope handles, 14"x5½", 1941 – 1943. $85.00 – 95.00.
#3560 basket, round rope handle, 12", 1941 – 1943. $85.00 – 95.00.
#3562 bowl, oblong leaf, 11½"x4½", 1941 – 1943. $35.00 – 45.00.
#3564 plate, 8" apple, 1941 – 1943. $22.00 – 28.00.
#3565 bowl, 9" apple, 1941 only. $60.00 – 75.00.
#3566 vase, oval pointed leaves, 9½"x9" (same as vase #3515), 1941 – 1942. $55.00 – 70.00.
#3567 vase, ruffled leaves, 11", 1941 – 1942. $65.00 – 80.00.
#3568 drape vase, 6¾"x7½", 1941 – 1942. $40.00 – 50.00.

Della-Ware Serve Ware, made for Fisher, Bruce & Co.

Not Shown:

#3571 relish, scroll leaf, 3-part, 12"x12", marked Della-Ware, made for Fisher, Bruce & Co., 1941 – 1942. $60.00 – 75.00.
#3573 relish, shell, 3-part, 11¼", marked Della-Ware, made for Fisher, Bruce & Co., 1941 – 1942. $50.00 – 60.00.
#3574 tray, 2 handles, 13½"x8", marked Della-Ware, made for Fisher, Bruce & Co., 1941 – 1942. $60.00 – 75.00.
#3575 tray, round, 12" with applied pear, marked Della-Ware, made for Fisher, Bruce & Co., 1941 – 1942. $50.00 – 60.00.
#3576 bowl, scalloped, 14"x2½", marked Della-Ware, made for Fisher, Bruce & Co., 1941 – 1942. $60.00 – 75.00.
#3577 bowl, scalloped, 12"x2½", marked Della-Ware, made for Fisher, Bruce & Co., 1941 – 1942. $55.00 – 65.00.
#3578 relish, with apple, 11½"x6½", marked Della-Ware, made for Fisher, Bruce & Co., 1941 – 1942. $45.00 – 55.00.
#3587 relish, apple triple, 1941 – 1942. $40.00 – 50.00.

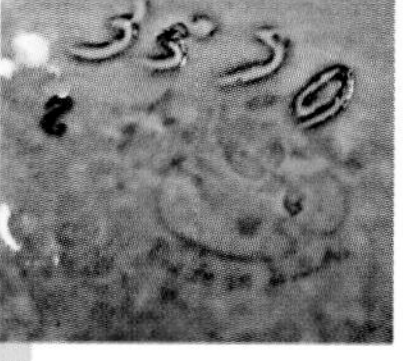

Terra Rose Mauve #3570 scroll leaf relish, 4-part, 12¾"x 9¼", marked Della-Ware, made for Fisher, Bruce & Co., 1941 – 1942. Inset shows carved shape number and underglaze ink stamp on back. $55.00 – 70.00.

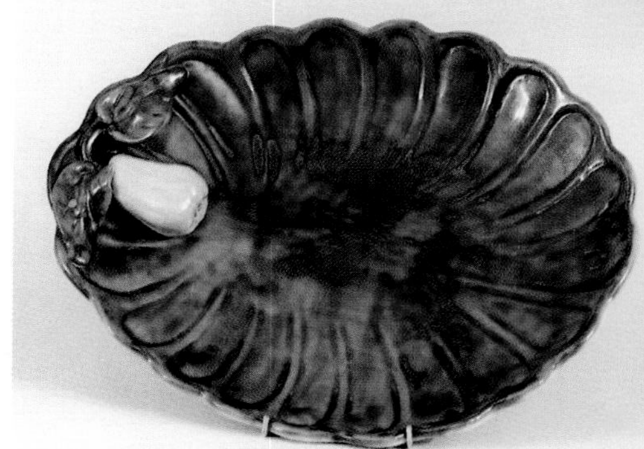

Terra Rose Green #3579 relish, with pear 13½"x11", marked Della-Ware, made for Fisher, Bruce & Co., 1941 – 1942. $55.00 – 65.00.

Indian Figure Book Blocks

Briefly during 1941 and 1942, the #3588 book blocks were mounted with hand-painted figurines representing Native American Indians. Three figurines were created during that time. The #3588 Indian Brave figurine was used during 1941; and the #3663 Indian Chief and #3664 Indian Squaw were added in 1942. Each was realistically decorated with vivid underglaze colors and stands approximately 5½" tall. The #3588 book block shapes were both plain and rippled in design.

Not Shown:

#3588 book blocks, 4¼"x5¼"x6¼" tall, plain or ripple design, no figurine, 1941 – 1942. $55.00 – 65.00 pair.

Bottom of book block with Terra Rose backstamp and "11" decorator's mark.

Terra Rose Mauve #3588 book blocks, plain design, with #3588 Indian Brave figures, 1941 – 1942. $800.00 – 900.00 pair.

Terra Rose Mauve #3588 book blocks, ripple design, with #3663 Indian Chief and #3664 Indian Squaw figures, 1941 – 1942. $800.00 – 900.00 pair. Courtesy of the Louis and Sarah DiPlacido collection.

Frederik Lunning, Inc. Terra Rose Art Ware

Not Shown:

#3601 ashtray, 3 corner, 3¾", made for Frederik Lunning, 1941 only. $25.00 – 30.00.

#3602 cigarette cup, 3 corner, 2¾", made for Frederik Lunning, 1941 only. $25.00 – 35.00.

#3603 cigarette holder, 2⅝", made for Frederik Lunning, 1941 only. $25.00 – 35.00.

#3604 cigarette box, 3¾" high, made for Frederik Lunning, 1941 only. $85.00 – 95.00.

#3605 candy jar, 4½" high, made for Frederik Lunning, 1941 only. $100.00 – 125.00.

#3606 vase, ribbed, 7⅝", made for Frederik Lunning, 1941 only. $55.00 – 70.00.

#3607 vase, 3 corner, 8⅝", made for Frederik Lunning, 1941 only. $70.00 – 85.00.

#3608 large salad bowl, 8"deep, 12½" diameter, made for Frederik Lunning, 1941 only. $100.00 – 125.00.

#3610 ashtray, 3 corner, 5½", made for Frederik Lunning, 1941 only. $25.00 – 35.00.

Terra Rose Green #3609 tray, hors d'oeuvres, 13" diameter, made for Frederik Lunning, 1941 (back, inset). $150.00.

Two-tone Terra Rose Blue #3611 Horse head vase, 13", 1942 – 1944. $500.00 – 600.00. Courtesy of the Jim and Barbara Nelson collection.

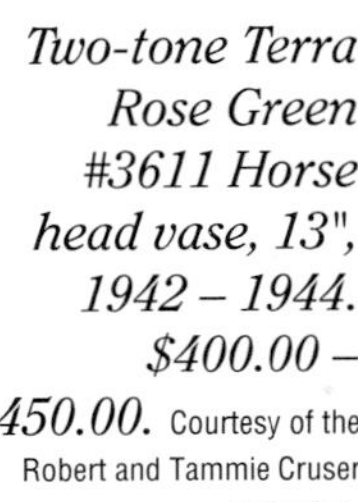

Two-tone Terra Rose Green #3611 Horse head vase, 13", 1942 – 1944. $400.00 – 450.00. Courtesy of the Robert and Tammie Cruser collection.

Solid Terra Rose Green #3611 Horse head vase, 13", 1944 – 1950. $290.00 – 325.00.

Terra Rose vases #3612 tall horn lily, 8", solid Mauve on left, 1944 – 1955. $18.00 – 22.00; Two-tone Blue on right, 1942 – 1944. $25.00 – 30.00.

Two-tone Terra Rose Blue #3613 low horn basket with fish, 5¼", 1942 – 1943. $60.00 – 75.00. Courtesy of the Jim and Barbara Nelson collection.

Two-tone Terra Rose Green #3614 shell vase, scroll base, 8½"x10½", 1942 – 1945 and again during 1951 for Flemington Outlet. $65.00 – 80.00.

Two-tone Terra Rose Blue #3615 scroll vase, 10½"x8¼", 1942 – 1943. $70.00 – 85.00.

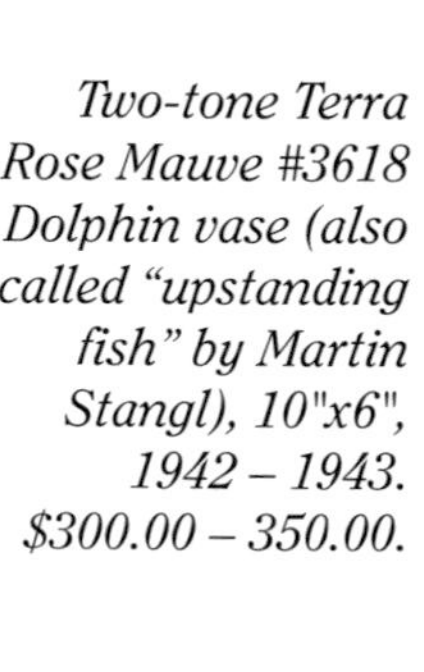

Two-tone Terra Rose Mauve #3618 Dolphin vase (also called "upstanding fish" by Martin Stangl), 10"x6", 1942 – 1943. $300.00 – 350.00.

Two-tone Terra Rose Green #3620 lily of the valley bowl, 5"x7", 1942 – 1943. $120.00 – 145.00. Courtesy of the Marcena North collection.

Terra Rose Mauve #3621 small basket with handle, 5½", 1942 – 1950. $25.00 – 35.00.

Two-tone Terra Rose Green #3618 Dolphin vase, 10"x6", 1942 – 1943. $350.00 – 375.00.

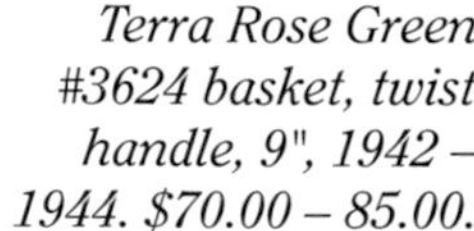

Terra Rose Green #3624 basket, twist handle, 9", 1942 – 1944. $70.00 – 85.00.

#3516 leaf basket, sweeping handle, 9½", Two-tone, 1942 – 1944. $65.00 – 80.00.
#3617 horn of plenty, 10½"x16", Two-tone, 1942 – 1945. $130.00 – 150.00.
#3619 vase, leaf horn, 9¼", Two-tone, 1942 – 1945. $70.00 – 85.00.
#3622 basket, flat handle, 7¾", 1942 only. $60.00 – 75.00.
#3623 basket, scalloped, 9", 1942 only. $70.00 – 85.00.

Saks Fifth Avenue Serve Ware

Not Shown:

#3640 serving dish with 3 handles, 16"x10"x 5", handmade for Saks Fifth Avenue, 1942 only. $70.00 – 85.00.

#3641 hors d'oeuvres, 4-part, 4½"x3", handmade for Saks Fifth Avenue, 1942 only. $40.00 – 50.00.

#3642 oval pear, 11"x9", handmade for Saks Fifth Avenue, 1942 only. $30.00 – 40.00.

#3643 double vegetable, 10"x5½", handmade for Saks Fifth Avenue, 1942 only. $40.00 – 50.00.

#3644 ovoid cup, handmade for Saks Fifth Avenue, 1942 only. $25.00 – 35.00.

#3646 saucer for shrimp cup, handmade for Saks Fifth Avenue, 1942 only. $15.00 – 20.00.

#3647 pitcher, handmade for Saks Fifth Avenue, 1942 only. $95.00 – 110.00.

#3648 bowl, salad, 10½"x3", handmade for Saks Fifth Avenue, 1942 only. $70.00 – 85.00.

#3649 casserole, pie crust, 8" with cover, handmade for Saks Fifth Avenue, 1942 only. $80.00 – 90.00.

#3651 mug, handmade for Saks Fifth Avenue, 1942 only. $40.00 – 50.00.

#3652 hors d'oeuvres 4-part plate, handmade for Saks Fifth Avenue, 1942 only. $60.00 – 75.00.

#3653 mayonnaise bowl for hors d'oeuvres plate, handmade for Saks Fifth Avenue, 1942 only. $30.00 – 40.00.

#3654 ladle for mayonnaise bowl, handmade for Saks Fifth Avenue, 1942 only. $30.00 – 35.00.

#3655 cover for 4-part plate, handmade for Saks Fifth Avenue, 1942 only. $30.00 – 40.00.

#3656 casserole, 9½" open, fluted, handmade for Saks Fifth Avenue, 1942 only. $40.00 – 50.00.

#3657 casserole, 8" open, fluted, handmade for Saks Fifth Avenue, 1942 only. $30.00 – 40.00.

#3658 casserole, 6¼" open, fluted, handmade for Saks Fifth Avenue, 1942 only. $25.00 – 35.00.

#3659 punch bowl, 14"x7¾", handmade for Saks Fifth Avenue, 1942 only. $150.00 – 175.00.

#3660 ladle, punch bowl, handmade for Saks Fifth Avenue, 1942 only. $60.00 – 75.00.

Handmade Terra Rose Green #3645 shrimp cup, for Saks Fifth Avenue, 1942 only. $45.00 – 55.00.

Handmade Terra Rose Green #3650 hors d'oeuvres boat, 12" with attached celery vase, for Saks Fifth Avenue, 1942 only. $130.00 – 150.00. Courtesy of the Hill-Fulper-Stangl Museum.

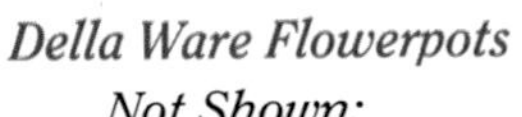

Della Ware Flowerpots

Not Shown:

#3661 flowerpot, plain collar, 8½", marked Della-Ware, made for Fisher, Bruce & Co., 1942 only. $35.00 – 45.00.

#3661 flowerpot, plain collar, 6½", marked Della-Ware, made for Fisher, Bruce & Co., 1942 only. $25.00 – 35.00.

#3661 flowerpot, plain collar, 5½", marked Della-Ware, made for Fisher, Bruce & Co., 1942 only. $20.00 – 25.00.

#3661 flowerpot, plain collar, 4½", marked Della-Ware, made for Fisher, Bruce & Co., 1942 only. $15.00 – 20.00.

#3661 flowerpot, fluted collar, 8½", marked Della-Ware, made for Fisher, Bruce & Co., 1942 only. $35.00 – 45.00.

#3661 flowerpot, fluted collar, 6½", marked Della-Ware, made for Fisher, Bruce & Co., 1942 only. $25.00 – 35.00.

#3661 flowerpot, fluted collar, 5½", marked Della-Ware, made for Fisher, Bruce & Co. 1942 only. $20.00 – 25.00.

#3661 flowerpot, fluted collar, 4½", marked Della-Ware, made for Fisher, Bruce & Co., 1942 only. $15.00 – 20.00.

#3672 double Shell vase, 7½"x12", 1942 only. $150.00 – 165.00.

Two-tone Terra Rose Mauve #3671 Sea Horse bowl, 6"x12", 1942 only. $165.00 – 190.00.

Two-tone Terra Rose Blue #3673 Tulip bowl, 9¼"x13", 1942 – 1944. $120.00 – 145.00.

Two-tone #3673 Tulip bowls, 9¼"x13", Terra Rose Green on left and Mauve on right, 1942 – 1944. $95.00 – 130.00 each.

Two-tone Terra Rose Green #3675 oval Morning Glory vase, 10", 1942 – 1945. $70.00 – 85.00.

Two-tone Terra Rose Green #3674 Tulip candleholders, 6½", 1942 – 1944. $85.00 – 95.00 pair.

Terra Rose Mauve #3688 milk can vase, 7", $30.00 – 40.00; Terra Rose Green #3684 candy jar, $35.00 – 45.00.

Terra Rose Mauve #3685 ovoid vase 7", $35.00 – 45.00; Terra Rose Green #3692 oval bowl 7", $20.00 – 25.00; and Terra Rose Mauve #3694 round vase 5", $30.00 – 40.00.

#3676 square candy jar, bird knob, 4½"x5½", 1942 – 1952. $40.00 – 50.00.
#3681 vase, 11", 1942 – 1948. $65.00 – 80.00.
#3682 ball vase, 5", 1942 – 1948. $30.00 – 40.00.
#3683, cup vase, 7", 1942 – 1948. $30.00 – 40.00.
#3684 round candy jar, tulip knob, 7", 1942 – 1955. $35.00 – 45.00.
#3685 ovoid vase 7", 1942 – 1948. $35.00 – 45.00.
#3686 low bowl, round, 10", 1942 – 1948. $40.00 – 50.00.
#3687 candleholder, 3½", 1942 – 1948. $25.00 – 35.00 pair.
#3688 vase, milk can, 7", 1942 – 1952. $30.00 – 40.00.
#3689 ovoid jar and cover, tulip knob, 4½", 1942 – 1945. $50.00 – 60.00.
#3690 scalloped vase, 9", 1942 – 1948. $50.00 – 60.00.
#3691 ovoid vase 5", 1942 – 1948. $40.00 – 50.00.
#3692 oval bowl, 7", 1942 – 1948. $20.00 – 25.00.
#3693 oval bowl, 9", 1942 – 1948. $25.00 – 30.00.
#3694 round vase 5", 1942 – 1948. $30.00 – 40.00.
#3695 oblong bowl, 11"x7", 1942 – 1945. $35.00 – 45.00.
#3696 large ovoid vase, 9", $35.00 – 45.00.

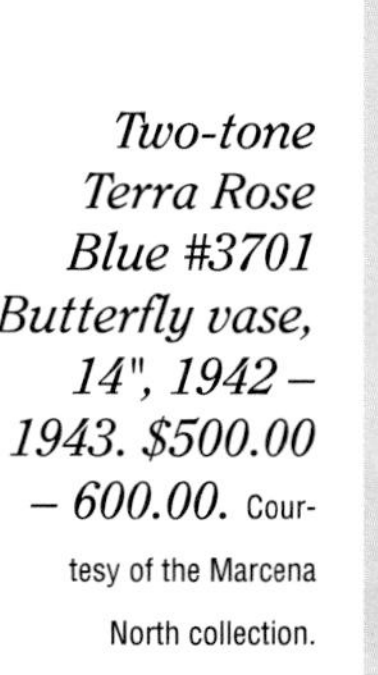

Two-tone Terra Rose Blue #3701 Butterfly vase, 14", 1942 – 1943. $500.00 – 600.00. Courtesy of the Marcena North collection.

Two-tone Terra Rose Mauve #3705 large scroll horn vase, 10", 1942 – 1944 and again during 1951 for Flemington Outlet. $70.00 – 85.00.

Terra Rose Green #3706 oblong leaf vase, 11"x16", 1942 – 1945 and again during 1951 for Flemington Outlet. $65.00 – 80.00.

Two-tone Terra Rose Blue #3708 Gazelle vase, 15", 1942 – 1944. $450.00 – 550.00. Courtesy of the Jim and Barbara Nelson collection.

Solid Terra Rose Blue #3708 Gazelle vase, 15", 1942 – 1946. $325.00 – 375.00.

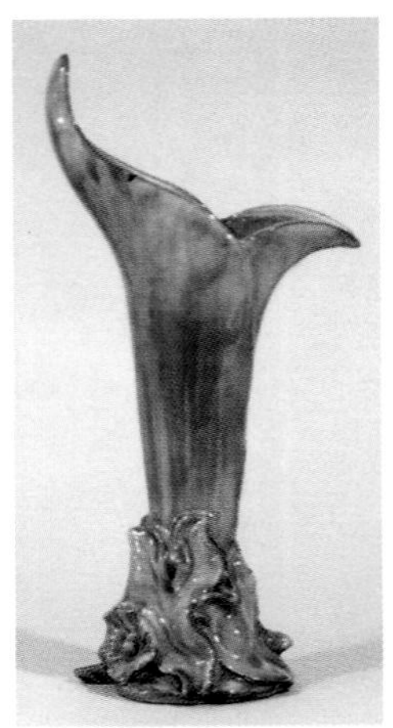

Solid Terra Rose Green #3709 tall lily vase, 14", 1942 – 1944 and again during 1951 for Flemington Outlet. $60.00 – 75.00.

Two-tone Terra Rose Mauve #3710 tall plume vase, 12", 1942 – 1944. $85.00 – 95.00.

Solid Terra Rose Green #3710 tall plume vase, 12", 1951 for Flemington Outlet. $60.00 – 75.00.

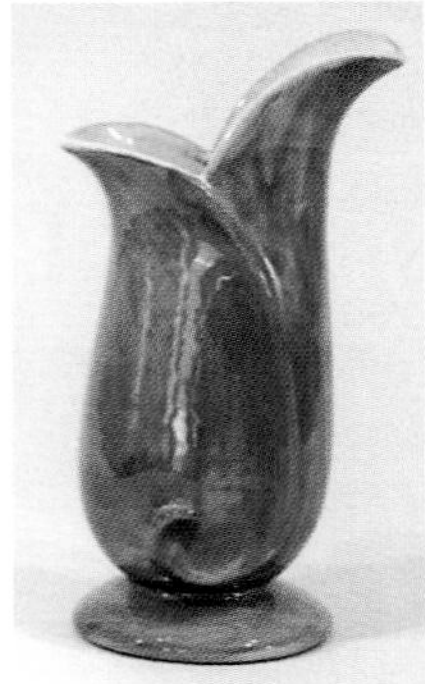

Terra Rose Blue #3730 vase, curl design, 6½", 1944 – 1946. $40.00 – 50.00.

Terra Rose Blue and Terra Rose Green #3731 tall tulip vases, 1944 – 1948. $30.00 – 40.00 each.

Two-tone Terra Rose Blue #3734 plume bowl, 13", 1944 – 1945, and in solid Terra Rose during 1951 for the Flemington Outlet. $85.00 – 95.00.

Two-tone Terra Rose Green #3732 vase with handle, 12", 1944 – 1945. $120.00 – 145.00.

Two-tone Terra Rose Green #3736 snail scroll shell bowl, 14", 1944 – 1946. $60.00 – 75.00.

Two-tone Terra Rose Blue #3735 shell bowl, 15", 1944 – 1945. $70.00 – 85.00.

#3707 double leaf vase, 15", 1942 – 1943. $120.00 – 145.00.

#3711 Conch Shell vase, 19"x10", 1942 – 1944. $135.00 – 175.00.

#3712 Starfish candleholders, 6", 1942 – 1944. $85.00 – 95.00 pair.

#3733 vase, large horn, 1944 only. $85.00 – 95.00.

Terra Rose Yellow #3787 6" heart dish, $15.00 – 20.00; Terra Rose Green #3779 leaf server, $25.00 – 35.00; and Terra Rose Green #3786 square snack dish, $20.00 – 25.00.

Terra Rose Yellow #3784 double apple dish, $18.00 – 22.00; #3779 leaf server, $25.00 – 35.00; and #3786 square snack dish, $20.00 – 25.00. Courtesy of the Marcena North collection.

#3766 Rose hors d'oeuvre platter, 14" round, 1947 only. $130.00 – 150.00.
#3779 leaf server, 7"x14½", 1948 – 1955. $25.00 – 35.00.
#3780 oval tray, 12", 1948 – 1952. $30.00 – 40.00.
#3781 triple shell relish, 12", 1948 – 1955. $30.00 – 45.00.
#3782 double pear dish, 7½"x7½", 1948 – 1959. $18.00 – 22.00.
#3783 single pear dish, 7½"x4", 1948 – 1959. $15.00 – 20.00.
#3784 double apple dish, 10"x5½", 1948 – 1959. $18.00 – 22.00.
#3785 single apple dish, 6", 1948 – 1959. $15.00 – 20.00.
#3786 square snack dish, 4½", 1948 – 1958. $20.00 – 25.00.
#3787 heart dish, 6", 1948 – 1960. $15.00 – 20.00.
#3788 heart dish, 8", 1948 – 1960. $20.00 – 25.00.
#3789 clam shell, 10½", 1948 – 1959. $25.00 – 35.00.
#3790 large leaf, 19" x 12", 1948 – 1952. $35.00 – 45.00.
#3816 ashtray, windproof, 8", 1949 – 1960 (Kay Hackett design). $18.00 – 22.00.
#3817 ashtray, windproof, 6", 1949 – 1960 (Kay Hackett design). $12.00 – 18.00.
#3846 long ashtray, 6¼"x2⅝", Terra Rose colors 1950 – 1960. $22.00 – 28.00 (see page 282 for photo).
#3855 scoop leaf server, 9¼"x5" (Kay Hackett design), 1951 – 1955. $25.00 – 30.00.
#3856 apple server, 7¼"x8" (Kay Hackett design), 1951 – 1955. $25.00 – 30.00.
#3857 clover server, 7"x7½" (Kay Hackett design), 1951 – 1955. $25.00 – 30.00.
#3858 footed compote, 8" (Kay Hackett design), 1951 – 1959. $20.00 – 25.00.
#3860 relish dish, footed, 11½"x4½" (Kay Hackett design), 1951 – 1955. $25.00 – 35.00.
#3873 round candle warmer, 1952 – 1955. $20.00 – 25.00.
#3889 large candleholder, 1953 – 1959. $25.00 – 35.00.
#3897S Pond ashtray, square, 4"x4" (Ed Pettingil design), 1954 – 1956. $20.00 – 25.00.
#3897M Pond ashtray, square, 5"x5" (Ed Pettingil design), 1954 – 1956. $22.00 – 28.00 (see page 282 for photo).
#3897L Pond ashtray, square, 6½"x6½" (Ed Pettingil design), 1954 – 1956. $25.00 – 35.00.
#3904 ashtray, free form, 7"x4½" (Ed Pettingil design), 1954 – 1956. $20.00 – 25.00.
#3905 ashtray, free form (same as #3904), 5"x3½" (Ed Pettingil design), 1954 – 1956. $15.00 – 20.00.
#3906 ashtray, notched, free form, 5½" (Ed Pettingil design), 1954 – 1956. $12.00 – 18.00.
#3914 ashtray, square with square well, 9" (Kay Hackett design), 1954 – 1956. $20.00 – 25.00.
#3915 ashtray, square with round well, 9" (Kay Hackett design), 1954 – 1956. $20.00 – 25.00.
#3926 ashtray, oval, plain, 10¾"x8" (Kay Hackett design), 1955 – 1956. $15.00 – 20.00.
#3927 ashtray, casual, 10½"x 7½" (Kay Hackett design), 1955 – 1956. $25.00 – 30.00.
#3937 ashtray, 7" diameter, 1955 – 1956. $25.00 – 30.00.
#3938 ashtray, free form, 7¼"x5⅞" (Ed Pettingil design), 1955 – 1956. $20.00 – 25.00.

Two-tone Terra Rose Mauve #3737 Bird vase, 13", 1944 only. $500.00 – 600.00. Courtesy of the Louis and Sarah DiPlacido collection.

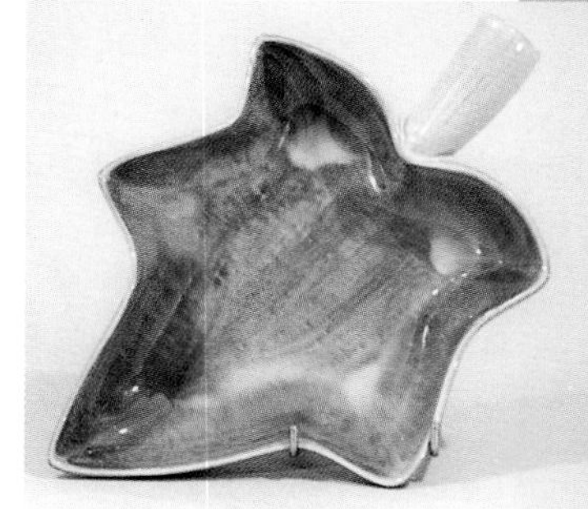

Terra Rose Blue #3859 ivy leaf server, 8"x7" (Kay Hackett design), 1951 – 1955. $25.00 – 30.00.

Terra Rose Green #3737 6" heart dish, $15.00 – 20.00; Terra Rose Blue #3860 relish dish, $25.00 – 35.00; Terra Rose Yellow #3855 leaf server, $25.00 – 30.00; and Terra Rose Green #3857 clover server, $25.00 – 30.00.

Terra Rose Green #3871 gladiola vase, 13" x 17", 1952 – 1953. $175.00 – 200.00.
Courtesy of the Hill-Fulper-Stangl Museum.

#3939 ashtray, rectangular, 9⅛"x9⅛" (Ed Pettingil design), 1955 – 1956. $20.00 – 25.00.
#3940 ashtray, irregular shape, 6½"x5"x8" (Ed Pettingil design), 1955 – 1956. $20.00 – 25.00.
#3941 ashtray, Safety, free form, 5⅜"x6¼"x7 (Ed Pettingil design), 1955 – 1956. $20.00 – 25.00.
#3942 ashtray, Safety, oval, 8½"x7" (Ed Pettingil design), 1955 – 1956. $15.00 – 20.00.
#3944 bowl, low footed 3-corner, 2½"x 10" (Ed Pettingil design), 1956 – 1958. $55.00 – 65.00.
#3945 bowl, semi-round, footed, 4"x10⅜" (Ed Pettingil design), 1956 – 1958. $55.00 – 65.00.
#3945 bowl, semi-round, 3¼"x 8¼" (Ed Pettingil design), 1956 – 1958. $35.00 – 45.00.
#3945 bowl, semi-round, 2½"x 6¼" (Ed Pettingil design), 1956 – 1958. $45.00 – 55.00.
#3952 cylinder vase, 10" (Kay Hackett design), 1956 – 1958. $40.00 – 50.00.
#3952 cylinder vase, 8" (Kay Hackett design), 1956 – 1958. $30.00 – 40.00.
#3952 cylinder vase, 6" (Kay Hackett design), 1956 – 1958. $25.00 – 30.00.
#3952 cylinder vase, 4" (Kay Hackett design), 1956 – 1958. $25.00 – 30.00.
#3953 pencil holder, made for Tri-Rex pencils, 1956 – 1958. $85.00 – 95.00.
#3954 square tray, 10¾"x2½" (Ed Pettingil design), 1956 – 1958. $45.00 – 55.00.
#3955 vase, square, 2"x8"x9", 1956 – 1958. $25.00 – 35.00.
#3955 vase, square, 4"x6"x7", 1956 – 1958. $25.00 – 35.00.
#3955 vase, square, 6"x4"x5", 1956 – 1958. $25.00 – 35.00.
#3955 vase, square, 8"x2"x3", 1956 – 1958. $25.00 – 35.00.
#3969 Jelly mold, swirl design, 7½"x2¾", 1957 only. $40.00 – 50.00.
#3970 Jelly mold, fish, 8½"x7⅞"x2", 1957 only. $45.00 – 55.00.
#3971 Jelly mold, artichoke, 7¾"x3½", 1957 only. $45.00 – 55.00.
#4032 ashtray, Oak leaf, 5½"x4" (orig. #3525), 1958 – 1960. $20.00 – 25.00.
#4033 ashtray, Cosmos, 5½" (orig. #3526), 1958 – 1960. $20.00 – 25.00.
#4034 ashtray, triangle leaf, 6½"x4" (orig. #3523), 1958 – 1960. $20.00 – 25.00.
#4035 ashtray, Ivy leaf, 5¼"x4¼" (orig. #3524), 1958 – 1960. $15.00 – 20.00.
#4036 ashtray, leaf, 6"x4½" (orig. #3532), 1958 – 1960. $15.00 – 20.00.
#4037 ashtray, shell dish, 5"x5½" (orig. #3522), 1958 – 1960. $20.00 – 25.00.
#4038 leaf server, Oak, 13½"x9" (orig. #3540), 1958 – 1960. $40.00 – 50.00.
#4039 leaf server, 12"x8½" (orig. #3496), 1958 – 1960. $55.00 – 65.00.
#4040 candleholder, curl flower 4¼" (orig. #3499), 1958 – 1960. $50.00 – 60.00 pair.
#4041 leaf server, 18½"x13" (orig. #3538), 1958 – 1960. $60.00 – 75.00.
#4042 leaf server, 16½"x10" (orig. #3429), 1958 – 1960. $50.00 – 60.00.
#4043 candleholder, Calla Lily, 3¼" (orig. #3428), 1958 – 1960. $40.00 – 50.00 pair.

James Teague's Stangl Stoneware, 1940 – 1941

During the late 1930s, the town of Flemington and Stangl's Flemington Outlet showroom became increasingly popular tourist destinations, and Martin Stangl was convinced that the Flemington Outlet should be more than just a retail store. He was continually initiating pottery demonstrations and displays at the outlet, with the pinnacle of his educational effort being the opening of the Stangl Museum in 1965.

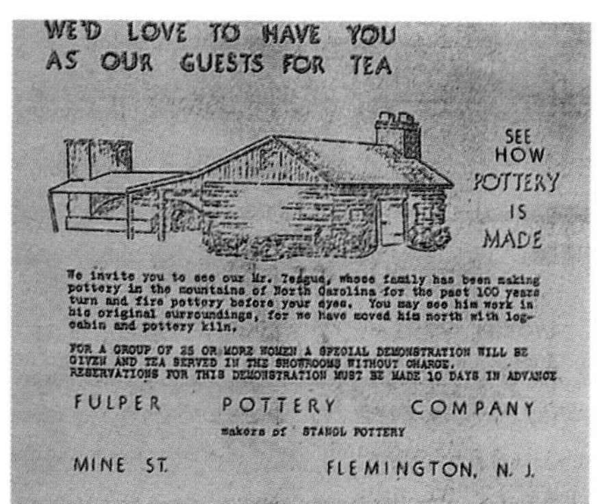
WE'D LOVE TO HAVE YOU AS OUR GUESTS FOR TEA

SEE HOW POTTERY IS MADE

We invite you to see our Mr. Teague, whose family has been making pottery in the mountains of North Carolina for the past 100 years turn and fire pottery before your eyes. You may see him work in his original surroundings, for we have moved him north with log-cabin and pottery kiln.

FOR A GROUP OF 25 OR MORE WOMEN A SPECIAL DEMONSTRATION WILL BE GIVEN AND TEA SERVED IN THE SHOWROOMS WITHOUT CHARGE. RESERVATIONS FOR THIS DEMONSTRATION MUST BE MADE 10 DAYS IN ADVANCE

FULPER POTTERY COMPANY

makers of STANGL POTTERY

MINE ST. FLEMINGTON, N. J.

Original Flemington Outlet mimeographed flyer advertising James Teague's pottery demonstrations. Courtesy of the Hill-Fulper-Stangl Museum.

Martin Stangl's first large-scale, "home-based" pottery demonstration was the installation of a full-time, truly American potter at the Flemington Outlet in 1940. Martin Stangl had considered establishing an authentic American potter at the Flemington Outlet for some time and had been greatly impressed by the folk potteries of the Steeds (now Seagrove), North Carolina pottery district. In 1939, Martin Stangl hired James Goodwin Teague, a third-generation North Carolina potter, to demonstrate pottery in Flemington. (See page 60 for more information.) Martin Stangl advertising of the Teague demonstrations stated: "See how pottery is made! We invite you to see our Mr. Teague, whose family has been making pottery in the mountains of North Carolina for the past 100 years, turn and fire pottery before your eyes."

Teague hand-turned a variety of shapes based on the same traditional early American pottery forms he and his family had been producing for generations. The shapes were made primarily of gray-colored Amboy stoneware clay, but occasionally Stangl's white artware clay was used. Teague produced all the shapes in the log cabin workshop and fired each one in the attached groundhog kiln. The shapes were standardized, and each one was assigned a shape number, but items of the same shape can vary by several inches or amount of finishing or detail.

Two sample jugs made by James Teague at the log cabin of white artware clay brushed with manganese oxide and glazed with clear dinnerware glaze, $250.00 – 300.00 each. From the Stangl and Fulper archival collection, courtesy the Wheaton Village Museum of American Glass.

Teague's salt glazing was achieved by adding common rock salt to the groundhog kiln when it reached approximately 2,300°. At that temperature, the salt vaporized and reacted with the silica in the stoneware clay and formed an impervious, glass-like finish on the pots. Because there was very little silica in Stangl's white artware clay, the sodium vapor did not react on those pieces so they would come from the kiln fired, but unglazed. Teague decorated many pieces with cobalt decorations. Simple dots, abstract florals, and unsophisticated designs were some of his typical cobalt motifs. One of Teague's most accomplished decorations was a variation of the Quaint Tree dinnerware motif he applied to a beer bottle shape. In addition to the salt glazed finish, some of the shapes made of white artware clay were sent to the Trenton factory where they were brushed with manganese or copper oxide stains and glazed with clear dinnerware glaze.

Large "STANGL STONEWARE" die-pressed mark.

Small "STANGL STONEWARE" die-pressed mark.

Die-pressed "STANGL" mark.

All of Teague's Flemington Outlet pottery was marked. The most common mark was a die-pressed "STANGL STONEWARE," which can be found in two sizes. A die-pressed "STANGL" was also used. The least common mark was a hand-inscribed "Stangl Stoneware" on the base.

Hand-inscribed "Stangl Stoneware," rarely used.

Teague was accustomed to firing his North Carolina kiln with pine knots, which burned fast, hot, and produced a high quality salt glaze. The Flemington groundhog kiln, however, was fired with used electric line poles, which also burned fast and seemed well-suited to stoneware firing. However, the creosote on the poles caused patchy oxidation and blackening of the salt glaze and cobalt decoration, which disturbed Teague. Martin Stangl was undaunted as usual, telling him, "Don't you worry, these are different and we will be able to charge more for them!" Always the consummate salesman, Martin Stangl was correct. The darkened salt glazed pots consistently sold more quickly and at higher prices than the pieces with even glaze color.

Teague conducted pottery demonstrations at the log cabin seven days a week and often produced several hundred pieces a day. Like John Kunsman before him, Teague was a distinguished-looking man and always performed his demonstrations dressed in a white shirt and necktie. One of the most popular features of his demonstrations was when he donned a blindfold and proceeded to turn pots blind.

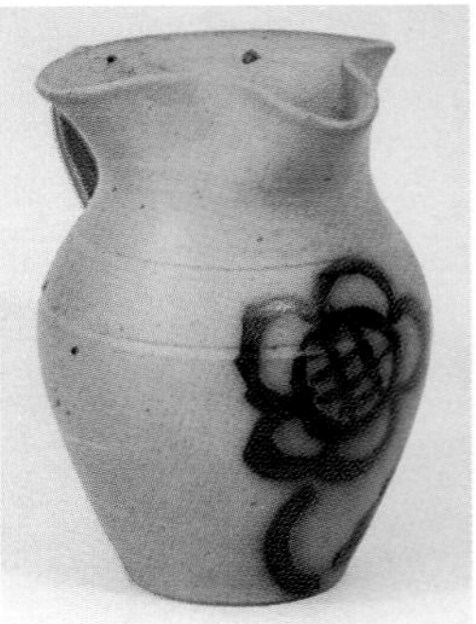

Nearly identical cobalt decorated #6007, 10" large water jugs, with creosote oxidation (left), and without (right), $150.00 – 180.00 each. Courtesy of the Brian and Cristi Hahn collection.

Teague produced a variety of Stangl Stoneware shapes that were fairly standard but could vary greatly in size. Many of the Stangl Stoneware shapes were assigned numbers only so that Fulper Pottery Company could comply with the ceiling price regulations of the early 1940s. Prices for these items ranged from 25¢ for 2" and 3" miniature jugs to $8.00 for the butter churn with cover and $12.00 for the largest 18" strawberry jar. Most items retailed in the 50¢ to $1.00 range, very realistic and reasonable for post-Depression, pre-war, touristy decorator ware.

Variations in size of the Stangl Stoneware Rebecca jugs, the two outer jugs are #6011, 3" and 4" tall, $60.00 – 95.00 each; the two inner jugs are #6000, 5½" tall, $70.00 – 95.00 each; the center jug is #6002, 11" tall, $125.00 – 200.00.

Teague produced Stangl Stoneware salt glazed pottery at the log cabin for nearly two years before moving his family back to North Carolina shortly after the start of World War II. Martin Stangl closed the log cabin in early 1942 and did not reopen it for pottery production again until the 1960s.

Sizes for these items are approximate as each shape was made in a variety of sizes. The shapes represented by numbers were somewhat standard but could vary in size. Teague also produced several shapes that were not assigned numbers. Stoneware shapes with clear, quality cobalt decoration always sell for more than items with murky or washed-out cobalt. Likewise, pieces with rich, dappled creosote oxidation are more desirable, just as Martin Stangl predicted.

Not Shown:

#6000 medium handled (Rebecca) jug, 5" to 8", 1940 – 1941 only. $70.00 – 145.00.

#6001 small hurricane lamp, 5" to 6", 1940 – 1941 only. $65.00 – 125.00.

#6002 tall handled (Rebecca) jug, 10" to 12", 1940 – 1941 only. $125.00 – 200.00.

#6003 elixir jug, tall, 10", 1940 – 1941 only. $200.00 – 250.00.

#6004 cup for elixir jug, 3", 1940 – 1941 only. $60.00 – 75.00.

#6005 large hurricane lamp, 8" to 9", 1940 – 1941 only. $130.00 – 175.00.

Stangl Stoneware #6000 medium Rebecca jug with cobalt decoration, 1940 – 1941 only. $120.00 – 145.00. Courtesy of the Ben and Floss Avila collection.

Stangl Stoneware #6003 low elixir jug, 6", 1940 – 1941 only. $175.00 – 200.00. Courtesy of the Hill-Fulper-Stangl Museum.

Stangl Stoneware hurricane lamps, #6001 small, 5", white artware clay with cobalt decoration, $100.00 – 125.00; #6005 large, 8½", Amboy stoneware clay with creosote oxidation and cobalt interior decoration, $150.00 – 175.00; #6001 small, 4½", Amboy stoneware clay, no cobalt, $60.00 – 70.00.

Stangl Stoneware #6006 medium water jug, 6", 1940 – 1941 only. $55.00 – 65.00.

Stangl Stoneware #6007 large water jug, 11", cobalt decorated, 1940 – 1941 only. $175.00 – 200.00.

Stangl Stoneware #6007 large water jug, 10", Amboy stoneware clay, undecorated, $120.00 – 145.00; and #6014 miniature water jug, 3", white artware clay, $60.00 – 75.00, 1940 – 1941 only.

Stangl Stoneware beer mug inscribed "Marni and Jack." About 150 of these were made by James Teague as wedding favors for Martin Stangl's eldest daughter Martha and Jack Bacheler in 1940. $190.00 – 225.00 each.

Stangl Stoneware #6008 handled mugs, 4" to 5", 1940 – 1941 only. $60.00 – 75.00 each. Courtesy of the Brian and Cristi Hahn collection.

Three Stangl Stoneware #6009 flared crimp vases showing the diversity of decorations and treatments used by Teague. The center vase is 6", white artware clay with cobalt decoration, the interior is glazed with Albany slip. The other two vases are 7¼" and 8", Amboy stoneware clay, $125.00 – 175.00 each. Courtesy of the Brian and Cristi Hahn collection.

Stangl Stoneware #6009 flared crimp vase, 6" to 8", 1940 – 1941 only. $150.00 – 175.00. Courtesy of the Brian and Cristi Hahn collection.

Stangl Stoneware #6010 flared vase, 6" to 8", cobalt decorated, 1940 – 1941 only. $150.00 – 175.00. Courtesy of the Brian and Cristi Hahn collection.

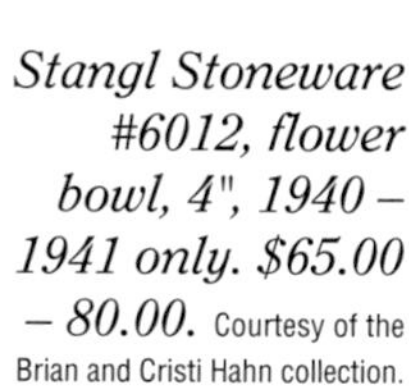

Stangl Stoneware #6012, flower bowl, 4", 1940 – 1941 only. $65.00 – 80.00. Courtesy of the Brian and Cristi Hahn collection.

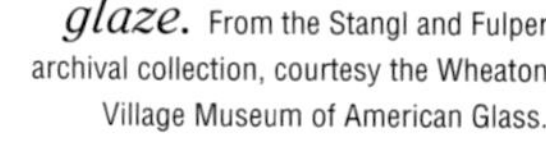

Stangl Stoneware #6013 flared vase, 7" to 8", 1940 – 1941 only. $160.00 – 195.00. This particular example is white artware clay, brushed with manganese oxide, and glazed with clear dinnerware glaze. From the Stangl and Fulper archival collection, courtesy the Wheaton Village Museum of American Glass.

Not Shown:

#6011 small handled (Rebecca) jug, 3" to 4", $60.00 – 95.00.

#6014 miniature water jug, 2" to 3", 1940 – 1941 only. $60.00 – 125.00.

#6015 miniature whiskey jug, 1½" to 3", 1940 – 1941 only. $75.00 – 125.00.

Stangl Stoneware #6015 miniature whiskey jug, 2", $85.00 – 95.00; and #6014 miniature water jug, 2". $100.00 – 125.00. Courtesy of the Robert and Tammie Cruser collection.

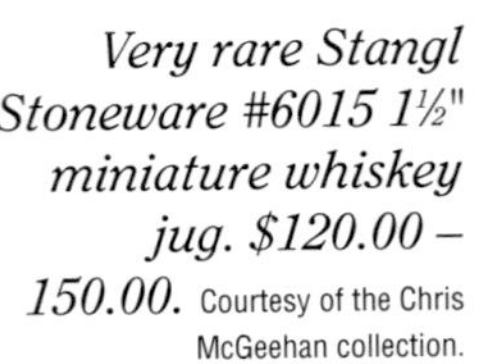

Very rare Stangl Stoneware #6015 1½" miniature whiskey jug. $120.00 – 150.00. Courtesy of the Chris McGeehan collection.

Stangl Stoneware #6019 urn, 18", 1940 – 1941 only. $375.00 – 400.00. From the Stangl and Fulper archival collection, courtesy the Wheaton Village Museum of American Glass.

Stangl Stoneware #6021 small whiskey jug, 4", cobalt decorated, 1940 – 1941 only. $80.00 – 100.00. Courtesy of the Hill-Fulper-Stangl Museum.

Stangl Stoneware #6023 butter churn & cover, 12", white artware clay with cobalt decoration and date, 1940 – 1941 only. $275.00 – 300.00.

Stangl Stoneware #6024 handled jar, 14", shaped like the butter churn, but no internal rim to support a cover, 1940 – 1941 only. $225.00 – 275.00. Courtesy of the Hill-Fulper-Stangl Museum.

Stangl Stoneware #6025 small bean pot & cover, 8"x4½", 1940 – 1941 only. $120.00 – 175.00. Courtesy of the Brian and Cristi Hahn collection.

Not Shown:

#6016 handled vase, 7" to 8", 1940 – 1941 only. $175.00 – 200.00.
#6017 small strawberry jar, 6" to 8", 1940 – 1941 only. $110.00 – 135.00.
#6018 medium strawberry jar, 10" to 12", 1940 – 1941 only. $175.00 – 200.00.
#6020 large strawberry jar, 16" to 18", 1940 – 1941 only. $375.00 – 400.00.
#6021 small whiskey jug, 4", undecorated, 1940 – 1941 only. $55.00 – 65.00.
#6022 large whiskey jug, 7", 1940 – 1941 only. $95.00 – 135.00.
#6023 butter churn & cover, 12", no decoration or date, 1940 – 1941 only. $190.00 – 225.00.
#6026 cookie jar & cover, 8", 1940 – 1941 only. $175.00 – 200.00.
#6027 large bean pot & cover, 10"x6", 1940 – 1941 only. $140.00 – 195.00.
#6028 flower pot with saucer, 5" to 6", 1940 – 1941 only. $85.00 – 95.00.
#6029 beer bottle, 8" to 9", 1940 – 1941 only. $120.00 – 165.00.
#6031 lamp base, 11", 1940 – 1941 only. $200.00 – 250.00.
#6032 lamp base, 9", 1940 – 1941 only. $170.00 – 195.00.
#6033 lamp base, handled, 8", 1940 – 1941 only. $150.00 – 175.00.
#6034 lamp base, 6", 1940 – 1941 only. $130.00 – 150.00.
#6035 lamp base, 6", 1940 – 1941 only. $130.00 – 150.00.
#6036 lamp base, handled, 11", 1940 – 1941 only. $275.00 – 300.00.
#6037 lamp base, handled, 7", 1940 – 1941 only. $130.00 – 160.00.
#6038 lamp base, 9", 1940 – 1941 only. $170.00 – 195.00.
#6039 lamp base, handled, 6", 1940 – 1941 only. $170.00 – 195.00.
#6040 lamp base, 10", 1940 – 1941 only. $175.00 – 200.00.

#6030 lamp base, 9", 1940 – 1941 only. $170.00 – 195.00. Courtesy of the Ben and Floss Avila collection.

Anné Fritsche's Log Cabin Pottery, 1965

In 1965, while Martin Stangl was planning the "50 Years of Pottery" celebration for the fiftieth anniversary of Fulper's winning the Award of Merit gold medal at the 1915 Panama Pacific Exposition, he decided to reinstate pottery-throwing demonstrations at the log cabin and hired local pottery major Anné Fritsche Martin. Like James Teague before her, Anné Fritsche Martin demonstrated turning pots to enthusiastic crowds at the Flemington Outlet log cabin during the summer of 1965.

Anné Fritsche Martin worked in Stangl's red-colored dinnerware clay that was shipped in large barrels from the Trenton factory. She turned small, simple shapes of an Oriental style that were appealing and could be sold inexpensively. Each item was marked with the word "STANGL" die-impressed into the wet clay near the base. Because these items were not stoneware in the true sense, the word "STONEWARE" had been removed from the die. Martin Stangl did not reopen James Teague's original groundhog kiln, so Anné Fritsche Martin's items were fired in the small electric kiln at Flemington or occasionally shipped back to the Trenton factory. Martin Stangl had developed a "stoneware" art glaze for Anné Fritsche's log cabin shapes, so most were covered in that glaze.

Small 4" bowl by Anné Fritsche Martin in cobalt Stoneware art glaze showing the "STANGL" mark, 1965 only. Inset shows base with original price of $1.50. $85.00 – 95.00.

The Stoneware art glazes featured a colored drip over a golden green-brown base glaze. The drip color was usually frosty copper green, but cobalt blue or yellow-gold was also used. The Stoneware art glazes were also applied to many lamp shapes during 1965, as well as to the large Blue Jay figurines. A very few examples of Anné Fritsche Martin's work were hand-decorated with the colored Stoneware art glazes and are quite rare.

In addition to turning pots at the log cabin, Anné Fritsche Martin also spent many hours demonstrating the art of hand-painting pansy and flower ashtrays. Please see Cigarette Boxes, Smoking Accessories, and Sportsmen's Giftware for more information on those items.

Pair of 3½" candleholders made by Anné Fritsche Martin, copper green Stoneware art glaze, 1965 only. $100.00 – 125.00 pair.

Not Shown:

large bowls, 8" to 10", 1965 only. $110.00 – 200.00.
small bowls, 4" to 6", 1965 only. $70.00 – 125.00.
jugs, 1965 only. $100.00 – 160.00.
covered jars, 1965 only. $150.00 – 200.00.

Small 6" bowl by Anné Fritsche Martin and hand-decorated with Stoneware art glaze colors, 1965 only. $150.00 – 165.00.

Log Cabin Pottery, 1967 – 1971

Two of Stangl's Flemington Outlet potters, Susan and Andrea, draw a crowd at the log cabin in 1970. Courtesy of the Hill-Fulper-Stangl Museum.

Each summer from 1967 to 1971, Martin Stangl hired college student potters to demonstrate at the Flemington Outlet log cabin. These students also used Stangl's red-colored dinnerware clay but with a goodly amount of grog added to give the clay a more stoneware-like appearance. Grog is a coarsely ground ceramic material used as an additive to add strength and texture to clay bodies. The grog is very evident in Stangl's red clay as miniscule grainy flecks. The grog clay was much less "plastic" than James Teague's Amboy stoneware or Anné Fritsche Martin's red dinnerware clays, so the shapes produced of it were by nature much heavier and more "clunky" than the Teague or Martin shapes.

Unglazed bisque 7" jug made of red grog clay during the late 1960s to early 1970s. $110.00 – 135.00.

The log cabin potters created a great variety of items during the late 1960s and early 1970s. The shapes were novel and daring and often featured boldly executed hand-painted decoration. The students were free to indulge in developing their own personal styles or to emulate the recognized studio potters of the day. Most of the log cabin items are marked only with the die-impressed "STANGL" mark, but a few were also hand-painted with the Stangl name. Several potters also discreetly marked their items with minute initials or ciphers. One potter earned herself the nickname "Daisy" because she marked all of her pieces with a tiny figure of a four-petal daisy.

Hand-thrown pig banks were a very novel log cabin item. These pigs were all handcrafted and decorated with bold abstract strokes of underglaze color. The poses and shapes of these pigs vary greatly and are nearly always larger than the #1076 pig shape, measuring from 6" to 8" long. They usually were marked with the "STANGL" die-pressed mark. These handcrafted pigs are quite rare, as very few were produced during the Flemington Outlet demonstrations.

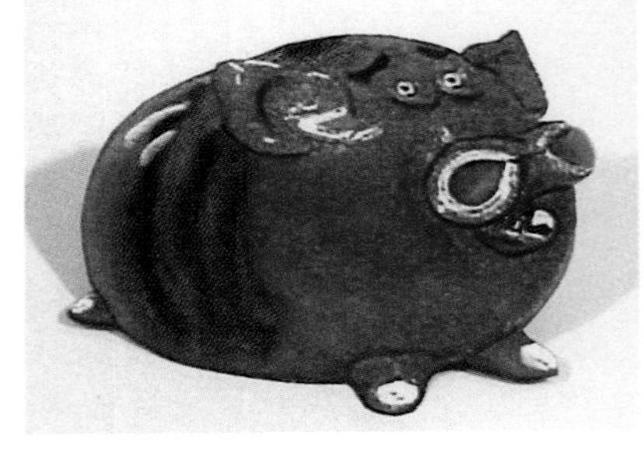

Hand-thrown pig bank with Dark Turquoise and Blue #95 stripes, die-pressed "STANGL" mark, made at the Flemington Outlet log cabin, 1967 – 1971 only. $350.00 – 450.00.

Items with appealing shapes and bold exciting decorations always sell for much more than plainer designs.

Not Shown:

large bowls, 10" to 12". $150.00 – 175.00.
small bowls, 6" to 8". $70.00 – 115.00.
covered candy jars, 4" to 6". $100.00 – 150.00.
covered cookie jars, 7" to 10". $175.00 – 200.00.
large jugs, 6" to 9". $125.00 – 185.00.
small jugs, 3" to 5". $65.00 – 125.00.
large lamps, 8" to 12". $120.00 – 225.00.
small lamps, 5" to 6". $90.00 – 145.00.
pig bank, 6" to 8". $350.00 – 450.00.
tiles and trivets. $160.00 – 180.00.

Log cabin-produced 5" covered candy jar, $140.00 – 150.00, 7" round pierced trivet, $160.00 – 180.00 (base, inset), and blossom-decorated jug, $110.00 – 125.00. The jug and candy jar were made by "Daisy." Courtesy of the Hill-Fulper-Stangl Museum.

The summer of 1971 was the last time potters demonstrated at the log cabin. After Martin Stangl's death in February 1972, the log cabin remained closed. The building now is home to the "Bee Happy Honey House."

Log cabin lamp, 9" tall with Dark turquoise and Blue #95 banded decoration (die-pressed mark on base, inset). $150.00 – 175.00. Courtesy of the Hill-Fulper-Stangl Museum.

Crudely-styled tile decorated with abstract toucans, 8½" by 5", $175.00 – 200.00. From the Stangl and Fulper archival collection, courtesy the Wheaton Village Museum of American Glass.

Between 1924 and 1934, Fulper Pottery Company designed and produced over 400 different lamp shapes for 20 different lamp, gift, and import companies. America's table lamp craze had its beginnings shortly after the turn of the nineteenth century, when many homes were being wired for electricity. However, only ceiling fixtures or wall brackets were used to provide light, as homes were not yet wired with electric outlets. As the bungalow-style of home construction spread, nearly all new homes were wired for electric lighting, and wall or floor outlets became commonplace. From 1911 to 1918, Fulper capitalized on this new, convenient electricity by producing Vasekraft table lamps and lighting fixtures.

Fulper Pottery Company 1916 catalog page showing a few of the Vasekraft lamps available.

By the mid 1910s, as electric outlets now provided power to nearly every corner of a room, top decorators were advocating greater use of table lamps. Glare-causing ceiling fixtures were becoming something to be shunned. This prompted a lamp craze that began just around World War I and lasted through the 1930s. Also fueling the lamp craze was the increasing availability of cheap electric power.

At the beginning of the table lamp craze, it was fashionable to own antique Chinese or Japanese vases drilled and fitted with sockets and mounted with silk shades. Carved Chinese jade or rose quartz statuary mounted on lamp bases were also popular. Many American import companies made their fortunes supplying America with Oriental antiques converted to lamps. As the true antiques became scarce, new Chinese reproductions were being imported as antiques and converted to lamps.

This page from the May 1922 issue of House and Garden *shows an assortment of decorative items converted to electric table lamps.*

Even Fulper Pottery was offering pre-drilled vases for use as lamps at that time. The 1925 catalog stated: "Drilling is done before firing, requiring special factory handling for which there is a charge of 20%." Fulper also sold lamp adapters in three sizes for "Instantly converting Vases into Lamps without drilling."

One of a variety of Fulper pottery lamp adapters available during the 1920s, shown installed in a vase. Courtesy of the Hill-Fulper-Stangl Museum.

As fewer Chinese lamp bases became available, decorators began to advocate using table lamps in a variety of materials and styles. Metal, glass, and ceramics companies began producing products made specifically as lamp bases and could not keep up with the demand. By the late 1920s, Chinese lamp styles were still reigning, but Jazz Modern and Modernism (as Art Deco was called then) and handmade Italian styles were also in vogue. Fulper Pottery Company produced lamp bases in all these styles in their Fayence, Porcelaine, and Pottery body and glazes. Fulper could provide nearly any type, style, body, glaze, or color needed. The jobbers assembled the lamps and marketed them to the gift and decorating shops and department stores. During the 1920s, Fulper Pottery sold only a handful of complete lamps; 95 percent of all lamp production was special-order for the lamp jobbers.

Some of the more prolific lamp body buyers during the 1920s included Daison, Inc., a New York gift shop specializing in hand-crafted American pottery; Katherine G. White's decorator shop on Lexington Ave, New York, specializing in Orientalia and other imports; and Fourman Bros. & Co. Inc., who imported furniture and decorative items.

Fulper's largest lamp account during the 1920s was L.D. Bloch Co. Bloch was yet another New York wholesaler of Orientalia, decorator items, giftwares, and home furnishings. Several of L.D. Bloch's lamp bodies were based on the glassware designs of René Lalique, the best known of which are the Lovebird, Dancing Nudes, and Archer lamps. These were styled after Lalique's Perruches, Bacchantes, and Archers glass vases. So popular were the Lovebird lamps, they were in continual production well into the 1930s. After L.D. Bloch Co. closed in 1929, three former

L.D. Bloch's #1183 Archers lamp was inspired by this René Lalique Archers vase of the 1920s. Courtesy of the Diana Bullock collection.

Bloch employees formed the Simon Jay-Willfred Co., which was Fulper's second largest lamp account during the 1930s.

Large companies that only occasionally bought special-order lamp bodies from Fulper were Macy's Department Store, S.S. Kresge Stores, International Light, Ligholier, Afton, and Vogue.

Martin Stangl's aggressive sales aptitude at procuring the extensive jobber accounts and capability to produce quality lamp bodies at a time when the country was clamoring for them not only "saved" Fulper Pottery Company during the early 1920s, but provided the dynamic force necessary to remain solvent throughout the Great Depression of the early 1930s. The Depression did have an effect on the lamp market, however. By the early 1930s, America's building boom was over. With no new construction, there was very little demand for household furnishings, and many of the gift and import companies supplied by Fulper Pottery during the 1920s had disappeared. Of the 20 lamp jobbers buying Fulper Pottery lamps at the height of the lamp craze during the 1920s, the only one actively ordering new lamp shapes in 1935 was Davart, a division of the Disabled American Veterans Association. The Davart and Simon Jay-Willfred companies were Fulper Pottery's most important lamp accounts of the 1930s.

By the mid 1930s, with so many of the old lamp jobbers gone, Martin Stangl began marketing Stangl Pottery brand lamps directly to the retailers and department stores. These lamps were assembled at the Trenton factory and sold in quantities of six per carton, complete with shades. An "exclusive" line of higher-priced lamps were introduced in 1938. Stangl called this group of lamps the "5000 Line." These lamps featured hand-painted decoration or specialty glazes such as crackle and antiqued finishes. To assure the customer that these lamps were indeed distinctive, the date of manufacture was hand-carved in the base of nearly every #5000 lamp.

By the early 1940s, interest in lamps had diminished, and very few new lamp shapes were introduced. Throughout the 1940s, Stangl Pottery was directing all manpower to the production of dinnerware and bird figurines.

In 1950, Stangl began a relationship manufacturing lamp bases for Mutual Sunset Lamp Co. that would last through the 1970s. Lamp production increased throughout the 1950s and 1960s, but never approached the quantities of the 1920s. Popular lamp finishes from the 1950s through the 1960s were Terra Rose and Antique Gold. At this time, Stangl was selling as many lamps at the Flemington Outlet as were being sold to lamp jobbers. By the 1970s, lamp production was again waning. Companies such as Mutual Sunset and Nelson Lebo Lamp were Stangl's only consistent lamp jobbers during the 1970s. Ironically, Stangl's most highly collectible lamp base figurines were produced for Mutual Sunset and Nelson Lebo during these waning years.

Fittings and Finials

A great variety of metal lamp fittings can be found on Stangl Pottery ceramic lamps. During the 1920s and 1930s, metal pedestals and bases were made of cast bronze and brass, brass-colored pot metal, or thin-stamped on spun-sheet brass. The better quality bases were bronze, but most of the bases used were of the pot metal variety. Larger table lamps normally had a long stem supporting the shade and two pull-chain sockets. A brass tube, usually embossed with a floral or leaf motif, covered the iron pipe that actually supported the sockets. Medium-sized lamps were usually fitted with a single socket and harp; small lamps that used clip-on shades had only a socket. Wood bases were also occasionally used and could be carved teak or ebonized wood.

Cast brass or iron stylized lotus finials in various finishes, usually found on L.D. Bloch and Fourman Bros. lamps, all approximately 3" tall. Courtesy of the Hill-Fulper-Stangl Museum.

Two different styles of cast brass bird finials used on the L.D. Bloch Lovebird lamps and an openwork diamond shaped finial from the #1081 Square Modern lamp, 3" to 4" tall.

Mutual Sunset lamps of the 1950s and 1960s were mounted on simple round or square antiqued metal bases. Maple or walnut bases with a long brass stem supporting the sockets were also used by Nelson Lebo and Mutual Sunset for figure lamps during the 1960s and 1970s. Stangl's Antique Gold and glazed lamps of the 1950s and 1960s were fitted with simple brass harps and sockets.

From the 1920s through the 1940s, bright polished brass was considered cheap and in bad taste. The metal bases and fittings, whether brass or pot metal, were always done in an antiqued finish. The antiqued finishes can range from a simple patina with lightly polished highlights to an overall dull charcoal gray. The antiqued finishes were very durable, and many survive intact today. Several lamp companies also used brass fittings painted to match or contrast the lamp bodies. The painted fittings are usually found worn and faded, but they retain more value in worn condition than if the original color has been removed.

Value of the 1920s and 1930s lamps is greatly affected by the condition of the metal parts. Lamps with metal parts that have lost their patina or antiquing due to polishing can be devalued by as much as 50 percent. This is particularly relevant to pot metal fittings that no longer resemble the antiqued brass they once emulated. Lamps that have been "updated" or "modernized" by having their original stem and double pull-chain sockets replaced with new harps and sockets can lose up to half their value. In addition, L.D. Bloch lamps of the 1920s missing their original heavy ornamental cast brass or iron harps are less desirable than lamps with original harps. While it is indeed wise to replace worn wiring and switches, all original metalwork should be retained. Lamp bodies that were originally fitted with a socket and harp lose only a portion of their value when the fittings are missing, as sockets and harps comparable to the originals can easily be found. However, large table lamps once fitted with a metal base and stem with double pull-chain sockets are a different situation. Because the pottery lamp body can outlast the relatively fragile pot metal fittings, lamp bodies (especially #1023 Lovebird lamp bodies) are often found without fittings. Since it is nearly impossible to find replacement fittings of the same style and quality as the originals, lamp bodies missing stems, sockets, and bases usually sell for about 25 to 50 percent of the value of an original complete lamp.

Lathe-turned brass finials in 1920s classical and modern styles, usually from 2" to 3½" tall.

A variety of metal finials was used through the years. L.D. Bloch lamps of the 1920s with heavy ornamented harps were usually surmounted by a large stylized cast brass or iron lotus finial painted or antiqued to match the harp. Cast brass bird finials were consistently mounted on the Lovebird lamps. Cast and lathe-turned brass finials in an appropriate style were used on other lamps. Simpler lamps of the 1930s were usually fitted with inexpensive brass or wood finials. The presence of original lotus or bird finials can add up to $25.00 to a lamp's value, but the value of other styles of brass or wood ball finials is negligible.

Throughout the 1930s, wood balls and eggs painted or stained to match the lamp bodies were used frequently, usually 2" to 3" tall.

In 1933, Martin Stangl developed a way to securely attach a ceramic lamp finial to its mounting screw, for which he was issued a patent on July 16, 1935. Stangl's new finial construction made possible the use of ceramic finials with ceramic lamps. Many of the lamps marketed directly to retailers by Stangl were available with coordinating finials.

Over 30 different styles of ceramic finials were designed, but only eight were used consistently. The ceramic finials often broke and were discarded, so are hard to find. An original matching ceramic finial can add up to $50.00 to the value of a lamp.

Bud lamp finial, 2", Dark Orchid glaze, 1930s.

Flame lamp finials, 2½", Oxblood and Satin White glazes, 1930s.

Chinese lamp finial, 2¼", Alice Blue glaze, 1930s.

Flower lamp finial, 2¾", Silver Green and Chinese Ivory combination glaze, 1930s.

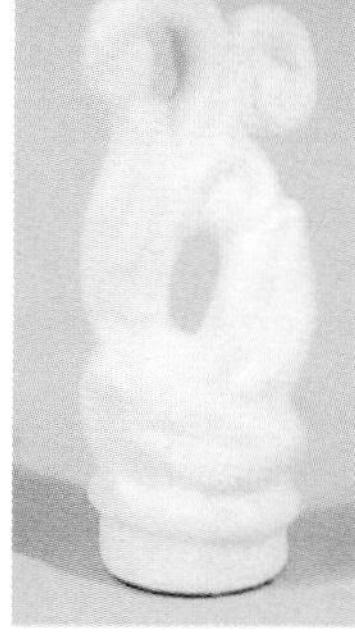

Fronds lamp finial, 3", Satin White glaze, 1930s.

Spiral Ball finials, 1½", Maize and Dark Green glazes, 1930s.

Briefly during the early 1960s, ceramic lamp finials in the Antique Gold finish were produced. Most lamp companies, however, simply used inexpensive brass finials. Ceramic Antique Gold lamp finials are extremely rare and can add up to $30.00 to the value of an Antique Gold lamp.

Globe Antique Gold lamp finial, 2".
Courtesy of Dave and Betty Stangl Thomas.

Lamp Glazes and Finishes

Because the lamp bodies were already special-order items, lamp jobbers could order them in any type of body, glaze, or finish. Martin Stangl developed a pricing structure based on cost per square-inch of pottery in addition to the base cost of the lamp shape. Cost prices often varied from one jobber to the next. Daison was charged 2¼¢ per inch for both glaze decorated and Fayence Crackle glazes, while Bloch was paying 1½¢ plus 10 percent per square-inch for glaze decorated lamps. Both companies paid 1½¢ plus 10 percent for Antiquing. All jobbers were charged 25 percent more for handmade lamps than mold-cast lamps and Multi-Color glaze was 1½¢ per square-inch plus 30 percent. Companies dealing in higher-grade lamps, such as Daison or L.D. Bloch, often ordered more costly finishes, such as crackled, decorated, and antiqued. Antiquing was simply a brown stain applied to glazed pottery then wiped off the piece's highlights, leaving the antiquing wash in the crevices of the design.

Detail of #1036 Boudoir Lovebird lamp with Chinese Ivory glaze with original antiquing finish.

Sadly, over the years, misguided lamp owners have removed a good deal of original antiquing by mistaking it for dirt. A lamp can always be identified as once being antiqued by the permanent stains on the unglazed ceramic foot left by the antiquing solution. Pristine, original antiquing on the pottery portion can add up to 25 percent to the value of an original lamp, but lamps with damaged or missing original antiquing can lose up to 25 percent of their value.

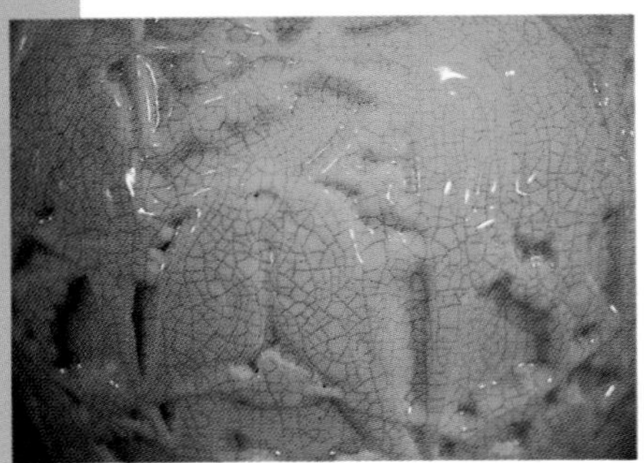

Close-up of #1023 Lovebird lamp in Persian Yellow Crackle glaze with accentuated crackling. Crackle glazes were washed with a staining solution resembling strong tea to produce the well-defined crackle figure.

Silver Green and Persian Yellow are the glazes most often found on 1920s lamps. Chinese Ivory and Rose were used more frequently on lamps than on vases. Colonial Blue is an ordinary glaze on vases and small lamps but is nearly nonexistent on large table lamps. All of these glazes could be had in a crackle finish at added cost. Crackled solid-color glazes are often mistaken for crazing, but crackling was a desired lamp finish in the 1920s and was usually antiqued to accentuate the crackle.

During the 1930s, Apple Green, Rust, and Oxblood were popular lamp glazes. Also during the 1930s, Martin Stangl glazed many lamp shapes in what he described as "cheap lamp glazes for Flemington." The Flemington colors were glossy dark green, tan, medium blue, and light yellow. Lamps with these inexpensive glazes were sold only at the Flemington Outlet.

Detail of the #1099 Girl and Dog lamp showing the fine crazing of the Rose Crackle glaze.

The value of highly detailed lamps is based on the crispness of modeling and detail. Lamps that were cast of worn molds that lack detail can lose up to 20 percent of the value of a lamp bearing excellent detail and crisp modeling. Values are based on lamps in pristine condition with original fittings, bases, harps, and sockets intact. The glaze colors in the photo captions describe the color of the lamp shown. Most lamps were produced in a variety of finishes, and the value listed is for lamps of similar finish. Measurements are for the ceramic parts only and do not include harps, stems, sockets or bases.

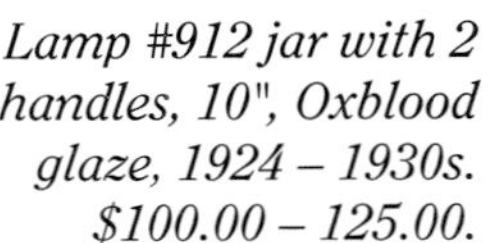

Lamp #912 jar with 2 handles, 10", Oxblood glaze, 1924 – 1930s. $100.00 – 125.00.

1924 Introductions

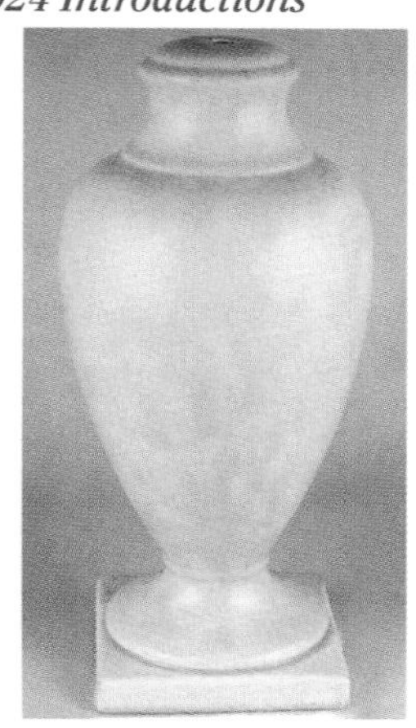

Lamp #918 Amphora, 16", square base, 1924 – late 1920s. $195.00 – 235.00. From the Stangl and Fulper archival collection, courtesy the Wheaton Village Museum of American Glass.

Lamp #941 Amphora, 6", with ceramic cap and wood base, Colonial Blue, 1924 – late 1920s. $70.00 – 85.00 each.

Lamp # 955, jar with metal cap and teak base, Rose glaze, made for Franklin, 1924 – late 1920s. $55.00 – 70.00.

Lamp #915 bottle, 12", Matte Blue glaze with original black-painted iron harp and finial, made for L.D. Bloch Co., 1924 – late 1920s. $170.00 – 195.00.

Not Shown:

#918 Amphora lamp, 14", solid-color glazes, 1920s. $175.00 – 200.00.
#918 Amphora lamp, 12", solid-color glazes, 1920s. $120.00 – 145.00.
#918 Amphora lamp, 10", solid-color glazes, 1920s. $95.00 – 110.00.
#918 Amphora lamp, 8", solid-color glazes, 1920s. $70.00 – 85.00.
#918 Amphora lamp, 6", solid-color glazes, 1920s. $55.00 – 65.00.
#923 Jug lamp base, 8", solid-color glazes, 1920s. $95.00 – 110.00.
#923 Jug lamp base, 8", Fulper Decorated, 1920s. $175.00 – 200.00.
#941 Amphora lamp, 13", with ceramic cap and wood base, solid-color glazes, 1920s. $130.00 – 160.00.
#941 Amphora lamp, 12", with ceramic cap and wood base, solid-color glazes, 1920s. $120.00 – 145.00.
#941 Amphora lamp, 10", with ceramic cap and wood base, solid-color glazes, 1920s. $100.00 – 125.00.

1925 Introductions

Not Shown:

#1004 Life Saver lamp base, 9", solid-color glazes, 1920s. $85.00 – 95.00.
#1010 Chinese lamp, 8½", solid-color glazes, made for L.D. Bloch Co. 1925 – 1930s. $275.00 – 300.00.

Lamp #970, 2 handles, 5½", Colonial Blue, 1925 – late 1920s. $60.00 – 75.00.

Lamp #972 Dancing Nudes with Faun, 12" Silver Green with antiquing, made for both L.D. Bloch Co. and Franklin, 1925 – late 1920s. $600.00 – 700.00.

Courtesy of the Hill-Fulper-Stangl Museum.

Lamp #980 bottle, 8", Colonial Blue with heavy cast brass fittings, made for L.D. Bloch Co. 1925 – late 1920s. $100.00 – 125.00.

Lamp #983 Egg shape, 4½", Colonial Blue with faux marble iron base and antiqued fittings, made for L.D. Bloch Co. 1925 – late 1920s. $85.00 – 95.00.

Lamp #1010 Chinese, 8½", Multi-Color glaze, made for L.D. Bloch Co., 1920s. $375.00 – 425.00. Courtesy of the Hill-Fulper-Stangl Museum.

Lamp #1011 flat bottle, 12", Silver Green with black-painted brass fittings and wood base, made for L.D. Bloch Co., 1925 – late 1920s. $200.00 – 250.00.

Lamp #1013 oval with Lion heads, 11", Persian Yellow, made for L.D. Bloch Co., 1925 – late 1920s. $200.00 – 250.00. Courtesy of the Hill-Fulper-Stangl Museum.

Lamp #1023 Lovebird, 9" Persian Yellow with original antiquing and fittings, made for L.D. Bloch Co., 1925 – 1930s. $255.00 – 295.00. Courtesy of the Hill-Fulper-Stangl Museum.

Lamp #1030 flat ovoid, 8½"x9¾", Persian Yellow with original fittings and lotus finial, made for L.D. Bloch Co., 1925 – late 1920s. $190.00 – 225.00.

Lamp #1032 four-sided jar, 5¾", Silver Green, made for L.D. Bloch Co. (matches the #1050 tobacco set also made for Bloch), 1925 – late 1920s. $65.00 – 80.00.

Lamp #1036 Boudoir Lovebird, 5½", Chinese Ivory with original antiquing and fittings, made for L.D. Bloch Co., 1925 – late 1920s. $85.00 – 95.00.

Lamp #1037 Oval Lovebird, 8", Silver Green with original shade and finial, made for L.D. Bloch Co., 1925 – 1930s. $200.00 – 250.00.

Lamp #1041 flat oval, 6", Persian Yellow, made for L.D. Bloch Co., 1925 – late 1920s. $70.00 – 85.00.

Lamp #1043 cone-shape base, 6½" Colonial Blue with original blue-painted iron and steel fittings and decorated glass shade, made for L.D. Bloch Co., 1925 – late 1920s. $95.00 – 110.00.

Lamp #1044 2-piece jar and square base, 8½", made for L.D. Bloch Co., 1925 – late 1920s. $110.00 – 135.00.

Lamp #1046 French oval, decorated, 8½"x7½", underglaze decorated, made for L.D. Bloch Co. 1925 – late 1920s. $350.00 – 375.00. Courtesy of the Hill-Fulper-Stangl Museum.

Lamp #1062 oval, 9½", Silver Green with original green-painted harp and lotus finial, made for Fourman Bros., 1925 – late 1920s. $150.00 – 175.00.

Lamp #1071 special square base, 11½", Persian Yellow, made for L.D. Bloch Co., 1925 – late 1920s. $225.00 – 275.00. Courtesy of the Hill-Fulper-Stangl Museum.

1926 Introductions

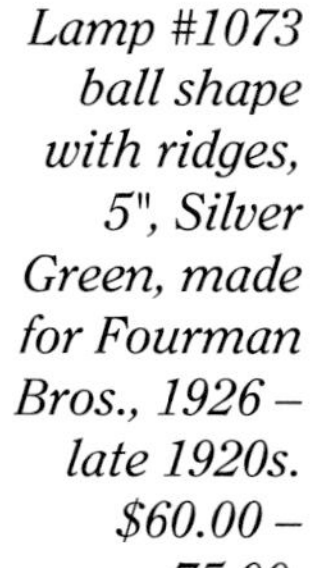

Lamp #1073 ball shape with ridges, 5", Silver Green, made for Fourman Bros., 1926 – late 1920s. $60.00 – 75.00.

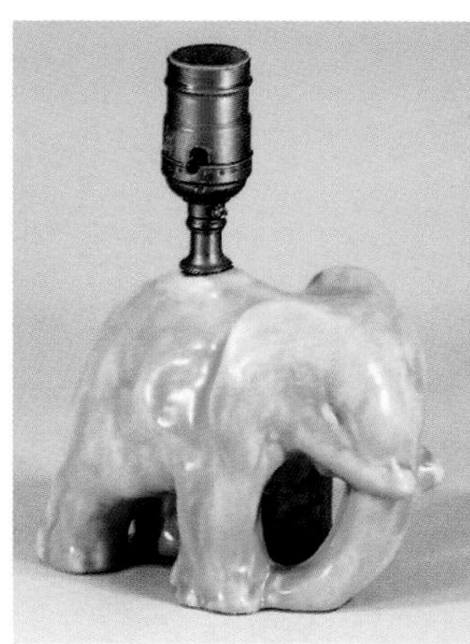

Lamp #1077 Large Elephant, 5½"x 6¼", Silver Green, made for Rena Rosenthal (also made as a figurine), 1926 – 1928. $300.00 – 350.00. Courtesy of the Hill-Fulper-Stangl Museum.

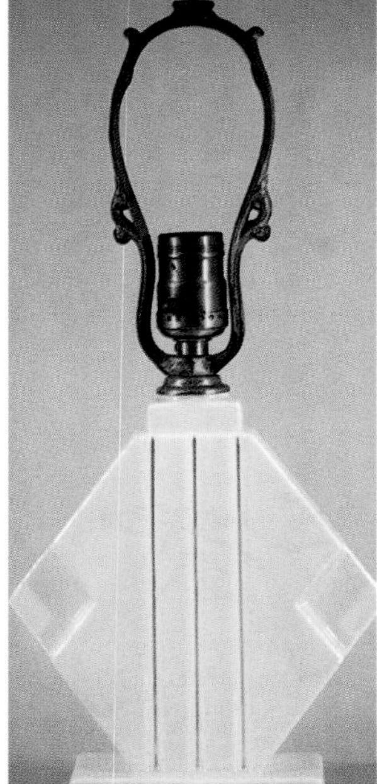

Lamp #1081 Square Modern, 8¼", Persian Yellow with original ornamental heavy cast brass harp. Matches dinnerware pattern #1081 Square Modern, 1926 – late 1920s. $500.00 – 600.00.

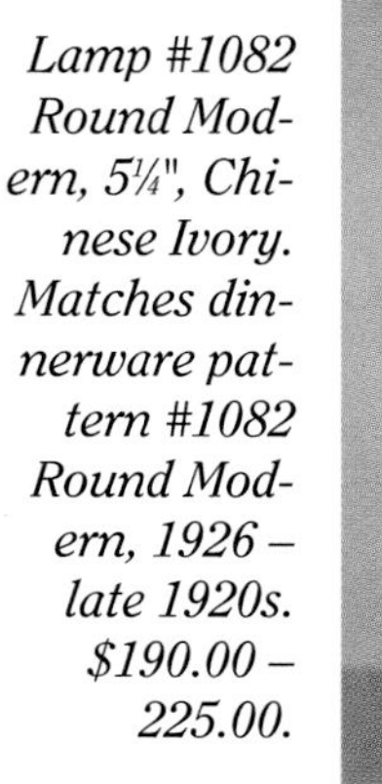

Lamp #1082 Round Modern, 5¼", Chinese Ivory. Matches dinnerware pattern #1082 Round Modern, 1926 – late 1920s. $190.00 – 225.00.

Lamp #1083 Colonial primitive, 7", Persian Yellow, $100.00 – 125.00; and #1084 Colonial primitive, 5", Colonial Blue, $85.00 – 95.00, 1926 – late 1920s. In 1927, these two shapes were also produced as #1156 and #1157 with Multi-Color glaze.

Lamp #1090 modern handle, 10¼", Oxblood glaze with original spun brass base and maroon-painted harp, made for Macy's Department Store, 1926 – 1930s. $190.00 – 225.00.

Lamp #1093 oval with designs, 8?", Apple Green, made for L.D. Bloch Co., 1926 – late 1920s. $50.00 – 60.00.

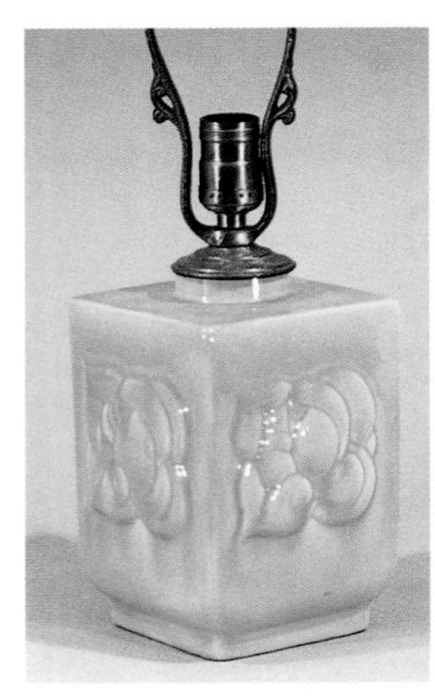

Lamp #1096 square with flat flowers, 8", Silver Green, made for L.D. Bloch Co., 1926 – late 1920s. $150.00 – 175.00.

Lamp #1099 oblong with girl and dog, 8", Persian Yellow, made for L.D. Bloch Co., 1926 – late 1920s. $175.00 – 200.00.

Lamp #1099 oblong with girl and dog, 8", Dark Rose Crackle, made for L.D. Bloch Co., 1926 – late 1920s. $225.00 – 250.00.

Lamp #1101 flat modern boudoir, 6¼", Silver Green, made for L.D. Bloch Co., 1926 – late 1920s. $100.00 – 125.00 each.

Lamp #1103 Moon and Stars, 7¼", solid-color glazes, made for L.D. Bloch Co., 1926 – late 1920s. $275.00 – 300.00. Original Flemington Outlet catalog drawing courtesy of Merrill and Christl Stangl Bacheler.

Lamp #1104 round diamond cut, 5¾", Rose Crackle, made for L.D. Bloch Co., 1926 – late 1920s. $130.00 – 150.00.

Lamp #1105 flat modern wheel, 5¾", Silver Green, made for L.D. Bloch Co., 1926 – late 1920s. $130.00 – 150.00. Courtesy of the Brian and Cristi Hahn collection.

1927 Introductions

Not Shown:

#1124 Primitive handmade slanting handle lamp, 7½", solid-color glazes, 1927 – early 1930s. $130.00 – 150.00.
#1126 Primitive handmade ball with rings lamp, 7", solid-color glazes, 1927 – early 1930s. $110.00 – 135.00.
#1128L Primitive handmade lamp, 4 double handles, 8", solid-color glazes, 1927 – early 1930s. $170.00 – 195.00.
#1128S Primitive handmade lamp, 4 double handles, 4", solid-color glazes, 1927 – early 1930s. $150.00 – 165.00.
#1129L Primitive handmade lamp, 3 double handles, 8¾" solid-color glazes, 1927 – early 1930s. $170.00 – 195.00.
#1129S Primitive handmade lamp, 3 double handles, 5¾", solid-color glazes, 1927 – early 1930s. $150.00 – 165.00.
#1177 Primitive lamp, 6" (same as vase #1153) solid-color glazes, made for Daison, 1927 – 1928. $70.00 – 85.00.
#1177 Primitive lamp, 6" (same as vase #1153) Multi-Color glaze, made for Daison, 1927 – 1928. $175.00 – 200.00.
#1178 Primitive lamp, 9" (same as vase #1153) solid-color glazes, made for Daison, 1927 – 1928. $130.00 – 150.00.
#1178 Primitive lamp, 9" (same as vase #1153) Multi-Color glaze, made for Daison, 1927 – 1928. $290.00 – 325.00.

Lamp #1130 square, dome top, 8½", Chinese Ivory with blue splatter, made for Franklin, 1927 only. $130.00 – 150.00. From the Stangl and Fulper archival collection, courtesy the Wheaton Village Museum of American Glass.

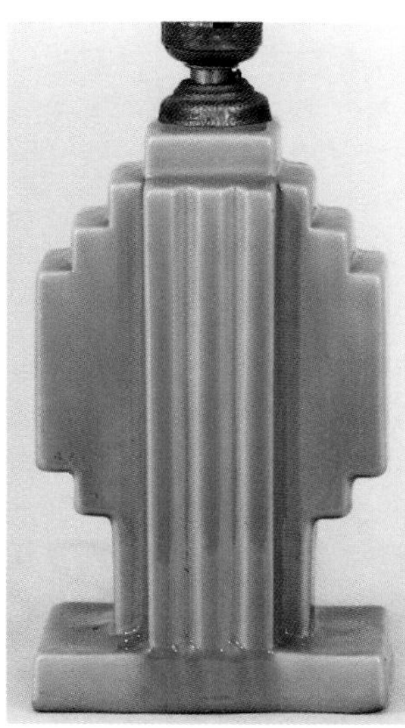

Lamp #1132 modern square blocks, 9" Turquoise glaze, made for Franklin, 1927 – 1928. $150.00 – 175.00. From the Stangl and Fulper archival collection, courtesy the Wheaton Village Museum of American Glass.

Lamp #1135 modern flat oval disk, 9", Persian Yellow, made for Franklin, 1927 – 1928. $150.00 – 175.00. Courtesy of the Brian and Cristi Hahn collection.

Lamp #1136 diamond cut ball, 10" Silver Green, made for Franklin, 1927 – 1928. $170.00 – 195.00. Courtesy of the Hill-Fulper-Stangl Museum.

Lamp #1156 Colonial primitive, 7", Multi-Color glaze, $195.00 – 235.00; and #1157 Colonial primitive, 5", Yellow Multi-Color glaze, $150.00 – 175.00, 1927 – late 1920s. In 1926, these two shapes were also produced as #1083 and #1084 with solid-color glazes.

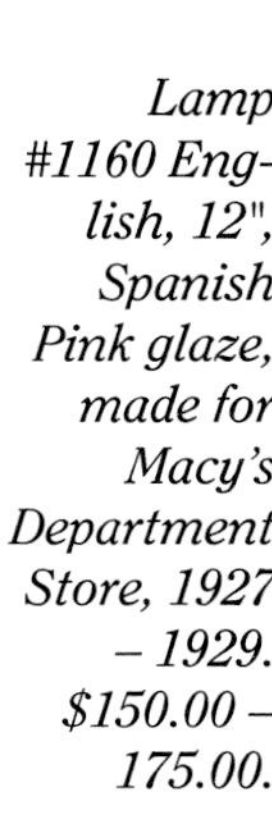

Lamp #1160 English, 12", Spanish Pink glaze, made for Macy's Department Store, 1927 – 1929. $150.00 – 175.00.

1928 Introductions

Lamp #1183 Archers, 10" Light Rose, made for L.D. Bloch Co., 1928 – 1929. $550.00 – 650.00.

Comparison of Silver Green and Dark Rose Crackle #1183 Archers lamps, made for L.D. Bloch Co., 1928 – 1929. Silver Green or Persian Yellow #1183 Archers lamps. $400.00 – 450.00. Courtesy of the Hill-Fulper-Stangl Museum.

Lamp #1185 Square Modern, 9", Silver Green, 1928 – 1930. $175.00 – 200.00.

1929 Introductions

Not Shown:

#1213 pleated flowerpot lamp, 8", solid-color glazes, 1929 – 1930. $100.00 – 125.00.
#1213 pleated flowerpot lamp, 6", solid-color glazes, 1929 – 1930. $70.00 – 85.00.
#1213 pleated flowerpot lamp, 4", solid-color glazes, 1929 – 1930. $70.00 – 85.00.
#1226 Primitive ball, indents, 8", Multi-Color glaze, 1929 – 1930. $375.00 – 400.00.
#1226 Primitive ball, indents, 8", solid-color glazes, 1929 – 1930. $130.00 – 150.00.
#1246 ball lamp, 10½", solid-color glazes, 1929 – 1930s. $95.00 – 110.00.
#1246 ball lamp, 8½", solid-color glazes, 1929 – 1930s. $80.00 – 90.00.
#1246 ball lamp, 7", solid-color glazes, 1929 – 1930s. $60.00 – 75.00.

Primitive ball lamp bases #1226 in Rose Multi-Color and Blue Multi-Color glazes, $375.00 – 400.00 each. From the Stangl and Fulper archival collection, courtesy the Wheaton Village Museum of American Glass.

Lamp #1228 ovoid, scroll handles, 9½", Leaf Green, 1929 – 1930s. $110.00 – 135.00. Courtesy of the Brian and Cristi Hahn collection.

Lamp #1232 German ball, 8½", Rust glaze, 1929 – 1930s. $150.00 – 165.00.

Lamp #1238 handmade jar, 3-handles, 9", Persian Yellow, 1929 – 1935. $130.00 – 150.00.

Lamp #643 vase, 2 handles, 8¼", Yellow Orange glaze, 1920s – 1930s. $95.00 – 130.00.

Lamp #1263 handmade, 2 handles, 13", Buff and Silver Green glaze (original bronze fittings have been replaced), made for Mario Studios, NY, Hubley Mfg. Co., 1930 only. $400.00 – 450.00. Courtesy of the Robert Sherman collection.

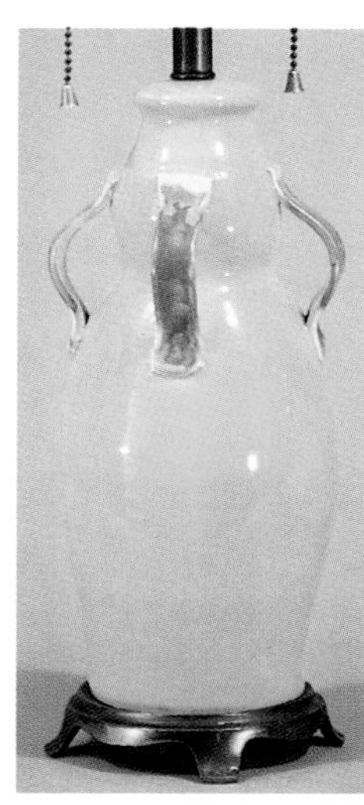

Lamp #1264 handmade, 4 handles, 13", Persian Yellow and Orange glaze with original bronze fittings marked "Hubley," made for Mario Studios, NY, Hubley Mfg. Co., 1930 only. $400.00 – 450.00. Courtesy of the Hill-Fulper-Stangl Museum.

Lamp #1267 French jar, 9", Persian Yellow with original fittings and wood base, styled after a Sabino of Paris art glass vase, 1930 – early 1930s. $165.00 – 185.00. Courtesy of the Brian and Cristi Hahn collection.

Lamp #1276, scroll handles, 9", Persian Yellow, made for Davart, 1930 – early 1930s. $125.00 – 145.00.

Lamp #1279 oval oblong, 6¾", Persian Yellow, made for Davart, 1930 – early 1930s. $150.00 – 175.00.

Lamp #1287 oval leaves, 9", Silver Green, made for Katherine White, 1930 – early 1930s. $95.00 – 110.00.

Lamp #1292 low bottle, 12", Black #35 glaze, made for Simon Jay-Willfred, 1930 – early 1930s. $120.00 – 145.00. Courtesy of the Hill-Fulper-Stangl Museum.

Lamp #1294 Diana and deer, 10", Silver Green, made for Daison, NY, 1930 – early 1930s. $175.00 – 200.00.

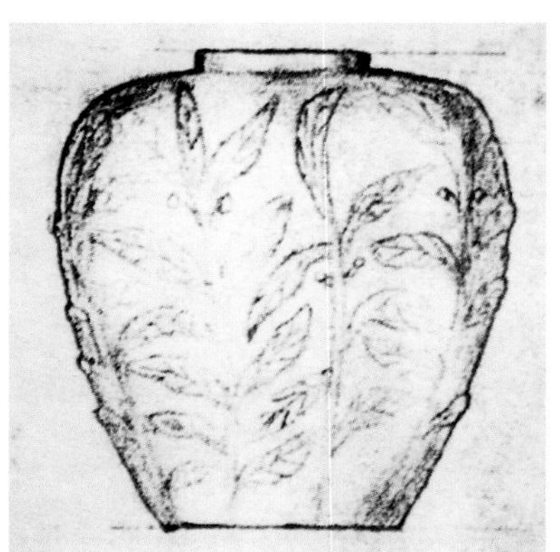

Lamp #1296 leaves, 9" solid-color glazes, 1930 – early 1930s. $170.00 – 195.00. Original Flemington Outlet catalog drawing courtesy of Merrill and Christl Stangl Bacheler.

Lamp #1341 Hunters, 10", Silver Green on left, antiqued Persian Yellow on right, made for Davart, 1930 – early 1930s. $350.00 – 375.00. Courtesy of the Hill-Fulper-Stangl Museum.

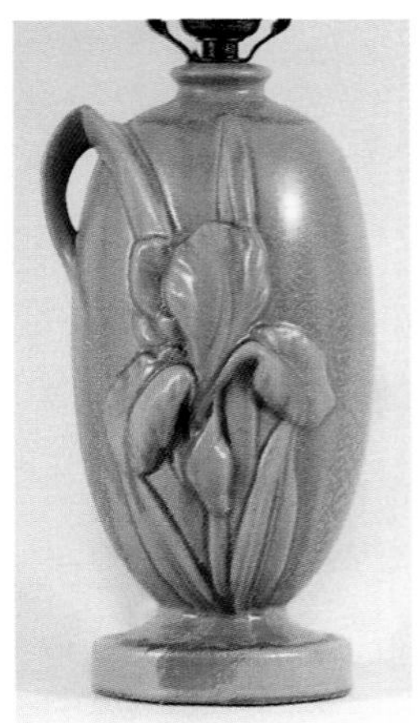

Lamp #1349 Oval Iris, 9¼", Apple Green, made for Katherine White, 1930 – early 1930s. $150.00 – 165.00. Courtesy of Kay Hackett.

Lamp #1350 cylinder with square base, 10"x4", Chinese Ivory and Silver Green combination glaze, made for Katherine White, 1930 – early 1930s. $150.00 – 175.00.

Lamp #1352 urn, 2 handles and base, 2 pieces, 8½", Dark Blue Matte, made for Katherine White, 1930 – early 1930s. $120.00 – 145.00.

Not Shown:

#1356-A plain lamp base, 10½", solid-color glazes, $50.00 – 60.00.

#1356-A plain lamp base, 10½", Terra Rose colors, 1950 – 1959, $50.00 – 60.00.

#1356 Musicians lamp base, 10½", Silver Green with raised motifs depicting a jazz orchestra and chorus line of nude dancers with an audience, 1930 only. $700.00 – 800.00. From the Stangl and Fulper archival collection, courtesy the Wheaton Village Museum of American Glass.

Lamp #1357 Bird lamp base, 9½", Oxblood glaze, each section is adorned with a different bird, flower or fruit motif, 1930 – 1933. $190.00 – 225.00. Courtesy of the Hill-Fulper-Stangl Museum.

Lamp #1360 twist candle, 10"x5", Black glaze, made for Davart, 1930 – early 1930s. $85.00 – 95.00.

Lamp #1371 round candle boudoir, 3"x4", Silver Green, made for Katherine White, 1930 – early 1930s. $60.00 – 75.00.

Lamp #1372 square base urn, 8¼", Apple Green, made for Katherine White, 1930 – early 1930s. $55.00 – 65.00.

Lamp #1377 fluted bottle, 10", Sunburst glaze, made for Simon Jay-Willfred, 1930 – early 1930s. $190.00 – 225.00.

#1377 fluted bottle, 10", solid-color glazes, made for Simon Jay-Willfred, 1930 – early 1930s. $100.00 – 125.00.

1931 Introductions

Not Shown:

#1381-B ivy ball stand lamp, 6½", solid-color glazes, $85.00 – 95.00.

#1381-B ivy ball stand lamp, 6½", Sunburst glaze, $200.00 – 250.00.

Lamp #1405 small ball, 6", glaze-decorated over pink bisque, with original hand-painted silk shade, made for Davart, 1931 – 1932. $175.00 – 200.00.
Courtesy of the Hill-Fulper-Stangl Museum.

Lamp #1409 small Moroccan design, 6½" Silver Green, made for Wilheim Co., 1931 – 1932. $95.00 – 110.00.

Lamp #1410 urn, square base, 2 handles, 12", Silver Green with original green-painted fittings, made for Wilheim Co. 1931 – 1932. $190.00 – 225.00.

Lamp #1424 4-footed base, fan handles, 8½", Light Oxblood glaze, made for Wilheim Co., 1931 – 1932. $120.00 – 145.00.

Lamp #1425 Moroccan allover design, 9½" Purple, made for Wilheim Co., 1931 – 1932. $170.00 – 195.00.

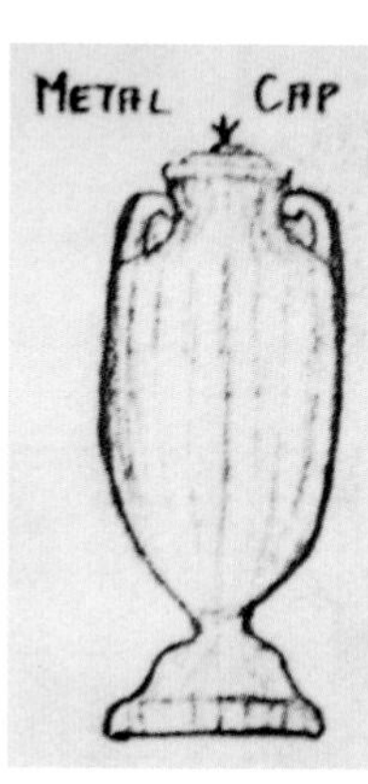

Lamp #1441 2 handle, 8", solid-color glazes, 1930s. $70.00 – 85.00.
Original Flemington Outlet catalog drawing courtesy of Merrill and Christl Stangl Bacheler.

Lamp #1448 long handles, 7", Persian Yellow, made for Davart, 1931 – 1935. $75.00 – 95.00.

Lamp #1474 concave fluted cone, 7½", Oxblood glaze on left, Butterscotch glaze on right, made for Davart, 1931 – 1935. $130.00 – 160.00 each.

Lamp #1475 Milano cone, handles and base, Silver Green (original stem and pull-chain sockets have been replaced), made for Davart, 1931 – 1935. $175.00 – 200.00.

Lamp #1481 square base, 2 pieces, 7", Dark Orchid glaze, made for Lighting Specialties, Co., 1931 – 1932. $95.00 – 110.00 each. Courtesy of the Hill-Fulper-Stangl Museum.

Lamp #1482 large barrel, 8", Apple Green glaze, 1931 – 1935. $85.00 – 95.00.

Lamp #1489 small barrel, 7½", Persian Yellow with original shade and finial, 1931 – 1935. $85.00 – 95.00 (add $75.00 – 100.00 for an original shade and finial).

Lamp #1492 Corinthian leaves, 9", Oxblood with Yellow leaves, 1931 – 1933, $150.00 – 165.00. Courtesy of the Hill-Fulper-Stangl Museum.

Lamp #1492 Corinthian leaves, 9", Rust with Leaf Green leaves, 1931 – 1933, $165.00 – 185.00. Courtesy of the Brian and Cristi Hahn collection.

Lamp #1493 natural design daisy, 11", Silver Green with Leaf Green and Yellow flowers, 1931 – 1933. $175.00 – 200.00. Courtesy of the Hill-Fulper-Stangl Museum.

Lamp #1503 urn, 2 handles, 8¾", Rust glaze, 1931 – 1933. $150.00 – 165.00.

Lamp #1505 garland, 2 handles, 8½", Ivory glaze, 1931 – 1933. $70.00 – 85.00.

Lamp #1509 large handles, 11½", Rust glaze, 1931 – 1935. $110.00 – 135.00.

Not Shown:

#1497 medium radio lamp, urn, 10", solid-color glazes, made for International Light, Inc., 1931 – 1933. $130.00 – 160.00.

Lamp #1510 large scroll handle, 8½", Satin White glaze, 1931 – 1935. $100.00 – 125.00.

Three #1524 large Modern radio lamps, 13", Oxblood, Sunburst, and Rust glazes, made for International Light, Inc., 1931 – 1933. Sunburst, $400.00 – 450.00; Oxblood or Rust glazes, $255.00 – 295.00 each. From the Stangl and Fulper archival collection, courtesy the Wheaton Village Museum of American Glass.

Lamp #1532 twisted top, 12", Stoneware art glaze, 1960s. $120.00 – 145.00. 1930s solid-color glazes, $95.00 – 110.00.

Radio Lamps #1525 small, 8", glazed in Stangl's gloss tan and Flemington Green glazes, made for International Light, Inc., 1931 – 1933. $80.00 – 90.00 each. Courtesy of the Ben and Pauline Jensen collection.

Lamp #1533 twist handle, 9", Apple Green, 1931 – 1935. $150.00 – 165.00.

Lamp #1534 Grecian, 2 handles, 8¼", Rust glaze, 1931 – 1935. $120.00 – 145.00. Courtesy of the Brian and Cristi Hahn collection.

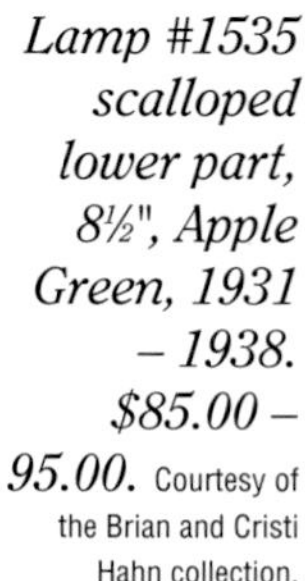

Lamp #1535 scalloped lower part, 8½", Apple Green, 1931 – 1938. $85.00 – 95.00. Courtesy of the Brian and Cristi Hahn collection.

Lamp #1536 shell top and base, 9", Apple Green glaze, 1931 – 1935. $110.00 – 135.00.

Lamp #1537 handled, Rust glaze, 1931 – 1933. $120.00 – 145.00.

Not Shown:

#1532 twisted top lamp, 12", solid-color glazes, 1931 – 1935. $95.00 – 110.00.

#1532 twisted top lamp, 12", Antique Gold, 1960s. $95.00 – 110.00.

#1535 scalloped lower part, 8½", Antique Gold, 1960s. $70.00 – 85.00.

#1535 scalloped lower part, 8½", Stoneware art glaze, 1960s. $85.00 – 95.00.

1932 Introductions

Lamp #1557 3-handle, mold-cast (same as #1124), Sunburst glaze, 1931 – 1934. $195.00 – 235.00. Courtesy of the Lewis/Servis collection.

Lamp #1560 melon, 6½", Silver Green, made for Davart, 1932 – 1935. $150.00 – 175.00.

Lamp #1563 fluted, grapes, 12", Apple Green glaze, 1931 – 1933. $175.00 – 200.00.

Lamp #1565 bottle, 4 handles, 10½", Oxblood with Ivory Antique handles, made for Davart, 1932 – 1935. $175.00 – 200.00.

Lamp #1566 cone bottle, 2 handles, 8½", Dark Tan glaze, made for Davart, 1932 – 1935. $150.00 – 165.00.

Lamp #1603 footed melon, handles, 8½", Apple Green glaze on left, Yellow Orange glaze on right, 1932 – 1936. $95.00 – 130.00 each.

Lamp #1607 4-sided, handles, 8½", Apple Green over Buff glaze, 1932 – 1935. $150.00 – 165.00.

Lamp #1608 grillwork on top, 9", Apple Green over Buff glaze, 1932 – 1935. $150.00 – 175.00. Courtesy of the Robert Sherman collection.

Lamp #1608 grillwork on top, 9", Terra Rose colors, 1950 – early 1960s. $95.00 – 110.00. Courtesy of the Marcena North collection.

Lamp #1608 grillwork on top, 9", Antique Gold, early 1960s. $100.00 – 125.00.

#1557 3-handle lamp, mold-cast (same as #1124), solid-color glazes, 1931 – 1935. $130.00 – 150.00.

#1565 bottle lamp, 4 handles, 10½", single solid-color glaze, made for Davart, 1932 – 1935. $130.00 – 160.00.

Lamp #1609 ring handles, 7", Black glaze, made for S.S. Kresge, 1932 – 1933. $85.00 – 95.00. Courtesy of the Frank and Elizabeth Kramar collection.

Lamp #1618 pedestal square, cut-out orchid, 6¾"x4½", Ivory Antique glaze, 1932 – 1933. $150.00 – 165.00.

Lamp #1619 4-footed square, bird and berries, 6"x4½", Silver Green, 1932 – 1935. $95.00 – 110.00.

Davart 2-piece lamps, #1620, 5½", Persian Yellow, on right, $100.00 – 125.00; #1622 7", Apple Green, on left, $130.00 – 150.00.

#1618 pedestal square, orchid (not cut-out), 6¾"x4½", solid-color glazes, 1932 – 1935. $85.00 – 95.00.

#1620, 2-piece, round, 5½", with socket and harp, solid-color glazes, made for Davart, 1932 – 1935. $100.00 – 125.00.

#1622, 2-piece, round, 7", with stem and pull-chain sockets, solid-color glazes, made for Davart, 1932 – 1935. $130.00 – 150.00.

1933 Introductions

Not Shown:

The following children's lamp bases were closely based on the Sir John Tenniel illustrations of Lewis Carroll's *Alice's Adventures in Wonderland*. The lamps were produced only during 1933, and were available in hand-painted colors under the tinted Parchment glaze. These lamps were also produced in solid-color glazes.

#1650 Alice lamp base, 7", hand-painted, 1933 only. $450.00 – 500.00.

#1650 Alice lamp base, 7", solid-color glazes, 1933 only. $300.00 – 350.00.

#1651 King lamp base, 7", hand-painted, 1933 only. $400.00 – 450.00.

#1651 King lamp base, 7", solid-color glazes, 1933 only. $300.00 – 350.00.

#1652 White Rabbit lamp base, 7¼", solid-color glazes, 1933 only. $300.00 – 350.00.

Lamp #1652 White Rabbit, 7¼", hand-painted, 1933 only. $400.00 – 450.00. Courtesy of the Hill-Fulper-Stangl Museum.

Lamp #1653 Mad Hatter, 6¾", 1933 only. Hand-painted (left), $400.00 – 450.00; Silver Green, $300.00 – 350.00. Courtesy of the Robert and Tammie Cruser collection.

Lamp #1655 handmade candleholder, 6", Apple Green over Buff glaze, 1932 – 1935. $85.00 – 95.00.

Lamp #1664 handmade double handles, 9", Satin White with Blue Satin handles, 1933 – 1934. $195.00 – 235.00.

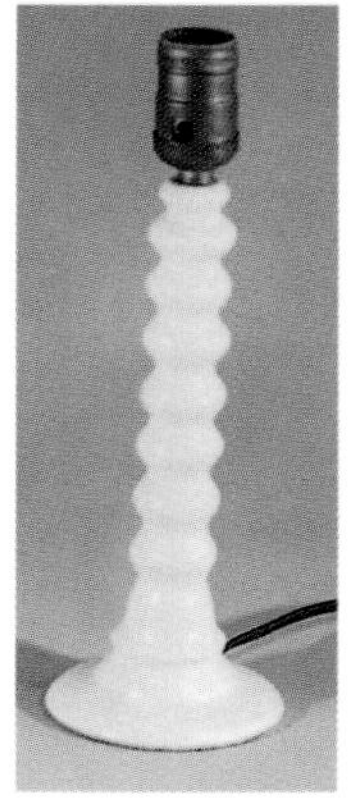

Lamp #1686 spool candles, 10", Satin White glaze (left), 1933 – 1940s, $65.00 – 80.00; Terra Rose colors (right), 1940s – 1950s, $65.00 – 80.00. Courtesy of Merrill and Christl Stangl Bacheler and the Brian and Cristi Hahn collection.

Lamp #1688 large candle, 2 handles, 10", hand-painted, blue underglaze color, 1950s – 1960s. $65.00 – 80.00. 1930s solid-color glazes, $60.00 – 75.00.
Courtesy of the Ben and Floss Avila collection.

Lamp #1709, large, 2 handles, 8½", Green Matte glaze, 1933 – 1940. $70.00 – 85.00.

Lamp #1713 "carved" decoration, 6¾", glaze-decorated, Gray with Ivory glaze, 1933 – 1934. $165.00 – 185.00.

Lamp #1706 "carved" decoration, 7¾", Silver Green glaze with silver-plated base and indirect socket, made for Rembrandt Lamp Co. 1933 – 1934. $100.00 – 125.00.

Lamp #1760 small base, curl handles, 6", Turquoise Blue glaze, 1933 – 1934. $70.00 – 85.00.
Courtesy of the Brian and Cristi Hahn collection.

#1688 large candle lamp, 2 handles, 10", solid-color glazes, 1933 – 1938. $60.00 – 75.00.
#1694 ringed ball lamp base (old #1126), 8½", solid-color glazes, 1933 – 1939. $100.00 – 125.00.
#1714 ball lamp (#1246) 7", Flemington colors (Stangl's "cheap" glazes), 1933 only. $60.00 – 75.00.
#1715 ball lamp (#1246) 8", Flemington colors (Stangl's "cheap" glazes), 1933 only. $80.00 – 90.00.
#1716 ball lamp (#1246) 10", Flemington colors (Stangl's "cheap" glazes), 1933 only. $95.00 – 110.00.
#1717 ball lamp (#1246) 15", Flemington colors (Stangl's "cheap" glazes), 1933 only. $130.00 – 160.00.
#1718 ball lamp (#1246) 7", solid platinum luster, 1933 only. $80.00 – 100.00.
#1719 ball lamp (#1246) 8", solid platinum luster, 1933 only. $95.00 – 130.00.
#1720 ball lamp (#1246) 9", solid platinum luster, 1933 only. $130.00 – 150.00.
#1721 ball lamp (#1246) 7", platinum luster bands, 1933 only. $80.00 – 100.00.
#1722 ball lamp (#1246) 8", platinum luster bands, 1933 only. $95.00 – 130.00.
#1723 ball lamp (#1246) 9", platinum luster bands, 1933 only. $130.00 – 150.00.

1934 Introductions

Not Shown:
#1832 large cylinder lamp, 10", solid-color glazes, 1930s. $85.00 – 95.00.

Lamp #1823, 2 scroll handles, 8", Green Matte glaze, 1934 – 1938. $95.00 – 110.00.

Lamp #1826, 2 flat handles, 8½", Yellow Orange glaze, 1934 – 1936. $95.00 – 110.00.

Lamps #1827, 3 ring handles, 8", Rust glaze on the left, Apple Green over Buff glaze on the right, 1934 – 1936. $150.00 – 175.00 each.

Lamp #1828 Modern 2 handles, 9", Rust glaze, 1934 – 1936. $130.00 – 150.00.

Lamp #1832 large cylinder, 10", Antique Gold, 1960s. $55.00 – 65.00. 1930s solid-color glazes, $85.00 – 95.00.

Lamp #1834 handmade ball (#1126) with rose, 7½", Rust glaze, 1934 – 1935. $170.00 – 195.00.

Lamp #1848 small bottle with handmade rose, 6", Yellow Orange glaze, 1934 – 1935. $110.00 – 135.00.

1935 Introductions

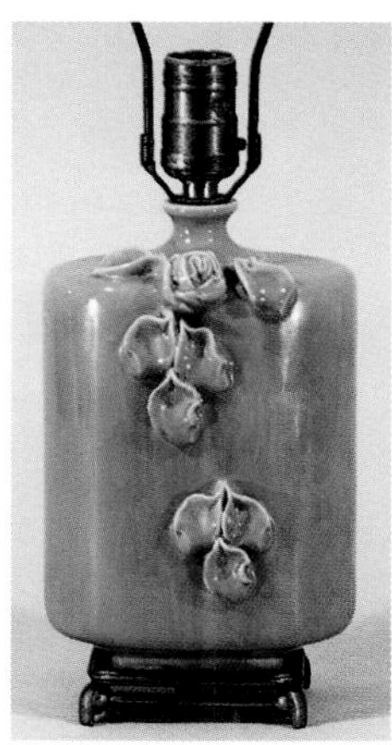

Lamp #1923 oval jar with handmade rose, 7", Silver Green, made for Davart, 1935 only. $170.00 – 195.00.

Lamp #1927 spool study lamp, 12", Rust glaze with original wiring, base switch, and indirect socket, 1935 – 1936. $150.00 – 175.00. From the Stangl and Fulper archival collection, courtesy the Wheaton Village Museum of American Glass.

Lamp #1936 square base column, 14", Alice Blue glaze with original indirect socket, 1935 – 1936. $195.00 – 235.00. From the Stangl and Fulper archival collection, courtesy the Wheaton Village Museum of American Glass.

Not Shown:

#1936 round base column lamp, 14", solid-color glazes, 1935 – 1936. $190.00 – 225.00.

#1942-L 4-handle lamp, 7", Tropical combination glazes, 1935 – 1936. $175.00 – 200.00.

#1959 Duck with sailor hat, 8", solid-color glazes, 1935 – 1936. $165.00 – 185.00.

#1963 lamp, swirled, 3 ball handles, 5", solid-color glazes, 1935 – 1938. $60.00 – 75.00.

#1964 lamp, 2 square handles, 5", Tropical combination glazes, 1935 only. $150.00 – 175.00.

#1964 lamp, 2 square handles, 5", solid-color glazes, 1935 – 1938. $60.00 – 75.00.

#1974 wheat and ribbon, square handles, 8½", solid-color glazes, 1935 – 1938. $150.00 – 165.00.

Lamp #1932 square base candleholder (#1584 candleholder), 7½" Apple Green glaze with original parchment shades, 1935 – 1937. $55.00 – 65.00 each.

Lamp #1963 swirled, 3 ball handles, 5", Ivory with Light Blue handles, 1935 only. $130.00 – 150.00. Courtesy of the Hill-Fulper-Stangl Museum.

Lamp #1968 with center insert, 9", Turquoise Blue glaze, 1935 – 1938. $120.00 – 145.00.

Lamp #1973 square base urn, curl handles, 9", Colonial Blue, 1935 – 1940. $95.00 – 110.00.

Lamp #1976 oval with flower handles, 10", Apple Green glaze, 1935 only. $150.00 – 165.00.

Lamp #1981 urn with flower, 8½", Stoneware art glaze, 1960s. $120.00 – 145.00.

Lamp #1978 tall Rococo lamp base, 14", Silver Green, 1935 – 1936. $175.00 – 200.00. Courtesy of the Hunterdon County Historical Society.

Lamp #1990 footed ball, 4 balls, 5", Oyster White & Eggplant Tropical combination glaze, 1935 only. $110.00 – 135.00. Courtesy of Primarily Pottery.

Lamp#1992 Duck, 5½", Colonial Blue, 1935 – 1938. $130.00 – 160.00.

Lamp #1991 Pig (old #1076), 4", Silver Green (left), 1935 – 1940, $120.00 – 145.00; Terra Rose Green (right), 1950s, $100.00 – 125.00.

Not Shown:

#1981 urn with flower lamp, 8½", solid-color glazes, 1935 – 1938. $120.00 – 145.00.
#1981 urn with flower lamp, 8½", Terra Rose colors, 1950s, $65.00 – 80.00.
#1981 urn with flower lamp, 8½", Antique Gold, 1960s. $65.00 – 80.00.
#1988 lamp, ball, 4 feet, 6", Tropical combination glazes, 1935 only. $120.00 – 145.00.
#1988 lamp, ball, 4 feet, 6", solid-color glazes, 1935 – 1938. $65.00 – 80.00.
#1988 lamp, ball, 4 feet, 6", Antique Gold, 1960s. $65.00 – 80.00.
#1988 lamp, ball, 4 feet, 6", Stoneware art glaze, 1960s. $60.00 – 75.00.
#1989 lamp, square lines, 6", Tropical combination glazes, 1935 only. $120.00 – 145.00.
#1989 lamp, square lines, 5", solid-color glazes, 1935 – 1938. $65.00 – 80.00.
#1990 footed ball, 4 balls, 5", solid-color glazes, 1935 – 1938. $60.00 – 75.00.
#1991 Pig lamp (old #1076), 4", Antique Gold, 1959 – 1960s. $100.00 – 125.00.

Lamp #1993 Elephant, 5", Colonial Blue, 1935 – 1938. $130.00 – 160.00.

Lamp #1995 rosettes, 5", Silver Green, 1935 – 1937. $55.00 – 65.00.

Not Shown:

#2033 urn, Greek band lamp, 12", solid-color glazes, 1935 – 1936. $150.00 – 165.00.

#2033 urn, Greek-band lamp, 12", Antique Gold, 1960s. $85.00 – 95.00.

1936 Introductions

Not Shown:

#3002 Scroll Ball lamp, 8½", solid-color glazes, 1936 – 1938. $110.00 – 135.00.

#3003 Scroll Leaf lamp, 8½", solid-color glazes, 1936 – 1938. $130.00 – 150.00.

#3012 Ginger Jar lamp, 7½", solid-color glazes, 1936 – 1938. $120.00 – 145.00.

Lamp #3001 Footed with Leaves, 8", Persian Yellow, $120.00 – 145.00.

Lamp #3003 Scroll Leaf, 8½", Matte Green, 1936 – 1938. $130.00 – 150.00. Courtesy of the Brian and Cristi Hahn collection.

1937 Introductions

Children's Lamp #3057 Child's Figures, 6½", Silver Green, 1937 – 1938. $120.00 – 145.00.

Children's Lamp #3058 Fish, 5¾", Satin White glaze, 1937 – 1941. $70.00 – 85.00.

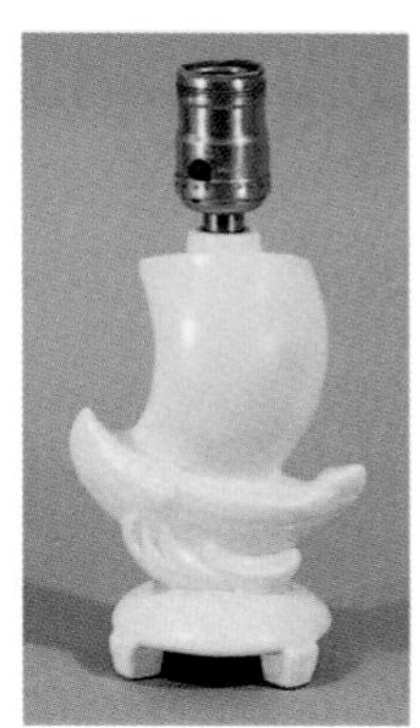

Children's Lamp #3059 Ship, 6", Satin White glaze, 1937 – 1938. $120.00 – 145.00.

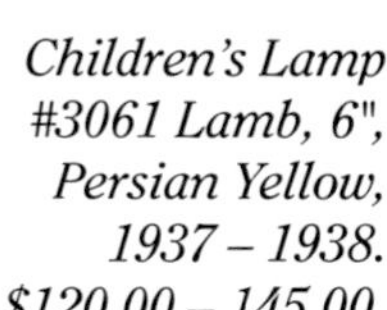

Children's Lamp #3061 Lamb, 6", Persian Yellow, 1937 – 1938. $120.00 – 145.00.

Not Shown:

#3058 Fish children's lamp, 5¾", Terra Rose colors, 1940s – 1950s. $55.00 – 65.00.

#3060 Old Mill children's lamp, 6½", solid-color glazes, 1937 – 1938. $120.00 – 145.00.

#3062 Urn & Scroll Handles, 8", solid-color glazes, 1937 – 1938. $110.00 – 135.00.

#3063 Chinese Handles, 7¾", solid-color glazes, 1937 – 1940. $100.00 – 125.00.

#3066 Six-Sided, 7", solid-color glazes, 1937 – 1940. $100.00 – 125.00.

#3066 Six-Sided, 7", Antique Gold, 1960s. $70.00 – 85.00.

#3066 Six-Sided, 7", Stoneware art glaze, 1960s. $85.00 – 95.00.

#3067 Chinese Flowers, 9", solid-color glazes, 1937 – 1940. $110.00 – 135.00.

#3068 Chrysanthemum, 8", solid-color glazes, 1937 – 1938. $100.00 – 125.00.

#3068 Chrysanthemum, 8", Antique Gold, 1960s. $80.00 – 90.00.

#3069 Animal Handles, 9", solid-color glazes, 1937 – 1938. $120.00 – 145.00.

#3070 Bird & Leaves, 8½", solid-color glazes, 1937 only. $120.00 – 145.00.

#3070 Bird & Leaves, 8½", Terra Rose colors, 1950s, $70.00 – 85.00.

#3070 Bird & Leaves, 8½", Antique Gold, 1960s, $85.00 – 95.00.

#3071 Chinese Low Jar, 8½", solid-color glazes, 1937 – 1938. $100.00 – 125.00.

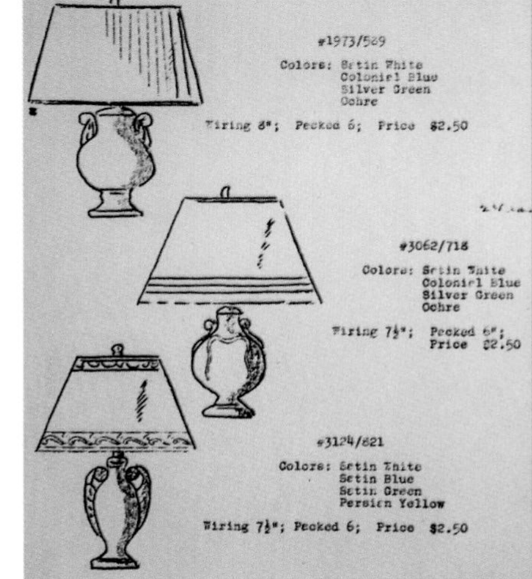

#1973/569
Colors: Satin White
Colonial Blue
Silver Green
Ochre
Wiring 8"; Packed 6; Price $2.50

#3062/718
Colors: Satin White
Colonial Blue
Silver Green
Ochre
Wiring 7½"; Packed 6"; Price $2.50

#3124/821
Colors: Satin White
Satin Blue
Satin Green
Persian Yellow
Wiring 7½"; Packed 6; Price $2.50

Original 1937 Stangl catalog page showing lamps #1973, #3062, and #3124. Courtesy of the Hill-Fulper-Stangl Museum.

Lamp #3063, Chinese Handles, 7¾", Colonial Blue, 1937 – 1940. $100.00 – 125.00.

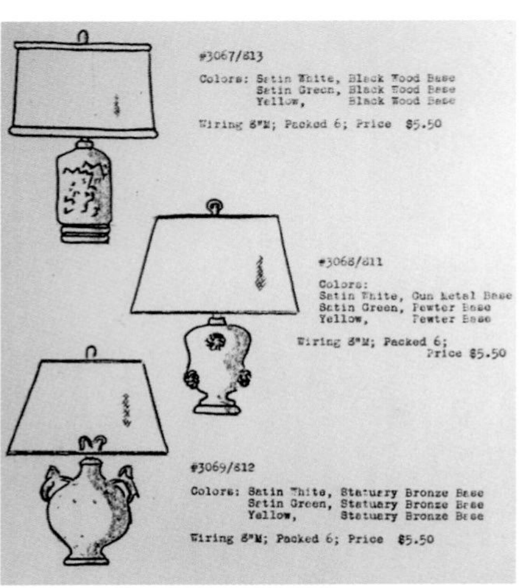

#3067/813

Colors: Satin White, Black Wood Base
Satin Green, Black Wood Base
Yellow, Black Wood Base

Wiring 8"M; Packed 6; Price $5.50

#3068/811

Colors:
Satin White, Gun Metal Base
Satin Green, Pewter Base
Yellow, Pewter Base

Wiring 8"M; Packed 6; Price $5.50

#3069/812

Colors: Satin White, Statuary Bronze Base
Satin Green, Statuary Bronze Base
Yellow, Statuary Bronze Base

Wiring 8"M; Packed 6; Price $5.50

Original Stangl catalog page showing lamps #3067, #3068, and #3069. Courtesy of the Hill-Fulper-Stangl Museum.

Lamp #3070 Bird & Leaves, 8½" Opaque Dark Green glaze, 1937 only. $120.00 – 145.00. Courtesy of the Hill-Fulper-Stangl Museum.

Children's Lamp #3119 Snow White, 7¾", Rose glaze, 1937 only. Detail of Snow White on front, $290.00 – 325.00. Courtesy of the Hill-Fulper-Stangl Museum.

Children's Lamp #3119 Snow White, 7¾", Colonial Blue glaze, 1937 only. Detail of Prince Charming on the back, $290.00 – 325.00.

Children's Lamp #3119 Snow White, 7¾", Colonial Blue with original printed paper shade.

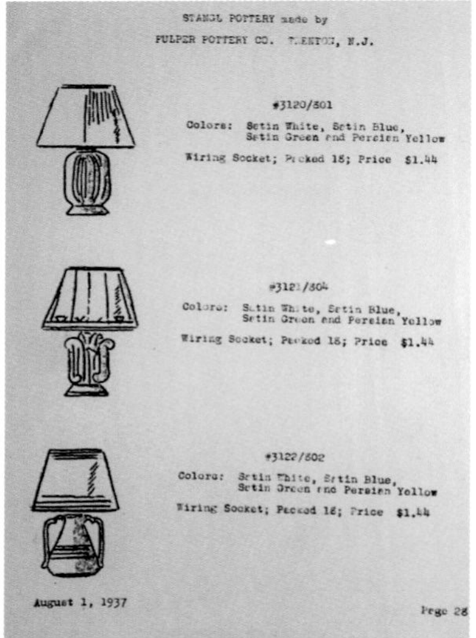

STANGL POTTERY made by
FULPER POTTERY CO. TRENTON, N.J.

#3120/801

Colors: Satin White, Satin Blue,
Satin Green and Persian Yellow

Wiring Socket; Packed 18; Price $1.44

#3121/804

Colors: Satin White, Satin Blue,
Satin Green and Persian Yellow

Wiring Socket; Packed 18; Price $1.44

#3122/802

Colors: Satin White, Satin Blue,
Satin Green and Persian Yellow

Wiring Socket; Packed 18; Price $1.44

August 1, 1937 Page 28

Original Stangl catalog page showing lamps #3120, #3121, and #3122. Courtesy of the Hill-Fulper-Stangl Museum.

Lamp #3120 Scalloped, 6", Satin White glaze with original shade, 1937 – 1945. $55.00 – 65.00.

Lamp #3121 Scroll, 6", Satin Blue glaze, 1937 – 1940. $60.00 – 75.00.

Lamps #3123 Vase, 2 handles, 6". Satin Blue on left, Persian Yellow glaze on right, 1937 – 1942. $65.00 – 80.00 each.

Original Stangl catalog page showing lamps #3125, #3126, and #3127. Courtesy of the Hill-Fulper-Stangl Museum.

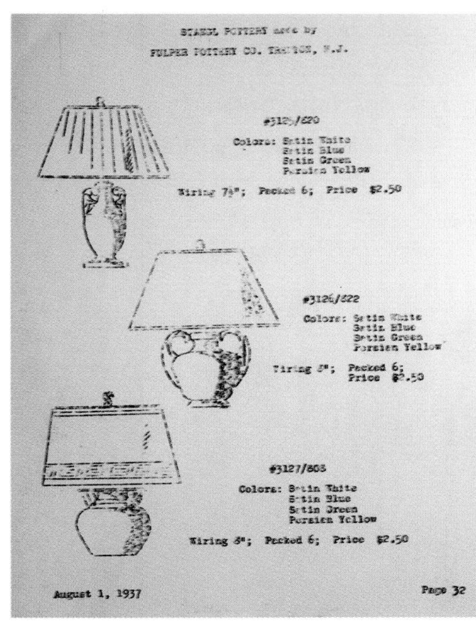

STANGL POTTERY made by
FULPER POTTERY CO. TRENTON, N.J.

#3125/620
Colors: Satin White
Satin Blue
Satin Green
Persian Yellow
Wiring 7½"; Packed 6; Price $2.50

#3126/622
Colors: Satin White
Satin Blue
Satin Green
Persian Yellow
Wiring 8"; Packed 6;
Price $2.50

#3127/808
Colors: Satin White
Satin Blue
Satin Green
Persian Yellow
Wiring 8"; Packed 6; Price $2.50

August 1, 1937 Page 32

Not Shown:

#3122 Bottle, 2 handles, 6", solid-color glazes, 1937 – 1938. $80.00 – 90.00.

#3123 Vase, 2 handles, 6", solid-color glazes, 1937 – 1942. $65.00 – 80.00.

#3124 Rosette handles, 9", solid-color glazes, 1937 – 1940. $130.00 – 150.00.

#3125 Scroll handles, 9", solid-color glazes, 1937 – 1938. $120.00 – 140.00.

Lamp #3126 Ovoid, 7½", Satin Blue glaze with original finial, 1937 – 1942. $110.00 – 135.00.

Original Stangl catalog page showing lamps #3128, #3129, and #3003. Courtesy of the Hill-Fulper-Stangl Museum.

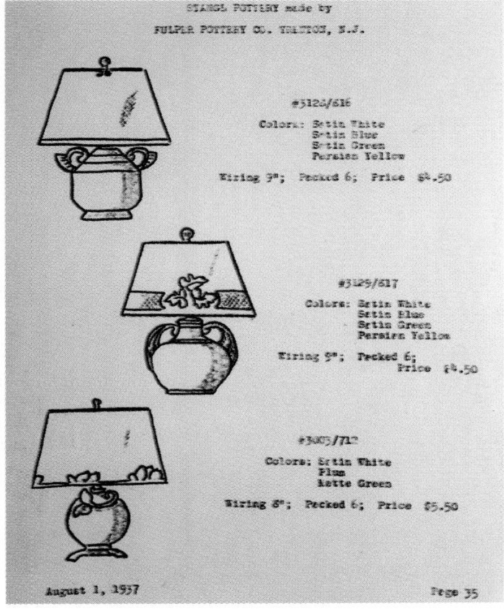

STANGL POTTERY made by
FULPER POTTERY CO. TRENTON, N.J.

#3128/616
Colors: Satin White
Satin Blue
Satin Green
Persian Yellow
Wiring 9"; Packed 6; Price $4.50

#3129/617
Colors: Satin White
Satin Blue
Satin Green
Persian Yellow
Wiring 9"; Packed 6;
Price $4.50

#3003/712
Colors: Satin White
Plum
Matte Green
Wiring 8"; Packed 6; Price $5.50

August 1, 1937 Page 35

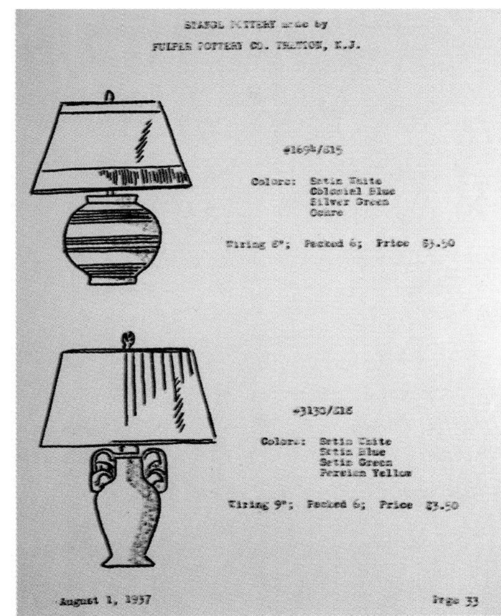

STANGL POTTERY made by
FULPER POTTERY CO. TRENTON, N.J.

#1694/615
Colors: Satin White
Colonial Blue
Silver Green
Ochre
Wiring 8"; Packed 6; Price $3.50

#3130/618
Colors: Satin White
Satin Blue
Satin Green
Persian Yellow
Wiring 9"; Packed 6; Price $3.50

August 1, 1937 Page 33

Original Stangl catalog page showing lamps #1694 and #3130.

1938 Introductions

Lamp #1388 coffee pot, 6½", Tangerine glaze with original cast metal base, 1938 – 1943. $95.00 – 110.00.

Lamp #1388 coffee pot, 6½", Tangerine glaze with original turned wood base, 1938 – 1943. $95.00 – 110.00. Courtesy of Primarily Pottery.

Not Shown:

#3127 Ovoid, solid handles, 7½", solid-color glazes, 1937 – 1938. $130.00 – 150.00.

#3128 Jar, Wing handles, 9", solid-color glazes, 1937 – 1938. $150.00 – 165.00.

#3129 Ovoid, 2 handles, solid-color glazes, 1937 – 1942. $130.00 – 150.00.

#3130 Amphora, 11", solid-color glazes, 1937 – 1938. $170.00 – 195.00.

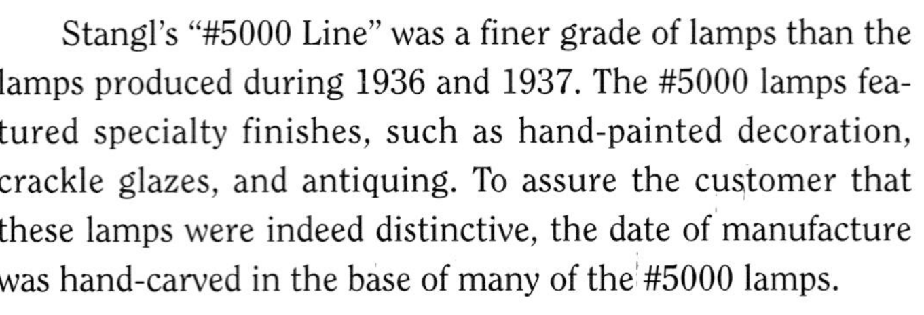

Stangl's "#5000 Line" was a finer grade of lamps than the lamps produced during 1936 and 1937. The #5000 lamps featured specialty finishes, such as hand-painted decoration, crackle glazes, and antiquing. To assure the customer that these lamps were indeed distinctive, the date of manufacture was hand-carved in the base of many of the #5000 lamps.

Lamp #5002 Chinese Bottle with handles, 9", Cobalt Blue glaze with gold striping, 1938 – 1939. $200.00 – 250.00.

Lamp #5004 Chinese Jar, 9", underglaze decorated in blue and yellow with antiqued Satin White Crackle glaze, 1938 only. $375.00 – 425.00. Courtesy of the Hill-Fulper-Stangl Museum.

Lamp #5004 Chinese Jar, 9", Silver Green. The #5004 shape was adapted from the old #1010 Chinese lamp. The #5004 shape has a closed top; the original #1010 shape had an open top and was fitted with a 4" brass cap, $290.00 – 325.00, complete with fittings. From the Stangl and Fulper archival collection, courtesy the Wheaton Village Museum of American Glass.

Lamp #5005 Centaur and Deer, 10¼", Silver Green with antiquing, 1938 – 1939. $290.00 – 325.00.

Lamp #5008 Lovebirds, 9" (based on the old #1023 Lovebirds shape, but with a closed top), Oxblood glaze with antiquing, 1938 only. $290.00 – 325.00.

Lamp #5010 Primitive, 10" (based on #1664 handmade shape), hand-painted underglaze color bands, 1938 – 1939. $175.00 – 200.00. Courtesy of the Vera Kaufman collection.

Lamp #5020 Flower Ball Stand, 7½", hand-painted motif, 1938 – 1939. $170.00 – 195.00.

Lamp #5031 Oval with Berries, 8", hand-painted motif, 1938 – 1939. $190.00 – 225.00.

Not Shown:
#5037 Primrose lamp, 9", hand-painted motif, 1938 – 1939. $190.00 – 225.00.
#5051 Starflower, solid handles lamp, 9", hand-painted motif, 1938 only. $190.00 – 225.00.
#5061 Oblong Flowers, solid handle lamp, 8½", hand-painted motif, 1938 – 1939. $190.00 – 225.00.
#5070 Leaf, ball handles lamp, 10", hand-painted motif, 1938 – 1939. $190.00 – 225.00.

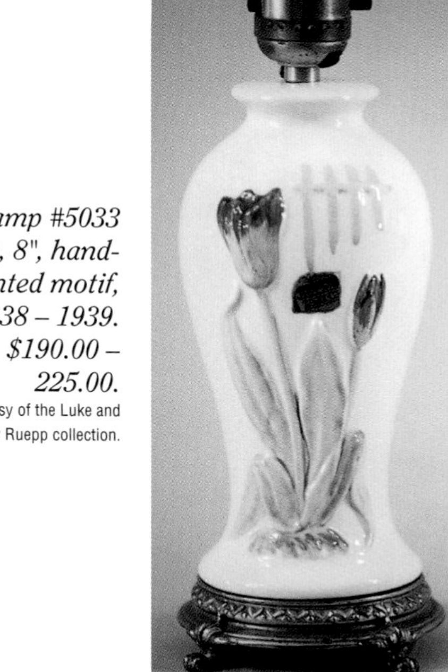

Lamp #5033 Tulips, 8", hand-painted motif, 1938 – 1939. $190.00 – 225.00. Courtesy of the Luke and Nancy Ruepp collection.

Lamp #5037 Primrose, 9", Oxblood glaze, 1938 – 1939. $110.00 – 135.00.

Lamp #5045 Lily Bells, 7½", Yellow hand-painted motif with original wood finial, 1938 – 1939. $175.00 – 200.00. Courtesy of the Bill Servis, Susan Lewis collection.

Lamp #5045 Lily Bells, 7½", Red hand-painted motif, 1938 – 1939. $175.00 – 200.00. Courtesy of the Bill Servis, Susan Lewis collection.

Lamp #5051 Starflower, solid handles, 9" Silver Green Crackle glaze, 1938 only. $130.00 – 160.00.

Lamp #5052 Grapevine, 8", hand-painted under Satin Blue glaze, 1938 – 1939. $160.00 – 180.00. Courtesy of the Wayne Weigand collection.

Lamp #5053 Torpedo Cone, 9", hand-painted under Satin White glaze, 1938 only. $300.00 – 350.00. Courtesy of the Jim Horner collection.

Lamp #5054 Handled Vase, 8½", hand-painted motif, 1938 – 1939. $190.00 – 225.00. Courtesy of the Hill-Fulper-Stangl Museum.

Lamp #5058 Trumpet Vine, 7½", hand-painted under Satin White glaze, 1938 – 1939. $190.00 – 225.00. Courtesy of the Jim and Barbara Nelson collection.

Lamp #5061 Oblong Flowers, solid handles, 8½", Oxblood glaze, 1938 – 1939. $120.00 – 145.00.

Lamp #5065 Pitcher, 7¼", hand-decorated, 1938 – 1939. $150.00 – 165.00.

Lamp #5070 Leaf, ball handles, 10", Oxblood glaze, 1938 – 1939. $150.00 – 165.00.
Courtesy of the Marcena North collection.

Lamp #5073 Modern Leaf Column, 10", hand-painted under Satin Blue glaze, 1938 – 1939. $190.00 – 225.00.

Lamp #5073 Modern Leaf Column, 10", hand-painted under Satin White glaze with matching finial, 1938 – 1939. $200.00 – 250.00.

1940s Introductions

Lamp #3509 Chinese urn, 13", hand-brushed engobe, carved and decorated under glaze, 1941 – 1943. $130.00 – 160.00.

Lamp #3690 scalloped vase, 9", Early Pennsylvania Artware vase converted to lamp, 1940s. $95.00 – 110.00.
Courtesy of the Chris McGeehan collection.

Verplex Plaque Pin-Up Lamps, 1949

During 1949, Stangl produced three styles of hand-painted plaques for the Verplex Lamp Co. The plaques were made with three motifs: Ribbon, Floral, and Bird. The Bird was usually painted in Mallard duck colors. The plaques measure 5½" by 3¼" and were mounted on brass pin-up wall lamps by Verplex. Produced only briefly, the ceramic plaques are quite hard to come by. The lamps were made of thin stamped brass, so surviving lamps are more scarce than the plaques. Value for a plaque mounted on a complete lamp in excellent condition is usually about $50.00 – 75.00 more than the plaque alone.

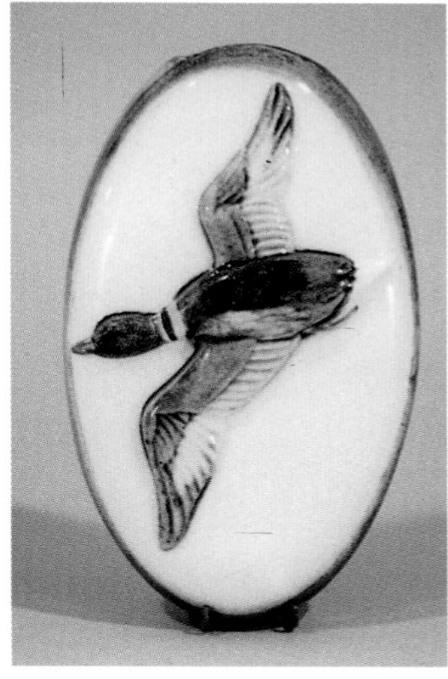

Verplex #3805 Bird plaque, 5½"x3¼", 1949 only. $100.00 – 125.00. Courtesy of the Marcena North collection.

Verplex pin-up lamp mounted with a #3805 Bird Plaque. $175.00 – 200.00 Courtesy of the Robert and Tammie Cruser collection.

Not Shown:

#3803 Ribbon Verplex plaque, 5½"x3¼", 1949 only. $95.00 – 110.00.

#3804 Floral Verplex plaque, 5½"x3¼", 1949 only. $95.00 – 110.00.

#3805 Bird Verplex plaque, 5½"x3¼", 1949 only. $100.00 – 125.00.

1950s Introductions

During the 1950s, Stangl's lamp shape numbers departed from the usual series of shape numbers and seemed to be assigned arbitrarily. Old shapes from the 1930s were brought back with new finishes, sometimes with new numbers, sometimes keeping the old. New lamp shapes were developed and assigned numbers already in use, while other shapes were never assigned numbers at all. The shape numbers and lamp names shown here are the ones with most common usage in original Stangl documents.

One particularly interesting shape that changed its number and size several times was the #1246 ball lamp. This shape started in 1929 in three sizes, 7", 8½", and 10½" in diameter. In 1933, the shape numbers were changed, and each size was assigned its own number: #1714 was 7", #1715 was 8", #1716 was 10", #1717 was 15", and #1720 was 9". In 1950 the shape became "Globe" instead of "Ball," and was assigned new numbers; the 7" became #3832, 9" became #3833, and 10½" became #3834. In 1965 the lamps changed size again, from 10½", 9", and 7" to 10", 8", and 6", and their name was returned to "Ball." All three sizes were lumped into the same shape, #3852. The number should have remained #3832, but a slip of a digit permanently recorded this lamp as #3852 (the number for the Cliff Swallow bird figurine). In 1967 the 6" ball lamp was discontinued; the 10" ball became #21, and the 8" ball, #22.

Original 1965 Stangl catalog page listing the #3852 Ball lamps. Courtesy of the Hill-Fulper-Stangl Museum.

Mutual Sunset Lamps

Stangl Pottery began producing a series of hand-carved, hand-painted lamp bodies for Mutual Sunset Lamp Co. in 1950. Mutual Sunset, also of Trenton, was Stangl's largest lamp account throughout the 1950s, 1960s, and 1970s. The initial motifs were designed by Kay Hackett, and many continued in production during the 1960s and 1970s with slight changes in color and style to reflect decorating trends. Stangl shipped the lamp bodies to Mutual Sunset where they were fitted with bases, harps, and sockets. 1950s-era Mutual Sunset bases were cast metal with a dark brown sprayed finish and are in-mold marked on the bottom with the initials "M S L C." During the late 1950s and through the 1970s, Mutual Sunset also mounted the lamps on bases of wood or spun brass.

Stangl's contract with Mutual Sunset allowed Stangl to sell Mutual Sunset lamp bodies at the Flemington Outlet. The Flemington Outlet Mutual Sunset lamps were usually not fitted with bases but simply have a harp and socket. Occasionally Mutual Sunset lamp shapes were decorated in non-Mutual Sunset motifs and finishes specifically for the Flemington Outlet. Decorations such as dinnerware patterns, Stoneware art glaze, or Antique Gold were typical.

Some of the Mutual Sunset wildlife lamp motifs were adapted to Sportsmen's ashtray shapes in 1955. In 1959, several #3834 10½" globe lamps were decorated with wildlife motifs on gray engobe to coordinate with the Sportsmen's Giftware line and sold at the Flemington Outlet. Unlike the Mutual Sunset lamps, the backs of many of the gray Sportsmen's lamps are undecorated. The dark background and lack of original Mutual Sunset base and fittings usually causes these lamps to sell for less than the white background Mutual Sunset wildlife lamps.

Not Shown:

#3832 globe, 7", leaf motif, made for Mutual Sunset Lamp Co., 1950 – 1955. $120.00 – 145.00.

#3832 globe, 7", floral motif, made for Mutual Sunset Lamp Co., 1950 – 1955. $165.00 – 185.00.

#3833 globe, 9", Pennsylvania Dutch bird motif, made for Mutual Sunset Lamp Co., 1950 – 1955. $290.00 – 325.00.

#3833 globe, 9", floral motif, made for Mutual Sunset Lamp Co., 1950 – 1955. $190.00 – 225.00.

#3834 globe, 10½", Goose motif, made for Mutual Sunset Lamp Co., 1950 – 1955. $350.00 – 375.00.

#3834 globe, 10½", Duck motif, made for Mutual Sunset Lamp Co., 1950 – 1955. $350.00 – 375.00.

Markings typically found on a Mutual Sunset Lamp Co. metal lamp base.

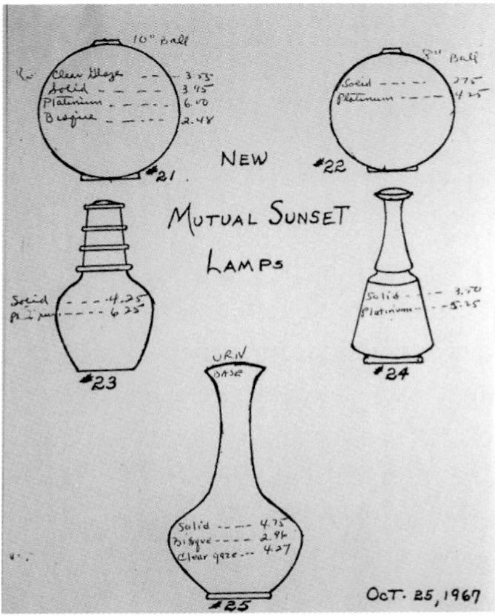

Original Stangl catalog page dated 1967, showing Mutual Sunset lamp body shapes. Courtesy of the Hill-Fulper-Stangl Museum.

Lamp #3832 globe, 7", Pennsylvania Dutch bird motif, made for Mutual Sunset Lamp Co. 1950 – 1955. $200.00 – 250.00. Courtesy of the Jim and Barbara Nelson collection.

Lamp #3833 globe, 9", leaf motif, made for Mutual Sunset Lamp Co. 1950 – 1955. $130.00 – 160.00. Courtesy of the Lewis/Servis collection.

Lamp #3834 globe, 10½", Floral motif with brushed engobe, made for Mutual Sunset Lamp Co. 1950 – 1955. $275.00 – 300.00. Courtesy of Dave and Betty Stangl Thomas.

Lamp #3834 globe, 10½", Pheasant motif, made for Mutual Sunset Lamp Co. 1950 – 1955. $350.00 – 375.00. Courtesy of the Hill-Fulper-Stangl Museum.

#3834 globe, 10½", Fish motif, made for Mutual Sunset Lamp Co., 1950 – 1955. $350.00 – 375.00.

#3834 globe, 10½", Pennsylvania Dutch bird motif, made for Mutual Sunset Lamp Co., 1950 – 1955. $350.00 – 375.00.

#3834 globe, 10½", leaf motif, made for Mutual Sunset Lamp Co., 1950 – 1955. $200.00 – 250.00.

#3837 5-tier coffee warmer, 11", brown and gold underglaze colors, late 1950s – 1960s, made for Mutual Sunset Lamp Co., $110.00 – 135.00.

#3837 5-tier coffee warmer, 11", red, yellow, and green underglaze colors, 1950 – 1955, made for Mutual Sunset Lamp Co., $175.00 – 200.00.

#3837 5-tier coffee warmer, 11", Fruit dinnerware motif, made for the Flemington Outlet, 1965 – 1968. $300.00 – 350.00.

#3838 ovoid, 11½", Willow motif, 1950 – 1955, made for Mutual Sunset Lamp Co., $175.00 – 200.00.

#3 small cylinder lamp, 10" floral motif, turquoise, blue, and green underglaze colors, made for Mutual Sunset Lamp Co., 1959 – 1960s. $100.00 – 125.00.

Coordinating motif on the back of the Pheasant lamp. Nearly all of the Mutual Sunset lamps produced during the early 1950s were decorated on both sides.

Lamp #3837 5-tier coffee warmer, 11", turquoise, blue, and green underglaze colors, late 1950s – 1960s, made for Mutual Sunset Lamp Co. $130.00 – 160.00. Courtesy of the Chris McGeehan collection.

Lamp #3839 ellipse, 14", red, yellow, and green underglaze colors, 1950 – 1955, made for Mutual Sunset Lamp Co. $190.00 – 225.00. Courtesy of Dave and Betty Stangl Thomas.

Lamp #3839 ellipse, 14", turquoise, blue, and green underglaze colors, late 1950s – 1960s, made for Mutual Sunset Lamp Co. $150.00 – 175.00. Courtesy of the Jim Horner collection.

Lamp #3434 teapot, 6¾", Lime motif, made for Mutual Sunset Lamp Co., 1950 – 1953. $150.00 – 165.00.

Lamp #2 large cylinder, 12", turquoise, blue, and green underglaze colors, made for Mutual Sunset Lamp Co., 1959 – 1970s. $95.00 – 110.00.

Lamp #2 large cylinder, 12", gold and brown underglaze colors, with original shade, made for Mutual Sunset Lamp Co., 1959 – 1970s. $80.00 – 90.00.

Lamp #2 large cylinder, 12", brown and green underglaze colors with fired-on decal of the Mayflower, made for Mutual Sunset Lamp Co., 1970s. $100.00 – 125.00. Courtesy of the Hill-Fulper-Stangl Museum.

Lamp #2 large cylinder, 12", Fruit dinnerware motif, made for the Flemington Outlet, 1960s. $275.00 – 300.00.

Lamp #3 small cylinder, 10" floral motif, gold and brown underglaze colors, made for Mutual Sunset Lamp Co., 1959 – 1960s. $95.00 – 110.00. Courtesy of Merrill and Christl Stangl Bacheler.

Lamp #11 coffee pot, 14", hand-carved decoration with turquoise, blue, and green underglaze colors, made for Mutual Sunset Lamp Co., 1963 – 1970s. $100.00 – 125.00. Courtesy of Primarily Pottery.

Lamp #11 coffee pot, 14", Antique Gold, made for the Flemington Outlet, 1960s. $100.00 – 125.00. Courtesy of Dave and Betty Stangl Thomas.

Lamp #11 coffee pot, 14", in-mold decoration (not hand-carved), Speckled Gold glaze, made for Mutual Sunset Lamp Co., 1960s – 1970s. $70.00 – 85.00.

Lamp #481 Large Rooster, 16", with original mountings and shade, made for Mutual Sunset Lamp Co., 1960s – 1970s. $1,500.00 – 1,800.00. For more information on Mutual Sunset Lamp Co.'s Rooster and other lamp figurines, please see the chapter on Bird Figurines.

Lamp #4014 Flemington, 6", brushed copper luster, made for the Flemington Outlet, 1958 only. $70.00 – 85.00.

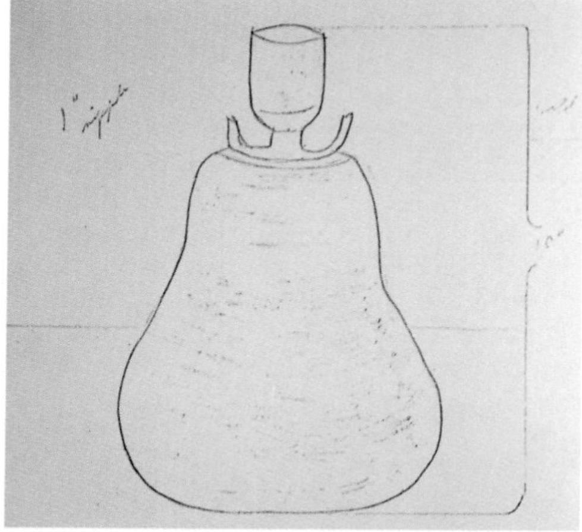

(Left) Lamp #4023 Flemington, 8", Antique Gold, made for the Flemington Outlet, 1958 – 1960s. $35.00 – 45.00. (Right) Lamp #4051 bud vase, 8¾", Antique Gold, 1958 – 1960s. $40.00 – 50.00. Original Stangl catalog pages courtesy of the Hill-Fulper-Stangl Museum.

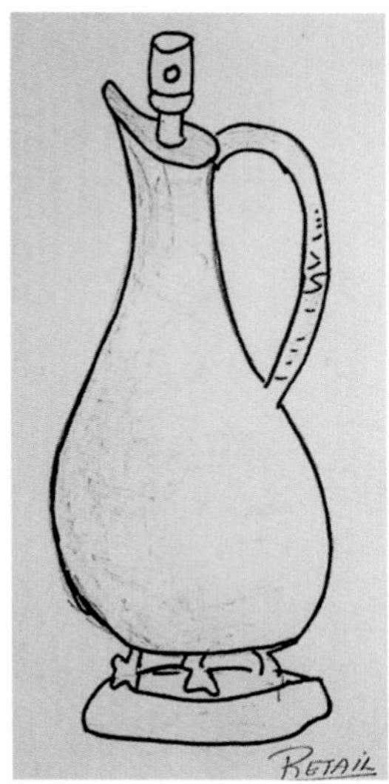

Lamp #4055 large pitcher, 14", Antique Gold, 1958 – 1960s. $40.00 – 50.00. Original Stangl catalog page courtesy of the Hill-Fulper-Stangl Museum.

Lamp #941 vase, 10", Antique Gold, 1958 – 1960s. $45.00 – 55.00. Courtesy of the Robert and Tammie Cruser collection.

Lamp #2033 urn, Greek band, 12", Antique Gold, 1958 – 1960s. $85.00 – 95.00.

Lamp #4041 decorated vase, 9", Antique Gold, 1958 – 1960s. $85.00 – 95.00. Courtesy of the Brian and Cristi Hahn collection.

#4014 Flemington lamp, 6", Antique Gold, made for the Flemington Outlet, 1958 – 1960s. $25.00 – 35.00.
#1832 large cylinder lamp, 10", Antique Gold, 1959 – 1960s. $55.00 – 65.00.
#1981 urn with flower lamp, 8½", Antique Gold, 1960s. $65.00 – 80.00.
#1991 Pig lamp (old #1076), 4", Terra Rose or Antique Gold, 1950s – 1960s. $100.00 – 125.00.
#5010 Primitive lamp, 10" Terra Rose or Antique Gold, 1950s – 1960s. $70.00 – 85.00.

1960s Introductions

Not Shown:

#5086 Pig lamp (old #1991), 4", pink or blue floral decoration, 1961 – 1962. $350.00 – 400.00.
#5087 Duck lamp, 4", pink or blue floral decoration, 1961 – 1962. $450.00 – 500.00.
#5180 Taper, 13½", Antique Gold, 1964 – 1970. $60.00 – 75.00.
#5181 Taper, 11½", Antique Gold, 1964 – 1970. $45.00 – 55.00.
#5182 Taper, 10", Antique Gold, 1964 – 1970. $40.00 – 50.00.
#5180 Taper, 13½", Mediterranean, 1964 – 1966. $110.00 – 135.00.
#5181 Taper, 11½", Mediterranean, 1964 – 1966. $85.00 – 95.00.
#5182 Taper, 10", Mediterranean, 1964 – 1966. $70.00 – 85.00.
#5180 Taper, 13½", Caughley, 1964 – 1970. $120.00 – 145.00.
#5181 Taper, 11½", Caughley, 1964 – 1970. $95.00 – 110.00.
#5182 Taper, 10", Caughley, 1964 – 1970. $85.00 – 95.00.
#5180 Taper, 13½", Scandinavia, 1965. $60.00 – 75.00.
#5181 Taper, 11½", Scandinavia, 1965. $55.00 – 65.00.
#5182 Taper, 10", Scandinavia, 1965. $40.00 – 50.00.
#5180 Taper, 13½", Stoneware art glaze, 1965. $110.00 – 135.00.
#5181 Taper, 11½", Stoneware art glaze, 1965. $95.00 – 110.00.
#5182 Taper, 10", Stoneware art glaze, 1965. $80.00 – 100.00.
#5184 Large Square, 11", Blue Caughley, 1964 – 1970. $175.00 – 200.00.

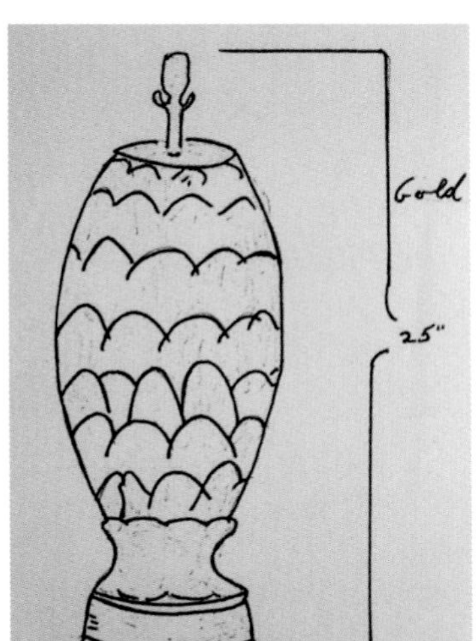

Lamp #5179 Pineapple, 22", Antique Gold or Black Gold, 1961 – 1970. $70.00 – 85.00. Original Stangl catalog page courtesy of the Hill-Fulper-Stangl Museum.

Lamp #5179 Pineapple, 22, Martin Stangl's personal lamp, brushed gold over gray glaze and Terra Rose Mauve. Martin Stangl liked gray and had a pair of Pineapple lamps decorated in this finish for his home. The Pineapple lamp shape was typically produced in Antique Gold or Black Gold. Courtesy of Dave and Betty Stangl Thomas.

#5184 Large Square, 11", Blue Town & Country, 1976 – 1977. $175.00 – 200.00.
#5184 Large Square, 11", Town & Country, 1976 – 1977. $130.00 – 150.00.
#637 jug, 10", Fruit Basket motif, 1965 – 1970. $110.00 – 135.00.
#637 jug, 10", Blue Caughley. $175.00 – 200.00.
#637 jug, 10", Caughley. $130.00 – 150.00.
#637 jug, 10", Blue Town & Country, 1976. $190.00 – 225.00.
#637 jug, 10", Town & Country, 1976. $130.00 – 150.00.
#1256 Fluted Jar, 14" Black Gold, 1968 – 1970. $55.00 – 70.00.
#1256 Fluted Jar, 14" fashion-color glazes, 1968 – 1977. $70.00 – 85.00.
#1532 twisted top, 12" Stoneware art glaze, 1965. $120.00 – 145.00.
#1850 Temple Jar, 18", Black Gold, 1968 – 1970. $65.00 – 80.00.
#1850 Temple Jar, 18", Stoneware art glaze, 1965. $130.00 – 160.00.
#1850 Temple Jar, 18", fashion-color glazes, 1968 – 1977. $70.00 – 85.00.
#1850 temple jar, 18", Blue Caughley, 1965 – 1972. $175.00 – 200.00.
#1850 temple jar, 18", Caughley, 1965 – 1972. $130.00 – 150.00.
#1850 Temple Jar, 18" Blue Town & Country, 1976 – 1977. $200.00 – 250.00.
#1850 Temple Jar, 18" Town & Country, 1976 – 1977. $150.00 – 175.00.
#3068 Chrysanthemum, 8", Black Gold, 1968 – 1970. $55.00 – 70.00.
#3068 Chrysanthemum, 8", Stoneware art glaze, 1965. $100.00 – 125.00.
#3774 coffee pot lamp, Fruit dinnerware motif, made for Mutual Sunset Lamp Co., 1965 – 1972. $175.00 – 200.00.
#3774 Coffee pot lamp, Orchard Song dinnerware motif, made for Mutual Sunset Lamp Co., 1965 – 1972. $100.00 – 125.00.
#3833 globe lamp 9", Stoneware art glaze, made for the Flemington Outlet, 1965. $130.00 – 160.00.
#3834 globe lamp 10½", Stoneware art glaze, made for the Flemington Outlet, 1965. $160.00 – 180.00.
#3832 globe lamp, 7", Antique Gold, 1965 – 1968. $40.00 – 50.00.
#3833 globe lamp 9", Antique Gold, 1965 – 1968. $50.00 – 60.00.
#3834 globe lamp 10½", Antique Gold, 1965 – 1968. $85.00 – 95.00.
Rembrandt pitcher lamp, 12½", Stoneware art glaze, 1965. $130.00 – 160.00.
Rembrandt pitcher lamp, 12½", White or fashion-color glazes, 1968 – 1975. $110.00 – 135.00.
#9051 Shouldered Jar, 20", Stoneware art glaze, 1965. $150.00 – 175.00.
#9051 Shouldered Jar, 20", Blue Caughley. $175.00 – 200.00.
#9051 Shouldered Jar, 20", Caughley. $130.00 – 150.00.
#9051 Shouldered Jar, 20", fashion-color glazes, 1970 – 1974. $100.00 – 125.00.
#9051 Shouldered Jar, 20", Blue Town & Country. $190.00 – 225.00.
#9051 Shouldered Jar, 20", Town & Country. $130.00 – 150.00.
#9098 Barrel, 10", Black Gold or Granada Gold, 1960s, $60.00 – 75.00.
#9098 Barrel, 10", Stoneware art glaze, 1965. $110.00 – 135.00.
Spirits Barrel lamp, 14", Black Gold or Granada Gold, 1960s. $85.00 – 95.00.
Spirits Barrel lamp, 14", Stoneware art glaze, 1965. $150.00 – 175.00.
#9103 Tyndale lamp, 12", unglazed bisque, Made for Tyndale Specialty Co. 1965. $70.00 – 85.00.
Basket Weave lamp, 10", 12", unglazed bisque, 1965. $60.00 – 75.00.
#9917 Ginger Jar, small, 9", Stoneware art glaze, 1965. $95.00 – 110.00.
#9917 Ginger Jar, small, 9", Pebblestone finish, 1965. $80.00 – 100.00.
#9917 Ginger Jar, small, 9", unglazed bisque, 1965. $65.00 – 80.00.
Ginger Jar, large, 22", Stoneware art glaze, 1965. $150.00 – 175.00.
Ginger Jar, large, 22", fashion-color glazes, 1970 – 1976. $100.00 – 125.00.

Lamp #5087 Duck, 4", natural color decoration, 1961 – 1962. $450.00 – 500.00.

Lamp #5088 Rabbit (old #3109), 8", pink or blue floral decoration, 1961 – 1962. $500.00 – 550.00. Courtesy of Merrill and Christl Stangl Bacheler.

Lamp #5086 Elephant, 6", pink or blue decoration, 1961 – 1962. $450.00 – 500.00.

Lamp #5181 Taper, 11½", Antique Gold, 1964 – 1970. $45.00 – 55.00.

Lamp #1832 large cylinder, 10", vibrant Blue Stoneware art glaze, 1965 only. $130.00 – 160.00. Courtesy of the Hill-Fulper-Stangl Museum.

Lamp #5184 Large Square, 11", Yellow Caughley, 1964 – 1970. $130.00 – 150.00. Courtesy of the Luke and Nancy Ruepp collection.

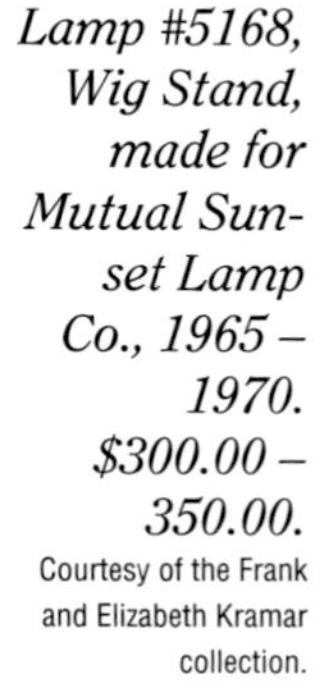

Lamp #5168, Wig Stand, made for Mutual Sunset Lamp Co., 1965 – 1970. $300.00 – 350.00. Courtesy of the Frank and Elizabeth Kramar collection.

(Left) Lamp #1 bottle, 12", Antique Gold or Stoneware art glaze, 1965 – 1968. $70.00 – 85.00. (Right) Lamp #43 Chinese, 10", Antique Gold or Stoneware art glaze, 1965 – 1968. $175.00 – 200.00. Original 1965 Stangl catalog pages courtesy of the Hill-Fulper-Stangl Museum.

Lamp #637 jug, 10", Fruit dinnerware motif, 1965 – 1974. $275.00 – 300.00. Courtesy of the David and Laura Solomon collection.

Lamp #637 jug, 10", Orchard Song dinnerware motif, 1965 – 1974. $175.00 – 200.00.

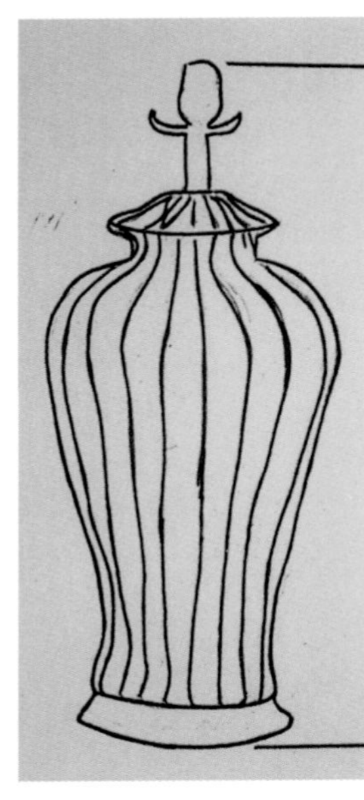

Lamp #1256 Fluted Jar, 14" Antique Gold, 1965 – 1970. $100.00 – 125.00. Original 1965 Stangl catalog page courtesy of the Hill-Fulper-Stangl Museum.

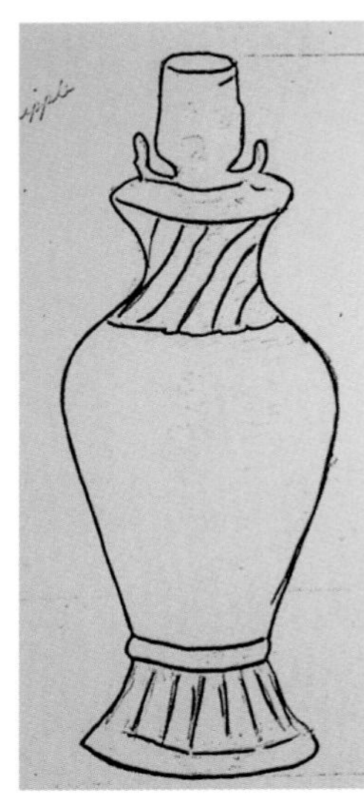

Lamp #1532 twisted top, 12" Antique Gold, 1965 – 1970s. $95.00 – 110.00. Original 1965 Stangl catalog page courtesy of the Hill-Fulper-Stangl Museum.

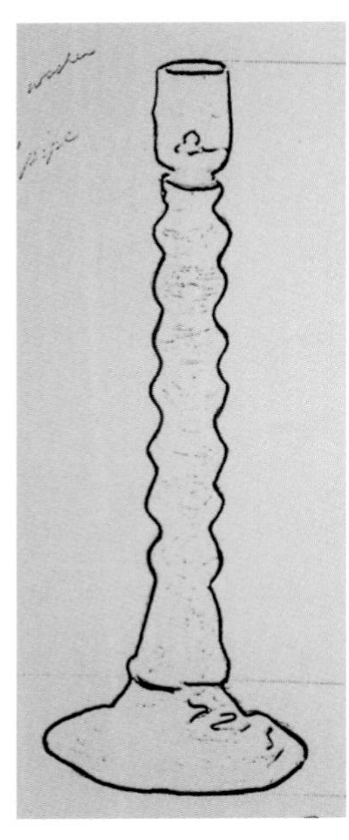

Lamp #1686 Spool Candle, 10", Antique Gold, 1960s. $60.00 – 75.00. Original 1965 Stangl catalog page courtesy of the Hill-Fulper-Stangl Museum.

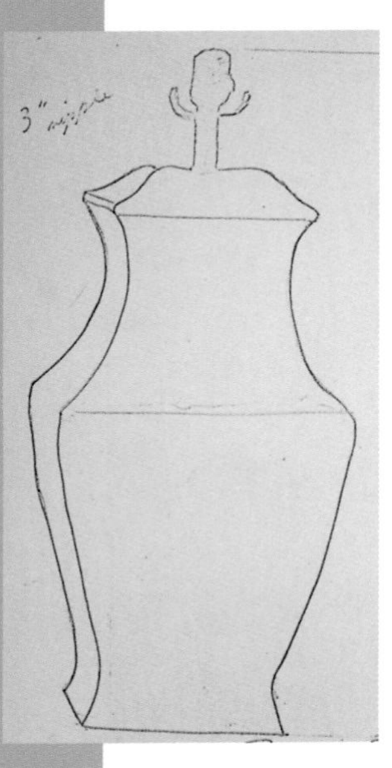

Lamp #1850 Temple Jar, 18", Antique Gold, 1965 – 1970. $130.00 – 150.00. Original 1965 Stangl catalog page courtesy of the Hill-Fulper-Stangl Museum.

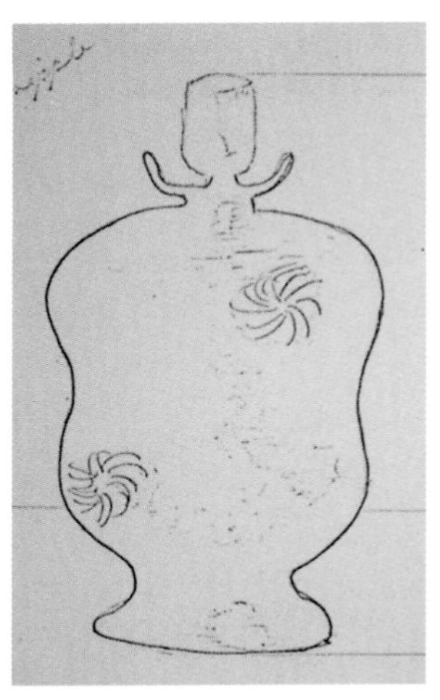

Lamp #3068 Chrysanthemum, 8", Antique Gold, 1965 – 1970. $80.00 – 90.00.

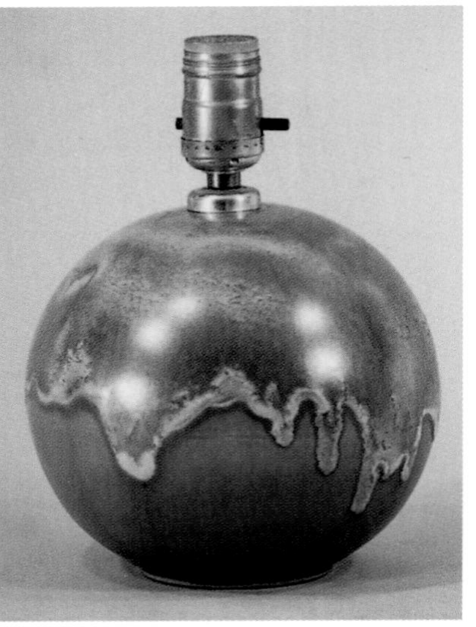

Lamp #3832 globe, 7", Green Stoneware art glaze, made for the Flemington Outlet, 1965. $110.00 – 135.00.

Cookie Jar lamp, 9", Antique Gold, 1965 – 1968. $100.00 – 125.00. Original 1965 Stangl catalog page courtesy of the Hill-Fulper-Stangl Museum.

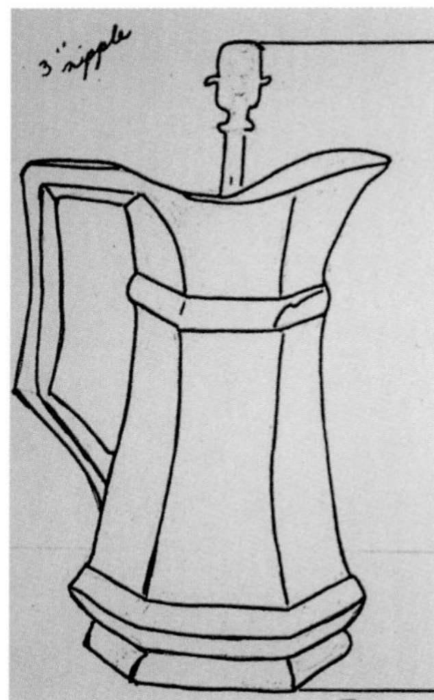

Rembrandt pitcher lamp, 12½", Antique Gold, 1965 – 1970. $120.00 – 145.00. Original 1965 Stangl catalog page courtesy of the Hill-Fulper-Stangl Museum.

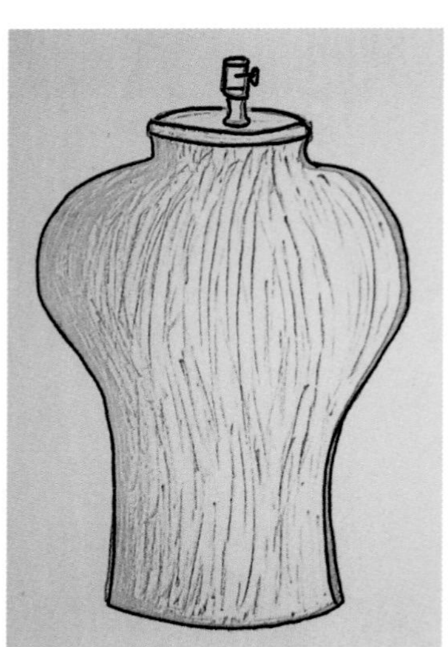

Lamp #9051 Shouldered Jar, 20", Antique Gold, $130.00 – 150.00. Original 1965 Stangl catalog page courtesy of the Hill-Fulper-Stangl Museum.

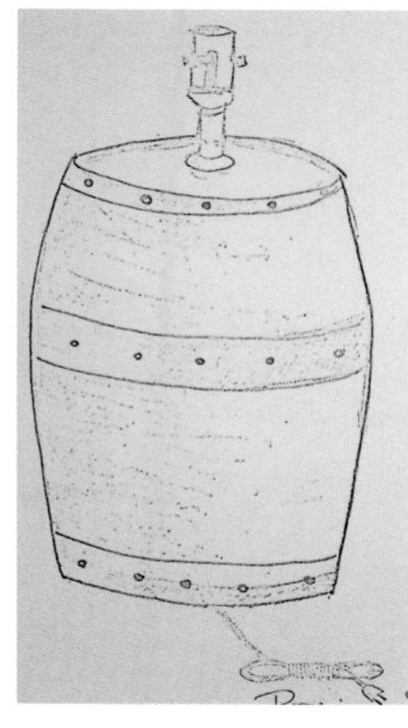

Lamp #9098 Barrel, 10", Antique Gold, $85.00 – 95.00. Original 1965 Stangl catalog page courtesy of the Hill-Fulper-Stangl Museum.

Spirits Barrel lamp, 14", Antique Gold, 1965 – 1970. $150.00 – 165.00. Original 1965 Stangl catalog page courtesy of the Hill-Fulper-Stangl Museum.

#9917 Ginger Jar, small, 9", Antique Gold, 1965 – 1968. $50.00 – 60.00. Original 1965 Stangl catalog page courtesy of the Hill-Fulper-Stangl Museum.

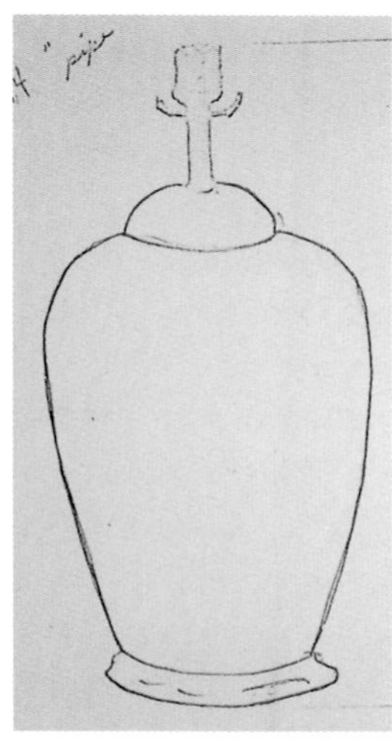

Ginger Jar, large, 22", Antique Gold, 1965 – 1968. $130.00 – 160.00. Original 1965 Stangl catalog page courtesy of the Hill-Fulper-Stangl Museum.

Two-part lamp, large, 14", Caribbean finish, made for Mutual Sunset Lamp Co., 1968 – 1970. $100.00 – 125.00.

Handled jar, large, 22", Caribbean or Pebblestone finish, made for Mutual Sunset Lamp Co., 1968 – 1972. $110.00 – 135.00.

Lamp #1185, Water Dog, 10¾", made for the Nelson Lebo Lamp Co., 1960s – 1970s. $450.00 – 600.00 For more information on Nelson Lebo Lamp Co.'s Water Dog and other lamp figurines, please see page 87.

Beginning in 1937, Fulper Pottery produced various salt and pepper shakers in novelty shapes. The first shakers originated as part of the bird and animal figurine line. Others were designed to coordinate with popular dinnerware patterns. Throughout the 1940s, several salt and pepper set shapes were produced for Stangl dealers, while others were special-orders for Howard L. Ross. During the 1950s and 1960, Stangl produced novelty salt and peppers for sales at the Flemington Outlet.

Percheron #3178F, 3" salt & pepper set. $300.00 – 350.00.
Courtesy of the Robert and Tammie Cruser collection.

1937 Introduction

Stangl's first novelty salt and pepper shaker set was adapted from the #3178F Percheron animal figurine. These retailed at the Flemington Outlet for 75¢ a pair during 1937 and 1938.

1939 Introductions

The novelty salt and pepper shakers introduced in 1939 were available in both hand-painted decoration and solid-color glazes. Nearly all of these shakers were discontinued by 1943.

Bluebird #3282 salt and pepper shakers were smaller versions of the #3276 Bluebird 5" figurine. The Bluebird #3282 shakers are 3" tall and decorated in the same natural colors as the larger figurine. The shakers shown were made for a tourist spot in Banff, Canada.

Rooster #3285 and Hen #3286 were hand-painted white with black stippling, French Green bases, pink #160 combs and orange beaks. These were the standard colors for these figures.

Bluebird #3282 salt and pepper, $175.00 – 200.00 set.

Hand-Painted Rooster #3285 and Hen #3286 shakers, $175.00 – 200.00 hen/rooster set.
Courtesy of the Frank and Elizabeth Kramar collection.

Two Rooster #3285 shaker figurines, Persian Yellow glaze. $160.00 – 220.00 hen/rooster set.
Courtesy of the Wayne Weigand collection.

Ranger Dudes Cowgirl #3294 pepper and Cowboy #3295 salt were hand-painted under Satin Yellow glaze to match the #3304 Ranger dinnerware pattern. Stangl advertised the #3294/95 shakers as Ranger Dudes. These shakers retailed for $1.50 per set in 1942. Occasionally these shakers are found with murky, muddy underglaze decoration or with no faces. The faces were painted under the glaze, so if the face is missing, that shaker was a hastily decorated second. Values for shakers with murky colors or lacking faces are nearly half that for well-decorated examples.

Jolly Tars Sailor Girl #3296 pepper and Sailor Boy #3297 salt were hand-painted in blue under Stangl's Satin Blue glaze to match dinnerware pattern #3333 Newport. Stangl advertised the #3296/97 shakers as Jolly Tars during the early 1940s. Like the Ranger Dudes, these shakers also retailed for $1.50 per set in 1942. Occasionally these shakers are found with murky colors or decorated with no faces; values for these are nearly half that for well-decorated examples.

The Daisy #3298 salt and pepper shakers were hand-painted in blue, yellow, or pink to match the #3306 Field Daisy, #3345 Brown-Eyed Daisy, #3346 Blue Mountain Daisy, or #3347 Pink Mountain Daisy dinnerware patterns. During the early 1960s, the same Daisy #3298 shaker shape was decorated to match the Blue Daisy dinnerware pattern.

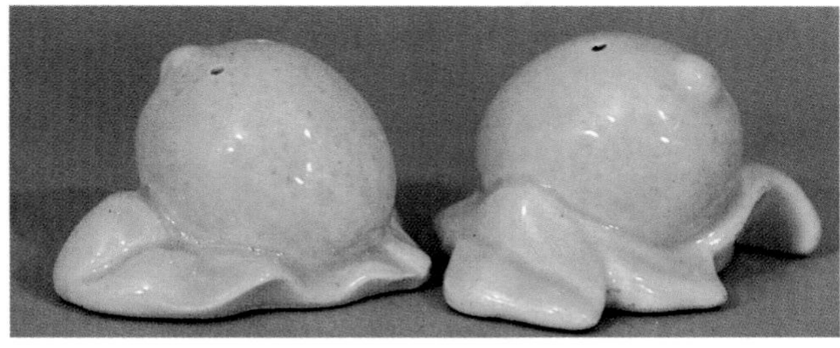

Lemon #3290 pepper, #3291 salt in Persian Yellow glaze. These shakers were also decorated in yellow and green under satin glaze to match the #3338 Tropic dinnerware pattern. Hand-painted, $150.00 – 175.00 set. Solid-color glazes, $100.00 – 125.00 set.

Fish #3292 pepper, #3293 salt in Silver Green glaze. The Fish shakers were also decorated with brown details under Satin Yellow glaze to match the #3336 Galley dinnerware pattern. Hand-painted, $150.00 – 200.00 set. Solid-color glazes, $175.00 – 200.00 set.

Hand-painted Ranger Dudes Cowgirl #3294 pepper and Cowboy #3295 salt $500.00 – 650.00 set. Solid-color glazes, $250.00 – 350.00 set.

Hand-painted Jolly Tars Sailor Girl #3296 pepper and Sailor Boy #3297 salt $450.00 – 550.00 set. Solid-color glazes, $200.00 – 275.00 set.

Hand-painted Daisy #3298 salt and pepper shakers $175.00 – 200.00 per set. Solid-color glazes, $125.00 – 150.00 set.

The Blue Bell #3290 salt and pepper shakers were decorated to match the #3334 Blue Bell and #3340 Sunflower dinnerware patterns. The shakers shown are decorated with Art Ware Blue and Orange under clear glaze. Hand-painted, $125.00 – 150.00 set. Solid-color glazes, $95.00 – 125.00 set.

1941 Introductions

In 1941, Fulper Pottery contracted with Howard L. Ross, gift and novelty inventor and jobber at 30 Rockefeller Plaza, New York, to produce a line of novelty stacking salt and pepper sets. Ross, who held the patents for each design, supplied the control drawings for the models and molds to be produced. Each shaker set was identified with the in-mold "ROSS-WARE" mark and sometimes an oval gold-foil paper label stamped "ROSSWARE, made in USA." These stacking shakers were greatly superior to the novelty Japanese stacking shakers that were available before and after World War II.

Large group of Ross-Ware stacking shakers.

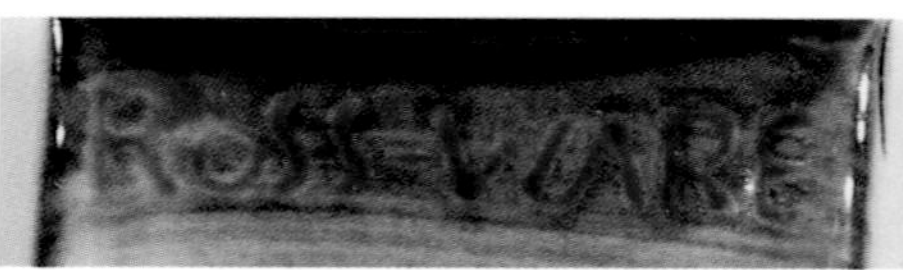

ROSS-WARE in-mold mark.

ROSSWARE gold-foil paper label.

Stangl produced several different stacking shaker shapes for Howard Ross throughout the 1940s and early 1950s. The Ross-Ware shakers were produced in a variety of bodies, finishes, and colors. Add $75.00 – 100.00 to the value of a complete set of Ross-Ware shakers in the original "Ross-Ware made by Stangl" box.

Showing two styles of Rossware gold-foil paper labels on Cherubim shaker bases.

The Comma-shape shakers were nearly always cast of red clay and glazed in the Terra Rose colors Green, Blue, or Mauve. The Commas also had a small ceramic button that was affixed to the cork stopper to conceal it when in place.

The Cherubim shakers were cast of red clay or white clay and painted with blonde, brunette, red, or black hair and wings of blue, gold, or white. The red clay Cherubim were considered black. Cherubim cast of white clay were either glazed with a flesh-colored glaze or simply left white with clear glaze.

Original Ross-Ware box with Cherubim shakers packed in original excelsior. Courtesy of the Horner collection.

Cherubim glazed with clear glaze will have hair and facial details painted in colors under the glaze. To achieve the bright yellow blonde on the red clay "Black" Cherubim, white engobe was brushed on the head before the yellow underglaze color was applied. Hair and facial details are done in fired-on overglaze colors on the Cherubim glazed with dark glazes.

Shortly after her introduction, the Cherubim's neck and wings were redesigned to better support her head. Heads on the original Cherubim tended to roll. To improve the situation, the top of the neck was recessed to accommodate the cork in the bottom of her head, and her wings were raised to support her hair so her head would not flop.

The Mexican Man was produced in a variety of finishes. He was cast of red clay with clear glaze, white clay with dark rose or flesh-colored glaze, and white clay with clear glaze. He can be found with his hair, teeth, and serape painted with fired-on overglaze color. Red clay versions had hair, mustache, and serape painted with underglaze colors with white engobe for teeth and under the color on the serape. White clay shakers are airbrushed with yellow underglaze color on the serape with overglaze color mustache and hair. Sometimes his hatband was decorated with gold.

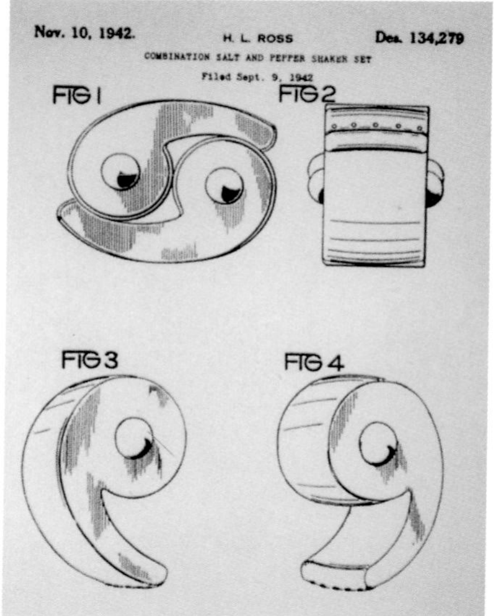

Ross-Ware Comma shakers, 1¾"x 3", showing the ceramic button attached to the stopper. $85.00 – 95.00 pair, with original stoppers.

Howard L. Ross's patent drawing for the Comma shakers, patent issued November 10, 1942.

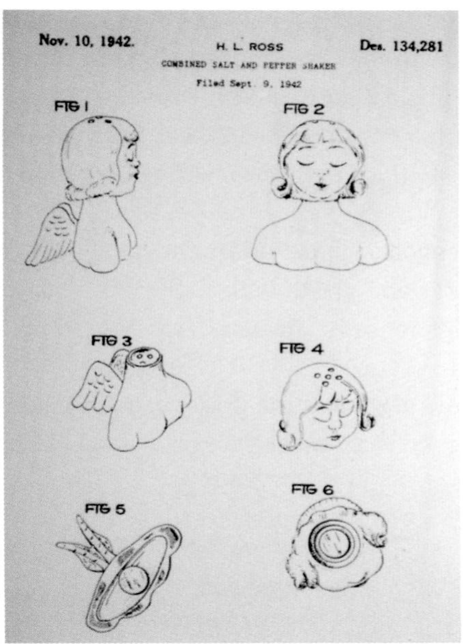

Group of Ross-Ware Cherubim shakers showing the variety of decorations produced, 3½". $150.00 – 175.00 set.

Howard L. Ross's patent drawing for the Cherubim shakers, patent issued November 10, 1942.

Ross-Ware Cherubim shakers with original gift box. Courtesy of the Jim Horner collection.

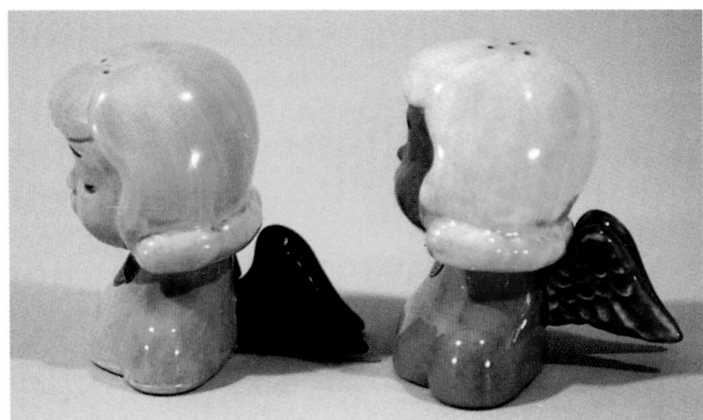

Cherubim shakers showing the original wing design on the left and redesigned wings on the right.

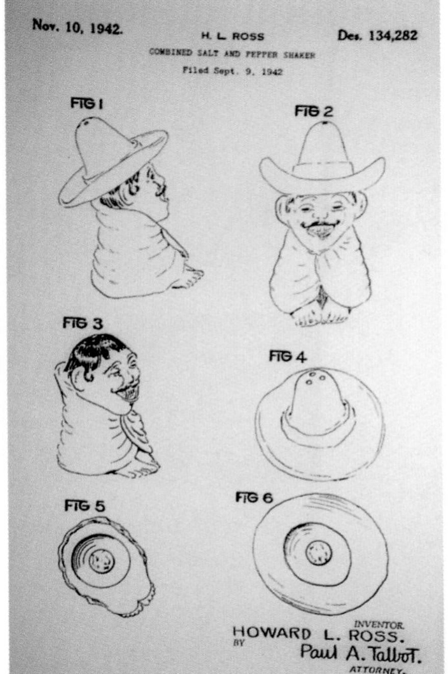

Group of Ross-Ware Mexican Man shakers showing the variety of decorations used, 4½". $190.00 – 225.00 set.

Howard L. Ross's patent drawing for the Mexican Man shakers, patent issued November 10, 1942.

The Hurricane Lamp bases were cast of white clay with colored glazes or cast of red clay with Terra Rose Blue, Green, or Mauve finish. The top "Chimney" shaker was cast of white clay and glazed in yellow. As with the Cherubim shakers, the Hurricane Lamp shakers were redesigned for stability shortly after introduction. The top of the base was slightly dished to accommodate the cork in the bottom of the "chimney." In addition, the flat top of the "chimney" was recessed to add dimension to the shaker. Shakers cast of red clay are about ⅛" larger than those cast of white clay due to the difference in shrinkage between Stangl's red and white clay bodies.

The Golf Tee shaker set was produced with the base cast of red clay with white engobe applied under the hand-painted grass, or cast of white clay with hand-painted green grass. The golf ball was white clay and glazed with Satin White glaze. Shakers cast of red clay are about ⅛" larger than those cast of white clay due to the difference in shrinkage between Stangl's red and white clay bodies.

The Mother Kangaroo and Joey shakers were usually white clay with flesh-colored glaze and the dress, hair, and facial details hand-painted in fired-on overglaze colors. This set was also produced hand-painted with underglaze colors and glazed with clear glaze.

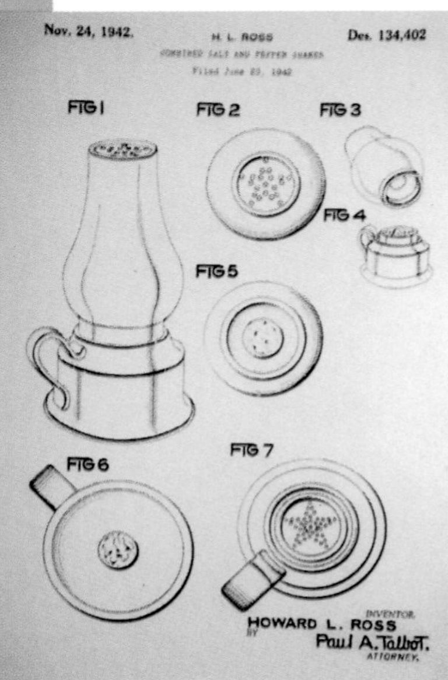

Howard L. Ross's patent drawing for the Hurricane Lamp shakers, patent issued November 10, 1942.

Three pair of Ross-Ware Hurricane Lamp shakers, 3½". $120.00 – 145.00 set.

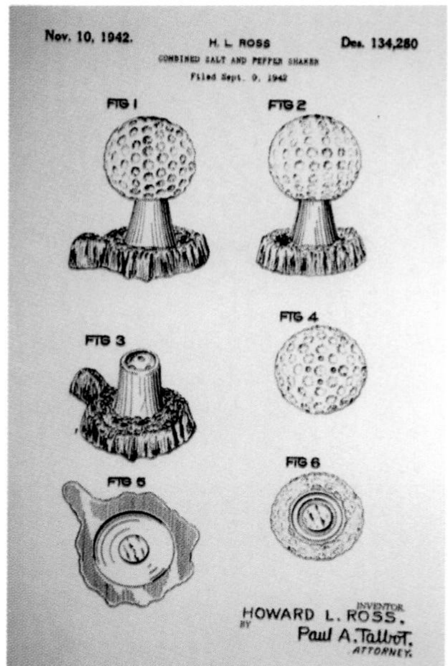

Howard L. Ross's patent drawing for the Golf Tee shakers, patent issued November 10, 1942.

Two pairs of Ross-Ware Golf Tee shakers, 3". $120.00 – 145.00 set.

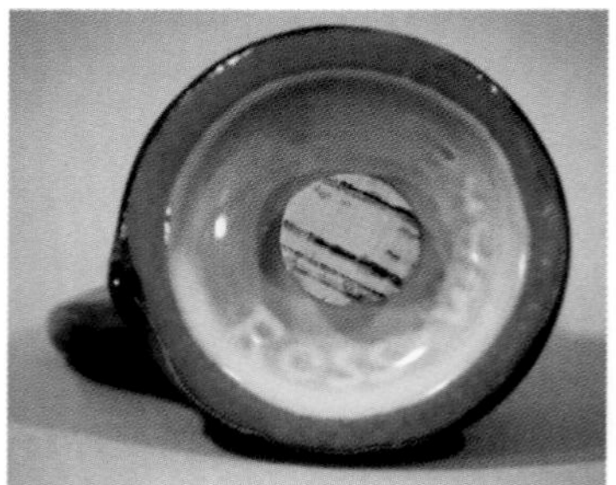

Ross-Ware in-mold mark on the base of the Golf Tee shakers.

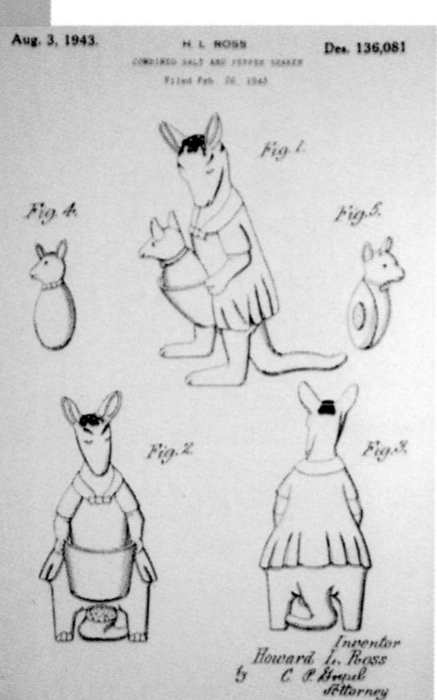

Howard L. Ross's patent drawing for the Kangaroo shakers, patent issued August 3, 1943.

Ross-Ware Kangaroo gold-foil paper label.

Ross-Ware Kangaroo shakers, red clay with underglaze color (left) and white clay with flesh clay on right, 5½", $190.00 – 225.00 set.

The Lily Pad shaker set was redesigned from a four-leaf style as shown in the patent drawing to a three-leaf design. The leaves were produced with either a red body and Terra Rose Green finish or white body with underglaze color decorated base. The blossom was white body glazed with Persian Yellow or hand-painted yellow or pink.

The Puppy shaker was cast of white clay with hand-painted details underglaze or cold paint. The Doghouse was red clay glazed in Terra Rose colors or white clay with colored glaze.

The Horse salt and pepper is very reminiscent of a modern-styled horse bust or knight chess piece. The base and head were glazed in bright contrasting colors, usually black and white. They were also glazed with cobalt blue and bright yellow.

Ross-Ware Lily Pad shakers, $160.00 – 180.00 set.
Courtesy of Trish Claar.

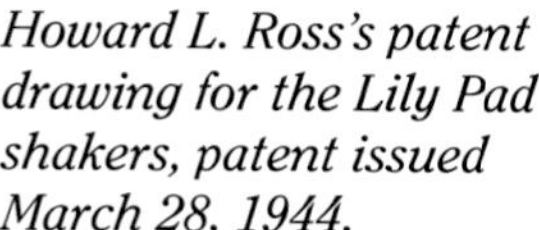

Howard L. Ross's patent drawing for the Lily Pad shakers, patent issued March 28, 1944.

Two sets of Ross-Ware Puppy and Doghouse shakers, $275.00 – 300.00 set.

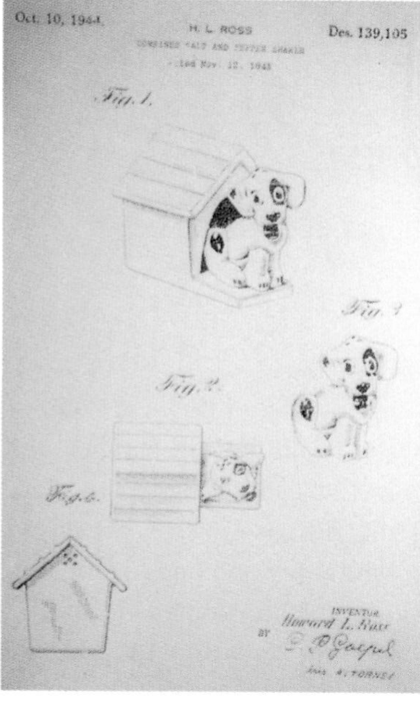

Howard L. Ross's patent drawing for the Doghouse shakers, patent issued October 10, 1944.

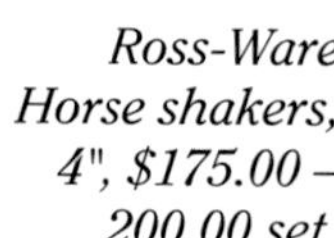

Ross-Ware Horse shakers, 4", $175.00 – 200.00 set.

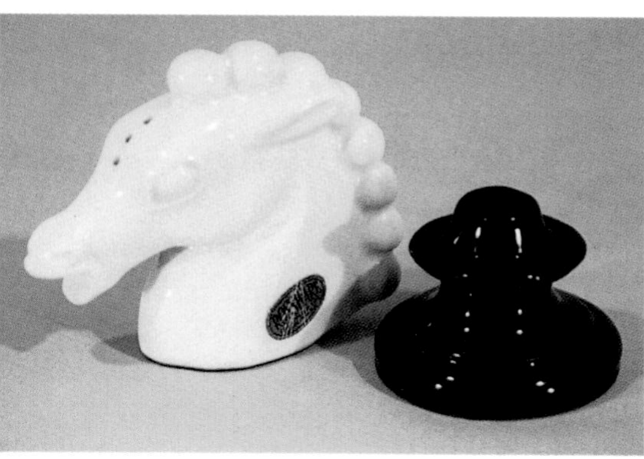

Ross-Ware Horse shakers, showing the base.

1943 Introductions

In 1943, two more novelty salt and pepper sets were introduced. One set was shaped liked a Pennsylvania Dutch boy and girl, and the other set was tulips. These shakers were produced of white or red clay and were decorated with solid-color glazes, Terra Rose glazes, or hand-painted decoration. The Tulip #3721 salt and pepper were usually decorated with Terra Rose Green, Blue, or Mauve, but can also be found hand-painted in yellow or blue to match the Blue Tulip and Yellow Tulip dinnerware patterns.

Not Shown:

Tulip #3721 shakers, Hand-painted, $175.00 – 200.00 per set. Solid-color glazes, $75.00 – 100.00 set.

Pennsylvania Dutch Boy and Girl #3718/19 salt and pepper shakers in Colonial Blue glaze. Hand-painted, $300.00 – 350.00 set. Solid-color glazes, $250.00 – 300.00 set.

Golf Ball salt and pepper, $85.00 – 95.00 set.

1958 Introduction:

The next novelty shakers came about during the early 1950s when the Golf Ball shakers were made for the Flemington Outlet. Golf Ball shakers were created from the same golf ball molds that had been used to cast the Ross-Ware Golf Tee stacking shaker set. Molds for the Golfer Sportsman and Antique Gold ashtray golf balls were also used to create golf ball shakers for the Flemington Outlet. The golf ball shakers can be found glazed with White Satin glaze or clear gloss glaze.

1965 Introductions

In spring 1965, apple-shape salt and pepper shakers were introduced for the Apple Delight dinnerware pattern, and the Daisy #3298 salt and pepper shakers were re-introduced, decorated to match the Blue Daisy dinnerware pattern. The Apple Delight shakers were cast of red clay and glazed with a gloss red Oxblood glaze or white clay and hand-painted in apple colors. The Blue Daisy shakers were white clay and hand-painted with the turquoise and brown Blue Daisy dinnerware colors. The Apple and Blue Daisy figural shakers were short-lived products as they were not produced after the fire in August 1965. These shakers usually only had Stangl's rubber stoppers to identify them.

Blue Daisy salt and pepper shakers, $130.00 – 150.00 set.

Apple Delight salt and pepper shakers in red clay and oxblood glaze, $80.00 – 110.00 set.

Apple Delight salt and pepper shakers, hand-painted in red and yellow, $130.00 – 150.00 set.

Stangl's rubber stoppers embossed with the name STANGL. These were designed by Kay Hackett during the 1950s and were used to identify Stangl shakers from the mid 1950s through 1978. $5.00 – 8.00 pair.

1967 Introductions

During the late 1960s, the Hen, Rooster, Duck, and Pig novelty salt and pepper shaker shapes were produced for the Flemington Outlet. The 1960s Hen and Rooster shakers used less color than the 1939 versions. Only the base (Pomona green), eyes (Eye black), beak (Orange), and comb (Pink #167) were decorated. The Ducks were more vibrantly decorated than the original #3250 figurines. The Pigs were decorated with either Black or Pink #160 spots. Often the Pig, Hen, and Rooster shakers were not marked. These pieces relied on the "Stangl" rubber stopper to identify them as Stangl products.

Ducks salt and pepper shakers with a Duck handled deviled egg dish. Duck salt and pepper, $240.00 – 270.00 pair; deviled egg dish, $200.00 – 250.00.

Rooster and Hen salt and pepper shakers produced during the 1960s. $150.00 – 200.00 set.

Bases of the Duck salts and peppers.

Pigs salt and pepper shakers. $130.00 – 160.00 set.

1978 Introduction

The last figural-novelty salt and pepper shakers introduced by Stangl were the corn-shaped shakers that were part of the Maize-Ware dinnerware pattern. Introduced in 1978, these shakers were available in the new solid-color glazes of Pioneer-Brown, Summer-Green, Harvest-Yellow, and Winter-Tan.

Not Shown:

Maize-Ware corn salt and pepper shakers, $15.00 – 20.00 set.

Cleo Salerno's Pottery Brooches

Cleo Crawford Salerno floral brooch, 3", $200.00 – 250.00. Courtesy of the Bullock collection.

Between 1945 and 1947, Stangl designer Cleo Crawford Salerno adapted many of her dinnerware designs to jewelry. She would cut the motif from a slab of red clay, brush on the engobe, then carve and paint the design. Once glazed and fired, standard bar pins were glued to the backs. Martin Stangl had asked her to create several of these to use as business gifts, and others she created for her own gift giving. The brooches were made in a variety of styles, including birds and insects, but were mostly floral motifs. They average in size from about 2" to 3" in diameter. Most are unmarked, but a few of them are signed "cleo."

Cleo brooch, floral motif, 2" to 3", 1945 – 1947. $200.00 – 300.00.

Cleo brooch, bird or insect motif, 2" to 3", 1945 – 1947. $250.00 – 350.00.

Flemington Outlet Necklace and Button Flowers

During the late 1940s, Stangl introduced pottery floral buttons for the Flemington Outlet. The diminutive blossoms were about 1" in diameter and were designed to be used as buttons or earrings, or strung as necklaces. Martin Stangl's official name for these shapes was "Necklace Flowers."

There were six blossom and two leaf shapes, which were decorated in a multitude of bright and pastel colors and color combinations. These items were produced at Trenton and at times were decorated at the Flemington Outlet during demonstrations. They were sold mounted on pasteboard cards. Buttons sold six for $1.00. Earrings were sold two pairs and one set of earring clips for $1.00. Necklaces were $2.50 to $4.00, depending on the number of flowers or leaves.

The buttons were fantastically popular during the late 1940s and into the 1950s, and literally thousands were sold at the Flemington Outlet. By the early 1960s, however, the necklace and buttons were no longer the vogue. By that time, the pansy and flower ashtrays were becoming the favorite inexpensive souvenir item of the Flemington Outlet.

"Necklace Flower" blossoms, $45.00 – 65.00 each.

"Necklace Flower" leaves, $35.00 – 50.00 each.

Assortment of blossoms and leaves showing just a small portion of the variety of decorations applied to these items. $35.00 – 65.00 each. Courtesy of the Hunterdon County Historical Society.

A pastel "Necklace Flower" necklace and pair of earrings. The necklaces were strung with bright green mercerized cotton cord. Necklace, $475.00 – 750.00; earrings, $90.00 – 130.00 pair. Courtesy of Merrill and Christl Stangl Bacheler.

Backs of a pair of buttons showing the style of earring clips used. Courtesy of Merrill and Christl Stangl Bacheler.

Another group of flower and leaf buttons. $35.00 – 65.00 each. Courtesy of Merrill and Christl Stangl Bacheler.

Kay Hackett's Hand-Painted Porcelain Jewelry

In 1954 Martin Stangl asked Kay Hackett to develop prototypes for a line of hand-painted jewelry he considered producing. Dave Thomas, Stangl's general manager, supplied Kay with blank porcelain cabochons purchased from Wenczel Tile, just down the street from Stangl Pottery. Dave Thomas also procured the overglaze colors and portable electric kiln to enable her to produce the samples.

Kay Hackett designed over a dozen motifs for the jewelry line. The designs featured various song birds and adaptations of Stangl dinnerware patterns. Samples on 2" round, oval, or rectangle cabochons were produced for each motif. Sample ¾" earrings were also created.

Kay Hackett's oval Holly brooch, 2", 1954 only. $175.00 – 200.00. Courtesy of Kay Hackett.

Martin Stangl decided not to produce the hand-painted jewelry line but allowed Kay to borrow the portable electric kiln and create a quantity of the brooch and earring sets on her own. She was able to sell the sets to various friends and acquaintances; some of her best customers were Stangl's own decorators. On average, Kay received $3.00 per brooch and earring set. Her most popular sets were decorated with the Cardinal and Holly motifs; she sold approximately 30 sets of each of those patterns.

Kay Hackett's Pennsylvania Flower 2" brooch and earring set, 1954 only. $300.00 – 350.00. Courtesy of Kay Hackett.

About a dozen each of the Fruit and Robin sets were produced. The Bluebird motif was popular, but very few Bluebird sets were created because it was difficult to control the dark blue overglaze color. Kay decorated nearly a dozen oval brooches with the Blue Rooster for a local social club. The Lyric-styled motifs were based on non-objective art and are all one-of-a-kind, since no two of those motifs were decorated alike.

Kay Hackett's rectangle Holly brooch, 2", 1954 only. $175.00 – 200.00. Courtesy of Kay Hackett.

Less than a dozen of some of the other motifs were decorated before Kay stopped producing the jewelry in late 1954.

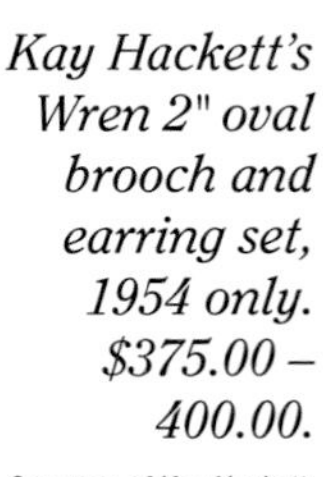

Kay Hackett's Wren 2" oval brooch and earring set, 1954 only. $375.00 – 400.00. Courtesy of Kay Hackett.

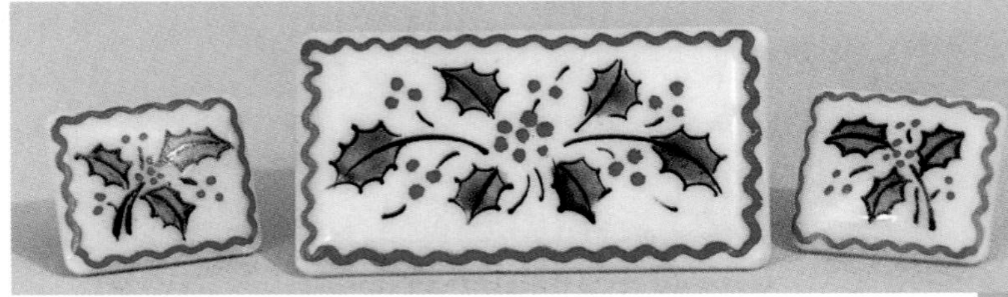

Kay Hackett's Holly rectangle brooch and earring set, 1954 only. $300.00 – 350.00. Courtesy of Kay Hackett.

Kay Hackett's Blue Rooster oval 2" brooch, 1954 only. $375.00 – 400.00. Courtesy of Kay Hackett.

Kay Hackett's Fruit round brooch and earring set, 1954 only. $400.00 – 450.00. Courtesy of Kay Hackett.

Kay Hackett's Blossom Time oval brooch and earring set, 1954 only. $225.00 – 275.00. Courtesy of Kay Hackett.

Kay Hackett's Cardinal oval brooch and earring set, 1954 only. $375.00 – 400.00. Courtesy of Kay Hackett.

Kay Hackett's oval 2" Bluebird brooch, 1954 only. $275.00 – 300.00. Courtesy of Kay Hackett.

Kay Hackett's Arabesque round 2" brooch, 1954 only. $300.00 – 350.00. Courtesy of Kay Hackett.

Kay Hackett's round non-objective Face 2" brooch, 1954 only. $375.00 – 400.00. Courtesy of Kay Hackett.

Kay Hackett's Robin oval brooch and earring set, 1954 only. $350.00 – 375.00. Courtesy of Kay Hackett.

Kay Hackett's Sandpiper oval 2" brooch, 1954 only. $375.00 – 400.00. Courtesy of Kay Hackett.

Employee Identification Badges

During the late 1930s and very early 1940s, Martin Stangl ordered employee photo badges from the Photo Art Co. Inc. of Trenton, New Jersey. The badges were typical 1½" round pin-back buttons with a photo of the employee and the employee's number along with "Fulper Pottery Company, Trenton, NJ." Employee badges were discontinued by the early 1940s.

Not Shown:

Fulper Pottery Company employee photo badge, late 1930s. $175.00 – 200.00.

Employee Service Pins

Martin Stangl commissioned two styles of 10k-gold service pins in the 1950s. Five-year pins measured ¾" and featured the Stangl name within a red enamel scrolled border. Ten-year pins were the same but set with a small ruby chip beneath the "n" in "Stangl." Twenty-year pins were set with a diamond chip. Martin Stangl generally awarded the service pins only to retiring employees. Employees that outlasted Mr. Stangl were denied the honor of receiving a pin. Altogether very few five-year service pins were issued and even fewer ten- and twenty-year pins.

Not Shown:

Five-year service pin. $150.00 – 175.00.

Ten-year service pin. $175.00 – 200.00.

Twenty-year service pin. $175.00 – 200.00.

Stangl Pottery five-year service pin. $150.00 – 175.00.

From the 1920s through the 1970s, Stangl produced dealer signs for retailers to use with Stangl displays. The signs were always decorated to match the Stangl products advertised at that time. Signs from the 1920s and 1930s were glazed with solid-color glazes; later signs were produced with popular hand-painted motifs or glaze finishes. Earlier dealer signs had a simple bracket stand, however, beginning in the late 1960s, many dealer signs were produced with a pocket on the back for holding dinnerware price lists.

Not Shown:

"Fulper Fayence" fan shape dealer sign, 1924 – 1929. $800.00 – 900.00.

"Stangl Rainbow Sets" dealer sign, rainbow shape, solid-color glazes, 1937 – 1940. $600.00 – 750.00.

"Stangl Pottery" individual display letters, Antique Gold, 1957. $850.00 – 1,200.00 per complete set.

"Tiffany Caughley" dealer sign, 1964 – 1978, Brown, Green. $200.00 – 250.00.

"Caughley" dealer sign, 1964 – 1978, Blue. $200.00 – 250.00.

"Caughley" dealer sign, 1964 – 1978, Brown, Green, Yellow. $175.00 – 200.00.

"Scandinavia" dealer sign, 1965. $100.00 – 125.00.

"Mediterranean" dealer sign, 1965 – 1972. $130.00 – 150.00.

"Antique French Crackle" dealer sign, 1970 – 1971. $120.00 – 135.00.

"Pompeii" dealer sign, 1971. $130.00 – 160.00.

"Pebblestone" dealer sign, 1972 – 1973. $100.00 – 125.00.

"Dainty-Ware" dealer sign, 1977 – 1978. $95.00 – 110.00.

"Indian Summer" dealer sign, 1977 – 1978. $110.00 – 135.00.

"Maize-ware" dealer sign, 1978. $95.00 – 110.00.

"Fulper Pottery" dealer sign, 1927 – 1935, Chinese Blue glaze. $1,000.00 – 1,200.00.

"Fulper" Fayence oblong dealer sign, 1924 – 1929, Turquoise Blue glaze. $500.00 – 600.00.

"Fulper-Stangl Pottery" dealer sign, Persian Yellow, 1927 – 1929. $700.00 – 800.00.

"Stangl Pottery" dealer sign, jar shape, solid-color glazes, late 1920s, Persian Yellow. $350.00 – 500.00.

"Stangl Pottery" individual display letters, edge motif, solid-color glazes, early 1930s. $850.00 – 1,200.00 complete set. From the Stangl and Fulper archival collection, courtesy the Wheaton Village Museum of American Glass.

"Stangl Pottery" dealer sign, vase motif, solid-color glazes, late 1920s – 1930s, Oxblood glaze. $350.00 – 500.00.

"Stangl Pottery" dealer sign, vase motif, black or ivory with gold or silver luster, 1933 only. $500.00 – 600.00.

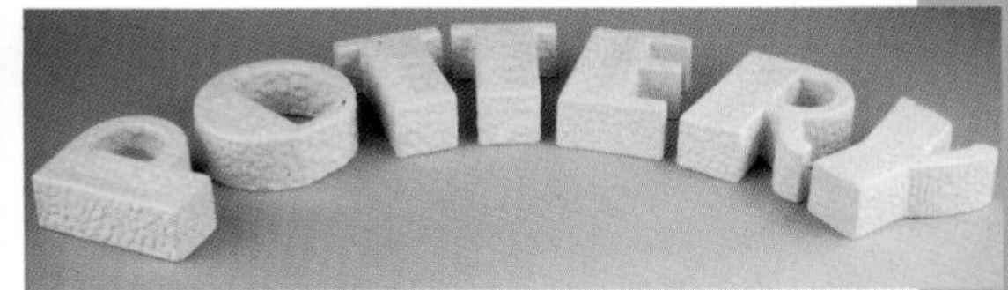

"Stangl Pottery" individual display letters, pebbly surface, solid-color glazes, early 1930s. $850.00 – 1,200.00 complete set. From the Stangl and Fulper archival collection, courtesy the Wheaton Village Museum of American Glass.

"Stangl Pottery" dealer sign, vase motif, hand-painted, 1938 – 1940. $450.00 – 550.00. From the Stangl and Fulper archival collection, courtesy the Wheaton Village Museum of American Glass.

"Stangl Pottery" dealer sign, vase motif, hand-painted, 1938 – 1940. $450.00 – 550.00.

"Della-Ware" dealer sign, palette shape, 1940 – 1950. $350.00 – 400.00.

"Stangl Pottery" individual display letters, Terra Rose, 1940. $850.00 – 1,200.00 per complete set. From the Stangl and Fulper archival collection, courtesy the Wheaton Village Museum of American Glass.

"Stangl Terra Rose" dealer sign, rose shape, 1940 – 1945. $300.00 – 350.00.

"Stangl Terra Rose" dealer sign, oval, 1940 – 1945. $375.00 – 400.00.

"Stangl Bird" dealer sign, 1944 – 1950s. $3,000.00 – 3,500.00. Courtesy of the Wayne Weigand collection.

(Left) "Stangl Dinnerware" dealer sign, hand-carved Tulip and Garden Flower motifs, 1945 – 1950. $375.00 – 400.00. (Right) "Lunning Peasant-ware" dealer sign, 1946 – 1948. $450.00 – 550.00.

"Stangl Dinnerware" dealer sign, hand-carved, Thistle and Blueberry motifs, 1950 – 1960. $500.00 – 600.00.

"Stangl" dealer sign, hand-carved, green letters, 1950 – 1960. $200.00 – 250.00.

"Stangl" dealer sign, cut-out ends, 1955 – 1960. $300.00 – 350.00.

Original "Antique Gold" dealer sign with crisp cross-hatching, 1958 – 1965. $120.00 – 145.00.

Re-styled "Antique Gold" dealer sign, 1965 – 1977. $85.00 – 95.00.

"Granada Gold" dealer sign, 1963 – 1977. $70.00 – 85.00.

"Appliqué" dealer sign, 1964 – 1965. $150.00 – 175.00.

"Tiffany Caughley" dealer sign, 1964 – 1978, Blue. $275.00 – 300.00.

"Stangl" dealer sign, raised lettering, cherry and floral motifs, 1965 – 1976. $200.00 – 250.00.

"Stangl" dealer sign, raised lettering, Golden Blossom motifs, 1965 – 1968. $200.00 – 250.00.

"Stangl" dealer sign, raised lettering, apple and blueberry motifs, 1965 – 1968. $250.00 – 300.00.

"Caribbean" dealer sign, 1968 – 1970. $160.00 – 180.00.

"Stangl Stoneware" dealer signs, redware with Dark Turquoise or Yellow lettering to coordinate with Stangl's Red Stoneware dinnerware patterns, 1971 – 1973. $110.00 – 135.00 each.

"Stangl Stoneware, Hand Painted" dealer sign, Hardened Blue lettering with Tan glaze, 1971 – 1973. $130.00 – 150.00.

"Stangl Stoneware, Hand Painted" dealer sign, Walnut Brown lettering with White Satin glaze, 1971 – 1973. $130.00 – 150.00.

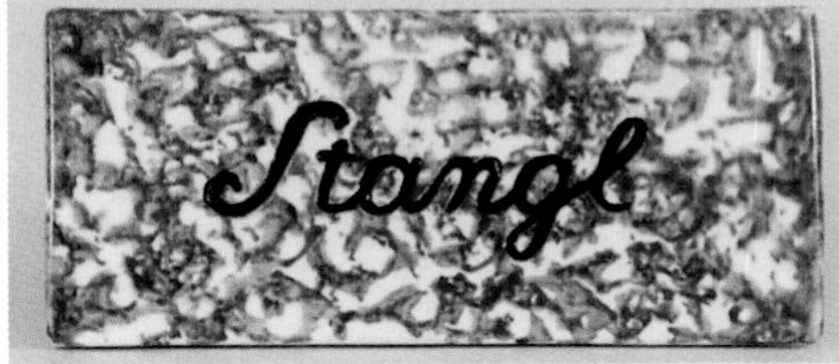

"Stangl" Town & Country Blue dealer sign, 1974 – 1978. $160.00 – 180.00.

"Stangl" Town & Country Brown, Green or Yellow dealer sign. $100.00 – 125.00.

"Patrician" dealer sign, 1978. $75.00 – 95.00.

As with many companies, Stangl printed a wide assortment of price lists, catalogs, booklets, and other paper items. Price lists for open stock dinnerware patterns were given to customers at department stores and the Flemington Outlet. Catalogs showing Stangl's general line of merchandise were usually available only to Stangl's sales force. Booklets, pamphlets, and advertising novelties were nearly always available only at the Flemington Outlet. Paper napkins and placemats matching popular dinnerware patterns were sold at department stores as well as the Flemington Outlet.

Stangl Pottery provided nearly any selling tool required by a retailer. During the 1940s, Stangl produced 12" plywood discs with dinnerware motifs for display at retail showrooms. This one featured Lunning's single Bird motif, which Lunning, Inc. would distribute to its various retail accounts. $85.00 – 145.00 each. Courtesy of the Luke and Nancy Ruepp collection.

Letterheads and Correspondence

The company used a variety of letterheads during its lifetime. The most available letterheads today date from the 1970s. These usually sell for $10.00 – 25.00 each, depending on how interesting the content might be. Earlier letterheads can sell for considerably more, particularly those from Fulper's Vasekraft era.

From the 1930s onward, Stangl Pottery mailed fliers listing sales, weekly specials, and upcoming events to patrons on the Flemington Outlet mailing list. These were usually mimeograph printing on 8½"x11" or 8½"x14" colored paper. Martin Stangl's daughters Christl and Martha were responsible for all the Flemington Outlet fliers and mailers, from designing the artwork to drafting the layouts and cutting the mimeograph stencils.

During the 1960s, postcards were used by the Flemington Outlet to advertise sales and specials. The postcards were chrome photos and featured Stangl products or views of the Outlet building.

(Above) Postcards were used throughout the 1920s for retailers to conveniently place orders for goods or Fulper Pottery literature. $18.00 – 25.00 each. (Below) Reverse of postcard.

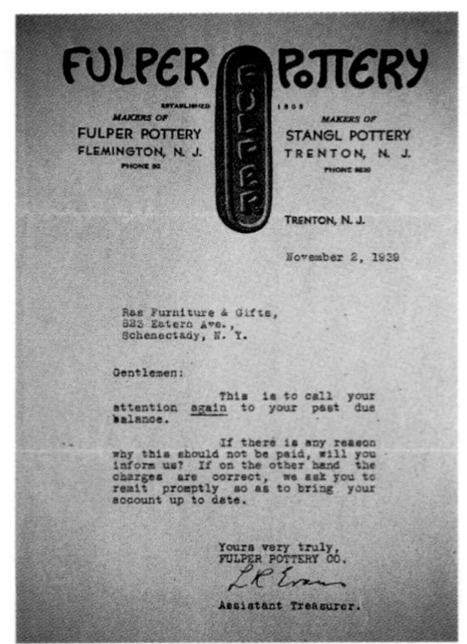
FULPER POTTERY

MAKERS OF FULPER POTTERY FLEMINGTON, N. J.

MAKERS OF STANGL POTTERY TRENTON, N. J.

TRENTON, N. J.

November 2, 1939

Ras Furniture & Gifts,
883 Eatern Ave.,
Schenectady, N. Y.

Gentlemen:

This is to call your attention again to your past due balance.

If there is any reason why this should not be paid, will you inform us? If on the other hand the charges are correct, we ask you to remit promptly so as to bring your account up to date.

Yours very truly,
FULPER POTTERY CO.

Assistant Treasurer.

A 1920s Fulper Pottery letterhead, used in 1939 to send a dunning notice to one of the company's past due accounts. $50.00 – 75.00.

A 1930s Flemington Outlet mailer drawn by Martha Stangl. $40.00 – 50.00. Courtesy of Gloria Logan.

Address side of a Flemington Outlet postcard, where the advertised specials would be printed.

Several 1940s mimeographed Flemington Outlet fliers and promotional leaflets, most drawn by Christl Stangl Bacheler. $25.00 – 50.00 each.

Stangl Pottery postcard showing an assortment of Antique Gold ashtrays. $8.00 – 12.00.

Four Stangl Pottery postcards featuring several dinnerware patterns. $10.00 – 15.00 each.

Postcard advertising Stangl's wig stands. $12.00 – 18.00.

One of the most popular views of the Flemington Outlet on a 1960s postcard. $12.00 – 18.00.

Stangl®

HAND-CRAFTED HAND PAINTED
DINNERWARE AND GIFTWARE

Padded Jiffy-Mailer imprinted with the Stangl Pottery logo, used for shipping promotional items such as 10" tidbits. $8.00 – 12.00.

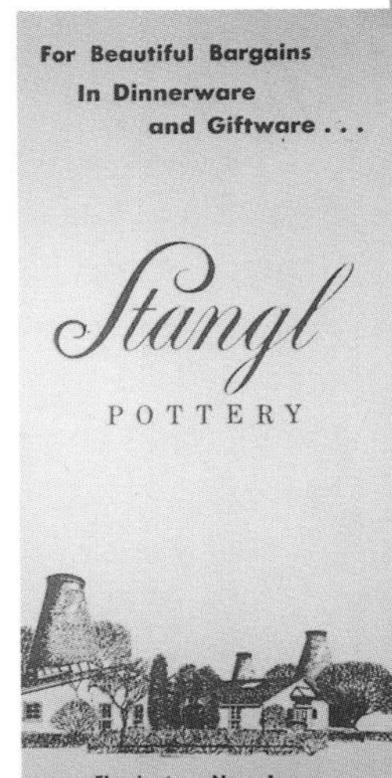

A 1973 tri-fold brochure advertising Stangl's Flemington Outlet, distributed around the country. $20.00 – 25.00.

Stangl

HAND PAINTED POTTERY

DINNER WARE

QUEENS FLOWER

Pattern No. 3319

Made in America by one of the oldest potteries. Noted for its tradition of fine Art Pottery this New Hand Painted Dinner Ware is an outstanding example of pottery craftsmanship at its best.

Captivating in warmth and character Queens Flower pattern shown above will enhance the attractiveness of your table setting. You will like it too for its rugged wearing qualities, for it is oven-proof and all colors are hand painted under the glaze.

And too, each piece is signed by the artist.

MADE IN AMERICA

PRICE LIST

10" Plates	F — 1.20 ea.	12" Chop	F — 2.25 ea.
9" Plates	F — 1.00 "	9½" Vegetable	F — 1.25 "
8" Plates	F — .80 "	10" Vegetable	F — 1.60 "
7" Plates	F — .60 "	12" Vegetable	F — 1.80 "
6" Plates	F — .40 "	12" Salad	F — 1.90 "
Cups, Coffee	F — .80 "	Sugar & Cover	F — 1.20 "
Cups, Tea	F — .60 "	Creamer	F — .80 "
Saucers	F — .35 "	Salt	F — .35 "
Bored Soups	F — .80 "	Pepper	F — .35 "
Fruits	F — .45 "	Candleholders	F — .75 "
14" Chop	F — 3.00 "	Coffee Carafe	F — 2.25 "

20 piece STARTER SETS
Service for four $11.20

THE FULPER POTTERY CO.
(Est. 1805)
Trenton - Flemington
New Jersey

A typical early 1940s price list for hand-painted dinnerware. $60.00 – 75.00.

Dinnerware and Artware Price Lists

Because Stangl's dinnerware patterns were open stock, multitudes of dinnerware price lists were printed to inform consumers of the pieces available and the retail prices. These lists were distributed to every Stangl Pottery retailer and given at the Flemington Outlet as well. Very few artware price lists were printed until the 1960s, when 8½"x11" glossy artware flyers were produced. A few exceptions were some printed cigarette set and pottery bird lists intended for retail level distribution.

Tri-fold flyer advertising Stangl's cigarette sets in 1946. $60.00 – 75.00.

Dinnerware price lists were usually printed for Stangl's most popular patterns only. Stangl rarely, if ever, made price lists available for private label patterns, salad sets or Flemington patterns. During the 1930s, price lists for hand-painted dinnerware patterns were usually 8½"x11" mat-finish, four-color single sheets. Beginning in 1942, hand-carved dinnerware pattern price lists were mat-finish, four-color 3½"x6¼" bi-fold sheets. From the 1950s through the 1970s, Stangl used glossy, full-color bi-fold, tri-fold, and single sheet price lists ranging from 3½"x6¼" to 8½"x11". Stangl's dinnerware price lists can sell from $5.00 to 35.00, depending on the pattern.

Various Stangl dinnerware price lists dating from the 1940s through 1978.

Booklets and Handouts

Several different booklets were printed from the 1940s through the 1970s describing Stangl's history, manufacturing processes, and decorative attributes. These items were distributed at department store demonstrations and the Flemington Outlet and could be requested by mail.

Not Shown:

Stangl Dinnerware and How They Do It, 1948; 2½"x5¼". $20.00 – 25.00.

History of Stangl Pottery, 1964; 8 pages 3½"x5½". $20.00 – 25.00.

Facts About Stangl, 1965. $10.00 – 15.00.

Stangl, A Portrait of Progress in Pottery, 1965; 32 pages. $40.00 – 50.00.

Attractive Settings for Your Table, *1946; 6 pages 7"x8½". $50.00 – 60.00.*

Stangl booklets, Stangl, A Portrait of Progress in Pottery, *$40.00 – 50.00, and* History of Stangl Pottery, *$20.00 – 25.00.*

Flemington Outlet Advertising and Novelties

In addition to promoting the Flemington Outlet with fliers and local newspaper ads, Stangl used assorted advertising give-away items. These were usually small and inexpensively produced.

bridge tally, 1940s; paper with tassel. $15.00 – 20.00.
canasta tally, 1940s; paper. $15.00 – 20.00.
litter bag, 1970s; printed vinyl. $20.00 – 25.00.
Fulper matchbook, 1930s. $80.00 – 125.00.
Stangl matchbooks, 1930s – 1950s. $18.00 – 22.00.
Stangl matchboxes, 1960s. $18.00 – 22.00.
memorandum booklet, 1970s; printed vinyl with calendar. $20.00 – 25.00.

Two Stangl Pottery advertising ballpoint pens, 1950s – 1970s, $15.00 – 20.00 each. Courtesy of the Wayne Weigand Collection.

memorandum booklet, 1940s – 1950s; printed paper. $25.00 – 35.00.
pen, 1950s – 1970s; ballpoint. $15.00 – 20.00.
pencil, 1950s; mechanical. $20.00 – 25.00.
pencil, 1950s; wood. $6.00 – 8.00.
ruler, 1950s; 6" with calendar, paper. $20.00 – 25.00.
ruler, 1950s; 18" metal. $30.00 – 40.00.
tumbler, 1976 employee Christmas Party souvenir, glass. $45.00 – 55.00.

Stangl Pottery advertising matchbox and matchbooks, 1940s – 1960s, $18.00 – 22.00 each; Fulper Pottery matchbook, 1930s, $80.00 – 125.00.

Vinyl memo booklet, $20.00 – 25.00; paper memo booklet, $25.00 – 35.00; wood memo pencil, $6.00 – 8.00.

Stangl paper 6" calendar rulers, 1950s, $20.00 – 25.00 each.

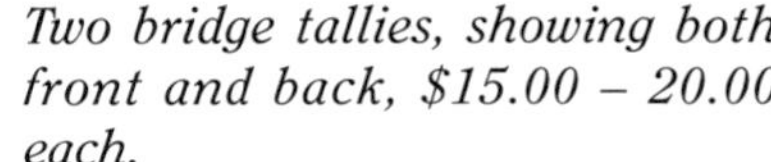

Two bridge tallies, showing both front and back, $15.00 – 20.00 each.

Stangl Pottery 1976 Christmas Party tumbler, $45.00 – 55.00.

Paper Napkins and Placemats

Stangl's first paper napkins were produced for a short time during the mid-1950s. These were dinner- and cocktail-sized napkins printed with motifs matching a few of the more popular dinnerware patterns. These napkins had a scalloped edge and were packed 100 to a pasteboard box or 25 in a cellophane package. This style of napkin was discontinued by the late 1950s. Stangl did not offer paper napkins again until the late 1960s when they were reintroduced by plant superintendent James Paul.

Paper placemats were produced only during the mid-1950s. The placemats measure 14"x10" and were sold in pasteboard boxes of 100. Paper placemats were available with the same motifs as the scalloped edge paper napkins.

1950s Blueberry and Thistle dinner and cocktail napkins, pasteboard napkin box. Napkins, $1.00 – 1.50 each.

The paper napkins developed by James Paul during the 1960s and 1970s had straight edges instead of scalloped and were sold in cellophane packs of 50.

Paper placemats with Thistle motif and pasteboard box. Placemats, $3.00 – 5.00 each.

1960s era Fruit pattern napkins in original cellophane package. Napkins, $1.00 each.

Several of the paper napkin patterns available during the late 1960s to mid – 1970s. Paper napkins usually sell between 50¢ – $1.00 each.

Because Martin Stangl was producing a product with a known reputation for high quality, he felt that every piece sold should bear a recognizable trademark. The earliest Fulper Fayence and Fulper-Stangl pieces usually bore only a paper label, and rarely an in-mold shape number was cast into the bases. Often a Fulper Fayence label was used in conjunction with a square Fulper label indicating the name of the item on the base. During the late 1920s and early 1930s, a steel die was used to impress the Fulper-Stangl or Stangl name into the base. Paper labels were always used in conjunction with these marks. During the 1930s, in-mold shape numbers in conjunction with the Stangl name came into prominence. Many solid-color articles produced from that time through the 1950s were marked in this fashion.

When Stangl began mass-producing underglaze decorated articles, rubber-stamped underglaze marks began to be used. Variations of underglaze backstamps were in use from 1937 until the close of the factory. The only exception to this was for a short time between 1946 and 1949 when underglaze decal marks were used.

During the 1950s, Stangl used rubber stamp marks with a date code. The code was a Roman numeral system. Beginning in 1953, three small slashes were used in conjunction with the oval backstamp. The three slashes represented 1953. In 1954, there were four slashes and five slashes during the first half of 1955. By the end of 1955, the five slashes were replaced with the Roman numeral "V." During the last half of the 1950s, Roman numerals represented the date for each year. The Roman numeral "X" represented 1960, which was the last year that a date code backstamp was used.

During the 1960s, various logos were added to the trademark, such as "Hand Painted," "Dura-Fired," and "Oven Proof." After the 1965 fire, the trademark was significantly modified. The word "Pottery" was removed, and the oval became somewhat flattened. The words "Since 1805" were added at this time. For marks used on the bird figurines, see page 96.

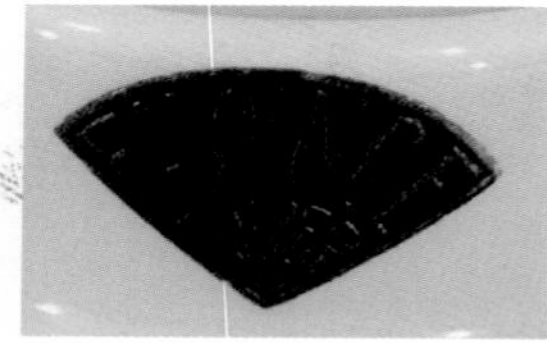

Fulper Fayence gold-foil paper label, 1924 – 1928.

Fulper square paper label with product information, 1924 – 1928.

Fulper square paper label with product information, 1924 – 1928.

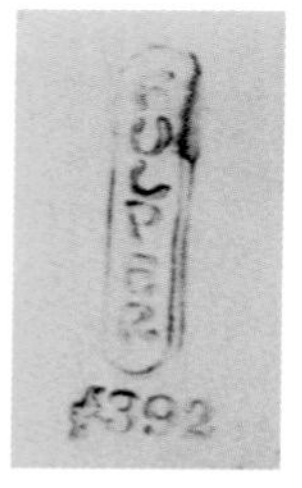

Fulper overglaze stamp used on Fulper Decorated items, 1920s.

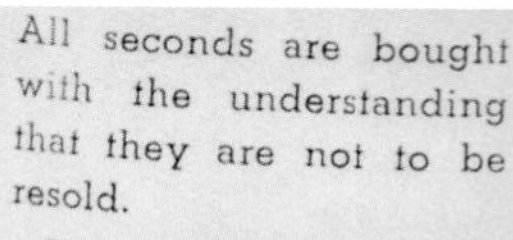
All seconds are bought with the understanding that they are not to be resold.

FULPER POTTERY COMPANY

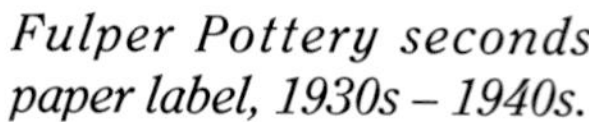

Fulper Pottery seconds paper label, 1930s – 1940s.

Fulper/Stangl paper label, 1926 – 1929.

Fulper/Stangl die-pressed oval mark, 1926 – 1929.

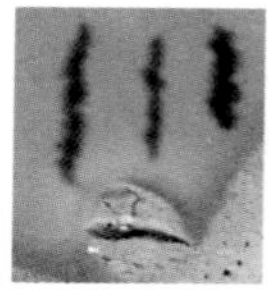

Finishers' marks, 1920s – 1930s

Stangl Pottery jar-shape gold-foil paper label, 1929 – early 1930s.

Stangl die-pressed mark, 1929 – 1940s.

In-mold shape number, 1920s – 1970s.

In-mold Selma Robb or Fisk with shape number, 1930s.

Gold-foil paper label, vase motif, 1930 – 1940s.

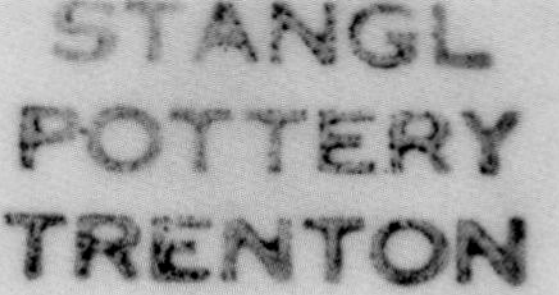

Underglaze stamp, block letters, 1937 – 1939.

Underglaze stamp, vase motif, dark letters, 1937 – 1939.

Underglaze stamp, vase motif, light letters, 1937 – 1939.

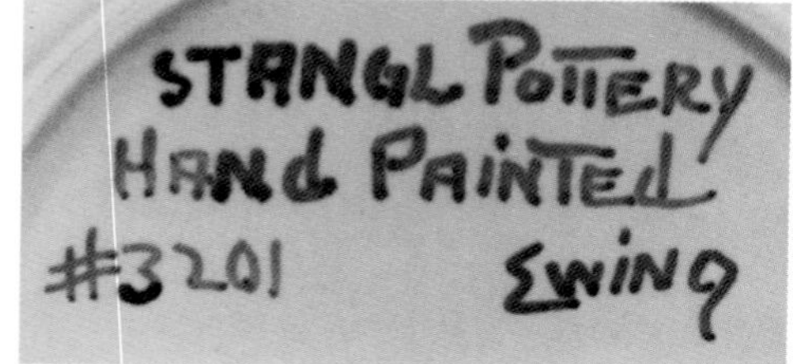

Hand painted dinnerware mark, 1938 – 1940.

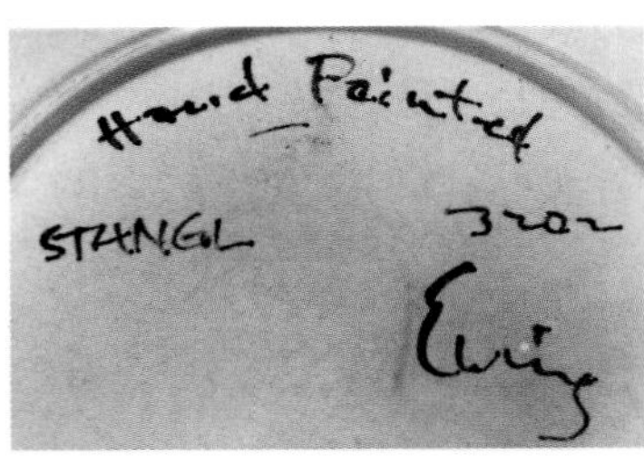

Hand painted dinnerware mark, 1938 – 1940.

Underglaze stamp, vase motif, 1938 – 1940s.

Underglaze stamp, vase motif, "Handpainted by," 1938 – 1940s.

American Way underglaze stamp, 1940 – 1942.

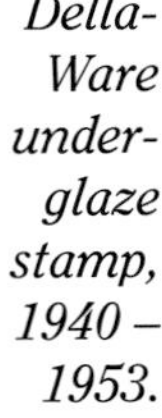

Della-Ware underglaze stamp, 1940 – 1953.

Carole Stupell Ltd. underglaze stamp, 1940 – 1945.

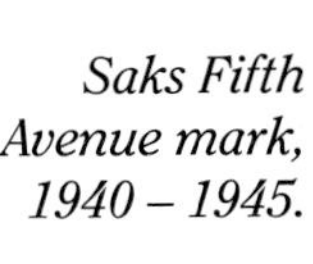

Saks Fifth Avenue mark, 1940 – 1945.

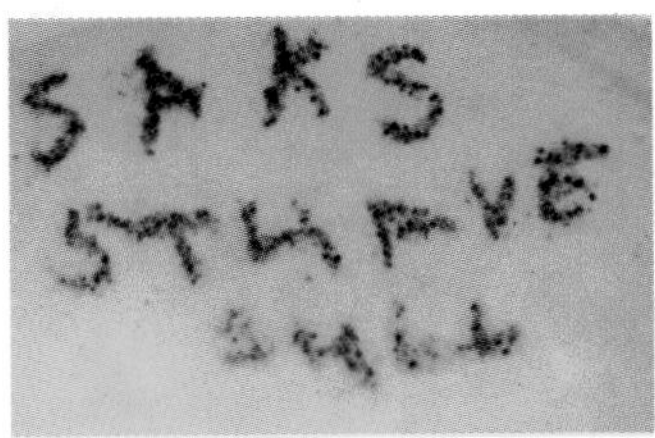

Terra Rose with Saks Fifth Avenue mark, 1940 – 1945.

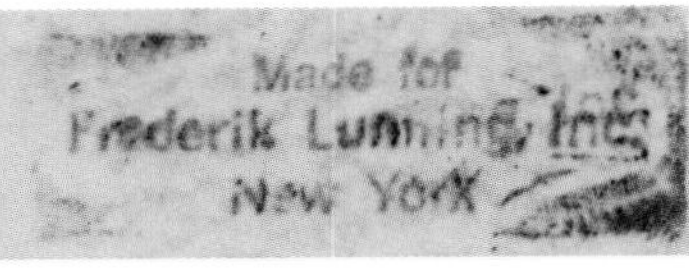

Frederik Lunning, Inc. underglaze stamp, 1940 – 1942.

Terra Rose underglaze stamp, block letters, 1940 – 1950.

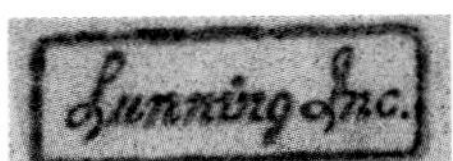

Lunning, Inc. underglaze stamp, 1942 – 1953.

Terra Rose gold-foil paper label, early 1940s.

Terra Rose gold-foil paper label, late 1940s – 1950s.

Terra Rose underglaze stamp, script letters, mid – 1940s.

Terra Rose underglaze decal, 1946 – 1949.

Stangl Pottery Birds underglaze decal, 1940s.

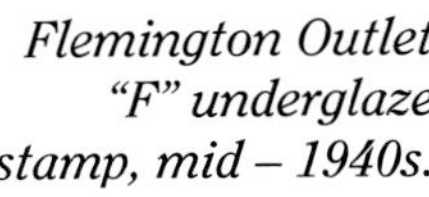

Flemington Outlet "F" underglaze stamp, mid – 1940s.

Oval Stangl Flemington Outlet underglaze stamp, sometimes used to mark seconds, late 1940s – 1978.

Made by Stangl gold-foil paper label, 1940s.

Stangl Pottery gold-foil paper label, black type, 1940s.

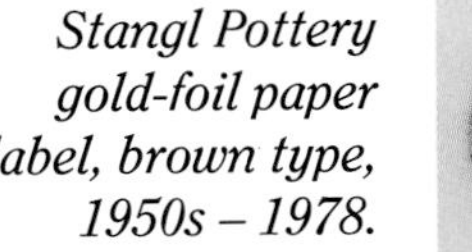

Stangl Pottery gold-foil paper label, brown type, 1950s – 1978.

Stangl Pottery underglaze decal, 1947 – 1949.

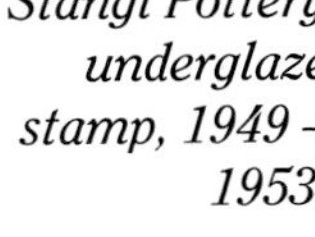

Stangl Pottery underglaze stamp, 1949 – 1953.

Underglaze stamp, dated "1954."

150th Anniversary underglaze stamp, 1955.

American Bone China gold luster stamp, 1955.

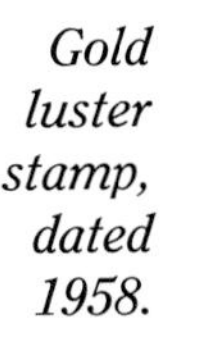

Gold luster stamp, dated 1958.

Patent Pending stamp, late 1950s – early 1960s.

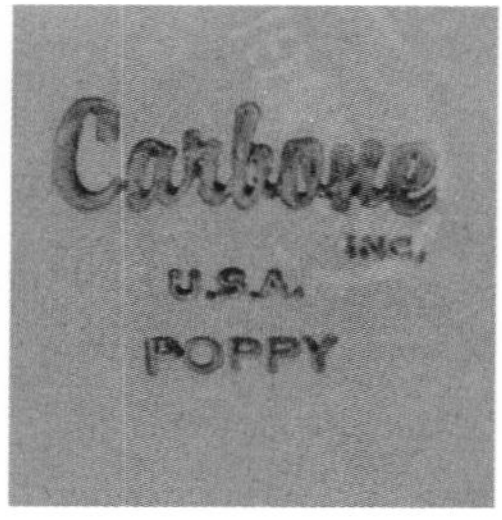

Carbone underglaze stamp, 1959 – 1963.

Oven Proof underglaze stamp, early 1960s.

Made For Jordan Marsh underglaze stamp, early 1960s.

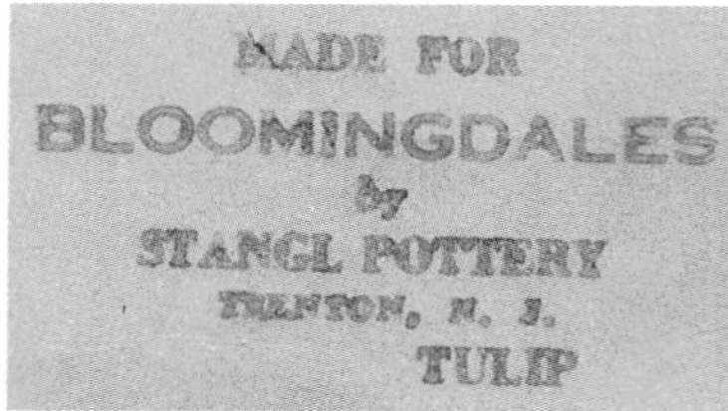

Made For Bloomingdale's underglaze stamp, early 1960s.

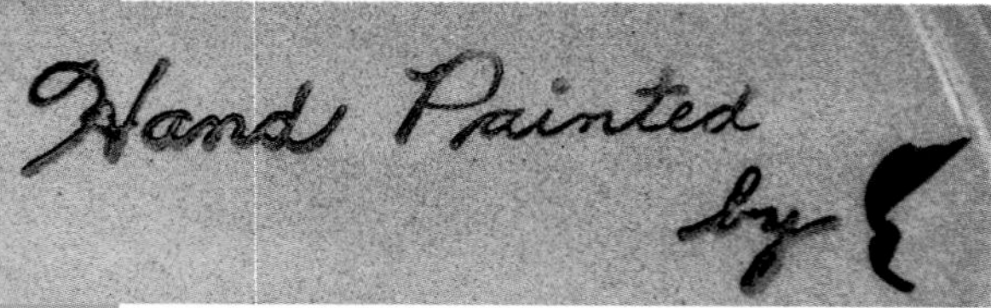

Hand Painted By... underglaze stamp, early 1960s.

Henri Bendel underglaze stamp, early 1960s.

Dura-Fired underglaze stamp, 1963 – 1965.

Caughley underglaze stamp, 1964 – 1978.

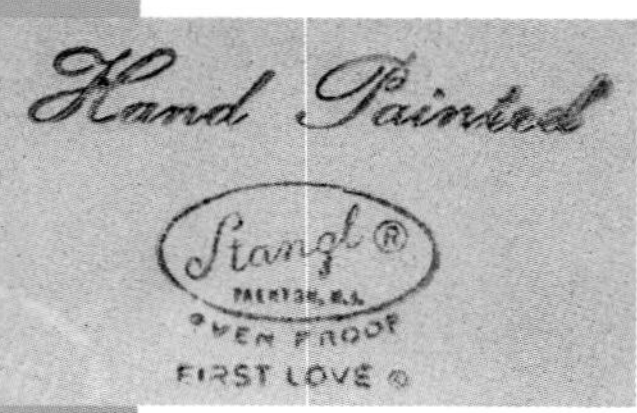

Large Hand Painted underglaze stamp, late 1960s.

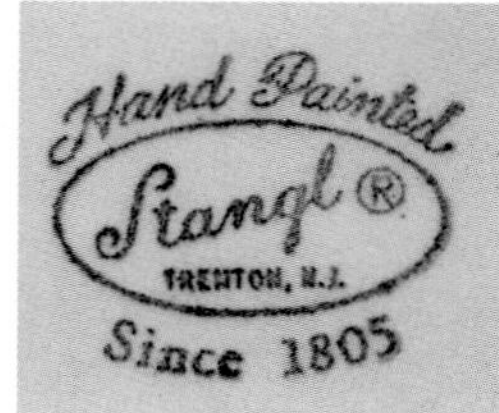

Hand Painted Since 1805 underglaze stamp, 1965 – 1978.

CAROLE STUPELL LTD gold luster stamp, 1970 – 1974.

Potter's Association underglaze stamp, early 1970s.

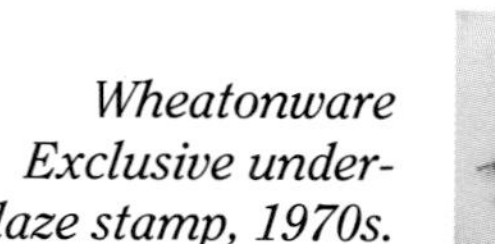
Wheatonware Exclusive underglaze stamp, 1970s.

PRESIDENT'S WEEK
WINNER 1970

President's Week Winner 1970 stamp, 1970.

HAND PAINTED BY
EXPERIENCED ARTISTS

Hand Painted by Experienced Artists underglaze stamp, early 1970s.

Large Stangl Stoneware underglaze stamp, 1971 – 1974.

Small Stangl Stoneware underglaze stamp, 1971 – 1974.

Genuine Handcrafted underglaze stamp, late 1977 – 1978.

TO OVEN ... underglaze stamp, late 1977 – 1978.

Maize-Ware underglaze stamp, 1978.

Micro-Oven-Table-Dishwasher underglaze stamp, 1978.

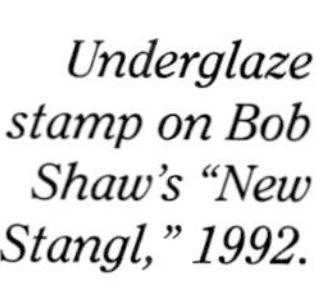
Underglaze stamp on Bob Shaw's "New Stangl," 1992.

Seconds Marks

Stangl marked second-quality items with special "second" marks for several reasons but primarily to prevent discounted items purchased at the Flemington Outlet from being returned to department stores for full value. This was why Lunning's contract with Stangl required that all Lunning seconds have the Lunning mark obliterated in some way. The Lunning marks were at first obliterated by grinding them with a grinding wheel. Beginning in 1942, the mark on Lunning seconds was covered with black glaze and the whole piece re-fired. This added considerable cost and labor to Lunning items sold at the Flemington Outlet.

Pieces that were determined to be seconds before glaze was applied were marked with one of several underglaze "second" rubber-stamps. Until the early 1950s, there was no truly effective way to permanently mark glazed pieces as second quality. By 1953, a sandblast marking system was developed which enabled the word "Stangl" to be indelibly etched into the glaze, indicating the piece as second quality. Most of the items marked with the sandblasted "seconds" mark were actually first quality. Martin Stangl often sold first quality items at the Flemington Outlet as seconds. He could get more money more quickly for seconds at discounted list price at the Flemington Outlet than he could selling firsts to department stores at wholesale; many first quality items would be sandblasted with a seconds mark so they could be sold at the Flemington Outlet.

Until the late 1960s, seconds were sold only at the Flemington Outlet. During the late 1960s and early 1970s, however, Stangl began selling "slightly imperfect" seconds to discount stores at reduced prices. This group of seconds was called the "A" Line or "A" Ware. Each piece was marked with a sandblasted "A" within a circle.

Frederik Lunning, Inc. ground-out underglaze stamp, 1940 – 1942.

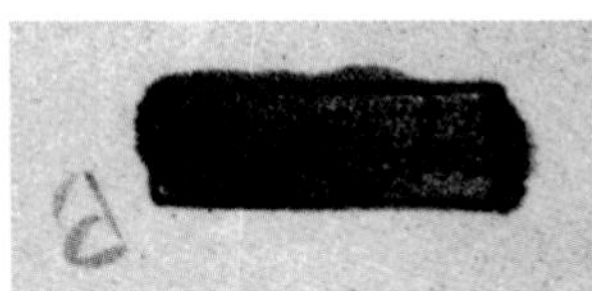

Lunning, Inc. blacked-out underglaze stamp, 1942 – 1953.

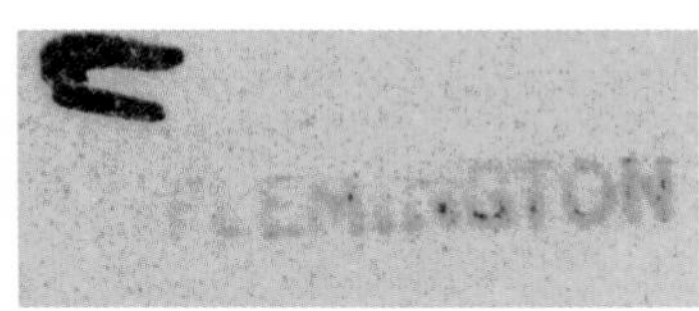

Flemington second underglaze stamp, mid – 1940s.

Oval Stangl Flemington Outlet underglaze stamp, sometimes used to mark seconds, late 1940s – 1978.

Stangl Sec. second underglaze stamp, 1950s – 1960s.

Sandblasted second mark, 1953 – 1978.

Sandblasted "A" Ware mark, late 1960s – early 1970s.

Bibliography

Binns, Charles F. *The Potter's Craft*. 1922, D. Van Nostrand Co., New York.

Blasberg, Robert W. "Twenty Years of Fulper," *Spinning Wheel*. October 1973.

Blasberg, Robert W., and Todd M. Volpe. "Fulper Art Pottery: Amazing Glazes," *American Art & Antiques*. July – August, 1978.

Blasberg, Robert W. *Fulper Art Pottery: An Aesthetic Appreciation 1909 – 1929*. 1979, The Jordan - Volpe Gallery, New York.

Branin, M. Lelyn. *The Early Makers of Handcrafted Earthenware and Stoneware in Central and Southern New Jersey*. 1988, Associated University Presses, Cranbury, New Jersey.

Cameron, Elisabeth. *Encyclopedia of Pottery and Porcelain: 1800 – 1960*. 1986, Cameron Books, London.

Carney, Margaret. "Daddy Binns: The Reason Why the Best Studied at Alfred," *Journal of the American Art Pottery Association*. November – December 1998.

Chappell, James. *The Potter's Complete Book of Clay and Glazes*. 1977, Watson-Guptill Publications, New York.

Cunningham, John T. "Railroading in New Jersey," *Newark Sunday News*. Associated Railroads of New Jersey, 1951, Newark, New Jersey.

De Beck, Ethel. *The State of New Jersey*. 1937, Ginn and Company, New York.

Evans, Paul. *Art Pottery of the United States*. Feingold & Lewis Publishing, New York.

Fort, Margaret H. "New Jersey's Oldest Art Pottery," *New Jersey Life*. June 1931

Gray, Gordon W. *Fulper! Form, Function, & Finance*. 1992, Clinton Historical Museum, Clinton, New Jersey.

Goldberg, David J. *Potteries: The Story of Trenton's Ceramic Industry*. 1983, 1998, Trenton, New Jersey.

Hennessey, William J. *Russel Wright: American Designer*. 1983, MIT Press.

Jacobs, Michel. *The Art of Color*. 1923, Doubleday, Doran & Company, Inc., Garden City, New York.

Lee, Warren F. *Down Along the Old Bel-Del*. 1987, Bel-Del Enterprises, Ltd., Albuquerque, New Mexico.

Lock, Robert C. *The Traditional Potters of Seagrove, North Carolina*. 1994, Robert C. Lock, Inc./The Antiques & Collectibles Press, Greensboro, North Carolina.

McManus Brothers. Auto Map of New Jersey. 1922, McManus Brothers Furniture Co., Elizabeth, New Jersey.

Nelson, Glenn C. *Ceramics, A Potter's Handbook*. 1960, 1966, Holt, Reinhart and Winston, Inc., New York.

Parmelee, Cullen W., *Ceramic Glazes*, 1951, Industrial Publications, Inc., Chicago, Illinois.

Ries, Heinrich and Henry B. Krummel. *The Clays and Clay Industry of New Jersey*. 1904, MacCrellish & Quigley, Book and Job Printers, Trenton, New Jersey.

Ricker, Ruth. "The Fulper Doll Head," *Spinning Wheel*, July 1956.

Schaltenbrand, Phil and Larry Rumble. *Ceramics Monthly*. September 1998.

Shuman, Eleanor Nolan. *The Trenton Story*. 1958.

Stern, Marc Jeffrey. *The Pottery Industry of Trenton – A Skilled Trade in Transition 1850 – 1929*. 1994, Rutgers University Press, New Brunswick, New Jersey.

Stuart, Evelyn Marie. "Pottery at the Panama-Pacific Exposition," *Fine Arts Journal*. 1914. Reprinted by Fulper Pottery Company, 1915.

_____. "Vasekraft – An American Art Pottery," *Fine Arts Journal*. 1914. Reprinted by Fulper Pottery Company, 1915.

Snell, James P. *History of Hunterdon and Somerset Counties, New Jersey*. 1881, Everts & Peck, Philadelphia, Pennsylvania.

Business Executives of America. 1950, Institute for Research Biography, Inc., New York.

Business Review of the Counties of Hunterdon, Morris and Somerset, New Jersey. 1891, Pennsylvania Publishing Co., Philadelphia.

First 250 Years of Hunterdon County, 1714 – 1964. 1964, Hunterdon County Board of Chosen Freeholders, Flemington, New Jersey.

From Teacups to Toilets. New Jersey Department of Transportation.

Industrial Trenton and Vicinity. 1900, George A. Wolf, Wilmington, Delaware.

The Industrial Directory of New Jersey. 1906, Trenton, New Jersey.

An Inventory of Historic Engineering and Industrial Sites: Trenton, New Jersey. 1975, Trenton, New Jersey.

New Industrial Digest of New Jersey. 1934. New Jersey Council, Trenton, New Jersey.

New Jersey: Life, Industries & Resources of a Great State. 1928, New Jersey State Chamber of Commerce, Newark, New Jersey.

Raritan Township, Flemington and Environs. 1976, Raritan Township, New Jersey.

Who's Who in the East. 1948, 1951, A.N. Marquis Co., Chicago 11, Illinois.

250th Anniversary of the Settlement of Trenton. 1929, Trenton Chamber of Commerce, Trenton, New Jersey.

Haeger: The Craftsmen for a Century. 1971, Haeger Potteries, Inc., Dundee, Illinois.

Stangl: A Portrait of Progress in Pottery. 1965, Stangl Pottery, Trenton, New Jersey.

History of Stangl Pottery. 1964, Stangl Pottery, Trenton, New Jersey.

Periodicals

Arts and Decoration. Issues 1918 – 1941.

Art-In-Trade. September 1929.

Bucks County Traveler. November 1957

Ceramic Age, The Ceramist. Issues 1921 – 1968.

China, Glass & Tablewares. Summer supplement, 1955.

The Craftsman. Issues 1902 – 1916.

Crockery and Glass Journal. Summer supplement, 1955.

Enamel – Glass – Whiteware. May 1955.

Exploring Hunterdon's Heritage. Vol. 1, No. 1, Winter 1981.

Giftwares & Decorative Furnishings. June 1931.

House and Garden. Issues 1910 – 1928.

House Beautiful. Issues 1912 – 1927.

Hunterdon County Democrat. Issues spanning 1914 – 1988, Flemington, New Jersey.

Hunterdon Historical Newsletter. Winter 1973. Hunterdon County Historical Society, Flemington, New Jersey.

Good Furniture Magazine. January – July 1923.

Keramic Studio. September 1913.

The News. February 6, 1969, Frenchtown, New Jersey.

Trenton Magazine. 1954.

The Trentonian. August 30, 1965, Trenton, New Jersey.

The Trenton Times. July 16, 1951; August 31, 1965, Trenton, New Jersey.

Sunday Times Advertiser. October 17, 1965; September 4, 1966, Trenton, New Jersey.

American Way sales catalog, Regional Handcraft Program, 1940.

Fulper Pottery sales catalogs, advertising, company records.

Stangl Pottery sales catalogs, dinnerware price lists, company records.

Martin Stangl's personal notebooks. 1927 – 1978, handwritten by Martin Stangl, Anne Pogranicy.

Interviews and conversations with Stangl family members, Stangl employees, descendants of employees, and Stangl business associates, conducted 1989 – 2001.

By Diana E. Bullock-Runge

Known to champion the cause of historic preservation, Rob Runge is fondly referred to as "Mr. Stangl." He is universally respected as the one person who possesses a "textbook" knowledge of the history, operation, personalities, and products of the Stangl Pottery Company.

Through his tireless research efforts spanning the last 20 years, Rob has delved into company files, as well as public and museum records. He has access to Martin Stangl's personal production notebooks and a wealth of file memos. He conducted countless interviews with former Stangl company employees. Martin Stangl's own daughter and son-in-law, Christl Stangl Bacheler and Merrill Bacheler, often quip that Rob knows more about the company than "Pop" Stangl himself!

Rob was born, raised, and educated in the Hunterdon County/Trenton, New Jersey area. He became quite interested in the area's industrial growth and the importance of the Trenton ceramics industry in New Jersey's economic structure.

Rob has been intensely involved with many civic activities aimed at advancing the interests of collectors today. He has organized major events to honor former Stangl employees. He designed and was instrumental in having historic markers erected in Flemington to designate important Fulper and Stangl sites in town. The most important feat was when Rob rescued the original Stangl molds from a warehouse slated for demolition. Today, they sit safely in storage. Always interested in sharing his knowledge, he has been responsible for presenting many exhibits and programs. He is well-known and frequently booked by local groups for his "Meet Me at the Kiln" program (page 69).

For the past 15 years or so, Rob has been accumulating examples of Fulper and Stangl pottery, amassing a huge collection. It was his dream to display as many examples as possible to show the length and breadth of the manufacturing process of these potteries. On April 15, 2000, the dream came to fruition, and Rob and I celebrated the grand opening of the Hill-Fulper-Stangl Potteries Museum (pages 67 – 69).

This *Collector's Encyclopedia of Stangl Artware, Lamps, and Birds* is an exciting book. It represents many years of research plus thousands of photos, which portray the color and quality of these wonderful pottery items. The collector who picks up this book will be utterly amazed to see so many previously undocumented items accurately identified. Through his extensive research, Rob has been able to identify pieces that one would never imagine to be Stangl.

Rob is once again entrenched in newly-discovered research material for his next book about Fulper Pottery artware.

Rob (center), Diana, and closest family and friends gathered in front of the great jug at the old Stangl Flemington Outlet.